chronological dictionary of quotations

chronological dictionary of quotations

Edited by Edmund Wright

BLOOMSBURY

First published 1988 as *Who Said What When*

Revised edition first published 1993

This paperback edition first published 1994

Copyright © 1993 by Bloomsbury Publishing Limited
Bloomsbury Publishing Limited, 2 Soho Square
London W1V 5DE

The moral right of the author has been asserted

Extracts from the Authorized King James Version of the Bible, which is Crown Copyright, are reproduced by permission of Eyre and Spottiswoode, Her Majesty's Printers.

A copy of the CIP entry for this book is available from the British Library

ISBN 0-7475-1512-3

Compiled and typeset by
Market House Books, Ltd., Aylesbury
Printed in Great Britain by
Clays Ltd, St Ives plc

contents

acknowledgments

Editors

Edmund Wright
Anne Stibbs
Ruth Salomon
Megan Remmer
John Daintith

Contributors

Elizabeth Bonham
Deborah Chapman
Sue Cope
Eve Daintith
Hazel Egerton
Rosalind Fergusson
Joanna Gosling
Jock Graham
Lawrence Holden
Alan Isaacs
Amanda Isaacs
Valerie Illingworth
Stephen Jones
Elizabeth Martin
David Pickering
Jessica Scholes
Gwynneth Shaw
Mary Shields
Kate Smith
Jean Wright

introduction

This is a unique collection of quotations arranged chronologically from earliest times to the present day. Many of these have been selected for their historical interest—that is for the light they throw on some important event or figure, or on some attitude current at the time. Quotations like these will not appear in more conventional dictionaries of quotations. But we have also included many well-known, and not so well-known, literary quotations, witty remarks, etc. Each chapter of the book is a historical period:

1 The Old Testament
2 The Ancient World (before 50 BC)
3 The New Testament
4 The Roman World (50 BC–399 AD)
5 The Early Middle Ages (400–1099)
6 The Later Middle Ages (1100–1517)
7 The Reformation and Counter-Reformation (1518–1659)
8 The Age of Enlightenment (1660–1788)
9 The French Revolution (1789–1815)
10 Liberalism, Nationalism, and Reaction (1816–69)
11 The Age of Imperialism (1870–1913)
12 The World Wars (1914–45)
13 The Post-War World (1946–)

History is a continuous process not necessarily designed for chopping into book chapters. However, we feel that this division is a useful and convenient way of presenting the information. The chapter titles are not, of course, exclusive. For example, the period from 1789 to 1815 has to be called *The French Revolution* because the revolution in France dominated European history in that time. But other things were happening during these years and quotations about these have been included. Similarly, the chapter on *The World Wars* includes quotations from 1914 before the outbreak of World War I, quotations from between the Wars, and quotations that are not connected with the Wars.

Each chapter begins with a short introductory article on the period, its importance, and the main events. There is also a list of contents in each chapter. Within each chapter the material is organized into four main sections:

Politics, Government, and World Events is the main historical section of the chapter. It includes quotations about specific events, politics, political figures, law and government, society, etc. Throughout the historical sections we have tried to include as much additional information as possible to place the quotations in context. This has been done by linking text for significant events (the Spanish Armada, the American Revolution, the Russian Revolution), or by explanatory notes attached to individual quotations (as in the Vicar of Bray or many nursery rhymes).

Attitudes contains a collection of quotations designed to show the attitudes of the time to various topics through quotations about them. The full list of topics used is:

Art, Literature, and Music
Daily Life
Death
Education, Knowledge, and Learning
History
Human Nature
Humour
Life
Love and Sex
Marriage and the Family
Men and Women
Morality, Vices, and Virtues
Other People
Religion
Wealth and Poverty
Work and Occupations

Sayings of the Time includes a few quotations that date from the period but do not fall into the two previous categories. These are usually well-known sayings, for example, 'Imitation is the sincerest form of flattery' (1820) or 'Tinker, Tailor, Soldier, Sailor' (1829).

With Hindsight gives a few later sayings about the period or about events or personalities in that period. Some of these are serious commentaries, but we have also included more light-hearted remarks. For instance, Alfonso the Wise commented on the complicated Ptolemaic model of the universe that had he been present at the Creation he would have recommended something simpler.

The quotations in the chapter are numbered sequentially throughout. Within each section, or sub-section, the quotations are arranged in date order. Note that most of the quotations were said or written in the year given, but we have also included quotations that are about the period—for example, Shakespeare on Elizabethan England.

Finally, in explaining the organization of the book, we have to say something about the difficulties in assigning dates to many of the quotations. There are two problems:

1. The quotation may be dateable, but we have been unable to find a reliable date reference.

2. The date of the quotation is unknown. Many quotations are 'Attributed' and nobody knows the exact year in which they were said (if they were said at all).

We have, generally, dated attributed quotations at the death date of the person involved, unless there is a logical reason for doing otherwise. For the others, we have made an arbitrary judgment about the year in order to put the quotation in some sort of historical context.

All quotations for which the date is uncertain, for whatever reason, are marked with an asterisk (*) after the quotation number. **These dates should be treated with caution.** If an asterisked quotation appears under the year 1805, it was not necessarily said in 1805. The asterisk means that it was probably said within a few years of 1805, and that 1805 is a convenient place to put it in the sequence. We feel that this is the best way of treating these 'problem' quotations. We would welcome any information from readers that would allow us to date these quotations more accurately.

We hope that the reader will find the book useful in a number of ways:

- To find quotations about a specific event, or things said in a certain year.
- To follow a period of history from what was said at the time.
- To look at the attitudes of people at a given time in the past to some subject.
- To compare the way that attitudes have changed to certain issues (or, perhaps more interestingly, how they have not changed).
- To trace the source of a known quotation, or the exact wording of a half-remembered one. We have included an extensive keyword-key phrase index in which the references are to chapter and quotation number (e.g. 6:230 is quotation number 230 in chapter 6).
- To find quotations by particular people. The name index has the same reference system as the keyword index.

But above all, we hope that the reader will find the book stimulating, sometimes amusing, and always interesting.

The Editors

1

The Old Testament

Attempting to date the events described in the Old Testament has led to the downfall of many theologians. It is now accepted by all but the most fundamental of fundamentalists that some biblical accounts, such as those of the creation of the world and of Eve from the rib of Adam, are no more than allegorical fables. Other incidents, such as the Flood, may or may not have been based on historical events — indeed, Noah may or may not have been a historical person. On the other hand, Kings Saul, David, and Solomon were undoubtedly historical iron-age monarchs; likewise the building and destruction of the first Temple can be fairly confidently dated. Nevertheless, it was felt that quotations from the Old Testament do not fit comfortably in a chronological sequence with quotations from less auspicious sources. For this reason, the following section lists the quotations taken from the Old Testament in book, chapter, and verse order, with no attempt to date the events described. It therefore follows that there will be some temporal overlap between the real biblical events and the events described in the quotations from the Ancient World, which appear in the next section.

1 In the beginning God created the heaven and
the earth.
And the earth was without form, and void; and
darkness was upon the face of the deep.
And the Spirit of God moved upon the face of
the waters.
And God said, Let there be light: and there
was light.
And God saw the light, that it was good: and
God divided the light from the darkness.
And God called the light Day, and the darkness he called Night. And the evening and
the morning were the first day.
Bible: Genesis
1:1–5

2 And God called the dry land Earth; and the
gathering together of the waters called he
Seas: and God saw that it was good.
And God said, Let the earth bring forth grass,
the herb yielding seed, and the fruit tree
yielding fruit after his kind, whose seed is in
itself, upon the earth: and it was so.
Bible: Genesis
1:10–11

3 And God made two great lights: the greater
light to rule the day, and the lesser light to rule
the night: he made the stars also.
Bible: Genesis
1:16

4 And God said, Let the earth bring forth the living creature after his kind, cattle, and creeping thing, and beast of the earth after his kind:
and it was so.
Bible: Genesis
1:24

5 And God said, Let us make man in our image,
after our likeness: and let them have dominion
over the fish of the sea, and over the fowl of
the air, and over the cattle, and over all the
earth, and over every creeping thing that
creepeth upon the earth.
So God created man in his own image, in the
image of God created he him; male and female created he them.
And God blessed them, and God said unto
them, Be fruitful, and multiply, and replenish
the earth, and subdue it: and have dominion over the fish of the sea, and over the
fowl of the air, and over every living thing that
moveth upon the earth.
Bible: Genesis
1:26–28

6 And on the seventh day God ended his work
which he had made; and he rested on the seventh day from all his work which he had
made.
Bible: Genesis
2:2

7 But there went up a mist from the earth, and
watered the whole face of the ground.
And the Lord God formed man of the dust of
the ground, and breathed into his nostrils
the breath of life; and man became a living
soul.
And the Lord God planted a garden eastward

in Eden; and there he put the man whom he
had formed.
And out of the ground made the Lord God to
grow every tree that is pleasant to the sight,
and good for food; the tree of life also in
the midst of the garden, and the tree of
knowledge of good and evil.
And a river went out of Eden to water the
garden.
Bible: Genesis
2:6–10

8 And the Lord God took the man, and put him
into the garden of Eden to dress it and to keep
it.
And the Lord God commanded the man, saying, Of every tree of the garden thou mayest
freely eat:
But of the tree of the knowledge of good and
evil, thou shalt not eat of it: for in the day
that thou eatest thereof thou shalt surely die.
Bible: Genesis
2:15–17

9 And the Lord God said, It is not good that the
man should be alone; I will make him an help
meet for him.
And out of the ground the Lord God formed
every beast of the field, and every fowl of
the air; and brought them unto Adam to see
what he would call them: and whatsoever
Adam called every living creature, that was
the name thereof.
Bible: Genesis
2:18–19

10 And the Lord God caused a deep sleep to fall
upon Adam, and he slept: and he took one of
his ribs, and closed up the flesh instead
thereof;
And the rib, which the Lord God had taken
from man, made he a woman, and brought her
unto the man.
And Adam said, This is now bone of my
bones, and flesh of my flesh: she shall be
called Woman, because she was taken out of
Man.
Therefore shall a man leave his father and his
mother, and shall cleave unto his wife: and
they shall be one flesh.
And they were both naked, the man and his
wife, and were not ashamed.
Bible: Genesis
2:21–25

11 Now the serpent was more subtil than any
beast of the field which the Lord God had
made.
Bible: Genesis
3:1

12 God doth know that in the day ye eat thereof,
then your eyes shall be opened, and ye shall
be as gods, knowing good and evil.
And when the woman saw that the tree was
good for food, and that it was pleasant to
the eyes, and a tree to be desired to make
one wise, she took of the fruit thereof, and
did eat, and gave also unto her husband
with her; and he did eat.
And the eyes of them both were opened, and

they knew that they were naked; and they sewed fig leaves together; and made themselves aprons.

And they heard the voice of the Lord God walking in the garden in the cool of the day: and Adam and his wife hid themselves from the presence of the Lord God amongst the trees of the garden.
Bible: Genesis
3:5–8

13 And the man said, The woman whom thou gavest to be with me, she gave me of the tree, and I did eat.

And the Lord God said unto the woman, What is this that thou hast done? And the woman said, The serpent beguiled me, and I did eat.

And the Lord God said unto the serpent, Because thou hast done this, thou art cursed above all cattle, and above every beast of the field; upon thy belly shalt thou go, and dust shalt thou eat all the days of thy life:

And I will put enmity between thee and the woman, and between thy seed and her seed; it shall bruise thy head, and thou shalt bruise his heel.

Unto the woman he said, I will greatly multiply thy sorrow and thy conception; in sorrow thou shalt bring forth children; and thy desire shall be to thy husband, and he shall rule over thee.

And unto Adam he said, Because thou hast hearkened unto the voice of thy wife, and has eaten of the tree, of which I commanded thee, saying, Thou shalt not eat of it: cursed is the ground for thy sake; in sorrow shalt thou eat of it all the days of thy life.
Bible: Genesis
3:12–17

14 In the sweat of thy face shalt thou eat bread, till thou return unto the ground; for out of it wast thou taken: for dust thou art and unto dust shalt thou return.

And Adam called his wife's name Eve; because she was the mother of all living.
Bible: Genesis
3:19–20

15 Abel was a keeper of sheep, but Cain was a tiller of the ground.
Bible: Genesis
4:2

16 And the Lord said unto Cain, Where is Abel thy brother? And he said, I know not: Am I my brother's keeper?

And he said, What hast thou done? the voice of thy brother's blood crieth unto me from the ground.
Bible: Genesis
4:9–10

17 When thou tillest the ground, it shall not henceforth yield unto thee her strength; a fugitive and a vagabond shalt thou be in the earth.

And Cain said unto the Lord, My punishment is greater than I can bear.
Bible: Genesis
4:12–13

18 And the Lord said unto him, Therefore whosoever slayeth Cain, vengeance shall be taken on him sevenfold. And the Lord set a mark upon Cain, lest any finding him should kill him.

And Cain went out from the presence of the Lord, and dwelt in the land of Nod, on the east of Eden.
Bible: Genesis
4:15–16

19 And they went in unto Noah into the ark, two and two of all flesh, wherein is the breath of life.

And they that went in, went in male and female of all flesh, as God had commanded him: and the Lord shut him in.

And the flood was forty days upon the earth; and the waters increased, and bare up the ark, and it was lift up above the earth.
Bible: Genesis
7:15–17

20 And the dove came in to him in the evening; and, lo, in her mouth was an olive leaf pluckt off: so Noah knew that the waters were abated from off the earth.
Bible: Genesis
8:11

21 And surely your blood of your lives will I require; at the hand of every beast will I require it, and at the hand of man; at the hand of every man's brother will I require the life of man.

Whoso sheddeth man's blood, by man shall his blood be shed: for in the image of God made he man.
Bible: Genesis
9:5–6

22 He was a mighty hunter before the Lord: wherefore it is said, Even as Nimrod the mighty hunter before the Lord.
Bible: Genesis
10:9

23 Therefore is the name of it called Babel; because the Lord did there confound the language of all the earth: and from thence did the Lord scatter them abroad upon the face of all the earth.
Bible: Genesis
11:9

24 Now the Lord had said unto Abram, Get thee out of thy country, and from thy kindred, and from thy father's house, unto a land that I will shew thee:

And I will make of thee a great nation, and I will bless thee, and make thy name great; and thou shalt be a blessing:

And I will bless them that bless thee, and curse him that curseth thee: and in thee shall all families of the earth be blessed.
Bible: Genesis
12:1–3

25 But his wife looked back from behind him, and she became a pillar of salt.
Bible: Genesis
19:26

26 And Abraham lifted up his eyes, and looked,

and behold behind him a ram caught in a thicket by his horns: and Abraham went and took the ram, and offered him up for a burnt of-fering in the stead of his son.
Bible: Genesis
22:13

27 And Jacob said to Rebekah his mother, Behold, Esau my brother a hairy man, and I am a smooth man.
Bible: Genesis
27:11

28 Now Israel loved Joseph more than all his chil-dren, because he was the son of his old age: and he made him a coat of many colours.
Bible: Genesis
37:3

29 And they said one to another, Behold, this dreamer cometh.
Come now therefore, and let us slay him, and cast him into some pit, and we will say, Some evil beast hath devoured him: and we shall see what will become of his dreams.
Bible: Genesis
37:19–20

30 And the seven thin ears devoured the seven rank and full ears. And Pharaoh awoke, and, be-hold, it was a dream.
Bible: Genesis
41:7

31 And when she could not longer hide him, she took for him an ark of bulrushes, and daubed it with slime and with pitch, and put the child therein; and she laid it in the flags by the river's brink.
Bible: Exodus
2:3

32 He called his name Gershom: for he said, I have been a stranger in a strange land.
Bible: Exodus
2:22

33 And the angel of the Lord appeared unto him in a flame of fire out of the midst of a bush: and he looked, and, behold, the bush burned with fire, and the bush was not consumed.
Bible: Exodus
3:2

34 And I am come down to deliver them out of the hand of the Egyptians, and to bring them up out of that land unto a good land and a large, unto a land flowing with milk and honey; unto the place of the Canaanites, and the Hit-tites, and the Amorites, and the Perizzites, and the Hivites, and the Jebusites.
Bible: Exodus
3:8

35 And God said unto Moses, I AM THAT I AM: and he said, Thus shalt thou say unto the chil-dren of Israel, I AM hath sent me unto you.
Bible: Exodus
3:14

36 And thus shall ye eat it; with your loins girded, your shoes on your feet, and your staff in your hand; and ye shall eat it in haste: it is the Lord's passover.

For I will pass through the land of Egypt this night, and will smite all the firstborn in the land of Egypt, both man and beast; and against all the gods of Egypt I will execute judgment: I am the Lord.
Bible: Exodus
12:11–12

37 And the Lord went before them by day in a pil-lar of a cloud, to lead them the way; and by night in a pillar of fire, to give them light; to go by day and night.
Bible: Exodus
13:21

38 And the children of Israel went into the midst of the sea upon the dry ground: and the waters were a wall unto them on their right hand, and on their left.
Bible: Exodus
14:22

39 And when the children of Israel saw it, they said one to another, It is manna: for they wist not what it was. And Moses said unto them, This is the bread which the Lord hath given you to eat.
Bible: Exodus
16:15

40 I am the Lord thy God, which have brought thee out of the land of Egypt, out of the house of bondage.
Thou shalt have no other gods before me.
Thou shalt not make unto thee any graven im-age, or any likeness of any thing that is in heaven above, or that is in the earth beneath, or that is in the water under the earth:
Thou shalt not bow down thyself to them, nor serve them: for Lord thy God am a jealous God, visiting the iniquity of the fathers upon the children unto the third and fourth gen-eration of them that hate me;
And shewing mercy unto thousands of them that love me, and keep my commandments.
Thou shalt not take the name of the Lord thy God in vain; for the Lord will not hold him guiltless that taketh his name in vain.
Remember the sabbath day, to keep it holy. Six days shalt thou labour, and do all thy work:
But the seventh day is the sabbath of the Lord thy God: in it thou shalt not do any work, thou, nor thy son, nor thy daughter, thy manservant, nor thy maidservant, nor thy cattle, nor thy stranger that is within thy gates:
For in six days the Lord made heaven and earth, the sea, and all that in them is, and rested the seventh day: wherefore the Lord blessed the sabbath day, and hallowed it.
Honour thy father and thy mother: that thy days may be long upon the land which the Lord thy God giveth thee.
Thou shalt not kill.
Thou shalt not commit adultery.
Thou shalt not steal.
Thou shalt not bear false witness against thy neighbour.
Thou shalt not covet thy neighbour's house, thou shalt not covet thy neighbour's wife,

nor his manservant, nor his maidservant, nor his ox, nor his ass, nor any thing that is thy neighbour's.
Bible: Exodus
20:2—17

41 And if any mischief follow, then thou shalt give life for life,
Eye for eye, tooth for tooth, hand for hand, foot for foot,
Burning for burning, wound for wound, stripe for stripe.
Bible: Exodus
21:23—25

42 Thou shalt not suffer a witch to live.
Bible: Exodus
22:18

43 And the Lord said unto Moses, Come up to me into the mount, and be there: and I will give thee tables of stone, and a law, and commandments which I have written; that thou mayest teach them.
Bible: Exodus
24:12

44 Take heed to yourselves, that your heart be not deceived, and ye turn aside, and serve other gods, and worship them.
Bible: Deuteronomy
11:16

45 Be strong and of a good courage, fear not, nor be afraid of them: for the Lord thy God, he it is that doth go with thee; he will not fail thee, nor forsake thee.
Bible: Deuteronomy
31:6

46 So the people shouted when the priests blew with the trumpets: and it came to pass, when the people heard the sound of the trumpet, and the people shouted with a great shout, that the wall fell down flat, so that the people went up into the city, every man straight before him, and they took the city.
Bible: Joshua
6:20

47 And the women answered one another as they played, and said, Saul hath slain his thousands, and David his ten thousands.
Bible: I Samuel
18:7

48 So David slept with his fathers, and was buried in the city of David.
Bible: I Kings
2:10

49 Then the king answered and said, Give her the living child, and in no wise slay it: she is the mother thereof.
And all Israel heard of the judgment which the king had judged; and they feared the king: for they saw that the wisdom of God was in him, to do judgment.
Bible: I Kings
The 'Judgment of Solomon'
3:27—28

50 And when the queen of Sheba heard of the fame of Solomon concerning the name of the Lord, she came to prove him with hard questions.
Bible: I Kings
10:1

51 And he said, Go forth, and stand upon the mount before the Lord. And, behold, the Lord passed by, and a great and strong wind rent the mountains, and brake in pieces the rocks before the Lord; but the Lord was not in the wind: and after the wind an earthquake; but the Lord was not in the earthquake:
And after the earthquake a fire; but the Lord was not in the fire: and after the fire a still small voice.
Bible: I Kings
19:11—12

52 And it came to pass, as they still went on, and talked, that, behold, there appeared a chariot of fire, and horses of fire, and parted them both asunder; and Elijah went up by a whirlwind into heaven.
And Elisha saw it, and he cried, My father, my father, the chariot of Israel, and the horsemen thereof. And he saw him no more: and he took hold of his own clothes, and rent them in two pieces.
Bible: II Kings
2:11—12

53 And he shall judge among the nations, and shall rebuke many people: and they shall beat their swords into plowshares, and their spears into pruning-hooks: nation shall not lift up sword against nation, neither shall they learn war any more.
Bible: Isaiah
2:4

54 Comfort ye, comfort ye my people, saith your God.
Speak ye comfortably to Jerusalem, and cry unto her, that her warfare is accomplished, that her iniquity is pardoned: for she hath received of the Lord's hand double for all her sins.
The voice of him that crieth in the wilderness, Prepare ye the way of the Lord, make straight in the desert a highway for our God.
Every valley shall be exalted, and every mountain and hill shall be made low: and the crooked shall be made straight, and the rough places plain:
And the glory of the Lord shall be revealed, and all flesh shall see it together: for the mouth of the Lord hath spoken it.
Bible: Isaiah
40:1—5

55 There is no peace, saith the Lord, unto the wicked.
Bible: Isaiah
48:22

56 Then the king commanded, and they brought Daniel, and cast him into the den of lions. Now the king spake and said unto Daniel, Thy God whom thou servest continually, he will deliver thee.
Bible: Daniel
6:16

57 For they have sown the wind, and they shall reap the whirlwind: it hath no stalk: the bud shall yield no meal: if so be it yield, the strangers shall swallow it up.
Bible: Hosea
8:7

58 Now the Lord had prepared a great fish to swallow up Jonah. And Jonah was in the belly of the fish three days and three nights.
Bible: Jonah
1:17

59 Behold, I will send my messenger, and he shall prepare the way before me: and the Lord, whom ye seek, shall suddenly come to his temple, even the messenger of the covenant, whom ye delight in: behold, he shall come, saith the Lord of hosts. But who may abide the day of his coming? and who shall stand when he appeareth? for he is like a refiner's fire, and like fullers' soap.
Bible: Malachi
3:2

Attitudes

Death

60 Whatsoever thy hand findeth to do, do it with thy might; for there is no work, nor device, nor knowledge, nor wisdom, in the grave, whither thou goest.
Bible: Ecclesiastes
9:10

Education, Knowledge, and Learning

61 With the ancient is wisdom; and in length of days understanding.
Bible: Job
12:12

62 No mention shall be made of coral, or of pearls: for the price of wisdom is above rubies.
Bible: Job
28:18

63 For in much wisdom is much grief: and he that increaseth knowledge increaseth sorrow.
Bible: Ecclesiastes
1:18

64 The words of wise men are heard in quiet more than the cry of him that ruleth among fools.
Bible: Ecclesiastes
9:17

65 Miss not the discourse of the elders: for they also learned of their fathers, and of them thou shalt learn understanding, and to give answer as need requireth.
Bible: Ecclesiasticus
8:9

66 The wisdom of a learned man cometh by opportunity of leisure: and he that hath little business shall become wise.
How can he get wisdom that holdeth the plough, and that glorieth in the goad, that driveth oxen, and is occupied in their labours, and whose talk is of bullocks?
Bible: Ecclesiasticus
38:24−25

67 For wisdom is more moving than any motion: she passeth and go through all things by reason of her pureness.
For she is the breath of the power of God, and a pure influence flowing from the glory of the Almighty: therefore can no defiled thing fall into her.
For she is the brightness of the everlasting light, the unspotted mirror of the power of God, and the image of his goodness.
And being but one, she can do all things: and remaining in herself, she maketh all things new: and in all ages entering into holy souls, she maketh them friends of God, and prophets.
For God loveth none but him that dwelleth with wisdom.
Bible: Wisdom
7:24−28

Human Nature

68 And I gave my heart to seek and search out by wisdom concerning all things that are done under heaven: this sore travail hath God given to the sons of man to be exercised therewith.
I have seen all the works that are done under the sun; and, behold, all is vanity and vexation of spirit.
Bible: Ecclesiastes
1:13−14

69 Two are better than one; because they have a good reward for their labour.
For if they fall, the one will lift up his fellow: but woe to him that is alone when he falleth; for he hath not another to help him up.
Bible: Ecclesiastes
4:9−10

70 Forsake not an old friend; for the new is not comparable to him: a new friend is as new wine; when it is old, thou shalt drink it with pleasure.
Bible: Ecclesiasticus
9:10

Humour

71 Then I commended mirth, because a man hath no better thing under the sun, than to eat, and to drink, and to be merry: for that shall abide with him of his labour the days of his life, which God giveth him under the sun.
Bible: Ecclesiastes
8:15

Life

72 For the world hath lost his youth, and the times
    begin to wax old.
    Bible: II Esdras
    14:10

73 Man that is born of a woman is of few days,
    and full of trouble.
    Bible: Job
    14:1

74 The thing that hath been, it is that which shall
    be; and that which is done is that which shall
    be done: and there is no new thing under the
    sun.
    Bible: Ecclesiastes
    1:7–9

75 To every thing there is a season, and a time to
    every purpose under the heaven:
    A time to be born, and a time to die; a time to
    plant, and a time to pluck up that which is
    planted;
    A time to kill, and a time to heal; a time to
    break down, and a time to build up;
    A time to weep, and a time to laugh; a time to
    mourn, and a time to dance;
    A time to cast away stones, and a time to
    gather stones together; a time to embrace,
    and a time to refrain from embracing;
    A time to get, and a time to lose; a time to
    keep, and a time to cast away;
    A time to rend, and a time to sew; a time to
    keep silence, and a time to speak;
    A time to love, and a time to hate; a time of
    war, and a time of peace.
    Bible: Ecclesiastes
    3:1–8

76 I returned, and saw under the sun, that the race
    is not to the swift, nor the battle to the strong,
    neither yet bread to the wise, nor yet riches
    to men of understanding, nor yet favour to men
    of skill; but time and chance happeneth to
    them all.
    For man also knoweth not his time: as the
    fishes that are taken in an evil net, and as the
    birds that are caught in the snare; so are the
    sons of men snared in an evil time, when it
    falleth suddenly upon them.
    Bible: Ecclesiastes
    9:11–12

77 If thou hast gathered nothing in thy youth, how
    canst thou find any thing in thine age?
    Bible: Ecclesiasticus
    25:3

78 And behold joy and gladness, slaying oxen, and
    killing sheep, eating flesh, and drinking wine:
    let us eat and drink; for tomorrow we shall
    die.
    Bible: Isaiah
    22:13
    A similar sentiment is expressed in Corinthians
    15:32–33

Marriage and the Family

79 He that spareth his rod hateth his son: but he
    that loveth him chasteneth him betimes.
    Bible: Proverbs
    13:24

80 Desire not a multitude of unprofitable children,
    neither delight in ungodly sons.
    Bible: Ecclesiasticus
    16:1

Men and Women

81 Who can find a virtuous woman? for her price
    is far above rubies
    The heart of her husband doth safely trust in
    her, so that he shall have no need of spoil.
    She will do him good and not evil all the days
    of her life.
    Bible: Proverbs
    31:10–12

Morality, Vices, and Virtues

82 Pride goeth before destruction, and an haughty
    spirit before a fall.
    Bible: Proverbs
    16:18

83 He that is slow to anger is better than the
    mighty; and he that ruleth his spirit than he that
    taketh a city.
    Bible: Proverbs
    16:32

84 Wine is a mocker, strong drink is raging: and
    whosoever is deceived thereby is not wise.
    Bible: Proverbs
    20:1

85 Let thy speech be short, comprehending much
    in few words; be as one that knoweth and yet
    holdeth his tongue.
    Bible: Ecclesiasticus
    32:8

86 Be not made a beggar by banqueting upon bor-
    rowing, when thou hast nothing in thy purse:
    for thou shalt lie in wait for thine own life,
    and be talked on.
    Bible: Ecclesiasticus
    18:33

87 Woe unto them that rise up early in the morn-
    ing, that they may follow strong drink; that
    continue until night, till wine inflame them!
    Bible: Isaiah
    5:11

88 There is no peace, saith the Lord, unto the
    wicked.
    Bible: Isaiah
    48:22

89 Blessed is the man that endureth temptation:
    for when he is tried, he shall receive the crown
    of life, which the Lord hath promised to them
    that love him.
    Bible: James
    1:12

90 Can the Ethiopian change his skin, or the leopard his spots? then may ye also do good, that are accustomed to do evil.
Bible: Jeremiah
13:23

91 For the ear of jealousy heareth all things: and the noise of murmurings is not hid.
Bible: Wisdom
1:10

Other People

92 One of themselves, even a prophet of their own, said, The Cretians are alway liars, evil beasts, slow bellies.
Bible: Titus
1:12

Religion

93 The Lord is a man of war: the Lord is his name.
Bible: Exodus
15:3

94 For I know that my redeemer liveth, and that he shall stand at the latter day upon the earth: And though after my skin worms destroy this body, yet in my flesh shall I see God.
Bible: Job
19:25–26

95 Let us hear the conclusion of the whole matter: Fear God, and keep his commandments: for this is the whole duty of man.
Bible: Ecclesiastes
12:13

96 In the year that king Uzziah died I saw also the Lord sitting upon a throne, high and lifted up, and his train filled the temple.
Above it stood the seraphims: each one had six wings; with twain he covered his face, and with twain he covered his feet, and with twain he did fly.
And one cried unto another, and said, Holy, holy, holy, is the Lord of hosts: the whole earth is full of his glory.
And the posts of the door moved at the voice of him that cried, and the house was filled with smoke.
Then said I, Woe is me! for I am undone; because I am a man of unclean lips, and I dwell in the midst of a people of unclean lips: for mine eyes have seen the King, the Lord of hosts.
Then flew one of the seraphims unto me, having a live coal in his hand, which he had taken with the tongs from off the altar:
And he laid it upon my mouth, and said, Lo, this hath touched thy lips; and thine iniquity is taken away, and thy sin purged.
Also I heard the voice of the Lord, saying, Whom shall I send, and who will go for us? Then said I, Here am I; send me.
Bible: Isaiah
6:1–8

97 Therefore the Lord himself shall give you a

sign; Behold, a virgin shall conceive, and bear a son, and shall call his name Immanuel.
Butter and honey shall he eat, that he may know to refuse the evil, and choose the good.
Bible: Isaiah
7:14–15

98 The people that walked in darkness have seen a great light: they that dwell in the land of the shadow of death, upon them hath the light shined.
Bible: Isaiah
9:2

99 For unto us a child is born, unto us a son is given: and the government shall be upon his shoulder: and his name shall be called Wonderful, Counsellor, The mighty God, The everlasting Father, The Prince of Peace.
Of the increase of his government and peace there shall be no end, upon the throne of David, and upon his kingdom, to order it, and to establish it with judgment and with justice from henceforth even for ever. The zeal of the Lord of hosts will perform this.
Bible: Isaiah
9:6–7

100 And there shall come forth a rod out of the stem of Jesse, and a Branch shall grow out of his roots:
And the spirit of the Lord shall rest upon him, the spirit of wisdom and understanding, the spirit of counsel and might, the spirit of knowledge and of the fear of the Lord.
Bible: Isaiah
11:1–2

Wealth and Poverty

101 A feast is made for laughter, and wine maketh merry: but money answereth all things.
Bible: Ecclesiastes
10:19

Sayings of the Time

102 Then Job answered and said, I have heard many such things: miserable comforters are ye all.
Bible: Job
16:1

103 Canst thou draw out leviathan with an hook? or his tongue with a cord which thou lettest down?
Bible: Job
41:1

104 Let us now praise famous men, and our fathers that begat us.
Bible: Ecclesiasticus
44:1

105 He calleth to me out of Seir, Watchman, what of the night? Watchman, what of the night?
The watchman said, The morning cometh, and

also the night: if ye will enquire, enquire ye: return, come.
Bible: Isaiah
21:11–12

106 Then the eyes of the blind shall be opened, and
the ears of the deaf shall be unstopped.
Bible: Isaiah
35:5

107 And he said unto me, Son of man, can these
bones live? And I answered, O Lord God, thou
knowest.
Again he said unto me, Prophesy upon these
bones, and say unto them, O ye dry bones,
hear the word of the Lord.
Bible: Ezekiel
37:3–4

With Hindsight

13th century

108 Had I been present at the Creation, I would
have given some useful hints for the better ordering of the universe.
Alfonso the Wise (c. 1221–84) King of Cas-
tile and Léon.
Referring to the complicated Ptolemaic model of
the universe; often quoted as, 'Had I been con-

sulted I would have recommended something
simpler'
Attrib.

14th century

109 Whan that the month in which the world bigan,
That highte March, whan God first maked
man.
Geoffrey Chaucer (c. 1342–1400) English
poet.
The Canterbury Tales, 'The Nun's Priest's Tale'

17th century

110 Which beginning of time according to our Chro-
nologie, fell upon the entrance of the night
preceding the twenty third day of *Octob.* in the
year of the Julian Calendar, 710.
James Ussher (1581–1656) Irish churchman.
Referring to the Creation, as described in Genesis, which, he had calculated, took place on 22
Oct 4004 BC
The Annals of the World

111 Of Man's first disobedience, and the fruit
Of that forbidden tree, whose mortal taste
Brought death into the World, and all our woe
. . .
John Milton (1608–74) English poet.
Paradise Lost, Bk. I

2

The Ancient World (before 50 BC)

While history goes back some 4000 years BC and the Hindu Vedas were being written in Sanskrit over 3500 years ago, the earliest quotable sources to have had a continuous and lasting influence on the western world are the Old Testament (see previous section) and the works of the ancient Greeks. Between the 6th and 4th centuries BC an astounding burst of creativity flourished throughout the ancient world. In China Lao Tse and Confucius, in India Guatama Buddha, and in Persia Zoroaster were roughly contemporary with the Jewish prophets and Pericles of Athens. But it was primarily the Greek city states that provided the starting points of western culture in history, philosophy, drama, and literature; it is, therefore, from this quarter that most of the quotations from the ancient world come.

When the rising Roman Republic absorbed Greece in the 2nd century BC, it also absorbed Greek culture and learning. Politically, Rome was a new phenomenon: a city-state that not only acquired an empire but eventually conquered most of the known world. Its political institutions were still those of a city-state, unsuited to controlling its vast territories. By 50 BC, when Julius Caesar completed his conquest of Gaul, they were ready to break.

Politics, Government, and World Events

6th century BC

1 Laws are like spider's webs: if some poor weak creature come up against them, it is caught; but a bigger one can break through and get away.
Solon (6th century BC) Athenian statesman.
Lives of the Eminent Philosophers (Diogenes Laertius), I

2 Recompense injury with justice, and recompense kindness with kindness.
Confucius (K'ung Fu-tzu; 551–479 BC) Chinese philosopher.
Analects

3 The people may be made to follow a course of action, but they may not be made to understand it.
Confucius
Analects

480 BC

4 Go, stranger, and tell the Lacedaemonians that here we lie, obedient to their commands.
Leonidas (died 480 BC) King of Sparta.
Epitaph over the tomb in which he and his followers were buried after their defeat at Thermopylae

430 BC

5 Our love of what is beautiful does not lead to extravagance; our love of the things of the mind does not make us soft.
Pericles (c. 495–429 BC) Greek statesman.
Part of the funeral oration, 430 BC, for the dead of the first year of the Peloponnesian War
Attrib. in *Histories* (Thucydides), Bk. II, Ch. 40

399 BC

6 Crito, we owe a cock to Aesculapius; please pay it and don't let it pass.
Socrates (469–399 BC) Athenian philosopher.
Before his execution by drinking hemlock
Phaedo (Plato), 118

4th century BC

7 Our object in the construction of the state is the greatest happiness of the whole, and not that of any one class.
Plato (429–347 BC) Greek philosopher.
Republic, Bk. IV

8 There will be no end to the troubles of states, or indeed, my dear Glaucon, of humanity itself, till philosophers become kings in this world, or till those we now call kings and rulers really and truly become philosophers.
Plato
Republic, Bk. V

9 I wonder if we could contrive . . . some magnificent myth that would in itself carry conviction to our whole community.
Plato
Republic, Bk. V

10 Democracy passes into despotism.
Plato
Republic, Bk. VIII

11 The difference between us is that my family begins with me, whereas yours ends with you.
Iphicrates (d. 353 BC) Athenian general.
Reply to a descendant of Harmodius (an Athenian hero), who had derided Iphicrates for being the son of a cobbler
Attrib.

12 If I were not Alexander, I would be Diogenes.
Alexander the Great (356–323 BC) King of Macedon.
Plutarch, *Life of Alexander*, Bk. XIV

13 Stand a little less between me and the sun.
Diogenes (412–322 BC) Greek philosopher.
When Alexander the Great asked if there was anything he wanted
Life of Alexander (Plutarch)

14 Man is by nature a political animal.
Aristotle (384–322 BC) Greek philosopher.
Politics, Bk. I

15 Where some people are very wealthy and others have nothing, the result will be either extreme democracy or absolute oligarchy, or despotism will come from either of those excesses.
Aristotle
Politics, Bk. IV

16 Inferiors revolt in order that they may be equal and equals that they may be superior. Such is the state of mind which creates revolutions.
Aristotle
Politics, Bk. V

279 BC

17 Such another victory and we are ruined.
Pyrrhus (319–272 BC) King of Epirus.
Commenting upon the costliness of his victory at the Battle of Asculum, 279 BC
Life of Pyrrhus (Plutarch)

2nd century BC

18 Carthage must be destroyed.
Cato the Elder (Marcius Porcius C.; 234–149 BC) Roman statesman.
Repeated on almost every possible occasion; war was declared on Carthage in 149 BC, and the city was destroyed in 146 BC.
Life of Cato (Plutarch)

19 Let them hate, so long as they fear.
Lucius Accius (170–c. 85 BC) Roman tragic playwright.
Atreus, 'Seneca'

---
63 BC
---

20   *O tempora! O mores!*
   What times! What customs!
   Cicero (106–43 BC) Roman orator and
   statesman.
   In Catilinam, I

---
62 BC

21* **Caesar's wife must be above suspicion.**
   Julius Caesar (100–44 BC) Roman general
   and statesman.
   Said in justification of his divorce from Pompeia,
   after she was unwittingly involved in a scandal
   Lives, 'Julius Caesar' (Plutarch)

---
51 BC

22* **All Gaul is divided into three parts.**
   Julius Caesar
   De Bello Gallico, Vol. I, Ch. 1

Attitudes

Art, Literature, and Music

5th century BC
---

23   **I depict men as they ought to be, but Euripides
   portrays them as they are.**
   Sophocles (c. 496–406 BC) Greek dramatist.
   Poetics (Aristotle)

4th century BC
---

24   **Now a whole is that which has a beginning, a
   middle, and an end.**
   Aristotle (384–322 BC) Greek philosopher.
   Referring specifically to the dramatic form of
   tragedy
   Poetics, Ch. 7

1st century BC
---

25   **For the godly poet must be chaste himself, but
   there is no need for his verses to be so.**
   Catullus (c. 84–c. 54 BC) Roman poet.
   Carmina, XVI

Death

4th century BC
---

26   **Whom the gods love dies young.**
   Menander (c. 341–c. 290 BC) Greek dramatist.
   Dis Exapaton

Education, Knowledge, and Learning

6th century BC
---

27   **Learning without thought is labour lost; thought
   without learning is perilous.**
   Confucius (K'ung Fu-tzu; 551–479 BC) Chinese philosopher.
   Analects

4th century BC
---

28   **What we have to learn to do, we learn by doing.**
   Aristotle (384–322 BC) Greek philosopher.
   Nicomachean Ethics, Bk. II

History

6th century BC
---

29   **Study the past, if you would divine the future.**
   Confucius (K'ung Fu-tzu; 551–479 BC) Chi-
   nese philosopher.
   Analects

5th century BC
---

30   **Even God cannot change the past.**
   Agathon (c. 446–401 BC) Athenian poet and
   playwright.
   Nicomachean Ethics (Aristotle), VI

4th century BC
---

31   **For this reason poetry is something more philosophical and more worthy of serious attention
   than history.**
   Aristotle (384–322 BC) Greek philosopher.
   Poetics, Ch. 9

Human Nature

6th century BC
---

32   **Don't count your chickens before they are
   hatched.**
   Aesop (6th century BC) Reputed Greek writer of
   fables.
   Fables, 'The Milkmaid and her Pail'

33   **The lamb that belonged to the sheep whose
   skin the wolf was wearing began to follow the
   wolf in the sheep's clothing.**
   Aesop
   Fables, 'The Wolf in Sheep's Clothing'

34   **It is not only fine feathers that make fine birds.**
   Aesop
   Fables, 'The Jay and the Peacock'

35   **I am sure the grapes are sour.**
   Aesop
   Fables, 'The Fox and the Grapes'

36   The boy cried 'Wolf, wolf!' and the villagers came out to help him.
Aesop
Fables, 'The Shepherd's Boy'

37   Have no friends not equal to yourself.
Confucius (K'ung Fu-tzu; 551–479 BC) Chinese philosopher.
Analects

38   Men's natures are alike; it is their habits that carry them far apart.
Confucius
Analects

39   When you have faults, do not fear to abandon them.
Confucius
Analects

40   The superior man is satisfied and composed; the mean man is always full of distress.
Confucius
Analects

41   The superior man is distressed by his want of ability.
Confucius
Analects

42   When you meet someone better than yourself, turn your thoughts to becoming his equal.
When you meet someone not as good as you are, look within and examine your own self.
Confucius
Analects

4th century BC

43   Either a beast or a god.
Aristotle (384–322 BC) Greek philosopher.
Politics, Bk. I

44   Obstinate people can be divided into the opinionated, the ignorant, and the boorish.
Aristotle
Nicomachean Ethics, Bk. VII

3rd century BC

45   It is not so much our friends' help that helps us as the confident knowledge that they will help us.
Epicurus (341–270 BC) Greek philosopher.

Life

6th century BC

46   The gods help them that help themselves.
Aesop (6th century BC) Reputed Greek writer of fables.
Fables, 'Hercules and the Waggoner'

47   Because there is no difference.
Thales (c. 624–547 BC) Greek philosopher and astronomer.
His reply when asked why he chose to carry on living after saying there was no difference between life and death
The Story of Civilization (W. Durant), Vol. 2

5th century BC

48   Everything flows and nothing stays.
Heraclitus (c. 535–c. 475 BC) Greek philosopher.
Cratylus (Plato), 402a

49   I am moved to pity, when I think of the brevity of human life, seeing that of all this host of men not one will still be alive in a hundred years' time.
Xerxes (d. 465 BC) King of Persia.
On surveying his army

50   To famous men all the earth is a sepulchre.
Thucydides (c. 460–c. 400 BC) Greek historian and general.
History of the Peloponnesian War, Bk. II, Ch. 43

51   I am not an Athenian or a Greek, but a citizen of the world.
Socrates (469–399 BC) Athenian philosopher.
Of Banishment (Plutarch)

52   The unexamined life is not worth living.
Socrates
Apology (Plato)

3rd century BC

53   I do not know whether I was then a man dreaming I was a butterfly, or whether I am now a butterfly dreaming I am a man.
Chuang Tse (or Zhuangzi; c. 369–286 BC) Chinese philosopher.
Chuang Tse (H. A. Giles), Ch. 2

Love and Sex

5th century BC

54   Someone asked Sophocles, 'How do you feel now about sex? Are you still able to have a woman?' He replied, 'Hush, man; most gladly indeed am I rid of it all, as though I had escaped from a mad and savage master.'
Sophocles (c. 496–406 BC) Greek dramatist.
Republic (Plato), Bk. I

Men and Women

5th century BC

55   It is a great glory in a woman to show no more weakness than is natural to her sex, and not be talked of, either for good or evil by men.
Thucydides (c. 460–c. 400 BC) Greek historian and general.
History of the Peloponnesian War, Bk. II, Ch. 45

Morality, Vices, and Virtues

6th century BC

56 Beware that you do not lose the substance by grasping at the shadow.
Aesop (6th century BC) Reputed Greek writer of fables.
Fables, 'The Dog and the Shadow'

57 Thinking to get at once all the gold that the goose could give, he killed it, and opened it only to find — nothing.
Aesop
Fables, 'The Goose with the Golden Eggs'

58 Wrongdoing can only be avoided if those who are not wronged feel the same indignation at it as those who are.
Solon (6th century BC) Athenian statesman.
Greek Wit (F. Paley)

59 Fine words and an insinuating appearance are seldom associated with true virtue.
Confucius (K'ung Fu-tzu; 551–479 BC) Chinese philosopher.
Analects

60 To be able to practise five things everywhere under heaven constitutes perfect virtue . . . gravity, generosity of soul, sincerity, earnestness, and kindness.
Confucius
Analects

61 What you do not want done to yourself, do not do to others.
Confucius
Analects

62 This Ariyan Eightfold Path, that is to say: Right view, right aim, right speech, right action, right living, right effort, right mindfulness, right contemplation.
Buddha (Gautama Siddhartha; c. 563–c. 483 BC) Indian religious teacher.
Some Sayings of the Buddha (F. L. Woodward)

5th century BC

63 Nothing can harm a good man, either in life or after death.
Socrates (469–399 BC) Athenian philosopher.
Apology (Plato)

4th century BC

64 The good is the beautiful.
Plato (429–347 BC) Greek philosopher.
Lysis

65 The man who gets angry at the right things and with the right people, and in the right way and at the right time and for the right length of time, is commended.
Aristotle (384–322 BC) Greek philosopher.
Nicomachean Ethics, Bk. IV

66 Plato is dear to me, but dearer still is truth.
Aristotle
Attrib.

Other People

1st century BC

67 To the Greeks the Muse gave native wit, to the Greeks the gift of graceful eloquence.
Horace
Ars Poetica

Religion

6th century BC

68 All things, oh priests, are on fire . . . The eye is on fire; forms are on fire; eye-consciousness is on fire; impressions received by the eye are on fire.
Buddha (Gautama Siddhartha; c. 563–c. 483 BC) Indian religious teacher.
The Fire Sermon

69 Ye must leave righteous ways behind, not to speak of unrighteous ways.
Buddha
Some Sayings of the Buddha (F. L. Woodward)

70 The Ethiopians say that their gods are snub-nosed and black, the Thracians that theirs have light blue eyes and red hair.
Xenophanes (c. 560–c. 478 BC) Greek poet and philosopher.
Fragment 15

5th century BC

71 Those whom God wishes to destroy, he first makes mad.
Euripides (c. 480–406 BC) Greek dramatist.
Fragment

Science, Medicine, and Technology

5th century BC

72 The life so short, the craft so long to learn.
Hippocrates (c. 460–c. 377 BC) Greek physician.
Describing medicine. It is often quoted in Latin as *Ars longa, vita brevis*, and interpreted as 'Art lasts, life is short'
Aphorisms, I

73 Extreme remedies are most appropriate for extreme diseases.
Hippocrates
Aphorisms, I

4th century BC

74 Let no one ignorant of mathematics enter here.
Plato (429–347 BC) Greek philosopher.
Inscription written over the entrance to the Academy
Biographical Encyclopedia (I. Asimov)

323 BC

75 I am dying with the help of too many
physicians.
Alexander the Great (356–323 BC) King of
Macedon.
Attrib.

3rd century BC

76 There is no 'royal road' to geometry.
Euclid (c. 300 BC) Greek mathematician.
Said to Ptolemy I Soter, King of Egypt, when
asked if there were an easier way to solve
theorems
Comment on Euclid (Proclus)

77 *Quod erat demonstrandum.*
Which was to be proved.
Euclid
Hence, of course, Q.E.D.
Elements, I:5

78 *Eureka!*
I have found it!
Archimedes (c. 287–212 BC) Greek
mathematician.
An exclamation of joy supposedly uttered as,
stepping into a bath and noticing the water over-
flowing, he saw the answer to a problem and
began the train of thought that led to his principle of buoyancy
Attrib.

79 Give me a firm place to stand, and I will move
the earth.
Archimedes
On the Lever

Wealth and Poverty

4th century BC

80 If only it were as easy to banish hunger by rub-
bing the belly as it is to masturbate.
Diogenes (412–322 BC) Greek philosopher.
Lives and Opinions of Eminent Philosophers
(Diogenes Laertius)

Sayings of the Time

7th century BC

81 The fox knows many things – the hedgehog
one *big* one.
Archilochus (c. 680–c. 640 BC) Greek poet.
Attrib.

With Hindsight

1st century BC

82 Many brave men lived before Agamemnon's
time; but they are all, unmourned and unknown,
covered by the long night, because they lack
their sacred poet.
Horace (Quintus Horatius Flaccus; 65–8 BC)
Roman poet.
Odes, IV

1st century AD

83 Now there are fields where Troy once was.
Ovid (Publius Ovidius Naso; 43 BC–17 AD) Ro-
man poet.
Heroides, Bk. I

20th century

84 The Romans and Greeks found everything
human. Everything had a face, and a human
voice. Men spoke, and their fountains piped an
answer.
D. H. Lawrence (1885–1930) British novelist.
Fantasia of the Unconscious, Ch. 4

85 I'm surprised that a government organization
could do it that quickly.
Jimmy Carter (1924–) US president.
Visiting Egypt, when told that it took twenty
years to build the Great Pyramid
Presidential Anecdotes (P. Boller)

3

The New Testament

The Romans first conquered Judaea in 63 BC. In 4 BC, following the death of their puppet king, Herod the Great, it became a Roman province.

Jesus of Nazareth, who had been born in Bethlehem during the reign of Herod, began his preaching in Galilee. In approximately 30 AD he was crucified by the Roman procurator Pontius Pilate.

Jesus was one of several religious and political agitators to cause the Romans concern in the period following Herod's death. He was, however, the only one to have profoundly changed, indeed shaped, western culture for the next 2000 years. Some 35 years after his crucifixion, St Mark's Gospel established the beginnings of the New Testament. In the ensuing section, quotations from this part of the Bible, derived from the Gospels and the other sources of the New Testament, are given in book, chapter, and verse order, without dates. However, as with the Old Testament, there is considerable temporal overlap with other events occurring in the Roman world, which appear in the following section.

1 And the angel came in unto her, and said, Hail, thou that art highly favoured, the Lord is with thee: blessed art thou among women.
And when she saw him, she was troubled at his saying, and cast in her mind what manner of salutation this should be.
Bible: Luke
1:28–29

2 And Mary said, My soul doth magnify the Lord, And my spirit hath rejoiced in God my Saviour.
For he hath regarded the low estate of his handmaiden: for, behold, from henceforth all generations shall call me blessed.
Bible: Luke
1:46–48

3 And it came to pass in those days, that there went out a decree from Caesar Augustus, that all the world should be taxed.
Bible: Luke
2:1

4 And she brought forth her firstborn son, and wrapped him in swaddling clothes, and laid him in a manger; because there was no room for them in the inn.
Bible: Luke
2:7

5 And there were in the same country shepherds abiding in the field, keeping watch over their flock by night.
And, lo, the angel of the Lord came upon them, and the glory of the Lord shone round about them: and they were sore afraid.
And the angel said unto them, Fear not: for, behold, I bring you good tidings of great joy, which shall be to all people.
Bible: Luke
2:8–10

6 Glory to God in the highest, and on earth peace, good will toward men.
Bible: Luke
2:14

7 But Mary kept all these things, and pondered them in her heart.
Bible: Luke
2:19

8 Lord, now lettest thou thy servant depart in peace, according to thy word:
For mine eyes have seen thy salvation,
Which thou hast prepared before the face of all people;
A light to lighten the Gentiles, and the glory of thy people Israel.
Bible: Luke
2:29–32

9 Now when Jesus was born in Bethlehem of Judaea in the days of Herod the king, behold, there came wise men from the east to Jerusalem,
Saying, Where is he that is born King of the Jews? for we have seen his star in the east, and are come to worship him.

When Herod the king had heard these things, he was troubled, and all Jerusalem with him.
Bible: Matthew
2:1–3

10 And when they were come into the house, they saw the young child with Mary his mother, and fell down, and worshipped him: and when they had opened their treasures, they presented unto him gifts; gold, and frankincense, and myrrh.
And being warned of God in a dream that they should not return to Herod, they departed into their own country another way.
Bible: Matthew
2:11–12

11 He it is, who coming after me is preferred before me, whose shoe's latchet I am not worthy to unloose.
Bible: John
1:27

12 The next day John seeth Jesus coming unto him, and saith, Behold the Lamb of God, which taketh away the sin of the world.
Bible: John
1:29

13 There is a lad here, which hath five barley loaves, and two small fishes: but what are they among so many?
And Jesus said, Make the men sit down. Now there was much grass in the place. So the men sat down, in number about five thousand.
Bible: John
6:9–10

14 Your fathers did eat manna in the wilderness, and are dead.
This is the bread which cometh down from heaven, that a man may eat thereof, and not die.
I am the living bread which came down from heaven: if any man eat of this bread, he shall live for ever: and the bread that I will give is my flesh, which I will give for the life of the world.
Bible: John
6:49–51

15 And the devil, taking him up into an high mountain, shewed unto him all the kingdoms of the world in a moment of time.
Bible: Luke
4:5

16 And Jesus answering said, A certain man went down from Jerusalem to Jericho, and fell among thieves, which stripped him of his raiment, and wounded him, and departed, leaving him half dead.
And by chance there came down a certain priest that way: and when he saw him, he passed by on the other side.
Bible: Luke
10:30–31

17 And there came a certain poor widow, and she threw in two mites, which make a farthing.
And he called unto him his disciples, and saith unto them, Verily I say unto you, That this

poor widow hath cast more in, than all they which have cast into the treasury: For all they did cast in of their abundance; but she of her want did cast in all that she had, even all her living.
Bible: Mark
12:42—44

18 From that time Jesus began to preach, and to say, Repent: for the kingdom of heaven is at hand.
Bible: Matthew
4:17

19 And he saith unto them, Follow me, and I will make you fishers of men.
Bible: Matthew
4:19

20 And his disciples came to him, and awoke him, saying, Lord, save us: we perish.
And he saith unto them, Why are ye fearful, O ye of little faith? Then he arose, and rebuked the winds and the sea; and there was a great calm.
But the men marvelled, saying, What manner of man is this, that even the winds and the sea obey him!
Bible: Matthew
8:25—27

21 But when Herod's birthday was kept, the daughter of Herodias danced before them, and pleased Herod.
Whereupon he promised with an oath to give her whatsoever she would ask.
And she, being before instructed of her mother, said, Give me John Baptist's head in a charger.
Bible: Matthew
14:6—8

22 And in the fourth watch of the night Jesus went unto them, walking on the sea.
And when the disciples saw him walking on the sea, they were troubled, saying, It is a spirit; and they cried out for fear.
But straightway Jesus spake unto them, saying, Be of good cheer; it is I; be not afraid.
Bible: Matthew
14:25—27

23 And I say also unto thee, That thou art Peter, and upon this rock I will build my church; and the gates of hell shall not prevail against it.
And I will give unto thee the keys of the kingdom of heaven: and whatsoever thou shalt bind on earth shall be bound in heaven: and whatsoever thou shalt loose on earth shall be loosed in heaven.
Bible: Matthew
16:18—19

24 Then said Jesus unto his disciples, If any man will come after me, let him deny himself, and take up his cross, and follow me.
Bible: Matthew
16:24

25 And a very great multitude spread their garments in the way; others cut down branches from the trees, and strawed them in the way.
And the multitudes that went before, and that followed, cried, saying, Hosanna to the Son of David: Blessed is he that cometh in the name of the Lord; Hosanna in the highest.
Bible: Matthew
21:8—9

26 And he answered and said, He that dippeth his hand with me in the dish, the same shall betray me.
The Son of man goeth as it is written of him: but woe unto that man by whom the Son of man is betrayed! it had been good for that man if he had not been born.
Then Judas, which betrayed him, answered and said, Master, is it I? He said unto him, Thou hast said.
Bible: Matthew
26:23—25

27 And as they were eating, Jesus took bread, and blessed it, and brake it, and gave it to the disciples, and said, Take, eat; this is my body.
And he took the cup, and gave thanks, and gave it to them, saying, Drink ye all of it;
For this is my blood of the new testament, which is shed for many for the remission of sins.
Bible: Matthew
26:26—28

28 Jesus said unto him, Verily I say unto thee, That this night, before the cock crow, thou shalt deny me thrice.
Peter said unto him, Though I should die with thee, yet will I not deny thee. Likewise also said all the disciples.
Bible: Matthew
26:34—35

29 And forthwith he came to Jesus, and said, Hail, master; and kissed him.
And Jesus said unto him, Friend, wherefore art thou come? Then came they, and laid hands on Jesus, and took him.
Bible: Matthew
26:49—50

30 Then cried they all again, saying, Not this man, but Barabbas. Now Barabbas was a robber.
Bible: John
18:40

31 Then came Jesus forth, wearing the crown of thorns, and the purple robe. And Pilate saith unto them, Behold the man!
Bible: John
19:5

32 Pilate answered, What I have written I have written.
Bible: John
19:22

33 When Pilate saw that he could prevail nothing, but that rather a tumult was made, he took water, and washed his hands before the multitude, saying, I am innocent of the blood of this just person: see ye to it.
Then answered all the people, and said, His blood be on us, and on our children.
Bible: Matthew
27:24—25

34　And when they were come to the place, which is called Calvary, there they crucified him, and the malefactors, one on the right hand, and the other on the left.
Bible: Luke
23:33

35　Then said Jesus, Father, forgive them; for they know not what they do. And they parted his raiment, and cast lots.
Bible: Luke
23:34

36　When Jesus therefore saw his mother, and the disciple standing by, whom he loved, he saith unto his mother, Woman, behold thy son! Then saith he to the disciple, Behold thy mother! And from that hour that disciple took her unto his own home.
Bible: John
19:26–27

37　And about the ninth hour Jesus cried with a loud voice, saying, Eli, Eli, lama sabachthani? that is to say, My God, my God, why hast thou forsaken me?
Bible: Matthew
27:46

38　When Jesus therefore had received the vinegar, he said, It is finished: and he bowed his head, and gave up the ghost.
Bible: John
19:30

39　Jesus, when he had cried again with a loud voice, yielded up the ghost.
And, behold, the veil of the temple was rent in twain from the top to the bottom; and the earth did quake, and the rocks rent;
And the graves were opened; and many bodies of the saints which slept arose.
Bible: Matthew
27:50–52

40　And when Jesus had cried with a loud voice, he said, Father, into thy hands I commend my spirit: and having said thus, he gave up the ghost.
Bible: Luke
23:46

41　*Consummatum est.*
It is finished.
Bible: John
Vulgate 19:30

42　Then saith he to Thomas, Reach hither thy finger, and behold my hands; and reach hither thy hand, and thrust it into my side: and be not faithless, but believing.
And Thomas answered and said unto him, My Lord and my God.
Bible: John
20:27–28

43　And when he had spoken these things, while they beheld, he was taken up; and a cloud received him out of their sight.
Bible: Acts
1:9

44　And when the day of Pentecost was fully come, they were all with one accord in one place.
And suddenly there came a sound from heaven as of a rushing mighty wind, and it filled all the house where they were sitting.
And there appeared unto them cloven tongues like as of fire, and it sat upon each of them.
And they were all filled with the Holy Ghost, and began to speak with other tongues, as the Spirit gave them utterance.
Bible: Acts
2:1–4

45　And as he journeyed, he came near Damascus: and suddenly there shined round about him a light from heaven:
And he fell to the earth, and heard a voice saying unto him, Saul, Saul, why persecutest thou me?
And he said, Who art thou, Lord? And the Lord said, I am Jesus whom thou persecutest: it is hard for thee to kick against the pricks.
Bible: Acts
9:3–5

46　But Peter took him up, saying, Stand up; I myself also am a man.
Bible: Acts
10:26

47　(For all the Athenians and strangers which were there spent their time in nothing else, but either to tell, or to hear some new thing.)
Then Paul stood in the midst of Mars' hill, and said, Ye men of Athens, I perceive that in all things ye are too superstitious.
For as I passed by, and beheld your devotions, I found an altar with this inscription, TO THE UNKNOWN GOD. Whom therefore ye ignorantly worship, him declare I unto you.
God that made the world and all things therein, seeing that he is Lord of heaven and earth, dwelleth not in temples made with hands.
Bible: Acts
17:21–24

48　And when they heard these sayings, they were full of wrath, and cried out, saying, Great is Diana of the Ephesians.
Bible: Acts
19:28

49　Then Festus, when he had conferred with the council, answered, Hast thou appealed unto Caesar? Unto Caesar shalt thou go.
Bible: Acts
25:12

50　Honour all men. Love the brotherhood. Fear God. Honour the king.
Bible: I Peter
2:17

51　And almost all things are by the law purged with blood; and without shedding of blood is no remission.
Bible: Hebrews
9:22

Attitudes

Daily Life

52 Drink no longer water, but use a little wine for
thy stomach's sake and thine often infirmities.
Bible: I Timothy
5:23

Death

53 Behold, I shew you a mystery; We shall not all
sleep, but we shall all be changed,
In a moment, in the twinkling of an eye, at the
last trump: for the trumpet shall sound, and
the dead shall be raised incorruptible, and
we shall be changed.
For this corruptible must put on incorruption,
and this mortal must put on immortality.
So when this corruptible shall have put on incorruption, and this mortal shall have put on
immortality, then shall be brought to pass
the saying that is written, Death is swallowed
up in victory.
O death, where is thy sting? O grave, where
is thy victory?
Bible: I Corinthians
15:51–55

54 And I looked, and behold a pale horse: and his
name that sat on him was Death, and Hell followed with him. And power was given unto
them over the fourth part of the earth, to kill
with sword, and with hunger, and with death,
and with the beasts of the earth.
Bible: Revelations
6:8

55 And I saw a great white throne, and him that
sat on it, from whose face the earth and the
heaven fled away; and there was found no
place for them.
And I saw the dead, small and great, stand
before God; and the books were opened: and
another book was opened, which is the book
of life: and the dead were judged out of
those things which were written in the books,
according to their works.
And the sea gave up the dead which were in
it; and death and hell delivered up the dead
which were in them: and they were judged
every man according to their works.
Bible: Revelations
20:11–13

Education, Knowledge, and Learning

56 Now as touching things offered unto idols, we
know that we all have knowledge. Knowledge
puffeth up, but charity edifieth.
Bible: I Corinthians
8:1

Human Nature

57 Judge not, that ye be not judged.
Bible: Matthew
7:1

58 Neither do men put new wine into old bottles:
else the bottles break, and the wine runneth
out, and the bottles perish: but they put new
wine into new bottles, and both are
preserved.
Bible: Matthew
9:17

59 Watch and pray, that ye enter not into temptation: the spirit indeed is willing, but the flesh
is weak.
Bible: Matthew
26:41

60 Greater love hath no man than this, that a man
lay down his life for his friends.
Bible: John
15:13

61 For ye suffer fools gladly, seeing ye yourselves
are wise.
Bible: II Corinthians
11:19

62 Beware lest any man spoil you through philosophy and vain deceit, after the tradition of
men, after the rudiments of the world, and not
after Christ.
Bible: Colossians
2:8

63 If we say that we have no sin, we deceive ourselves, and the truth is not in us.
If we confess our sins, he is faithful and just
to forgive us our sins, and to cleanse us
from all unrighteousness.
Bible: I John
1:8–9

64 Grudge not one against another, brethren, lest
ye be condemned: behold, the judge standeth
before the door.
Bible: James
5:9

Life

65 But many that are first shall be last; and the
last shall be first.
Bible: Matthew
19:30

66 What? know ye not that your body is the temple of the Holy Ghost which is in you, which
ye have of God, and ye are not your own?
Bible: I Corinthians
6:19

67 And they that use this world, as not abusing it:
for the fashion of this world passeth away.
Bible: I Corinthians
7:31

68 For the earth is the Lord's, and the fulness
thereof.
Bible: I Corinthians
10:26

69 For we walk by faith, not by sight.
Bible: II Corinthians
5:7

70 Be not deceived: God is not mocked: for whatsoever a man soweth, that shall he also reap. For he that soweth to his flesh shall of the flesh reap corruption; but he that soweth to the Spirit shall of the Spirit reap life everlasting.
And let us not be weary in well doing: for in due season we shall reap, if we faint not.
Bible: Galatians
6:7–9

71 For we brought nothing into this world, and it is certain we carry nothing out.
Bible: I Timothy
6:7

Love and Sex

72 Beloved, let us love one another: for love is of God; and every one that loveth is born of God, and knoweth God.
He that loveth not knoweth not God; for God is love.
Bible: I John
4:7–8

Marriage and the Family

73 Wherefore they are no more twain, but one flesh. What therefore God hath joined together, let not man put asunder.
Bible: Matthew
19:6

74 But if they cannot contain, let them marry: for it is better to marry than to burn.
Bible: I Corinthians
7:9

75 Children, obey your parents in the Lord: for this is right.
Bible: Ephesians
6:1

Men and Women

76 A woman when she is in travail hath sorrow, because her hour is come: but as soon as she is delivered of the child, she remembereth no more the anguish, for joy that a man is born into the world.
Bible: John
16:21

77 Even as Sara obeyed Abraham, calling him lord: whose daughters ye are, as long as ye do well, and are not afraid with any amazement. Likewise, ye husbands, dwell with them according to knowledge, giving honour unto the wife, as unto the weaker vessel, and as being heirs together of the grace of life; that your prayers be not hindered.
Bible: I Peter
3:6–7

Morality, Vices, and Virtues

78 Then was Jesus led up of the Spirit into the wilderness to be tempted of the devil.
And when he had fasted forty days and forty nights, he was afterward an hungred.
And when the tempter came to him, he said, If thou be the Son of God, command that these stones be made bread.
But he answered and said, It is written, Man shall not live by bread alone, but by every word that proceedeth out of the mouth of God.
Bible: Matthew
4:1–4

79 Blessed are the poor in spirit: for theirs is the kingdom of heaven.
Blessed are they that mourn: for they shall be comforted.
Blessed are the meek: for they shall inherit the earth.
Blessed are they which do hunger and thirst after righteousness: for they shall be filled.
Blessed are the merciful: for they shall obtain mercy.
Blessed are the pure in heart: for they shall see God.
Blessed are the peacemakers: for they shall be called the children of God.
Blessed are they which are persecuted for righteousness' sake: for theirs is the kingdom of heaven.
Bible: Matthew
5:3–10

80 Blessed are the meek: for they shall inherit the earth.
Bible: Matthew
5:5

81 Ye are the salt of the earth: but if the salt have lost his savour, wherewith shall it be salted? it is thenceforth good for nothing, but to be cast out, and to be trodden under foot of men. Ye are the light of the world. A city that is set on an hill cannot be hid.
Neither do men light a candle, and put it under a bushel, but on a candlestick; and it giveth light unto all that are in the house. Let your light so shine before men, that they may see your good works, and glorify your Father which is in heaven.
Bible: Matthew
5:13–16

82 And if thy right eye offend thee, pluck it out, and cast it from thee: for it is profitable for thee that one of thy members should perish, and not that thy whole body should be cast into hell.
Bible: Matthew
5:29

83 But I say unto you, That ye resist not evil: but whosoever shall smite thee on thy right cheek, turn to him the other also.
And if any man will sue thee at the law, and take away thy coat, let him have thy cloke also.

And whosoever shall compel thee to go a
mile, go with him twain.
Bible: Matthew
5:39–41

84 But I say unto you, Love your enemies, bless
them that curse you, do good to them that
hate you, and pray for them which despitefully
use you, and persecute you;
That ye may be the children of your Father
which is in heaven: for he maketh his sun to
rise on the evil and on the good, and
sendeth rain on the just and on the unjust.
For if ye love them which love you, what reward have ye? do not even the publicans
the same?
Bible: Matthew
5:44–46

85 Lay not up for yourselves treasures upon earth,
where moth and rust doth corrupt, and where
thieves break through and steal:
But lay up for yourselves treasures in heaven,
where neither moth nor rust doth corrupt,
and where thieves do not break through nor
steal:
For where your treasure is, there will your
heart be also.
Bible: Matthew
6:19–21

86 Behold the fowls of the air: for they sow not,
neither do they reap, nor gather into barns; yet
your heavenly Father feedeth them. Are ye
not much better than they?
Which of you by taking thought can add one
cubit unto his stature?
And why take ye thought for raiment? Consider the lilies of the field, how they grow;
they toil not, neither do they spin:
And yet I say unto you, That even Solomon in
all his glory was not arrayed like one of
these.
Wherefore, if God so clothe the grass of the
field, which today is, and tomorrow is cast into
the oven, shall he not much more clothe you,
O ye of little faith?
Therefore take no thought, saying, What shall
we eat? or, What shall we drink? or, Where-
withal shall we be clothed?
Bible: Matthew
6:26–31

87 But seek ye first the kingdom of God, and his
righteousness; and all these things shall be
added unto you.
Take therefore no thought for the morrow: for
the morrow shall take thought for the things
of itself. Sufficient unto the day is the evil
thereof.
Bible: Matthew
6:33–34

88 And why beholdest thou the mote that is in thy
brother's eye, but considerest not the beam
that is in thine own eye?
Bible: Matthew
7:3

89 Give not that which is holy unto the dogs,
neither cast ye your pearls before swine, lest

they trample them under their feet, and turn
again and rend you.
Bible: Matthew
7:6

90 Then came Peter to him, and said, Lord, how
oft shall my brother sin against me, and I forgive him? till seven times?
Jesus saith unto him, I say not unto thee, Until seven times: but, Until seventy times
seven.
Bible: Matthew
18:21–22

91 Then said Jesus unto his disciples, Verily I say
unto you, That a rich man shall hardly enter
into the kingdom of heaven.
And again I say unto you, It is easier for a
camel to go through the eye of a needle, than
for a rich man to enter into the kingdom of
God.
Bible: Matthew
19:23–24

92 Woe unto you, scribes and Pharisees, hypo-
crites! for ye are like unto whited sepulchres,
which indeed appear beautiful outward, but are
within full of dead men's bones, and of all
uncleanness.
Bible: Matthew
23:27

93 For what shall it profit a man, if he shall gain
the whole world, and lose his own soul? Or
what shall a man give in exchange for his soul?
Bible: Mark
8:36–37

94 So when they continued asking him, he lifted
up himself, and said unto them, He that is without sin among you, let him first cast a stone
at her.
Bible: John
8:7

95 Though I speak with the tongues of men and of
angels, and have not charity, I am become as
sounding brass, or a tinkling cymbal.
And though I have the gift of prophecy, and
understand all mysteries, and all knowledge; and though I have all faith, so that I
could remove mountains, and have not charity, I am nothing.
And though I bestow all my goods to feed the
poor, and though I give my body to be
burned, and have not charity, it profiteth me
nothing.
Charity suffereth long, and is kind; charity en-
vieth not; charity vaunteth not itself, is not
puffed up,
Doth not behave itself unseemly, seeketh not
her own, is not easily provoked, thinketh no
evil;
Rejoiceth not in iniquity, but rejoiceth in the
truth;
Beareth all things, believeth all things, hopeth
all things, endureth all things.
Charity never faileth: but whether there be
prophecies, they shall fail; whether there be
tongues, they shall cease; whether there
be knowledge, it shall vanish away.
For we know in part, and we prophesy in part.

But when that which is perfect is come, then
that which is in part shall be done away.
When I was a child, I spake as a child, I understood as a child, I thought as a child: but
when I became a man, I put away childish
things.
For now we see through a glass, darkly; but
then face to face: now I know in part; but
then shall I know even as also I am known.
And now abideth faith, hope, charity, these
three; but the greatest of these is charity.
Bible: I Corinthians
13:1–13

96   Wherefore putting away lying, speak every man
truth with his neighbour: for we are members
one of another.
Be ye angry, and sin not: let not the sun go
down upon your wrath:
Neither give place to the devil.
Let him that stole steal no more: but rather let
him labour, working with his hands the thing
which is good, that he may have to give to
him that needeth.
Bible: Ephesians
4:25–28

97   For the love of money is the root of all evil:
which while some coveted after, they have
erred from the faith, and pierced themselves
through with many sorrows.
Bible: I Timothy
6:10

98   Let brotherly love continue.
Be not forgetful to entertain strangers: for
thereby some have entertained angels
unawares.
Bible: Hebrews
13:1–2

99   Submit yourselves therefore to God. Resist the
devil, and he will flee from you.
Draw nigh to God, and he will draw nigh to
you. Cleanse your hands, ye sinners; and purify your hearts, ye double minded.
Bible: James
4:7–8

100   And the woman was arrayed in purple and scarlet colour, and decked with gold and precious
stones and pearls, having a golden cup in
her hand full of abominations and filthiness of
her fornication:
And upon her forehead was a name written,
MYSTERY, BABYLON THE GREAT, THE
MOTHER OF HARLOTS AND ABOMINA-
TIONS OF THE EARTH.
And I saw the woman drunken with the blood
of the saints, and with the blood of the martyrs of Jesus: and when I saw her, I wondered with great admiration.
Bible: Revelations
17:4–6

Religion

101   For I say unto you, That except your righteousness shall exceed the righteousness of the
scribes and Pharisees, ye shall in no case
enter into the kingdom of heaven.
Bible: Matthew
5:20

102   But when ye pray, use not vain repetitions, as
the heathen do: for they think that they shall
be heard for their much speaking.
Be not ye therefore like unto them: for your
Father knoweth what things ye have need
of, before ye ask him.
After this manner therefore pray ye: Our Father which art in heaven, Hallowed be thy
name.
Thy kingdom come. Thy will be done in earth,
as it is in heaven.
Give us this day our daily bread.
And forgive us our debts, as we forgive our
debtors.
And lead us not into temptation, but deliver
us from evil: For thine is the kingdom, and the
power, and the glory, for ever. Amen.
Bible: Matthew
6:7–13

103   Jesus said unto him, Thou shalt love the Lord
thy God with all thy heart, and with all thy
soul, and with all thy mind.
This is the first and great commandment.
And the second is like unto it, Thou shalt love
thy neighbour as thyself.
On these two commandments hang all the
law and the prophets.
Bible: Matthew
22:37–40

104   Verily I say unto you, Except ye be converted,
and become as little children, ye shall not
enter into the kingdom of heaven.
Bible: Matthew
18:3

105   Heaven and earth shall pass away, but my
words shall not pass away.
Bible: Matthew
24:35

106   He hath shewed strength with his arm; he hath
scattered the proud in the imagination of their
hearts.
He hath put down the mighty from their seats,
and exalted them of low degree.
He hath filled the hungry with good things;
and the rich he hath sent empty away.
Bible: Luke
1:51–53

107   For God so loved the world, that he gave his
only begotten Son, that whosoever believeth in
him should not perish, but have everlasting
life.
Bible: John
3:16

108   And this is the condemnation, that light is come
into the world, and men loved darkness rather
than light, because their deeds were evil.
Bible: John
3:19

109   And Jesus said unto them, I am the bread of
life: he that cometh to me shall never hunger;

and he that believeth on me shall never
thirst.
Bible: John
6:35

110 Then spake Jesus again unto them, saying, I
am the light of the world: he that followeth me
shall not walk in darkness, but shall have the
light of life.
Bible: John
8:12

111 I am the door: by me if any man enter in, he
shall be saved, and shall go in and out, and find
pasture.
Bible: John
10:9

112 I am the good shepherd: the good shepherd
giveth his life for the sheep.
Bible: John
10:11

113 Jesus said unto her, I am the resurrection, and
the life: he that believeth in me, though he
were dead, yet shall he live.
Bible: John
11:25

114 In my Father's house are many mansions: if it
were not so, I would have told you. I go to
prepare a place for you.
Bible: John
14:2

115 Jesus saith unto him, I am the way, the truth,
and the life: no man cometh unto the Father,
but by me.
Bible: John
14:6

116 And said unto them, It is written, My house
shall be called the house of prayer; but ye have
made it a den of thieves.
Bible: Matthew
21:13

117 And he saith unto them, Whose is this image
and superscription?
They say unto him, Caesar's. Then saith he
unto them, Render therefore unto Caesar the
things which are Caesar's; and unto God
the things that are God's.
Bible: Matthew
22:20−21

118 For the kingdom of God is not in word, but in
power.
Bible: I Corinthians
4:20

119 Now faith is the substance of things hoped for,
the evidence of things not seen.
Bible: Hebrews
11:1

120 Behold, he cometh with clouds; and every eye
shall see him, and they also which pierced
him: and all kindreds of the earth shall wail because of him. Even so, Amen.
I am Alpha and Omega, the beginning and the
ending, saith the Lord, which is, and which
was, and which is to come, the Almighty.
I John, who also am your brother, and companion in tribulation, and in the kingdom
and patience of Jesus Christ, was in the isle
that is called Patmos, for the word of God,
and for the testimony of Jesus Christ.
Bible: Revelations
1:7−9

121 And I saw in the right hand of him that sat on
the throne a book written within and on the
backside, sealed with seven seals.
And I saw a strong angel proclaiming with a
loud voice, Who is worthy to open the book,
and to loose the seals thereof?
Bible: Revelations
5:1−2

122 And I beheld, and, lo, in the midst of the throne
and of the four beasts, and in the midst of the
elders, stood a Lamb as it had been slain,
having seven horns and seven eyes, which are
the seven Spirits of God sent forth into all the
earth.
Bible: Revelations
5:6

123 And he hath on his vesture and on his thigh a
name written, KING OF KINGS, AND LORD
OF LORDS.
Bible: Revelations
19:16

124 And I saw a new heaven and a new earth: for
the first heaven and the first earth were
passed away; and there was no more sea.
And I John saw the holy city, new Jerusalem,
coming down from God out of heaven, prepared as a bride adorned for her husband.
And I heard a great voice out of heaven saying, Behold, the tabernacle of God is with
men, and he will dwell with them, and they
shall be his people, and God himself shall be
with them, and be their God.
And God shall wipe away all tears from their
eyes; and there shall be no more death,
neither sorrow, nor crying, neither shall there
be any more pain: for the former things are
passed away.
And he that sat upon the throne said, Behold,
I make all things new. And he said unto me,
Write: for these words are true and faithful.
Bible: Revelations
21:1−5

Work and Occupations

125 Woe unto you, lawyers! for ye have taken away
the key of knowledge: ye entered not in yourselves, and them that were entering in ye
hindered.
Bible: Luke
11:52

126 For even when we were with you, this we commanded you, that if any would not work,
neither should he eat.
Bible: II Thessalonians
3:10

127 This is a true saying, If a man desire the office
of a bishop, he desireth a good work.
A bishop then must be blameless, the hus-

band of one wife, vigilant, sober, of good behaviour, given to hospitality, apt to teach;
Not given to wine, no striker, not greedy of
filthy lucre; but patient, not a brawler, not
covetous.
Bible: I Timothy
3:1–3

Sayings of the Time

128 *Quo vadis*?
Whither goest thou?
Bible: John
Vulgate 16:5

129 Ask, and it shall be given you; seek, and ye
shall find; knock, and it shall be opened unto
you:
For every one that asketh receiveth; and he
that seeketh findeth; and to him that knocketh
it shall be opened.
Bible: Matthew
7:7–8

130 Enter ye in at the strait gate: for wide is the
gate, and broad is the way, that leadeth to destruction, and many there be which go in
thereat:
Because strait is the gate, and narrow is the
way, which leadeth unto life, and few there
be that find it.
Bible: Matthew
7:13–14

131 He that hath ears to hear, let him hear.
Bible: Matthew
11:15

132 And immediately Jesus stretched forth his
hand, and caught him, and said unto him, O
thou of little faith, wherefore didst thou doubt?
Bible: Matthew
14:31

133 Then said Jesus unto him, Put up again thy
sword into his place: for all they that take the
sword shall perish with the sword.
Bible: Matthew
26:52

134 And he asked him, What is thy name? And he
answered, saying. My name is Legion: for we
are many.
Bible: Mark
5:9

135 And that no man might buy or sell, save he that
had the mark, or the name of the beast, or the
number of his name.
Here is wisdom. Let him that hath understanding count the number of the beast: for it
is the number of a man; and his number is
Six hundred threescore and six.
Bible: Revelations
13:17–18

With Hindsight

136 It was just one of those parties which got out of
hand.
Lenny Bruce (1925–66) US comedian.
Referring to the Crucifixion
The Guardian, 10 May 1979

4

The Roman World (50 BC–399 AD)

Julius Caesar completed his conquest of Gaul in 50 BC; a year later, refusing to resign his command, he initiated the Roman Civil War. The conflicts of the following years ended with the decisive victory of Caesar's great-nephew Augustus over Mark Antony at the battle of Actium (31 BC). Augustus nominally restored the republic, but, by ensuring that he held enough key positions for his authority to be unquestioned, he came to be regarded as the first emperor of Rome.

This empire – within roughly the boundaries Augustus had established – endured for 400 years. During its evolution the image of the empire changed: from a city-state on the Tiber that had subjugated the peoples of the Mediterranean, it became a state that encompassed the known world. Distinctions between Roman citizens and subject peoples were removed, so that by 330 AD, the capital itself was able to move from Rome to Constantinople. The office of emperor itself changed over the years. Initially, Augustus was merely the first citizen of the state; by the time of Diocletian (reigned 284–305), who restored the empire after anarchy in the 3rd century, the emperor had acquired not only monarchical but also divine attributes. With the adoption of Christianity – personally by Constantine (reigned 312–337) and as the sole religion of the empire by Theodosius (in 391) – the emperor became God's representative on earth. Rome bequeathed to the Middle Ages the concept of a universal empire coterminous with Christendom, ruled by an emperor whose power derived directly from God.

In fact, the empire had passed its prime by 200 AD. Wealth declined and pressure on its frontiers from tribal peoples increased. As it evolved into a world state, it was found to be too large to administer effectively. Diocletian and his successors experimented with dividing it into two parts, each with its own emperor. After the death of Theodosius (395), this division became permanent. The Eastern Empire continued, with varying degrees of success, for another thousand years; but the Western – poorer and with longer frontiers – soon succumbed to barbarian invasions.

Politics, Government, and World Events

1st century BC

1 **The good of the people is the chief law.**
Cicero (106–43 BC) Roman orator and
statesman.
De Legibus, III

2 **Necessity knows no law.**
Publilius Syrus (1st century BC) Roman
dramatist.
Attrib.

49 BC

3 *Alea jacta est.*
The die is cast.
Julius Caesar (100–44 BC) Roman general
and statesman.
Said on crossing the River Rubicon, N Italy (49
BC), at the start of the civil war against Pompey
Attrib.

47 BC

4 *Veni, vidi, vici.*
I came, I saw, I conquered.
Julius Caesar
Referring to his campaign against Pharnaces,
King of the Cimmerian Bosporus
The Twelve Caesars (Suetonius)

44 BC

5 **Beware the ides of March.**
William Shakespeare (1564–1616) English
dramatist.
Julius Caesar, I:2 (1599)

6 *Et tu, Brute?*
You too, Brutus?
William Shakespeare
Said by Julius Caesar
Julius Caesar, III:1 (1599)

7 **Friends, Romans, countrymen, lend me your
ears
I come to bury Caesar, not to praise him.
The evil that men do lives after them;
The good is oft interred with their bones.**
William Shakespeare
Said by Mark Antony
Julius Caesar, III:2 (1599)

8 **His life was gentle; and the elements
So mix'd in him that Nature might stand up
And say to all the world 'This was a man!'**
William Shakespeare
Referring to Brutus
Julius Caesar, V:5 (1599)

9 **This was the noblest Roman of them all.
All the conspirators save only he
Did that they did in envy of great Caesar.**
William Shakespeare
Julius Caesar, V:5 (1599)

30 BC

10 **Dost thou not see my baby at my breast
That sucks the nurse asleep?**
William Shakespeare
Said by Cleopatra, holding the asp to her breast
Antony and Cleopatra, V:2 (1607)

23 BC

11 **Force, if unassisted by judgement, collapses
through its own mass.**
Horace (Quintus Horatius Flaccus; 65–8 BC)
Roman poet.
Odes, III

12 **What do the ravages of time not injure? Our
parents' age (worse than our grandparents')
has produced us, more worthless still, who will
soon give rise to a yet more vicious
generation.**
Horace
Odes, III

13 *Dulce et decorum est pro patria mori.*
**It is a sweet and seemly thing to die for one's
country.**
Horace
Odes, III

14 **Undeservedly you will atone for the sins of your
fathers.**
Horace (Quintus Horatius Flaccus; 65–8 BC)
Roman poet.
Odes, III

20 BC

15 *Nullius addictus iurare in verba magistri,
Quo me cumque rapit tempestas, deferor
hospes.*
**Not bound to swear allegiance to any master,
wherever the wind takes me I travel as a
visitor.**
Horace
Nullius in verba is the motto of the Royal
Society
Epistles, I

19 BC

16 **Maybe one day we shall be glad to remember
even these hardships.**
Virgil (Publius Vergilius Maro; 70–19 BC) Roman poet.
Aeneid, Bk. I

2 BC

17 **He sometimes forgets that he is Caesar, but I
always remember that I am Caesar's
daughter.**
Julia (39 BC–AD 14) Daughter of Augustus.
Replying to suggestions that she should live in
the simple style of her father, which contrasted
with her own extravagance
Saturnalia (Macrobius)

1st century AD

18   *Ave Caesar, morituri te salutant.*
Hail Caesar; those who are about to die salute you.
Anonymous
Greeting to the Roman Emperor by gladiators

40 AD

19* Would that the Roman people had but one neck!
Caligula (Gaius Caesar; 12—41 AD) Roman emperor.
Life of Caligula (Suetonius), Ch. 30

79 AD

20   Dear me, I believe I am becoming a god. An emperor ought at least to die on his feet.
Vespasian (9—79 AD) Roman emperor.
Lives of the Caesars (Suetonius)

84 AD

21   They make a wilderness and call it peace.
Tacitus (c. 55—c. 120 AD) Roman historian.
Agricola, 30

100 AD

22   I will have this done, so I order it done; let my will replace reasoned judgement.
Juvenal (Decimus Junius Juvenalis; 60—130 AD) Roman satirist.
Satires, VI

23   *Quis custodiet ipsos custodes?*
Who is to guard the guards themselves?
Juvenal
Satires, VI

24   The people long eagerly for just two things — bread and circuses.
Juvenal
Satires, X

2nd century AD

25   Remember that to change your mind and follow him who sets you right is to be none the less free than you were before.
Marcus Aurelius (121—180 AD) Roman emperor.
Meditations, Bk. VIII, Ch. 16

4th century AD

26   Let him who desires peace, prepare for war.
Vegetius (Flavius Vegetius Renatus; 4th century AD) Roman writer.
Epitoma Rei Militaris, 3, 'Prologue'

Attitudes

Art, Literature, and Music

23 BC

27   And if you include me among the lyric poets, I'll hold my head so high it'll strike the stars.
Horace (Quintus Horatius Flaccus; 65—8 BC) Roman poet.
Odes, I

8 BC

28   If you believe Cratinus from days of old, Maecenas, (as you must know) no verse can give pleasure for long, nor last, that is written by drinkers of water.
Horace
Epistles, I

29   I'm aggrieved when sometimes even excellent Homer nods.
Horace
Ars Poetica

30   Not gods, nor men, nor even booksellers have put up with poets' being second-rate.
Horace
Ars Poetica

31   Many terms which have now dropped out of favour, will be revived, and those that are at present respectable will drop out, if usage so choose, with whom resides the decision and the judgement and the code of speech.
Horace
Ars Poetica

32   You will have written exceptionally well if, by skilful arrangement of your words, you have made an ordinary one seem original.
Horace
Ars Poetica

33   'Painters and poets alike have always had licence to dare anything.' We know that, and we both claim and allow to others in their turn this indulgence.
Horace
Ars Poetica

2nd century AD

34   Many suffer from the incurable disease of writing, and it becomes chronic in their sick minds.
Juvenal (Decimus Junius Juvenalis; 60—130 AD) Roman satirist.
Satires, VII

270 AD

35   It is bad enough to be condemned to drag around this image in which nature has impris-

oned me. Why should I consent to the perpetuation of the image of this image?
Plotinus (205–270 AD) Egyptian-born Greek philosopher.
Refusing to have his portrait painted
Attrib.

Daily Life

36 *In vino veritas.*
Truth comes out in wine.
Pliny the Elder (Gaius Plinius Secundus; 23–79 AD) Roman scholar.
Natural History, XIV

Death

23 BC

37 Pale Death kicks his way equally into the cottages of the poor and the castles of kings.
Horace (Quintus Horatius Flaccus; 65–8 BC) Roman poet.
Odes, I

1st century AD

38 He's gone to join the majority.
Petronius Arbiter (1st century AD) Roman satirist.
Referring to a dead man
Satyricon: Cena Trimalchionis, 42

Education, Knowledge, and Learning

161 BC

39 Nothing has yet been said that's not been said before.
Terence (Publius Terentius Afer; c. 190–159 BC) Roman poet.
Eunuchus, Prologue

20 BC

40 And seek for truth in the groves of Academe.
Horace (Quintus Horatius Flaccus; 65–8 BC) Roman poet.
Epistles, II

History

1st century BC

41 History is philosophy teaching by examples.
Dionysius of Halicarnassus (40–8 BC) Greek historian.
Ars rhetorica, XI:2

150 AD

42 All things from eternity are of like forms and come round in a circle.
Marcus Aurelius (121–180 AD) Roman emperor.
Meditations, Bk. II, Ch. 14

Human Nature

2nd century BC

43 I am a man, I count nothing human foreign to me.
Terence (Publius Terentius Afer; c. 190–159 BC) Roman poet.
Heauton Timorumenos

44 So many men, so many opinions.
Terence
Phormio

1st century BC

45 What is food to one man is bitter poison to others.
Lucretius (Titus Lucretius Carus; c. 99–55 BC) Roman philosopher.
On the Nature of the Universe, IV

43 BC

46 To like and dislike the same things, that is indeed true friendship.
Sallust (Gaius Sallustius Crispus; c. 86–c. 34 BC) Roman historian and politician.
Bellum Catilinae

37 BC

47 Everyone is dragged on by their favourite pleasure.
Virgil (Publius Vergilius Maro; 70–19 BC) Roman poet.
Eclogue, Bk. II

20 BC

48 To marvel at nothing is just about the one and only thing, Numicius, that can make a man happy and keep him that way.
Horace (Quintus Horatius Flaccus; 65–8 BC) Roman poet.
Epistles, I

49 You may drive out nature with a pitchfork, yet she'll be constantly running back.
Horace
Epistles, I

13 BC

50 Not the owner of many possessions will you be right to call happy: he more rightly deserves the name of happy who knows how to use the gods' gifts wisely and to put up with rough

poverty, and who fears dishonour more than death.
Horace
Odes, IV

1st century AD

51 Love of fame is the last thing even learned men can bear to be parted from.
Tacitus (c. 55–c. 120 AD) Roman historian.
Histories, IV, 6

---

98 AD

52 It is part of human nature to hate the man you have hurt.
Tacitus (c. 55–c. 120 AD) Roman historian.
Agricola, 42

2nd century AD

53 If you hear that someone is speaking ill of you, instead of trying to defend yourself you should say: 'He obviously does not know me very well, since there are so many other faults he could have mentioned'.
Epictetus (c. 60–110 AD) Stoic philosopher.
Enchiridion

54 Whatever this is that I am, it is a little flesh and breath, and the ruling part.
Marcus Aurelius (121–180 AD) Roman emperor.
Meditations, Bk. II, Ch. 2

Humour

1st century AD

55 It's hard not to write satire.
Juvenal (Decimus Junius Juvenalis; 60–130 AD) Roman satirist.
Satires, I

Life

3rd century BC

56 Each man the architect of his own fate.
Appius Caecus (4th–3rd century BC) Roman statesman.
De Civitate (Sallust), Bk. I

1st century BC

57 Constant dripping hollows out a stone.
Lucretius (Titus Lucretius Carus; c. 99–55 BC) Roman philosopher.
On the Nature of the Universe, I.

58 *Inque brevi spatio mutantur saecla animantum*

Et quasi cursores vitai lampada tradunt.
The generations of living things pass in a short time, and like runners hand on the torch of life.
Lucretius
On the Nature of the Universe, II

---

29 BC

59 But meanwhile it is flying, irretrievable time is flying.
Virgil (Publius Vergilius Maro; 70–19 BC) Roman poet.
Georgics, Bk. III

---

23 BC

60 Believe each day that has dawned is your last.
Horace (Quintus Horatius Flaccus; 65–8 BC) Roman poet.
Epistles, I

61 We are just statistics, born to consume resources.
Horace
Epistles, I

62 Drop the question what tomorrow may bring, and count as profit every day that Fate allows you.
Horace
Odes, I

63 *Carpe diem.*
Seize the day.
Horace
Odes, I

64 Life's short span forbids us to enter on far-reaching hopes.
Horace
Odes, I

1st century AD

65 Woe to the vanquished.
Livy (Titus Livius; 59 BC–17 AD) Roman historian.
History, V:48

---

77 AD

66 There is always something new out of Africa.
Pliny the Elder (Gaius Plinius Secundus; 23–79 AD) Roman scholar.
Natural History, VIII

---

100 AD

67 *Orandum est ut sit mens sana in corpore sano.*
Your prayer must be for a sound mind in a sound body.
Juvenal (Decimus Junius Juvenalis; 60–130 AD) Roman satirist.
Satires, X

2nd century AD

68 And thou wilt give thyself relief, if thou doest every act of thy life as if it were the last.
Marcus Aurelius (121 – 180 AD) Roman emperor.
Meditations, Bk. II, Ch. 5

69 The universe is transformation; our life is what our thoughts make it.
Marcus Aurelius
Meditations, Bk. IV, Ch. 3

70 Everything that happens happens as it should, and if you observe carefully, you will find this to be so.
Marcus Aurelius
Meditations, Bk. IV, Ch. 10

71 Time is like a river made up of the events which happen, and its current is strong; no sooner does anything appear than it is swept away, and another comes in its place, and will be swept away too.
Marcus Aurelius
Meditations, Bk. IV, Ch. 43

72 Nothing happens to any man that he is not formed by nature to bear.
Marcus Aurelius
Meditations, Bk. V, Ch. 18

73 Whatever may happen to you was prepared for you from all eternity; and the implication of causes was from eternity spinning the thread of your being.
Marcus Aurelius
Meditations, Bk. X, Ch. 5

Love and Sex

37 BC

74 Love conquers all things: let us too give in to Love.
Virgil (Publius Vergilius Maro; 70 – 19 BC) Roman poet.
Eclogue, Bk. X

23 BC

75 My life with girls has ended, though till lately I was up to it and soldiered on not ingloriously; now on this wall will hang my weapons and my lyre, discharged from the war.
Horace (Quintus Horatius Flaccus; 65 – 8 BC) Roman poet.
Odes, III

Marriage and the Family

65 AD

76 I have a wife, I have sons: all of them hostages given to fate.
Lucan (Marcus Annaeus Lucanus; 39 – 65 AD) Roman poet.
Works, VII

Men and Women

19 BC

77 Woman is always fickle and changing.
Virgil (Publius Vergilius Maro; 70 – 19 BC) Roman poet.
Aeneid, Bk. IV

1st century AD

78 No one delights more in vengeance than a woman.
Juvenal (Decimus Junius Juvenalis; 60 – 130 AD) Roman satirist.
Satires, XIII

8 AD

79 Whether a pretty woman grants or withholds her favours, she always likes to be asked for them.
Ovid (Publius Ovidius Naso; 43 BC – 17 AD) Roman poet.
Ars Amatoria

Morality, Vices, and Virtues

1st century BC

80 He gives twice who gives promptly.
Publilius Syrus (1st century BC) Roman dramatist.
Attrib.

19 BC

81 What do you not drive human hearts into, cursed craving for gold!
Virgil (Publius Vergilius Maro; 70 – 19 BC) Roman poet.
Aeneid, Bk. III

8 BC

82 To save a man's life against his will is the same as killing him.
Horace (Quintus Horatius Flaccus; 65 – 8 BC) Roman poet.
Ars Poetica

1st century AD

83 Live among men as if God beheld you; speak to God as if men were listening.
Seneca (c. 4 BC – 65 AD) Roman author.
Epistles

3rd century AD

84 Give me chastity and continence, but not yet.
St Augustine of Hippo (354 – 430) Bishop of Hippo.
Confessions, Bk. VIII, Ch. 7

85 We make ourselves a ladder out of our vices if
we trample the vices themselves underfoot.
St Augustine of Hippo
Sermons, Bk. III, 'De Ascensione'

Religion

23 BC

86 Do not try to find out — we're forbidden to
know — what end the gods have in store for
me, or for you.
Horace (Quintus Horatius Flaccus; 65–8 BC)
Roman poet.
Odes, I

2nd century AD

87 I believe because it is impossible.
Tertullian (c. 160–225 AD) Carthaginian father
of the church.
The usual misquotation of 'It is certain because it
is impossible.'
De Carne Christi, V

88 See how these Christians love one another.
Tertullian
Apologeticum, XXXIX

89 The blood of the martyrs is the seed of the
Church.
Tertullian
Traditional misquotation: more accurately, 'Our
numbers increase as often as you cut us down:
the blood of Christians is the seed.'
Apologeticum, L

5th century AD

90 There is no salvation outside the church.
St Augustine of Hippo (354–430) Bishop
of Hippo.
De Bapt., IV

Wealth and Poverty

1st century BC

91 If possible honestly, if not, somehow, make
money.
Horace (Quintus Horatius Flaccus; 65–8 BC)
Roman poet.
Epistles, I

23 BC

92 Hard to train to accept being poor.
Horace
Odes, I

1st century AD

93 The misfortunes of poverty carry with them

nothing harder to bear than that it exposes men
to ridicule.
Juvenal (Decimus Junius Juvenalis; 60–130
AD) Roman satirist.
Satires, III

94 It's not easy for people to rise out of obscurity
when they have to face straitened circumstances at home.
Juvenal
Satires, III

Work and Occupations

1st century BC

95 There is nothing so absurd but some philosopher has said it.
Cicero (106–43 BC) Roman orator and
statesman.
De Divinatione, II

Sayings of the Time

1st century BC

96 *Atque in perpetuum, frater, ave atque vale.*
And for ever, brother, hail and farewell!
Catullus (c. 84–c. 54 BC) Roman poet.
Carmina, CI

With Hindsight

17th century

97 Had Cleopatra's nose been shorter, the whole
face of the world would have changed.
Blaise Pascal (1623–62) French philosopher
and mathematician.
Pensées, II

18th century

98 When the British warrior queen,
Bleeding from the Roman rods,
Sought, with an indignant mien,
Counsel of her country's gods.
William Cowper (1731–1800) British poet.
Boadicea

99 The various modes of worship, which prevailed
in the Roman world, were all considered by
the people as equally true; by the philosopher,
as equally false; and by the magistrate, as
equally useful. And thus toleration produced
not only mutual indulgence, but even religious
concord.
Edward Gibbon (1737–94) British historian.
Decline and Fall of the Roman Empire, Ch. 2

19th century

100 'How different, how very different from the home life of our own dear Queen!'
Anonymous
Remark by Victorian lady about the character of Cleopatra as performed by Sarah Bernhardt

101 **A man of great common sense and good taste, — meaning thereby a man without originality or moral courage.**
George Bernard Shaw (1856–1950) Irish dramatist and critic.
Referring to Julius Caesar
Caesar and Cleopatra, Notes

20th century

102 **The Roman Conquest was, however, a *Good Thing*, since the Britons were only natives at the time.**
W. C. Sellar (1898–1951) British humorous writer.
1066 And All That

5

The Earlier Middle Ages (400–1099)

The division of the Roman Empire in 395 effectively sounded the death knell for the Western Empire. Soon Germanic tribes were settling freely in imperial territory, and Rome itself was sacked in 410; in 476 the last emperor was deposed. However, the idea of the empire persisted. The Germans had not wanted to destroy it; rather, they had wished to settle in it and participate in its superior civilization. Christianity, the religion of the empire, was adopted by successive waves of invaders; and the universal, if conveniently remote, sovereignty of the Eastern Emperor in Constantinople was acknowledged. In 800, after Charlemagne had built up the greatest of the Germanic kingdoms, the pope crowned him as emperor — the beginning of what later became known as the Holy Roman Empire.

In a wider perspective, these successor states in the west were crude barbarian kingdoms. Always there was the threat not only of further invasions from outside, but also of political anarchy. Not until the 11th century were the beginnings of permanent stability achieved. Most ancient knowledge was lost and learning of any kind was scarce. Charlemagne's capital, Aachen, was a mere village when compared to Constantinople or the cities of the Arabic world, such as Baghdad. Indeed, after the great Moslem expansion of the 7th century, the Arabic Caliphate that stretched from Spain to Persia was more civilized and cultured than any Christian kingdom.

Politics, Government, and World Events

5th century

1 They came from three very powerful nations of the Germans; that is, from the *Saxones, Angli,* and *Iutae.*
St Bede (The Venerable Bede; c. 673–735 AD) English churchman and historian.
Referring to the Anglo-Saxon invaders of Britain
Historia Ecclesiastica, Bk. I

533

2 Justice is the constant and perpetual wish to render to every one his due.
Justinian I (482–565 AD) Byzantine emperor.
Institutes, I

596

3* *Non Angli sed Angeli*
Not Angles, but angels.
Gregory I (540–604) Pope and saint.
On seeing child slaves in Rome and being told that they were Angles
Attrib.

7th century

4 ... of middle stature, neither tall nor short. His complexion was rosy white; his eyes black; his hair, thick, brilliant, and beautiful, fell to his shoulders. His profuse beard fell to his breast ... There was such sweetness in his visage that no one, once in his presence, could leave him. If I hungered, a single look at the Prophet's face dispelled the hunger. Before him all forgot their griefs and pains.
Ali (c. 600–661) Son-in-law of Mohammed and fourth caliph
Describing Mohammed (570–632)
Chronique (Abu Jafar Mohammed al-Tabari), Pt. III, Ch. 46

770

5* *Vox populi, vox dei.*
The voice of the people is the voice of God.
Alcuin (c. 735–804) Anglo-Saxon scholar.
Letter to Charlemagne

796

6* But above all things I strive to train them to be useful to the Holy Church of God and for the glory of your kingdom.
Alcuin
Referring to his school at Tours
Letter to Charlemagne, c. 796

799

7 If many people follow your enthusiastic en-deavours, perhaps a new Athens might be created in the land of the Franks, or rather a much better one.
Alcuin
Letter to Charlemagne, Mar 799

800

8 I should never have entered the church on that day, though it was an important feast, could I have known the Pope's intention in advance.
Charlemagne (742–814) Holy Roman Emperor.
Referring to his coronation as emperor, 25 Dec 800
Attrib.

962

9 Nevertheless, this measure is to be common to all the nation, whether Englishmen, Danes or Britons, and every province of my dominion to the end that poor men and rich may possess what they rightly acquire and that a thief may not find a place to bring what he has stolen.
Edgar (944–75) King of England.
Law, 96263

1061

10 As these two, the kingdom and the priesthood, are brought together by divine mystery, so are their two heads, by the force of mutual loves; the King may be found in the Roman pontiff, and the Roman pontiff be found in the King.
St Peter Damian (1007–72) Bishop of Ostia.
Written just after the enthronement of Pope Alexander II (1061)
Disceptatio synodalis

1066

11 He will give him seven feet of English ground, or as much more as he may be taller than other men.
Harold II (1022–1066) King of England.
Offer to Harald, King of Norway, who invaded England immediately before William the Conqueror (1066)
Heimskringla (Snorri Sturluson)

12 By the splendour of God I have taken possession of my realm; the earth of England is in my two hands.
William the Conqueror (1027–87) King of England.
Said after falling over when coming ashore at Pevensey with his army of invasion
Attrib.

1077

13 There for three days, before the castle gate, he laid aside all his royal gear; barefoot and wearing coarse wool, he stood pitifully, and did not stop begging for our apostolic help and compassion, until he had moved everyone

there, or who heard tell of this, to great reverence and pity.
Gregory VII (c. 1020–85) Pope and saint.
Referring to the excommunicate Emperor Henry IV's submission at Canossa, N Italy; he received absolution on 28 Jan 1077
Letter

1087

14 He caused castles to be built
Which were a sore burden to the poor,
A hard man was the king
And took from his subjects many marks
In gold and many more hundreds of pounds in silver.
These sums he took by weight from his people,
Most unjustly and for little need.
He was sunk in greed
And utterly given up to avarice.
He set apart a vast deer preserve and imposed laws concerning it.
Whoever slew a hart or a hind
Was to be blinded.
He forbade the killing of boars
Even as the killing of harts.
For he loved the stags as dearly
As though he had been their father.
Hares, also, he decreed should go unmolested.
The rich complained and the poor lamented,
But he was too relentless to care though all might hate him,
And they were compelled, if they wanted
To keep their lives and their lands
And their goods and the favour of the king,
To submit themselves wholly to his will.
Alas! that any man should bear himself so proudly
And deem himself exalted above all other men!
May Almighty God shew mercy to his soul
And pardon him his sins.
Written on the death of William the Conqueror
The Peterborough Chronicle (part of *The Anglo-Saxon Chronicle*)

1089

15 . . . belching from daily excess he came hiccupping to the war.
William of Malmesbury (c. 1080–c. 1143)
English cleric and historian.
Referring to Philip I of France
Gesta Regum, Bk. II

1093

16 . . . no one before Anselm became a bishop or abbot who did not first become the king's man and from his hand receive investiture by the gift of the pastoral staff.
Eadmer (c. 1055–c. 1124) English cleric and historian.
Historia Novorum in Anglia

1097

17 The mounted knight is irresistible; he would bore his way through the walls of Babylon.
Anna Comnena
Describing the French knights of the First Crusade, who passed through Constantinople in 1097
The Alexiad

1098

18 Since it is neither right nor natural for Frenchmen to be subject to Englishmen, but rather for Englishmen to be subject to Frenchmen, the outcome of the event mocked his vile expectation.
Suger, Abbot of St Denis (1081–1152)
French monk and diplomat.
Referring to William II of England's campaigns in Normandy
Life of Louis VI

Attitudes

Daily Life

839

19 . . . the illustrious place, built by the skill of the ancient Romans, called throughout the world the great city of London.
Bishop Helmstan of Winchester
Cartularium Saxonicum

926

20 We declare . . . that there shall be one coinage throughout the king's dominions and that there shall be no minting except in a *port*. And if a minter be convicted of striking bad money, the hand with which he was guilty shall be cut off and set up on the mint-smithy.
Athelstan (d. 939) King of Wessex and Mercia and later of England.
The Laws of Athelstan

1020

21 We give warning that a festival must be observed on Sunday and honoured with full intent from noon on Saturday until dawn on Monday, and that no person shall presume either to practise trade or attend any meeting on this Holy Day; and all men, poor and rich, shall go to their church and offer supplication for their sins and observe zealously every appointed fast and honour readily those saints whose feasts shall be commended by the priests.
Canute (995–1035) King of England, Denmark and Norway.
Letter to the Archbishops and people of England

Education, Knowledge, and Learning

894

22 ...all the youth now in England of free men, who are rich enough to be able to devote themselves to it, be set to learn as long as they are not fit for any other occupation, until they are able to read English writing well.
Alfred the Great (849–901) King of Wessex
Cura Pastoralis, Preface

Human Nature

524

23* In every adversity of fortune, to have been happy is the most unhappy kind of misfortune.
Boethius (c. 480–524) Roman statesman, philosopher, and scholar.
The Consolation of Philosophy

Life

731

24 The present life of men on earth, O king, as compared with the whole length of time which is unknowable to us, seems to me to be like this: as if, when you are sitting at dinner with your chiefs and ministers in wintertime, ... one of the sparrows from outside flew very quickly through the hall; as if it came in one door and soon went out through another. In that actual time it is indoors it is not touched by the winter's storm; but yet the tiny period of calm is over in a moment, and having come out of the winter it soon returns to the winter and slips out of your sight. Man's life appears to be more or less like this; and of what may follow it, or what preceded it, we are absolutely ignorant.
St Bede (The Venerable Bede; c. 673–735 AD) English churchman and historian.
Ecclesiastical History of the English People, Bk. II, Ch. 13

Marriage and the Family

7th century

25 Marry those who are single among you, and such as are honest of your men-servants and your maid-servants: if they be poor, God will enrich them of his abundance; for God is bounteous and wise.
Koran
Ch. XXIV

26 Suffer the women whom ye divorce to dwell in some part of the houses wherein ye dwell; according to the room and conveniences of the habitations which ye possess; and make them not uneasy, that ye may reduce them to straits.
Koran
Ch. LXV

Morality, Vices, and Virtues

7th century

27 The whore, and the whoremonger, shall ye scourge with a hundred stripes.
Koran
Ch. XXIV

Religion

5th century

28 *Roma locuta est; causa finita est.*
Rome has spoken; the case is concluded.
St Augustine of Hippo (354–430) Bishop of Hippo.
Sermons, Bk. I

29 *Da mihi castitatem et continentiam, sed noli modo.*
Give me chastity and continence, but not yet.
St Augustine of Hippo
Confessions

30 If this man is not faithful to his God, how can he be faithful to me, a mere man?
Theodoric (c. 445–526) King of the Ostrogoths.
Explaining why he had had a trusted minister, who had said he would adopt his master's religion, beheaded
Dictionnaire Encyclopédique (E. Guérard)

7th century

31 The month of Ramadan shall ye fast, in which the Koran was sent down from heaven, a direction unto men, and declarations of direction, and the distinction between good and evil.
Koran
Ch. II

11th century

32 Hail Mary, full of grace, the Lord is with thee: Blessed art thou among women, and blessed is the fruit of thy womb, Jesus.
Anonymous
Ave Maria, 11th century

1078

33 It is the custom of the Roman Church which I unworthily serve with the help of God, to tolerate some things, to turn a blind eye to some, following the spirit of discretion rather than the rigid letter of the law.
Gregory VII (c. 1020–85) Pope and saint.
Letter, 9 Mar 1078

Science, Medicine, and Technology

10th century

34 The sciences were transmitted into the Arabic language from different parts of the world; by it they were embellished and penetrated the hearts of men, while the beauties of the language flowed in their veins and arteries.
Al-Biruni (973–1048) Arabic scholar.
Kitab as-Saidana

With Hindsight

20th century

35 Unlike Christianity, which preached a peace that it never achieved, Islam unashamedly came with a sword.
Steven Runciman (1903–   ) British academic and diplomat.
A History of the Crusades, 'The First Crusade'

6

The Later Middle Ages (1100–1517)

Late in the 11th century, learning in western Europe began to revive; the clouds that caused the period known as the Dark Ages began to lift as the knowledge of the ancient world was rediscovered. This quickly flowered into the twelfth-century Renaissance. Aristotle's philosophy and science, when reconciled with Christianity, were held in great esteem; indeed, Aristotelian logic was seized upon as the essential tool with which to rationalize a thousand years of Christian canon law and theology. This 12th-century enthusiasm for knowledge did not last, however. As knowledge and correct doctrine were defined ever more clearly and closely, so previously acceptable beliefs came to be regarded as unacceptable and even, in some cases, heretical. There was, moreover, an influx of heretical ideas, such as those adopted by the Cathars, from outside western Europe. Such extremes of ideology made the Church nervous; its reaction was to set up the Inquisition (in 1231). Even St Thomas Aquinas, whose *Summa Theologica* was regarded as the high point of medieval scholastic theology, had some of his doctrines posthumously condemned. As the Church became more defensive, intellectual emphasis moved to secular learning. The Renaissance proper, which began in Italy in the 14th century, was a secular movement based on a reappraisal, uninfluenced by the theological preconceptions, of all forms of classical art and learning. Mankind's potential for positive achievement was emphasized. In painting, religious subjects were treated with an emphasis on human feelings. Renaissance architecture, with its domed structures and classical pediments, brought to Europe a revitalized form of the best building techniques of the ancient world.

Politics, Government, and World Events

12th century

1 Were the world all mine
From the sea to the Rhine
I'd give it all
If so be the Queen of England
Lay in may arms.
Anonymous
Referring to Eleanor of Aquitaine
Wandering Scholars (Helen Waddell); a free
translation of *Carmina Burana* (ed. Schmeller),
108a

1100

2 By intermarriage and by every means in his
power he bound the two peoples into a firm
union
Walter Map (c. 1140–c. 1209) Welsh cleric
and writer.
Referring to Henry I of England, and specifically
to his marriage (1100) to Matilda, a descendant of the Anglo-Saxon royal family
De Nugis Curialium, Pt. V, Ch. 5

3 Who killed Cock Robin?
I, said the Sparrow,
With my bow and arrow,
I killed Cock Robin.
Who saw him die?
I, said the Fly,
With my little eye,
I saw him die.
Thought to refer to William II, who was killed by
a stray arrow while hunting in the New Forest
Tommy Thumb's Pretty Song Book

1135

4* He who was strongest got most, and everyone
held on to what he had seized as if by right.
Referring to the anarchy of King Stephen's reign,
1135–1154
Chronicon Monasterii de Bello

5 In this king's time there was nothing but dis-
turbance and wickedness and robbery, for
forthwith the powerful men who were traitors
rose against him
Referring to the reign of Stephen, 1135–54
Anglo-Saxon Chronicle

1147

6* The Christian glories in the death of a pagan
because thereby Christ himself is glorified.
St Bernard (1090–1153) French monk and
theologian.
Richard the Lionheart (J. Gillingham), Ch. 9

7* Oh mighty soldier, O man of war, at last you
have a cause for which you can fight without
endangering your soul; a cause in which to win
is glorious and for which to die is but gain.
Are you a shrewd businessman, quick to see

the profits of this world? If you are, I can offer you a bargain which you cannot afford to
miss. Take the sign of the cross. At once you
will have an indulgence for all the sins
which you confess with a contrite heart. The
cross is cheap and if you wear it with
humility you will find that you have obtained the
Kingdom of Heaven.
St Bernard
Referring in particular to the second Crusade
Richard the Lionheart (J. Gillingham), Ch. 6

1157

8 Our kingdom and whatever anywhere is subject
to our rule we place at your disposal and commit to your power, that everything may be arranged at your nod, and that the will of your
empire may be carried out in all respects. Let
there be between us and our peoples an undivided unity of love and peace and safety of
commerce, in such a way that to you, who
are pre-eminent in dignity, be given the authority of command, and to us the will to obey
shall not be lacking.
Henry II (1133–89) King of England.
Letter to the Emperor Frederick Barbarossa,
1157

1160

9* Your lord the King of England, who lacks nothing, has men, horses, gold, silk, jewels, fruits,
game and everything else. We in France
have nothing but bread and wine and gaiety.
Louis VII (c. 1120–80) King of France.
By 'France' Louis meant the comparatively small
area around Paris that he ruled directly
Remark to Walter Map; cited in *Richard the
Lionheart* (J. Gillingham), Ch. 4

1162

10 . . . a patron of play-actors and a follower of
hounds to become a shepherd of souls.
Herbert of Bosham (fl. 1162–86) Chaplain
and biographer of Thomas Becket.
Referring to Becket
Vita Sancti Thomae

1170

11 Will no one rid me of this turbulent priest?
Henry II (1133–89) King of England.
Referring to Thomas Becket, Archbishop of Canterbury; four of Henry's household knights took
these words literally, hurried to Canterbury,
and killed Becket in the cathedral (Dec 1170)
Attrib.

12 I am ready to die for my Lord, that in my blood
the Church may obtain liberty and peace.
Thomas Becket (c. 1118–70) English
churchman.
One version of his last words
*Vita S. Thomae, Cantuariensis Archiepiscopi et
Martyris* (Edward Grim)

1173

13 This is how war is begun: such is my advice.
First destroy the land, deal after with the foe.
Philip, Count of Flanders
Advice to William, King of Scotland
Chronique de la guerre entre les Anglois et les Ecossois en 1173 et 1174 (Jordan Fantosme)

14 I order you to hold a free election, but forbid
you to elect anyone but Richard my clerk.
Henry II (1133–89) King of England.
Writ to the electors of the See of Winchester regarding the election of a new bishop; Richard d'Ilchester was one of the king's trusted servants
Recueil des Historiens des Gaules et de la France, XIV

15 St. Thomas, guard for me my kingdom! To you I
declare myself guilty of that for which others
bear the blame.
Henry II
Said at the outbreak of the Great Rebellion, 1173–74; one of Henry's first actions was to perform a public penance for Thomas Becket's murder
Chronique de la guerre entre les Anglois et les Ecossais en 1173 et 1174 (Jordan Fantosme)

16* . . . now in Ireland, now in England, now in Normandy, he must fly rather than travel by horse
or ship.
Louis VII (c. 1120–80) King of France.
Referring to Henry II of England
Imagines Historiarum (Ralph de Diceto)

1181

17 . . . the rustics vie with each other in bringing
up their ignoble and degenerate offspring to
the liberal arts.
Walter Map (c. 1140–c. 1209) Welsh cleric
and writer.
Drawing a comparison with the aristocracy, who were 'too poud or too lazy to put their children to learning'
De Nugis Curialium, Pt. I, Ch. 10

1183

18 Rich, noble, lovable, eloquent, handsome, gallant, every way attractive, a little lower than
the angels — all these gifts he turned to the
wrong side.
Walter Map
Referring to Henry, 'The Young King', eldest son of Henry II
De Nugis Curialium, Pt. I, Ch. 1

1189

19* I would sell London, if I could find a suitable
purchaser.
Richard I (1157–1199) King of England.
Comment while raising money for the third Crusade.
Historia Rerum Anglicarum (William of Newburgh), Bk. IV, Ch. 5

20* The four eaglets are my four sons who cease
not to persecute me even unto death. The
youngest of them, whom I now embrace with so
much affection, will sometime in the end insult me more grievously and more dangerously
than any of the others.
Henry II (1133–89) King of England.
Describing a painting of four eaglets preying on their parent. 'The youngest' refers to the future King John
De Principis Instructione (Gerald of Wales)

1190

21* The laity found him more than a king, the clergy
more than a pope, and both an intolerable
tyrant.
William of Newburgh (1136–c. 1198) English monk and historian.
Referring to William Longchamp, Justiciar and Chancellor of England during Richard I's absence on Crusade
Historia Rerum Anglicarum, Bk. IV, Ch. 14

1192

22 I have long since been aware that your king is a
man of the greatest honour and bravery, but
he is imprudent.
Saladin (1137–93) Sultan of Egypt and Syria.
Referring to Richard I
Remark to the Bishop of Salisbury, 1192

1193

23* My brother John is not the man to conquer a
country if there is anyone to offer even the
feeblest resistance.
Richard I (1157–99) King of England.
From Domesday Book to Magna Carta (A. L. Poole)

1194

24 Think no more of it, John; you are only a child
who has had evil counsellors.
Richard I
Said at his reconciliation, at Lisieux in May 1294, with his brother John, who had attempted to overthrow him while he was held prisoner in Germany (1193–94)
Histoire de Guillaume le Maréchal

1198

25 Just as the moon receives its light from the
sun, . . . so the royal power takes all its reputation and prestige from the pontifical power.
Innocent III (1160–1216) Pope.
Letter to recteurs of Tuscany, 1198

26 Thus we have defeated the king of France at
Gisors but it is not we who have done it, but
God and our right through us.
Richard I (1157–99) King of England.
Letter to the Bishop of Durham, 1198

27 *Dieu et mon droit.*

God and my right.
Richard I
Motto on the royal arms of Great Britain; originally used as a war-cry, Sept 1198

13th century

28   So passes the glory of the world.
Anonymous
Referring to the large number of ruined castles in England, Normandy, and Anjou, which had been demolished after the rebellion (1173–74) against Henry II
Histoire de Guillaume le Maréchal

29   ...hanged privily by night or in the luncheon hour.
Anonymous
Referring to abuses of the procedure for trying clerics
From Domesday Book to Magna Carta (A. L. Poole)

1207

30   Any service rendered to the temporal king to the prejudice of the eternal king is, without doubt, an act of treachery.
Stephen Langton (c. 1150–1228) Archbishop of Canterbury.
Letter to the barons of England, 1207

1209

31   I have two huge lions tearing at my flanks, the so-called Emperor Otto and John, King of England. Both try with all their might to upset the Kingdom of France. I cannot leave the country myself or do without my son here.
Philip II (1165–1223) King of France.
Explaining, to Pope Innocent III, his refusal to crusade against the Albigensian heretics

1215

32   This charter has been forced from the king. It constitutes an insult to the Holy See, a serious weakening of the royal power, a disgrace to the English nation, a danger to all Christendom, since this civil war obstructs the crusade.
Innocent III (1160–1216) Pope.
Referring to Magna Carta
Papal Bull, 24 Aug 1215

1216

33   A certain versifier, a false one, said, 'Just as England has been filthy with the defiler John, so now the filth of Hell is fouled by his foul presence'; but it is dangerous to write against a man who can easily do you wrong.
Matthew Paris (fl. 1235–50) Chronicler.
Referring to King John of England (r. 1199–1216); this quotation is better known in the form used by J. R. Green in his *Short History of the*

English People (1875): "Foul as it is, Hell itself is defiled by the fouler presence of King John."
Chronica Majora, 1216

1238

34   They illuminate our whole country with the bright light of their preaching and teaching.
Robert Grosseteste (c. 1175–1253) Bishop of Lincoln.
Referring to the Franciscans
Letter to Pope Gregory IX, 1238

1260

35*   Human law is law only by virtue of its accordance with right reason, and by this means it is clear that it flows from Eternal law. In so far as it deviates from right reason it is called an Unjust law; and in such a case, it is no law at all, but rather an assertion of violence.
St Thomas Aquinas (1225–74) Italian theologian.
Summa Theologiae

1264

36   So whether it is that the King, misled
By flattering talk to giving his consent,
And truly ignorant of their designs
Unknowingly approves such wrongs as these
Whose only end can be destruction, and
The ruin of his land; or whether he,
With malice in his heart, and ill-intent,
Commits these shameful crimes by raising up
His royal state and power far beyond
The reach of all his country's laws, so that
His whim is satisfied by the abuse
Of royal privilege and strength; if thus
Or otherwise this land of ours is brought
To total rack and ruin, and at last
The kingdom is left destitute, it is
The duty of the great and noble men
To rescue it, to purge the land of all
Corruption and all false authority.
Roger de Berksted
Referring to Henry III
The Song of Lewes

1297

37   By God, O King, I will neither go nor hang!
Roger Bigod, Earl of Norfolk (1245–1306) Marshal of England.
Reply to Edward I's 'By God, Earl, you shall either go or hang!'; Edward had ordered Norfolk and other barons to invade France from Gascony
Hemingburgh's Chronicle, Bk. II

1298

38*   The whole city is arrayed in squares just like a chess-board, and disposed in a manner so

perfect and masterly that it is impossible to
give a description that should do it justice.
Marco Polo (c. 1254–1324) Venetian traveller.
Referring to Kublai Khan's capital, Cambaluc
(later Peking)
The Book of Marco Polo

14th century

39   ...whenever kingship approaches tyranny it is
near its end, for by this it becomes ripe for
division, change of dynasty, or total destruction, especially in a temperate climate...
where men are habitually, morally and naturally
free.
Nicholas of Oresme (c. 1320–82) Chaplain
to Charles V of France.
De Moneta

1301

40   In this year King Edward of England made Lord
Edward, his son and heir, Prince of Wales and
Earl of Chester. When the Welsh heard this,
they were overjoyed, thinking him their lawful
master, as he was born in their lands.
Thomas of Walsingham (d. 1419) English
monk and chronicler.
Edward of Caernarfon, later Edward II, began the
tradition that male heirs to the English throne
were invested with these titles
Historia Anglicana

1327

41   The king is incompetent to govern in person.
Throughout his reign he has been controlled
and governed by others who have given him
evil counsel.
John de Stratford (d. 1348) Archbishop of
Canterbury.
Referring to Edward II
Historiae Anglicanae Scriptores (Twysden)

1337

42   ...the king of France, hardened in his malice,
would assent to no peace or treaty, but called
together his strong host to take into his hand
the duchy of Aquitaine, declaring against all
truth that it was forfeit to him.
Edward III (1312–77) King of England.
Proclamation on the outbreak of the Hundred
Years War
Foedera (ed. T. Rymer), Vol. IV

1344

43   *Honi soit qui mal y pense*
Evil be to him who evil thinks.
Edward III
Reputedly said on retrieving the Countess of Sal-
isbury's garter, which had fallen off
Attrib. in later tradition; associated with the foun-
dation of the Order of the Garter (1344)

1346

44   Let the boy win his spurs.
Edward III
Replying to a suggestion that he should send
reinforcements to his son, the Black Prince, dur-
ing the Battle of Crécy, 1346
Attrib.

1348

45   In scarcely any house did only one die, but all
together, man and wife with their children and
household, traversed the same road, the
road of death...I leave the parchment for the
work to be continued in case in the future any
human survivor should remain, or someone
of the race of Adam should be able to escape
this plague and continue what I have begun.
John of Clyn Irish friar.
Recording the effects of the Black Death in
Kilkenny
Annals of Ireland

1363

46   ...his lieges who from their hearts entirely
thank God who has given them such a lord and
governor, who has delivered them from servitude to other lands and from the charges
sustained by them in times past.
A tribute by the Commons to Edward III
Rotuli Parliamentorum, Vol. II

1376

47   It is neither fitting nor safe that all the keys
should hang from the belt of one woman.
Thomas Brinton (c. 1320–89) Bishop of
Rochester.
Criticizing the influence of Alice Perrers over the
ageing Edward III
Sermon, Westminister Abbey, 18 May 1376

1377

48   For, he said, albeit unworthy, he was a king's
son and one of the greatest lords in the kingdom after the king: and what had been so evilly
spoken of him could rightly be called plain
treason...And if any man were so bold as to
charge him with treason or other disloyalty or
with anything prejudicial to the realm, he was
ready to defend himself with his body as
though he were the poorest bachelor in the
land.
John of Gaunt (1340–99) Duke of Lancaster.
Report of a speech to Richard II's first parliament
Rotuli Parliamentorum, Vol. III

1381

49* When Adam delved and Eve span,
Who was then the gentleman?
John Ball (d. 1381) English priest.
Text of sermon

50   From the beginning all were created equal by

nature, slavery was introduced through the injust oppression of worthless men, against the will of God; for, if God had wanted to create slaves, he would surely have decided at the beginning of the world who was to be slave and who master.
John Ball
Sermon, Blackheath, 1381

51   No man should be a serf, nor do homage or any manner of service to any lord, but should give fourpence rent for an acre of land, and that no one should work for any man but as his own will, and on terms of a regular covenant.
Wat Tyler (d. 1381) English rebel.
Anonimalle Chronicle

52   I believe that in the end the truth will conquer.
John Wycliffe (1329–84) English religious reformer.
Said to John of Gaunt, Duke of Lancaster, 1381
Short History of the English People (J. R. Green)

1399

53   My God! this is a wonderful land and a faithless one; for she has exiled, slain, destroyed and ruined so many Kings, so many rulers, so many great men, and she is always diseased and suffering from differences, quarrels and hatred between her people.
Richard II (1365–99) King of England.
Attrib. remark, Tower of London, 21 Sept 1399

54   I did not usurp the crown, but was duly elected.
Henry IV (1367–1413) King of England.
Reply when accused by Richard Frisby, a Franciscan on trial for plotting (1402) to overthrow him
Eulogium Historiarum

55   For God's sake let us sit upon the ground
And tell sad stories of the death of kings:
How some have been depos'd, some slain in war,
Some haunted by the ghosts they have depos'd,
Some poison'd by their wives, some sleeping kill'd,
All murder'd – for within the hollow crown
That rounds the mortal temples of a king
Keeps Death his court.
William Shakespeare (1564–1616) English dramatist.
Said by Richard II
Richard II, III:2 (1597)

15th century

56   Baa, baa, black sheep,
Have you any wool?
Yes, sir, yes, sir,
Three bags full;
One for the master,
And one for the dame,
And one for the little boy
Who lives down the lane.
Possibly a reference to the perceived iniquities of the medieval wool trade in England: the

king (the 'master') and a small group of wool merchants (the 'dame') made large profits, from which the rest of the kingdom (the 'little boy') was excluded
Tommy Thumb's Pretty Song Book

57   A great ship which sailed for many a day in the sea of prosperity is that plenteous realm, the realm of England. The forecastle of this ship is the clergy, prelates, religious, and priests; the hindcastle is the barony, the king with his nobles; the body of the ship is the commons, merchants, craftsmen and labourers.
From a sermon preached in the reign of Henry V (1413–22)
Literature and Pulpit in Medieval England (G. R. Owst)

1402

58   It was not, as our enemies say, our intention to kill the king and his sons, but to make him the duke of Lancaster, which is what he ought to be.
Referring to Henry IV; said by one of the Franciscans condemned for plotting (1402) to overthrow him
Eulogium Historiarum

1403

59   The whole of the Welsh nation in these parts are concerned in this rebellion.
John Fairfield Receiver of Brecon.
Referring to the rebellion of Owen Glendower
Letter to Henry IV

1407

60   You have gold and I want gold; where is it?
Henry IV (1367–1413) King of England.
Said to merchants at a Great Council (Apr–June 1407) when trying to borrow money to pay the garrison at Calais, which had mutinied because of arrears in its wages
Attrib. in *Eulogium Historiarum*

1415

61   Once more unto the breach, dear friends, once more;
Or close the wall up with our English dead.
William Shakespeare (1564–1616) English dramatist.
Henry V exhorting his troops at the seige of Harfleur
Henry V, III:1 (1600)

62   Fair stood the wind for France
When we our sails advance.
Michael Drayton (1563–1631) English poet.
Agincourt

1418

63   Everyone knows that I act in everything with kindness and mercy, for I am forcing Rouen

into submission by starvation, not by fire,
sword or bloodshed.
Henry V (1387–1422) King of England.
Remark to an envoy from Rouen, 1418

1429

64* . . . a disciple and limb of the fiend, called the
Pucelle, that used false enchantments and
sorcery.
John of Lancaster, Duke of Bedford
(1389–1435) Brother of Henry V.
Referring to Joan of Arc
Proceeding and Ordinances of the Privy Council (ed. N. H. Nicolas), Vol. IV

1430

65* It is much safer to obey than to rule.
Thomas à Kempis (Thomas Hemmerken;
c. 1380–1471) German monk.
The Imitation of Christ, I

1431

66 If I said that God did not send me, I should condemn myself; truly God did send me.
St Joan of Arc (c. 1412–31) French patriotic
leader.
Said at her trial

1433

67 Daily many warantis come to me of paiementz
. . . of much more than all youre revenuz wold
come to, thowe they were not assigned afore
. . . the which warrantes yf I shuld paye hem,
youre Household, chambre and warderope
and youre werkes, shuld be unservid and unpaide and yf I paye hem not, I renne in grete
indignation of my lordes and grete sclandre,
noyse and maugre of all youre peple.
Lord Cromwell (c. 1394–1456) Treasurer of
England.
Rotuli Parliamentorum, Vol. IV

1440s

68 Myn hert ys set and all myn hole entent,
To serve this flour in my most humble wyse
As faythfully as can be thought or ment,
Wythout feynyng or slouthe in my servyse;
For wytt the wele, yt ys a paradyse
To se this floure when yt begyn to sprede,
Wyth colours fressh ennewyd, white and
rede.
Duke of Suffolk (1396–1450) English
nobleman.
Poem dedicated to Margaret of Anjou, Queen of
England
Secular Lyrics of XIVth and XVth Centuries (ed.
R. H. Robbins)

1452

69 It would be better to see the royal turban of the

Turks in the midst of the city than the Latin
mitre.
Michael Ducas (?1400–?70) Byzantine
historian.
Referring to Emperor Constantine XI's reunification of the Orthodox and Roman Churches
(1452), in an attempt to save the Byzantine Empire from the Turks
Attrib.

1453

70 Of the two lights of Christendom, one has been
extinguished.
Aeneas Silvius (1405–64) Bishop of Trieste.
Remark on hearing of the fall of Constantinople
to the Turks (29 May 1453)

1460

71 I know of no one in the realm who would not
more fitly to come to me than I to him.
Richard, Duke of York (1411–60) Father of
Edward IV.
Reply when asked, in parliament, whether he
wished to go and see the king; York formally
claimed the throne six days later
Remark, 10 Oct 1460

1461

72 And in that journey was Owen Tudor taken and
brought unto Haverfordwest, and he was beheaded at the market place, and his head set
upon the highest grice of the market cross,
and a mad woman combed his hair and washed
away the blood of his face, and she got candles and set about him burning more than a
hundred.
William Gregory (d. 1467) Chronicler.
Owen Tudor was the grandfather of Henry VII
Gregory's Chronicle

1468

73 Hence it comes about that there is scarcely a
man learned in the laws to be found in the
realm who is not noble or sprung of noble
lineage.
Sir John Fortescue (c. 1394–c. 1476) Chief
justice of the King's Bench.
The Governance of England

74 The greatest harm that cometh of a king's poverty is, that he shall by necessity be forced to
find exquisite means of getting goods, as to
put in default some of his subjects that be innocent, and upon the rich men more than the
poor, because they may the better pay.
Sir John Fortescue
The Governance of England

75 The king's council was wont to be chosen of
the great princes, and of the greatest lords of
the land, both spiritual and temporal . . .
Wherethrough, when they came together they
were so occupied with their own matters that

they attended but little, and other whiles nothing, to the king's matters.
John Fortescue
The Governance of England

1469

76* And much more am I sorrier for my good knights' loss than for the loss of my fair queen; for queens I might have enough, but such a fellowship of good knights shall never be together in no company.
Thomas Malory (1400–71) English writer.
Morte d'Arthur, Bk. XX, Ch. 9

1478

77 This year, that is to mean ye 18 day of February, the Duke of Clarence and second brother to the king, then being prisoner in ye Tower, was secretly put to death and drowned in a barrel of malvesye within the said Tower.
Robert Fabyan (d. 1513) English chronicler.
This account is apocryphal and reflects popular rumour
Chronicle

1482

78 I'll bell the cat.
Archibald Douglas (1449–1514) Scottish nobleman.
Of his proposed capture of Robert Cochrane (executed 1482); the phrase 'bell the cat' was earlier used by Eustache Deschamps in his
Ballade: Le Chat et les souris

1483

79 He used towardes every men of highe and low degree more than mete famylyarytie which trade of life he never changed.
Polydore Vergil (c. 1470–c. 1555) Italian historian.
Referring to Edward IV
Anglica Historia

80 Of hearte couragious, politique in counsaile in adversitie nothynge abashed, in peace juste and mercifull, in warre sharpe and fyerce, in the fielde bolde and hardye and natheless no farther than wysedome woulde adventurouse. Whose warres whoso will consyder, hee shall no lesse commende hys wysedome where he voyded thys by hys mannehode where he vanquished. He was of visage louelye, of body myghtie, strong and cleane made.
Thomas More (1478–1535) English lawyer and scholar.
Referring to Edward IV
The Historie of Kyng Rycharde the Thirde

81 Now is the winter of our discontent Made glorious summer by this sun of York.
William Shakespeare (1564–1616) English dramatist.
Said by Richard III
Richard III, I:1 (1597)

1484

82* The Cat, the Rat, and Lovell our dog Rule all England under a hog.
William Collingbourne (d. 1484) English landowner.
The cat was Sir William Catesby; the rat Sir Richard Ratcliffe; the dog Lord Lovell, who had a dog on his crest. The wild boar refers to the emblem of Richard III.
Chronicles (R. Holinshed), III

83 He contents the people where he goes best that ever did Prince, for many a poor man that hath suffered wrong many days has been relieved and helped by him.
Thomas Langton (c. 1440–1501) Bishop of St David's.
Referring to Richard III
Remark

1485

84 A horse! a horse ! my kingdom for a horse.
William Shakespeare (1564–1616) English dramatist.
Said by Richard III at the Battle of Bosworth (22 Aug 1485)
Richard III, V:4 (1597)

1499

85 He was my crowned King, and if the Parliamentary authority of England set the Crown upon a stock, I will fight for that stock: And as I fought then for him, I will fight for you, when you are established by the said authority.
Earl of Surrey
Reply when asked by Henry VII why he had fought for Richard III at the Battle of Bosworth (22 Aug 1485)
Remains Concerning Britain (W. Camden)

86 In the midst stood Prince Henry, who showed already something of royalty in his demeanour, in which there was a certain dignity combined with singular courtesy.
Erasmus (c. 1466–1536) Dutch humanist, scholar, and writer.
Remark on first meeting the future Henry VIII

16th century

87 . . . the state of things and the dispositions of men were then such, that a man could not well tell whom he might trust or whom he might fear.
Thomas More (1478–1535) English lawyer and scholar.
Refering to England
The English Works of Sir Thomas More, Vol. I

1500

88 I believe that the earthly Paradise lies here, which no one can enter except by God's leave. I believe that this land which your Highnesses have commanded me to discover is very great, and that there are many other lands in

the south of which there have never been reports.
Christopher Columbus (1451–1506) Italian navigator.
From the narrative of his third voyage, on which he discovered South America

1509

89   Oh, my Erasmus, if you could see how all the world here is rejoicing in the possession of so great a prince, how his life is all their desire, you could not contain your tears for joy. The heavens laugh, the earth exults, all things are full of milk, of honey and of nectar! Avarice is expelled the country. Liberality scatters wealth with bounteous hand. Our king does not desire gold or gems or precious metals, but virtue, glory, immortality . . . The other day he wished he was more learned. I said, that is not what we expect of your Grace, but that you will foster and encourage learned men. Yea, surely, said he, for indeed without them we should scarcely exist at all.
Lord Mountjoy (d. 1534) English statesman.
Referring to Henry VIII
Letter to Erasmus, 27 May 1509

1513

90* Since God has given us the papacy, let us enjoy it.
Leo X (Giovanni de' Medici; 1475–1521) Pope (1513–21).
Men of Art (T. Craven)

91   We Italians then owe to the Church of Rome and to her priests our having become irreligious and bad, but we owe her a still greater debt, and one that will be the cause of our ruin, namely that the Church has kept and still keeps our country divided.
Niccolò Machiavelli (1469–1527) Italian statesman and writer.
Discourses on First Ten Books of Livy

Attitudes

Art, Literature, and Music

12th century

92   The wanton and effeminate sound produced by caressing, chiming and intertwining melodies, a veritable harmony of sirens.
John of Salisbury (c. 1115–80) English churchman and scholar.
Referring to polyphony in music, contrasted with unison of Gregorian chant
Richard the Lionheart (J. Gillingham), Ch. 3

1385

93* And for ther is so greet diversitee
In English and in wryting of our tonge

So preye I God that noon miswryte thee
Ne thee mismetre for defaute of tonge.
And red wherso thou be, or elles songe,
That thou be understonde, I God beseche.
Geoffrey Chaucer (c. 1342–1400) English poet.
Troilus and Criseyde

Daily Life

1176

94   . . . the sanctuary and special delight of kings, where, laying aside their cares, they withdraw to refresh themselves with a little hunting; there, away from the turmoils inherent in a court, they breathe the pleasure of natural freedom.
Richard FitzNigel Treasurer of England and Bishop of London.
Referring to the royal forests
Dialogus de Scaccario, Bk. I, Ch. 11

1182

95* If die I must, let me die drinking in an inn.
Walter Map (c. 1140–c. 1209) Welsh cleric and writer.
De Nugis Curialium

13th century

96   I love the gay Eastertide, which brings forth leaves and flowers; and I love the joyous song of the birds, re-echoing through the copse. But I also love to see, admist the meadows, tents and pavilions spread; it gives me great joy to see, drawn up on the field, knights and horses in battle array.
Bertrand le Born French troubadour.

1250

97* Sumer is icumen in,
Lhude sing cuccu!
Groweth sed, and bloweth med,
And springth the wude nu.
Anonymous
Cuckoo Song

1390

98   So was hir joly whistle wel y-wet.
Geoffrey Chaucer (c. 1342–1400) English poet.
The Canterbury Tales, 'The Reve's Tale'

1501

99   Strong be thy wallis that about thee standis;
Wise be the people that within thee dwellis;
Fresh be thy ryver with his lusty strandis;
Blithe by thy chirches, wele swonyng be thy bellis;
Riche by they merchauntis in substaunce that excellis;

Fair be their wives, right lovesom, white and small;
Clere by thy virgyns, lusty under kellis:
London, thou art the flour of Cities all.
William Dunbar (1460–1530)
Referring to London
The Earlier Tudors (J. D. Mackie)

Education, Knowledge, and Learning

13th century

100   This dumb ox will fill the whole world with his bellowing.
Albertus Magnus (c. 1200–80) German bishop.
Referring to his pupil Thomas Aquinas, whose nickname was "The Dumb Ox"
Aquinas (A. Kenny)

1224

101   We keep the students within view of their parents; we save them many toils and long foreign journeys; we protect them from robbers. They used to be pillaged while travelling abroad; now, they may study at small cost and short wayfaring, thanks to our liberality.
Frederick II (1194–1250) Holy Roman Emperor.
Foundation charter of Naples University

14th century

102   Entities should not be multiplied unnecessarily. No more things should be presumed to exist than are absolutely necessary.
William of Okham (c. 1280–1349) English philosopher.
'Okham's Razor'. Despite its attribution to William of Okham, it was in fact a repetition of an ancient philosophical maxim

1323

103*   There are as many miracles as there are articles of the *Summa*.
John XXII (Jacques d'Euse; c. 1249–1334) Pope.
Referring to the *Summa Theologiae* of Thomas Aquinas, who was in the process of being canonized
Attrib.

1390

104   A Clerk ther was of Oxenford also,
That un-to logik hadde longe y-go.
Geoffrey Chaucer (c. 1342–1400) English poet.
The Canterbury Tales, Prologue

105   This is to seyn, to syngen and to rede,
As smale children doon in hire childhede.
Geoffrey Chaucer
The Canterbury Tales, 'The Prioress's Tale'

Human Nature

14th century

106   Manners maketh man.
William of Wykeham (1324–1404) English churchman.
Motto of Winchester College and New College, Oxford

107   Only do always in health what you have often promised to do when you are sick.
Sigismund (1368–1437) Holy Roman Emperor (1411–37).
His advice on achieving happiness
Biographiana, Vol. I

1307

108   There is no greater sorrow than to recall a time of happiness when in misery.
Dante Alighieri (1265–1321) Italian poet.
Divine Comedy, Inferno, V

15th century

109   If you cannot mould yourself as you would wish, how can you expect other people to be entirely to your liking?
Thomas à Kempis (Thomas Hemmerken; c. 1380–1471) German monk.
The Imitation of Christ, I

1513

110   It is the nature of men to be bound by the benefits they confer as much as by those they receive.
Machiavelli (1469–1527) Italian statesman.
The Prince

Life

1145

111   ...how, not many years before, one John, King and Priest, who dwells in the extreme Orient beyond Persia and Armenia ... is said to be of the ancient race of those Magi who are mentioned in the Gospel.
Otto, Bishop of Freising (c. 1111–58) German chronicler.
The first mention of Prester John; the legend of a great Christian Priest-King in Asia persisted throughout the Middle Ages
Chronicle, 1145

1390

112   This world nis but a thurghfare ful of wo,
And we ben pilgrimes, passinge to and fro;
Deeth is an ende of every worldly sore.
Geoffrey Chaucer (c. 1342–1400) English poet.
The Canterbury Tales, 'The Knight's Tale'

15th century

113 *O quam cito transit gloria mundi.*
**Oh how quickly the glory of the world passes
away.**
Thomas à Kempis (Thomas Hemmerken;
c. 1380–1471) German monk.
Generally misquoted as 'Sic transit gloria mundi
(Thus passes the glory of the world)' – a
formula spoken during papal coronations from
1409
The Imitation of Christ, I

1508

114 **While I thought that I was learning how to live,
I have been learning how to die.**
Leonardo da Vinci (1452–1519) Italian artist.
Notebooks

1516

115 **Nature made him, and then broke the mould.**
Ludovico Ariosto (1474–1533) Italian poet.
Referring to Charlemagne's paladin, Roland
Orlando furioso

Love and Sex

1469

116* **For love that time was not as love is nowadays.**
Thomas Malory (1400–71) English writer.
Morte d'Arthur, Bk. XX, Ch. 3

16th century

117 **Love of honour and honour of love.**
Philip Sidney (1554–86) English poet and
courtier.
Referring to the ideal of chivalry
English Literature: Mediaeval (W. P. Ker)

Marriage and the Family

1390

118 **She was a worthy womman al hir lyve,
Housbondes at chirche-dore she hadde fyve,
Withouten other companye in youthe.**
Geoffrey Chaucer (c. 1342–1400) English
poet.
Referring to the wife of Bath
The Canterbury Tales, Prologue

Morality, Vices, and Virtues

1367

119 **Dowel, Dobet and Dobest.**
William Langland (c. 1330–c. 1400) English
poet.
Do well, Do better, and Do Best: three concepts

central to the search for Truth in *Piers Plowman*, in which they appear as allegorical
characters
The Vision of Piers Plowman

1370

120 **A Knyght ther was and that a worthy man,
That fro the tyme that he first bigan
To riden out, he loved chivalrie,
Trouthe and honour, fredom and curteisie.**
. . .
He was a verray parfit, gentil knyght.
Geoffrey Chaucer (c. 1342–1400) English
poet.
The Canterbury Tales, Prologue

1390

121 **Mordre wol out, that see we day by day.**
Geoffrey Chaucer
The Canterbury Tales, 'The Nun's Priest's Tale'

Religion

12th century

122 **. . . kept a hearth-girl in his house who kindled
his fire but extinguished his virtue.**
Gerald of Wales (c. 1146–c. 1220) Welsh to-
pographer, archdeacon, and writer.
Referring to the parish priest
Gemma Ecclesiastica

1307

123 **Abandon hope, all ye who enter here.**
Dante Alighieri (1265–1321) Italian poet.
The inscription at the entrance to Hell
Divine Comedy, Inferno, III

1390

124 **Ful wel she song the service divyne,
Entuned in hir nose ful semely.**
Geoffrey Chaucer (c. 1342–1400) English
poet.
Referring to the prioress
The Canterbury Tales, Prologue

15th century

125 **Man proposes but God disposes.**
Thomas à Kempis (Thomas Hemmerken;
c. 1380–1471) German monk.
The Imitation of Christ, I

16th century

126 **I believe firmly what I read in the holy Scriptures, and the Creed, called the Apostles', and I
don't trouble my head any farther: I leave the
rest to be disputed and defined by the clergy,
if they please; and if any Thing is in common
use with Christians that is not repugnant to the**

holy Scriptures, I observe it for this Reason, that I may not offend other people.
Erasmus (c. 1466–1536) Dutch humanist, scholar, and writer.
Commenting on the teachings of John Colet
The Colloquies of Erasmus, Vol. I

Science, Medicine, and Technology

1267

127 All science requires mathematics
Roger Bacon (c. 1214–c. 1292) English monk, scholar, and scientist.
Opus Maius, Pt. IV

1380

128* That lyf so short, the craft so long to lerne,
Th' assay so hard, so sharp the conquerynge.
Geoffrey Chaucer (c. 1342–1400) English poet.
Referring to medicine
The Parliament of Fowls

1505

129 A man with wings large enough and duly attached might learn to overcome the resistance of the air, and conquering it succeed in subjugating it and raise himself upon it.
Leonardo da Vinci (1452–1519) Italian artist.
Flight of Birds

Wealth and Poverty

1380

130* For of fortunes sharp adversitee
The worst kinde of infortune is this,
A man to have ben in prosperitee,
And it remembren, what is passed is.
Geoffrey Chaucer (c. 1342–1400) English poet.
Troilus and Criseyde, 3

Work and Occupations

1390

131 No-wher so bisy a man as he ther nas,
And yet he semed bisier than he was.
Geoffrey Chaucer
Referring to the man of law
The Canterbury Tales, Prologue

132 For gold in phisik is a cordial,
Therfore he lovede gold in special.
Geoffrey Chaucer
Referring to the doctor
The Canterbury Tales, Prologue

Sayings of the Time

12th century

133 *Rex illiteratus, asinus coronatus.*
An unlettered king is a crowned ass.
A saying common in the 12th century; also said, by William of Malmesbury, to have been used by Henry I of England in his youth

With Hindsight

17th century

134 . . . it was ordained that the winding ivy of a Plantagenet should kill the true tree itself.
Francis Bacon (1561–1626) English philosopher.
Referring to the execution (1499) of Perkin Warbeck, who claimed to be Edward V's brother, and the Earl of Warwick, the true heir of the house of York
The Life of Henry VII

135 Being a king that loved wealth and treasure, he could not endure to have trade sick.
Francis Bacon
Referring to Henry VII
The Life of Henry VII

19th century

136 There may have been disillusionments in the lives of the medieval saints, but they would scarcely have been better pleased if they could have foreseen that their names would be associated nowadays chiefly with racehorses and the cheaper clarets.
Saki (Hector Hugh Munro; 1870–1916) British writer.
Reginald at the Carlton

20th century

137 . . . the pulpit was the cradle of English prose.
A. G. Little (1863–1945) British historian.
English Historical Review, xlix (1934)

138 In essence the Renaissance was simply the green end of one of civilization's hardest winters.
John Fowles (1926–   ) British novelist.
The French Lieutenant's Woman, Ch. 10

139 Compared with this revolution the Renaissance is a mere ripple on the surface of literature.
C. S. Lewis (1898–1963) British academic and writer.
Referring to the appearance of the concept of courtly love in the 12th century
The Allegory of Love

7

The Reformation and Counter-Reformation (1518–1659)

On 31 October, 1517, Martin Luther nailed to the door of the castle church at Wittenburg. 95 theses attacking abuses in the Roman Catholic Church. These complaints were not new, but because the time was ripe they set off the Reformation of the Catholic Church. Within a few years Protestant ideas had spread widely and several rulers had renounced the authority of the Pope. Notably, Henry VIII of England defied the Pope to divorce his first queen; thereafter he assumed full religious authority within his kingdom. For the next century and more, religious conflicts played a central role in politics and diplomacy, and most disputes acquired a religious dimension. In this period the Catholic Church attempted, notably at the Council of Trent (1545–63), to put its own house in order. This became known as the Counter-Reformation. Only in the later stages of the Thirty Years War (1618–48) did religion's political importance decline; and by 1661, when Louis XIV began his personal government of France, dynastic and national ambitions were again paramount.

Politics, Government, and World Events

1518

1 The King has a way of making every man feel that he is enjoying his special favour, just as the London wives pray before the image of Our Lady by the Tower till each of them believes it is smiling upon her.
Thomas More (1478–1535) English lawyer and scholar.
Referring to Henry VIII
Letter to Bishop John Fisher, 1518

2 I shall never be a heretic, I may err in dispute; but I do not wish to decide anything finally; on the other hand, I am not bound by the opinions of men.
Martin Luther (1483–1546) German Protestant.
Letter to the chaplain to the Elector of Saxony, 28 Aug 1518

1519

3 This cardinal is the person who rules both the king and the entire kingdom.
Sebastian Giustiniani Venetian ambassador to England.
Referring to Cardinal Wolsey
Wolsey (A. F. Pollard)

4 Nothing pleased him more than to be styled the arbitrator of the affairs of Christendom.
Sebastian Giustiniani
Referring to Cardinal Wolsey
Letters and Papers of Henry VIII, Vol. III

1520

5* My cousin Francis and I are in perfect accord – he wants Milan, and so do I.
Charles V (1500–58) Holy Roman Emperor.
Referring to his dispute with Francis I of France over Italian territory
The Story of Civilization (W. Durant), Vol. 5

6 Arise, O Lord, plead Thine own cause; remember how the foolish man reproacheth Thee daily; the foxes are wasting Thy vineyard, which Thou hast given to Thy Vicar Peter, the boar out of the wood doth waste it, and the wild beast of the field doth devour it.
Leo X (Giovanni de' Medici; 1475–1521) Pope (1513–21).
Papal Bull, Exsurge, Domine, Preface

1521

7 Here stand I. I can do no other. God help me. Amen.
Martin Luther (1483–1546) German Protestant.
Speech, Diet of Worms, 18 Apr 1521

8 A single friar who goes counter to all Christianity for a thousand years must be wrong.
Charles V (1500–58) Holy Roman Emperor.
Referring to Martin Luther
Remark, Diet of Worms, 19 Apr 1521

9 If I had heard that as many devils would set on me in Worms as there are tiles on the roofs, I should none the less have ridden there.
Martin Luther (1483–1546) German Protestant.
Referring to the Diet of Worms
Luthers Sämmtliche Schriften

10 We are so much bounden to the See of Rome that we cannot do too much honour to it . . . for we received from that See our Crown Imperial.
Henry VIII (1491–1547) King of England.
Remark to Thomas More

11 As time requireth, a man of marvellous mirth and pastimes, and sometimes of as sad gravity, as who say: a man for all seasons.
Robert Whittington (16th century) English writer.
Referring to Sir Thomas More; after Erasmus
Vulgaria, Pt. II, 'De constructione nominum'

1525

12 Of all I had, only honour and life have been spared.
Francis I (1494–1547) King of France.
Referring to his defeat and capture by the forces of the Emperor Charles V at the Battle of Pavia, 24 Feb 1525; usually misquoted as 'All is lost save honour'
Letter to Louise of Savoy (his mother), 1525

13 Anyone who can be proved to be a seditious person is an outlaw before God and the emperor; and whoever is the first to put him to death does right and well.
Martin Luther (1483–1546) German Protestant.
Referring to the 'Peasants' War', an uprising (1524–25) of peasants in Germany partly inspired by Luther's teachings
Against the Robbing and Murdering Hordes of Peasants (Broadsheet, May 1525)

14 In my opinion it is better that all of these peasants should be killed rather than that the sovereigns and magistrates should be destroyed, because the peasants take up the sword without God's authorization.
Martin Luther
Letter to Nicholas von Ansdorf, 30 May 1525

1529

15 I perceive that that man hath the sow by the right ear.
Henry VIII (1491–1547) King of England.
Referring to Cranmer
Letter to Edward Foxe and Stephen Gardiner, 3 Aug 1529

1530

16 I speak Spanish to God, Italian to women, French to men, and German to my horse.
Charles V (1500–58) Holy Roman Emperor.
Attrib.

17 Had I but served God as diligently as I have served the king, he would not have given me over in my gray hairs.
Cardinal Wolsey (1475–1530) English churchman.
Remark to Sir William Kingston; Wolsey, Henry VIII's chief minister from 1515 to 1529, had been discarded following his failure to secure Henry's divorce from Catherine of Aragon
Negotiations of Thomas Wolsey (Cavendish)

18 He is a prince of royal courage and hath a princely heart; and rather than he will miss or want part of his appetite, he will hazard the loss of one-half of his kingdom.
Cardinal Wolsey
Referring to Henry VIII
Remark, Nov 1530

1534

19 Is not this house as nigh heaven as my own?
Thomas More (1478–1535) English lawyer and scholar.
Referring to the Tower of London; More was imprisoned here, and in 1535 executed, for treason arising from his defiance of Henry VIII's religious policies
Life of Sir Thomas More (Roper)

1535

20 I cumber you goode Margaret muche, but I woulde be sorye, if it shoulde be any lenger than to morrowe, for it is S. Thomas evin and the vtas of Sainte Peter and therefore to morowe longe I to goe to God, it were a daye very meete and conveniente for me. I neuer liked your maner towarde me better then when you kissed me laste for I loue when doughterly loue and deere charitie hathe no laisor to looke to worldely curtesye. Fare well my deere childe and praye for me, and I shall for you and all your friendes that we maie merily meete in heaven.
Thomas More
Last letter to Margaret Roper, his daughter, on the eve of his execution on 6 July 1535

21 I pray you, Master Lieutenant, see me safe up, and for coming down let me shift for myself.
Thomas More
On climbing onto the scaffold prior to his execution
Life of Sir Thomas More (William Roper)

22 Pluck up thy spirits, man, and be not afraid to do thine office; my neck is very short; take heed therefore thou strike not awry, for saving of thine honesty.
Thomas More
Said to the headsman
Life of Sir Thomas More (Roper)

23 This hath not offended the king.
Thomas More
Said as he drew his beard aside before putting his head on the block

1536

24 The king has been very good to me. He promoted me from a simple maid to be a marchioness. Then he raised me to be a queen. Now he will raise me to be a martyr.
Anne Boleyn (1507–36) Second wife of Henry VIII.
Notable Women in History (W. Abbot)

1537

25* Little Jack Horner
Sat in the corner,
Eating a Christmas pie;
He put in his thumb,
And pulled out a plum,
And said, What a good boy am I!
Thought to relate to an incident when the Abbot of Glastonbury, in an attempt to pacify Henry VIII, sent his steward, John Horner, to the king with a pie containing the title deeds to 12 Somerset manors. John Horner is believed to have discovered these deeds in the pie and kept them himself
Namby Pamby (Henry Carey)

26 We should easily convert even the Turks to the obedience of our gospel, if only we would agree among ourselves and unite in some holy confederacy.
Thomas Cranmer (1489–1556) English churchman.
Letter to the Swiss scholar, Joachim Vadian, 1537

27 Pity it is that the folly of one brainsick Pole – or, to say better, of one witless fool – should be the ruin of so great a family.
Thomas Cromwell (c. 1485–1540) English statesman.
Referring to the denunciation of Reginald Pole (the King's cousin) for siding with the Pope in the disputes of the English Reformation
Letter to Michael Throgmorton (Pole's confidant), Sept 1537

1539

28 You have sent me a Flanders mare.
Henry VIII (1491–1547) King of England.
Remark on meeting his fourth wife, Anne of Cleves, for the first time; generally assumed to have been said to Thomas Cromwell
Attrib.

1540

29 It much grieves me that I should be noted a traitor when I always had your laws on my breast, and that I should be a sacramenty.

God he knoweth the truth, and that I am of the one and the other guiltless.
Thomas Cromwell (c. 1485–1540) English statesman.
On being condemned to death for treason and heresy
Letter to Henry VIII, 30 June 1540

30* Junker Henry means to be God and do as he pleases.
Martin Luther (1483–1546) German Protestant.
Referring to Henry VIII's religious policy
The Earlier Tudors (J. D. Mackie)

1543
---

31 We at no time stand so highly in our estate royal as in the time of Parliament, wherein we as head and you as members are conjoined and knit together into one body politic.
Henry VIII (1491–1547) King of England.
Speech to a deputation from the House of Commons, 31 Mar 1543

1545
---

32 I am very sorry to know and hear how unreverently that most precious jewel, the Word of God, is disputed, rhymed, sung and jangled in every ale-house and tavern, contrary to the true meaning and doctrine of the same.
Henry VIII
Commenting on the translation of the Bible into English
Speech, Parliament, 24 Dec 1545

1546
---

33 I make war on the living, not on the dead.
Charles V (1500–58) Holy Roman Emperor.
After the death of Martin Luther, when it was suggested that he hang the corpse on a gallows
Attrib.

1547
---

34 I came, I saw, God conquered.
Charles V
Remark after the Battle of Mühlberg, 23 Apr 1547

1550

35* My father made the most part of you almost out of nothing.
Mary I (1516–58) Queen of England.
Reply when threatened, during the reign of Edward VI, because of her Catholicism
The Earlier Tudors (J. D. Mackie)

1555
---

36 England's chief defence depends upon the navy

being always ready to defend the realm against invasion.
Philip II (1527–98) King of Spain.
Philip, as husband of Mary I, was King-Consort of England (1554–58)
Submission to the Privy Council

1556
---

37 Three blind mice, see how they run!
They all run after the farmer's wife,
Who cut off their tails with a carving knife,
Did you ever see such a thing in your life,
As three blind mice?
The 'three blind mice' are thought to be Archbishop Cranmer, Bishop Ridley, and Bishop Latimer, who were executed in the reign of Mary I (the 'farmer's wife') for heresy
Deuteromelia (Thomas Ravenscroft)

38 Be of good comfort, Master Ridley, and play the man; we shall this day light such a candle, by God's grace, in England as I trust shall never be put out.
Hugh Latimer (1485–1555) English churchman.
Said to Nicholas Ridley as they were about to be burnt at the stake for heresy
Famous Last Words (B. Conrad)

1558
---

39 When I am dead and opened, you shall find 'Calais' lying in my heart.
Mary I (1516–58) Queen of England.
Chronicles (Holinshed), III

40 After all the stormy, tempestuous, and blustering windy weather of Queen Mary was overblown, the darksome clouds of discomfort dispersed, the palpable fogs and mist of the most intolerable misery consumed, and the dashing showers of persecution overpast: it pleased God to send England calm and quiet season, a clear and lovely sunshine, a quietest from former broils of a turbulent estate, and a world of blessings by good Queen Elizabeth.
Raphael Holinshed (d. 1580) English chronicler.
Chronicles

41 The First Blast of the Trumpet Against the Monstrous Regiment of Women.
John Knox (c. 1514–72) Scottish religious reformer.
Title of pamphlet, 1558

42 This judgment I have of you, that you will not be corrupted with any manner of gift and that you will be faithful to the state, and that, without respect of my private will, you will give me that counsel that you think best.
Elizabeth I (1533–1603) Queen of England.
To William Cecil, 1558

1559
---

43 To me it shall be a full satisfaction both for the memorial of my name, and for the glory also, if

when I shall let my last breath, it be engraven upon my marble tomb, 'Here lieth Elizabeth, who reigned a virgin and died a virgin'.
Elizabeth I
Reply to a petition from the House of Commons.
6 Feb 1559

1564

44 Let justice be done, though the world perish.
Ferdinand I (1503–64) Holy Roman Emperor.
Attrib.

1565

45* In old time we had treen chalices and golden priests, but now we have treen priests and golden chalices.
John Jewel (1522–71) English bishop.
Certain Sermons Preached Before the Queen's Majesty

1566

46 The queen of Scots is this day leichter of a fair son, and I am but a barren stock.
Elizabeth I (1533–1603) Queen of England.
Memoirs of Sir James Melville (1549–93)

47 No more tears now; I will think upon revenge.
Mary Stuart (1542–87) Queen of Scots.
Remark on hearing of the murder (9 March 1566) of her secretary, David Riccio, by her husband, Lord Darnley

48 I muse how men of wit can so hardly use that gift they hold.
Elizabeth I (1533–1603) Queen of England.
Speech to a delegation from parliament, 5 Nov 1566

49 Most excellent Royall Majesty, of our *Elizabeth* (sitting at the *Helm* of this Imperiall Monarchy: or rather, at the Helm of the Imperiall Ship).
John Dee (1527–1608) English mathematician and astrologer.
General and Rare Memorials pertaining to the Perfect Arte of Navigation

50 Those who follow their conscience directly are of my religion; and, for my part, I am of the same religion as all those who are brave and true.
Henri IV (1553–1610) King of France.
Henri had become a Roman Catholic, as a political move, in 1576
Letter to M. de Batz, 1577

1579

51 Be assured on the faith of a monkey that your frog lives in hope.
Jean de Simier
The 'monkey' was Elizabeth I's pet name for Simier, who tried unsuccessfully to arrange a marriage between Elizabeth and his master, the Duke of Anjou (the 'frog')

1580s

52* Hey diddle diddle,
The cat and the fiddle,
The cow jumped over the moon;
The little dog laughed
To see such sport,
And the dish ran away with the spoon.
Believed to depict the Elizabethan court; the characters represented are Elizabeth I (the cat), Sir Francis Walsingham (the moon), and Earl of Leicester (the dog)
Mother Goose's Melody

1580

53* I am your anointed Queen. I will never be by violence constrained to do anything. I thank God that I am endued with such qualities that if I were turned out of the Realm in my petticoat I were able to live in any place in Christome.
Elizabeth I (1533–1603) Queen of England.
Sayings of Queen Elizabeth (Chamberlin)

1584

54 My question is not whether there be witches or nay; but whether they can do such marvellous works as are imputed to them. Good Master Dean, is it possible for a man to break his fast with you at Rochester, and to dine that day at Durham with Master Doctor Matthew; or can your enemy maim you, when the Ocean sea is betwixt you? May a spiritual body become temporal at his pleasure? Or may a carnal body become invisible? . . . Alas, I am sorry and ashamed to see how many die, that being said to be bewitched, only seek for magical cures, whom wholesome diet and good medicines would have recovered.
Reginald Scot
The Discoverie of Witchcraft

1586

55 As for me, I see no such great cause why I should either be fond to live or fear to die. I have had good experience of this world, and I know what it is to be a subject and what to be a sovereign. Good neighbours I have had, and I have met with bad: and in trust I have found treason.
Elizabeth I (1533–1603) Queen of England.
Speech to Parliament, 1586

56* A dead woman bites not.
Lord Gray (d. 1612) Scottish nobleman.
Advocating the execution of Mary, Queen of Scots
Attrib.

57 The daughter of debate, that eke discord doth sow.
Elizabeth I (1533–1603) Queen of England.
Referring to Mary Queen of Scots
Sayings of Queen Elizabeth (Chamberlin)

1587

58* **God may pardon you, but I never can.**
Elizabeth I
To the Countess of Nottingham
History of England under the House of Tudor
(Hume), Vol. II, Ch. 7

59 **I have singed the Spanish king's beard.**
Francis Drake (1540–96) British navigator.
Referring to the raid on Cadiz harbour, 1587
Attrib.

1588
---

60 **Here lies a valiant warrior**
Who never drew a sword;
Here lies a noble courtier
Who never kept his word;
Here lies the Earl of Leicester
Who governed the estates
Whom the earth could never living love,
And the just heaven now hates.
Ben Jonson (1573–1637) English dramatist.
Attrib. in *Collection of Epitaphs* (Tissington)

The Spanish Armada (1588)

Philip II of Spain sent a fleet of 130 ships to transport
his army across the Channel to invade England and
overthrow the 'heretical' Queen Elizabeth I. Disrupted
by English fireships and defeated off Gravelines, it suffered further losses from Atlantic storms and returned
to Spain with only 86 ships.

61 **The advantage of time and place in all practical**
actions is half a victory; which being lost is
irrecoverable.
Francis Drake (1540–96) British navigator.
Letter to Elizabeth I, 1588

62 **There is plenty of time to win this game, and to**
thrash the Spaniards too.
Francis Drake
Referring to the sighting of the Armada during a
game of bowls, 20 July 1588
Attrib.

63 **Drake he's in his hammock till the great Arma-**
das come.
(Capten, art tha sleepin' there below?)
Slung atween the round shot, listenin' for the
drum,
An dreamin' arl the time o' Plymouth Hoe.
Henry John Newbolt (1862–1938) British
poet.
Drake's Drum

64 **'Take my drum to England, hang et by the**
shore,
Strike et when your powder's runnin' low;
If the Dons sight Devon, I'll quit the port o'
Heaven,
An' drum them up the Channel as we
drummed them long ago.'
Henry John Newbolt
Drake's Drum

65 **I know I have the body of a weak and feeble**
woman, but I have the heart and stomach of a
King, and of a King of England too.
Elizabeth I (1533–1603) Queen of England.
Speech at Tilbury on the approach of the Spanish
Armada

66 *Flavit deus et dissipati sunt.*
God blew and they were scattered.
Inscription on the medallion minted to com-
memorate the defeat of the Spanish Armada

67 **They did not, in all their sailing round about**
England, so much as sink or take one ship,
bark, pinnace, or cockboat of ours, or even
burn so much as one sheepcote in this land.
Anonymous
Referring to the Spanish Armada
The Reign of Elizabeth (J. D. Black), Ch. 10

1594
---

68 **Paris is worth a mass.**
Henri IV (1553–1610) King of France.
Said on entering Paris (March 1594), having se-
cured its submission to his authority by becom-
ing a Roman Catholic
Attrib.

1596
---

69 **This royal throne of kings, this sceptred isle,**
This earth of majesty, this seat of Mars,
This other Eden, demi-paradise,
This fortress built by Nature for herself
Against infection and the hand of war,
This happy breed of men, this little world,
This precious stone set in the silver sea,
Which serves it in the office of a wall,
Or as a moat defensive to a house,
Against the envy of less happier lands;
This blessed plot, this earth, this realm, this
England,
This nurse, this teeming womb of royal kings,
Fear'd by their breed, and famous by their
birth.
William Shakespeare (1564–1616) English
dramatist.
Richard II, II:1

70 **Not all the water in the rough rude sea**
Can wash the balm from an anointed king;
The breath of worldly men cannot depose
The deputy elected by the Lord.
William Shakespeare
Richard II, III:2

1598
---

71 **. . . her face oblong, fair but wrinkled; her eyes**
small, yet black and pleasant; her nose a little
hooked, her lips narrow and her teeth black
(a defect the English seem subject to from their
too great use of sugar) . . . She wore false hair
and that red.
Paul Hentzner (fl. 1590s) German tutor.
Referring to Elizabeth I
Journey into England

72 Uneasy lies the head that wears a crown.
    William Shakespeare (1564–1616) English
    dramatist.
    Henry IV, Part Two, III:1

73 The sun does not set in my dominions.
    Friedrich von Schiller (1759–1805) German
    dramatist.
    Said by Philip II of Spain
    Don Carlos, I:6

1599

74* That realm cannot be rich whose coin is poor or
    base.
    William Cecil, Lord Burghley (1520–98)
    English statesman
    Referring to Elizabeth I's reform of coinage
    Attrib.

75 Every subject's duty is the King's; but every
    subject's soul is his own.
    William Shakespeare (1564–1616) English
    dramatist.
    Henry V, IV:1

1600

76 Perhaps your fear in passing judgement is
    greater than mine in receiving it.
    Giordano Bruno (1548–1600) Italian
    philosopher.
    Said on being sentenced to death for heresy, 8
    Feb 1600
    Attrib.

77 Cry 'Havoc!' and let slip the dogs of war.
    William Shakespeare (1564–1616) English
    dramatist.
    Julius Caesar, III:1

78 I want there to be no peasant in my kingdom so
    poor that he is unable to have a chicken in his
    pot every Sunday.
    Henri IV (1553–1610) King of France.
    Hist. de Henry le Grand (Hardouin de Péréfixe)

1601

79 I have been, though unworthy, a member of this
    House in six or seven Parliaments, yet never
    did I see the House in so great confusion. This
    is more fit for a grammar school than a Court
    of Parliament.
    Robert Cecil, 1st Earl of Salisbury (1563–
    1612) English statesman.
    Speech, House of Commons, 24 Nov 1601

80 Though God hath raised me high, yet this I
    count the glory of my crown: that I have
    reigned with your loves.
    Elizabeth I (1533–1603) Queen of England.
    Speech to a deputation from the House of Com-
    mons (the Golden Speech), 30 Nov 1601

81 Of myself I must say this, I never was any
    greedy, scraping grasper, nor a strait fast-hold-
    ing prince, nor yet a waster; my heart was

never set on wordly goods, but only for my
subjects' good.
Elizabeth I
Speech to a deputation from the House of Commons (the Golden Speech), 30 Nov 1601

82 There's such divinity doth hedge a king
    That treason can but peep to what it would.
    William Shakespeare (1564–1616) English
    dramatist.
    Hamlet, IV:5

1603

83 Must! Is *must* a word to be addressed to
    princes? Little man, little man! thy father, if he
    had been alive, durst not have used that word.
    Elizabeth I (1533–1603) Queen of England.
    Said to Robert Cecil, on her death bed
    A Short History of the English People (J. R.
    Green). Ch. 7

84 I will that a king succeed me, and who but my
    kinsman the king of Scots.
    Elizabeth I
    Said shortly before she died, when pressed con-
    cerning the succession
    The Reign of Elizabeth (J. D. Black). Ch. 13

85 . . . by putting her hand to her head, when the
    King of Scots was named to succeed her, they
    all knew he was the man she desired should
    reign after her.
    Sir Robert Carey (c. 1560–1639) English
    courtier.
    Referring to the death of Elizabeth I
    Memoirs

1604

86 No Bishop, no King.
    James I (1566–1625) King of England.
    An expression, at a conference on doctrinal re-
    form, of his belief that a non-episcopal form of
    church government was incompatible with
    monarchy
    Remark, Hampton Court, 14 Jan 1604; reported
    by William Barlow

1605

87 Please to remember the Fifth of November,
    Gunpowder Treason and Plot.
    We know no reason why gunpowder treason
    Should ever be forgot.
    Anonymous
    Traditional

88 A desperate disease requires a dangerous
    remedy.
    Guy Fawkes (1570–1606) English conspirator.
    In justification of the Gunpowder Plot; said when
    questioned by the King and council immediately
    after his arrest (5 Nov 1605)
    Dictionary of National Biography

89 . . . to blow the Scots back again into Scotland.
    Guy Fawkes
    One of his professed objectives for the Gunpow-
    der Plot, referring to the Scottish-born King
    James I; said when questioned by the King and

council immediately after his arrest. 5 Nov
1605
Dictionary of National Biography

90　On the 5th of November we began our Parliament, to which the King should have come in
person, but refrained, through a practice but
that morning discovered. The plot was to have
blown up the King.
Sir Edward Hoby (1560–1617) English
politician.
Letter to Sir Thomas Edmondes, 19 Nov 1605

91　... in general sorrow that so monstrous a
wickedness should be found harboured with in
the breast of any of their religion.
Charles Cornwallis (c. 1580–1629) British
ambassador in Madrid.
Describing Spanish reaction to the Gunpowder
Plot
Letter to Lord Salisbury, Nov 1605

92　The law of the realm cannot be changed but by
Parliament.
Edward Coke (1552–1634) English lawyer
and politician.
Dictum, in the case *Articuli Cleri*, 1605

93　The king reigns, but does not govern.
Jan Zamoyski (1541–1605) Grand chancellor
of Poland.
Speech, Polish Parliament, 1605

94　That in the captain's but a choleric word
Which in the soldier is flat blasphemy.
William Shakespeare (1564–1616) English
dramatist.
Measure for Measure, II:2

95　Farewell the neighing steed and the shrill
trump,
The spirit-stirring drum, th'ear piercing fife,
The royal banner, and all quality,
Pride, pomp, and circumstance, of glorious
war!
William Shakespeare
Othello, III:3

1609

96　The state of monarchy is the supremest thing
upon earth; for kings are not only God's
Lieutenants upon earth, and sit upon God's
throne, but even by God himself they are called
Gods.
James I (1566–1625) King of England.
Speech, Parliament, 21 Mar 1609

97　Kings are earth's gods; in vice their law's their
will.
William Shakespeare (1564–1616) English
dramatist.
Pericles, I:1

1610

98*　Mahomet made the people believe that he
would call a hill to him ... when the hill stood
still, he was never a whit abashed, but said,

'If the hill will not come to Mahomet, Mahomet
will go to the hill.'
Francis Bacon (1561–1626) English
philosopher.
Often misquoted as 'If the mountain will not
come to Mohammed'
Essays, 'Of Boldness'

99*　Nothing destroyeth authority so much as the
unequal and untimely interchange of power
pressed too far, and relaxed too much.
Francis Bacon
Essays, 'Of Empire'

100　The wisest fool in Christendom.
Henri IV (1553–1610) King of France.
Referring to James I of England
Attrib.

1611

101　Who but my father would keep such a bird in a
cage?
Henry, Prince of Wales (1594–1612) Firstborn son of James I.
Referring to Sir Walter Raleigh, who was imprisoned in the Tower of London for treason from
1603
Remark

102　Though authority be a stubborn bear, yet he is
oft led by the nose with gold.
William Shakespeare (1564–1616) English
dramatist.
The Winter's Tale, IV:3

1615

103　There are only two families in the world, my old
grandmother used to say, The *Haves* and the
Have-Nots.
Miguel de Cervantes (1547–1616) Spanish
novelist.
Don Quixote, Pt. II, Ch. 20

1618

104　Treason doth never prosper: what's the reason?
For if it prosper, none dare call it treason.
John Harington (1561–1612) English writer.
Epigrams, 'Of Treason'

105　So the heart be right, it is no matter which way
the head lies.
Walter Raleigh.
On laying his head on the executioner's block
Attrib.

106　Tis a sharp remedy, but a sure one for all ills.
Walter Raleigh (1554–1618) English explorer.
Referring to the executioner's axe just before he
was beheaded
Attrib.

1620

107　May not and ought not the children of these fathers rightly say: 'Our fathers were English-

men which came over this great ocean, and were ready to perish in this wilderness.'
William Bradford (1590–1657) Pilgrim Father.
Referring to the Pilgrim Fathers, after their arrival at Cape Cod
Of Plymouth Plantation, Ch. 10

1621

108 I will govern according to the common weal, but not according to the common will.
James I (1566–1625) King of England.
History of the English People (J. R. Green)

1623

109* He that makes a good war makes a good peace.
George Herbert (1593–1633) English poet.
Outlandish Proverbs, 420

1624

110 One of the Seven was wont to say: 'That laws were like cobwebs; where the small flies were caught, and the great brake through.'
Francis Bacon (1561–1626) English philosopher.
Apothegms

1628

111 Magna Charta is such a fellow, that he will have no sovereign.
Edward Coke (1552–1634) English lawyer and politician.
Speaking on the Lords' Amendment to the Petition of Right, 17 May 1628
Hist. Coll. (Rushworth), I

1635

112 That pig of a Henry VIII committed such sacrilege by profaning so many ecclesiastical benefices in order to give their goods to those who being so rewarded might stand firmly for the King in the Lower House; and now the King's greatest enemies are those who are enriched by these benefices.
Sir Francis Windebank (1582–1646) English politician.
Remark to the Papal envoy, Apr 1635

1636

113 Never make a defence or apology before you be accused.
Charles I (1600–49) King of England.
Letter to Lord Wentworth, 3 Sept 1636

1640

114 They say princes learn no art truly, but the art of horsemanship. The reason is, the brave

beast is no flatterer. He will throw a prince as soon as his groom.
Ben Jonson (1573–1637) English dramatist.
Timber, or Discoveries made upon Men and Matter

1641

115 To know how to dissimulate is the knowledge of kings.
Cardinal Richelieu (1585–1642) French statesman.
Testament Politique, Maxims

116 Not least among the qualities in a great King is a capacity to permit his ministers to serve him.
Cardinal Richelieu
Testament Politique, Maxims

117 Secrecy is the first essential in affairs of the State.
Cardinal Richelieu
Testament Politique, Maxims

1642

118 Richelieu leaned to the good whenever his interests did not draw him towards evil.
Cardinal de Retz (1614–79) French churchman.
Mémoires

119 Stone walls do not a prison make,
Nor iron bars a cage.
Richard Lovelace (1618–58) English poet.
To Althea, from Prison

The English Civil War, the Commonwealth, and the Protectorate (1642–59)

The English Civil War was the conflict between royalists (Cavaliers) and parliamentarians (Roundheads) which began on 22 August 1642 when King Charles I raised his standard at Nottingham. At first finely balanced, it tilted decisively against the king from c. 1645. He was captured in 1646, but escaped in 1647; he was recaptured and, in 1649, executed. Oliver Cromwell formed the Commonwealth and overcame residual resistance to end the warfare in 1651. In 1653, he dismissed Parliament, set up the Protectorate, and assumed power himself. He ruled until his death (1658), and was briefly succeeded by his son until the Restoration of King Charles II (1660).

120 Well, since I see all the birds are flown, I do expect from you that you shall send them unto me as soon as they return hither.
Charles I (1600–49) King of England.
On entering the House of Commons to arrest five MPs
Remark, 4 Jan 1642

121 I have neither eye to see, nor tongue to speak

here, but as the House is pleased to direct me.
William Lenthall (1591–1662) English parliamentarian.
A succinct restatement of the Speaker's traditional role; said on 4 Jan 1642 in the House of Commons, when asked by Charles I if he had seen five MPs whom the King wished to arrest
Historical Collections (Rushworth)

122 O Lord! thou knowest how busy I must be this day: if I forget thee, do not thou forget me.
Lord Astley (1579–1652) English Royalist general.
Prayer before taking part in the Battle of Edgehill
Memoires (Sir Philip Warwick)

1643

123 Tell me not, Sweet, I am unkind,
That from the nunnery
Of thy chaste breast and quiet mind
To war and arms I fly.

True, a new mistress now I chase,
The first foe in the field;
And with a stronger faith embrace
A sword, a horse, a shield.

Yet this inconstancy is such
As thou too shalt adore;
I could not love thee, Dear, so much,
Loved I not Honour more.
Richard Lovelace
To Lucasta, Going to the Wars

124* Humpty Dumpty sat on a wall,
Humpty Dumpty had a great fall.
All the king's horses,
And all the king's men,
Couldn't put Humpty together again.
Believed to be based on an incident in the Civil War; Charles I attempted to bridge the river Severn at Gloucester using a huge machine, nicknamed 'Humpty Dumpty' by the troops. The machine collapsed in the middle of the river
Gammer Gurton's Garland

1644

125 I laboured nothing more than that the external public worship of God, too much slighted in most parts of this kingdom, might be preserved.
William Laud (1573–1645) Archbishop of Canterbury.
Remark at his trial, 12 Mar 1644

126 The State, in choosing men to serve it, takes no notice of their opinions. If they be willing faithfully to serve it, that satisfies.
Oliver Cromwell (1599–1658) English soldier and statesman.
Said before the Battle of Marston Moor, 2 July 1644

127 If we beat the King ninety and nine times yet he is King still, and so will his posterity be after

him; but if the King beat us once we shall all be hanged, and our posterity made slaves.
Earl of Manchester
Remark

128 My lord, if this be so, why did we take up arms at first? This is against fighting ever hereafter.
Oliver Cromwell (1599–1658) English soldier and statesman.
Reply to the Earl of Manchester (above)
Remark

1645

129* New Presbyter is but old Priest writ large.
John Milton (1608–74) English poet.
Sonnet: 'On the New Forcers of Conscience under the Long Parliament'

130* The parliament intended to have hanged him; and he expected no less, but resolved to be hanged with the Bible under one arm and Magna Carta under the other.
John Aubrey (1626–1697) English antiquary.
David Jenkins (1582–1663), a Welsh judge and royalist, was imprisoned by parliament (1645–60)
Brief Lives, 'David Jenkins'

1646

131 Every old woman with a wrinkled face, a furr'd brow, a hairy lip, a gobber tooth, a squint eye, a squeaking voice, or a scolding tongue . . . a dog or cat by her side, is not only suspected but pronounced for a witch.
John Gaule (fl. 1660) Vicar of Great Stoughton (Huntingdonshire).
Sermons on Witchcraft

1647

132 The poorest he that is in England hath a life to live as the greatest he.
Thomas Rainborowe (d. 1648) English soldier and vice-admiral.
Life of Rainborowe (Peacock)

1648

133 'Twixt kings and tyrants there's this difference known;
Kings seek their subjects' good: tyrants their own.
Robert Herrick (1591–1674) English poet.
Hesperides, 'Kings and Tyrants'

134 Do you not know, my son, with how little wisdom the world is governed?
Axel Oxenstierna (1583–1654) Swedish statesman.
Letter to his son, 1648

1649

135 A Subject and a Sovereign are clean different things.
Charles I (1600–49) King of England.
Speech on the scaffold, 30 Jan 1649

136 I die a Christian, according to the Profession of
the Church of England, as I found it left me by
my Father.
Charles I
Speech on the scaffold, 30 Jan 1649

137 He nothing common did or mean
Upon that memorable scene,
But with his keener eye
The axe's edge did try.
Andrew Marvell (1621–78) English poet.
Referring to the execution of Charles I
*An Horatian Ode upon Cromwell's Return from
Ireland*

138 Oh let that day from time be blotted quite,
And let belief of't in next age be waived.
In deepest silence th'act concealed might,
So that the Kingdom's credit might be saved.

But if the Power Divine permitted this,
His Will's the law and ours must acquiesce.
Lord Thomas Fairfax (1612–71) General.
Referring to the execution of Charles I
The Faber Book of English History in Verse
(Kenneth Baker)

139 I paid a visit of condolence to the Queen of
England. Her husband had been beheaded by
order of the British parliament. The court did
not go into general mourning on this occasion,
for want of funds. I found her not so deeply
affected as she should have been.
Duchess of Montpensier (1627–93) Niece
of Louis XIII.
Referring to the French court
Mémoires, Feb 1649

140 You noble Diggers all, stand up now,
The waste land to maintain, seeing Cavaliers
by name
Your digging do disdain and persons all
defame.
Gerrard Winstanley (c. 1609–c. 1660)
Leader of the Diggers.
The Diggers were a radical group that believed in
land reform and practised a primitive agrarian
communism. Important in 1649, they were dispersed by the Commonwealth government in
1650
The Diggers' Song

141 Seeing the common people of England by joint
consent of person and purse have cast out
Charles our Norman oppressor, we have by
this victory recovered ourselves from under his
Norman yoke.
Gerrard Winstanley
Remark to Lord Fairfax, 8 Dec 1649

142 None ought to be lords or landlords over another, but the earth is free for every son and
daughter of mankind to live free upon.
Gerrard Winstanley
Letter to Lord Fairfax, 1649

143 None can love freedom heartily, but good men;
the rest love not freedom, but licence.
John Milton (1608–74) English poet.
Tenure of Kings and Magistrates

144 The power of kings and magistrates is nothing

else, but what only is derivative, transformed
and committed to them in trust from the
people to the common good of them all, in
whom the power yet remains fundamentally,
and cannot be taken from them, without a viola-
tion of their natural birthright.
John Milton
The Tenure of Kings and Magistrates

1650
---

145 I beseech you, in the bowels of Christ, think it
possible you may be mistaken.
Oliver Cromwell (1599–1658) English soldier
and statesman.
Letter to the General Assembly of the Church of
Scotland, 3 Aug 1650

146 So restless Cromwell could not cease
In the inglorious arts of peace.
Andrew Marvell (1621–78) English poet.
*An Horatian Ode upon Cromwell's Return from
Ireland*

1651
---

147 The condition of man . . . is a condition of war
of everyone against everyone.
Thomas Hobbes (1588–1679) English
philosopher.
Leviathan, Pt. I, Ch. 4

148 They that approve a private opinion, call it opinion; but they that mislike it, heresy: and yet
heresy signifies no more than private opinion.
Thomas Hobbes
Leviathan, Pt. I, Ch. 11

149 No arts; no letters; no society; and which is
worst of all, continual fear and danger of violent
death; and the life of man, solitary, poor,
nasty, brutish, and short.
Thomas Hobbes
Leviathan, Pt. I, Ch. 13

150 The only way to erect such a common power,
as may be able to defend them from the invasion of foreigners, and the injuries of one another . . . is, to confer all their power and
strength upon one man, or upon one assembly
of men, that may reduce all their wills, by plu-
rality of voices, unto one will . . . This is the
generation of that great Leviathan, or rather (to
speak more reverently) of that *Mortal God*, to
which we owe under the *Immortal God*, our
peace and defence.
Thomas Hobbes
Leviathan, Pt. II, Ch. 17

151 Covenants without the sword are but words
and of no strength to secure a man at all.
Thomas Hobbes
Leviathan, Pt. II, Ch. 17

152 They that are discontented under *monarchy*,
call it *tyranny* ; and they that are displeased
with *aristocracy*, call it *oligarchy*: so also, they
which find themselves grieved under a *democracy*, call it *anarchy*, which signifies the want
of government; and yet I think no man believes,

that want of government, is any new kind of government.
Thomas Hobbes
Leviathan, Pt. II, Ch. 19

153 The Papacy is not other than the Ghost of the deceased Roman Empire, sitting crowned upon the grave thereof.
Thomas Hobbes
Leviathan, Pt. IV, Ch. 37

1652

154 It is upon the navy under the Providence of God that the safety, honour, and welfare of this realm do chiefly attend.
Charles II (1630–1685) King of England.
Articles of War

155 Peace hath her victories
No less renowned than war.
John Milton (1608–74) English poet.
Sonnet: 'To the Lord General Cromwell, May 1652'

1653

156 Take away that fool's bauble, the mace.
Oliver Cromwell (1599–1658) English soldier and statesman.
Speech dismissing the Rump Parliament, 20 Apr 1653

157 It is not fit that you should sit here any longer!
...you shall now give place to better men.
Oliver Cromwell
Speech dismissing the Rump Parliament, 20 Apr 1653

1654

158 The people would be just as noisy if they were going to see me hanged.
Oliver Cromwell
Referring to a cheering crowd

159 Necessity hath no law.
Oliver Cromwell
Speech, Parliament, 12 Sept 1654

1655

160* Mr Lely, I desire you would use all your skill to paint my picture truly like me, and not flatter me at all; but remark all these roughnesses, pimples, warts, and everything as you see me, otherwise I will never pay a farthing for it.
Oliver Cromwell
The origin of the expression 'warts and all'
Anecdotes of Painting (Horace Walpole), Ch. 12

1656

161 For the Colonies in the Indies, they are yet babes that cannot live without sucking the breasts of their mother-Cities, but such as, I

mistake, if when they come of age they do not wean themselves.
James Harrington (1611–77) English political writer.
The Commonwealth of Oceana

1660

162* Christianity is part of the Common Law of England.
Matthew Hale (1609–76) English judge.
Historia Placitorum Coronae (ed. Sollom Emlyn)

163 He will be looked upon by posterity as a brave bad man.
Edward Hyde, Earl of Clarendon (1609–74) English statesman and historian.
Referring to Cromwell
History of the Great Rebellion

164 Here out of the window it was a most pleasant sight to see the City from one end to the other with a glory about it, so high was the light of the bonfires, and so thick round the City, and the bells rang everywhere.
Samuel Pepys (1633–1703) English diarist.
Describing the celebrations in London at the end of the Commonwealth
Diary, 21 Feb 1660

165 Of this you may be assured, that you shall none of you suffer for your opinions or religion, so long as you live peaceably, and you have the word of a king for it.
Charles II (1630–85)
Said to a deputation of quakers
Works (R. Hubberthorn)

Attitudes

Art, Literature, and Music

1595

166 There have been many most excellent poets that have never versified, and now swarm many versifiers that need never answer to the name of poets.
Philip Sidney (1554–86) English poet and courtier.
The Defence of Poesy

1597

167 The man that hath no music in himself,
Nor is not mov'd with concord of sweet sounds,
Is fit for treasons, stratagems, and spoils.
William Shakespeare (1564–1616) English dramatist.
The Merchant of Venice, V:1

1600

168* Good painters imitate nature, bad ones spew it up.
Miguel de Cervantes (1547–1616) Spanish novelist.
El Licenciado Vidriera

169 O that Ocean did not bound our style
Within these strict and narrow limits so:
But that the melody of our sweet isle
Might now be heard to Tiber, Arne, and Po:
That they might know how far Thames doth outgo
The music of declined Italy.
Michael Drayton
Referring to the English Language
The Reign of Elizabeth (J. B. Black), Ch. 8

170 The truest poetry is the most feigning.
William Shakespeare (1564–1616) English dramatist.
As You Like It, III:3

1601

171 The play, I remember, pleas'd not the million; 'twas caviare to the general.
William Shakespeare
Hamlet, II:2

1602

172 If music be the food of love, play on,
Give me excess of it, that, surfeiting,
The appetite may sicken and so die.
William Shakespeare
Twelfth Night, I:1

1609

173 Not marble, nor the gilded monuments
Of princes, shall outlive this powerful rhyme.
William Shakespeare
Sonnet 55

1612

174 Our revels now are ended. These our actors,
As I foretold you, were all spirits, and
Are melted into air, into thin air;
And, like the baseless fabric of this vision,
The cloud-capp'd towers, the gorgeous palaces,
The solemn temples, the great globe itself,
Yea, all which it inherit, shall dissolve,
And, like this insubstantial pageant faded,
Leave not a rack behind. We are such stuff
As dreams are made on; and our little life
Is rounded with a sleep.
William Shakespeare
The Tempest, IV:1

1616

175 Sweet Swan of Avon!
Ben Jonson (1573–1637) English dramatist.
To the Memory of William Shakespeare

176 He was not of an age, but for all time!
Ben Jonson
To the Memory of William Shakespeare

1621

177 From this it is clear how much more cruel the pen is than the sword.
Robert Burton (1577–1640) English scholar and explorer.
Anatomy of Melancholy, Pt. I

1624

178 In *Architecture* as in all other *Operative* Arts, the *end* must direct the *Operation*. The end is to build well. Well building hath three Conditions. *Commodity, Firmness,* and *Delight*.
Henry Wotton (1568–1639) English poet and diplomat.
Elements of Architecture, Pt. I

1630

179 My soul; sit thou a patient looker-on;
Judge not the play before the play is done:
Her plot hath many changes, every day
Speaks a new scene; the last act crowns the play.
Francis Quarles (1592–1644) English poet.
Epigram, Respice Finem

1632

180 Or sweetest Shakespeare, Fancy's child,
Warble his native wood-notes wild.
John Milton (1608–74) English poet.
L'Allegro

1637

181 The reading of all good books is like a conversation with the finest men of past centuries.
René Descartes (1596–1650) French philosopher.
Le Discours de la méthode

1644

182 Who kills a man kills a reasonable creature, God's image; but he who destroys a good book, kills reason itself, kills the image of God, as it were in the eye.
John Milton (1608–74) English poet.
Areopagitica

183 A good book is the precious life-blood of a master spirit, embalmed and treasured up on purpose to a life beyond life.
John Milton
Areopagitica

Daily Life

1530

184 Who loves not wine, woman and song,
Remains a fool his whole life long.
Martin Luther (1483–1546) German
Protestant.
Attrib.

1531

185 ...wherein is nothing but beastly fury and extreme violence, whereof proceedeth hurt; and consequently rancour and malice do remain with them that be wounded.
Thomas Elyot (?1450–1522) English diplomat.
Referring to football
Boke called the Governour

1534

186 I drink for the thirst to come.
François Rabelais (1483–1553) French
satirist.
Gargantua, Bk. I, Ch. 5

1550

187* For when the wine is in, the wit is out.
Thomas Becon (1512–67) English Protestant
churchman.
Catechism, 375

1557

188 At Christmas play and make good cheer,
For Christmas comes but once a year.
Thomas Tusser (1524–80) English farmer.
Five Hundred Points of Good Husbandry, 'The Farmer's Daily Diet'

189 Seek home for rest,
For home is best.
Thomas Tusser
Five Hundred Points of Good Husbandry, 'Instructions to Housewifery'

1583

190 Footeball ... causeth fighting, brawling, contention, quarrel picking, murder, homicide and great effusion of bloode, as daily experience teacheth.
Philip Stubbs (fl. 1583–91) English puritan
pamphleteer.
The Anatomie of Abuses

1584

191 ...many thousands of idle persons are within this realm which, being no way to be set on work, be either mutinous and seek alteration in the state or at least very burdensome to the common wealth and often fall to pilfering and thieving and other lewdness, whereby all the prisons of the land are daily pestered and stuffed full of them.
Richard Hakluyt (c. 1552–1616) Geographer.
Particular Discourse of Western Planting

1598

192 Ods me, I marvel what pleasure or felicity they have in taking their roguish tobacco. It is good for nothing but to choke a man, and fill him full of smoke and embers.
Ben Jonson (1573–1637) English dramatist.
Every Man in His Humour, III:5

1604

193 A branch of the sin of drunkenness, which is the root of all sins.
James I (1566–1625) King of England, Scotland, and Ireland.
A Counterblast to Tobacco

194 A custom loathsome to the eye, hateful to the nose, harmful to the brain, dangerous to the lungs, and in the black, stinking fume thereof, nearest resembling the horrible Stygian smoke of the pit that is bottomless.
James I
A Counterblast to Tobacco

1610

195* Houses are built to live in and not to look on; therefore let use be preferred before uniformity, except where both may be had.
Francis Bacon (1561–1626) English
philosopher.
Essays, 'Of Building'

1611

196 I would there were no age between ten and three and twenty, or that youth would sleep out the rest; for there is nothing in the between but getting wenches with child, wronging the ancientry, stealing, fighting.
William Shakespeare (1564–1616) English
dramatist.
The Winter's Tale, III:3

1614

197 Neither do thou lust after that tawney weed tobacco.
Ben Jonson (1573–1637) English dramatist.
Bartholomew Fair, II:6

1616

198 And he that will go to bed sober,
Falls with the leaf still in October.
John Fletcher (1579–1625) English dramatist.
The Bloody Brother, II:2

1622

199* The house of every one is to him as his castle and fortress.
Edward Coke (1552–1634) English lawyer and politician.
Semayne's Case

1632

200 Popular stage-plays are sinful, heathenish, lewd, ungodly Spectacles and most pernicious Corruptions, condemned in all ages as intolerable Mischiefs to Churches, to Republics, to the manners, minds and souls of men.
William Prynne (1600–69) English Puritan.
Histriomastix

Death

1589

201 Sleep after toil, port after stormy seas, Ease after war, death after life does greatly please.
Edmund Spenser (1552–99) English poet.
The Faerie Queene, I:9

1598

202 I care not; a man can die but once; we owe God a death.
William Shakespeare (1564–1616) English dramatist.
Henry IV, Part Two, III:2

1600

203 I have often thought upon death, and I find it the least of all evils.
Francis Bacon (1561–1626) English philosopher.
An Essay on Death

204 I do not believe that any man fears to be dead, but only the stroke of death.
Francis Bacon
An Essay on Death

205 Men fear death, as children fear to go in the dark; and as that natural fear in children is increased with tales, so is the other.
Francis Bacon
An Essay on Death

206 It is natural to die as to be born; and to a little infant, perhaps, the one is as painful as the other.
Francis Bacon
An Essay on Death

207 Why, he that cuts off twenty years of life Cuts off so many years of fearing death.
William Shakespeare (1564–1616) English dramatist.
Julius Caesar, III:1

1601

208 The dread of something after death –
The undiscover'd country, from whose bourn No traveller returns.
William Shakespeare
Hamlet, III:1

209 To be, or not to be – that is the question;
Whether 'tis nobler in the mind to suffer
The slings and arrows of outrageous fortune,
Or to take arms against a sea of troubles,
And by opposing end them? To die, to sleep –
No more; and by a sleep to say we end
The heart-ache and the thousand natural shocks
That flesh is heir to, 'tis a consummation
Devoutly to be wish'd. To die, to sleep;
To sleep, perchance to dream. Ay, there's the rub;
For in that sleep of death what dreams may come,
When we have shuffled off this mortal coil,
Must give us pause.
William Shakespeare
Hamlet, III:1

1606

210 As flies to wanton boys are we to th' gods –
They kill us for their sport.
William Shakespeare
King Lear, IV:1

1609

211 Like as the waves make towards the pebbled shore,
So do our minutes hasten to their end.
William Shakespeare
Sonnet 60

1610

212 Fear no more the heat o' th' sun
Nor the furious winter's rages;
Thou thy worldly task hast done,
Home art gone, and ta'en thy wages.
Golden lads and girls all must,
As chimney-sweepers, come to dust.
William Shakespeare
Cymbeline, IV:2

1615

213 Well, now, there's a remedy for everything except death.
Miguel de Cervantes (1547–1616) Spanish novelist.
Don Quixote, Pt. II, Ch. 10

1623

214 Any man's death diminishes me, because I am involved in Mankind; And therefore never

send to know for whom the bell tolls; it tolls for thee.
John Donne (1573–1631) English poet.
Devotions, 17

Education, Knowledge, and Learning

1570

215   I remember when I was young, in the north, they went to the grammar school little children: they came from thence great lubbers: always learning, and little profiting: learning without book everything, understanding within the book little or nothing.
Roger Ascham (1515–68)
The Scholemaster

1595

216   Wisely and slow; they stumble that run fast.
William Shakespeare (1564–1616) English dramatist.
Romeo and Juliet, II:3

1605

217   If a man will begin with certainties, he shall end in doubts, but if he will be content to begin with doubts, he shall end in certainties.
Francis Bacon (1561–1626) English philosopher.
The Advancement of Learning, Bk. I, Ch. 5

218   For all knowledge and wonder (which is the seed of knowledge) is an impression of pleasure in itself.
Francis Bacon
The Advancement of Learning, Bk. I, Ch. 1

1610

219*   A wise man will make more opportunities than he finds.
Francis Bacon
Essays, 'Of Ceremonies and Respects'

220*   *Nam et ipsa scientia potestas est.*
Knowledge itself is power.
Francis Bacon
Religious Meditations, 'Of Heresies'

221*   Reading maketh a full man; conference a ready man; and writing an exact man.
Francis Bacon
Essays, 'Of Studies'

1642

222   Learning hath gained most by those books by which the printers have lost.
Thomas Fuller (1608–61) English historian.
The Holy State and the Profane State

223   Many have been the wise speeches of fools,

though not so many as the foolish speeches of wise men.
Thomas Fuller
The Holy State and the Profane State

Human Nature

1579

224   And he that strives to touch the stars,
Oft stumbles at a straw.
Edmund Spenser (1552–99) English poet.
The Shepherd's Calendar, 'July'

1580

225   Unless a man feels he has a good enough memory, he should never venture to lie.
Michel de Montaigne (1533–92) French essayist.
Also quoted in *Le Menteur*, IV:5 by Pierre Corneille (1606–84)
Essais, I

226   A man who fears suffering is already suffering from what he fears.
Michel de Montaigne
Essais, III

227   The dark night of the soul.
St John of the Cross (Juan de Yepes y Alvarez; 1542–91) Spanish churchman and poet.
English translation of *Noche obscura del alma*, the title of a poem

1583

228   We are as near to heaven by sea as by land.
Humphrey Gilbert (c. 1539–83) English navigator.
Remark made shortly before he went down with his ship *Squirrel*
A Book of Anecdotes (D. George)

1595

229   What's in a name? That which we call a rose By any other name would smell as sweet.
William Shakespeare (1564–1616) English dramatist.
Romeo and Juliet, II:2

1597

230   The devil can cite Scripture for his purpose.
William Shakespeare
The Merchant of Venice, I:3

231   Hath not a Jew eyes? Hath not a Jew hands, organs, dimensions, senses, affections, passions, fed with the same food, hurt with the same weapons, subject to the same diseases, healed by the same means, warmed and cooled by the same winter and summer, as a Christian is? If you prick us, do we not bleed? If you tickle us, do we not laugh? If you

poison us, do we not die? And if you wrong us,
shall we not revenge?
William Shakespeare
The Merchant of Venice, III:1

1598

232 Care I for the limb, the thews, the stature, bulk,
and big assemblance of a man! Give me the
spirit.
William Shakespeare
Henry IV, Part Two, III:2

1599

233 Friendship is constant in all other things
Save in the office and affairs of love.
William Shakespeare
Much Ado About Nothing, II:1

234 Men of few words are the best men.
William Shakespeare
Henry V, III:2

235 To be a well-favoured man is the gift of fortune;
but to write and read comes by nature.
William Shakespeare
Much Ado About Nothing, III:3

1600

236 A friend should bear his friend's infirmities,
But Brutus makes mine greater than they are.
William Shakespeare
Julius Caesar, IV:3

237 Most friendship is feigning, most loving mere
folly.
William Shakespeare
As You Like It, II:7

1601

238 Costly thy habit as thy purse can buy,
But not express'd in fancy; rich, not gaudy;
For the apparel oft proclaims the man.
William Shakespeare
Hamlet, I:3

239 To be honest, as this world goes, is to be one
man pick'd out of ten thousand.
William Shakespeare
Hamlet, II:2

240 What a piece of work is a man! How noble in
reason! how infinite in faculties! in form and
moving, how express and admirable! in action,
how like an angel! in apprehension, how like a
god! the beauty of the world! the paragon of
animals! And yet, to me, what is this quintessence of dust? Man delights not me – no,
nor woman neither.
William Shakespeare
Hamlet, II:2

1603

241 Our remedies oft in ourselves do lie,

Which we ascribe to heaven.
William Shakespeare
All's Well that Ends Well, I:1

1605

242 The miserable have no other medicine
But only hope.
William Shakespeare
Measure for Measure, III:1

1606

243 This is the excellent foppery of the world, that,
when we are sick in fortune, often the surfeits
of our own behaviour, we make guilty of our
disasters the sun, the moon, and stars.
William Shakespeare
King Lear, I:2

244 Yet do I fear thy nature;
It is too full o' th' milk of human kindness
To catch the nearest way.
William Shakespeare
Macbeth, I:5

1609

245 3RD FISHERMAN. Master, I marvel how the fishes
live in the sea.
1ST FISHERMAN. Why, as men do a-land – the
great ones eat up the little ones.
William Shakespeare
Pericles, II:1

1610

246 There is in human nature generally more of the
fool than of the wise.
Francis Bacon (1561–1626) English
philosopher.
Essays, 'Of Boldness'

247* A man's nature runs either to herbs, or to
weeds; therefore let him seasonably water the
one; and destroy the other.
Francis Bacon
Essays, 'Of Nature in Men'

248 Nature is often hidden, sometimes overcome,
seldom extinguished.
Francis Bacon
Essays, 'Of Nature in Men'

249 You are no better than you should be.
Francis Beaumont (1584–1616) English
dramatist.
The Coxcomb, IV:3

1611

250 It is the wisdom of the crocodiles, that shed
tears when they would devour.
Francis Bacon (1561–1626) English
philosopher.
Essays, 'Of Wisdom for a Man's Self'

1612

251 When they will not give a doit to relieve a lame beggar, they will lay out ten to see a dead Indian.
William Shakespeare (1564–1616) English dramatist.
The Tempest, II:2

1615

252 Every man is as Heaven made him, and sometimes a great deal worse.
Miguel de Cervantes (1547–1616) Spanish novelist.
Don Quixote, Pt. II, Ch. 4

1623

253 He that would govern others, first should be The master of himself.
Philip Massinger (1583–1640) English dramatist.
The Bondman, I

1632

254 Hence, vain deluding Joys,
The brood of Folly without father bred!
John Milton (1608–74) English poet.
Il Penseroso

1637

255 We triumph without glory when we conquer without danger.
Pierre Corneille (1606–84) French dramatist.
Le Cid, II:2

1641

256 Talking and eloquence are not the same: to speak, and to speak well, are two things.
Ben Jonson (1573–1637) English dramatist.
Timber, or Discoveries made upon Men and Matter

257 One often calms one's grief by recounting it.
Pierre Corneille (1606–84) French dramatist.
Polyeucte, I:3

1642

258 If you give me six lines written by the most honest man, I will find something in them to hang him.
Cardinal Richelieu (1585–1642) French statesman.
Exact wording uncertain
Attrib.

259 Anger is one of the sinews of the soul.
Thomas Fuller (1608–61) English historian.
The Holy State and the Profane State

Humour

1595

260 A jest's prosperity lies in the ear
Of him that hears it, never in the tongue
Of him that makes it.
William Shakespeare (1564–1616) English dramatist.
Love's Labour's Lost, V:2

Life

1530

261 Nature abhors a vacuum.
François Rabelais (1483–1553) French satirist.
Attrib.

1549

262 The drop of rain maketh a hole in the stone, not by violence, but by oft falling.
Hugh Latimer (1485–1555) English churchman.
Sermon preached before Edward VI

1580

263 Change is not made without inconvenience, even from worse to better.
Richard Hooker (c. 1554–1600) English theologian.
English Dictionary (Johnson), Preface

264 The world is but a school of inquiry.
Michel de Montaigne (1533–92) French essayist.
Essais, III

265 A man must keep a little back shop where he can be himself without reserve. In solitude alone can he know true freedom.
Michel de Montaigne
Essais, I

1592

266 When all the world dissolves,
And every creature shall be purified,
All place shall be hell that is not heaven.
Christopher Marlowe (1564–93) English dramatist.
Doctor Faustus, II:1

1596

267 The purest treasure mortal times afford
Is spotless reputation; that away,
Men are but gilded loam or painted clay.
William Shakespeare (1564–1616) English dramatist.
Richard II, I:1

268 How sour sweet music is
When time is broke and no proportion kept!

So is it in the music of men's lives.
William Shakespeare
Richard II, V:5

269   Things sweet to taste prove in digestion sour.
William Shakespeare
Richard II, I:3

270   Teach thy necessity to reason thus:
There is no virtue like necessity.
William Shakespeare
Richard II, I:3

1597

271   Life is as tedious as a twice-told tale
Vexing the dull ear of a drowsy man.
William Shakespeare
King John, III:4

1599

272   I think the King is but a man as I am: the violet
smells to him as it doth to me.
William Shakespeare
Henry V, IV:1

273   Crabbed age and youth cannot live together:
Youth is full of pleasure, age is full of care;
Youth like summer morn, age like winter
weather;
Youth like summer brave, age like winter
bare.
William Shakespeare (1564–1616) English
dramatist.
The Passionate Pilgrim, XII

1600

274   All the world's a stage,
And all the men and women merely players;
They have their exits and their entrances;
And one man in his time plays many parts,
His acts being seven ages.
William Shakespeare
As You Like It, II:7

275   Last scene of all,
That ends this strange eventful history,
Is second childishness and mere oblivion;
Sans teeth, sans eyes, sans taste, sans every
thing.
William Shakespeare
As You Like It, II:7

276   And so, from hour to hour, we ripe and ripe,
And then, from hour to hour, we rot and rot;
And thereby hangs a tale.
William Shakespeare
As You Like It, II:7

277   There is a tide in the affairs of men
Which, taken at the flood, leads on to fortune;
Omitted, all the voyage of their life
Is bound in shallows and in miseries.
On such a full sea are we now afloat,
And we must take the current when it serves,
Or lose our ventures.
William Shakespeare
Julius Caesar, IV:3

1601

278   When sorrows come, they come not single
spies,
But in battalions!
William Shakespeare
Hamlet, IV:5

279   Why, then the world's mine oyster,
Which I with sword will open.
William Shakespeare
The Merry Wives of Windsor, II:2

280   There are more things in heaven and earth, Ho-
ratio,
Than are dreamt of in your philosophy.
William Shakespeare
Hamlet, I:5

281   How weary, stale, flat, and unprofitable,
Seem to me all the uses of this world!
William Shakespeare
Hamlet, I:2

1602

282   Some are born great, some achieve greatness,
and some have greatness thrust upon 'em.
William Shakespeare
Twelfth Night, II:5

1603

283   The world itself is but a large prison, out of
which some are daily led to execution.
Walter Raleigh (1554–1618) English explorer.
Said after his trial for treason, 1603
Attrib.

284   The web of our life is of a mingled yarn, good
and ill together.
William Shakespeare (1564–1616) English
dramatist.
All's Well that Ends Well, IV:3

1605

285   Reputation, reputation, reputation! O, I have
lost my reputation! I have lost the immortal part
of myself, and what remains is bestial.
William Shakespeare
Othello, II:3

286   To mourn a mischief that is past and gone
Is the next way to draw new mischief on.
William Shakespeare
Othello, I:3

1606

287   Tomorrow, and tomorrow, and tomorrow,
Creeps in this petty pace from day to day
To the last syllable of recorded time,
And all our yesterdays have lighted fools
The way to dusty death. Out, out, brief
candle!
Life's but a walking shadow, a poor player,
That struts and frets his hour upon the stage,
And then is heard no more; it is a tale
Told by an idiot, full of sound and fury,

Signifying nothing.
William Shakespeare
Macbeth, V:5

288 When we are born, we cry that we are come
To this great stage of fools.
William Shakespeare
King Lear, IV:6

289 The worst is not
So long as we can say 'This is the worst'.
William Shakespeare
King Lear, IV:1

290 Come what come may,
Time and the hour runs through the roughest
day.
William Shakespeare
Macbeth, I:3

1607

---

291 My salad days,
When I was green in judgment, cold in blood,
To say as I said then!
William Shakespeare
Antony and Cleopatra, I:5

1610

292* There is no excellent beauty that hath not some
strangeness in the proportion.
Francis Bacon (1561–1626) English
philosopher.
Essays, 'Of Beauty'

293* He that will not apply new remedies must expect new evils: for time is the greatest
innovator.
Francis Bacon
Essays, 'Of Innovations'

294 Dreams and predictions ought to serve but for
winter talk by the fireside.
Francis Bacon (1561–1626) English
philosopher.
Essays, 'Of Prophecies'

1612

---

295 Misery acquaints a man with strange
bedfellows.
William Shakespeare (1564–1616) English
dramatist.
The Tempest, II:2

1613

---

296 Farewell, a long farewell, to all my greatness!
This is the state of man: to-day he puts forth
The tender leaves of hopes: to-morrow
blossoms
And bears his blushing honours thick upon
him;
The third day comes a frost, a killing frost,
And when he thinks, good easy man, full
surely
His greatness is a-ripening, nips his root,

And then he falls, as I do.
William Shakespeare
Henry VIII, III:2

1620

297* A man that is young in years may be old in
hours, if he have lost no time.
Francis Bacon (1561–1626) English
philosopher.
Essays, 'Of Youth and Age'

1621

---

298 If there is a hell upon earth, it is to be found in
a melancholy man's heart.
Robert Burton (1577–1640) English scholar
and explorer.
Anatomy of Melancholy, Pt. I

1623

---

299 No man is an Island, entire of itself; every man
is a piece of the Continent, a part of the main.
John Donne (1573–1631) English poet.
Devotions, 17

1625

---

300 For my name and memory, I leave it to men's
charitable speeches, and to foreign nations,
and the next ages.
Francis Bacon (1561–1626) English
philosopher.
Will, 19 Dec 1625

1630

---

301 Tempt not the stars, young man, thou canst not
play
With the severity of fate.
John Ford (c. 1586–c. 1640) English
dramatist.
The Broken Heart, I:3

1635

---

302 For man's greatest crime is to have been born.
Pedro Calderón de la Barca (1600–81)
Spanish dramatist.
La Vida es Sueño, I

303 For I see now that I am asleep that I dream
when I am awake.
Pedro Calderón de la Barca
La Vida es Sueño, II

1637

---

304 *Cogito, ergo sum.*
I think, therefore I am.
René Descartes (1596–1650) French
philosopher.
Le Discours de la méthode

305   Travelling is almost like talking with men of
other centuries.
René Descartes
Le Discours de la méthode

306   Fame is the spur that the clear spirit doth raise
(That last infirmity of noble mind)
To scorn delights, and live laborious days.
John Milton (1608–74) English poet.
Lycidas

1642

307   All things are artificial, for nature is the art of
God.
Thomas Browne (1605–82) English physician
and writer.
Religio Medici, Pt. I

308   There is surely a piece of divinity in us, something that was before the elements, and owes
no homage unto the sun.
Thomas Browne
Religio Medici, Pt. II

309   For the world, I count it not an inn, but an hos-
pital, and a place, not to live, but to die in.
Thomas Browne
Religio Medici, Pt. II

310   Fame is sometimes like unto a kind of mushroom, which Pliny recounts to be the greatest
miracle in nature, because growing and having no root.
Thomas Fuller (1608–61) English historian.
The Holy State and the Profane State

Love and Sex

1580

311   The daughter-in-law of Pythagoras said that a
woman who goes to bed with a man ought to
lay aside her modesty with her skirt, and put it
on again with her petticoat.
Michel de Montaigne (1533–92) French
essayist.
Essais, I

1590

312*   Love built on beauty, soon as beauty, dies.
John Donne (1573–1631) English poet.
Elegies, 2. 'The Anagram'

1595

313   Therefore love moderately: long love doth so;
Too swift arrives as tardy as too slow.
William Shakespeare (1564–1616) English
dramatist.
Romeo and Juliet, II:6

1596

314   For aught that I could ever read,
Could ever hear by tale or history,

The course of true love never did run smooth.
William Shakespeare
A Midsummer Night's Dream, I:1

315   Love looks not with the eyes, but with the
mind;
And therefore is wing'd Cupid painted blind.
William Shakespeare
A Midsummer Night's Dream, I:1

1597

316   But love is blind, and lovers cannot see
The pretty follies that themselves commit.
William Shakespeare
The Merchant of Venice, II:6

1598

317   Who ever loved, that loved not at first sight?
Christopher Marlowe (1564–93) English
dramatist.
Hero and Leander, I

1600

318   If thou rememb'rest not the slightest folly
That ever love did make thee run into,
Thou hast not lov'd.
William Shakespeare (1564–1616) English
dramatist.
As You Like It, II:4

319   Men have died from time to time, and worms
have eaten them, but not for love.
William Shakespeare
As You Like It, IV:1

1602

320   What is love? 'Tis not hereafter;
Present mirth hath present laughter;
What's to come is still unsure.
In delay there lies no plenty,
Then come kiss me, sweet and twenty;
Youth's a stuff will not endure.
William Shakespeare
Twelfth Night, II:3

321   Love sought is good, but given unsought is
better.
William Shakespeare
Twelfth Night, III:1

322   To be wise and love
Exceeds man's might.
William Shakespeare
Troilus and Cressida, III:2

323   Lechery, lechery! Still wars and lechery! Noth-
ing else holds fashion.
William Shakespeare
Troilus and Cressida, V:2

1609

324   Let me not to the marriage of true minds
Admit impediments. Love is not love
Which alters when it alteration finds,
Or bends with the remover to remove.

O, no! it is an ever-fixed mark,
That looks on tempests and is never shaken.
William Shakespeare
Sonnet 116

325 Th' expense of spirit in a waste of shame
Is lust in action; and till action, lust
Is perjur'd, murd'rous, bloody, full of blame,
Savage, extreme, rude, cruel, not to trust;
Enjoy'd no sooner but despised straight.
William Shakespeare
Sonnet 129

1610

326* Nuptial love maketh mankind; friendly love
perfecteth it; but wanton love corrupteth and
embaseth it.
Francis Bacon (1561–1626) English
philosopher.
Essays, 'Of Love'

1611

327 Those have most power to hurt us that we love.
Francis Beaumont (1584–1616) English
dramatist.
The Maid's Tragedy, V:6

1614

328 Love is a sickness full of woes,
All remedies refusing;
A plant that with most cutting grows,
Most barren with best using.
Why so?
More we enjoy it, more it dies;
If not enjoyed, it sighing cries,
Hey ho.
Samuel Daniel (c. 1562–1619) English poet
and dramatist.
Hymen's Triumph, I

1616

329 Drink to me only with thine eyes,
And I will pledge with mine;
Or leave a kiss but in the cup,
And I'll not look for wine.
The thirst that from the soul doth rise
Doth ask a drink divine;
But might I of Jove's nectar sup,
I would not change for thine.

I sent thee late a rosy wreath,
Not so much honouring thee,
As giving it a hope that there
It could not wither'd be.
Ben Jonson (1573–1637) English dramatist.
The Forest, IX, 'To Celia'

1648

330 Gather ye rosebuds while ye may,
Old time is still a-flying:
And this same flower that smiles today

Tomorrow will be dying.
Robert Herrick (1591–1674) English poet.
Hesperides, 'To the Virgins, to Make Much of
Time'

Marriage and the Family

1580

331 Marriage is like a cage; one sees the birds
outside desperate to get in, and those inside
equally desperate to get out.
Michel de Montaigne (1533–92) French
essayist.
Essais, III

1597

332 It is a wise father that knows his own child.
William Shakespeare (1564–1616) English
dramatist.
The Merchant of Venice, II:2

1606

333 Ingratitude, thou marble-hearted fiend,
More hideous when thou show'st thee in a
child
Than the sea-monster!
William Shakespeare
King Lear I:4

1610

334* Wives are young men's mistresses, companions for middle age, and old men's nurses.
Francis Bacon (1561–1626) English
philosopher.
Essays, 'Of Marriage and Single Life'

335* Children sweeten labours, but they make mis-
fortunes more bitter.
Francis Bacon
Essays, 'Of Parents and Children'

336* He that hath wife and children hath given hostages to fortune; for they are impediments to
great enterprises, either of virtue or
mischief.
Francis Bacon
Essays, 'Of Marriage and Single Life'

337* He was reputed one of the wise men, that made
answer to the question, when a man should
marry? A young man not yet, an elder man not
at all.
Francis Bacon
Essays, 'Of Marriage and Single Life'

1650

338* He that loves not his wife and children, feeds a
lioness at home and broods a nest of sorrows.
Jeremy Taylor (1613–67) English Anglican
theologian.
Sermons, 'Married Love'

1662

339 To have and to hold from this day forward, for better for worse, for richer for poorer, in sickness and in health, to love and to cherish, till death us do part.
The Book of Common Prayer
Solemnization of Matrimony

Men and Women

1558

340 To promote a Woman to bear rule, superiority, dominion or empire, above any Realm, Nation, or City, is repugnant to Nature; contumely to God, a thing most contrarious to his revealed will and approved ordinance, and finally it is the subversion of good Order, of all equity and justice.
John Knox (c. 1514–72) Scottish religious reformer.
Opening words
First Blast of the Trumpet against the Monstrous Regiment of Women

1583

341 A ship is sooner rigged than a gentlewoman made ready.
Philip Stubbes
The Anatomie of Abuses

1595

342 I have no other but a woman's reason:
I think him so, because I think him so.
William Shakespeare (1564–1616) English dramatist.
The Two Gentlemen of Verona, I:2

1600

343 Do you not know I am a woman? When I think, I must speak.
William Shakespeare
As You Like It, III:2

1601

344 Frailty, thy name is woman!
William Shakespeare
Hamlet, I:2

1607

345 Were't not for gold and women, there would be no damnation.
Cyril Tourneur (1575–1626) English dramatist.
The Revenger's Tragedy, II:1

1610

346* These are rare attainments for a damsel, but pray tell me, can she spin?
James I (1566–1625) King of England.
On being introduced to a young girl proficient in Latin, Greek, and Hebrew
Attrib.

1632

347 ...it being natural and comely to women to nourish their hair, which even God and nature have given them for a covering, a token of subjection, and a natural badge to distinguish them from men.
William Prynne (1600–69) English Puritan.
Histriomastix

Morality, Vices, and Virtues

1534

348 In their rules there was only one clause: Do what you will.
François Rabelais (1483–1553) French satirist.
Referring to the fictional Abbey of Thélème
Gargantua, Bk. I, Ch. 57

1550

349* To give and not to count the cost;
To fight and not to heed the wounds;
To toil and not to seek for rest;
To labour and not ask for any reward
Save that of knowing that we do Thy will.
St Ignatius Loyola (1491–1556) Spanish priest.
Prayer for Generosity

1594

350 Our purses shall be proud, our garments poor;
For 'tis the mind that makes the body rich;
And as the sun breaks through the darkest clouds,
So honour peereth in the meanest habit.
William Shakespeare (1564–1616) English dramatist.
The Taming of the Shrew, IV:3

1597

351 Bell, book, and candle, shall not drive me back,
When gold and silver becks me to come on.
William Shakespeare
King John, III:3

352 How far that little candle throws his beams!
So shines a good deed in a naughty world.
William Shakespeare
The Merchant of Venice, V:1

1598

353 Honour pricks me on. Yea, but how if honour prick me off when I come on? How then? Can honour set to a leg? No. Or an arm? No. Or take away the grief of a wound? No. Honour hath no skill in surgery, then? No. What is honour? A word. What is in that word? Honour. What is that honour? Air.
William Shakespeare
Henry IV, Part One, V:1

354 The better part of valour is discretion; in the which better part I have saved my life.
William Shakespeare
Henry IV, Part One, V:4

355 Anger makes dull men witty, but it keeps them poor.
Elizabeth I (1533–1603) Queen of England.
Apophthegms (Bacon)

1599

356 Though patience be a tired mare, yet she will plod.
William Shakespeare (1564–1616) English dramatist.
Henry V, II:1

1600

357 Blow, blow, thou winter wind,
Thou art not so unkind
As man's ingratitude.
William Shakespeare
As You Like It, II:7

358 Ambition should be made of sterner stuff.
William Shakespeare
Julius Caesar, III:2

1601

359 There is nothing either good or bad, but thinking makes it so.
William Shakespeare
Hamlet, II:2

360 Neither a borrower nor a lender be;
For loan oft loses both itself and friend,
And borrowing dulls the edge of husbandry.
This above all: to thine own self be true,
And it must follow, as the night the day,
Thou canst not then be false to any man.
William Shakespeare
Hamlet, I:3

361 Murder most foul, as in the best it is;
But this most foul, strange, and unnatural.
William Shakespeare
Hamlet, I:5

1602

362 Dost thou think, because thou art virtuous, there shall be no more cakes and ale?
William Shakespeare
Twelfth Night, II:3

363 I hate ingratitude more in a man

Than lying, vainness, babbling drunkenness,
Or any taint of vice whose strong corruption
Inhabits our frail blood.
William Shakespeare
Twelfth Night, III:4

1605

364 Just as it is always said of slander that something always sticks when people boldly slander, so it might be said of self-praise (if it is not entirely shameful and ridiculous) that if we praise ourselves fearlessly, something will always stick.
Francis Bacon (1561–1626) English philosopher.
The Advancement of Learning

365 I have always heard, Sancho, that doing good to base fellows is like throwing water into the sea.
Miguel de Cervantes (1547–1616) Spanish novelist.
Don Quixote, Pt. I, Ch. 23

366 O, beware, my lord, of jealousy;
It is the green-ey'd monster which doth mock
The meat it feeds on.
William Shakespeare (1564–1616) English dramatist.
Othello, III:3

1607

367 Celerity is never more admir'd
Than by the negligent.
William Shakespeare
Antony and Cleopatra, III:7

1610

368* Be so true to thyself, as thou be not false to others.
Francis Bacon (1561–1626) English philosopher.
Essays, 'Of Wisdom for a Man's Self'

369* A man that studieth revenge keeps his own wounds green.
Francis Bacon
Essays, 'Of Revenge'

370* As in nature things move violently to their place and calmly in their place, so virtue in ambition is violent, in authority settled and calm.
Francis Bacon
Essays, 'Of Great Place'

371* Revenge is a kind of wild justice; which the more man's nature runs to, the more ought law to weed it out.
Francis Bacon
Essays, 'Of Revenge'

372* Suspicions amongst thoughts are like bats amongst birds, they ever fly by twilight.
Francis Bacon
Essays, 'Of Suspicion'

373* It is always good

When a man has two irons in the fire.
Francis Beaumont (1584 – 1616) English
dramatist.
The Faithful Friends, I:2

1611
---

374   Though I am not naturally honest, I am so
sometimes by chance.
William Shakespeare (1564 – 1616) English
dramatist.
The Winter's Tale, IV:3

1613
---

375   Men's evil manners live in brass; their virtues
We write in water.
William Shakespeare
Henry VIII, IV:2

1614

376* Good thoughts his only friends,
His wealth a well-spent age,
The earth his sober inn
And quiet pilgrimage.
Thomas Campion (1567 – 1620) English poet.
The Man of Life Upright

1615
---

377   A private sin is not so prejudicial in the world
as a public indecency.
Miguel de Cervantes (1547 – 1616) Spanish
novelist.
Don Quixote, Pt. II, Ch. 22

1623
---

378   Other sins only speak; murder shrieks out.
John Webster (1580 – 1625) English dramatist.
The Duchess of Malfi, IV:2

1633
---

379   Only a sweet and virtuous soul,
Like season'd timber, never gives;
But though the whole world turn to coal,
Then chiefly lives.
George Herbert (1593 – 1633) English poet.
Virtue

1642
---

380   No man can justly censure or condemn another, because indeed no man truly knows
another.
Thomas Browne (1605 – 82) English physician
and writer.
Religio Medici, Pt. II

1644
---

381   Let her and Falsehood grapple; who ever knew

Truth put to the worse, in a free and open
encounter?
John Milton (1608 – 74) English poet.
Areopagitica

Other People

1591
---

382   England is the paradise of women, the purga-
tory of men, and the hell of horses.
John Florio (c. 1553 – 1625) English
lexicographer.
Second Fruits

1598
---

383   Well, I cannot last ever; but it was always yet
the trick of our English nation, if they have a
good thing, to make it too common.
William Shakespeare (1564 – 1616) English
dramatist.
Henry IV, Part Two, I:2

1606
---

384   The Englishman's dress is like a traitor's body
that hath been hanged, drawn, and quartered,
and is set up in various places; his cod-
piece is in Denmark, the collar of his doublet
and the belly in France; the wing and narrow
sleeve in Italy; the short waist hangs over a
Dutch butcher's stall in Utrecht; his huge slops
speak Spanishly . . . And thus we that mock
every nation for keeping of one fashion, yet
steal patches from every one of them to piece
out our pride.
Thomas Dekker (c. 1570 – 1632) English
writer.
Seven Deadly Sins of London

1615
---

385   The French are wiser than they seem, and the
Spaniards seem wiser than they are.
Francis Bacon (1561 – 1626) English
philosopher.
Essays, 'Of Seeming Wise'

1621
---

386   England is a paradise for women, and hell for
horses: Italy a paradise for horses, hell for
women.
Robert Burton (1577 – 1640) English scholar
and explorer.
Anatomy of Melancholy, Pt. III

1630

387* The English take their pleasures sadly after the
fashion of their country.
Duc de Sully (1560 – 1641) French statesman.
Memoirs

1638

388 For howbeit the Irish might do very good Service, being a People removed from the Scottish, as well in Affections as Religion; yet is not safe to train them up more than needs must in the military Way.
Thomas Wentworth (1593–1641) English statesman.
Letter to King Charles I, from Ireland, 28 July 1638

Religion

1522

389 To arrive at the truth in all things, we ought always to be ready to believe that what seems to us white is black if the hierarchical Church so defines it.
St Ignatius Loyola (1491–1556) Spanish priest.
Spiritual Exercises

1530

390* I have a Catholic soul, but a Lutheran stomach.
Erasmus (c. 1466–1536) Dutch humanist, scholar, and writer.
Replying to criticism of his failure to fast during Lent
Dictionnaire Encyclopédique

391* Be a sinner and sin strongly, but more strongly have faith and rejoice in Christ.
Martin Luther (1483–1546) German Protestant.
Letter to Melanchthon

1532

392 Man never found the deities so kindly
As to assure him that he'd live tomorrow.
François Rabelais (1483–1553) French satirist.
Pantagruel, Bk. III, Ch. 2

1572

393 A man with God is always in the majority.
John Knox (c. 1514–72) Scottish religious reformer.
Inscription, Reformation Monument, Geneva, Switzerland

1577

394 Alas, O Lord, to what a state dost Thou bring those who love Thee!
St Teresa of Ávila (1515–82) Spanish mystic.
The Interior Castle, VI

1580

395 I die because I do not die.
St John of the Cross (Juan de Yepes y Alvarez; 1542–91) Spanish churchman and poet.
Coplas del alma que pena por ver a dios

396 Man is quite insane. He wouldn't know how to create a maggot and he creates Gods by the dozen.
Michel de Montaigne (1533–92) French essayist.
Essais, II

1592

397* I count religion but a childish toy,
And hold there is no sin but ignorance.
Christopher Marlowe (1564–93) English dramatist.
The Jew of Malta, Prologue

1601

398 Do not, as some ungracious pastors do,
Show me the steep and thorny way to heaven,
Whiles, like a puff'd and reckless libertine,
Himself the primrose path of dalliance treads
And recks not his own rede.
William Shakespeare (1564–1616) English dramatist.
Hamlet, I:3

399 There's a divinity that shapes our ends,
Rough-hew them how we will.
William Shakespeare
Hamlet, V:2

1610

400* God never wrought miracle to convince atheism, because his ordinary works convince it.
Francis Bacon (1561–1626) English philosopher.
Essays, 'Of Atheism'

401* For none deny there is a God, but those for whom it maketh that there were no God.
Francis Bacon
Essays, 'Of Atheism'

402* Take heed of thinking. *The farther you go from the church of Rome, the nearer you are to God.*
Henry Wotton (1568–1639) English poet and diplomat.
Reliquiae Wottonianae (Izaak Walton)

403* It were better to have no opinion of God at all, than such an opinion as is unworthy of him.
Francis Bacon (1561–1626) English philosopher.
Essays, 'Of Superstition'

1621

404 One religion is as true as another.
Robert Burton (1577–1640) English scholar and explorer.
Anatomy of Melancholy, Pt. III

Science, Medicine, and Technology

1610

405* Books must follow sciences, and not sciences
books.
Francis Bacon (1561–1626) English
philosopher.
Proposition touching Amendment of Laws

406* Cure the disease and kill the patient.
Francis Bacon
Essays, 'Of Friendship'

407* And new Philosophy calls all in doubt,
The Element of fire is quite put out;
The Sun is lost, and th' earth, and no man's
wit
Can well direct him where to look for it.
John Donne (1573–1631) English poet.
An Anatomy of the World, 205

1615

408 . . . in my studies of astronomy and philosophy
I hold this opinion about the universe, that the
Sun remains fixed in the centre of the circle
of heavenly bodies, without changing its place;
and the Earth, turning upon itself, moves
round the Sun.
Galileo Galilei (1564–1642) Italian scientist.
Letter to Cristina di Lorena, 1615

1632

409 *Eppur si muove.*
Yet it moves.
Galileo Galilei
Referring to the Earth. Remark supposedly made
after his recantation (1632) of belief in the Co-
pernican system
Attrib.

Wealth and Poverty

1530

410 So our Lord God commonly gives riches to
those gross asses to whom he vouchsafes
nothing else.
Martin Luther (1483–1546) German
Protestant.
Colloquia (J. Aurifaber), Ch. XX

1597

411 Well, whiles I am a beggar, I will rail
And say there is no sin but to be rich;
And being rich, my virtue then shall be
To say there is no vice but beggary.
William Shakespeare (1564–1616) English
dramatist.
King John, II:1

1610

412* Riches are for spending.
Francis Bacon (1561–1626) English
philosopher.
Essays, 'Of Expense'

413* Money is like muck, not good except it be
spread.
Francis Bacon
Essays, 'Of Seditions and Troubles'

Work and Occupations

1604

414 An ambassador is an honest man sent to lie
abroad for the good of his country.
Henry Wotton (1568–1639) English poet and
diplomat.
Life (Izaak Walton)

Sayings of the Time

1570

415 Thirty days hath September,
April, June, and November;
All the rest have thirty-one,
Excepting February alone
And that has twenty-eight days clear
And twenty-nine in each leap year.
Abridgement of the Chronicles of England
(Richard Grafton)

1611

416 A frog he would a-wooing go,
Heigh ho! says Rowley,
A frog he would a-wooing go,
Whether his mother would let him or no.
With a rowley, powley, gammon and spinach,
Heigh ho! says Anthony Rowley.
Melismata (Thomas Ravenscroft)

1616

417 I'll put a spoke among your wheels.
Francis Beaumont (1584–1616) English
dramatist.
The Mad Lover, III:6

With Hindsight

19th century

418 Persecution produced its natural effect on

them. It found them a sect; it made them a faction.
Lord Macaulay (1800–59) British historian.
Referring to the early Puritans
History of England

20th century

419 Burnings of people and (what was more valuable) works of art.
A. L. Rowse (1903–) British historian and critic.
Historical Essays (H. R. Trevor-Roper)

420 If Galileo had said in verse that the world moved, the Inquisition might have let him alone.
Thomas Hardy (1840–1928) British novelist.
The Later Years of Thomas Hardy (F. E. Hardy)

421 The Cavaliers (wrong but Wromantic) and the Roundheads (Right but Repulsive).
W. C. Sellar (1898–1951) British humorous writer.
1066 And All That

8

The Age of Enlightenment (1660–1788)

With Louis XIV of France, absolute monarchy reached its zenith. Regarding the monarchy as a status ordained by God, he permitted no challenge to his authority; he was, moreover, imitated throughout western Europe. Even in England, where the king had been beheaded not many years before and parliament was strong, there lingered a fear – or in some quarters a hope – that the king would assert himself and dispense with parliament. When James II showed real signs of doing so, the Glorious Revolution (1688) deposed him.

At the same time scientific progress, led by such men as Newton, Pascal, and Descartes, was beginning to suggest that at least some events in the world could be predicted. The view that everything that happened was the result of God's capricious will became less acceptable; instead, the belief grew that the world was governed by natural laws, amenable to rational inquiry. During the 18th century this spirit of Enlightenment spread into other fields, notably political thought. Philosophers such as Locke and Voltaire criticized both society and established authority on the grounds of reason, establishing what was later called the Age of Reason. The response of rulers was mixed. Some Enlightened Despots, such as Frederick the Great of Prussia and Joseph II of Austria, claimed to follow rational principles in the formulation of their policies, without actually lessening the absolute and arbitrary authority they exercised over their subjects; others, notably the kings of France, were more conservative. However, all monarchs continued to draw a fine line between permissible speculation and seditious thinking.

The period ended with the revolt of Britain's American colonies (1775–83), Europe's first experience from the New World of aspirations aimed at substituting nationhood for a colonial status. The ideas of liberty, fostered by the Enlightenment in Europe, had a profound influence on the revolutionaries, whose case was now based on emerging notions of human rights as well as the traditionally English view of liberty.

Politics, Government, and World Events

1661

1 I owe you everything, Sire, but I believe I can pay some of my debt with this gift – Colbert.
Cardinal Mazarin (1602–61) Italian-born French statesman.
Remark to Louis XIV, shortly before Mazarin's death; referring to Jean-Baptiste Colbert

---

1664

2 You will have heard of our taking of New Amsterdam ... It did belong to England heretofore, but the Dutch by degrees drove our people out and built a very good town, but we have got the better of it, and 'tis now called New York.
Charles II (1630–85) King of England.
Letter, 24 Oct 1664

1665

3 Pretty witty Nell.
Samuel Pepys (1633–1703) English diarist.
Referring to Nell Gwynne
Diary, 3 Apr 1665

4 Thence I walked to the Tower; but Lord! how empty the streets are and how melancholy, so many poor sick people in the streets full of sores ... in Westminster, there is never a physician and but one apothecary left, all being dead.
Samuel Pepys
Written during the Great Plague – the last major outbreak of bubonic plague in England, and the worst since the Black Death of 1348
Diary, 16 Sept 1665

5 Ring-a-ring o'roses,
A pocket full of posies,
A-tishoo! A-tishoo!
We all fall down.
Thought to refer to plague: 'ring o'roses' was the skin-marking indicating a victim of the disease; 'posies' were the herbs carried in an attempt to ward off the disease
Mother Goose (Kate Greenway)

6 Oh what a pity were the greatest and most virtuous of kings, of that real virtue which makes the greatest of princes, to be measured by the yardstick of Versailles!
Jean-Baptiste Colbert (1619–83) French statesman.
Letter to Louis XIV, 28 Sept 1665

7 The love of justice in most men is simply the fear of suffering injustice.
Duc de la Rochefoucauld (1613–80) French writer.
Maximes, 78

1666

8 This fatal night about ten, began that deplorable fire near Fish Street in London ... all the sky were of a fiery aspect, like the top of a burning Oven, and the light seen above 40 miles round about for many nights.
John Evelyn (1620–1706) English diarist.
The Fire of London (2–5 Sept 1666) began in a bakehouse in Pudding Lane and spread to two-thirds of the city
Diary, 23 Sept 1666

9 The fire, mean time, walks in a broader gross,
To either hand his wings he opens wide:
He wades the streets, and straight he reaches cross,
And plays his longing flames on th'other side.

At first they warm, then scorch, and then they take:
Now with long necks from side to side they feed:
At length, grown strong, their Mother fire forsake,
And a new collony of flames succeed.
John Dryden (1631–1700) British poet and dramatist.
Annus Mirabilis

1667

10 Who overcomes
By force, hath overcome but half his foe.
John Milton (1608–74) English poet.
Paradise Lost, Bk. I

11 To reign is worth ambition, though in Hell:
Better to reign in Hell than serve in Heaven.
John Milton
Paradise Lost, Bk. I

12 ... always with right reason dwells
Twinn'd, and from her hath no dividual being.
John Milton
Referring to liberty
Paradise Lost, Bk. XII

1670

13* Not a religion for gentlemen.
Charles II (1630–85) King of England.
Referring to Presbyterianism
History of My Own Time (Burnet), Vol. I, Bk. II, Ch. 2

14 Better than a play.
Charles II
Referring to House of Lords debate on the Divorce Bill
Attrib.

1672

15* Our business is to break with them and yet to lay the breache at their door.
Earl of Arlington (1618–85)
Referring to the diplomacy that preceded the third Dutch War (1672–74)
Arlington (Violet Barbour)

16   I will drive a coach and six horses through the
     Act of Settlement.
     Stephen Rice (1637–1715) English politician.
     State of the Protestants of Ireland (W. King),
     Ch. 3

1675

17   **God is always on the side of the big battalions.**
     Vicomte de Turenne (1611–75) French
     marshal.
     Attrib.

1676

18* **A merry monarch, scandalous and poor.**
     Earl of Rochester (1647–80) English poet.
     Referring to Charles II
     A Satire on King Charles II

1678

The Exclusion Crisis (1678–81)

In 1678, a 'Jesuit conspiracy' to kill Charles II and replace him with his Catholic brother James was 'revealed' by Titus Oates and Israel Tonge. Although
quickly exposed as a fabrication, the anti-Catholic fer-
vour aroused by this 'Popish Plot' led to the execution
of 35 people and persistent demands in parliament that
James be excluded from the succession to the throne
in favour of the Duke of Monmouth, an illegitimate but
Protestant son of Charles. Charles resisted these demands, which were encouraged by men such as the
Earl of Shaftesbury for their own political purposes.
The crisis abated in 1681, when an annual subsidy
from Louis XIV of France enabled Charles to rule without parliament; but the issues it raised resurfaced in
Monmouth's rebellion (1685) and the Glorious Revolution (1688).

19* **I am sure no man in England will take away my
     life to make you King.**
     Charles II (1630–85) King of England.
     To his brother James following the revelation of
     the Popish Plot
     Attrib.

20   **Pray, good people, be civil. I am the Protestant
     whore.**
     Nell Gwyn (1650–87) English actress.
     On being surrounded in her coach by an angry
     mob in Oxford at the time of the Popish Plot. The
     mob, thinking that the coach contained the
     King's Catholic mistress, Louise de Kérouoille,
     shouted 'It is the Catholic whore!'
     Nell Gwyn (Bevan), Ch. 13

1679

21   **If His Majesty shall come by any violent death,**

it shall be revenged to the utmost upon all
Papists.
Resolution of the House of Commons, 1679

1680

22* **Here lies our sovereign lord the King
     Whose word no man relies on;
     He never said a foolish thing,
     Nor ever did a wise one.**
     Lord Rochester (1647–80) English courtier
     and poet.
     Suggested epitaph for Charles II

23* **This is very true: for my words are my own, and
     my actions are my ministers'.**
     Charles II (1630–85) King of Great Britain and
     Ireland.
     Replying to Lord Rochester
     King Charles II (A. Bryant)

24* **Brother, I am too old to go again to my travels.**
     Charles II
     Referring to his exile, 1651–60
     History of Great Britain (Hume), Vol. II, Ch. 7

25   **Whatever he may promise me he will break
     everything to get a regular income from his
     parliament.**
     Louis XIV (1638–1715) King of France.
     Referring to Charles II of England
     Letter to Barillon, 1680

26   **He only treats with me to derive an advantage
     in his future negotiations with his subjects.**
     Louis XIV
     Referring to Charles II of England
     Letter to Barillon, 1680

27* **I have forgotten more law than you ever knew,
     but allow me to say, I have not forgotten
     much.**
     John Maynard (1602–90) English judge.
     Replying to Judge Jeffreys' suggestion that he
     was so old he had forgotten the law

1681

28   **No Popery, No Slavery.**
     Slogan of the London MPs at the Oxford Parlia-
     ment (Mar 1681)

29   **You had better have one King than five
     hundred.**
     Charles II (1630–85) King of England.
     Remark after dissolving the Oxford Parliament,
     28 Mar 1681; he did not summon parliament
     again

30   **Then, my lord, be his blood on your own con-
     science. You might have saved him if you
     would. I cannot pardon him because I dare not.**
     Charles II
     Reply to the Earl of Essex, who had protested St
     Oliver Plunket's innocence of the treason for
     which he had been sentenced to death
     The Later Stuarts (Sir George Clark)

31 Government has no other end but the preservation of property.
John Locke (1632–1704) English philosopher.
Second Treatise on Civil Government

1681
---

32 The people's prayer, the glad diviner's theme,
The young men's vision, and the old men's dream!
John Dryden (1631–1700) British poet and dramatist.
John Dryden's poem, written at the request of Charles II, is a satire of the Exclusion Crisis: 'Absolom' is the Duke of Monmouth, and 'Achitophel' is the Earl of Shaftesbury.
Absalom and Achitophel, I

33 Nor is the Peoples Judgment always true:
The Most may err as grossly as the Few.
John Dryden
Absalom and Achitophel, I

34 In pious times, e'r Priest-craft did begin,
Before Polygamy was made a Sin.
John Dryden
Absalom and Achitophel, I

35 During his Office, Treason was no Crime.
The Sons of Belial had a Glorious Time.
John Dryden
Absalom and Achitophel, I

36 To die for faction is a common evil,
But to be hanged for nonsense is the Devil.
John Dryden
Absalom and Achitophel, II

1683
---

37 I came; I saw; God conquered.
John III Sobieski (1624–96) King of Poland.
Announcing his victory over the Turks at Vienna to the pope (paraphrasing Caesar's 'veni, vidi, vici')
Attrib.

38 'Tis not necessary to light a candle to the sun.
Algernon Sidney (1622–83) English statesman.
Discourses concerning Government, Ch. 2

1684
---

39 The multitude is always in the wrong.
Earl of Roscommon (1633–85) Irish-born English poet.
Essay on Translated Verse

1685
---

40 He had been, he said, a most unconscionable time dying; but he hoped that they would excuse it.
Charles II (1630–85) King of England.
History of England (Macaulay), Vol. I, Ch. 4

41 Let not poor Nelly starve.
Charles II
Referring to Nell Gwynne
Said on his death bed

42 He said once to myself that he was no atheist but he could not think God would make a man miserable only for taking a little pleasure out of the way.
Gilbert Burnet (1643–1715) English bishop and historian.
Referring to Charles II
History of My Own Times

43 I have often heretofore ventured my life in defence of this nation; and I shall go as far as any man in preserving it in all its just rights and liberties.
James II (1633–1701)
Address to the Privy Council on becoming King (1685)

44 Do not hack me as you did my Lord Russell.
Duke of Monmouth (1649–85) An illegitimate son of Charles II.
Said to the headsman before his execution
History of England (Macaulay), Vol. I, Ch. 5

45 I was not half bloody enough for him who sent me thither.
Judge Jeffreys (George, Baron J.; 1648–89) English Chief Justice and Lord Chancellor.
Referring to his 'Bloody Assizes' following Monmouth's rebellion (1685)
Remark made later (Apr 1689) to the chaplain of the Tower of London

46 When the People contend for their Liberty, they seldom get anything by their Victory but new masters.
George Saville Halifax (1633–95) English statesman.
Political, Moral, and Miscellaneous Thoughts and Reflections

47 Power is so apt to be insolent and Liberty to be saucy, that they are seldom upon good Terms.
George Saville Halifax
Political, Moral, and Miscellaneous Thoughts and Reflections

48 Men are not hanged for stealing horses, but that horses may not be stolen.
George Saville Halifax
Political, Moral and Miscellaneous Thoughts and Reflections

1687
---

49 ... establish such a politie of civil and military power and create and secure such a large revenue ... as may be the foundation of a large, well-grounded sure English dominion in India for all time to come.
Dispatch from the East India Company to its chief executive in Surat

---
1688
---

50 The Duke of Buckingham gave me once a short but severe character of the two brothers. It was the more severe, because it was true: the

King (he said) could see things if he would,
and the Duke would see things if he could.
Gilbert Burnet (1643–1715) English bishop
and historian.
Referring to Charles II and James II
History of My Own Times

51 One of the strangest catastrophes that is in any
history. A great king, with strong armies and
mighty fleets, a great treasure and powerful allies, fell all at once, and his whole strength,
like a spider's web, was . . . irrecoverably broken at a touch.
Gilbert Burnet
Referring to the Glorious Revolution, 1688
History of My Own Times

52 This is a standard of rebellion.
James II (1633–1701) King of England.
Referring to a petition from seven bishops
against his Declaration of Indulgence (1687; re-
issued 7 May 1688); the bishops were pros-
ecuted for sedititious libel, but acquitted
Remark, 2 June 1688

53 . . . to long for and desire the landing of that
Prince, whom they looked on as their deliverer
from Popish tyranny, praying incessantly for
an Easterly wind . . .
John Evelyn (1620–1706) English diarist.
Referring to William III
Diary, 6 Oct 1688

54 If the circumstances stand so with your Highness, that you believe you can get here time
enough, in a condition to give assistance this
year sufficient for a relief under these circumstances which have been now represented,
we, who subscribe this, will not fail to attend
your Highness upon your landing.
Letter from seven English notables to William of
Orange, 10 July 1688

55 Party loyalty lowers the greatest of men to the
petty level of the masses.
Jean de La Bruyère (1645–96) French
satirist.
Les Caractères

56 If by the people you understand the multitude,
the *hoi polloi*, 'tis no matter what they think;
they are sometimes in the right, sometimes
in the wrong; their judgement is a mere lottery.
John Dryden (1631–1700) British poet and
dramatist.
Essay of Dramatic Poesy

1689
---

57 She came into Whitehall laughing and jolly, as
to a wedding, so as to seem quite transported.
John Evelyn (1620–1706) English diarist.
Referring to Mary II's arrival in London
Diary, 21 Feb 1689

58 In Hide Park he rides like a hog in armour,
In Whitehall he creeps like a country farmer,
Old England may boast of a godly reformer;

A dainty fine king indeed.
Anonymous
Referring to William III
The Faber Book of English History in Verse
(Kenneth Baker)

59 Good People come buy
The Fruit that I cry,
That now is in Season, tho' Winter is nigh;
'Twill do you all good
And sweeten your Blood,
I'm sure it will please when you've once
understood
'Tis an *Orange*.
Anonymous
Referring to William III
The Faber Book of English History in Verse
(Kenneth Baker)

60 Ignorance of the law excuses no man; not that
all men know the law, but because 'tis an excuse every man will plead, and no man can
tell how to confute him.
John Selden (1584–1654) English historian.
Table Talk

61 Every law is a contract between the king and
the people and therefore to be kept.
John Selden
Table Talk

1690
---

62 Most men were in fear that the French would
invade, but I was always of another opinion,
for I always said that, whilst we had a fleet in
being, they would not dare to make an
attempt.
Earl of Torrington English admiral.
Justifying his refusal to give battle to a numeri-
cally superior French fleet; when subsequently
ordered to do so, he was defeated off Beachy
Head (10 July 1690)
The Later Stuarts (Sir George Clark)

63 When a King has Dethron'd himself and put
himself in a state of War with his People, what
shall hinder them from prosecuting him who is
no King?
John Locke (1632–1704) English philosopher.
Second Treatise on Civil Government

1692

64* . . . was apt to suffer things to run on till there
was a great heap of papers laid before him, so
then he signed them a little too precipitately.
Gilbert Burnet (1643–1715) Scottish-born
English bishop.
Referring to William III; his authorization of the
Glencoe Massacre (1692) may have been one
consequence of this habit
History of My Own Times

65 Our dear King James is good and honest, but
the most incompetent man I have ever seen

in my life. A child of seven years would not
make such silly mistakes as he does.
Duchess of Orleans (1652–1722) Sister-in-
law to Louis XIV.
Referring to James II, who was in exile in France
Letter to the Electress Sophia, 6 June 1692

1693

66 Let the people think they govern and they will
be governed.
William Penn 1644–1718
Some Fruits of Solitude, 337

1694

67 Your peoples die of hunger. Agriculture is almost stationary, industry languishes everywhere, all commerce is destroyed. . . . You
relate everything to yourself as though you
were God on earth.
François Fénelon (1651–1715) French writer
and prelate.
Letter to Louis XIV

1698

68 The rights of parliament should be preserved
sacred and inviolable, wherever they are found.
This kind of government, once so universal
all over Europe, is now almost vanished from
amongst the nations thereof. Our king's dominions are the only supporters of this noble
Gothic constitution, save only what little remains may be found thereof in Poland.
William Molyneux
*The Case of Ireland's being Bound by Acts of
Parliament in England stated* (Pamphlet, 1698)

18th century

69 In good King Charles's golden days,
When loyalty no harm meant,
A zealous High Churchman was I,
And so I got preferment.

And this is law, that I'll maintain,
Unto my dying day, Sir,
That whatsoever King shall reign,
I'll be the Vicar of Bray, Sir.
Anonymous
Thought to refer to Symon Symonds, who was
vicar of Bray in the reigns of Henry VIII, Ed-
ward VI, Mary, and Elizabeth I. He was twice a
Papist and twice a Protestant, but when accused
of time-serving replied, 'Not so, neither, for if I
changed my religion, I am sure that I kept true to
my principle, which is to live and die the vicar
of Bray.'
The Vicar of Bray

70 Certainty is the Mother of Repose, and therefore the Law aims at Certainty.
A maxim used by Lord Hardwicke (Lord Chancellor, 1737–1756)

71 The King over the Water.
Anonymous
Jacobite toast

1700

72* Every time I make an appointment, I make one
ungrateful person and a hundred with a
grievance.
Louis XIV (1638–1715) French king.
Siècle de Louis XIV (Voltaire), Ch. 26

73* Let us consider the reason of the case. For
nothing is law that is not reason.
John Powell (1645–1713) English judge.
Coggs v. Bernard, 2 Lord Raymond, 911

74 Il n'y a plus de Pyrénées.
There are no more Pyrenees.
Louis XIV (1638–1715) French king.
On the accession of his grandson to the Spanish
throne (1700); attributed by Voltaire

1701

75 And of all plagues with which mankind are
curst,
Ecclesiastic tyranny's the worst.
Daniel Defoe (1660–1731) British journalist
and writer.
The True-Born Englishman, Pt. II

1702

76 I know my own heart to be entirely English.
Anne (1665–1714)
Drawing a contrast with her predecessor, the
Dutch William III
Speech on opening parliament, 1702

1704

77 I have not time to say more, but to beg you will
give my duty to the Queen, and let her know
her army has had a glorious victory. Monsieur Tallard and two other generals are in my
coach, and I am following the rest . . .
Duke of Marlborough (1650–1722) British
military commander.
Referring to the Battle of Blenheim, 13 Aug 1704
Note to his wife, written on a tavern bill

78 How could God do this to me after all I have
done for him?
Louis XIV (1638–1715) French king.
On receiving news of the French army's defeat at
the Battle of Blenheim
Saint-Simon at Versailles (L. Norton)

1705

79 Neither is money the sinews of war (as it is triv-
ially said).
John Aubrey (1626–1697) English antiquary.
Essays, 'Of the True Greatness of Kingdoms'

80 Neither will it be, that a people overlaid with
taxes should ever become valiant and martial.
John Aubrey
Essays, 'Of the True Greatness of Kingdoms'

1707

81 Justice is such a fine thing that we cannot pay too dearly for it.
Alain-René Lesage (1668–1747) French writer.
Crispin rival de son maître, IX

1709

82 Now indeed with God's help the final stone has been laid in the foundation of St Petersburg.
Peter the Great (1672–1725) Tsar of Russia.
Referring to his victory over Charles XII of Sweden at the Battle of Poltava (28 June 1709)
Letter to Admiral Apraksin, 27 June 1709

83 Laws are like cobwebs, which may catch small flies, but let wasps and hornets break through.
Jonathan Swift (1667–1745) Irish-born Anglican priest and writer.
A Tritical Essay upon the Faculties of the Mind

1710

84 In the first place, I have only five guineas in my pocket; and in the second, they are very much at your service.
Lord Peterborough (1658–1735) English military and naval commander.
Persuading an angry mob that he was not the Duke of Marlborough, notorious for his meanness
Dictionary of National Biography

1711

85 I have changed my ministers, but I have not changed my measures; I am still for moderation and will govern by it.
Anne (1665–1714) Queen of Great Britain
To members of the new Tory ministry, Jan 1711

86 It is folly of too many to mistake the echo of a London coffee-house for the voice of the kingdom.
Jonathan Swift (1667–1745) Irish-born Anglican priest and writer.
The Conduct of the Allies

1712

87 He warns the heads of parties against believing their own lies.
John Arbuthnot (1667–1735) Scottish writer and physician.
The Art of Political Lying

88 The hungry judges soon the sentence sign,
And wretches hang that jury-men may dine.
Alexander Pope (1688–1744) British poet.
The Rape of the Lock, III

1713

89 What pity is it

That we can die but once to serve our country!
Joseph Addison (1672–1719) British essayist.
Cato, IV:4

1715

90 *L'État c'est moi.*
I am the State.
Louis XIV (1638–1715) French king.
Attrib.

91 I almost had to wait.
Louis XIV
Attrib.

92* Try to keep peace with your neighbours. I have loved war too much; do not copy me in that nor in my extravagance.
Louis XIV
Remark to his great-grandson, the future Louis XV

93 Why are you weeping? Did you imagine that I was immortal?
Louis XIV
Noticing as he lay on his deathbed that his attendants were crying
Louis XIV (V. Cronin)

94* . . . for the most part the worst instructed, and the least knowing of any of their rank, I ever went amongst.
Gilbert Burnet (1643–1715) Scottish-born English bishop.
Referring to the English gentry
History of My Own Times, Conclusion

1722

95 Let pride be taught by this rebuke,
How very mean a thing's a Duke;
From all his ill-got honours flung,
Turn'd to that dirt from whence he sprung.
Jonathan Swift (1667–1745) Irish-born Anglican priest and writer.
Referring to the Duke of Marlborough
A Satirical Elegy on the Death of a Late Famous General

1723

96 *Si monumentum requiris, circumspice.*
If you seek my monument, look around you.
Sir Christopher Wren (1632–1723) English architect.
Inscription in St Paul's Cathedral, London

1726

97 I cannot but conclude the bulk of your natives to be the most pernicious race of little odious vermin that nature ever suffered to crawl upon the surface of the earth.
Jonathan Swift (1667–1745) Irish-born Anglican priest and writer.
Gulliver's Travels, 'Voyage to Brobdingnag'. Ch. 6

98   Whoever could make two ears of corn or two blades of grass to grow upon a spot of ground where only one grew before would deserve better of mankind and do more essential service to his country than the whole race of politicians put together.
Jonathan Swift
Gulliver's Travels, 'Voyage to Brobdingnag', Ch. 7

1728
---

99   The right divine of kings to govern wrong.
Alexander Pope (1688–1744) British poet.
The Dunciad, IV

1730

100*   For God's sake, madam, don't say that in England for if you do, they will surely tax it.
Jonathan Swift (1667–1745) Irish-born Anglican priest and writer.
Responding to Lady Carteret's admiration for the quality of the air in Ireland
Lives of the Wits (H. Pearson)

1731
---

101   With favour and fortune fastidiously blest,
He's loud in his laugh and he's coarse in his jest;
. . .
Though I name not the wretch you know who I mean –
'Tis the cur dog of Britain and spaniel of Spain.
Jonathan Swift
Referring to Sir Robert Walpole
Two Character Studies

1733
---

102   Order is heaven's first law.
Alexander Pope (1688–1744) British poet.
An Essay on Man, IV

1734
---

103   An empire founded by war has to maintain itself by war.
Baron de Montesquieu (1688–1755) French writer.
Considérations sur les causes de la grandeur et de la décadence des romains, Ch. 8

104   Madam, there are fifty thousand men slain this year in Europe, and not one Englishman.
Robert Walpole (1676–1745) British statesman.
Referring to his determination not to involve Britain in the War of Polish Succession (1733–35), despite considerable political pressure
Remark to Queen Caroline, 1734

105*   I took the right sow by the ear.
Robert Walpole
Commenting on his perception that, to influence George II, the correct woman to cultivate was Queen Caroline, not any of the King's mis-

tresses – a mistake made by his political opponents
Remark to a friend, c. 1734

1736
---

106   Lost or strayed out of this house, a man who left a wife and six children on the parish; whoever will give any tidings of him to the churchwardens of St. James's Parish, so he may be got again, shall receive four shillings and sixpence. N.B. This reward will not be increased, nobody judging him to deserve a Crown.
Anonymous
Referring to George II, whose frequent absences in Hanover made him unpopular
Notice posted on the gate of St. James's Palace

1737
---

107   No, I shall have mistresses.
George II (1683–1760) King of Great Britain and Ireland.
Reply to Queen Caroline's suggestion, as she lay on her deathbed, that he should marry again after her death
Memoirs of George the Second (Hervey), Vol. II

1738
---

108   Faction is to party what the superlative is to the positive: party is a political evil and faction is the worst of all parties.
Bolingbroke, Henry St John, Viscount (1678–1751) British politician and writer.
The Patriot King

1739
---

109   I have lived long enough in the world, Sir, . . . to know that the safety of a minister lies in his having the approbation of this House. Former ministers, Sir, neglected this, and therefore they fell; I have always made it my first study to obtain it, and therefore I hope to stand.
Robert Walpole (1676–1745) British statesman.
Speech, House of Commons, 21 Nov 1739

110   All those men have their price.
Robert Walpole
Memoirs of Sir Robert Walpole (W. Coxe)

111   They now *ring* the bells, but they will soon *wring* their hands.
Robert Walpole
Said when war was declared with Spain, against Walpole's wishes
Memoirs of Sir Robert Walpole (W. Coxe)

1740

112*   Great lords have their pleasures, but the people have fun.
Baron de Montesquieu (1688–1755) French writer.
Pensées diverses

113* A crown is merely a hat that lets the rain in.
Frederick the Great (1712–86) King of
Prussia.
Remark

114 God save our Gracious King,
Long live our noble King,
God save the King.
Send him victorious,
Happy and glorious.
Henry Carey (c. 1690–1743) English poet and
musician.
God Save the King

115 When Britain first, at heaven's command,
Arose from out the azure main,
This was the charter of the land,
And guardian angels sung this strain:
'Rule, Britannia, rule the waves;
Britons never will be slaves.'
James Thomson (1700–48) British poet.
Alfred: a Masque, Act II

1741
---

116 The balance of power.
Robert Walpole (1676–1745) British
statesman.
Speech, House of Commons, 13 Feb 1741

1742
---

117 It is now apparent that this great, this powerful,
this formidable Kingdom is considered only as
a province of a despicable Electorate.
William Pitt the Elder (1708–78) British
statesman.
Referring to Hanover, which Pitt accused George
II of favouring over England
Speech, House of Commons, 10 Dec 1742

118 My Lord Bath, you and I are now two as insignificant men as any in England.
Robert Walpole (1676–1745) British
statesman.
Said to William Pulteney, Earl of Bath, when they
were promoted to the peerage (1742)
Political & Literary Anecdotes (W. King)

1743
---

119 Our supreme governors, the mob.
Horace Walpole (1717–97) British writer.
Letter to Sir Horace Mann, 7 Sept 1743

1745
---

120 Gentlemen of the French Guard, fire first!
Lord Charles Hay (d. 1760) British soldier.
Said at the Battle of Fontenoy, 1745
Attrib.

121 I'll be at your Board, when at leisure from
cricket.
John Montagu, Earl of Sandwich (1718–
92) British politician.
Message on being appointed a lord commissioner of the Admiralty, June 1745

1748
---

122 It must be owned, that the Graces do not seem
to be natives of Great Britain; and I doubt, the
best of us here have more of rough than polished diamond.
Earl of Chesterfield (1694–1773) English
statesman.
Letter to his son, 18 Nov 1748

123 Liberty is the right to do everything which the
laws allow.
Baron de Montesquieu (1688–1755) French
writer.
L'Esprit des lois

124 See, the conquering hero comes!
Sound the trumpets, beat the drums!
Thomas Morell (1703–84) British classicist.
The libretto for Handel's oratorio
Joshua, Pt. III

1750
---

125 It is impossible that a man who is false to his
friends and neighbours should be true to the
public.
Bishop Berkeley (1685–1753) Irish churchman and philosopher.
Maxims Concerning Patriotism

1751
---

126 Here lies Fred,
Who was alive and is dead:
Had it been his father,
I had much rather;
Had it been his brother,
Still better than another;
Had it been his sister,
No one would have missed her;
Had it been the whole generation,
Still better for the nation:
But since 'tis only Fred,
Who was alive and is dead, –
There's no more to be said.
Referring to Frederick, Prince of Wales (d.
1751), eldest son of George II and father of
George III.
Memoirs of George II (Horace Walpole)

1755
---

127 There are kings enough in England. I am nothing there, I am old and want rest and should
only go to be plagued and teased there
about that D—d House of Commons.
George II (1683–1760) King of Great Britain
and Ireland.
George II's reply when urged to leave Hanover
and return to England
Letter from the Earl of Holderness to the Duke of
Newcastle, 3 Aug 1755

1756

128　I know that I can save this country and that no
one else can.
William Pitt the Elder (1708–78) British
statesman.
Remark, Nov 1756, during the political crisis at
the start of the Seven Years War; Pitt became
secretary of state for the southern department,
and effective head of the government, on 4
Dec 1756

1757

129　Rascals, would you live for ever?
Frederick the Great (1712–86) King of
Prussia.
Addressed to reluctant soldiers at the Battle of
Kolin, 18 June 1757

130　*Après nous le déluge.*
After us the deluge.
Madame de Pompadour (1721–64) The
mistress of Louis XV of France.
After the Battle of Rossbach, 5 Nov 1757

1758

131　*Laissez faire, laissez passer.*
Liberty of action, liberty of movement.
Jean Claude Vincent de Gournay (1712–
59) French economist.
Speech, Sept 1758

1759

132　Come cheer up, my lads! 'tis to glory we steer,
To add something more to this wonderful
year;
To honour we call you, not press you like
slaves,
For who are so free as the sons of the waves?
Heart of oak are our ships,
Heart of oak are our men:
We always are ready;
Steady, boys, steady;
We'll fight and we'll conquer again and again.
David Garrick (1717–79) British actor and
manager.
Heart of Oak

133*　Oh! he is mad, is he? Then I wish he would bite
some other of my generals.
George II (1683–1760) King of Great Britain
and Ireland.
Replying to advisors who told him that General
James Wolfe (1727–59) was mad
Attrib.

134　I would rather have written those lines than
take Quebec.
James Wolfe (1727–59) British general.
Referring to Gray's Elegy, on the eve of the Bat-
tle of Quebec (13 Sept 1759)
Attrib.

135　Now God be praised, I will die in peace.
James Wolfe
After being mortally wounded at the Battle of
Quebec, 1759
Historical Journal of Campaigns, 1757–60 (J.
Knox), Vol. II

136　*Dans ce pays-ci, il est bon de tuer de temps en
temps un amiral pour encourager les autres.*
**In this country it is good to kill an admiral
from time to time, to encourage the others.**
Voltaire (François-Marie Arouet; 1694–1778)
French writer.
Referring to England: Admiral Byng was executed
for failing to engage the French at Minorca
(1757)
Candide, Ch. 23

1760s

137　Taxation without representation is tyranny.
James Otis (1725–83) US political activist.
As 'No taxation without representation' this be-
came the principal slogan of the American
Revolution
Attrib.

1760

138*　A cow is a very good animal in the field; but we
turn her out of a garden.
Samuel Johnson (1709–84) British
lexicographer.
Responding to Boswell's objections to the expul-
sion of six Methodists from Oxford University
The Personal History of Samuel Johnson (C.
Hibbert)

139　Born and educated in this country I glory in the
name of Briton.
George III (1738–1820) King of Great Britain
and Ireland.
Speech on opening parliament, 18 Nov 1760

140　I think for my part one half of the nation is mad
– and the other not very sound.
Tobias Smollett (1721–71) British novelist.
The Adventures of Sir Launcelot Greaves

141　True patriotism is of no party.
Tobias Smollett
The Adventures of Sir Launcelote Greaves

1761

142　George, be a King.
**Augusta of Saxe-Gotha, Princess of
Wales** (1719–72) Mother of King George III.
Attrib.

1762

143*　I shall be an autocrat: that's my trade. And the
good Lord will forgive me: that's his.
Catherine the Great (1729–96) Empress of
Russia (1762–96).
Attrib.

144 Man was born free and everywhere he is in chains.
Jean Jacques Rousseau (1712–78) French philosopher.
Du contrat social, Ch. 1

1763

145 In vain will such a minister, or the foul dregs of his power, the tools of despotism and corruption, preach up 'the spirit of concord...' They have sent the spirit of discord through the land and I will prophesy it will never be distingushed but by the extinction of their power.
John Wilkes (1725–97) British politician.
Part of a libellous article on George III's speech (which was drafted by George Grenville, the 'minister') at the opening of parliament. This article led to a celebrated legal battle
North Briton, 45 (23 Apr 1763)

146* Wilkes and Liberty.
Slogan of the London mob

147 Your levellers wish to level *down* as far as themselves; but they cannot bear levelling *up* to themselves.
Samuel Johnson (1709–84) British lexicographer.
Life of Johnson (J. Boswell), Vol. I

1764

148* The poorest man may in his cottage bid defiance to all the forces of the Crown. It may be frail – its roof may shake – the wind may blow through it – the storm may enter – the rain may enter – but the King of England cannot enter! –all his force dares not cross the threshold of the ruined tenement!
William Pitt the Elder (1708–78) British statesman.
Statesmen in the Time of George III (Lord Brougham), Vol. I

149 Be England what she will,
With all her faults, she is my country still.
Charles Churchill (1731–64) British poet.
The Farewell

150 Where wealth and freedom reign, contentment fails,
And honour sinks where commerce long prevails.
Oliver Goldsmith (1728–74) Irish-born British writer.
The Traveller

151 Laws grind the poor, and rich men rule the law.
Oliver Goldsmith
The Traveller

152 Laws are generally found to be nets of such a texture, as the little creep through, the great break through, and the middle-sized are alone entangled in.
William Shenstone (1714–63) British poet and writer.
Essays on Men, Manners, and Things, 'On Politics'

1765

153 Caesar had his Brutus – Charles the First, his Cromwell – and George the Third – ('Treason,' cried the Speaker) ... *may profit by their example.* If *this* be treason, make the most of it.
Patrick Henry (1736–99) US statesman.
Speech, Virginia Convention, May 1765

154 Man was formed for society.
William Blackstone (1723–80) British jurist.
Commentaries on the Laws of England, Introduction

155 The king never dies.
William Blackstone
Commentaries on the Laws of England, Bk. I, Ch. 7

156 The Royal Navy of England has ever been its greatest defence and ornament; it is its ancient and natural strength, the floating bulwark of the island.
William Blackstone
Commentaries on the Laws of England, Bk. I, Ch. 13

157 Time whereof the memory of man runneth not to the contrary.
William Blackstone
Commentaries on the Laws of England, Bk. I, Ch. 18

158 That the king can do no wrong, is a necessary and fundamental principle of the English constitution.
William Blackstone
Commentaries on the Laws of England, Bk. III, Ch. 17

159 It is better that ten guilty persons escape than one innocent suffer.
William Blackstone
Commentaries on the Laws of England, Bk. IV, Ch. 27

160 No vote can be given by lunatics, idiots, minors, aliens, females, persons convicted of perjury, subornation of perjury, bribery treating or undue influence, or by those tainted of felony or outlawed in a criminal suit.
William Blackstone
Commentaries on the Laws of England

161 The British parliament has no right to tax the Americans ... Taxation and representation are inseparably united.
Charles Pratt (1714–94) Lord Chancellor.
Speech, House of Lords, Dec 1765

1766

162 I rejoice that America has resisted. Three millions of people, so dead to all the feelings of liberty, would have been fit instruments to make slaves of the rest.
William Pitt the Elder (1708–78) British statesman.
Speech, House of Commons, 14 Jan 1766

163 Once the people begin to reason, all is lost.
Voltaire (François-Marie Arouet; 1694–1778)
French writer.
Letter to Damilaville, 1 Apr 1766

1767

164 The sovereign is absolute; for, in a state whose
expanse is so vast, there can be no other appropriate authority except that which is con-
centrated in him.
Catherine II (1729–96) Empress of Russia
(1762–96).
Nakaz

165 I am not like a lady at the court of Versailles,
who said: 'What a dreadful pity that the
bother at the tower of Babel should have got
language all mixed up, but for that, everyone
would always have spoken French.
Voltaire (François-Marie Arouet; 1694–1778)
French writer.
Letter to Catherine the Great, Empress of Russia, 26 May 1767

1768

166 The best sun we have is made of Newcastle
coal.
Horace Walpole (1717–97) British writer.
Letter to Montagu, 15 June 1768

1769

167* The Liberty of the press is the *Palladium* of all
the civil, political and religious rights of an
Englishman.
Junius An unidentified writer of letters (1769–
72) to the *London Public Advertiser*.
Letters, 'Dedication'

168 There is a holy, mistaken zeal in politics, as
well as religion. By persuading others we convince ourselves.
Junius
Letter, 19 Dec 1769

169 This agglomeration which was called and which
still calls itself the Holy Roman Empire was
neither holy, nor Roman, nor an empire.
Voltaire (François-Marie Arouet; 1694–1778)
French writer.
Essai sur les moeurs et l'esprit des nations,
LXX

170 Why, Sir, most schemes of political improvement are very laughable things.
Samuel Johnson (1709–84) British
lexicographer.
Life of Johnson (J. Boswell), Vol. II

1770

171* Consider what you think justice requires, and
decide accordingly. But never give your rea-

sons; for your judgement will probably be right,
but your reasons will certainly be wrong.
Lord Mansfield (1705–93) British judge and
politician.
Advice given to a new colonial governor
Lives of the Chief Justices (Campbell), Ch. 40

172 Unlimited power is apt to corrupt the minds of
those who possess it.
William Pitt the Elder (1708–78) British
statesman.
Speech, House of Lords, 9 Jan 1770

173 Where laws end, tyranny begins.
William Pitt the Elder
Referring to the case of John Wilkes, who had
been elected to parliament four times but, because of government opposition, not allowed to
take his seat
Speech, House of Lords, 9 Jan 1770

174 There is something behind the throne greater
than the King himself.
William Pitt the Elder
Speech, House of Lords, 2 Mar 1770

175 At daylight in the morning we discovered a bay,
which appeared to be tolerably well sheltered
from all winds, into which I resolved to go
with the ship.
James Cook (1728–79) British navigator and
cartographer.
On the discovery of Botany Bay
Journal, 28 Apr 1770

176 Upon the whole New Holland, tho' in every respect the most barren country I have seen, is
not so bad that between the products of sea
and land, a company of people who should
have the misfortune of being shipwrecked upon
it might support themselves.
Sir Joseph Banks (1744–1820) British
scientist.
Note, as a participant in Captain Cook's circum-
navigation of the world (1768–71), on leaving
New South Wales.
Journal, Aug 1770

177 When bad men combine, the good must associate; else they will fall one by one, an unpitied
sacrifice in a contemptible struggle.
Edmund Burke (1729–97) British politician.
*Thoughts on the Cause of the Present Discon-
tents*

178 My people and I have come to an agreement
which satisfies us both. They are to say what
they please, and I am to do what I please.
Frederick the Great (1712–86) King of
Prussia.
Attrib.

179 Everybody talks of the constitution, but all sides
forget that the constitution is extremely well,
and would do very well, if they would but let it
alone.
Horace Walpole (1717–97) British writer.
Letter to Sir Horace Mann, 1770

180 Ill fares the land, to hast'ning ills a prey,
Where wealth accumulates, and men decay;
Princes and lords may flourish, or may fade;

A breath can make them, as a breath has made;
But a bold peasantry, their country's pride,
When once destroy'd, can never be supplied.
Oliver Goldsmith (1728–74) Irish-born British writer.
The Deserted Village

1771

181 The greater the power, the more dangerous the abuse.
Edmund Burke (1729–97) British politician.
Speech, House of Commons, 7 Feb 1771

1772

182 Walpole was a minister given by the King to the people: — Pitt was a minister given by the people to the King.
Samuel Johnson (1709–84) British lexicographer.
Life of Johnson (J. Boswell)

183 It was easier to conquer it than to know what to do with it.
Horace Walpole (1717–97) British writer.
Referring to the East
Letter to Sir Horace Mann, 27 Mar 1772

184 Every man who comes to England is entitled to the protection of the English law, whatever oppression he may heretofore have suffered, and whatever may be the colour of his skin, whether it is black or whether it is white.
Lord Mansfield (1705–93) British judge and politician.
From the judgment in the case of James Somersett, a fugitive negro slave (May 1772); it established the principle that slaves enjoyed the benefits of freedom while in England

185 I would not give half a guinea to live under one form of government rather than another. It is of no moment to the happiness of an individual.
Samuel Johnson (1709–84) British lexicographer.
Life of Johnson (J. Boswell), Vol. II

186 Much may be made of a Scotchman, if he be *caught* young.
Samuel Johnson
Referring to Lord Mansfield
Life of Johnson (J. Boswell), Vol. II

1773

187 By God, Mr Chairman, at this moment I stand astonished at my own moderation!
Clive of India (1725–74) British soldier and governor of Bengal.
Referring to allegations of corruption and extortion in India for personal gain
Reply to House of Commons select committee, Mar 1773

188 No, Sir; there were people who died of drop-

sies, which they contracted in trying to get drunk.
Samuel Johnson (1709–84) British lexicographer.
Scornfully criticizing the strength of the wine in Scotland before the Act of Union in response to Boswell's claim that there had been a lot of drunkenness
Tour to the Hebrides (J. Boswell)

1774

189 Your representative owes you, not his industry only, but his judgement; and he betrays instead of serving you if he sacrifices it to your opinion.
Edmund Burke (1729–97) British politician.
Speech to the electors of Bristol, 3 Nov 1774

190 A savage old Nabob, with an immense fortune, a tawny complexion, a bad liver and a worse heart.
Lord Macaulay (1800–59) British historian.
Referring to Clive of India (1725–74)
Historical Essays, 'Lord Clive'

191 I am not a Virginian, but an American.
Patrick Henry (1736–99) US statesman.
Speech, Continental Congress, 5 Sept 1774

1775

192 *Excise*. A hateful tax levied upon commodities.
Samuel Johnson (1709–84) British lexicographer.
Dictionary of the English Language

193 Politics are now nothing more than a means of rising in the world.
Samuel Johnson
Life of Johnson (J. Boswell), Vol. II

194 I think the full tide of human existence is at Charing-Cross.
Samuel Johnson
Life of Johnson (J. Boswell), Vol. II

195 Patriotism is the last refuge of a scoundrel.
Samuel Johnson
Life of Johnson (J. Boswell), Vol. II

The American Revolution (1775–83)

Claiming equality with their British kinsmen, they jealously guarded their way of life, resenting any interference with their large measure of *de facto* independence. In the 1760s their discontent focused on attempts by the British government to tax them effectively – primarily to pay for their defence. Various ill-considered acts culminated in armed revolution breaking out in 1775, and a formal Declaration of Independence was issued on 4 July 1776. In the war that followed, the British had some successes; but disasters at Saratoga (1777) and Yorktown (1781), and the entry of France (1788) and other European countries into the conflict on the American side, led to disheartenment in Britain. The war ended in 1783, with the recognition of American independence.

196   I do not know the method of drawing up an indictment against an whole people.
Edmund Burke (1729–97) British politician.
Speech on Conciliation with America (House of Commons, 22 Mar 1775)

197   All government, indeed every human benefit and enjoyment, every virtue, and every prudent act, is founded on compromise and barter.
Edmund Burke
Speech on Conciliation with America (House of Commons, 22 Mar 1775)

198   The use of force alone is but *temporary*. It may subdue for a moment; but it does not remove the necessity of subduing again: and a nation is not governed, which is perpetually to be conquered.
Edmund Burke
Speech on Conciliation with America (House of Commons, 22 Mar 1775)

199   The concessions of the weak are the concessions of fear.
Edmund Burke
Speech on Conciliation with America (House of Commons, 22 Mar 1775)

200   I know not what course others may take; but as for me, give me liberty or give me death.
Patrick Henry (1736–99) US statesman.
Speech, Virginia Convention, 23 Mar 1775

201   Stand your ground. Don't fire unless fired upon, but if they mean to have a war, let it begin here!
John Parker (1729–75) US general.
Command given at the start of the Battle of Lexington (19 Apr 1775)
Familiar Quotations (J. Bartlett)

202   By the waters of Babylon we sit down and weep, when we think of thee, O America!
Horace Walpole (1717–97) British writer.
On the eve of the American Revolution
Letter to Mason, 12 June 1775

203   Don't fire until you see the whites of their eyes.
William Prescott (1726–95) US revolutionary soldier.
Command given at the Battle of Bunker Hill (17 June 1775)

1776
---

204   That these United Colonies are, and of right ought to be, free and independent states.
Richard Henry Lee (1732–94) US Revolutionary patriot and Senator.
Motion, Continental Congress, Philadelphia, 7 June 1776

205   The second day of July 1776 will be the most memorable epoch in the history of America ... It ought to be solemnized with pomp and parade, with shows, games, sports, guns, bells, bonfires and illuminations from one end of this continent to the other, from this time forward, for ever more.
John Adams (1735–1826) Second president of the USA.
The Continental Congress voted for independence from Britain on 2 July
Letter to his wife, 3 July 1776

206   When in the course of human events, it becomes necessary for one people to dissolve the political bonds which have connected them with another, and to assume among the powers of the earth the separate and equal station to which the laws of nature and of Nature's God entitle them, a decent respect to the opinions of mankind requires that they should declare the causes which impel them to the separation.
Thomas Jefferson (1743–1826) US statesman.
Declaration of Independence, Preamble

207   We hold these truths to be self-evident: that all men are created equal; that they are endowed by their Creator with certain unalienable rights; that among these are life, liberty, and the pursuit of happiness.
Thomas Jefferson
Declaration of American Independence, 4 July 1776

208   We must indeed all hang together, or most assuredly, we shall all hang separately.
Benjamin Franklin (1706–90) US scientist and statesman.
Remark on signing the Declaration of Independence, 4 July 1776

209   There, I guess King George will be able to read that.
John Hancock (1737–93) US revolutionary.
Referring to his signature, written in a bold hand, on the US Declaration of Independence
The American Treasury (C. Fadiman)

210   A nation of shop-keepers are very seldom so disinterested.
Samuel Adams (1722–1803) US revolutionary leader.
Referring to Britain, following the Declaration of Independence, 4 July 1776
Speech, Philadelphia, 1 Aug 1776

211   I only regret that I have but one life to lose for my country.
Nathan Hale (1755–76) US revolutionary hero.
Speech before his execution, 22 Sept 1776

212*   Yankee Doodle came to town,
Riding on a pony;
He stuck a feather in his cap
And called it macaroni.
Believed to have been sung by British troops ridiculing the Americans in the American Revolution. The Americans adopted the song and added new verses telling of their victories in the war
Gammer Gurton's Garland

213   There is no art which one government sooner

learns of another than that of draining money from the pockets of the people.
Adam Smith (1723–90) Scottish economist.
The Wealth of Nations

214 People of the same trade seldom meet together but the conversation ends in a conspiracy against the public, or in some diversion to raise prices.
Adam Smith
The Wealth of Nations

215 Government, even in its best state, is but a necessary evil; in its worst state, an intolerable one.
Thomas Paine (1737–1809) British writer.
Common Sense, Ch. 1

216 As to religion, I hold it to be the indispensable duty of government to protect all conscientious professors thereof, and I know of no other business which government hath to do therewith.
Thomas Paine
Common Sense, Ch. 4

217 A man who has not been in Italy, is always conscious of an inferiority, from his not having seen what it is expected a man should see. The grand object of travelling is to see the shores of the Mediterranean.
Samuel Johnson (1709–84) British lexicographer.
Life of Johnson (J. Boswell), Vol. III

218 Sir, it is not so much to be lamented that Old England is lost, as that the Scotch have found it.
Samuel Johnson
Life of Johnson (J. Boswell), Vol. III

219 The principles of a free constitution are irrecoverably lost, when the legislative power is nominated by the executive.
Edward Gibbon (1737–94) British historian.
Decline and Fall of the Roman Empire, Ch. 3

1777

220 Yonder are the Hessians. They were bought for seven pounds and tenpence a man. Are you worth more? Prove it. Tonight the American flag floats from yonder hill or Molly Stark sleeps a widow!
John Stark (1728–1822) US general.
Urging on his troops at the Battle of Bennington in 1777
The American Treasury (C. Fadiman)

221 You cannot conquer America.
William Pitt the Elder (1708–78) British statesman.
Speech, House of Lords, 18 Nov 1777

222 I invoke the genius of the Constitution.
William Pitt the Elder
Referring to the American Revolution
Speech, House of Lords, 18 Nov 1777

223 If I were an American, as I am an Englishman, while a foreign troop was landed in my country, I never would lay down my arms, – never – never – never!
William Pitt the Elder
Speech, House of Lords, 18 Nov 1777

224 Liberty, too, must be limited in order to be possessed.
Edmund Burke (1729–97) British politician.
Letter to the Sheriffs of Bristol, 1777

225 Among a people generally corrupt, liberty cannot long exist.
Edmund Burke
Letter to the Sheriffs of Bristol, 1777

226 When a man is tired of London, he is tired of life; for there is in London all that life can afford.
Samuel Johnson (1709–84) British lexicographer.
Life of Johnson (J. Boswell), Vol. III

1778

227 I will rather risk my Crown than do what I think personally disgraceful, and whilst I have no wish but for the good and prosperity of my country, it is impossible that the nation shall not stand by me; if they will not, they shall have another King.
George III (1738–1820) King of Great Britain and Ireland.
Letter to Lord North, 17 Mar 1778

228 I am willing to love all mankind, *except an American*.
Samuel Johnson (1709–84) British lexicographer.
Life of Johnson (J. Boswell), Vol. III

229 A country governed by a despot is an inverted cone.
Samuel Johnson
Life of Johnson (J. Boswell), Vol. III

230 When I forget my sovereign, may God forget me!
Lord Thurlow (1731–1806) British lawyer.
Speech, House of Lords, 15 Dec 1778

231 I disapprove of what you say, but I will defend to the death your right to say it.
Voltaire (François-Marie Arouet; 1694–1778) French writer.
Attrib.

232 Governments needs to have both shepherds and butchers.
Voltaire
Notebooks

1779

233 I have not yet begun to fight.
John Paul Jones (1747–92) Scottish-born US naval commander.
Retort when informed his ship was sinking
Life and Letters of J. P. Jones (De Koven), Vol. I

234   **Worth seeing? yes; but not worth going to see.**
Samuel Johnson (1709–84) British lexicographer.
Referring to the Giant's Causeway
Life of Johnson (J. Boswell), Vol. III

1780

235   **I can never suppose this country so far lost to all ideas of self-importance as to be willing to grant America independence; if that could ever be adopted I shall despair of this country being ever preserved from a state of inferiority and consequently falling into a very low class among the European States.**
George III (1738–1820) King of Great Britain and Ireland.
Letter to Lord North, 7 Mar 1780

236   **The influence of the Crown has increased, is increasing, and ought to be diminished.**
John Dunning (1731–83) British lawyer and politician.
Motion passed by the House of Commons, 1780

237   **The people are the masters.**
Edmund Burke (1729–97) British politician.
Speech on the Economical Reform (House of Commons, 11 Feb 1780)

238   **Kings are naturally lovers of low company.**
Edmund Burke
Speech on the Economical Reform (House of Commons, 11 Feb 1780)

239   **One man shall have one vote.**
John Cartwright (1740–1824) British writer.
People's Barrier Against Undue Influence

240*   **Dublin, though a place much worse than London, is not so bad as Iceland.**
Samuel Johnson (1709–84) British lexicographer.
Letter to Mrs Christopher Smart
Life of Johnson (J. Boswell), Vol. IV

241*   **I have got no further than this: Every man has a right to utter what he thinks truth, and every other man has a right to knock him down for it. Martyrdom is the test.**
Samuel Johnson
Life of Johnson (J. Boswell), Vol. IV

242   **No man could be so wise as Thurlow looked.**
Charles James Fox (1749–1806) British Whig politician.
Lives of the Lord Chancellors (Campbell), Vol. V

243   **When security and equality are in conflict, it will not do to hesitate a moment. Equality must yield.**
Jeremy Bentham (1748–1832) British philosopher.
Principles of Legislation

1781

244   **The whole commerce between master and slave is a perpetual exercise of the most bois-**

terous passions, the most unremitting despotism on the one part, and degrading submissions on the other.
Thomas Jefferson (1743–1826) US statesman.
Notes on the State of Virginia

245*   **He snatched the lightning shaft from heaven, and the sceptre from tyrants.**
Anne-Robert-Jacques Turgot (1727–81) French economist.
An inscription for a bust of Benjamin Franklin, alluding both to Franklin's invention of the lightning conductor and to his role in the American Revolution
Vie de Turgot (A. N. de Condorcet)

246   **. . . we are moved to grant the right of private worship to the Lutheran, Calvinist and non-Uniat Greek religions everywhere.**
Joseph II (1741–90) Holy Roman Emperor.
Edict of Toleration, 13 Oct 1781

247   **He was not merely a chip of the old block, but the old block itself.**
Edmund Burke (1729–97) British politician.
Referring to William Pitt the Younger's first speech in the House of Commons, 26 Feb 1781
Attrib.

1782

248   **My opinion is, that power should always be distrusted, in whatever hands it is placed.**
Sir William Jones (1746–1794) British jurist, linguist and orientalist.
Letter to Lord Althorpe, 5 Oct 1782

1783

249   **There never was a good war or a bad peace.**
Benjamin Franklin (1706–90) US scientist and statesman.
Letter to Josiah Quincy, 11 Sept 1783

250   **Necessity is the plea for every infringement of human freedom. It is the argument of tyrants; it is the creed of slaves.**
William Pitt the Younger (1759–1806) British statesman.
Speech, House of Commons, 18 Nov 1783

251   **The King of England changes his ministers as often as he changes his shirts.**
Frederick the Great (1712–86) King of Prussia.
Referring to George III
Attrib.

1784

252   **If a man were to go by chance at the same time with Burke under a shed, to shun a shower, he would say – 'this is an extraordinary man.'**
Samuel Johnson (1709–84) British lexicographer.
Referring to Edmund Burke
Life of Johnson (J. Boswell), Vol. IV

1785

253 The summer soldier and the sunshine patriot will, in this crisis, shrink from the service of their country.
Thomas Paine (1737–1809) British writer.
Pennsylvania Journal, 'The American Crisis'

254* He was uniformly of an opinion which, though not a popular one, he was ready to aver, that the right of governing was not property but a trust.
Charles James Fox (1749–1806) British Whig politician.
Referring to William Pitt's plans for parliamentary reform
C.J. Fox (J. L. Hammond)

255 Mountains interposed
Make enemies of nations, who had else,
Like kindred drops, been mingled into one.
William Cowper (1731–1800) British poet.
The Task

256 Slaves cannot breathe in England; if their lungs Receive our air, that moment they are free;
They touch our country, and their shackles fall.
William Cowper
A situation resulting from a judicial decision in 1772
The Task

1787

257 Let Americans disdain to be the instruments of European greatness. Let the Thirteen States, bound together in a strict and indissoluble union, concur in erecting one great American system.
Alexander Hamilton (1755–1804) American statesman.
Federalist Papers, XI

258 A little rebellion now and then is a good thing.
Thomas Jefferson (1743–1826) US statesman
Letter to James Madison, 30 Jan 1787

259 The tree of liberty must be refreshed from time to time with the blood of patriots and tyrants. It is its natural manure.
Thomas Jefferson
Letter to W. S. Smith, 13 Nov 1787

260 A bill of rights is what the people are entitled to against every government on earth, general or particular and what no just government should refuse to rest on inference.
Thomas Jefferson
Letter to James Madison, 20 Dec 1787

1788

261 There is not a single crowned head in Europe whose talents or merits would entitle him to be elected a vestryman by the people of any parish in America.
Thomas Jefferson
Written from Paris
Letter to George Washington, 2 May 1788

262 A thing may look specious in theory, and yet be ruinous in practice; a thing may look evil in theory, and yet be in practice excellent.
Edmund Burke (1729–97) British politician.
Impeachment of Warren Hastings, 19 Feb 1788

1789

263 The King bathes, and with great success; a machine follows the Royal one into the sea, filled with fiddlers, who play *God Save the King* as his Majesty takes his plunge.
Fanny Burney (Frances Burney D'Arblay; 1752–1840) British novelist.
Referring to George III at Weymouth
Diary, 8 July 1789

1790

264 Here lies Joseph, who failed in everything he undertook.
Joseph II (1741–90) Holy Roman Emperor.
Suggesting his own epitaph when reflecting upon the disappointment of his hopes for reform
Attrib.

265 The condition upon which God hath given liberty to man is eternal vigilance.
John Philpot Curran (1750–1817) Irish judge.
Speech on the Right of Election of Lord Mayor of Dublin, 10 July 1790

1793

266 Let them eat cake.
Marie-Antoinette (1755–93) Queen of France.
On being told that the people had no bread to eat; in fact she was repeating a much older saying
Attrib.

Attitudes

Art, Literature, and Music

17th century

267 Blest pair of Sirens, pledges of Heaven's joy, Sphere-born harmonious sisters, Voice and Verse.
John Milton (1608–74) English poet.
At a Solemn Music

1666

268 I could also have stepped into a style much higher than this in which I have here discoursed, and could have adorned all things more than here I have seemed to do, but I dare not. God did not play in convincing of me, the devil did not play in tempting of me neither did I play when I sunk into a bottomless pit,

when the pangs of hell caught hold upon me;
wherefore I may not play in my relating of
them, but be plain and simple, and lay down the
thing as it was.
John Bunyan (1628–88)
Referring to literary style
Grace Abounding to the Chief of Sinners,
Preface

1667
---

269 Rhyme being no necessary adjunct or true ornament of poem or good verse, in longer
works especially, but the invention of a barbarous age, to set off wretched matter and lame
metre.
John Milton (1608–74) English poet.
Paradise Lost, The Verse. Preface to 1668 ed.

1668
---

270 He was the man who of all modern, and perhaps ancient poets had the largest and most
comprehensive soul.
John Dryden (1631–1700) British poet and
dramatist.
Referring to Shakespeare
Essay of Dramatic Poesy

1675
---

271 Words may be false and full of art,
Sighs are the natural language of the heart.
Thomas Shadwell (1642–92) English
dramatist.
Psyche, III

1683
---

272 ... just imitation of the most fam'd Italian masters: principally, to bring the seriousness and
gravity of that sort of musick into vogue and
reputation among our countrymen, whose hu-
mor, 'tis time now, should begin to loath the
levity, and balladry of our neighbours.
Henry Purcell (1659–95) English composer.
Preface to a volume of sonatas

1693
---

273 When he killed a calf he would do it in a high
style, and make a speech.
John Aubrey (1626–1697) English antiquary.
Brief Lives, 'William Shakespeare'

274 He was so fair that they called him *the lady of
Christ's College.*
John Aubrey
Brief Lives, 'John Milton'

1697
---

275 Music has charms to soothe a savage breast.
William Congreve (1670–1729) British Res-
toration dramatist.
The Mourning Bride, I

18th century
---

276 The secret of the arts is to correct nature.
Voltaire (François-Marie Arouet; 1694–1778)
French writer.
Épîtres, 'À M. de Verrière'

1711
---

277 A reader seldom peruses a book with pleasure
until he knows whether the writer of it be a
black man or a fair man, of a mild or choleric
disposition, married or a bachelor.
Joseph Addison (1672–1719) British
essayist.
The Spectator, 1

278 Nothing is capable of being well set to music
that is not nonsense.
Joseph Addison
The Spectator, 18

279 True ease in writing comes from art, not
chance,
As those move easiest who have learn'd to
dance.
'Tis not enough no harshness gives offence,
The sound must seem an echo to the sense.
Alexander Pope (1688–1744) British poet.
An Essay on Criticism

1723

280* Architecture has its political use; publick buildings being the ornament of a country; it estab-
lishes a nation, draws people and commerce;
makes the people love their native country,
which passion is the original of all great actions
in a commonwealth.
Sir Christopher Wren (1632–1723) English
architect and scientist.
Parentalia

1734
---

281 For painters, poets and builders have very high
flights, but they must be kept down.
Sarah, Duchess of Marlborough (1660–
1744) Wife of John Churchill, 1st Duke of
Marlborough.
Letter to the Duchess of Bedford, 21 June 1734

1736
---

282 There's sure no passion in the human soul,
But finds its food in music.
George Lillo (1693–1739) English dramatist.
Fatal Curiosity, I:2

1745
---

283 Ah, a German and a genius! a prodigy, admit
him!
Jonathan Swift (1667–1745) Irish-born
Anglican priest and writer.
Learning of the arrival of Handel; Swift's last
words
Attrib.

284 Words are men's daughters, but God's sons
     are things.
     Samuel Madden (1686–1765) Irish writer.
     Boulter's Monument

1750

285 Was there ever yet anything written by mere
     man that was wished longer by its readers, ex-
     cepting *Don Quixote*, *Robinson Crusoe*, and
     the *Pilgrim's Progress*?
     Samuel Johnson (1709–84) British
     lexicographer.
     Johnsonian Miscellanies (ed. G. B. Hill), Vol. I

1752

286 I have laboured to refine our language to gram-
     matical purity, and to clear it from colloquial
     barbarisms, licentious idioms, and irregular
     combinations.
     Samuel Johnson
     The Rambler

1755

287* I suffer from the disease of writing books and
      being ashamed of them when they are
      finished.
      Baron de Montesquieu (1688–1755) French
      writer.
      Pensées diverses

1756

288 The reciprocal civility of authors is one of the
     most risible scenes in the farce of life.
     Samuel Johnson (1709–84) British
     lexicographer.
     Life of Sir Thomas Browne

1759

289 That great Cham of literature, Samuel Johnson.
     Tobias Smollett (1721–71) British novelist.
     Letter to John Wilkes, 16 Mar 1759

290 Writing, when properly managed, (as you may
     be sure I think mine is) is but a different
     name for conversation.
     Laurence Sterne (1713–68) Irish-born British
     writer.
     Tristram Shandy

1763

291 It is burning a farthing candle at Dover, to shew
     light at Calais.
     Samuel Johnson (1709–84) British
     lexicographer.
     Referring to the impact of Sheridan's works upon
     the English language
     Life of Johnson (J. Boswell), Vol. I

1764

292 There can hardly be a stranger commodity in
     the world than books. Printed by people who
     don't understand them; sold by people who
     don't understand them; bound, criticized and
     read by people who don't understand them; and
     now even written by people who don't under-
     stand them.
     Georg Christoph Lichtenberg (1742–99)
     German physicist and writer.
     Aphorisms

293 One of the greatest geniuses that ever existed,
     Shakespeare, undoubtedly wanted taste.
     Horace Walpole (1717–97) British writer.
     Letter to Wren, 9 Aug 1764

1769

294 There is no arguing with Johnson; for when his
     pistol misses fire, he knocks you down with
     the butt end of it.
     Oliver Goldsmith (1728–74) Irish-born British
     writer.
     Life of Johnson (J. Boswell)

1769

295 Shakespeare never had six lines together with-
     out a fault. Perhaps you may find seven, but
     this does not refute my general assertion.
     Samuel Johnson (1709–84) British
     lexicographer.
     Life of Johnson (J. Boswell), Vol. II

1770

296 A mere copier of nature can never produce any-
     thing great.
     Joshua Reynolds (1723–92) British portrait
     painter.
     Discourse to Students of the Royal Academy, 14
     Dec 1770

1772

297 For instrumental music there is a certain
     Haydn, who has some peculiar ideas, but he is
     only just beginning.
     Maria Theresa (1717–80) Empress and ruler
     of the Habsburg dominions.
     Letter to Archduchess Marie Beatrix, 1772

1773

298 Read over your compositions, and where ever
     you meet with a passage which you think is
     particularly fine, strike it out.
     Samuel Johnson (1709–84) British
     lexicographer.
     Recalling the advice of a college tutor
     Life of Johnson (J. Boswell), Vol. II

1775

299 He was dull in a new way, and that made many
     people think him *great*.
     Samuel Johnson
     Referring to the poet Thomas Gray
     Life of Johnson (J. Boswell), Vol. II

1776

300 No man but a blockhead ever wrote, except for money.
Samuel Johnson
Life of Johnson (J. Boswell), Vol. III

301 *Sturm und Drang.*
Storm and stress.
Friedrich Maximilian von Klinger (1752–1831) German dramatist and novelist.
Used to designate a late 18th-century literary movement in Germany
Play title

1778

302 I do not think this poem will reach its destination.
Voltaire (François-Marie Arouet; 1694–1778) French writer.
Reviewing Rousseau's poem 'Ode to Posterity'
Attrib.

1780

303 They are forced plants, raised in a hot-bed; and they are poor plants; they are but cucumbers after all.
Samuel Johnson (1709–84) British lexicographer.
Referring to Gray's *Odes*
Life of Johnson (J. Boswell), Vol. IV

1781

304 Classical quotation is the *parole* of literary men all over the world.
Samuel Johnson
Life of Johnson (J. Boswell), Vol. IV

1784

305* The only sensual pleasure without vice.
Samuel Johnson
Referring to music
Johnsonian Miscellanies (ed. G. B. Hill), Vol. II

306* What is written without effort is in general read without pleasure.
Samuel Johnson
Johnsonian Miscellanies (ed. G. B. Hill), Vol. II

307* Now that the old lion is dead, every ass thinks he may kick at him.
Samuel Parr (1747–1825) British writer and scholar.
Referring to Dr Johnson
Life of Johnson (J. Boswell)

1786

308 All his own geese are swans, as the swans of others are geese.
Horace Walpole (1717–97) British writer.
Referring to Sir Joshua Reynolds
Letter to the Countess of Upper Ossory, 1 Dec 1786

1788

309 Another damned, thick, square book! Always scribble, scribble, scribble! Eh! Mr Gibbon?
William, Duke of Gloucester (1743–1805) The brother of George III.
Addressing Edward Gibbon, author of *The History of the Decline and Fall of the Roman Empire*; also attributed to George III
Literary Memorials (Best)

Daily Life

1674

310 'Tis to be wondered at our ancestors who were given so much to eat spices. Wee now, since the pox came up, eat none and will suffer none to be in meat.
Anthony Wood
Life and Times, Vol. II

1682

311* I have often seen the King consume four plates of different soups, a whole pheasant, a partridge, a large plate of salad, two big slices of ham, a dish of mutton in garlic sauce, a plateful of pastries followed by fruit and hard-boiled eggs. The King and Monsieur greatly like hard-boiled eggs.
Duchess of Orleans (1652–1722) Sister-in-law to Louis XIV.
Letter, ?1682

1689

312 'Tis not the drinking that is to be blamed, but the excess.
John Selden (1584–1654) English historian.
Table Talk

1729

313 Where's Troy, and where's the Maypole in the Strand?
Pease, cabbages and turnips once grew where
Now stands New Bond Street and a newer Square;
Such piles of buildings now rise up and down,
London itself seems going out of Town.
Our Fathers crossed from Fulham in a Wherry,
Their sons enjoy a Bridge at Putney Ferry.
James Bramston (c. 1694–1744) British poet.
The Whig Supremacy (Basil Williams), Ch. 15

1774

314 The way to ensure summer in England is to have it framed and glazed in a comfortable room.
Horace Walpole (1717–97) British writer.
Letter to Cole, 28 May 1774

1776

315 There is nothing which has yet been contrived by man, by which so much happiness is produced as by a good tavern or inn.
Samuel Johnson (1709–84) British lexicographer.
Life of Johnson (J. Boswell), Vol. II

Death

1668

316 Rather suffer than die is man's motto.
Jean de La Fontaine (1621–95) French poet.
Fables, I, 'La Mort et le Bûcheron'

1732

317 How often are we to die before we go quite off this stage? In every friend we lose a part of ourselves, and the best part.
Alexander Pope (1688–1744) British poet.
Letter to Jonathan Swift, 5 Dec 1732

1751

318 It hath been often said, that it is not death, but dying, which is terrible.
Henry Fielding (1707–54) British novelist.
Amelia, Bk. III, Ch. 4

319 Can storied urn or animated bust
Back to its mansion call the fleeting breath?
Can honour's voice provoke the silent dust,
Or flatt'ry soothe the dull cold ear of death?
Thomas Gray (1716–71) British poet.
Elegy Written in a Country Churchyard

320 The boast of heraldry, the pomp of pow'r,
And all that beauty, all that wealth e'er gave,
Awaits alike th' inevitable hour,
The paths of glory lead but to the grave.
Thomas Gray
Elegy Written in a Country Churchyard

1769

321 It matters not how a man dies, but how he lives. The act of dying is not of importance, it lasts so short a time.
Samuel Johnson (1709–84) British lexicographer.
Life of Johnson (J. Boswell), Vol. II

1785

322* What argufies pride and ambition?
Soon or late death will take us in tow:
Each bullet has got its commission,
And when our time's come we must go.
Charles Dibdin (1745–1814) British actor and dramatist.
Each Bullet has its Commission

Education, Knowledge, and Learning

1662

323 A proverb is much matter decorated into few words.
Thomas Fuller (1608–61) English historian.
The History of the Worthies of England, Ch. 2

1665

324 The intellect is always fooled by the heart.
Duc de la Rochefoucauld (1613–80) French writer.
Maximes, 102

1667

325 Vain wisdom all, and false philosophy.
John Milton (1608–74) English poet.
Paradise Lost, Bk. II

1685

326 Most men make little use of their speech than to give evidence against their own understanding.
Lord Halifax (1633–95) English statesman.
Political, Moral, and Miscellaneous Thoughts and Reflections

1688

327 There are some who speak one moment before they think.
Jean de La Bruyère (1645–96) French satirist.
Les Caractères

1690

328 New opinions are always suspected, and usually opposed, without any other reason but because they are not already common.
John Locke (1632–1704) English philosopher.
An Essay Concerning Human Understanding, dedicatory epistle

329 It is one thing to show a man that he is in an error, and another to put him in possession of truth.
John Locke (1632–1704) English philosopher.
An Essay Concerning Human Understanding, Bk. IV, Ch. 7

18th century

330 From ignorance our comfort flows,
The only wretched are the wise.
Matthew Prior (1664–1721) British poet.
To the Hon. Charles Montague

331 ...it a great error to waste young gentlemen's years so long in learning Latin by so tedious a grammar.
Gilbert Burnet (1643–1715) Scottish-born English bishop
The Later Stuarts (Sir George Clark)

332 Reading is to the mind what exercise is to the body.
Richard Steele (1672–1729) Dublin-born British essayist.
The Tatler, 147

333 Some for renown, on scraps of learning dote,
And think they grow immortal as they quote.
Edward Young (1683–1765) British poet.
Love of Fame, I

334 The King, observing with judicious eyes
The state of both his universities,
To Oxford sent a troop of horse, and why?
That learned body wanted loyalty;
To Cambridge books, as very well discerning
How much that loyal body wanted learning.
Joseph Trapp (1679–1747) English churchman and academic.
Written after George I donated the Bishop of Ely's library to Cambridge
Literary Anecdotes (Nichols), Vol. III

335 The King to Oxford sent a troop of horse,
For Tories own no argument but force:
With equal skill to Cambridge books he sent,
For Whigs admit no force but argument.
William Browne (1692–1774) English physician.
Literary Anecdotes (Nichols), Vol. III

336 Beware you be not swallowed up in books! An ounce of love is worth a pound of knowledge.
John Wesley (1703–91) British religious leader.
Life of Wesley (R. Southey), Ch. 16

1711

337 For fools rush in where angels fear to tread.
Alexander Pope (1688–1744) British poet.
An Essay on Criticism

338 Words are like leaves; and where they most abound,
Much fruit of sense beneath is rarely found.
Alexander Pope
An Essay on Criticism

1731

339 'Tis education forms the common mind,
Just as the twig is bent, the tree's inclined.
Alexander Pope
Moral Essays, I

1742

340 Public schools are the nurseries of all vice and immorality.
Henry Fielding (1707–54) British novelist.
Joseph Andrews, Bk. III, Ch. 5

1745

341 Be wiser than other people if you can, but do not tell them so.
Earl of Chesterfield (1694–1773) English statesman.
Letter to his son, 19 Nov 1745

1748

342 If we take in our hand any volume; of divinity or school metaphysics, for instance; let us ask, *Does it contain any abstract reasoning concerning quantity or number?* No. *Does it contain any experimental reasoning, concerning matter of fact and existence?* No. commit it then to the flames: for it can contain nothing but sophistry and illusion.
David Hume (1711–76) Scottish philosopher.
An Enquiry Concerning Human Understanding

343 Some folk are wise, and some are otherwise.
Tobias Smollett (1721–71) British novelist.
Roderick Random, Ch. 6

1749

344 Due attention to the inside of books, and due contempt for the outside, is the proper relation between a man of sense and his books.
Earl of Chesterfield (1694–1773) English statesman.
Letter to his son, 10 Jan 1749

345 There mark what ills the scholar's life assail
Toil, envy, want, the patron, and the jail.
Samuel Johnson (1709–84) British lexicographer.
Vanity of Human Wishes

1759

346 The true system of the World has been recognized, developed and perfected . . . Everything has been discussed and analysed, or at least mentioned.
Jean d'Alembert (1717–83) French philosopher and mathematician.
Referring to the *Encyclopédie* (1751–80), which he helped to edit
Elements of Philosophy

347 Integrity without knowledge is weak and useless, and knowledge without integrity is dangerous and dreadful.
Samuel Johnson (1709–84) British lexicographer.
Rasselas, Ch. 41

1764

348 Superstition sets the whole world in flames; philosophy quenches them.
Voltaire (François-Marie Arouet; 1694–1778) French writer.
Dictionnaire philosophique, 'Superstition'

349 I never approved either the errors of his book, or the trivial truths he so vigorously laid down. I have, however, stoutly taken his side when absurd men have condemned him for these same truths.
Voltaire
Referring to Helvetius's *De L'Esprit,* which was publicly burnt in 1758; usually misquoted as 'I disapprove of what you say, but I will defend to the death your right to say it'
Dictionnaire Philosophique Portaif, 'Homme'

350* Education made us what we are.
Claude-Adrien Helvétius (1715–71) French philosopher.
Discours XXX, Ch. 30

351 Let schoolmasters puzzle their brain,
With grammar, and nonsense, and learning,
Good liquor, I stoutly maintain,
Gives genius a better discerning.
Oliver Goldsmith (1728–74) Irish-born British writer.
She Stoops to Conquer, I

352 He who resolves never to ransack any mind but his own, will be soon reduced, from mere barrenness, to the poorest of all imitations; he will be obliged to imitate himself, and to repeat what he has before often repeated.
Joshua Reynolds (1723–92) British portrait painter.
Discourse to Students of the Royal Academy, 10 Dec 1774

353 All knowledge is of itself of some value. There is nothing so minute or inconsiderable, that I would not rather know it than not.
Samuel Johnson (1709–84) British lexicographer.
Life of Johnson (J. Boswell)

354 I am not yet so lost in lexicography, as to forget that words are the daughters of earth, and that things are the sons of heaven. Language is only the instrument of science, and words are but the signs of ideas: I wish, however, that the instrument might be less apt to decay, and that signs might be permanent, like the things which they denote.
Samuel Johnson
Dictionary of the English Language

355 The true genius is a mind of large general powers, accidentally determined to some particular direction.
Samuel Johnson
Lives of the English Poets, 'Cowley'

356 My dear friend, clear your *mind* of cant . . . You may *talk* in this manner; it is a mode of talking in Society: but don't *think* foolishly.
Samuel Johnson (1709–84) British lexicographer.
Life of Johnson (J. Boswell), Vol. IV

357 Knowledge dwells
In heads replete with thoughts of other men;
Wisdom in minds attentive to their own.
William Cowper (1731–1800) British poet.
The Task

358* To the University of Oxford I acknowledge no obligation; and she will as cheerfully renounce me for a son, as I am willing to disclaim her for a mother. I spent fourteen months at Magdalen College: they proved the fourteen months the most idle and unprofitable of my whole life.
Edward Gibbon (1737–94) British historian.
Autobiography

History

18th century

359 A good historian is timeless; although he is a patriot, he will never flatter his country in any respect.
François Fénelon (1651–1715) French writer and prelate.
Letter to M. Dacier

360* Anything but history, for history must be false.
Robert Walpole (1676–1745) British statesman.
Walpoliana

361 Great abilities are not requisite for an Historian . . . Imagination is not required in any high degree.
Samuel Johnson (1709–84) British lexicographer.
Life of Johnson (J. Boswell), Vol. I

362 All our ancient history, as one of our wits remarked, is no more than accepted fiction.
Voltaire (François-Marie Arouet: 1694–1778) French writer.
Jeannot et Colin

363 Indeed, history is nothing more than a tableau of crimes and misfortunes.
Voltaire
L'Ingénu, Ch. 10

364 His reign is marked by the rare advantage of furnishing very few materials for history; which

is, indeed, little more than the register of the
crimes, follies, and misfortunes of mankind.
Edward Gibbon (1737-94) British historian.
Referring to the reign of Antoninus Pius
Decline and Fall of the Roman Empire, Ch. 3

1778

365* We owe respect to the living; to the dead we
owe only truth.
Voltaire (François-Marie Arouet; 1694-1778)
French writer.
Oeuvres, 'Première lettre sur Oedipe'

Human Nature

1656

366 I have made this letter longer than usual, only
because I have not had the time to make it
shorter.
Blaise Pascal (1623-62) French philosopher
and mathematician.
Lettres provinciales, XVI

1662

367 We have erred, and strayed from thy ways like
lost sheep.
The Book of Common Prayer
Morning Prayer, General Confession

368 We have left undone those things which we
ought to have done; and we have done those
things we ought not to have done.
The Book of Common Prayer
Morning Prayer, General Confession

1663

369 When civil fury first grew high,
And men fell out they knew not why.
Samuel Butler (1612-80) English satirist.
Hudibras, Pt. I

1665

370 He who lives without tobacco is not worthy to
live.
Molière (Jean Baptiste Poquelin; 1622-73)
French dramatist.
Don Juan, I:1

371 We are never so happy nor so unhappy as we
imagine.
Duc de la Rochefoucauld (1613-80) French
writer.
Maximes, 49

372 It is more shameful to distrust one's friends
than to be deceived by them.
Duc de la Rochefoucauld
Maximes, 84

373 Silence is the best tactic for him who distrusts
himself.
Duc de la Rochefoucauld
Maximes, 79

374 In the misfortune of our best friends, we always
find something which is not displeasing to us.
Duc de la Rochefoucauld
Maximes, 99

375 There is scarcely a single man sufficiently
aware to know all the evil he does.
Duc de la Rochefoucauld
Maximes, 269

376 The accent of one's birthplace lingers in the
mind and in the heart as it does in one's
speech.
Duc de la Rochefoucauld
Maximes, 342

377 Nothing prevents us from being natural so
much as the desire to appear so.
Duc de la Rochefoucauld
Maximes, 431

1667

378 Accuse not Nature, she hath done her part;
Do thou but thine.
John Milton (1608-74) English poet.
Paradise Lost, Bk. VIII

379 In solitude
What happiness? who can enjoy alone,
Or, all enjoying, what contentment find?
John Milton
Paradise Lost, Bk. VIII

1668

380 One should oblige everyone to the extent of
one's ability. One often needs someone smaller
than oneself.
Jean de La Fontaine (1621-95) French poet.
Fables, II, 'Le Lion et le Rat'

381 Patience and passage of time do more than
strength and fury.
Jean de La Fontaine
Fables, II, 'Le Lion et le Rat'

382 He told me never to sell the bear's skin before
one has killed the beast.
Jean de La Fontaine
Fables, V, 'L'Ours et les deux Compagnons'

1669

383 The more intelligence one has the more people
one finds original. Commonplace people see
no difference between men.
Blaise Pascal (1623-62) French philosopher
and mathematician.
Pensées, I

384 The heart has its reasons which reason does
not know.
Blaise Pascal
Pensées, IV

1670

385 I have striven not to laugh at human actions,

not to weep at them, nor to hate them, but to understand them.
Benedict Spinoza (Baruch de Spinoza; 1632–77) Dutch philosopher.
Tractatus Theologico-Politicus, Ch. 1

1677
---

386   Desire is the very essence of man.
Benedict Spinoza
Ethics

387   Man is a social animal.
Benedict Spinoza
Ethics

1678
---

388   Men are but children of a larger growth;
Our appetites as apt to change as theirs,
And full as craving too, and full as vain.
John Dryden (1631–1700) British poet and dramatist.
All for Love, IV

389   People must help one another; it is nature's law.
Jean de La Fontaine (1621–95) French poet.
Fables, VIII, 'L'Âne et le Chien'

1680
---

390   But words once spoke can never be recall'd.
Earl of Roscommon (1633–85) Irish-born English poet.
Art of Poetry

1681
---

391   Beware the Fury of a Patient Man.
John Dryden (1631–1700) British poet and dramatist.
Absalom and Achitophel, I

1685
---

392   It is a general mistake to think the men we like are good for everything, and those we do not, good for nothing.
Lord Halifax (1633–95) English statesman.
Political, Moral and Miscellaneous Thoughts and Reflections

393   It is flattering some men to endure them.
Lord Halifax
Political, Moral and Miscellaneous Thoughts and Reflections

1687
---

394   For present joys are more to flesh and blood
Than a dull prospect of a distant good.
John Dryden (1631–1700) British poet and dramatist.
The Hind and the Panther, III

1688
---

395   One must laugh before one is happy, or one may die without ever laughing at all.
Jean de La Bruyère (1645–96) French satirist.
Les Caractères

1689
---

396   Pleasures are all alike simply considered in themselves . . . He that takes pleasure to hear sermons enjoys himself as much as he that hears plays.
John Selden (1584–1654) English historian.
Table Talk

397   Pleasure is nothing else but the intermission of pain.
John Selden
Table Talk

1701
---

398   Nature has left this tincture in the blood,
That all men would be tyrants if they could.
Daniel Defoe (1660–1731) British journalist and writer.
The Kentish Petition, Addenda

1706
---

399   A man should never be ashamed to own he has been in the wrong, which is but saying, in other words, that he is wiser to-day than he was yesterday.
Alexander Pope (1688–1744) British poet.
Thoughts on Various Subjects

400   I never wonder to see men wicked, but I often wonder to see them not ashamed.
Jonathan Swift (1667–1745) Irish-born Anglican priest and writer.
Thoughts on Various Subjects

1711
---

401   To err is human, to forgive, divine.
Alexander Pope (1688–1744) British poet.
An Essay on Criticism

402   Most sorts of diversion in men, children, and other animals, are an imitation of fighting.
Jonathan Swift (1667–1745) Irish-born Anglican priest and writer.
Thoughts on Various Subjects

1716
---

403   They do most by Books, who could do much without them, and he that chiefly owes himself unto himself, is the substantial Man.
Thomas Browne (1605–82) English physician and writer.
Christian Morals, Pt. II

1718

404   For hope is but the dream of those that wake.
Matthew Prior (1664–1721) British poet.
Solomon, II

1728

405   A moment of time may make us unhappy for ever.
John Gay (1685–1732) English poet and dramatist.
The Beggar's Opera

1733

406   And hence one master-passion in the breast,
Like Aaron's serpent, swallows up the rest.
Alexander Pope (1688–1744) British poet.
An Essay on Man, II

407   Know then thyself, presume not God to scan,
The proper study of Mankind is Man.
Alexander Pope
An Essay on Man, II

408   The ruling passion, be it what it will
The ruling passion conquers reason still.
Alexander Pope
Moral Essays, III

1735

409   Three may keep a secret, if two of them are dead.
Benjamin Franklin (1706–90) US scientist and statesman.
Poor Richard's Almanack

1736

410   A really intelligent man feels what other men only know.
Baron de Montesquieu (1688–1755) French writer.
Essai sur les causes qui peuvent affecter les esprits et les caractères

1739

411   We never remark any passion or principle in others, of which, in some degree or other, we may not find a parallel in ourselves.
David Hume (1711–76) Scottish philosopher.
A Treatise of Human Nature

412   Everyone has observed how much more dogs are animated when they hunt in a pack, than when they pursue their game apart. We might, perhaps, be at a loss to explain this phenomenon, if we had not experience of a similar in ourselves.
David Hume
A Treatise of Human Nature

413   There are two things for which animals are to be envied: they know nothing of future evils, or of what people say about them.
Voltaire (François-Marie Arouet; 1694–1778) French writer.
Letter, 1739

1741

414   Beauty in things exists in the mind which contemplates them.
David Hume (1711–76) Scottish philosopher.
Essays, 'Of Tragedy'

1743

415*   Whoever would lie usefully should lie seldom.
Lord Hervey (1696–1743) English writer and pamphleteer.
Memoirs of the Reign of George II, Vol. I

1751

416   These are called the pious frauds of friendship.
Henry Fielding (1707–54) British novelist.
Amelia, Bk. III, Ch. 4

1755

417   If a man does not make new acquaintance as he advances through life, he will soon find himself left alone. A man, Sir, should keep his friendship in constant repair.
Samuel Johnson (1709–84) British lexicographer.
Life of Johnson (J. Boswell), Vol. I

1757

418   I am convinced that we have a degree of delight, and that no small one, in the real misfortunes and pains of others.
Edmund Burke (1729–97) British politician.
On the Sublime and Beautiful, Pt. I

1758

419   Pleasure is very seldom found where it is sought; our brightest blazes of gladness are commonly kindled by unexpected sparks.
Samuel Johnson (1709–84) British lexicographer.
The Idler

420   We are inclined to believe those whom we do not know because they have never deceived us.
Samuel Johnson
The Idler

1762

421   The true use of speech is not so much to express our wants as to conceal them.
Oliver Goldsmith (1728–74) Irish-born British writer.
Essays, 'The Use of Language'

1766

422 That all who are happy, are equally happy, is
     not true. A peasant and a philosopher may be
     equally *satisfied*, but not equally *happy*. Hap-
     piness consists in the multiplicity of agree-
     able consciousness.
     Samuel Johnson (1709–84) British
     lexicographer.
     Life of Johnson (J. Boswell), Vol. II

1772

423 A man who does not lose his reason over cer-
     tain things has none to lose.
     Gotthold Ephraim Lessing (1729–81) Ger-
     man dramatist.
     Emilia Galotti, IV:7

1776

424 All that is human must retrograde if it does not
     advance.
     Edward Gibbon (1737–94) British historian.
     Decline and Fall of the Roman Empire, Ch. 71

1778

425 Drinking when we are not thirsty and making
     love all year round, madam; that is all there is
     to distinguish us from other animals.
     Beaumarchais (1732–99) French dramatist.
     Le Mariage de Figaro, II:21

426 All censure of a man's self is oblique praise. It
     is in order to shew how much he can spare.
     Samuel Johnson (1709–84) British
     lexicographer.
     Life of Johnson (J. Boswell), Vol. III

1779

427 If it is abuse – why one is always sure to hear
     of it from one damned good-natured friend or
     other!
     Richard Brinsley Sheridan (1751–1816)
     British dramatist.
     The Critic, I

1781

428 Always, Sir, set a high value on spontaneous
     kindness. He whose inclination prompts him to
     cultivate your friendship of his own accord,
     will love you more than one whom you have
     been at pains to attach to you.
     Samuel Johnson (1709–84) British
     lexicographer.
     Life of Johnson (J. Boswell), Vol. IV

1782

429 Society, friendship, and love,
     Divinely bestowed upon man,
     Oh, had I the wings of a dove,

How soon would I taste you again!
William Cowper (1731–1800) British poet.
*Verses supposed to be written by Alexander
Selkirk*

1783

430 As I know more of mankind I expect less of
     them, and am ready now to call a man *a good
     man*, upon easier terms than I was formerly.
     Samuel Johnson (1709–84) British
     lexicographer.
     Life of Johnson (J. Boswell), Vol. IV

431 There is a wicked inclination in most people to
     suppose an old man decayed in his intellects.
     If a young or middle-aged man, when leaving
     a company, does not recollect where he laid
     his hat, it is nothing; but if the same inatten-
     tion is discovered in an old man, people will
     shrug up their shoulders, and say, 'His memory
     is going.'
     Samuel Johnson
     Life of Johnson (J. Boswell), Vol. IV

1784

432 Sir, I look upon every day to be lost, in which I
     do not make a new acquaintance.
     Samuel Johnson
     Life of Johnson (J. Boswell), Vol. IV

433 No man is a hypocrite in his pleasures.
     Samuel Johnson
     Life of Johnson (J. Boswell), Vol. IV

1785

434* Out of the crooked timber of humanity no
     straight thing can ever be made.
     Immanuel Kant (1724–1804) German
     philosopher.
     *Idee zu einer allgemeinen Geschichte in
     weltbürgerlicher Absicht*

435 Happiness is not an ideal of reason but of
     imagination.
     Immanuel Kant
     Grundlegung zur Metaphysik der Sitten, II

Humour

1704

436 Satire is a sort of glass, wherein beholders do
     generally discover everybody's face but their
     own.
     Jonathan Swift (1667–1745) Irish-born
     Anglican priest and writer.
     The Battle of the Books, 'Preface'

1711

437 True wit is nature to advantage dress'd;
     What oft was thought, but ne'er so well
     express'd.
     Alexander Pope (1688–1744) British poet.
     An Essay on Criticism

1733

438 Satire should, like a polished razor keen,
Wound with a touch that's scarcely felt or
seen.
Lady Mary Wortley Montagu (1689–1762)
English writer.
To the Imitator of the First Satire of Horace.
Bk. II

1759

439 An ounce of a man's own wit is worth a ton of
other people's.
Laurence Sterne (1713–68) Irish-born British
writer.
Tristram Shandy

1763

440 A joke's a very serious thing.
Charles Churchill (1731–64) British poet.
The Ghost, Bk. IV

1778

441* God is on the side not of the heavy battalions,
but of the best shots.
Voltaire (François-Marie Arouet; 1694–1778)
French writer.
Notebooks

1784

442* Every man has, some time in his life, an ambition to be a wag.
Samuel Johnson (1709–84) British
lexicographer.
Diary and Letters (Mme D'Arblay), Vol. III, Ch.
46

Life

1651

443 As our life is very short, so it is very miserable,
and therefore it is well it is short.
Jeremy Taylor (1613–67) English Anglican
theologian.
The Rule and Exercise of Holy Dying, Ch. 1

1656

444 Life is an incurable disease.
Abraham Cowley (1618–67) English poet.
To Dr Scarborough

1665

445 To succeed in the world, we do everything we
can to appear successful.
Duc de la Rochefoucauld (1613–80) French
writer.
Maximes, 50

1666

446 It is a stupidity second to none, to busy oneself
with the correction of the world.
Molière (Jean Baptiste Poquelin; 1622–73)
French dramatist.
Le Misanthrope, I:1

1681

447 Great Wits are sure to Madness near alli'd
And thin Partitions do their Bounds divide.
John Dryden (1631–1700) British poet and
dramatist.
Absalom and Achitophel, I

1684

448 He that is down needs fear no fall;
He that is low, no pride.
John Bunyan (1628–88) English writer.
The Pilgrim's Progress, 'Shepherd Boy's Song'

449 As I walked through the wilderness of this
world.
John Bunyan
The Pilgrim's Progress, Pt. I

1688

450 There are only three events in a man's life;
birth, life, and death; he is not conscious of being born, he dies in pain, and he forgets to
live.
Jean de La Bruyère (1645–96) French
satirist.
Les Caractères

451 If poverty is the mother of crime, stupidity is its
father.
Jean de La Bruyère
Les Caractères

1706

452 The vanity of human life is like a river, constantly passing away, and yet constantly coming on.
Alexander Pope (1688–1744) British poet.
Thoughts on Various Subjects

453 When men grow virtuous in their old age, they
only make a sacrifice to God of the devil's
leavings.
Alexander Pope
Thoughts on Various Subjects

454 When a true genius appears in the world, you
may know him by this sign, that the dunces
are all in confederacy against him.
Jonathan Swift (1667–1745) Irish-born
Anglican priest and writer.
Thoughts on Various Subjects

1711

455 Thus I live in the world rather as a Spectator of
mankind, than as one of the species, by which
means I have made myself a speculative
statesman, soldier, merchant, and artisan, with-

out ever meddling with any practical part of life.
Joseph Addison (1672–1719) British essayist.
The Spectator, 1

1712
---

456 We are always doing something for posterity, but I would fain see posterity do something for us.
Joseph Addison
The Spectator, 583

1713
---

457 'Tis not in mortals to command success, But we'll do more, Sempronius; we'll deserve it.
Joseph Addison
Cato, I:2

1715
---

458 Lord, I ascribe it to Thy grace, And not to chance, as others do, That I was born of Christian race, And not a Heathen, or a Jew.
Isaac Watts (1674–1748) English theologian and hymn writer.
Divine Songs for Children, 'Praise for the Gospel'

1726
---

459 A little rule, a little sway, A sunbeam in a winter's day, Is all the proud and mighty have Between the cradle and the grave.
John Dyer (1700–58) British poet.
Grongar Hill

1732
---

460 Life is a jest; and all things show it. I thought so once; but now I know it.
John Gay (1685–1732) English poet and dramatist.
My Own Epitaph

1741
---

461 The atrocious crime of being a young man ... I shall neither attempt to palliate nor deny.
William Pitt the Elder (1708–78) British statesman.
Speech, House of Commons, 27 Jan 1741

1742
---

462 Time flies, death urges, knells call, heaven invites, Hell threatens.
Edward Young (1683–1765) British poet.
Night Thoughts

1746
---

463 To achieve great things we must live as though we were never going to die.
Marquis de Vauvenargues (1715–47) French soldier and writer.
Réflexions et maximes

1747
---

464 I recommend you to take care of the minutes: for hours will take care of themselves.
Earl of Chesterfield (1694–1773) English statesman.
Letter to his son, 6 Nov 1747

465 Not all that tempts your wand'ring eyes And heedless hearts, is lawful prize; Nor all, that glisters, gold.
Thomas Gray (1716–71) British poet.
Ode on the Death of a Favourite Cat

1748
---

466 Custom, then, is the great guide of human life.
David Hume (1711–76) Scottish philosopher.
An Enquiry Concerning Human Understanding

1757
---

467 Beauty in distress is much the most affecting beauty.
Edmund Burke (1729–97) British politician.
On the Sublime and Beautiful, Pt. III

1759
---

468 True genius walks along a line, and, perhaps, our greatest pleasure is in seeing it so often near falling, without being ever actually down.
Oliver Goldsmith (1728–74) Irish-born British writer.
The Bee, 'The Characteristics of Greatness'

469 A man should know something of his own country, too, before he goes abroad.
Laurence Sterne (1713–68) Irish-born British writer.
Tristram Shandy

470 All is for the best in the best of possible worlds.
Voltaire (François-Marie Arouet; 1694–1778) French writer.
Candide, Ch. 30

471 What a fine comedy this world would be if one did not play a part in it!
Denis Diderot (1713–84) French writer.
Letters to Sophie Volland

1764
---

472 Just as the meanest and most vicious deeds require spirit and talent, so even the greatest deeds require a certain insensitiveness which on other occasions is called stupidity.
Georg Christoph Lichtenberg (1742–99) German physicist and writer.
Aphorisms

1766

473   Man wants but little here below,
Nor wants that little long.
Oliver Goldsmith (1728–74) Irish-born British writer.
Edwin and Angelina, or the Hermit

1769

474   If you have great talents, industry will improve them: if you have but moderate abilities, industry will supply their deficiency.
Joshua Reynolds (1723–92) British portrait painter.
Discourse to Students of the Royal Academy, 11 Dec 1769

475   The world is a comedy to those who think, a tragedy to those who feel.
Horace Walpole (1717–97) British writer.
Letter to Sir Horace Mann, 1769

1776

476   It is better that some should be unhappy than that none should be happy, which would be the case in a general state of equality.
Samuel Johnson (1709–84) British lexicographer.
Life of Johnson (J. Boswell), Vol. III

1778

477   All argument is against it; but all belief is for it.
Samuel Johnson
Referring to the ghost of a dead person
Life of Johnson (J. Boswell), Vol. III

1785

478   God made the country, and man made the town.
William Cowper (1731–1800) British poet.
The Task

479   Oh for a lodge in some vast wilderness,
Some boundless contiguity of shade,
Where rumour of oppression and deceit,
Of unsuccessful or successful war,
Might never reach me more!
William Cowper
The Task

1787

480   A useless life is an early death.
Goethe (1749–1832) German poet and dramatist.
Iphegenie, I:2

1788

481   Two things fill the mind with ever new and increasing wonder and awe, the more often and the more seriously reflection concentrates upon them: the starry heaven above me and the moral law within me.
Immanuel Kant (1724–1804) German philosopher.
Critique of Practical Reason, Conclusion

Love and Sex

1665

482   There are very few people who are not ashamed of having been in love when they no longer love each other.
Duc de la Rochefoucauld (1613–80) French writer.
Maximes, 71

483   If one judges love by its visible effects, it looks more like hatred than like friendship.
Duc de la Rochefoucauld
Maximes, 72

1666

484   Age will bring all things, and everyone knows, Madame, that twenty is no age to be a prude.
Molière (Jean Baptiste Poquelin; 1622–73) French dramatist.
Le Misanthrope, III:4

1667

485   Oh, I have loved him too much to feel no hate for him.
Jean Racine (1639–99) French dramatist.
Andromaque, II:1

1680

486*   For, Heaven be thanked, we live in such an age, When no man dies for love, but on the stage.
John Dryden (1631–1700) British poet and dramatist.
Mithridates, Epilogue

1692

487   It is with our passions as it is with fire and water, they are good servants, but bad masters.
Roger L'Estrange (1616–1704) English journalist and writer.
Aesop's Fables, 38

1700

488   Say what you will, 'tis better to be left than never to have been loved.
William Congreve (1670–1729) British Restoration dramatist.
The Way of the World, II:1

1712

489   What dire offence from am'rous causes springs,

What mighty contests rise from trivial things.
Alexander Pope (1688–1744) British poet.
The Rape of the Lock, I

1743

490 He in a few minutes ravished this fair creature,
or at least would have ravished her, if she had
not, by a timely compliance, prevented him.
Henry Fielding (1707–54) British novelist.
Jonathan Wild, Bk. III, Ch. 7

1749

491 What is commonly called love, namely the desire of satisfying a voracious appetite with a
certain quantity of delicate white human flesh.
Henry Fielding
Tom Jones, Bk. VI, Ch. 1

1768

492 Friendship is a disinterested commerce between equals; love, an abject intercourse between tyrants and slaves.
Oliver Goldsmith (1728–74) Irish-born British
writer.
The Good-Natured Man, I

1778

493* It is one of the superstitions of the human mind
to have imagined that virginity could be a
virtue.
Voltaire (François-Marie Arouet; 1694–1778)
French writer.
Notebooks

1785

494* *Plaisir d'amour ne dure qu'un moment,
Chagrin d'amour dure toute la vie.*
Love's pleasure lasts but a moment; love's
sorrow lasts all through life.
Jean-Pierre Claris de Florian (1755–94)
French writer of fables.
Celestine

Marriage and the Family

1662

495 If any of you know cause, or just impediment.
The Book of Common Prayer
Solemnization of Matrimony

1665

496 Strange to say what delight we married people
have to see these poor fools decoyed into our
condition.
Samuel Pepys (1633–1703) English diarist.
Diary, 25 Dec 1665

1672

497 A mistress should be like a little country retreat
near the town, not to dwell in constantly, but
only for a night and away.
William Wycherley (1640–1716) English
dramatist.
The Country Wife, I:1

1678

498 Love is a boy, by poets styl'd,
Then spare the rod, and spoil the child.
Samuel Butler (1612–80) English satirist.
Hudibras, Pt. II

1689

499 Marriage is nothing but a civil contract.
John Selden (1584–1654) English historian.
Table Talk

1693

500 SHARPER. Thus grief still treads upon the heels of
pleasure:
Marry'd in haste, we may repent at leisure.
SETTER. Some by experience find those words
mis-plac'd:
At leisure marry'd, they repent in haste.
William Congreve (1670–1729) British Res-
toration dramatist.
The Old Bachelor, V:8

501 Men are generally more careful of the breed of
their horses and dogs than of their children.
William Penn (1644–1718) English preacher.
*Some Fruits of Solitude, in Reflections and
Maxims relating to the conduct of Humane Life*,
Pt. I, No 52

1696

502 No man worth having is true to his wife, or can
be true to his wife, or ever was, or ever will be
so.
John Vanbrugh (1664–1726) English architect and dramatist.
The Relapse, III:2

1706

503 What they do in heaven we are ignorant of;
what they do *not* we are told expressly, that
they neither marry, nor are given in marriage.
Jonathan Swift (1667–1745) Irish-born
Anglican priest and writer.
Thoughts on Various Subjects

1749

504 His designs were strictly honourable, as the
phrase is; that is, to rob a lady of her fortune by
way of marriage.
Henry Fielding (1707–54) British novelist.
Tom Jones, Bk. XI, Ch. 4

1759

505 **Marriage has many pains, but celibacy has no pleasures.**
Samuel Johnson (1709–84) British lexicographer.
Rasselas. Ch. 26

1770

506 **The triumph of hope over experience.**
Samuel Johnson (1709–84) British lexicographer.
Referring to the hasty remarriage of an acquaintance following the death of his first wife, with whom he had been most unhappy
Life of Johnson (J. Boswell), Vol. II

Men and Women

1660

507 **The souls of women are so small,**
That some believe they've none at all.
Samuel Butler (1612–80) English satirist.
Miscellaneous Thoughts

1662

508 **My wife, who, poor wretch, is troubled with her lonely life.**
Samuel Pepys (1633–1703) English diarist.
Diary, 19 Dec 1662

509 **One tongue is sufficient for a woman.**
John Milton (1608–74) English poet.
On being asked whether he would allow his daughters to learn foreign languages
Attrib.

1675

510 **Vain man is apt to think we were meerly intended for the world's propagation and to keep its humane inhabitants sweet and clean; but, by their leaves, had we the same literature he would find our brains as fruitful as our bodies.**
Hanna Woolley
Gentlewoman's Companion, 1675

1676

511 **Well, a widow, I see, is a kind of sinecure.**
William Wycherley (1640–1716) English dramatist.
The Plain Dealer, V:3

1688

512 **Women run to extremes; they are either better or worse than men.**
Jean de La Bruyère (1645–96) French satirist.
Les Caractères

1696

513 **Once a woman has given you her heart you can never get rid of the rest of her.**
John Vanbrugh (1664–1726) English architect and dramatist.
The Relapse. II:1

1697

514 **Heaven has no rage like love to hatred turned,**
Nor hell a fury like a woman scorned.
William Congreve (1670–1729) British Restoration dramatist.
The Mourning Bride, III

1712

515 **A woman seldom asks advice until she has bought her wedding clothes.**
Joseph Addison (1672–1719) British essayist.
The Spectator, 475

1728

516 **How, like a moth, the simple maid**
Still plays about the flame!
John Gay (1685–1732) English poet and dramatist.
The Beggar's Opera

1732

517 **Most women have no characters at all.**
Alexander Pope (1688–1744) British poet.
Moral Essays, II

518 **Men, some to business, some to pleasure take;**
But every woman is at heart a rake.
Alexander Pope
Moral Essays, II

1749

519 **Women are much more like each other than men: they have, in truth, but two passions, vanity and love; these are their universal characteristics.**
Earl of Chesterfield (1694–1773) English statesman.
Letter to his son, 19 Dec 1749

1752

520 **Every woman is infallibly to be gained by every sort of flattery, and every man by one sort or other.**
Earl of Chesterfield
Letter to his son, 16 Mar 1752

1763

521 **A woman's preaching is like a dog's walking on**

his hinder legs. It is not done well; but you are
surprised to find it done at all.
Samuel Johnson (1709–84) British
lexicographer.
Life of Johnson (J. Boswell), Vol. I

1784

522 A man is in general better pleased when he has
a good dinner upon his table, than when his
wife talks Greek.
Samuel Johnson
Johnsonian Miscellanies (ed. G. B. Hill), Vol. II

Morality, Vices, and Virtues

1664

523 The manner of giving is worth more than the
gift.
Pierre Corneille (1606–84) French dramatist.
Le Menteur, I:1

524 It is a public scandal that gives offence, and it
is no sin to sin in secret.
Molière (Jean Baptiste Poquelin; 1622–73)
French dramatist.
Tartuffe, IV:5

1665

525 We need greater virtues to sustain good fortune than bad.
Duc de la Rochefoucauld (1613–80) French
writer.
Maximes, 25

526 If we had no faults of our own, we would not
take so much pleasure in noticing those of
others.
Duc de la Rochefoucauld
Maximes, 31

527 Self-interest speaks all sorts of tongues, and
plays all sorts of roles, even that of
disinterestedness.
Duc de la Rochefoucauld
Maximes, 39

528 To refuse praise reveals a desire to be praised
twice over.
Duc de la Rochefoucauld
Maximes, 149

529 Hypocrisy is the homage paid by vice to virtue.
Duc de la Rochefoucauld
Maximes, 218

530 Most usually our virtues are only vices in
disguise.
Duc de la Rochefoucauld
Maximes, added to the 4th edition

1666

531 One should examine oneself for a very long
time before thinking of condemning others.
Molière (Jean Baptiste Poquelin; 1622–73)
French dramatist.
Le Misanthrope, III:4

1667

532 For neither man nor angel can discern
Hypocrisy, the only evil that walks
Invisible, except to God alone.
John Milton (1608–74) English poet.
Paradise Lost, Bk. III

533 Revenge, at first though sweet,
Bitter ere long back on itself recoils.
John Milton
Paradise Lost, Bk. IX

1669

534 If you want people to think well of you, do n
speak well of yourself.
Blaise Pascal (1623–62) French philosophe
and mathematician.
Pensées, I

1671

535 Most men admire
Virtue, who follow not her lore.
John Milton (1608–74) English poet.
Paradise Regained, Bk. I

1674

536 Often the fear of one evil leads us into a wors
Nicolas Boileau (1636–1711) French writer
L'Art poétique, I

1677

537 Crime, like virtue, has its degrees.
Jean Racine (1639–99) French dramatist.
Phèdre, IV:2

1678

538 Errors, like Straws, upon the surface flow;
He who would search for Pearls must dive
below.
John Dryden (1631–1700) British poet and
dramatist.
All for Love, Prologue

1684

539 It beareth the name of Vanity Fair, because th
town where 'tis kept is lighter than vanity.
John Bunyan (1628–88) English writer.
The Pilgrim's Progress, Pt. I

1685

540 Popularity is a crime from the moment it is
sought; it is only a virtue where men have it
whether they will or no.
Lord Halifax (1633–95) English statesman.
*Political, Moral and Miscellaneous Thoughts
and Reflections*

541 Our virtues and vices couple with one anothe

and get children that resemble both their parents.
Lord Halifax
Political, Moral and Miscellaneous Thoughts and Reflections

1688
---

542 Liberality lies less in giving liberally than in the timeliness of the gift.
Jean de La Bruyère (1645–96) French satirist.
Les Caractères

1693
---

543 The dreadful burden of having nothing to do.
Nicolas Boileau (1636–1711) French writer.
Épitres, XI

1694
---

544 See how love and murder will out.
William Congreve (1670–1729) British Restoration dramatist.
The Double Dealer, IV:6

1711
---

545 Fondly we think we honour merit then,
When we but praise ourselves in other men.
Alexander Pope (1688–1744) British poet.
An Essay on Criticism

546 Of all the causes which conspire to blind
Man's erring judgment, and misguide the mind,
What the weak head with strongest bias rules,
Is Pride, the never-failing vice of fools.
Alexander Pope
An Essay on Criticism

547 To err is human, to forgive, divine.
Alexander Pope
An Essay on Criticism

1715
---

548 For Satan finds some mischief still
For idle hands to do.
Isaac Watts (1674–1748) English theologian and hymn writer.
Divine Songs for Children, 'Against Idleness and Mischief'

1725
---

549 That action is best, which procures the greatest happiness for the greatest numbers.
Francis Hutcheson (1694–1746) Scottish philosopher.
Inquiry into the Original of our Ideas of Beauty and Virtue, Treatise II, 'Concerning Moral Good and Evil'

1739
---

550 Grief and disappointment give rise to anger, anger to envy, envy to malice, and malice to grief again, till the whole circle be completed.
David Hume (1711–76) Scottish philosopher.
A Treatise of Human Nature

1742
---

551 Procrastination is the thief of time.
Edward Young (1683–1765) British poet.
Night Thoughts

1746
---

552 Whatever is worth doing at all is worth doing well.
Earl of Chesterfield (1694–1773) English statesman.
Letter to his son, 10 Mar 1746

1747
---

553 Do as you would be done by is the surest method that I know of pleasing.
Earl of Chesterfield
Letter to his son, 16 Oct 1747

1749
---

554 Idleness is only the refuge of weak minds.
Earl of Chesterfield
Letter to his son, 20 July 1749

1759
---

555 Integrity without knowledge is weak and useless, and knowledge without integrity is dangerous and dreadful.
Samuel Johnson (1709–84) British lexicographer.
Rasselas, Ch. 41

556 'Tis known by the name of perseverance in a good cause, – and of obstinacy in a bad one.
Laurence Sterne (1713–68) Irish-born British writer.
Tristram Shandy

1763
---

557 The danger chiefly lies in acting well,
No crime's so great as daring to excel.
Charles Churchill (1731–64) British poet.
Epistle to William Hogarth

558 But if he does really think that there is no distinction between virtue and vice, why, Sir, when he leaves our houses let us count our spoons.
Samuel Johnson (1709–84) British lexicographer.
Life of Johnson (J. Boswell), Vol. I

1764

559 The best is the enemy of the good.
Voltaire (François-Marie Arouet; 1694–1778)
French writer.
Dictionnaire philosophique, 'Art dramatique'

1768

560 We must touch his weaknesses with a delicate
hand. There are some faults so nearly allied to
excellence, that we can scarce weed out the
fault without eradicating the virtue.
Oliver Goldsmith (1728–74) Irish-born British
writer.
The Good-Natured Man, I

1769

561 There is, however, a limit at which forbearance
ceases to be a virtue.
Edmund Burke (1729–97) British politician.
Observations on a Publication, 'The Present
State of the Nation'

1776

562 Corruption, the most infallible symptom of con-
stitutional liberty.
Edward Gibbon (1737–94) British historian.
Decline and Fall of the Roman Empire, Ch. 21

1777

563 He who praises everybody praises nobody.
Samuel Johnson (1709–84) British
lexicographer.
Life of Johnson (J. Boswell), Vol. III

1779

564 The bud may have a bitter taste,
But sweet will be the flower.
William Cowper (1731–1800) British poet.
Olney Hymns, 35

1782

565 I am not over-fond of resisting temptation.
William Beckford (1759–1844) British writer.
Vathek

1785

566 Finally, there is an imperative which commands
a certain conduct immediately . . . This imperative is Categorical . . . This imperative may be
called that of Morality.
Immanuel Kant (1724–1804) German
philosopher.
Grundlegung zur Metaphysik der Sitten, II

567 All universal moral principles are idle fancies.
Marquis de Sade (1740–1814) French
novelist.
The 120 Days of Sodom

Other People

1662

568 But Lord! to see the absurd nature of Englishmen, that cannot forbear laughing and jeering
at everything that looks strange.
Samuel Pepys (1633–1703) English diarist.
Diary, 27 Nov 1662

1688

569 If we heard it said of Orientals that they habitually drank a liquor which went to their heads,
deprived them of reason and made them
vomit, we should say: 'How very barbarous!'
Jean de La Bruyère (1645–96) French
satirist.
Les Caractères

1734

570 The English nation is the only one on earth
which has successfully regulated the power of
its kings by resisting them; and which, after
repeated efforts, has established that beneficial government under which the Prince, all
powerful for good, is restrained from doing ill.
Voltaire (François Marie Arouet; 1694–1778)
French writer.
Lettres philosophiques

1755

571 The Englishman . . . always has in his hands an
accurate pair of scales in which he scrupu-
lously weighs up the birth, the rank, and above
all, the wealth of the people he meets, in order to adjust his behaviour towards them
accordingly.
Jean Rouquet
The Reign of George III (J. Steven Watson),
Ch. 3

1758

572 When two Englishmen meet, their first talk is of
the weather.
Samuel Johnson (1709–84) British
lexicographer.
The Idler

1763

573 Norway, too, has noble wild prospects; and
Lapland is remarkable for prodigious noble wild
prospects. But, Sir, let me tell you, the noblest
prospect which a Scotchman ever sees, is
the high road that leads him to England!
Samuel Johnson
Life of Johnson (J. Boswell), Vol. I

1768

574 They are a loyal, a gallant, a generous, an inge-
ious, and good-temper'd people as is under

heaven – if they have a fault, they are too *serious*.
Laurence Sterne (1713–68) Irish-born British writer.
A Sentimental Journey, 'The Character. Versailles'

1773

575   Come, let me know what it is that makes a Scotchman happy!
Samuel Johnson
Ordering for himself a glass of whisky
Tour to the Hebrides (J. Boswell)

1774

576* I hate the French because they are all slaves, and wear wooden shoes.
Oliver Goldsmith (1728–74) Irish-born British writer.
Essays, 'Distresses of a Common Soldier'

1775

577   The Irish are a fair people; – they never speak well of one another.
Samuel Johnson
Life of Johnson (J. Boswell), Vol. II

1780

578   A Frenchman must be always talking, whether he knows anything of the matter or not; an Englishman is content to say nothing, when he has nothing to say.
Samuel Johnson (1709–84) British lexicographer.
Life of Johnson (J. Boswell), Vol. IV

1782

579   When you see how in this happy country the lowest and poorest member of society takes an interest in all public affairs; when you see how high and low, rich and poor, are all willing to declare their feelings and convictions; when you see how a carter, a common sailor, a beggar is still a man, nay, even more, an Englishman – then, believe me, you find yourself very differently affected from the experience you feel when staring at our soldiers drilling in Berlin.
Karl Philipp Moritz (1756–93) German Lutheran pastor.
Reaction to a by-election at Westminster
Letter to a friend, 1782

1787

580   I do not dislike the French from the vulgar antipathy between neighbouring nations, but for their insolent and unfounded airs of superiority.
Horace Walpole (1717–97) British writer.
Letter to Hannah More, 14 Oct 1787

Religion

1651

581   The Papacy is no other than the ghost of the deceased Roman empire, sitting crowned upon the grave thereof.
Thomas Hobbes (1588–1679) English philosopher.
Leviathan, Pt. IV, Ch. 47

1652

582   God doth not need
Either man's work or his own gifts. Who best
Bear his mild yoke, they serve him best: his state
Is kingly; thousands at his bidding speed,
And post o'er land and ocean without rest;
They also serve who only stand and wait.
John Milton (1608–74) English poet.
Sonnet: 'On his Blindness'

1653

583   Though the mills of God grind slowly, yet they grind exceeding small;
Though with patience He stands waiting, with exactness grinds He all.
Friedrich von Logau (1604–55) German poet and writer.
Sinngedichte, III

1662

584   Renounce the devil and all his works.
The Book of Common Prayer
Publick Baptism of Infants

1667

585   What in me is dark
Illumine, what is low raise and support;
That, to the height of this great argument,
I may assert Eternal Providence,
And justify the ways of God to men.
John Milton (1608–74) English poet.
Paradise Lost, Bk. I

586   Long is the way
And hard, that out of hell leads up to light.
John Milton
Paradise Lost, Bk. II

587   Which way I fly is Hell; myself am Hell;
And, in the lowest deep, a lower deep
Still threat'ning to devour me opens wide,
To which the Hell I suffer seems a Heaven.
John Milton
Paradise Lost, Bk. IV

1669

588   I cannot forgive Descartes; in all his philosophy he did his best to dispense with God. But he could not avoid making Him set the world in

motion with a flip of His thumb; after that he had no more use for God.
Blaise Pascal (1623–62) French philosopher and mathematician.
Pensées. II

1677
---

589 We feel and know that we are eternal.
Benedict Spinoza (Baruch de Spinoza; 1632–77) Dutch philosopher.
Ethics

1688
---

590 A pious man is one who would be an atheist if the king were.
Jean de La Bruyère (1645–96) French satirist.
Les Caractères

591 The Puritan hated bear-baiting, not because it gave pain to the bear, but because it gave pleasure to the spectators.
Lord Macaulay (1800–59) British historian.
History of England, Vol. I, Ch. 2

1689
---

592 For a priest to turn a man when he lies a-dying, is just like one that has a long time solicited a woman, and cannot obtain his end; at length makes her drunk, and so lies with her.
John Selden (1584–1654) English historian.
Table Talk

1700
---

593 While shepherds watch'd their flocks by night,
All seated on the ground,
The Angel of the Lord came down,
And 'Glory shone around.
Nahum Tate (1652–1715) Irish-born English poet.
Supplement to the New Version of the Psalms, 'While Shepherds Watched'

1701
---

594 Wherever God erects a house of prayer,
The Devil always builds a chapel there;
And 'twill be found, upon examination,
The latter has the largest congregation.
Daniel Defoe (1660–1731) British journalist and writer.
The True-Born Englishman, Pt. I

1721
---

595 No kingdom has ever had as many civil wars as the kingdom of Christ.
Baron de Montesquieu (1688–1755) French writer.
Lettres persanes

596 There is a very good saying that if triangles in-

vented a god, they would make him three-sided.
Baron de Montesquieu (1688–1755) French writer.
Lettres persanes

1739
---

597 I look upon all the world as my parish.
John Wesley (1703–91) British religious leader.
Journal, 11 June 1739

1741
---

598 The Christian religion not only was at first attended with miracles, but even at this day cannot be believed by any reasonable person without one. Mere reason is insufficient to convince us of its veracity: and whoever is moved by faith to assent to it, is conscious of a continued miracle in his own person, which subverts all the principles of his understanding, and gives him a determination to believe what is most contrary to custom and experience.
David Hume (1711–76) Scottish philosopher.
Essays, 'Of Miracles'

1743
---

599 Many a long dispute among divines may be thus abridged: It is so. It is not so. It is so. It is not so.
Benjamin Franklin (1706–90) US scientist and statesman.
Poor Richard's Almanack

1750
---

600 Religion is by no means a proper subject of conversation in a mixed company.
Earl of Chesterfield (1694–1773) English statesman.
Letter to his godson

1759
---

601 Whenever a man talks loudly against religion, – always suspect that it is not his reason, but his passions which have got the better of his creed.
Laurence Sterne (1713–68) Irish-born British writer.
Tristram Shandy

1762

602* Wandering in a vast forest at night, I have only a faint light to guide me. A stranger appears and says to me: 'My friend, you should blow out your candle in order to find your way more clearly.' This stranger is a theologian.
Denis Diderot (1713–84) French writer.
Addition aux Pensées philosophiques

1763

603   Truth, Sir, is a cow, which will yield such people no more milk, and so they are gone to milk the bull.
Samuel Johnson (1709–84) British lexicographer.
Referring to sceptics
Life of Johnson (J. Boswell), Vol. I

1764

604*   Probably no invention came more easily to man than Heaven.
Georg Christoph Lichtenberg (1742–99) German physicist and writer.
Aphorisms

1768

605   I never saw, heard, nor read, that the clergy were beloved in any nation where Christianity was the religion of the country. Nothing can render them popular, but some degree of persecution.
Jonathan Swift (1667–1745) Irish-born Anglican priest and writer.
Thoughts on Religion

606   I am positive I have a soul; nor can all the books with which materialists have pestered the world ever convince me of the contrary.
Laurence Sterne (1713–68) Irish-born British writer.
A Sentimental Journey, 'Maria, Moulines'

1769

607   There is no idolatry in the Mass. They believe God to be there, and they adore him.
Samuel Johnson (1709–84) British lexicographer.
Life of Johnson (J. Boswell), Vol. II

1773

608   As I take my shoes from the shoemaker, and my coat from the tailor, so I take my religion from the priest.
Oliver Goldsmith (1728–74) Irish-born British writer.
Life of Johnson (J. Boswell)

1778

609*   Faith consists in believing when it is beyond the power of reason to believe. It is not enough that a thing be possible for it to be believed.
Voltaire (François-Marie Arouet; 1694–1778) French writer.
Questions sur l'encyclopédie

610*   If God made us in His image, we have certainly returned the compliment.
Voltaire
Le Sottisier

611   Everything is good when it leaves the Creator's hands; everything degenerates in the hands of man.
Jean Jacques Rousseau (1712–78) French philosopher.
Attrib.

1788

612*   If God did not exist, it would be necessary to invent Him.
Voltaire
Épîtres, 'À l'auteur du livre des trois Imposteurs'

Science, Medicine, and Technology

1661

613   It is my intent to beget a good understanding between the chymists and the mechanical philosophers who have hitherto been too little acquainted with one another's learning.
Robert Boyle (1627–91) British scientist.
The Sceptical Chymist

1675

614   If I have seen further it is by standing on the shoulders of giants.
Isaac Newton (1642–1727) British scientist.
Letter to Robert Hooke, 5 Feb 1675

1704

615   Nature is very consonant and conformable with herself.
Isaac Newton
Opticks, Bk. III

1727

616   I do not know what I may appear to the world, but to myself I seem to have been only like a boy playing on the sea-shore, and diverting myself in now and then finding a smoother pebble or a prettier shell than ordinary, whilst the great ocean of truth lay all undiscovered before me.
Isaac Newton
Isaac Newton (L. T. More)

617*   O Diamond! Diamond! thou little knowest the mischief done!
Isaac Newton
Said to a dog that set fire to some papers, representing several years' work, by knocking over a candle
Wensley-Dale . . . a Poem (Thomas Maude)

618*   Nature, and Nature's laws lay hid in night:
God said, *Let Newton be!* and all was light.
Alexander Pope (1688–1744) British poet.
Epitaphs, 'Intended for Sir Isaac Newton'

1762

619   Men will always be mad and those who think
      they can cure them are the maddest of all.
      Voltaire (François-Marie Arouet: 1694–1778)
      French writer.
      Letter, 1762

1778

620   Man is a tool-making animal.
      Benjamin Franklin (1706–90) US scientist
      and statesman.
      Life of Johnson (J. Boswell), 7 Apr 1778

1779

621   We are perpetually moralists, but we are geo-
      metricians only by chance. Our intercourse
      with intellectual nature is necessary; our spec-
      ulations upon matter are voluntary, and at
      leisure.
      Samuel Johnson (1709–84) British
      lexicographer.
      Lives of the English Poets, 'Milton'

1788

622   The art of medicine consists of amusing the pa-
      tient while Nature cures the disease.
      Voltaire (1694–1788) French writer.
      Attrib.

Wealth and Poverty

1673

623   He must have killed a lot of men to have made
      so much money.
      Molière (Jean Baptiste Poquelin: 1622–73)
      French dramatist.
      Le Malade imaginaire, I:5

1688

624   The shortest and best way to make your fortune
      is to let people see clearly that it is in their
      interests to promote yours.
      Jean de La Bruyère (1645–96) French
      satirist.
      Les Caractères

1707

625   There's no scandal like rags, nor any crime so
      shameful as poverty.
      George Farquhar (1678–1707) Irish
      dramatist.
      The Beaux' Stratagem, I:1

1747

626   I knew once a very covetous, sordid fellow, who

used to say, 'Take care of the pence, for the
pounds will take care of themselves.'
Earl of Chesterfield (1694–1773) English
statesman.
Possibly referring to William Lowndes
Letter to his son, 6 Nov 1747

1751

627   Let not Ambition mock their useful toil,
      Their homely joys, and destiny obscure;
      Nor Grandeur hear with a disdainful smile,
      The short and simple annals of the poor.
      Thomas Gray (1716–71) British poet.
      Elegy Written in a Country Churchyard

1753

628   I am rich beyond the dreams of avarice.
      Edward Moore (1712–57) British dramatist.
      The Gamester, II

1775

629   There are few ways in which a man can be
      more innocently employed than in getting
      money.
      Samuel Johnson (1709–84) British
      lexicographer.
      Life of Johnson (J. Boswell), Vol. II

1776

630   With the great part of rich people, the chief em-
      ployment of riches consists in the parade of
      riches.
      Adam Smith (1723–90) Scottish economist.
      The Wealth of Nations

1778

631   Sir, the insolence of wealth will creep out.
      Samuel Johnson (1709–84) British
      lexicographer.
      Life of Johnson (J. Boswell), Vol. III

1782

632   Resolve not to be poor: whatever you have,
      spend less. Poverty is a great enemy to human
      happiness; it certainly destroys liberty, and it
      makes some virtues impracticable and
      others extremely difficult.
      Samuel Johnson
      Life of Johnson (J. Boswell), Vol. IV

1785

633   Riches have wings, and grandeur is a dream.
      William Cowper (1731–1800) British poet.
      The Task

Work and Occupations

1660

634 A client is fain to hire a lawyer to keep from the injury of other lawyers – as Christians that travel in Turkey are forced to hire Janissaries, to protect them from the insolencies of other Turks.
Samuel Butler (1835–1902) British writer.
Prose Observations

1669

635 Not to care for philosophy is to be a true philosopher.
Blaise Pascal (1623–62) French philosopher and mathematician.
Pensées, I

1681

636 For Politicians neither love nor hate.
John Dryden (1631–1700) British poet and dramatist.
Absalom and Achitophel, I

1715

637 How doth the little busy bee
Improve each shining hour,
And gather honey all the day
From every opening flower!
Isaac Watts (1674–1748) English theologian and hymn writer.
Divine Songs for Children, 'Against Idleness and Mischief'

1734

638 I am as sober as a Judge.
Henry Fielding (1707–54) British novelist.
Don Quixote in England, III:14

1742

639 For clergy are men as well as other folks.
Henry Fielding (1707–54) British novelist.
Joseph Andrews, Bk II, Ch. 6

1756

640 The booksellers are generous liberal-minded men.
Samuel Johnson (1709–84) British lexicographer.
Life of Johnson (J. Boswell), Vol. I

1759

641 Work banishes those three great evils, boredom, vice, and poverty.
Voltaire (François-Marie Arouet; 1694–1778) French writer.
Candide, Ch. 30

1762

642 To a philosopher no circumstance, however trifling, is too minute.
Oliver Goldsmith (1728–74) Irish-born British writer.
The Citizen of the World

1770

643 I do not care to speak ill of any man behind his back, but I believe the gentleman is an *attorney*.
Samuel Johnson (1709–84) British lexicographer.
Life of Johnson (J. Boswell), Vol. II

1772

644 A man who is good enough to go to heaven, is good enough to be a clergyman.
Samuel Johnson
Life of Johnson (J. Boswell), Vol. II

1773

645 A lawyer has no business with the justice or injustice of the cause which he undertakes, unless his client asks his opinion, and then he is bound to give it honestly. The justice or injustice of the cause is to be decided by the judge.
Samuel Johnson
Tour to the Hebrides (J. Boswell)

1776

646 We would all be idle if we could.
Samuel Johnson
Life of Johnson (J. Boswell), Vol. III

1780

647 Remember that time is money.
Benjamin Franklin (1706–90) US scientist and statesman.
Advice to a Young Tradesman

Sayings of the Time

1660

648 And so to bed.
Samuel Pepys (1633–1703) English diarist.
Diary, 6 May 1660 and *passim*

1684

649 The gentleman's name that met him was Mr Worldly Wiseman.
John Bunyan (1628–88) English writer.
The Pilgrim's Progress, Pt. I

1707

650   Spare all I have, and take my life.
George Farquhar (1678–1707) Irish
dramatist.
The Beaux' Strategem, V:2

651   Lady Bountiful.
Bernard de Fontenelle (1657–1757) French
philosopher.
The Beaux' Strategem, I:1

1708

652   Boys and girls come out to play,
The moon doth shine as bright as day.
Useful Transactions in Philosophy (William
King)

1719

653   I takes my man Friday with me.
Daniel Defoe (1660–1731) British journalist
and writer.
Robinson Crusoe, Pt. I

1725

654   London Bridge is broken down,
My fair lady.
Namby Pamby (Henry Carey)

1735

655   Some are weather-wise, some are otherwise.
Benjamin Franklin (1706–90) US scientist
and statesman.
Poor Richard's Almanack

656   Damn with faint praise, assent with civil leer,
And, without sneering, teach the rest to
sneer.
Alexander Pope (1688–1744) British poet.
Epistle to Dr. Arbuthnot

1742

657   Far from the madding crowd's ignoble strife,
Their sober wishes never learn'd to stray;
Along the cool sequester'd vale of life
They kept the noiseless tenor of their way.
Thomas Gray (1716–71) British poet.
Elegy Written in a Country Churchyard

1763

658   The distance doesn't matter; it is only the first
step that is difficult.
Marquise du Deffand (Marie de Vichy-
Chamrond; 1697–1780) French noblewoman.
Referring to the legend of St Denis, who is tradi-
tionally believed to have carried his severed
head for six miles after his execution
Letter to d'Alembert, 7 July 1763

With Hindsight

18th century

659   'And everybody praised the Duke,
Who this great fight did win.'
'But what good came of it at last?'
Quoth little Peterkin.
'Why that I cannot tell,' said he,
'But 'twas a famous victory.'
Robert Southey (1774–1843) British poet.
The Battle of Blenheim

660   His views and affections were singly confined
to the narrow compass of the Electorate;
England was too big for him.
Earl of Chesterfield (1694–1773) English
statesman.
Referring to George I
Letters

661   George the First knew nothing, and desired to
know nothing; did nothing, and desired to do
nothing; and the only good thing that is told
of him is, that he wished to restore the crown
to its hereditary successor.
Samuel Johnson (1709–84) British
lexicographer.
Life of Johnson (J. Boswell)

19th century

662   Better lo'ed ye canna be,
Will ye no come back again?
Carolina Nairne (1766–1845) Scottish
songwriter.
Referring to Bonnie Prince Charlie
Bonnie Charlie's now awa!

663   Charlie is my darling, my darling, my darling,
Charlie is my darling, the young Chevalier.
Carolina Nairne
Referring to Bonnie Prince Charlie
Charlie is my Darling

664   Wi' a hundred pipers an' a', an' a'.
Carolina Nairne
A romantic glorification of the 1745 Jacobite
Rebellion
The Hundred Pipers

665   . . . this haughty, vigilant, resolute, sagacious
blue-stocking, half Mithridates and half Trisso-
tin, bearing up against a world in arms
Lord Macaulay (1800–59) British historian.
Referring to Frederick the Great
Historical Essays, 'Frederick the Great'

666   Dr Johnson's morality was as English an article
as a beefsteak.
Nathaniel Hawthorne (1804–64) US novelist and writer.
Our Old Home, 'Lichfield and Uttoxeter'

667   Throughout the greater part of his life George
III was a kind of 'consecrated obstruction'.
Walter Bagehot (1826–1877) British econo-
mist and journalist.
The English Constitution, 'The Monarchy'

20th century

668   I'm glad you like my Catherine. I like her too. She ruled thirty million people and had three thousand lovers. I do the best I can in two hours.
Mae West (1892–1980) US actress.
After her performance in *Catherine the Great*
Speech from the stage

669   Too much counterpoint; what is worse, Protestant counterpoint.
Thomas Beecham (1879–1961) British conductor.
Said of J. S. Bach
The Guardian, 8 Mar 1971

670   It is sobering to consider that when Mozart was my age he had already been dead for a year.
Tom Lehrer (1928–) US university teacher and songwriter.
An Encyclopedia of Quotations about Music
(N. Shapiro)

671   The sonatas of Mozart are unique; they are too easy for children, and too difficult for artists.
Artur Schnabel (1882–1951) Austrian concert pianist.
An Encyclopedia of Quotations about Music
(N. Shapiro)

9

The French Revolution (1789–1815)

the 18th century, the French monarchy represented the *ancien régime*. Vast, intricate, and archaic, its power
d authority rested on a web of expedients woven over the centuries. By 1788, it was financially and politically
nkrupt; yet it dared not initiate any far-reaching reforms for fear of undermining its whole structure. In despera-
n Louis XVI summoned the States General, the medieval assembly of the realm, which had not met since 1614.
wever, his shaky control of the political process combined with an increasing radicalism throughout the country
destroy the monarchy. By 1793, when Louis XVI was executed, France had taken an unprecedented step: the
sic continuity of political and social institutions, together with the legitimacy offered by the past, had been
plicitly rejected. In their place the revolutionaries sought to construct a state based on the rational principles of
e Enlightenment, epitomized by the slogan 'Liberty, Equality, Fraternity'.
ar with the rest of Europe began in 1792. The revolutionaries were keen to export their ideas, which, not unnatu-
y, were anathema to the remaining traditional monarchies of Europe. From late 1792, the French were every-
ere victorious. The emergence of a soldier of genius, Napoleon Bonaparte, added a new dimension to this
uation. In 1799 he seized control of France and in 1804 declared himself emperor. France now became an
porter of Bonapartist imperialism rather than revolution. Invincible in battle, Napoleon was the arbiter of Europe
til his disastrous attack on Russia in 1812. When France was finally defeated in 1815, Napoleon was exiled;
vertheless the ideas of the French Revolution lived on to terrify the traditional monarchies for another half
ntury.
Britain during this period, a quite separate, but equally profound, change was beginning – the Industrial Revolu-
n. The exploitation of technological discoveries, especially the steam engine, encouraged the concentration of
oduction in factories. This revolution made industry more efficient, enabling larger volumes of goods to be pro-
ced at low prices. By 1815 Britain had acquired a decisive industrial advantage over the rest of the world.
hough this continued to increase, it brought with it a number of new social problems, particularly the large-scale
ovement of the population from the countryside to the towns and the appalling working conditions in the new
:tories. The industrial methods of production pioneered in Britain were not made use of in the rest of Europe and
America until the middle of the 19th century.

Politics, Government, and World Events

1788

1 No National Assembly ever threatened to be so stormy as that which will decide the fate of the monarchy, and which is gathering in such haste, and with so much distrust on both sides.
Comte de Mirabeau (1749–91) French statesman.
Letter, 6 Dec 1788

1789

2 *Liberté! Égalité! Fraternité!*
Freedom! Equality! Brotherhood!
Anonymous
Motto for French Revolutionaries

3 Let us take as our emblem green cockades, green the colour of hope!
Camille Desmoulins (1760–94) French Revolutionary leader.
Le Vieux Cordelier

4 Who will dare deny that the Third Estate contains within itself all that is needed to constitute a nation?
Abbé de Sieyès (1748–1836) French churchman.
The 'Third Estate' comprised all the French people except the nobility (the First Estate) and the clergy (the Second Estate)
Qu'est-ce que le Tiers État? (pamphlet, Jan 1789)

5 *Rien*
Nothing.
Louis XVI (1754–93) King of France.
Diary, 14 July 1789 – the day the Bastille fell

6 How much the greatest event it is that ever happened in the world! and how much the best!
Charles James Fox (1749–1806) British Whig politician.
Referring to the fall of the Bastille, 14 July 1789
Letter to Fitzpatrick, 30 July 1789

7 Every law is an evil, for every law is an infraction of liberty.
Jeremy Bentham (1748–1832) British philosopher.
An Introduction to the Principles of Morals and Legislation

1790s

8 Oh! the grand old Duke of York
He had ten thousand men;
He marched them up to the top of the hill,
And he marched them down again.
And when they were up they were up,
And when they were down they were down,
And when they were only half way up,
They were neither up nor down.
Anonymous
Referring to Frederick Augustus, son of George

III and Duke of York, who commanded two unsuccessful campaigns against the French (1793 and 1799)
Traditional

1790

9 To tell the truth, Napoleone is a dangerous man in a free country. He seems to me to have the makings of a tyrant.
Lucien Bonaparte (1775–1840) Brother of Napoleon I.
Letter to Joseph Bonaparte, 1790

10 But the age of chivalry is gone. That of sophisters, economists, and calculators, has succeeded; and the glory of Europe is extinguished for ever.
Edmund Burke (1729–97) British politician.
Reflections on the Revolution in France

11 Vice itself lost half its evil, by losing all its grossness.
Edmund Burke
Reflections on the Revolution in France

12 Kings will be tyrants from policy when subjects are rebels from principle.
Edmund Burke
Reflections on the Revolution in France

1791

13 The Commons, faithful to their system, remained in a wise and masterly inactivity.
James Mackintosh (1765–1832) Scottish lawyer, philosopher, and historian.
Vindiciae Gallicae

1792

14 Unquestionably there never was a time in the history of this country when, from the situation of Europe, we might more reasonably expect fifteen years of peace, than we may at this present moment.
William Pitt the Younger (1759–1806) British statesman.
Revolutionary France declared war on Britain on 1 Feb 1793
Speech, House of Commons, 17 Feb 1792

15 Dangers by being despised grow great.
Edmund Burke (1729–97) British politician.
Speech, House of Commons, 11 May 1792

16 *Allons, enfants, de la patrie,*
Le jour de gloire est arrivé.
Come, children of our native land,
The day of glory has arrived.
Rouget de Lisle (Claude Joseph Rouget de Lisle; 1760–1836) French military engineer and composer.
La Marseillaise (French national anthem)

17 The tocsin you hear today is not an alarm but an alert: it sounds the charge against our enemies. To conquer them we must dare, and

dare again, and dare for ever; and thus will France be saved
Georges Jacques Danton (1759–94) French political activist.
Speech, Paris, 2 Sept 1792

18 From today and from this place there begins a new epoch in the history of the world.
Goethe (1749–1832) German poet and dramatist.
On witnessing revolutionary France's first military victory, at the battle of Valmy (20 Sept 1792)
The Story of Civilization (W. Durant), Vol. II

19 How, indeed, may we judge a king as a citizen? For judging means applying the law. But law implies a common foundation of justice. And what common foundation of justice is there between humanity and kings?
Louis de Saint-Just (1767–94) French politician.
Speech, Convention, 18 Nov 1792

20 Citizens, we are talking of a republic, and yet Louis lives! We are talking of a republic, and the person of the King still stands between us and liberty.
Robespierre (1758–94) French lawyer and revolutionary.
Speech, Convention, 3 Dec 1792

1793

21 Any institution which does not suppose the people good, and the magistrate corruptible is evil.
Robespierre
Déclaration des Droits de l'homme, 24 Apr 1793

22 Son of Saint Louis, ascend to heaven.
Abbé Edgeworth de Firmont (1745–1807) Irish-born confessor to Louis XVI.
Said to Louis XVI as he climbed up to the guillotine: Saint Louis was Louis IX of France (1226–79)
Attrib.

23 'O liberté! O liberté! Que de crimes on commet en ton nom!'
Oh liberty! Oh liberty! What crimes are committed in thy name!
Madame Roland (1754–93) French revolutionary.
Said as she mounted the steps of the guillotine
Attrib.

24 There has been reason to fear that the Revolution may, like Saturn, devour each of her children one by one.
Pierre Vergniaud (1753–93) French revolutionary.
Said at his trial, Nov 1793
Attrib.

25 Prisons are built with stones of Law, brothels with bricks of Religion.
William Blake (1757–1827) British poet.
The Marriage of Heaven and Hell, 'Proverbs of Hell'

1794

26 Thou wilt show my head to the people: it i[s] worth showing.
Georges Jacques Danton (1759–94) French political activist.
Said as he mounted the scaffold, 5 Apr 179[4]
French Revolution (Carlyle), Bk. VI, Ch. 2

27* J'ai vécu.
I survived.
Abbé de Sieyès (1748–1836) French churchman.
Replying to an enquiry concerning what he h[ad] done during the Terror
Dictionnaire Encyclopédique (E. Guérard)

1795

28 Somebody has said, that a king may make a [no]bleman, but he cannot make a gentleman.
Edmund Burke (1729–97) British politicia[n]
Letter to William Smith, 29 Jan 1795

29 Harris, I am not well; pray get me a glass [of] brandy.
George IV (1762–1830) King of the Unite[d] Kingdom.
On seeing Caroline of Brunswick (his future w[ife]) for the first time
Diaries (Earl of Malmesbury)

30 In *this* country, my Lords, . . . the individual subject . . . 'has nothing to do with the laws [but] to obey them.'
Samuel Horsley (1733–1806) British bish[op]
House of Lords, 13 Nov 1795

31 The courtiers who surrounded him have for[got]ten nothing and learnt nothing.
Charles-François Dumouriez (1739–18[?]) French general.
Referring to Louis XVIII. This remark is also [at]tributed to Talleyrand
Attrib.

32* A whiff of grapeshot.
Thomas Carlyle (1795–1881) Scottish historian.
Describing how Napoleon, early in his career [?] quelled a minor riot in Paris
History of the French Revolution, Pt. I, Bk. [?] Ch. 3

1796

33 The French Revolution is merely the herald [of] far greater and much more solemn revolutio[n] which will be the last . . . The hour has com[e] for founding the Republic of Equals, that gr[eat] refuge open to every man.
François-Noël Babeuf (1760–97) French revolutionary.
Conjuration des Egaux

1797

34 In Scotland there is no shadow even of rep[re]sentation. There is neither a representation [of]

property for the counties, nor of population
for the towns.
Charles James Fox (1749–1806) British
politician.
Parliamentary History of England (W. Cobbett),
Vol. XXXIII

1798

5 Think of it, soldiers; from the summit of these
pyramids, forty centuries look down upon
you.
Napoleon I (Napoleon Bonaparte; 1769–
1821) French emperor.
Speech before the Battle of the Pyramids, 21
July 1798

6 The perpetual struggle for room and food.
Thomas Robert Malthus (1766–1834) British clergyman and economist.
Essays on the Principle of Population

1799

7 His taxes now prove
His great love for the people,
So wisely they're managed
To starve the poor souls.
Charles Morris (1745–1838) Song-writer.
Referring to William Pitt the Younger
The Faber Book of English History in Verse
(Kenneth Baker)

1800

8* You must hate a Frenchman as you hate the
devil.
Lord Nelson (1758–1805) British admiral.
Life of Nelson (Southey), Ch. 3

39 Providence has given to the French the empire
of the land, to the English that of the sea, and
to the Germans that of the air.
Jean Paul Richter (Johann Paul Friedrich
Richter; 1763–1825) German novelist.
Quoted by Thomas Carlyle

1801

40 I have only one eye: I have a right to be blind
sometimes: I really do not see the signal.
Lord Nelson (1758–1805) British admiral.
Remark, Battle of Copenhagen, 2 Apr 1801; Nelson ignored Admiral Parker's order to disengage by placing his telescope to his blind eye;
an hour later, he was victorious

41 He clapped the glass to his sightless eye,
And 'I'm damned if I see it', he said.
Henry John Newbolt (1862–1938) British
poet.
Referring to Lord Nelson at the Battle of
Copenhagen
Admirals All

42 Ye Mariners of England
That guard our native seas,

Whose flag has braved, a thousand years,
The battle and the breeze –
Your glorious standard launch again
To match another foe!
And sweep through the deep,
While the stormy winds do blow, –
While the battle rages loud and long,
And the stormy winds do blow.
Thomas Campbell (1777–1844) British poet.
Ye Mariners of England

1802

43 Think of your forefathers! Think of your
posterity!
John Quincy Adams (1767–1848) Sixth
president of the USA.
Speech, Plymouth, Massachusetts, 22 Dec 1802

44 We must be free or die, who speak the tongue
That Shakspeare spake; the faith and morals
hold
Which Milton held.
William Wordsworth (1770–1850) British
poet.
Sonnets, 'It is not to be thought of'

1803

45* Pitt is to Addington
As London is to Paddington.
George Canning (1770–1827) British
statesman.
Henry Addington had become Prime Minister
when Pitt resigned (1801) over George III's refusal to accept Catholic emancipation; Pitt returned as Prime Minister in 1804
The Oracle

46 I do not say the French cannot come, I only say
they cannot come by sea.
John Jervis, Earl St Vincent (1735–1823)
British admiral.
Remark to the Cabinet, 1803

47 The strongest poison ever known
Came from Caesar's laurel crown.
William Blake (1757–1827) British poet.
Auguries of Innocence

1804

48 He is an ordinary human being after all! . . . now
he will put himself above everyone else and
become a tyrant.
Ludwig van Beethoven (1770–1827) German composer.
Referring to Napoleon, on hearing that he had
declared himself emperor
Remark to Ferdinand Ries, a pupil

49 It is worse than a crime, it is a blunder.
Antoine Boulay de la Meurthe (1761–
1840) French politician.
Referring to the summary execution of the Duc
d'Enghien by Napoleon, 1804
Attrib.

1805

Battle of Trafalgar (1805)

The naval battle (21 October 1805), during the Napoleonic wars, in which the British, led by Nelson in the *Victory*, defeated the French and ended the threat of an invasion of Britain. The success was marred by the death of Nelson.

50 The Nelson touch.
Lord Nelson (1758–1805) British admiral.
Diary, 9 Oct 1805

51 Now, gentlemen, let us do something today which the world may talk of hereafter.
Lord Collingwood (1750–1810) British admiral.
Said before Trafalgar, 21 Oct 1805
Correspondence and Memoir of Lord Collingwood (G. L. Newnham; ed. Collingwood)

52 In case signals can neither be seen nor perfectly understood, no captain can do very wrong if he places his ship alongside that of an enemy.
Lord Nelson (1758–1805) British admiral.
Memorandum before Trafalgar, 9 Oct 1805

53 England expects every man will do his duty.
Lord Nelson
Signal hoisted prior to the Battle of Trafalgar, 1805

54 Kiss me, Hardy.
Lord Nelson
Spoken to Sir Thomas Hardy, captain of the *Victory*, during the Battle of Trafalgar, 1805

55 The death of Nelson was felt in England as something more than a public calamity; men started at the intelligence and turned pale, as if they had heard of the loss of a dear friend.
Robert Southey (1774–1843) British poet.
The Life of Nelson

56 England has saved herself by her exertions, and will, as I trust, save Europe by her example.
William Pitt the Younger (1759–1806) British statesman.
Speech, Guildhall, 1805

57 Roll up that map: it will not be wanted these ten years.
William Pitt the Younger
On learning that Napoleon had won the Battle of Austerlitz (2 Dec 1805)
Attrib.

58 Venice, the eldest Child of Liberty.
She was a maiden City, bright and free.
William Wordsworth (1770–1850) British poet.
Venice, a republic since the Middle Ages, was conquered by Napoleon in 1797 and absorbed into his Kingdom of Italy in 1805
Sonnets, 'Once did she hold'

59 O Caledonia! stern and wild,
Meet nurse for a poetic child!
Land of brown heath and shaggy wood,
Land of the mountain and the flood,
Land of my sires! what mortal hand
Can e'er untie the filial band
That knits me to thy rugged strand!
Walter Scott (1771–1832) Scottish novelis
The Lay of the Last Minstrel, VI

1806

60 I think I could eat one of Bellamy's veal pie
William Pitt the Younger (1759–1806) B
ish statesman.
Last words
Attrib.

61 Oh, my country! How I leave my country!
William Pitt the Younger

62 With death doomed to grapple,
Beneath this cold slab, he
Who lied in the chapel
Now lies in the Abbey.
Byron, George Gordon, 6th Baron (178
1824) British poet.
Epitaph for William Pitt

63* England is a nation of shopkeepers.
Napoleon I (Napoleon Bonaparte; 1769–18
French emperor.
Attrib.

64 Another year! – another deadly blow!
Another mighty empire overthrown!
And we are left, or shall be left, alone.
William Wordsworth (1770–1850) British poet.
Napoleon defeated Prussia at the Battles of Je
and Anerstädt, 14 Oct 1806
Sonnets, 'Another year!'

1807

65 The wealth of our island may be diminished, b
the strength of mind of the people cannot eas
ly pass away . . . We cannot lose our liberty,
because we cannot cease to think.
Humphry Davy (1778–1829) British chemi
Letter to Thomas Poole, 28 Aug 1807

66 A more virtuous man, I believe, does not exi
nor one who is more enthusiastically devote
to better the condition of mankind.
Thomas Jefferson (1743–1826) US
statesman.
Referring to Tsar Alexander I
Letter to William Duane, 20 July 1807

67 A power is passing from the earth
To breathless Nature's dark abyss;
But when the great and good depart,
What is it more than this –

That Man who is from God sent forth,
Doth yet again to God return? –
Such ebb and flow must ever be,

Then wherefore should we mourn?
William Wordsworth (1770–1850) British poet.
Referring to Charles James Fox, the hero of the liberal Whigs, who died in 1806
Lines on the Expected Dissolution of Mr. Fox

8 The moment the very name of Ireland is mentioned, the English seem to bid adieu to common feeling, common prudence, and common sense, and to act with the barbarity of tyrants, and the fatuity of idiots.
Sydney Smith (1771–1845) British clergyman and essayist.
The Letters of Peter Plymley

9 The harp that once through Tara's halls
The soul of music shed,
Now hangs as mute on Tara's walls
As if that soul were fled. –
So sleeps the pride of former days,
So glory's thrill is o'er;
And hearts, that once beat high for praise,
Now feel that pulse no more.
Thomas Moore (1779–1852) Irish poet.
Irish Melodies, 'The Harp that Once'

0 Me this unchartered freedom tires;
I feel the weight of chance-desires:
My hopes no more must change their name,
I long for a repose that ever is the same.
William Wordsworth (1770–1850) British poet.
Ode to Duty

1 Milton! thou shouldst be living at this hour:
England hath need of thee; she is a fen
Of stagnant waters: altar, sword, and pen,
Fireside, the heroic wealth of hall and bower,
Have forfeited their ancient English dower
Of inward happiness.
William Wordsworth
Sonnets, 'Milton! thou shouldst'

2 I travelled among unknown men
In lands beyond the sea;
Nor, England! did I know till then
What love I bore to thee.
William Wordsworth
I Travelled among Unknown Men

1808
---

3 And did those feet in ancient time
Walk upon England's mountains green?
And was the holy lamb of God
On England's pleasant pastures seen?
...
I will not cease from mental fight,
Nor shall my sword sleep in my hand,
Till we have built Jerusalem
In England's green and pleasant land.
William Blake (1757–1827) British poet.
Better known as the hymn 'Jerusalem', with music by Sir Hubert Parry; not to be confused with Blake's longer poem *Jerusalem*
Milton, Preface

4 *Noblesse oblige.*

Nobility has its own obligations.
Duc de Lévis (1764–1830) French writer and soldier.
Maximes et Réflexions

1809
---

75 I still love you, but in politics there is no heart, only head.
Napoleon I (Napoleon Bonaparte; 1769–1821) French emperor.
Referring to his divorce, for reasons of state, from the Empress Josephine (1809)
Bonaparte (C. Barnett)

76 Not a drum was heard, not a funeral note,
As his corse to the rampart we hurried.
Charles Wolfe (1791–1823) Irish poet.
The Burial of Sir John Moore at Corunna, I

77 We carved not a line, and we raised not a stone –
But we left him alone with his glory.
Charles Wolfe
The Burial of Sir John Moore at Corunna, VIII

1810
---

78 My principle is: France before everything.
Napoleon I (Napoleon Bonaparte; 1769–1821) French emperor.
Letter to Eugène Beauharnais, 23 Aug 1810

79* Every French soldier carries in his cartridge-pouch the baton of a marshal of France.
Napoleon I
La Vie Militaire sous l'Empire (E. Blaze)

80* Maybe it would have been better if neither of us had been born.
Napoleon I
Said while looking at the tomb of the philosopher Jean-Jacques Rousseau, whose theories had influenced the French Revolution
The Story of Civilization (W. Durant), Vol. II

81 I don't know what effect these men will have on the enemy, but, by God, they frighten me.
Duke of Wellington (1769–1852) British general and statesman.
Referring to his soldiers
Attrib.

82* What His Royal Highness most particularly prides himself upon, is the excellent harvest.
Richard Brinsley Sheridan (1751–1816) British dramatist.
Lampooning George IV's habit of taking credit for everything good in England
The Fine Art of Political Wit (L. Harris)

83* Who's your fat friend?
'Beau' Brummell (George Bryan Brummell; 1778–1840) British dandy.
Referring to George, Prince of Wales
Reminiscences (Gronow)

84* Shut the door, Wales.
'Beau' Brummell
Said to the Prince of Wales
Attrib.

1811

85 If I were asked at this moment for a summary opinion of what I have seen in England, I might probably say that its political institutions present a detail of corrupt practices, of profusion, and of personal ambition, under the mask of public spirit very carelessly put on, more disgusting than I should have expected. ...On the other hand, I should admit very readily that I have found the great mass of the people richer, happier, and more respectable than any other with which I am acquainted.
L. Simond French traveller and diarist.
Journal of a Tour and Residence in Great Britain during 1810 and 1811 by a French Traveller

86 Every country has the government it deserves.
Joseph de Maistre (1753–1821) French monarchist.
Lettres et Opuscules Inédits, 15 Aug 1811

87 As it will be the right of all, so it will be the duty of some, definitely to prepare for a separation, amicably if they can, violently if they must.
Josiah Quincy (1772–1864) US statesman.
Abridgement of Debates of Congress, Vol. IV, 14 Jan 1811

1812

88 It's the most beautiful battlefield I've ever seen.
Napoleon I (Napoleon Bonaparte; 1769–1821) French emperor.
Referring to carnage on the field of Borodino, near Moscow, after the battle (7 Sept 1812)
Attrib.

89 There rises the sun of Austerlitz.
Napoleon I
Said at the Battle of Borodino (7 Sept 1812), near Moscow; the Battle of Austerlitz (2 Dec 1805) was Napoleon's great victory over the Russians and Austrians

90 It is only a step from the sublime to the ridiculous.
Napoleon I
Remark following the retreat from Moscow, 1812
Attrib.

91 Napoleon is a torrent which as yet we are unable to stem. Moscow will be the sponge that will suck him dry.
Mikhail Kutuzov (1745–1813) Russian marshal.
Address to the commanders of the Russian army, 13 Sept 1812

92* Then was seen with what a strength and majesty the British soldier fights.
Sir William Napier (1785–1860) British general and historian.
History of the War in the Peninsula Bk. XII, Ch. 6

93 Never under the most despotic of infidel governments did I behold such squalid wretch-

edness as I have seen since my return in very heart of a Christian country.
Lord Byron (1788–1824) British poet.
Speaking against the death penalty for mach wrecking
Speech, House of Lords, 27 Feb 1812

94 Hereditary bondsmen! know ye not
Who would be free themselves must strik the blow?
Lord Byron
Childe Harold's Pilgrimage, I

95 This delightful, blissful, wise, pleasurable, honourable, virtuous, true and immortal Pri was a violator of his word, a libertine over head and ears in debt and disgrace, and de spiser of domestic ties, the companion of g blers and demireps, a man who has just closed half a century without one single cla on the gratitude of his country or the respec of posterity.
Leigh Hunt (1784–1859) British poet.
Referring to the Prince Regent. Hunt was imp oned for two years for this libellous attack
The Examiner, 22 Mar 1812

1813

96 It is the beginning of the end.
Talleyrand (Charles Maurice de Talleyrand-P igord; 1754–1838) French politician.
Referring to Napoleon's defeat at Borodino, 1813
Attrib.

97 France has more need of me than I have n of France.
Napoleon I (Napoleon Bonaparte; 1769–1821) French emperor.
Speech, 31 Dec 1813

98 We have met the enemy, and they are ours
Oliver Hazard Perry (1785–1819) US na officer.
Message sent reporting his victory in a naval tle on Lake Erie
Familiar Quotations (J. Bartlett)

99 I am my own ancestor.
Duc d'Abrantes (1771–1813) French gene
Said on being made a duke
Attrib.

1814

100 One could forgive the fiend for becoming a rent, but to become an earthquake was real too much.
Charles-Joseph, Prince de Ligne (1735 1814) Austrian diplomat.
Referring to Napoleon I
Attrib.

101 The bullet that is to kill me has not yet bee moulded.
Napoleon I (Napoleon Bonaparte; 1769–1821) French emperor.
In reply to his brother Joseph, King of Spain

who had asked whether he had ever been hit by a cannonball
Attrib.

102   The Congress is getting nowhere, it dances.
Le Congrès ne marche pas, il danse.
Charles-Joseph, Prince de Ligne (1735–1814) Austrian diplomat.
Referring to the Congress of Vienna
Remark, Nov 1814

103   'Tis the star-spangled banner; O long may it wave
O'er the land of the free, and the home of the brave!
Francis Scott Key (1779–1843) US lawyer.
The Star-Spangled Banner

1815

104   Metternich and Talleyrand held forth in their usual way, while I sensed as never before the futility of human endeavour, the failings of men who hold the fate of the world in their hands.
Friedrich von Gentz (1764–1832) Austrian bureaucrat.
Referring to a dinner at the Congress of Vienna
Diary, 12 Jan 1815

Battle of Waterloo (1815)

The battle (18 June 1815) in which the Duke of Wellington and the Prussian marshal von Blücher defeated Napoleon Bonaparte, leading to his second, and final, abdication and exile.

105   An army marches on its stomach.
Napoleon I (Napoleon Bonaparte; 1769–1821) French emperor.
Attrib.

106   I have got an infamous army, very weak and ill-equipped, and a very inexperienced staff.
Duke of Wellington (1769–1852) British general and statesman.
Written at the beginning of the Waterloo campaign
Letter to Lord Stewart, 8 May 1815

107   Our troops are all moving from this place at present. Lord Wellington was at the ball tonight as composed as ever.
Thomas Creevey (1768–1838) British politician and diarist.
Written at Brussels
Journal, 16 June 1815

108   It all depends upon that article there.
Duke of Wellington (1769–1852) British general and statesman.
Indicating a passing infantryman when asked if he would be able to defeat Napoleon
The Age of Elegance (A. Bryant)

109   Not upon a man from the colonel to the private in a regiment –both inclusive. We may pick up a marshal or two perhaps; but not worth a damn.
Duke of Wellington
Said during the Waterloo campaign, when asked whether he anticipated any desertions from Napoleon's army
Creevey Papers, Ch. X

110   It is not the business of generals to shoot one another.
Duke of Wellington
Refusing an artillery officer permission to fire upon Napoleon himself during the Battle of Waterloo, 1815
Attrib.

111   Up, Guards, and at 'em.
Duke of Wellington
Order given at the battle of Waterloo, 18 June 1815
Attrib.

112   It has been a damned serious business – Blücher and I have lost 30,000 men. It has been a damned nice thing – the nearest run thing you ever saw in your life . . . By God! I don't think it would have done if I had not been there.
Duke of Wellington
Referring to the Battle of Waterloo
Creevey Papers, Ch. X

113   Yes, and they went down very well too.
Duke of Wellington
Replying to the observation that the French cavalry had come up very well during the Battle of Waterloo
The Age of Elegance (A. Bryant)

114   Oh well, no matter what happens, there's always death.
Napoleon I (Napoleon Bonaparte; 1769–1821) French emperor.
Attrib.

115   I used to say of him that his presence on the field made the difference of forty thousand men.
Duke of Wellington (1769–1852) British general and statesman.
Referring to Napoleon
Notes of Conversations with the Duke of Wellington (Stanhope), 2 Nov 1831

116*   A battle of giants.
Duke of Wellington
Referring to the Battle of Waterloo; said to Samuel Rogers
Attrib.

Attitudes

Art, Literature, and Music

1790

117 I should desire that the last words which I should pronounce in this Academy, and from this place, might be the name of – Michael Angelo.
Joshua Reynolds (1723–92) British portrait painter.
Discourse to Students of the Royal Academy, 10 Dec 1790

1791

118 One of Edward's Mistresses was Jane Shore, who has had a play written about her, but it is a tragedy and therefore not worth reading.
Jane Austen (1775–1817) British novelist.
The History of England

1798

119 Poetry is the spontaneous overflow of powerful feelings: it takes its origin from emotion recollected in tranquillity.
William Wordsworth (1770–1850) British poet.
Lyrical Ballads, Preface

1800

120 There neither is, nor can be, any *essential* difference between the language of prose and metrical composition.
William Wordsworth
Lyrical Ballads, Preface

121 Every great and original writer, in proportion as he is great and original, must himself create the taste by which he is to be relished.
William Wordsworth
Lyrical Ballads, Preface

1802

122 An original writer is not one who imitates nobody, but one whom nobody can imitate.
Vicomte de Chateaubriand (1768–1848) French diplomat and writer.
Génie du Christianisme

123 But as we went along there were more and yet more and there at last under the boughs of the trees, we saw that there was a long belt of them along the shore, about the breadth of a country turnpike road. I never saw daffodils so beautiful they grew among the mossy stones about and about them, some rested their heads upon these stones as on pillow for weariness and the rest tossed and reeled and danced and seemed as if they verily laughed

with the wind that blew upon them over the lake.
Dorothy Wordsworth (1771–1855) British diarist and sister of William Wordsworth.
The Grasmere Journals, 15 Apr 1802

1805

124 For ne'er
Was flattery lost on poet's ear:
A simple race! they waste their toil
For the vain tribute of a smile.
Walter Scott (1771–1832) Scottish novelist.
The Lay of the Last Minstrel, IV

1809

125 A man may surely be allowed to take a glass of wine by his own fireside.
Richard Brinsley Sheridan (1751–1816) British dramatist.
As he sat in a coffeehouse watching his Drury Lane Theatre burn down
Memoirs of the Life of the Rt. Hon. Richard Brinsley Sheridan (T. Moore)

1810

126* The faults of great authors are generally excellences carried to an excess.
Samuel Taylor Coleridge (1772–1834) British poet.
Miscellanies, 149

1812

127 Mad, bad, and dangerous to know.
Lady Caroline Lamb (1785–1828) The wife of William Lamb (later Lord Melbourne).
Said of Byron in her journal
Journal, March 1812

128 I awoke one morning and found myself famous.
Lord Byron (1788–1824) British poet.
Remark made after the publication of *Childe Harold's Pilgrimage* (1812)
Entry in Memoranda

Daily Life

1796

129 What dreadful hot weather we have! It keeps me in a continual state of inelegance.
Jane Austen (1775–1817) British novelist.
Letter, 18 Sept 1796

1802

130 Earth has not anything to show more fair:
Dull would he be of soul who could pass by
A sight so touching in its majesty:
The City now doth, like a garment, wear
The beauty of the morning; silent, bare,
Ships, towers, domes, theatres, and temples lie
Open unto the fields, and to the sky;

All bright and glittering in the smokeless air.
William Wordsworth (1770–1850) British poet.
Sonnets, 'Composed upon Westminster Bridge'

1810

131* No perfumes, but very fine linen, plenty of it, and country washing.
'Beau' Brummell (George Bryan Brummell; 1778–1840) British dandy.
Memoirs (Harriette Wilson), Ch. 2

132* They hated everybody, and abused everybody, and would sit together in White's bay window, or the pit boxes at the Opera, weaving tremendous crammers. They swore a good deal, never laughed, looked hazy after dinner, and had most of them been patronized at one time or other by Brummell and the Prince Regent.
Rees Howell Gronow (1795–1865) MP and social observer.
Referring to Regency 'dandies'
Reminiscences, Vol. I

1814

133* There is nothing good to be had in the country, or, if there is, they will not let you have it.
William Hazlitt (1778–1830) British essayist.
Observations on Wordsworth's 'Excursion'

Death

1798

134 We are laid asleep
In body, and become a living soul:
While with an eye made quiet by the power
Of harmony, and the deep power of joy,
We see into the life of things.
William Wordsworth (1770–1850) British poet.
Lines composed a few miles above Tintern Abbey

1814

135 The good die first,
And they whose hearts are dry as summer dust
Burn to the socket.
William Wordsworth
The Excursion

Education, Knowledge, and Learning

1793

136 What is now proved was once only imagined.
William Blake (1757–1827) British poet.
The Marriage of Heaven and Hell, 'Proverbs of Hell'

137 A fool sees not the same tree that a wise man sees.
William Blake
The Marriage of Heaven and Hell, 'Proverbs of Hell'

1801

138 Against stupidity the gods themselves struggle in vain.
Friedrich von Schiller (1759–1805) German dramatist.
Die Jungfrau von Orleans, III:6

1804

139 I care not whether a man is Good or Evil; all that I care
Is whether he is a Wise Man or a Fool. Go! put off Holiness,
And put on Intellect.
William Blake (1757–1827) British poet.
Jerusalem

1808

140 Dear friend, theory is all grey,
And the golden tree of life is green.
Goethe (1749–1832) German poet and dramatist.
Faust, Pt. I

1815

141* The battle of Waterloo was won on the playing fields of Eton.
Duke of Wellington (1769–1852) British general.
Attrib.

History

1789

142 The history of the World is the World's court of justice.
Friedrich von Schiller (1759–1805) German dramatist.
Lecture, Jena, 26 May 1789

1798

143 A historian is a prophet in reverse.
Friedrich von Schlegel (1772–1829) German diplomat, writer, and critic.
Das Athenäum

1799

144 What millions died — that Caesar might be great!
Thomas Campbell (1777–1844) British poet.
Pleasures of Hope, II

Human Nature

1790
---

145   Talent develops in quiet places, character in the full current of human life.
Goethe (1749–1832) German poet and dramatist.
Torquato Tasso, I

1798
---

146   I do not want people to be very agreeable, as it saves me the trouble of liking them a great deal.
Jane Austen (1775–1817) British novelist.
Letter, 24 Dec 1798

147   If this belief from heaven be sent,
If such be Nature's holy plan,
Have I not reason to lament
What man has made of man?
William Wordsworth (1770–1850) British poet.
Lines written in Early Spring

1800

148* Pleasures newly found are sweet
When they lie about our feet.
William Wordsworth
To the Small Celandine

1803
---

149   Every tear from every eye
Becomes a babe in Eternity.
William Blake (1757–1827) British poet.
Auguries of Innocence

1806
---

150   Mankind are always happy for having been happy, so that if you make them happy now, you make them happy twenty years hence by the memory of it.
Sydney Smith (1771–1845) British clergyman and essayist.
Elementary Sketches of Moral Philosophy

1807
---

151   I wandered lonely as a cloud
That floats on high o'er vales and hills,
When all at once I saw a crowd,
A host, of golden daffodils;
Beside the lake, beneath the trees,
Fluttering and dancing in the breeze.
William Wordsworth (1770–1850) British poet.
I Wandered Lonely as a Cloud

1810

152* There is not a more mean, stupid, dastardly, pitiful, selfish, spiteful, envious, ungrateful

animal than the public. It is the greatest of cowards, for it is afraid of itself.
William Hazlitt (1778–1830) British essayist.
On Living to Oneself

153* The art of pleasing consists in being pleased.
William Hazlitt
On Manner

154* Men are we, and must grieve when even the shade
Of that which once was great is passed away.
William Wordsworth (1770–1850) British poet.
Sonnets, 'Once did she hold'

1813
---

155   For what do we live, but to make sport for our neighbours, and laugh at them in our turn?
Jane Austen (1775–1817) British novelist.
Pride and Prejudice, Ch. 57

156   I have been a selfish being all my life, in practice, though not in principle.
Jane Austen
Pride and Prejudice, Ch. 58

Life

1790
---

157   Superstition is the religion of feeble minds.
Edmund Burke (1729–97) British politician.
Reflections on the Revolution in France

1793
---

158   Without Contraries is no progression. Attraction and Repulsion, Reason and Energy, Love and Hate, are necessary to Human existence.
William Blake (1757–1827) British poet.
The Marriage of Heaven and Hell, 'The Argument'

159   For everything that lives is holy, life delights in life.
William Blake
America

1794
---

160   The sublime and the ridiculous are often so nearly related that it is difficult to class them separately. One step above the sublime makes the ridiculous; and one step above the ridiculous makes the sublime again.
Thomas Paine (1737–1809) British writer.
The Age of Reason, Pt. 2

1796
---

161   Example is the school of mankind, and they will learn at no other.
Edmund Burke
Letters on a Regicide Peace, letter 1

1798

162   I have learned
To look on nature, not as in the hour
Of thoughtless youth; but hearing often-times
The still, sad music of humanity.
William Wordsworth (1770–1850) British poet.
Lines composed a few miles above Tintern Abbey

163   Nor greetings where no kindness is, nor all
The dreary intercourse of daily life,
Shall e'er prevail against us, or disturb
Our cheerful faith, that all which we behold
Is full of blessings.
William Wordsworth
Lines composed a few miles above Tintern Abbey

1799

164   'Tis distance lends enchantment to the view,
And robes the mountain in its azure hue.
Thomas Campbell (1777–1844) British poet.
Pleasures of Hope, I

1800

165*   The good old rule
Sufficeth them, the simple plan,
That they should take, who have the power,
And they should keep who can.
William Wordsworth (1770–1850) British poet.
Rob Roy's Grave

166*   No young man believes he shall ever die.
William Hazlitt (1778–1830) British essayist.
On the Feeling of Immortality in Youth

167   The wiser mind
Mourns less for what age takes away
Than what it leaves behind.
William Wordsworth (1770–1850) British poet.
The Fountain

1803

168   To see a World in a grain of sand,
And a Heaven in a wild flower,
Hold Infinity in the palm of your hand,
And Eternity in an hour.
William Blake (1757–1827) British poet.
Auguries of Innocence

1805

169   Breathes there the man, with soul so dead,
Who never to himself hath said,
This is my own, my native land!
Whose heart hath ne'er within him burn'd,
As home his footsteps he hath turn'd
From wandering on a foreign strand!
Walter Scott (1771–1832) Scottish novelist.
The Lay of the Last Minstrel, VI

1806

170   The sight of it gave me infinite pleasure, as it proved that I was in a civilized society.
Mungo Park (1771–1806) Scottish explorer.
Remark on finding a gibbet in an unexplored part of Africa
Attrib.

1807

171   Though nothing can bring back the hour
Of splendour in the grass, of glory in the flower;
We will grieve not, rather find
Strength in what remains behind . . .
William Wordsworth (1770–1850) British poet.
Ode. Intimations of Immortality, IX

172   The world is too much with us; late and soon,
Getting and spending, we lay waste our powers:
Little we see in Nature that is ours.
William Wordsworth
Sonnets, 'The world is too much with us'

1808

173   Dear friend, theory is all grey,
And the golden tree of life is green.
Goethe (1749–1832) German poet and dramatist.
Faust, Pt. I

1812

174   Live as long as you may, the first twenty years are the longest half of your life.
Robert Southey (1774–1843) British poet.
The Doctor, Ch. 130

1814

175*   Lift not the painted veil which those who live Call life.
Percy Bysshe Shelley (1792–1822) British poet.
Lift not the Painted Veil

1816

176   One does not love a place the less for having suffered in it unless it has all been suffering, nothing but suffering.
Jane Austen (1775–1817) British novelist.
Persuasion, Ch. 20

Marriage and the Family

1790

177   What is your fortune, my pretty maid?
My face is my fortune, sir, she said.
Then I can't marry you, my pretty maid.

Nobody asked you, sir, she said.
Archaeologia Cornu-Britannica (William Pryce)

1800

178* It doesn't much signify whom one marries, for one is sure to find next morning that it was someone else.
Samuel Rogers (1763–1855) British poet.
Recollections of the Table Talk of Samuel Rogers (ed. Alexander Dyce)

1813

179 It is a truth universally acknowledged, that a single man in possession of a good fortune must be in want of a wife.
Jane Austen (1775–1817) British novelist.
The opening words of the book
Pride and Prejudice, Ch. 1

180 Happiness in marriage is entirely a matter of chance.
Jane Austen
Pride and Prejudice, Ch. 6

Men and Women

1792

181 I do not wish them to have power over men; but over themselves.
Mary Wollstonecraft (1759–97) British writer.
Referring to women
A Vindication of the Rights of Woman, Ch. 4

182 The *divine right* of husbands, like the divine right of kings, may, it is hoped, in this enlightened age, be contested without danger.
Mary Wollstonecraft
A Vindication of the Rights of Woman, Ch. 3

183 A king is always a king — and a woman always a woman: his authority and her sex ever stand between them and rational converse.
Mary Wollstonecraft
A Vindication of the Rights of Woman, Ch. 4

1800

184* Can anything be more absurd than keeping women in a state of ignorance, and yet so vehemently to insist on their resisting temptation?
Vicesimus Knox (1752–1821) British essayist.
Liberal Education, Vol. I, 'On the Literary Education of Women'

1813

185 One cannot be always laughing at a man without now and then stumbling on something witty.
Jane Austen (1775–1817) British novelist.
Pride and Prejudice, Ch. 40

186 Next to being married, a girl likes to be crossed in love a little now and then.
Jane Austen (1775–1817) British novelist.
Pride and Prejudice, Ch. 24

Morality, Vices, and Virtues

1798

187 That best portion of a good man's life,
His little, nameless, unremembered acts
Of kindness and of love.
William Wordsworth (1770–1850) British poet.
Lines composed a few miles above Tintern Abbey

1803

188 A truth that's told with bad intent
Beats all the lies you can invent.
William Blake (1757–1827) British poet.
Auguries of Innocence

1804

189 He who would do good to another must do it in Minute Particulars.
General Good is the plea of the scoundrel, hypocrite, and flatterer.
William Blake
Jerusalem

1810

190* One impulse from a vernal wood
May teach you more of man,
Of moral evil and of good,
Than all the sages can.
William Wordsworth (1770–1850) British poet.
The Tables Turned

191* We can scarcely hate any one that we know.
William Hazlitt (1778–1830) British essayist.
On Criticism

Other People

1806

192* England is a nation of shopkeepers.
Napoleon I (Napoleon Bonaparte; 1769–1821) French emperor.
Attrib.

1810

193* Scratch the Russian and you will find the Tartar.
Joseph de Maistre (1753–1821) French monarchist.
Attributed also to Napoleon and Prince de Ligne

1814

194   **What a place to plunder!**
Gebhard Blücher (1742–1819) Prussian general.
Referring to London
Attrib.

1815

195   I look upon Switzerland as an inferior sort of Scotland.
Sydney Smith (1771–1845) British clergyman and essayist.
Letter to Lord Holland, 1815

Religion

1790

196   Man is by his constitution a religious animal.
Edmund Burke (1729–97) British politician.
Reflections on the Revolution in France

1793

197   Man has no Body distinct from his Soul; for that called Body is a portion of Soul discerned by the five Senses, the chief inlets of Soul in this age.
William Blake (1757–1827) British poet.
The Marriage of Heaven and Hell, 'The Voice of the Devil'

1795

198   Nothing is so fatal to religion as indifference, which is, at least, half infidelity.
Edmund Burke (1729–97) British politician.
Letter to William Smith, 29 Jan 1795

1807

199   Whither is fled the visionary gleam?
Where is it now, the glory and the dream?

Our birth is but a sleep and a forgetting:
The Soul that rises with us, our life's Star,
Hath had elsewhere its setting,
And cometh from afar;
Not in entire forgetfulness,
And not in utter nakedness,
But trailing clouds of glory do we come
From God, who is our home:
Heaven lies about us in our infancy!
Shades of the prison-house begin to close
Upon the growing boy.
William Wordsworth (1770–1850) British poet.
Ode. Intimations of Immortality, IV

Science, Medicine, and Technology

1801

200   I believe the souls of five hundred Sir Isaac Newtons would go to the making up of a Shakespeare or a Milton.
Samuel Taylor Coleridge (1772–1834) British poet.
Letter to Thomas Poole, 23 Mar 1801

1810

201*   I have no need of that hypothesis.
Marquis de Laplace (1749–1827) French mathematician and astronomer.
On being asked by Napoleon why he had made no mention of God in his book about the universe, *Mécanique céleste*.
Men of Mathematics (E. Bell)

Wealth and Poverty

1795

202*   The only infallible criterion of wisdom to vulgar minds — success.
Edmund Burke (1729–97) British politician.
Letter to a Member of the National Assembly

Work and Occupations

1810

203*   Now Barabbas was a publisher.
Thomas Campbell (1777–1844) British poet.
Attrib.

Sayings of the Time

1800

204   I came home ... hungry as a hunter.
Charles Lamb (1775–1834) British essayist.
Letter to Coleridge, Apr 1800

1806

205   Twinkle, twinkle, little star,
How I wonder what you are!
Up above the world so high,
Like a diamond in the sky!
Jane Taylor (1783–1824) British writer.
Rhymes for the Nursery (with Ann Taylor), 'The Star'

With Hindsight

19th century

206 France was a long despotism tempered by epigrams.
Thomas Carlyle (1795–1881) Scottish historian and essayist.
History of the French Revolution, Pt. I, Bk. I, Ch. 1

207 The seagreen Incorruptible.
Thomas Carlyle
Referring to Robespierre
History of the French Revolution, Pt. II, Bk. IV, Ch. 4

208 Bliss was it in that dawn to be alive,
But to be young was very heaven!
William Wordsworth (1770–1850) British poet.
The Prelude, XI

209 The three-o'-clock in the morning courage, which Bonaparte thought was the rarest.
Henry David Thoreau (1817–62) US writer.
Walden, 'Sounds'

210 It was the best of times, it was the worst of times, it was the age of wisdom, it was the age of foolishness, it was the epoch of belief, it was the epoch of incredulity, it was the season of Light, it was the season of Darkness, it was the spring of hope, it was the winter of despair, we had everything before us, we had nothing before us, we were all going direct to Heaven, we were all going direct the other way.

Charles Dickens (1812–70) British novelist.
The opening words of the book
A Tale of Two Cities, Bk. I, Ch. 1

211 It has been said, not truly, but with a possible approximation to truth, 'that in 1802 every hereditary monarch was insane'.
Walter Bagehot (1826–1877) British economist and journalist.
The English Constitution, 'The House of Lords'

20th century

212 Napoleon's armies used to march on their stomachs, shouting: 'Vive l'intérieur!'
W. C. Sellar (1898–1951) British humorous writer.
1066 And All That

213 If the French noblesse had been capable of playing cricket with their peasants, their chateaux would never have been burnt.
George Macaulay Trevelyan (1876–1962) British historian.
English Social History, Ch. XIII

214 It is still too early to form a final judgement on the French Revolution.
George Macaulay Trevelyan
Speech, National Book League, 30 May 1945

215 No visit to Dove Cottage, Grasmere, is complete without examining the outhouse where Hazlitt's father, a Unitarian minister of strong liberal views, attempted to put his hand up Dorothy Wordsworth's skirt.
Alan Coren (1938–   ) British humorist and writer.
All Except the Bastard, 'Bohemia'

10

Liberalism, Nationalism, and Reaction (1816—69)

Even after Napoleonic France had been finally defeated, the two dominant themes of the revolutionary period continued to loom over European politics and diplomacy: Liberalism, the idea that a king's power should not be so absolute that his subjects have no say in how they are governed; and Nationalism, the desire of each nationality to govern itself, which had been encouraged to undermine Napoleon's empire. From 1815, the Great Powers, led by Austria and Russia, pursued a policy of reaction in which the first sign of popular discontent was sharply and instantly repressed. Even in Britain, reform of any kind was resisted until well into the 1820s. In 1848 a series of revolutions broke out in Europe (France, Italy, Prussia, Austria); although all were eventually repressed, they nevertheless marked the end of reaction. As the dread of revolution faded, rulers felt able to accommodate at least some of their subjects' aspirations. Exploiting the tide of nationalism, Victor Emmanuel created the kingdom of Italy (1861) and Bismarck achieved his ambition for a German Empire (1871).

The USA was unaffected by these European concerns, but tensions, epitomized by the issue of slavery, grew between the very different Northern and Southern states. This culminated in the American Civil War (1861—65). In this period Britain continued to forge ahead in industrial production, becoming the 'workshop of the world'. The Great Exhibition of 1851 celebrated her supremacy.

Politics, Government, and World Events

1816

1 Our country! In her intercourse with foreign nations, may she always be in the right; but our country, right or wrong.
Stephen Decatur (1779–1820) US naval officer.
Speech, Norfolk, Virginia, Apr 1816

1817

2 The interest of the landlord is always opposed to the interests of every other class in the community.
David Ricardo (1772–1823) English political economist.
Principles of Political Economy and Taxation

3 The natural price of labour is that price which is necessary to enable the labourers, one with another, to subsist and perpetuate their race, without either increase or diminution.
David Ricardo
Principles of Political Economy and Taxation

1819

4 An old, mad, blind, despised and dying king, –
Princes, the dregs of their dull race, who flow
Through public scorn.
Percy Bysshe Shelley (1792–1822) British poet.
Referring to George III and his sons
England in 1819

5 The fault of our younger politicians – who have never seen the Indian States in the days of their power – is a contempt for the natives, and an inclination to carry everything with a high hand.
Mountstuart Elphinstone (1779–1859) Governor of Bombay.
Letter to Sir John Malcolm

6 The mountains look on Marathon –
And Marathon looks on the sea:
And musing there an hour alone,
I dream'd that Greece might still be free.
Lord Byron (1788–1824) British poet.
Byron later died, of fever, while fighting in the war for Greek independence from Turkey (1821–32) – a cause that caught the imagination of cultured circles in Britain
Don Juan, III

1820

7* Don't quote Latin; say what you have to say, and then sit down.
Duke of Wellington (1769–1852) British general and statesman.
Advice to a new Member of Parliament
Attrib.

8* The greatest happiness of the greatest number is the foundation of morals and legislation.
Jeremy Bentham (1748–1832) British philosopher.
The Commonplace Book

9 This is THE MAN – all shaven and shorn,
All cover'd with Orders – and all forlorn;
THE DANDY OF SIXTY, who bows with a grace,
And has *taste* in wigs, collars, cuirasses and lace;
Who, to tricksters, and fools, leaves the State and its treasure,
And, when Britain's in tears, sails about at his pleasure;
Who spurn'd from his presence the Friends of his youth,
And now has not one who will tell him the truth;
Who took to his counsels, in evil hour,
The Friends to the Reasons of lawless Power;
That back the Public Informer, who
Would put down the *Thing*, that, in spite of new Acts,
And attempts to restrain it, by Soldiers of Tax,
Will *poison* the Vermin,
That plunder the Wealth,
That lay in the House,
That Jack built.
William Hone (1780–1842) Author and bookseller.
Referring to George IV
The Political House that Jack Built

10 A better farmer ne'er brushed dew from lawn,
A worse king never left a realm undone!
Lord Byron (1788–1824) British poet.
Referring to George III
The Vision of Judgment, VIII

11 I take it for granted that the present question is a mere preamble – a title-page to a great tragic volume.
John Quincy Adams (1767–1848) Sixth president of the USA.
Referring to the Missouri Compromise – a measure in the US Congress allowing Missouri to be admitted as the 24th state of the Union. At the time Congress was equally divided between 'slave states' and 'free states'. Missouri applied for admission as a slave state, and the North feared that this would upset the balance of power. The compromise involved the admission of Maine as a free state
Diary, Mar 1820

12 This momentous question, like a firebell in the night, awakened and filled me with terror. I considered it at once as the knell of the Union.
Thomas Jefferson (1743–1826) US statesman.
Referring to the Missouri Compromise
Letter to John Adams, Apr 1820

1821

13 The prison inspector would have a good salary; that, in England, is never omitted. It is equally a matter of course that he would be taken

from among Treasury retainers, and that he would never look at a prison.
Sydney Smith (1771–1845) British clergyman and essayist.
English Prisons under Local Government (S. and B. Webb)

14 I wish...that the Greeks were put in possession of their whole patrimony and that the Sultan were driven, bag and baggage, into the heart of Asia.
Stratford Canning (1786–1880) British diplomat.
Letter to George Canning, 29 Sept 1821

15 Whenever books are burned men also in the end are burned.
Heinrich Heine (1797–1856) German poet and writer.
Almansor

1822

16 Let there be light! said Liberty,
And like sunrise from the sea,
Athens arose!
Percy Bysshe Shelley (1792–1822) British poet.
Hellas, I

17* I met Murder on the way –
He had a mask like Castlereagh.
Percy Bysshe Shelley
Viscount Castlereagh (1769–1822) was British foreign secretary (1812–22); he was highly unpopular and became identified with such controversial events as the Peterloo massacre (16 Aug 1819) – an incident at a rally at St Peter's Field, Manchester, when hussars killed 11 people and wounded hundreds. The name 'Peterloo' is a reference to Waterloo
The Mask of Anarchy, 5

1823

18 The land self-interest groans from shore to shore,
For fear that plenty should attain the poor.
Lord Byron (1788–1824) British poet.
The Age of Bronze, XIV

19 Our first and fundamental maxim should be never to entangle ourselves in the broils of Europe. Our second, never to suffer Europe to intermeddle with cis-Atlantic affairs.
Thomas Jefferson (1743–1826) US president.
Letter to James Monroe, 24 Oct 1823

20 The American continents, by the free and independent condition which they have assumed and maintain, are henceforth not to be considered as subjects for future colonization by any European powers...In the wars of the European powers in matters relating to themselves we have never taken any part, nor does it comport with our policy to do so.
James Monroe (1758–1831) US president.
A statement of principle that, as the 'Monroe Doctrine', became a cornerstone of US foreign policy
Message to Congress, 2 Dec 1823

1824

21 States, like men, have their growth, their manhood, their decrepitude, their decay.
Walter Savage Landor (1775–1864) British poet and writer.
Imaginary Conversations, 'Pollio and Calvus'

1825

22 Many politicians of our time are in the habit of laying it down as a self-evident proposition, that no people ought to be free till they are fit to use their freedom. The maxim is worthy of the fool in the old story, who resolved not to go into the water till he had learnt to swim. If men are to wait for liberty till they become wise and good in slavery, they may indeed wait for ever.
Lord Macaulay (1800–59) British historian.
Literary Essays Contributed to the 'Edinburgh Review', 'Milton',

1826

23 I called the New World into existence to redress the balance of the Old.
George Canning (1770–1827) British statesman.
Speech, 12 Dec 1826

24 It is said to be hard on His Majesty's Ministers to raise objections to this proposition. For my part, I think it no more hard on His Majesty's Opposition to compel th⁻ . to take this course.
John Cam Hobhouse (1786–1869) British radical politician.
First recorded use of the phrase 'His Majesty's Opposition'
Speech, House of Commons, 27 Apr 1826

1828

25* That prig Peel seems as deeply bitten by "liberality"...as any of his fellows.
Thomas Creevey (1768–1838) British politician.
Referring to the question of the corn laws
The Creevey Papers (ed. Sir H. Maxwell)

26 The reluctant obedience of distant provinces generally costs more than it is worth.
Lord Macaulay (1800–59) British historian.
Historical Essays Contributed to the 'Edinburgh Review', 'Lord Mahon's War of the Succession'

27 There never was such a humbug as the Greek affair altogether. However, thank God it never cost us a shilling, and never shall.
Duke of Wellington (1769–1852) British general and statesman.
Referring to the Greek War of Independence
Remark, Feb 1828

28   The gallery in which the reporters sit has become a fourth estate of the realm.
Lord Macaulay (1800–59) British historian.
Referring to the press gallery in the House of Commons
Historical Essays Contributed to the 'Edinburgh Review', 'Hallam's 'Constitutional History''

29   As for rioting, the old Roman way of dealing with that is always the right one; flog the rank and file, and fling the ringleaders from the Tarpeian rock.
Thomas Arnold (1795–1842) British educator.
Cornhill Magazine, Aug 1868

1829

30   His Majesty's dominions, on which the sun never sets.
Christopher North (John Wilson; 1785–1854) Scottish writer.
Noctes Ambrosianae, 20 Apr 1829

31   What all the wise men promised has not happened, and what all the d—d fools said would happen has come to pass.
Lord Melbourne (1779–1848) British statesman.
Referring to Catholic Emancipation
Lord Melbourne (H. Dunckley)

32   There is no middle course between the throne and the scaffold.
Charles X (1757–1836) King of France.
Remark to Talleyrand, Dec 1829; Talleyrand is said to have replied, 'You are forgetting the postchaise'

33   I am very far from being prepared to admit that the improvement of the situation of a common police constable by the giving him more money would increase the efficiency of the establishment
Robert Peel (1788–1850) British Conservative prime minister.
Letter to John Croker, 10 Oct 1829

1830

34   We now are, as we always have been, decidedly and conscientiously attached to what is called the Tory, and which might with more propriety be called the Conservative, party.
John Wilson Croker (1780–1857) British Tory politician.
The first use of the term 'Conservative Party'
In *Quarterly Review*, Jan 1830

35   I will be good.
Victoria (1819–1901) Queen of the United Kingdom.
On learning that she would succeed to the throne
Remark to her governess, Louise (afterwards Baroness) Lehzen, 11 Mar 1830

36   Beginning reform is beginning revolution.
Duke of Wellington (1769–1852) British general and statesman.
Remark to Mrs Arbuthnot, 7 Nov 1830

37   But what is to be the fate of the great wen of all?
William Cobbett (1763–1835) British journalist and writer.
Referring to London; a wen is a sebaceous cyst
Rural Rides

38   The king reigns, and the people govern themselves.
Louis Adolphe Thiers (1797–1877) French statesman and historian.
In an unsigned article attributed to Thiers
Le National, 20 Jan 1830

39   We are dancing on a volcano.
Comte de Salvandy (1795–1856) French nobleman.
A remark made before the July Revolution in 1830

40   When Paris sneezes, Europe catches cold.
Clement Metternich (1773–1859) Austrian diplomat and Chancellor.
Remark, reflecting European anxiety at the July Revolution in France (1830)
Liberalism

41   The people's government, made for the people, made by the people, and answerable to the people.
Daniel Webster (1782–1852) US statesman.
Second speech on Foote's resolution, 26 Jan 1830

42*   Absolutism tempered by assassination.
Ernst Friedrich Herbert Münster (1766–1839) Hanoverian statesman.
Referring to the Russian Constitution
Letter

43   The spirit of revolution, the spirit of insurrection is a spirit radically opposed to liberty.
François Guizot (1787–1874) French statesman and historian.
Speech, Paris, 29 Dec 1830

1831

44   It is impossible that the whisper of a faction should prevail against the voice of a nation.
Lord John Russell (1792–1878)
Following the rejection in the House of Lords of the Reform Bill
Letter to T. Attwood, Oct 1831

45   So here is a pretty fly out of the King of the Netherlands! Who has bit him I cannot guess; we have some suspicion of France.
Lord Palmerston (1784–1865) British statesman.
Comment on the French invasion of Belgium, 1831
Life of Viscount Palmerston (H. W. Bulwer), Vol. II

46   I always say that, next to a battle lost, the greatest misery is a battle gained.
Duke of Wellington (1769–1852) British general and statesman.
Diary (Frances, Lady Shelley)

1832

47 War is the continuation of politics by other
    means.
    Karl von Clausewitz (1780–1831) Prussian
    general.
    The usual misquotation of 'War is nothing but a
    continuation of politics with the admixture of
    other means'.
    Vom Kriege

48 From a very early age, I had imbibed the opin-
    ion, that it was every man's duty to do all that
    lay in his power to leave his country as good
    as he had found it.
    William Cobbett (1763–1835) British journal-
    ist and writer.
    Political Register, 22 Dec 1832

49 A nation is the universality of citizens speaking
    the same tongue.
    Giuseppe Mazzini (1805–72) Italian republi-
    can leader and political theorist.
    La Giovine Italia

1833

50 And if it be true anywhere that such enact-
    ments are forced on the legislature by public
    opinion is Apostasy too hard a word to describe
    the temper of the nation?
    John Keble (1792–1866) British poet and
    clergyman.
    Assize Sermon, Oxford, 14 July 1833

51 We were meeting together to preserve our-
    selves, our wives, and our children, from utter
    degradation and starvation.
    George Loveless (b. 1805) Dorset farm-
    labourer and Trade Unionist.
    Defending the activities of the 'Tolpuddle Mar-
    tyrs', six members of an agricultural labourers'
    union. Convicted of administering unlawful
    oaths and transported to Australia, they were
    pardoned in 1836
    Statement, Dorchester Assizes, Mar 1833

52 God is our guide! from field, from wave,
    From plough, from anvil, and from loom;
    We come, our country's rights to save,
    And speak a tyrant faction's doom:
    We raise the watchword liberty;
    We will, we will, we will be free!

    God is our guide! no swords we draw,
    We kindle not war's battle fires;
    By reason, union, justice, law,
    We claim the birthright of our sires:
    We raise the watchword liberty;
    We will, we will, we will be free!!!
    George Loveless
    Referring to the Tolpuddle Martyrs
    The Faber Book of English History in Verse
    (Kenneth Baker)

53 A broken head in Cold Bath Fields produces a
    greater sensation among us than three
    pitched battles in India.
    Lord Macaulay (1800–59) British historian.
    Speech, 10 July 1833

54 Every time I come near him, I pray God to pre-
    serve me from the Devil.
    Nicholas I (1796–1855) Tsar of Russia.
    Referring to Metternich
    Letter to his wife, Sept 1833

55 But what is Freedom? Rightly understood,
    A universal licence to be good.
    Hartley Coleridge (1796–1849) British poet.
    Liberty

1834

56* It is as difficult to elevate the poor as it is easy
    to depress the rich. In human affairs ... it is
    much easier to do harm than good.
    Nassau Senior (1790–1864) British
    economist.
    Nassau Senior (M. Bowley)

57 By the workhouse system is meant having all
    relief through the workhouse, making this work-
    house an uninviting place of wholesome
    restraint.
    Edwin Chadwick (1800–90) British social
    reformer.
    Report of the Royal Commission on the Poor
    Laws

58 Unfortunately almost all trades unions hitherto
    formed have relied for success upon extorted
    oaths and physical force. The fault and de-
    struction of all trades unions has hitherto been
    that they have copied the vices which they
    professed to condemn ... Hence their failure
    was inevitable.
    **Committee of the London Compositors'
    Society**
    History of Trade Unionism (S. and B. Webb)

59 I have always thought complaints of ill-usage
    contemptible, whether from a seduced disap-
    pointed girl or a turned out Prime Minister.
    Lord Melbourne (1779–1848) British
    statesman.
    Following his dismissal by William IV
    Miss Eden's Letters (ed. V. Dickinson)

60* You must build your House of Parliament upon
    the river: so ... that the populace cannot ex-
    act their demands by sitting down round you.
    Duke of Wellington (1769–1852) British gen-
    eral and statesman.
    Words on Wellington (Sir William Fraser)

61 Equality may perhaps be a right, but no power
    on earth can ever turn it into a fact.
    Honoré de Balzac (1799–1850) French
    novelist.
    La Duchesse de Langeais

1835

62 The Public is an old woman. Let her maunder
    and mumble.
    Thomas Carlyle (1795–1881) Scottish histo-
    rian and essayist.
    Journal, 1835

63 The worst of the present day is that men hate

one another so damnably. For my part I love them all.
Lord Melbourne (1779–1848) British statesman.
Attrib.

64 Peel's smile: like the silver plate on a coffin.
Daniel O'Connell (1775–1847) Irish politician.
Referring to Sir Robert Peel; quoting J. P. Curran (1750–1817)
Hansard, 26 Feb 1835

65 An army is a nation within a nation; it is one of the vices of our age.
Alfred de Vigny (1797–1863) French writer.
Servitude et grandeur militaire, 1

1836

66 I know you do not make the laws but I also know that you are the wives and mothers, the sisters and daughters of those who do . . .
Angelina Grimké (1805–79) US writer.
The Anti-Slavery Examiner (Sep 1836), 'Appeal to the Christian Women of the South'

1837

67 . . . nothing could be more amiable and agreeable than she was. Can you wish for a better account of a little tit of 18 made all at once into a Queen?
Thomas Creevey (1768–1838) British politician and diarist.
Letter to Elizabeth Ord, 5 Aug 1837

68 I will sit down now, but the time will come when you will hear me.
Benjamin Disraeli (1804–81) British statesman.
Maiden Speech, House of Commons, 7 Dec 1837

69 In no country, I believe, are the marriage laws so iniquitous as in England, and the conjugal relation, in consequence, so impaired.
Harriet Martineau (1802–76) British writer.
Society in America, Vol. III, 'Marriage'

70 Our country is the world – our countrymen are all mankind.
William Lloyd Garrison (1805–79) US abolitionist.
The Liberator, 15 Dec 1837

1838

71 All reform except a moral one will prove unavailing.
Thomas Carlyle (1795–1881) Scottish historian and essayist.
Critical and Miscellaneous Essays, 'Corn Law Rhymes'

72 Oliver Twist has asked for more.
Charles Dickens (1812–70) British novelist.
Oliver Twist, Ch. 2

73 'If the law supposes that,' said Mr Bumble . . . , 'the law is a ass – a idiot.'
Charles Dickens
In reply to Mr Brounlow's statement that 'the law supposes that your wife acts under your direction'
Oliver Twist, Ch. 51

74 The Continent will not suffer England to be the workshop of the world.
Benjamin Disraeli (1804–81) British statesman.
Speech, House of Commons, 15 Mar 1838

75 Property has its duties as well as its rights.
Thomas Drummond (1797–1840) British engineer and statesman.
Letter to the Earl of Donoughmore, 22 May 1838

1839

76 The rising hope of those stern and unbending Tories.
Lord Macaulay (1800–59) British historian.
Referring to Gladstone
Historical Essays, 'Gladstone on Church and State'

77 Dear Uncle is given to believe that he must rule the roast everywhere. However that is not a necessity.
Victoria (1819–1901) Queen of the United Kingdom.
Referring to Leopold of Belgium

1840

78* Now, is it to lower the price of corn, or isn't it? It is not much matter which we say, but mind, we must all say *the same*.
Lord Melbourne (1779–1848) British statesman.
Said at a cabinet meeting
The English Constitution (Bagehot), Ch. 1

79* While I cannot be regarded as a pillar, I must be regarded as a buttress of the church, because I support it from the outside.
Lord Melbourne
Attrib.

80* If a traveller were informed that such a man was leader of the House of Commons, he may well begin to comprehend how the Egyptians worshipped an insect.
Benjamin Disraeli (1804–81) British statesman.
Referring to Lord John Russell
Attrib.

81* For God's sake, ma'am, let's have no more of that. If you get the English people into the way of making kings, you'll get them into the way of *un*making them.
Lord Melbourne (1779–1848) British statesman.
Advising Queen Victoria against granting Prince Albert the title of King Consort
Lord M. (Lord David Cecil)

82 I am a cousin to the Queen,
And our mothers they are cronies,

My father lives at home,
And deals in nice polonies.
Anonymous
Referring to Prince Albert
The Faber Book of English History in Verse
(Kenneth Baker)

83* Accidentally.
Talleyrand (Charles Maurice de Talleyrand-Pér-
igord; 1754–1838) French politician.
Replying, during the reign of Louis Philippe, to
the query 'How do you think this government will
end?'
The Wheat and the Chaff (F. Mitterand)

84 The truth is that Louis Philippe is the prime
mover of the foreign relations of France, and
one must admit in one's own mind that if he
had been a very straightforward, scrupulous
and high-minded man, he would not now have
been sitting on the French throne.
Lord Palmerston (1784–1865) British
statesman.
Life of Viscount Palmerston (H. L. Bulwer),
Vol. II

85 All Frenchmen want to encroach and extend
their territorial possessions at the expense of
other nations. Their rarity prompts them to be
the first nation in the world.
Lord Palmerston
Life of Viscount Palmerston (H. L. Bulmer),
Vol. II

86 Property is theft.
Pierre Joseph Proudhon (1809–65) French
socialist.
Qu'est-ce que la Propriété?, Ch. 1

1841

87 When I first came into Parliament, Mr Tierney,
a great Whig authority, used always to say
that the duty of an Opposition was very simple
– it was, to oppose everything, and propose
nothing.
Edward Stanley, Earl of Derby (1799–
1869) British Conservative prime minister.
Speech, House of Commons, 4 June 1841

88 I was totally ignorant both of political economy
and of the commerce of the country . . . In a
spirit of ignorant mortification I said to myself
at the moment: the science of politics deals
with the government of men, but I am set to
govern packages.
William Ewart Gladstone (1809–98) British
statesman.
Referring to his appointment as vice-president of
the board of trade
Life of Gladstone (Morley), Vol. I

89 *Deutschland, Deutschland über alles.*
Germany, Germany before all else.
Heinrich Hoffmann von Fallersleben
(1798–1876) German poet.
German national anthem

90 Let wealth and commerce, laws and learning
die,

But leave us still our old nobility
Lord John Manners (1818–1906) British
politician.
England's Trust, Pt. III, Ch. 1

91 Such grace had kings when the world begun!
Robert Browning (1812–89) British poet.
Pippa Passes, Pt. I

1842

92 Not in vain is Ireland pouring itself all over the
earth . . . The Irish, with their glowing hearts
and reverent credulity, are needed in this cold
age of intellect and skepticism.
Lydia M. Child (1802–80) US abolitionist
campaigner.
Letters from New York, Vol. I, No. 33, 8 Dec
1842

1843

93 The compact which exists between the North
and the South is a covenant with death and an
agreement with hell.
William Lloyd Garrison (1805–79) US
abolitionist.
Resolution, Massachusetts Anti-Slavery Society,
27 Jan 1843

94 *La cordiale entente qui existe entre mon
gouvernement et le sien.*
The friendly understanding that exists between my government and hers.
Louis Philippe (1773–1850) King of France.
Referring to an informal understanding reached
between Britain and France in 1843. The more
familiar phrase, 'entente cordiale', was first
used in 1844
Speech, 27 Dec 1843

95 Oh! God! that bread should be so dear,
And flesh and blood so cheap!
Thomas Hood (1799–1845) British poet.
The Song of the Shirt

1844

96 Thus you have a starving population, an absen-
tee aristocracy, and an alien Church, and in
addition the weakest executive in the world.
That is the Irish Question.
Benjamin Disraeli (1804–81) British
statesman.
Speech, House of Commons, 16 Feb 1844

97 Trial by jury itself, instead of being a security to
persons who are accused, will be a delusion,
a mockery, and a snare.
Thomas Denman (1779–1854) British judge.
Judgment in O'Connell v The Queen, 4 Sept
1844

98 Fifty-four forty or fight!
William Allen US Senator.
Slogan widely used in the 1844 US presidential
election campaign, referring to the northern
boundary of Oregon, which was disputed with
Britain; the 49th parallel was agreed as the frontier in 1846

1845

99   The right honourable gentleman caught the Whigs bathing, and walked away with their clothes.
Benjamin Disraeli (1804–81) British statesman.
Referring to Sir Robert Peel
Speech, House of Commons, 28 Feb 1845

100   A Conservative government is an organized hypocrisy.
Benjamin Disraeli
Speech, 17 Mar 1845

101   O let us love our occupations,
Bless the squire and his relations,
Live upon our daily rations,
And always know our proper stations.
Charles Dickens (1812–70) British novelist.
The Chimes, '2nd Quarter'

102   'Two nations; between whom there is no intercourse and no sympathy; who are as ignorant of each other's habits, thoughts, and feelings, as if they were dwellers in different zones, or inhabitants of different planets; who are formed by a different breeding, are fed by a different food, are ordered by different manners, and are not governed by the same laws.'
'You speak of –' said Egremont, hesitatingly 'THE RICH AND THE POOR.'
Benjamin Disraeli (1804–81) British statesman.
Sybil, Bk. II, Ch. 5

1846

103   Deprive me of power tomorrow, you can never deprive me of the consciousness that I have exercised the powers committed to me from no corrupt or interested motives, from no desire to gratify ambition, or attain any personal object.
Robert Peel (1788–1850) British Conservative prime minister.
Referring to the proposed repeal of the Corn Laws, which split the Conservative party; Peel resigned on 29 June, four days after the repeal was passed
Speech, House of Commons, 15 May 1846

104*   I know he is, and he adores his maker.
Benjamin Disraeli (1804–81) British statesman.
Replying to a remark made in defence of John Bright that he was a self-made man; often also attributed to Bright referring to Disraeli
The Fine Art of Political Wit (L. Harris)

105   He is so vain that he wants to figure in history as the settler of all the great questions; but a Parliamentary constitution is not favourable to such ambitions: things must be done by parties, not by persons using parties as tools.
Benjamin Disraeli
Referring to Sir Robert Peel
Letter to Lord John Manners, 17 Dec 1846

1847

106   A majority is always the best repartee.
Benjamin Disraeli
Tancred, Bk. II, Ch. 14

107   It is enough. That is the right place.
Brigham Young (1801–77) US Mormon leader.
Referring to the Great Salt Lake Valley, Utah; the Mormons settled there after a fifteen-week journey westwards to escape persecution
Remark, 24 July 1847

108   Whenever he met a great man he grovelled before him, and my-lorded him as only a free-born Briton can do.
William Makepeace Thackeray (1811–63) British novelist.
Vanity Fair, Ch. 13

1848

109   I think that your being the leader of the Tory party is the greatest triumph that Liberalism has ever achieved.
François Guizot (1787–1874) French historian and statesman.
Letter to Disraeli upon his appointment as leader of the Tory party in the House of Commons
Life of Disraeli (W. F. Monypenny and G. E. Buckle), Vol. III

110*   We have used the Bible as if it was a constable's handbook – an opium-dose for keeping beasts of burden patient while they are being overloaded.
Charles Kingsley (1819–75) British writer.
Letters to the Chartists, 2

111   *Italia farà da se.*
Italy will do it alone.
Charles Albert (1798–1849) King of Piedmont.
Referring to the movement to liberate and unify Italy
Proclamation, Mar 1848

112*   Anyone who wants to carry on the war against the outsiders, come with me. I can't offer you either honours or wages; I offer you hunger, thirst, forced marches, battles and death. Anyone who loves his country, follow me.
Giuseppe Garibaldi (1807–82) Italian general and political leader.
Garibaldi (Guerzoni)

113   Let me pass, I have to follow them, I am their leader.
Alexandre Auguste Ledru-Rollin (1807–74) French lawyer and politician.
Trying to force his way through a mob during the Revolution of 1848, of which he was one of the chief instigators. A similar remark is attributed to Bonar Law
The Fine Art of Political Wit (L. Harris)

114   Henceforth Prussia merges into Germany.
Frederick William IV (1795–1861) King of Prussia.
Proclamation, 21 Mar 1848

115 I am the emperor, and I want dumplings.
Ferdinand I (1793–1875) Emperor of Austria.
The Fall of the House of Habsburg (E. Crankshaw)

116 A spectre is haunting Europe – the spectre of communism.
Karl Marx (1818–83) German philosopher and revolutionary.
Opening words
Communist Manifesto

117 The history of all hitherto existing society is the history of class struggles.
Karl Marx
The Communist Manifesto, 1

118 The workers have nothing to lose but their chains. They have a world to gain. Workers of the world, unite.
Karl Marx
The Communist Manifesto, 4

1849
---

119 Misery generates hate; these sufferers hated the machines which they believed took their bread from them; they hated the buildings which contained these machines; they hated the manufacturers who owned those buildings.
Charlotte Brontë (1816–55) British novelist.
Referring to the effect of the introduction of knitting frames into the mills of northern England
Shirley, Ch. 2

120 In every age the vilest specimens of human nature are to be found among demagogues.
Lord Macaulay (1800–59) British historian.
History of England, Vol. I, Ch. 5

121 Under a government which imprisons any unjustly, the true place for a just man is also a prison.
Henry David Thoreau (1817–62) US writer.
Civil Disobedience

1850
---

122 No man has come so near our definition of a constitutional statesman – the powers of a first-rate man and the creed of a second-rate man.
Walter Bagehot (1826–77) British economist and journalist.
Historical Essays, 'The Character of Sir Robert Peel'

123 As the Roman, in days of old, held himself free from indignity when he could say *Civis Romanus sum*, so also a British subject in whatever land he may be, shall feel confident that the watchful eye and the strong arm of England will protect him against injustice and wrong.
Lord Palmerston (1784–1865) British statesman.
Speech, House of Commons, 26 June 1850

124 The object of oratory alone is not truth, but persuasion.
Lord Macaulay (1800–59) British historian.
Works (1898), Vol. XI, 'Essay on Athenian Orators'

125* Conquering kings their titles take.
John Chandler (1806–76) British clergyman and writer.
Poem title

126* Austria will astound the world with the magnitude of her ingratitude.
Prince Schwarzenberg (1800–52) Austrian statesman.
On being asked whether Austria was under any obligation to Russia for help received previously
The Fall of the House of Habsburg (E. Crankshaw)

127 From each according to his abilities, to each according to his needs.
Karl Marx (1818–83) German philosopher and revolutionary.
Criticism of the Gotha Programme

128 The dictatorship of the proletariat.
Karl Marx
Attrib.

1851
---

129 This is the negation of God erected into a system of Government.
William Ewart Gladstone (1809–98) British statesman.
First *Letter to Earl of Aberdeen on State Persecutions of Neapolitan Government*

130 The cause of which my name is the symbol – that is to say, France regenerated by the Revolution and organised by the Emperor.
Napoleon III (1808–73) French emperor.
Proclamation to the French people and army, 2 Dec 1851; issued during his *coup d'état*

131 The works of art, by being publicly exhibited and offered for sale, are becoming articles of trade, following as such the unreasoning laws of markets and fashion; and public and even private patronage is swayed by their tyrannical influence.
Prince Albert (1819–61) The consort of Queen Victoria.
Referring to the Great Exhibition, a display of the industrial products of Britain and Europe that he had organized
Speech, Royal Academy Dinner, 3 May 1851

132 An enchanted pile, which the sagacious taste and prescient philanthropy of an accomplished and enlightened Prince have raised for the glory of England and the instruction of two hemispheres.
Benjamin Disraeli (1804–81) British statesman.
Referring to the Crystal Palace, built in Hyde Park to house the Great Exhibition
The Faber Book of English History in Verse (Kenneth Baker)

133 **Sparrowhawks, Ma'am.**
Duke of Wellington (1769–1852) British general and statesman.
Advice when asked by Queen Victoria how to remove sparrows from the Crystal Palace
Attrib.

1852

---

134 **The Duke of Wellington had exhausted nature and exhausted glory. His career was one unclouded longest day.**
Written on Wellington's death
The Times, 16 Sept 1852

135 **For too long Society has resembled a pyramid which has been turned upside down and made to rest on its summit. I have replaced it on its base.**
Napoleon III (1808–73) French emperor.
Speech, 29 Mar 1852

136 **In a mood of defiance certain people are saying, 'The Empire means War'. Personally I say, 'The Empire means Peace'**
Napoleon III
Speech, Bordeaux, 15 Oct 1852; the Second Empire was established on 2 Dec 1852

137 **Hegel says somewhere that all great events and personalities in world history reappear in one fashion or another. He forgot to add: the first time as tragedy, the second as farce.**
Karl Marx (1818–83) German philosopher and revolutionary.
The Eighteenth Brumaire of Louis Napoleon

138 **Whipping and abuse are like laudanum: You have to double the dose as the sensibilities decline.**
Harriet Beecher Stowe (1811–96) US novelist.
Uncle Tom's Cabin, Ch. 20

139* **I did not write it. God wrote it. I merely did his dictation.**
Harriet Beecher Stowe
Referring to *Uncle Tom's Cabin*
Attrib.

The Crimean War (1853–56)

Caused by Russian expansionist ambitions in the Turkish-ruled Balkans, the main activity of the war was an Anglo-French-Turkish punitive expedition to capture Sevastopol in the Crimea. The British contribution was characterized by incompetence in almost every field. The famous charge of the Light Brigade, for example, was the result of a misunderstanding; and Florence Nightingale made her name by reforming the appalling conditions in the military hospitals. Eventually the war faded out without resolving its causes.

1853

---

140 **We have on our hands a sick man – a very sick man.**
Nicholas I (1796–1855) Tsar of Russia.
Referring to Turkey, the 'sick man of Europe'; said to Sir G. H. Seymour, British envoy to St Petersburg, Jan 1853
Attrib.

141 **Russia has two generals in whom she can confide – Generals Janvier and Février.**
Nicholas I
Referring to the Russian winter. Nicholas himself succumbed to a February cold in 1855 – the subject of the famous *Punch* Cartoon, 'General Février turned traitor', 10 Mar 1855
Attrib.

142 **If peace cannot be maintained with honour, it is no longer peace.**
Lord John Russell (1792–1878) British statesman.
Speech, Greenock, 19 Sep 1853

1854

143* **I think there is a certain basis of truth in the fear which the Russian government is beginning to have of communism: for communism is Tsarist autocracy turned upside down.**
Alexander Herzen (1812–70) Russian writer.
My Past and Thoughts

144 **Lads, war is declared with a numerous and bold enemy. Should they meet and offer battle, you know how to dispose of them. Should they remain in port, we must try and get at them. Success depends upon the quickness and precision of your firing. Also, lads, sharpen your cutlasses, and the day is your own.**
Sir Charles Napier (1786–1860) British admiral.
Referring to the declaration of war against Russia, 1854
Signal to his command

145 **Is it that war is a luxury? Is it that we are fighting – to use a cant phrase of Mr Pitt's time – to secure indemnity for the past and security for the future? Are we to be the Don Quixotes of Europe, to go about fighting for every cause where we find that someone has been wronged?**
Richard Cobden (1804–65) British politician.
Referring to the Crimean War
Speech, House of Commons, 22 Dec 1854

146 **Lord Raglan wishes the cavalry to advance rapidly to the front and try to prevent enemy carrying away the guns. Troop of Horse Artillery may accompany. French cavalry is on your left. Immediate.**
Lord Raglan (1788–1855) British field marshal.
Order to Lord Lucan, Battle of Balaclava, 25 Oct 1854; the result was the charge of the Light Brigade.

147   Half a league, half a league,
      Half a league onward,
      All in the valley of Death
      Rode the six hundred.
      Alfred, Lord Tennyson (1809–92) British
      poet.
      The Charge of the Light Brigade

148   Into the jaws of Death,
      Into the mouth of Hell.
      Alfred, Lord Tennyson
      The Charge of the Light Brigade

149   'Forward the Light Brigade!'
      Was there a man dismay'd?
      Not tho' the soldier knew
      Some one had blunder'd:
      Their's not to make reply,
      Their's not to reason why,
      Their's but to do and die:
      Into the valley of Death
      Rode the six hundred.
      Alfred, Lord Tennyson
      The Charge of the Light Brigade

150   *C'est magnifique, mais ce n'est pas la guerre.*
      It is magnificent, but it is not war.
      Pierre Bosquet (1810–61) French marshal.
      Referring to the Charge of the Light Brigade
      Attrib.

151   They dashed on towards that *thin red line
      tipped with steel.*
      William Howard Russell (1820–1907) British journalist.
      Description of the Russian charge against the
      British at the Battle of Balaclava, 25 Oct 1854
      The British Expedition to the Crimea

152   No man is good enough to govern another man
      without that other's consent.
      Abraham Lincoln (1809–65) US statesman.
      Speech, 1854

1855
---

153   The Angel of Death has been abroad throughout the land: you may almost hear the beating
      of his wings.
      John Bright (1811–89) British radical
      politician.
      Referring to the Crimean War
      Speech, House of Commons, 23 Feb 1855

154   The army is the true nobility of our country.
      Napoleon III (1808–73) French emperor.
      Speech, 20 Mar 1855

155   That knuckle-end of England — that land of Calvin, oat-cakes, and sulphur.
      Sydney Smith (1771–1845) British clergyman
      and essayist.
      Referring to Scotland
      Memoir (Lady Holland)

156   When one has been threatened with a great injustice, one accepts a smaller as a favour.
      Jane Welsh Carlyle (1801–66) The wife of
      Thomas Carlyle.
      Journal, 21 Nov 1855

157   His majesty, King Cotton, is forced to continue

the employment of his slaves; and, by their
toil, is riding on, conquering and to conquer.
David Christy (1802–c. 59) American writer.
Cotton is King: or Slavery in the Light of Political Economy

158   The almighty dollar, that great object of universal devotion throughout our land, seems to
      have no genuine devotees in these peculiar
      villages.
      Washington Irving (1783–1859) US writer.
      Wolfert's Roost, 'The Creole Village'

1856
---

159   Knight of the Crimean Burial Grounds, I
      suppose?
      Florence Nightingale (1820–1910) British
      nurse.
      Referring to the KCB awarded to Dr John Hall,
      the British Chief of Medical Staff in the Crimea
      Remark

160* Sir, it was said of Augustus that he found Rome
      brick and left it marble. May it be said of you
      that you found Paris stinking and left it
      sweet.
      Edwin Chadwick (1800–90) British social
      reformer.
      Remark to Napoleon III

161   It is better to begin to abolish serfdom from
      above than to wait for it to abolish itself from
      below.
      Alexander II (1818–81) Tsar of Russia.
      Speech, 30 Mar 1856

162   Those who deny freedom to others, deserve it
      not for themselves.
      Abraham Lincoln (1809–65) US statesman.
      Speech, 19 May 1856

163   The ballot is stronger than the bullet.
      Abraham Lincoln
      Speech, 19 May 1856

164   Where the populace rise at once against the
      never-ending audacity of elected persons.
      Walt Whitman (1819–92) US poet.
      Referring to revolution
      Song of the Broad Axe, 5

1857

165* Had any Christian bishop visited that scene of
      butchery when I saw it, I verily believe that he
      would have buckled on his sword.
      Sir G. Wolseley (1833–1913) British soldier
      and writer.
      Referring to the massacres at Delhi during the Indian Mutiny

166   Accidental and fortuitous concurrence of
      atoms.
      Lord Palmerston (1784–1865) British
      statesman.
      Referring to rumours of an impending coalition
      with Disraeli
      Speech, House of Commons, 1857

167   Whatever was required to be done, the Circumlocution Office was beforehand with all the

public departments in the art of perceiving –
HOW NOT TO DO IT.
Charles Dickens (1812–70) British novelist.
Little Dorrit, Bk. I, Ch. 10

1858

168   I see no prospect of the formation of an efficient party, let alone Government, out of the chaos on the Opposition benches. No one reigns over or in it, but discord and antipathy.
Sidney Herbert (1810–61) British statesman.
Referring to the Whigs
Memoir of Sydney Herbert (Lord Stanmore), Vol. II

169   I believe this government cannot endure permanently, half slave and half free.
Abraham Lincoln (1809–65) US statesman.
Speech, Springfield, Illinois, 16 June 1858

170   . . . slavery cannot exist a day or an hour anywhere unless it is supported by local police regulations . . .
Stephen A. Douglas (1813–61) US senator.
Speech, 27 Aug 1858

171   It is an irrepressible conflict between opposing and enduring forces, and it means that the United States must and will, sooner or later, become either entirely a slave-holding nation, or entirely a free-labour nation.
William Henry Seward (1801–72) US senator.
Speech, Rochester (New York), 25 Oct 1858

1859

172   I am as content to die for God's eternal truth on the scaffold as in any other way.
John Brown (1800–59) American slave abolitionist.
On the day before his execution
Letter to his children, 2 Dec 1859

173   That new saint, than whom nothing purer or more brave was ever led by love of men into conflict and death . . . will make the gallows glorious like the cross.
Ralph Waldo Emerson (1803–82) US poet and essayist.
Referring to John Brown's execution (Dec 1859)

174   John Brown's body lies a-mouldering in the grave,
His soul is marching on!
Charles Sprague Hall (19th century) US songwriter.
The song commemorates the American hero who died in the cause of abolishing slavery
John Brown's Body

175   The best thing I know between France and England is – the sea.
Douglas William Jerrold (1803–57) British dramatist.
Wit and Opinions of Douglas Jerrold, 'The Anglo-French Alliance'

176   I don't care for war, there's far too much luck in it for my liking.
Napoleon III (1808–73) French emperor.
Said after the narrow but bloody French victory at Solferino (24 June 1859)
The Fall of the House of Habsburg (E. Crankshaw)

177   England is one of the greatest powers of the world, no event or series of events bearing on the balance of power, or on probabilities of peace or war can be matters of indifference to her, and her right to have and to express opinions on matters thus bearing on her interests is unquestionable.
Lord Palmerston (1784–1865) British statesman.
Letter to Queen Victoria, 23 Aug 1859

178   If all mankind minus one, were of one opinion, and only one person were of the contrary opinion, mankind would be no more justified in silencing that one person, than he, if he had the power, would be justified in silencing mankind.
John Stuart Mill (1806–73) British philosopher.
On Liberty, Ch. 2

179   A party of order or stability, and a party of progress or reform, are both necessary elements of a healthy state of political life.
John Stuart Mill
On Liberty, Ch. 2

180   The liberty of the individual must be thus far limited; he must not make himself a nuisance to other people.
John Stuart Mill
On Liberty, Ch. 3

181   The worth of a State in the long run is the worth of the individuals composing it.
John Stuart Mill
On Liberty, Ch. 5

182   Every man meets his Waterloo at last.
Wendell Phillips (1811–84) US reformer.
Speech, Brooklyn, 1 Nov 1859

183   Authority forgets a dying king.
Alfred, Lord Tennyson (1809–92) British poet.
Idylls of the King, 'The Passing of Arthur'

1860

184*   He believes, with all his heart and soul and strength, that there *is* such a thing as truth; he has the soul of a martyr with the intellect of an advocate.
Walter Bagehot (1826–77) British economist and journalist.
Referring to Gladstone
Historical Essays, 'Mr Gladstone'

185*   Your dexterity seems a happy compound of the smartness of an attorney's clerk and the intrigue of a Greek of the lower empire.
Benjamin Disraeli (1804–81) British statesman.
Speaking to Lord Palmerston
Attrib.

186* England, we love thee better than we know.
Richard Trench (1807–86) Archbishop of
Dublin.
Gibraltar

187 If we were to do for ourselves what we have
done for our country, we should indeed be very
great rogues.
Camillo Cavour (1810–61) Italian statesman.
Remark, Sept 1860

188* You can fool some of the people all the time
and all the people some of the time; but you
can't fool all the people all the time.
Abraham Lincoln (1809–65) US statesman.
Attrib.

189* Die when I may, I want it said of me by those
who know me best, that I have always
plucked a thistle and planted a flower where I
thought a flower would grow.
Abraham Lincoln
Presidential Anecdotes (P. Boller)

190 What is conservatism? Is it not adherence to
the old and tried, against the new and untried?
Abraham Lincoln
Speech, 27 Feb 1860

191 Let us have faith that right makes might; and in
that faith let us to the end, dare to do our duty
as we understand it.
Abraham Lincoln
Speech, 27 Feb 1860

1861

The American Civil War
(1861–65)

The result of deep-seated tensions between the Northern and Southern states, war broke out after 11 states
seceded from the USA. Fought at first over the right of
states to secede from the Union, the war's main
theme, the emancipation of all slaves, was adopted as
a Northern war aim by President Abraham Lincoln in
1862. Initially the war was an even contest, but the
greater resources of the North eventually proved
decisive.

192 All we ask is to be let alone.
Jefferson Davis (1808–89) President of the
rebel Confederate States of America.
Inaugural address, 18 Feb 1861

193 This country, with its institutions, belongs to
the people who inhabit it. Whenever they shall
grow weary of the existing government, they
can exercise their constitutional right of
amending it, or their revolutionary right to dis-
member or overthrow it.
Abraham Lincoln (1809–65) US statesman.
First Inaugural Address, 4 Mar 1861

194 I think the necessity of being *ready* increases –
Look to it.
Abraham Lincoln (1809–65) US
statesman.
Letter to Andrew Curtin, Governor of Penn-
sylvania, 8 Apr 1861

195 Let us determine to die here, and we will
conquer.
There is Jackson standing like a stone wall.
Rally behind the Virginians.
Barnard Elliot Bee (1824–61) US soldier.
Said at the First Battle of Bull Run, 1861; hence
Gen Thomas Jackson's nickname, 'Stonewall
Jackson'
Reminiscences of Metropolis (Poore), II

196* There they are cutting each other's throats, because one half of them prefer hiring their servants for life, and the other by the hour.
Thomas Carlyle (1795–1881) Scottish historian and essayist.
Referring to the American Civil War
Attrib.

197 Rome must be the capital of Italy because with-
out Rome Italy cannot be constituted.
Camillo Cavour (1810–61) Italian statesman.
Speech, Turin, 25 Mar 1861

1862

198* So you're the little woman who wrote the book
that made this great war!
Abraham Lincoln (1809–65) US statesman.
Said on meeting Harriet Beecher Stowe, the au-
thor of *Uncle Tom's Cabin* (1852), which stimu-
lated opposition to slavery before the US Civil
War
Abraham Lincoln: The War Years (Carl
Sandburg), Vol. II, Ch. 39

199* 'Shoot, if you must, this old gray head,
But spare your country's flag,' she said.

A shade of sadness, a blush of shame,
Over the face of the leader came.
John Greenleaf Whittier (1807–92) US
poet.
Barbara Frietchie

200 No terms except unconditional and immediate
surrender can be accepted. I propose to
move immediately upon your works.
Ulysses Simpson Grant (1822–85) US
general.
Message to opposing commander, Simon Bolivar
Buckner, during siege of Fort Donelson, 16 Feb
1862

201 My paramount object in this struggle is to save
the Union ... If I could save the Union without
freeing any slave, I would do it; and if I could
save it by freeing all the slaves, I would do it;
... I have here stated my purpose according
to my views of official duty and I intend no

modification of my oft-expressed personal wish that all men everywhere could be free.
Abraham Lincoln (1809–65) US statesman.
Letter to Horace Greeley, 22 Aug 1862

202 A Star for every State and a State for every Star.
Robert Charles Winthrop (1809–94)
Speech, Boston Common, 27 Aug 1862

203 In giving freedom to the slave, we assure freedom to the free – honourable alike in what we give and what we preserve.
Abraham Lincoln (1809–65) US statesman.
Annual Message to Congress, 1 Dec 1862

204 If you don't want to use the army, I should like to borrow it for a while. Yours respectfully,
A. Lincoln.
Abraham Lincoln
Letter to General George B. McClellan, whose lack of activity during the US Civil War irritated Lincoln

205 It is well that war is so terrible; else we would grow too fond of it.
Robert E. Lee (1807–70) US general.
Speaking to another general during the battle of Fredericksburg
The American Treasury (C. Fadiman)

206 Mine eyes have seen the glory of the coming of the Lord:
He is trampling out the vintage where the grapes of wrath are stored.
Julia Ward Howe (1819–1910) US writer.
Battle Hymn of the American Republic

207 The great questions of our day cannot be solved by speeches and majority votes . . . but by iron and blood.
Bismarck (1815–98) German statesman.
Usually misquoted as 'blood and iron' – a form Bismarck himself used in 1886
Speech, Prussian Chamber, 30 Sept 1862

208 Whereas it has long been known and declared that the poor have no right to the property of the rich, I wish it also to be known and declared that the rich have no right to the property of the poor.
John Ruskin (1819–1900) British art critic and writer.
Unto this Last, Essay III

1863

209 In a larger sense we cannot dedicate, we cannot consecrate, we cannot hallow this ground. The brave men, living and dead, who struggled here, have consecrated it far above our power to add or detract. The world will little note, nor long remember, what we say here, but it can never forget what they did here. It is for us, the living, rather to be dedicated here to the unfinished work which they who fought here have thus far so nobly advanced. It is rather for us to be here dedicated to the great task remaining before us . . . that we here highly resolve that the dead shall not have died in vain, that this nation, under God, shall

have a new birth of freedom; and that government of the people, by the people, and for the people, shall not perish from the earth.
Abraham Lincoln (1809–65) US statesman.
Report of Lincoln's address at the dedication (19 Nov 1863) of the national cemetery on the site of the Battle of Gettysburg

210 Give them the cold steel, boys!
Lewis Addison Arminstead (1817–63) US general.
Exhortation given to his troops during the US Civil War
Attrib.

211* I got there fustest with the mostest.
Nathan Bedford Forrest (1821–77) Confederate general.
Popular misquotation of his explanation of his success in capturing Murfreesboro; his actual words were, 'I just took the short cut and got there first with the most men'
A Civil War Treasury (B. Botkin)

212 There are only three men who have ever understood it: one was Prince Albert, who is dead; the second was a German professor, who became mad. I am the third – and I have forgotten all about it.
Lord Palmerston (1784–1865) British statesman.
Referring to the Schleswig-Holstein question
Attrib.

213 Politics is not an exact science.
Bismarck (1815–98) German statesman.
Speech, Prussian Chamber, 18 Dec 1863

1864

214 I claim not to have controlled events, but confess plainly that events have controlled me.
Abraham Lincoln (1809–65) US statesman.
Letter to A. G. Hodges, 4 Apr 1864

215 I purpose to fight it out on this line, if it takes all summer.
Ulysses Simpson Grant (1822–85) US general.
Dispatch to Washington, 11 May 1864

216 An old Dutch farmer, who remarked to a companion once that it was not best to swap horses in mid-stream.
Abraham Lincoln (1809–65) US statesman.
Speech, 9 June 1864

217* I can't spare this man; he fights.
Abraham Lincoln
Resisting demands for the dismissal of Ulysses Grant
Attrib.

218 Nonsense, they couldn't hit an elephant at this distance
John Sedgwick (1813–64) US general.
In response to a suggestion that he should not show himself over the parapet during the Battle of the Wilderness
Attrib.

219* 'Hurrah! hurrah! we bring the Jubilee!

Hurrah! hurrah! the flag that makes you free!'
So we sang the chorus from Atlanta to the
sea
As we were marching through Georgia.
Henry Clay Work (1832–84) US songwriter.
Commemorating the march (Nov–Dec 1864) by
a Union army under General Sherman through
Confederate Georgia
Marching Through Georgia

220 The foreign policy of the noble Earl . . . may be
summed up in two truly expressive words:
'meddle' and 'muddle'.
Edward Stanley, Earl of Derby (1799–
1869) British statesman.
Referring to Lord Russell's policy towards the
American Civil War
Speech, House of Lords, Feb 1864

221 I venture to say that every man who is not pre-
sumably incapacitated by some consideration
of personal unfitness or of political danger,
is morally entitled to come within the pale of
the constitution.
William Ewart Gladstone (1809–98) British
statesman.
Referring to the reform of the franchise
Speech, House of Commons, 11 May 1864

1865

222* As President, I have no eyes but constitutional
eyes, I cannot see you.
Abraham Lincoln (1809–65) US statesman.
Reply to the South Carolina Commissioners
Attrib.

223 I don't know who my grandfather was; I am
much more concerned to know what his grand-
son will be.
Abraham Lincoln
Taking part in a discussion on ancestry
Attrib.

224 The much talked of surrendering of Lee's sword
and my handing it back, this and much more
that has been said about it is the purest
romance.
Ulysses Simpson Grant (1822–85) US general and president.
Personal Memoirs of Ulysses S. Grant

225* Go West, young man, and grow up with the
country.
Horace Greeley (1811–72) US politician and
journalist.
Also attributed to the US writer John Soule
(1815–91), *Terre Haute* (Indiana) *Express*, 1851
Hints toward Reform

226 With malice toward none; with charity for all;
with firmness in the right, as God gives us to
see the right, let us strive on to finish the work
we are in: to bind up the nation's wounds; to
care for him who shall have borne the battle,
and for his widow and his orphan, to do all
which may achieve and cherish a just and lasting peace among ourselves, and with all
nations.
Abraham Lincoln (1809–65) US statesman.
Second Inaugural Address, 4 Mar 1865

227 England is the mother of parliaments.
John Bright (1811–89) British radical
politician.
Speech, Birmingham, 18 Jan 1865

228 I think . . . that it is the best club in London.
Charles Dickens (1812–70) British novelist.
Mr Tremlow describing the House of Commons
Our Mutual Friend, Bk. II, Ch. 3

229 When I invented the phrase 'His Majesty's Opposition' he paid me a compliment on the fortunate hit.
John Cam Hobhouse (1786–1869) British
radical politician.
Speaking about Canning
Recollections of a Long Life, II, Ch. 12

230 Home of lost causes, and forsaken beliefs, and
unpopular names, and impossible loyalties!
Matthew Arnold (1822–88) British poet and
critic.
Referring to Oxford
Essays in Criticism, First Series, Preface

231 My fellow citizens, the President is dead, but
the Government lives and God Omnipotent
reigns.
James A. Garfield (1831–81) US statesman.
Speech following the assassination of Lincoln

232 Assassination has never changed the history of
the world.
Benjamin Disraeli (1804–81) British
statesman.
Speech, House of Commons, 1 May 1865

1866

233 You cannot fight against the future. Time is on
our side.
William Ewart Gladstone (1809–98) British
statesman.
Advocating parliamentary reform
Speech, 1866

234 The right hon. Gentleman . . . has retired into
what may be called his political Cave of
Adullam.
John Bright (1811–89) British radical
politician.
Referring to Robert Lowe, the leader of the Liberals who opposed Parliamentary Reform;
hence their name, the 'Adullamites'
Speech, House of Commons, 13 Mar 1866

1867

235 We have dished the Whigs.
Edward Stanley, Earl of Derby (1799–
1869) British statesman.
Referring to the Parliamentary Reform Act, 1867
Remark

236 A severe though not unfriendly critic of our in-
stitutions said that 'the cure for admiring the
House of Lords was to go and look at it.'
Walter Bagehot (1826–77) British economist
and journalist.
The English Constitution, 'The House of Lords'

237 The Sovereign has, under a constitutional mon-

archy such as ours, three rights — the right to be consulted, the right to encourage, the right to warn.
Walter Bagehot
The English Constitution, 'The Monarchy'

238 It has been said that England invented the phrase, 'Her Majesty's Opposition'.
Walter Bagehot
The English Constitution, 'The Monarchy'

239 The characteristic of the English Monarchy is that it retains the feelings by which the heroic kings governed their rude age, and has added the feeling by which the constitutions of later Greece ruled in more refined ages.
Walter Bagehot
The English Constitution, 'The Monarchy'

240 But of all nations in the world the English are perhaps the least a nation of pure philosophers.
Walter Bagehot
The English Constitution, 'The Monarchy'

241 The best reason why Monarchy is a strong government is that it is an intelligible government. The mass of mankind understand it, and they hardly anywhere in the world understand any other.
Walter Bagehot
The English Constitution, 'The Monarchy'

242 *The Times* has made many ministries.
Walter Bagehot
The English Constitution, 'The Cabinet'

243 Capitalist production begets, with the inexorability of a law of nature, its own negation.
Karl Marx (1818–83) German philosopher and revolutionary.
Das Kapital, Ch. 15

244 The centralization of the means of production and the socialization of labour reach a point where they prove incompatible with their capitalist husk. This bursts asunder. The knell of private property sounds. The expropriators are expropriated.
Karl Marx
Das Kapital

1868

245 Yes, I have climbed to the top of the greasy pole.
Benjamin Disraeli (1804–81) British statesman.
On being appointed prime minister
Remark, Feb 1868

246 The great Unwashed.
Henry Peter Brougham (1778–1868) Scottish lawyer and politician.
Attrib.

247 Let us have peace.
Ulysses Simpson Grant (1822–85) US general.
On accepting nomination
Letter, 29 May 1868

248 I do not have to forgive my enemies, I have had them all shot.
Ramón Maria Narváez (1800–68) Spanish general and political leader.
Said on his deathbed, when asked by a priest if he forgave his enemies
Famous Last Words (B. Conrad)

1869

249 The Common Law adapts itself by a perpetual process of growth to the perpetual roll of the tide of circumstances as society advances.
Sir William Erle (1793–1880) Judge.
Memorandum on Trade Union Law

250 Our society distributes itself into Barbarians, Philistines, and Populace; and America is just ourselves, with the Barbarians quite left out, and the Populace nearly.
Matthew Arnold (1822–88) British poet and critic.
Culture and Anarchy, Preface

251 One has often wondered whether upon the whole earth there is anything so unintelligent, so unapt to perceive how the world is really going, as an ordinary young Englishman of our upper class.
Matthew Arnold
Culture and Anarchy, Ch. 2

252 I often, therefore, when I want to distinguish clearly the aristocratic class from the Philistines proper, or middle class, name the former, in my own mind *the Barbarians*.
Matthew Arnold
Culture and Anarchy, Ch. 3

253 But that vast portion, lastly, of the working-class which, raw and half-developed, has long lain half-hidden amidst its poverty and squalor, and is now issuing from its hiding-place to assert an Englishman's heaven-born privilege of doing as he likes, and is beginning to perplex us by marching where it likes, meeting where it likes, bawling what it likes, breaking what it likes — to this vast residuum we may with great propriety give the name of Populace.
Matthew Arnold
Culture and Anarchy, Ch. 3

254 I know no method to secure the repeal of bad or obnoxious laws so effective as their stringent execution.
Ulysses Simpson Grant (1822–85) US president.
Inaugural address, 4 Mar 1869

255 The only good Indians I ever saw were dead.
Philip H. Sheridan (1831–88) US general.
The People's Almanac 2 (D. Wallechinsky)

256* I should be trading on the blood of my men.
Robert E. Lee (1807–70) US general.
Refusing to write his memoirs
Nobody Said It Better (M. Ringo)

Attitudes

Art, Literature, and Music

1816

257 Then felt I like some watcher of the skies
When a new planet swims into his ken;
Or like stout Cortez when with eagle eyes
He star'd at the Pacific — and all his men
Look'd at each other with a wild surmise —
Silent, upon a peak in Darien.
John Keats (1795–1821) British poet.
On first looking into Chapman's Homer

1817

258 Our myriad-minded Shakespeare.
Samuel Taylor Coleridge (1772–1834) British poet.
Biographia Literaria, Ch. 15

259 The excellence of every art is its intensity, capable of making all disagreeables evaporate, from their being in close relationship with beauty and truth.
John Keats (1795–1821) British poet.
Letter to G. and T. Keats, 21 Dec 1817

1818

260 Poetry is not the proper antithesis to prose, but to science. Poetry is opposed to science, and prose to metre.
Samuel Taylor Coleridge (1772–1834) British poet.
Lectures and Notes of 1818, I

261 We hate poetry that has a palpable design upon us — and if we do not agree, seems to put its hand in its breeches pocket. Poetry should be great and unobtrusive, a thing which enters into one's soul, and does not startle or amaze it with itself, but with its subject.
John Keats (1795–1821) British poet.
Letter to J. H. Reynolds, 3 Feb 1818

262 If poetry comes not as naturally as leaves to a tree it had better not come at all.
John Keats
Letter to John Taylor, 27 Feb 1818

263 I think I shall be among the English Poets after my death.
John Keats
Letter to George and Georgiana Keats, 14 Oct 1818

264 Art for art's sake.
Victor Cousin (1792–1867) French philosopher.
Lecture, Sorbonne, 1818

265 He talked on for ever; and you wished him to talk on for ever.
William Hazlitt (1778–1830) British essayist.
Referring to Coleridge
Lectures on the English Poets, Lecture VIII, 'On the Living Poets'

1820

266* With Donne, whose muse on dromedary trots,
Wreathe iron pokers into true-love knots.
Samuel Taylor Coleridge (1772–1834) British poet.
On Donne's Poetry

267* His worst is better than any other person's best.
William Hazlitt (1778–1830) British essayist
English Literature, Ch. XIV, 'Sir Walter Scott'

1821

268 Poetry is the record of the best and happiest moments of the happiest and best minds.
Percy Bysshe Shelley (1792–1822) British poet.
A Defence of Poetry

269 I weep for Adonais — he is dead!
O, weep for Adonais! though our tears
Thaw not the frost which binds so dear a head!
Percy Bysshe Shelley
Prompted by the death of Keats
Adonais, I

1822

270 I love to lose myself in other men's minds. When I am not walking, I am reading; I cannot sit and think. Books think for me.
Charles Lamb (1775–1834) British essayist
Last Essays of Elia, 'Detached Thoughts on Books and Reading'

1824

271 If they had said the sun and the moon was gone out of the heavens it could not have struck me with the idea of a more awful and dreary blank in the creation than the words: Byron is dead.
Jane Welsh Carlyle (1801–66) The wife of Thomas Carlyle.
Letter to Thomas Carlyle, 1824

272 Prose on certain occasions can bear a great deal of poetry: on the other hand, poetry sinks and swoons under a moderate weight of prose.
Walter Savage Landor (1775–1864) British poet and writer.
Imaginary Conversations, 'Archdeacon Hare and Walter Landor'

273 Clear writers, like clear fountains, do not seem so deep as they are; the turbid look the most profound.
Walter Savage Landor
Imaginary Conversations, 'Southey and Porson'

1825

274 We know no spectacle so ridiculous as the Brit

ish public in one of its periodical fits of morality.
Lord Macaulay (1800–59) British historian.
Literary Essays Contributed to the 'Edinburgh Review', 'Moore's 'Life of Lord Byron''

275 As civilization advances, poetry almost necessarily declines.
Lord Macaulay
Literary Essays Contributed to the 'Edinburgh Review', 'Milton'

276 Perhaps no person can be a poet, or can even enjoy poetry, without a certain unsoundness of mind.
Lord Macaulay
Literary Essays Contributed to the 'Edinburgh Review', 'Milton'

277 Romanticism is the art of presenting people with the literary works which are capable of affording them the greatest possible pleasure, in the present state of their customs and beliefs.
Classicism, on the other hand, presents them with the literature that gave the greatest possible pleasure to their great-grandfathers.
Stendhal (Henri Beyle; 1783–1842) French novelist.
Racine et Shakespeare, Ch. 3

1826

278 The Big Bow-Wow strain I can do myself like any now going; but the exquisite touch, which renders ordinary commonplace things and characters interesting, from the truth of the description and the sentiment, is denied to me.
Walter Scott (1771–1832) Scottish novelist.
In praise of Jane Austen
Journal, 14 Mar 1826

1830

279 A novel is a mirror walking along a main road.
Stendhal (Henri Beyle; 1783–1842) French novelist.
Le Rouge et le noir, Ch. 49

1831

280 Ancient sculpture is the true school of modesty. But where the Greeks had modesty, we have cant; where they had poetry, we have cant; where they had patriotism, we have cant; where they had anything that exalts, delights, or adorns humanity, we have nothing but cant, cant, cant.
Thomas Love Peacock (1785–1866) British novelist.
Crotchet Castle, Ch. 7

281 A book that furnishes no quotations is, *me judice*, no book – it is a plaything.
Thomas Love Peacock
Crotchet Castle, Ch. 9

1833

282 I wish our clever young poets would remember

my homely definitions of prose and poetry; that is, prose = words in their best order; – poetry = the best words in the best order.
Samuel Taylor Coleridge (1772–1834) British poet.
Table Talk

283 The misfortune is, that he has begun to write verses without very well understanding what metre is.
Samuel Taylor Coleridge
Referring to Tennyson
Table Talk

284 I hate the whole race . . . There is no believing a word they say – your professional poets, I mean – there never existed a more worthless set than Byron and his friends for example.
Duke of Wellington (1769–1852) British general and statesman.
Lady Salisbury's diary, 26 Oct 1833

1837

285 Poetry's unnat'ral; no man ever talked poetry 'cept a beadle on boxin' day.
Charles Dickens (1812–70) British novelist.
Pickwick Papers, Ch. 33

1838

286 A poet without love were a physical and metaphysical impossibility.
Thomas Carlyle (1795–1881) Scottish historian and essayist.
Critical and Miscellaneous Essays, 'Burns'

287 Literary men are . . . a perpetual priesthood.
Thomas Carlyle
Critical and Miscellaneous Essays, 'The State of German Literature'

288 A good book is the best of friends, the same today and for ever.
Martin Farquhar Tupper (1810–89) British writer.
Proverbial Philosophy, 'Of Reading'

1839

289 Beneath the rule of men entirely great,
The pen is mightier than the sword.
Edward Bulwer-Lytton (1803–73) British novelist and politician.
Richelieu, II:2

290 Rules and models destroy genius and art.
William Hazlitt (1778–1830) British essayist.
On Taste

1840

291* In my situation as Chancellor of the University of Oxford, I have been much exposed to authors.
Duke of Wellington (1769–1852) British general and statesman.
Collections and Recollections (G. W. E. Russell)

292   A good book is the purest essence of a human soul.
Thomas Carlyle (1795–1881) Scottish historian and essayist.
Speech made in support of the London Library
Carlyle and the London Library (F. Harrison)

1841

293   I shall not be satisfied unless I produce something that shall for a few days supersede the last fashionable novel on the tables of young ladies.
Lord Macaulay (1800–59) British historian.
Letter to Macvey Napier, 5 Nov 1841

1842

294   When once the itch of literature comes over a man, nothing can cure it but the scratching of a pen.
Samuel Lover (1797–1868) Irish novelist.
Handy Andy, Ch. 36

295   Whatever sentence will bear to be read twice, we may be sure was thought twice.
Henry David Thoreau (1817–62) US writer.
Journal, 1842

1845

296*   My business is to paint not what I know, but what I see.
Joseph Turner (1775–1851) British painter.
Responding to a criticism of the fact that he had painted no portholes on the ships in a view of Plymouth
Proust: The Early Years (G. Painter)

1848

297   The *Pall Mall Gazette* is written by gentlemen for gentlemen.
William Makepeace Thackeray (1811–63) British novelist.
This fictional journal inspired a real counterpart, founded in 1855
Pendennis, Ch. 32

1849

298   When we build let us think that we build for ever.
John Ruskin (1819–1900) British art critic and writer.
The Seven Lamps of Architecture, Ch. 6, 'The Lamp of Memory'

1850

299*   It always seems to me that the right sphere for Shelley's genius was the sphere of music, not of poetry.
Matthew Arnold (1822–88) British poet and critic.
Maurice de Guérin, Footnote

300   . . . essentially a cold, hard, silent, practical man . . . a man of an immense head, and great jaws like a crocodile's, cast in a mould designed for prodigious work.
Thomas Carlyle (1795–1881) Scottish historian and essayist.
Referring to William Wordsworth
Attrib.

301*   If people only knew as much about painting as I do, they would never buy my pictures.
Edwin Landseer (1802–73) British painter and sculptor.
Said to W. P. Frith
Landseer the Victorian Paragon (Campbell Lennie), Ch. 12

302*   Great artists have no country.
Alfred de Musset (1810–57) French dramatist and poet.
Lorenzaccio, I:5

303*   A picture has been said to be something between a thing and a thought.
Samuel Palmer (1805–81) British landscape painter.
Life of Blake (Arthur Symons)

1852

304   . . . a bottle of beautiful soda-water . . . very pleasant company now and then.
Thomas Carlyle (1795–1881) Scottish historian and essayist.
Referring to Ruskin
Attrib.

1853

305*   He spoke, and loos'd our heart in tears.
He laid us as we lay at birth
On the cool flowery lap of earth.
Matthew Arnold (1822–88) British poet and critic.
Referring to Wordsworth
Memorial Verses

306   Time may restore us in his course
Goethe's sage mind and Byron's force:
But where will Europe's latter hour
Again find Wordsworth's healing power?
Matthew Arnold
Memorial Verses

307   All one's inventions are true, you can be sure of that. Poetry is as exact a science as geometry.
Gustave Flaubert (1821–80) French novelist.
Letter to Louise Colet, 14 Aug 1853

308   No person who is not a great sculptor or painter can be an architect. If he is not a sculptor or painter, he can only be a *builder*.
John Ruskin (1819–1900) British art critic and writer.
Lectures on Architecture and Painting

309   I expect a judgment. Shortly.
Charles Dickens (1812–70) British novelist.
An overoptimistic hope: the case, *Jarndyce vs. Jarndyce*, lasted for many years and formed a satire on the abuses of the court of Chancery.
Bleak House, Ch. 3

1854

310 Books, we are told, propose to *instruct* or to *amuse*. Indeed! . . . The true antithesis to knowledge, in this case, is not *pleasure*, but *power*. All that is literature seeks to communicate power; all that is not literature, to communicate knowledge.
Thomas De Quincey (1785–1859) British writer.
Letters to a Young Man

1856

311 . . . the most honourable thing that man, as a gregarious animal, has ever produced.
John Ruskin (1819–1900) British art critic and writer.
Referring to a ship of the line
Attrib.

1858

312 Writers, like teeth, are divided into incisors and grinders.
Walter Bagehot (1826–77) British economist and journalist.
Estimates of some Englishmen and Scotchmen, 'The First Edinburgh Reviewers'

1859

313 Nobody cares much at heart about Titian, only there is a strange undercurrent of everlasting murmur about his name, which means the deep consent of all great men that he is greater than they.
John Ruskin (1819–1900) British art critic and writer.
The Two Paths, Lecture II

314 Fine art is that in which the hand, the head, and the heart of man go together.
John Ruskin
The Two Paths, Lecture II

1860

315* Talent alone cannot make a writer. There must be a man behind the book.
Ralph Waldo Emerson (1803–82) US poet and essayist.
Goethe

316* I have tried lately to read Shakespeare, and found it so intolerably dull that it nauseated me.
Charles Darwin (1809–82) British life scientist.
Autobiography

317* When I want to read a novel I write one.
Benjamin Disraeli (1804–81) British statesman.
Attrib.

1862

318 With the aid of a few columns stuck here and there, or rich window dressings and rustications in another place, and aided by the fatal facility of stucco, they managed to get over an immense amount of space with a very slight expenditure of thought.
James Fergusson (1808–86) British writer on architecture.
Referring to contemporary architects, such as Nash
History of Architecture, Vol. III

1865

319 All books are divisible into two classes, the books of the hour, and the books of all time.
John Ruskin (1819–1900) British art critic and writer.
Sesame and Lilies, 'Of Kings' Treasuries'

1867

320 Wagner has lovely moments but awful quarters of an hour.
Gioacchino Rossini (1792–1868) Italian operatic composer.
Remark made to Emile Naumann, April 1867
Italienische Tondichter (Naumann)

321 Not that the story need be long, but it will take a long while to make it short.
Henry David Thoreau (1817–62) US writer.
Letter, 16 Nov 1867

1868

322 Give me a laundry-list and I'll set it to music.
Gioacchino Rossini (1792–1868) Italian operatic composer.
Attrib.

1869

323 Historians tell the story of the past, novelists the story of the present.
Edmond de Goncourt (1822–96) French novelist.
Journal

324 For this class we have a designation which now has become pretty well known, and which we may as well still keep for them, the designation of Philistines.
Matthew Arnold (1822–88) British poet and critic.
Referring to the middle class
Culture and Anarchy, Ch. 3

Daily Life

1816

325 Nobody is healthy in London, nobody can be.
Jane Austen (1775–1817) British novelist.
Emma, Ch. 12

326 One has no great hopes from Birmingham. I al-

ways say there is something direful in the
sound.
Jane Austen
Emma, Ch. 36

1818

327 Oh! who can ever be tired of Bath?
Jane Austen
Northanger Abbey, Ch. 10

328 I like the weather, when it is not rainy,
That is, I like two months of every year.
Lord Byron (1788–1824) British poet.
Beppo

1819

329 Man, being reasonable, must get drunk;
The best of life is but intoxication.
Lord Byron
Don Juan, II

330 Give me books, fruit, French wine and fine
weather and a little music out of doors, played
by somebody I do not know.
John Keats (1795–1821) British poet.
Letter to Fanny Keats, 29 Aug 1819

1820

331 London, that great sea, whose ebb and flow
At once is deaf and loud, and on the shore
Vomits its wrecks, and still howls on for
more.
Percy Bysshe Shelley (1792–1822) British
poet.
Letter to Maria Gisborne, I

1822

332 Newspapers always excite curiosity. No one
ever lays one down without a feeling of
disappointment.
Charles Lamb (1775–1834) British essayist.
Last Essays of Elia, 'Detached Thoughts on
Books and Reading'

1823

333 'Twas the night before Christmas, when all
through the house
Not a creature was stirring, not even a
mouse;
The stockings were hung by the chimney with
care,
In hopes that St Nicholas soon would be
there.
Clement Clarke Moore (1779–1863) US
writer.
In *Troy Sentinel*, 23 Dec 1823, 'A Visit from St.
Nicholas'

1826

334 Summer has set in with its usual severity.
Samuel Taylor Coleridge (1772–1834) British poet.
Quoted in Lamb's letter to V. Novello, 9 May
1826

1827

335 The trivial round, the common task,
Would furnish all we ought to ask;
Room to deny ourselves; a road
To bring us, daily, nearer God.
John Keble (1792–1866) British poet and
clergyman.
The Christian Year, 'Morning'

1830

336* They will steal the very teeth out of your mouth
as you walk through the streets. I know it from
experience.
William Arabin (1773–1841) British judge.
Referring to the people of Uxbridge
Arabinesque at Law (Sir R. Megarry)

1834

337 He who drinks a tumbler of London water has
literally in his stomach more animated beings
than there are men, women and children on
the face of the globe.
Sydney Smith (1771–1845) British clergyman
and essayist.
Letter

1835

338 The loco-motive Monster, carrying *eighty* tons
of goods, and navigated by a tail of smoke
and sulphur, coming thro' every man's grounds
between Manchester and Liverpool.
Thomas Creevey (1768–1838) British
politician.
The Creevey Papers (ed. Sir H. Maxwell)

1836

339 ... I *too well* know its truth, from experience,
that whenever any poor Gipsies are en-
camped anywhere and crimes and robberies
&c. occur, it is invariably laid to their account,
which is shocking; and if they are always
looked upon as vagabonds, how *can* they become good people?
Victoria (1819–1901) Queen of the United
Kingdom.
Journal, 29 Dec 1836

1847

340 What a blessing this smoking is! perhaps the
greatest that we owe to the discovery of
America.
Arthur Helps (1813–75) British historian.
Friends in Council

1851

341 There are no countries in the world less known by the British than these selfsame British Islands.
George Henry Borrow (1803–81) British writer.
Lavengro, Preface

1853

342 This is a London particular . . . A fog, miss.
Charles Dickens (1812–70) British novelist.
Bleak House, Ch. 3

1854

343 The blue ribbon of the turf.
Benjamin Disraeli (1804–81) British statesman.
Describing the Derby
Life of Lord George Bentinck, Ch. 26

1857

344 It's more than a game. It's an institution.
Thomas Hughes (1822–96) British novelist.
Referring to cricket
Tom Brown's Schooldays, Pt. II, Ch. 7

1858

345 The comic almanacs give us dreadful pictures of January and February; but, in truth, the months which should be made to look gloomy in England are March and April. Let no man boast himself that he has got through the perils of winter till at least the seventh of May.
Anthony Trollope (1815–82) British novelist.
Doctor Thorne, Ch. 47

1859

346 . . . that old monkish place which I have a horror of.
Victoria (1819–1901) Queen of the United Kingdom
Referring to Oxford
Letter to Princess Victoria, 31 Oct 1859

1860

347* This vice brings in one hundred million francs in taxes every year. I will certainly forbid it at once – as soon as you can name a virtue that brings in as much revenue.
Napoleon III (1808–73) French emperor.
Reply when asked to ban smoking
Anekdotenschatz (H. Hoffmeister)

1865

348 Jolly boating weather,
And a hay harvest breeze,
Blade on the feather,
Shade off the trees
Swing, swing together

With your body between your knees.
William Johnson Cory (1823–92) British schoolmaster and poet.
Eton Boating Song

1867

349 That sweet City with her dreaming spires
She needs not June for beauty's heightening.
Matthew Arnold (1822–88) British poet and critic.
Referring to Oxford
Thyrsis

Death

1820

350 Darkling I listen; and, for many a time
I have been half in love with easeful Death,
Call'd him soft names in many a mused rhyme,
To take into the air my quiet breath;
Now more than ever seems it rich to die,
To cease upon the midnight with no pain,
While thou art pouring forth thy soul abroad
In such an ecstasy!
John Keats (1795–1821) British poet.
Ode to a Nightingale

351 Death is the veil which those who live call life:
They sleep, and it is lifted.
Percy Bysshe Shelley (1792–1822) British poet.
Prometheus Unbound, III

1821

352 I shall soon be laid in the quiet grave – thank God for the quiet grave – O! I can feel the cold earth upon me – the daisies growing over me – O for this quiet – it will be my first.
John Keats (1795–1821) British poet.
In a letter to John Taylor by Joseph Severn, 6 Mar 1821

1839

353 Grieve not that I die young. Is it not well
To pass away ere life hath lost its brightness?
Lady Flora Hastings (1806–39) British poet.
Swan Song

354 There is a Reaper whose name is Death,
And, with his sickle keen,
He reaps the bearded grain at a breath,
And the flowers that grow between.
Henry Wadsworth Longfellow (1807–82) US poet.
The Reaper and the Flowers

1844

355 He'd make a lovely corpse.
Charles Dickens (1812–70) British novelist.
Martin Chuzzlewit, Ch. 25

1859

356 It is a far, far, better thing that I do, than I have ever done; it is a far, far, better rest that I go to, than I have ever known.
Charles Dickens
Said by Sydney Carton
A Tale of Two Cities, Bk. II, Ch. 15

1862

357 Go and try to disprove death. Death will disprove you, and that's all!
Ivan Turgenev (1818–83) Russian novelist.
Fathers and Sons, Ch. 27

1865

358 The bitterest tears shed over graves are for words left unsaid and deeds left undone.
Harriet Beecher Stowe (1811–96) US novelist.
Little Foxes, Ch. 3

Education, Knowledge, and Learning

1817

359 The primary imagination I hold to be the living power and prime agent of all human perception, and as a repetition in the finite mind of the eternal act of creation in the infinite I AM.
Samuel Taylor Coleridge (1772–1834) British poet.
Biographia Literaria, Ch. 13

1818

360 Axioms in philosophy are not axioms until they are proved upon our pulses; we read fine things but never feel them to the full until we have gone the same steps as the author.
John Keats (1795–1821) British poet.
Letter to J. H. Reynolds, 3 May 1818

361 He was sent, as usual, to a public school, where a little learning was painfully beaten into him, and from thence to the university, where it was carefully taken out of him.
Thomas Love Peacock (1785–1866) British novelist.
Nightmare Abbey, Ch. 1

1820

362* You will hear more good things on the outside of a stagecoach from London to Oxford than if you were to pass a twelvemonth with the undergraduates, or heads of colleges, of that famous university.
William Hazlitt (1778–1830) British essayist.
The Ignorance of the Learned

1823

363 Man is an intellectual animal, and therefore an everlasting contradiction to himself. His senses centre in himself, his ideas reach to the ends of the universe; so that he is torn in pieces between the two, without a possibility of its ever being otherwise.
William Hazlitt
Characteristics

1828

364 My object will be, if possible to form Christian men, for Christian boys I can scarcely hope to make.
Thomas Arnold (1795–1842) British educator.
Letter on appointment as Headmaster of Rugby, 1828

365 Knowledge advances by steps, and not by leaps.
Lord Macaulay (1800–59) British historian.
Essays and Biographies, 'History'. *Edinburgh Review*

1830

366* Intellect is invisible to the man who has none.
Arthur Schopenhauer (1788–1860) German philosopher.
Aphorismen zur Lebensweisheit

1832

367 He never knew prosperity and adversity, passion nor satiety; he never had even the experiences which sickness gives . . . He knew no dejection, no heaviness of heart . . . He was a boy to the last.
John Stuart Mill (1806–73) British philosopher.
Referring to Jeremy Bentham
Dissertations

1835

368 What we must look for here is, first, religious and moral principles; secondly, gentlemanly conduct; thirdly, intellectual ability.
Thomas Arnold (1795–1842) British educator.
Address to the Scholars at Rugby

369 The highest intellects, like the tops of mountains, are the first to catch and to reflect the dawn.
Lord Macaulay (1800–59) British historian.
Historical Essays Contributed to the 'Edinburgh Review', 'Sir James Mackintosh'

1836

370 Be not the slave of Words.
Thomas Carlyle (1795–1881) Scottish historian and essayist.
Sartor Resartus, Bk. I, Ch. 8

1837

371 The difference between Orthodoxy or My-doxy and Heterodoxy or Thy-doxy.
Thomas Carlyle
A similar remark is attributed to the British churchman William Warburton (1698–1779)
History of the French Revolution, Pt. II, Bk. IV, Ch. 2

1839

372 When he has learnt that bottinney means a knowledge of plants, he goes and knows 'em. That's our system, Nickleby; what do you think of it?
Charles Dickens (1812–70) British novelist.
Said by Mr Squeers
Nicholas Nickleby, Ch. 8

373 There is an unseemly exposure of the mind, as well as of the body.
William Hazlitt (1778–1830) British essayist.
On Disagreeable People

1841

374 The true University of these days is a collection of books.
Thomas Carlyle (1795–1881) Scottish historian and essayist.
Heroes and Hero-Worship, 'The Hero as Man of Letters'

375 A foolish consistency is the hobgoblin of little minds, adored by little statesmen and philosophers and divines. With consistency a great soul has simply nothing to do.
Ralph Waldo Emerson (1803–82) US poet and essayist.
Essays, 'Self-reliance'

1845

376 Little things affect little minds.
Benjamin Disraeli (1804–81) British statesman.
Sybil, Bk. III, Ch. 2

1847

377 Reading is sometimes an ingenious device for avoiding thought.
Arthur Helps (1813–75) British historian.
Friends in Council

1848

378 I don't know, Ma'am, why they make all this fuss about education; none of the Pagets can read or write, and they get on well enough.
Lord Melbourne (1779–1848) British statesman.
Said to Queen Victoria
Attrib.

1850

379* A stand can be made against invasion by an army; no stand can be made against invasion by an idea.
Victor Hugo (1802–85) French writer.
Histoire d'un Crime, 'La Chute'

1851

380 To expect a man to retain everything that he has ever read is like expecting him to carry about in his body everything that he has ever eaten.
Arthur Schopenhauer (1788–1860) German philosopher.
Parerga and Paralipomena

1857

381 A thought is often original, though you have uttered it a hundred times.
Oliver Wendell Holmes (1809–94) US writer.
The Autocrat of the Breakfast Table, Ch. 1

1859

382 On earth there is nothing great but man; in man there is nothing great but mind.
William Hamilton (1788–1856) Scottish philosopher.
Lectures on Metaphysics

383 All good things which exist are the fruits of originality.
John Stuart Mill (1806–73) British philosopher.
On Liberty, Ch. 3

1860

384 A moment's insight is sometimes worth a life's experience.
Oliver Wendell Holmes (1809–94) US writer.
The Professor at the Breakfast Table, Ch. 10

1864

385 The true God, the mighty God, is the God of ideas.
Alfred de Vigny (1797–1863) French writer.
La Bouteille à la mer

1867

386 To make your children *capable of honesty* is the beginning of education.
John Ruskin (1819–1900) British art critic and writer.
Time and Tide, Letter VIII

History

1820

387* If men could learn from history, what lessons it
might teach us! But passion and party blind
our eyes and the light which experience gives
is a lantern on the stern, which shines only
on the waves behind us!
Samuel Taylor Coleridge (1772–1834) British poet.
Recollections (Allsop)

1825

388* What experience and history teach is this —
that people and governments never have
learned anything from history, or acted on principles deduced from it.
Hegel (1770–1831) German philosopher.
Philosophy of History, Introduction

1830

389 The past, at least, is secure.
Daniel Webster (1782–1852) US statesman.
Speech, US Senate, 26 Jan 1830

1838

390 History is the essence of innumerable
biographies.
Thomas Carlyle (1795–1881) Scottish historian and essayist.
Critical and Miscellaneous Essays, 'History'

1840

391 There is properly no history; only biography.
Ralph Waldo Emerson (1803–82) US poet
and essayist.
Essays, 'History'

1841

392 No great man lives in vain. The history of the
world is but the biography of great men.
Thomas Carlyle (1795–1881) Scottish histo-
rian and essayist.
Heroes and Hero-Worship, 'The Hero as
Divinity'

1848

393 The history of England is emphatically the his-
tory of progress.
Lord Macaulay (1800–59) British historian.
History of England

Human Nature

1816

394 Human nature is so well disposed towards
those who are in interesting situations, that a
young person, who either marries or dies, is
sure to be kindly spoken of.
Jane Austen (1775–1817) British novelist.
Emma, Ch. 22

1817

395 But with the morning cool repentance came.
Walter Scott (1771–1832) Scottish novelist.
Rob Roy, Ch. 12

1818

396 Scenery is fine — but human nature is finer.
John Keats (1795–1821) British poet.
Letter to Benjamin Bailey, 13 Mar 1818

1820

397* Speech was given to man to disguise his
thoughts.
Talleyrand (Charles Maurice de Talleyrand-Pér-
igord; 1754–1838) French politician.
Attrib.

398 Upon the whole I dislike mankind: whatever
people on the other side of the question may
advance, they cannot deny that they are always
surprised at hearing of a good action and
never of a bad one.
John Keats (1795–1821) British poet.
Letter, 1820

399* Nobody ever did anything very foolish except
from some strong principle.
Lord Melbourne (1779–1848) British
statesman.
The Young Melbourne (Lord David Cecil)

1822

400 To great evils we submit; we resent little
provocations.
William Hazlitt (1778–1830) British essayist.
On Great and Little Things

401 The human species, according to the best theory I can form of it, is composed of two distinct races, the men who borrow, and the men
who lend.
Charles Lamb (1775–1834) British essayist.
Essays of Elia, 'The Two Races of Men'

402 Credulity is the man's weakness, but the
child's strength.
Charles Lamb
Essays of Elia, 'Witches and other Night Fears'

403 Man is a gaming animal. He must always be
trying to get the better in something or other.
Charles Lamb
Essays of Elia, 'Mrs Battle's Opinions on Whist'

404 How sickness enlarges the dimensions of a
man's self to himself.
Charles Lamb
Last Essays of Elia, 'The Convalescent'

1827

405 What though the spicy breezes

Blow soft o'er Ceylon's isle;
Though every prospect pleases,
And only man is vile . . .
Reginald Heber (1783–1826) British bishop
and hymn writer .
From Greenland's Icy Mountains

1829

406 I do not know myself, and God forbid that I
should.
Goethe (1749–1832) German poet and
dramatist.
Conversations with Eckermann, 10 Apr 1829

1830

407 Woodman, spare that tree!
Touch not a single bough!
In youth it sheltered me,
And I'll protect it now.
George Pope Morris (1802–64) US
journalist.
Woodman, Spare That Tree

1836

408 There are three things which the public will al-
ways clamour for, sooner or later: namely,
Novelty, novelty, novelty.
Thomas Hood (1799–1845) British poet.
Announcement of *Comic Annual*, 1836

1839

409 The most fluent talkers or most plausible rea-
soners are not always the justest thinkers.
William Hazlitt (1778–1830) British essayist.
On Prejudice

410 When men understand what each other mean,
they see, for the most part, that controversy
is either superfluous or hopeless.
Cardinal Newman (1801–90) British
theologian.
Sermon, Oxford, Epiphany 1839

1840

411* Happiness is no laughing matter.
Richard Whately (1787–1863) British
churchman.
Apophthegms

412* A Friend may well be reckoned the masterpiece
of Nature.
Ralph Waldo Emerson (1803–82) US poet
and essayist.
Essays, 'Friendship'

413 You must not think me necessarily foolish because I am facetious, nor will I consider you
necessarily wise because you are grave.
Sydney Smith (1771–1845) British clergyman
and essayist.
Letter to Bishop Blomfield

1841

414 To be great is to be misunderstood.
Ralph Waldo Emerson (1803–82) US poet
and essayist.
Essays, 'Self-Reliance'

1844

415 Here's the rule for bargains: 'Do other men, for
they would do you.' That's the true business
precept.
Charles Dickens (1812–70) British novelist.
Martin Chuzzlewit, Ch. 11

1847

416 It is impossible, in our condition of society, not
to be sometimes a Snob.
William Makepeace Thackeray (1811–63)
British novelist.
The Book of Snobs, Ch. 3

417 Tears, idle tears, I know not what they mean,
Tears from the depth of some divine despair.
Alfred, Lord Tennyson (1809–92) British
poet.
The Princess, IV

418 He who meanly admires mean things is a Snob.
William Makepeace Thackeray (1811–63)
British novelist.
The Book of Snobs, Ch. 2

1849

419 Job endured everything — until his friends
came to comfort him, then he grew impatient.
Søren Kierkegaard (1813–55) Danish
philosopher.
Journal

1850

420 For words, like Nature, half reveal
And half conceal the Soul within.
Alfred, Lord Tennyson (1809–92) British
poet.
In Memoriam A.H.H., V

421 'Tis held that sorrow makes us wise.
Alfred, Lord Tennyson (1809–92)
In Memoriam A.H.H., CXIII

422* Tyndall, I must remain plain Michael Faraday to
the last; and let me now tell you, that if I accepted the honour which the Royal Society
desires to confer upon me, I would not answer
for the integrity of my intellect for a single
year.
Michael Faraday (1791–1867) British
scientist.
Said when Faraday was offered the Presidency
of the Royal Society
Faraday as a Discoverer (J. Tyndall), 'Illustra-
tions of Character'

1852

423 It is almost a definition of a gentleman to say
     that he is one who never inflicts pain.
     Cardinal Newman (1801–90) British
     theologian.
     The Idea of a University, 'Knowledge and Reli-
     gious Duty'

1854

424 I never found the companion that was so com-
     panionable as solitude.
     Henry David Thoreau (1817–62) US writer.
     Walden, 'Solitude'

1855

425 Best be yourself, imperial, plain and true!
     Robert Browning (1812–89) British poet.
     Bishop Blougram's Apology

426 You find people ready enough to do the Samari-
     tan, without the oil and twopence.
     Sydney Smith (1771–1845) British clergyman
     and essayist.
     Memoir (Lady Holland)

1858

427 Errors look so very ugly in persons of small
     means – one feels they are taking quite a lib-
     erty in going astray; whereas people of for-
     tune may naturally indulge in a few
     delinquencies.
     George Eliot (Mary Ann Evans; 1819–80) Brit-
     ish novelist.
     Janet's Repentance, Ch. 25

1860

428* The earth does not argue,
     Is not pathetic, has no arrangements,
     Does not scream, haste, persuade, threaten,
     promise,
     Makes no discriminations, has no conceivable
     failures,
     Closes nothing, refuses nothing, shuts none
     out.
     Walt Whitman (1819–92) US poet.
     To the sayers of words

429* One is happy as a result of one's own efforts,
     once one knows the necessary ingredients of
     happiness – simple tastes, a certain degree
     of courage, self denial to a point, love of work,
     and, above all, a clear conscience. Happiness
     is no vague dream, of that I now feel certain.
     George Sand (Aurore Dupin, Baronne Dude-
     vant; 1804–76) French novelist.
     Correspondence, Vol. V

430 A person seldom falls sick, but the bystanders
     are animated with a faint hope that he will die.
     Ralph Waldo Emerson (1803–82) US poet
     and essayist.
     Conduct of Life, 'Considerations by the Way'

431 The louder he talked of his honour, the faster
     we counted our spoons.
     Ralph Waldo Emerson
     Conduct of Life, 'Worship'

432* If a man make a better mouse-trap than his
     neighbour, though he build his house in the
     woods, the world will make a beaten path to his
     door.
     Ralph Waldo Emerson
     Attrib.

1862

433 I agree with no man's opinion. I have some of
     my own.
     Ivan Turgenev (1818–83) Russian novelist.
     Fathers and Sons, Ch. 13

1863

434 He did not know that a keeper is only a poacher
     turned outside in, and a poacher a keeper
     turned inside out.
     Charles Kingsley (1819–75) British writer.
     The Water Babies, Ch. 1

1865

435* Resolve to be thyself: and know, that he
     Who finds himself, loses his misery.
     Matthew Arnold (1822–88) British poet and
     critic.
     Self-Dependence

436* The gentleman will please remember that when
     his half-civilized ancestors were hunting the
     wild boar in Silesia, mine were princes of the
     earth.
     Judah Philip Benjamin (1811–84) US
     politician.
     Replying to a senator of Germanic origin who
     had made an antisemitic remark
     Attrib.

Humour

1833

437 No mind is thoroughly well organized that is
     deficient in a sense of humour.
     Samuel Taylor Coleridge (1772–1834) Brit-
     ish poet.
     Table Talk

1836

438 Sarcasm I now see to be, in general, the lan-
     guage of the devil.
     Thomas Carlyle (1795–1881) Scottish histo-
     rian and essayist.
     Sartor Resartus, Bk. II, Ch. 4

1843

439 *Peccavi!*

I have sinned!
Charles James Napier (1782–1853) British general.
Reporting his subjugation of Sind, N India (Feb 1843)
Attrib.

1857

440   Sir, you are like a pin, but without either its head or its point.
Douglas William Jerrold (1803–57) British dramatist.
Speaking to a small thin man who was boring him
Attrib.

Life

1816

441   One half of the world cannot understand the pleasures of the other.
Jane Austen (1775–1817) British novelist.
Emma, Ch. 9

442   Nothing can be more obvious than that all animals were created solely and exclusively for the use of man.
Thomas Love Peacock (1785–1866) British novelist.
Headlong Hall, Ch. 2

1817

443   O for a life of sensations rather than of thoughts!
John Keats (1795–1821) British poet.
Letter to Benjamin Bailey, 22 Nov 1817

1819

444   Society is now one polish'd horde,
Form'd of two mighty tribes, the *Bores* and *Bored*.
Lord Byron (1788–1824) British poet.
Don Juan, XIII

445   Superstition is the poetry of life.
Goethe (1749–1832) German poet and dramatist.
Sprüche in Prosa, III

446   'Beauty is truth, truth beauty,' – that is all
Ye know on earth, and all ye need to know.
John Keats (1795–1821) British poet.
Ode on a Grecian Urn

447   Nothing ever becomes real till it is experienced – even a proverb is no proverb to you till your life has illustrated it.
John Keats
Letter to George and Georgiana Keats, 19 Mar 1819

448   There is a Southern proverb, – fine words butter no parsnips.
Walter Scott (1771–1832) Scottish novelist.
The Legend of Montrose, Ch. 3

1820

449   When you have nothing to say, say nothing.
Charles Caleb Colton (?1780–1832) British clergyman and writer.
Lacon, Vol. I

450   Is there another life? Shall I awake and find all this a dream? There must be, we cannot be created for this sort of suffering.
John Keats (1795–1821) British poet.
Letter, 1820

1821

451   He hath awakened from the dream of life –
'Tis we, who lost in stormy visions, keep
With phantoms an unprofitable strife,
And in mad trance, strike with our spirit's knife
Invulnerable nothings.
Percy Bysshe Shelley (1792–1822) British poet.
Adonais, XXXIX

1822

452   We are nothing; less than nothing, and dreams. We are only what might have been, and must wait upon the tedious shores of Lethe millions of ages before we have existence, and a name.
Charles Lamb (1775–1834) British essayist.
In Greek mythology, Lethe was a river in the underworld, whose waters were drunk by souls about to be reborn in order to forget their past lives
Essays of Elia, 'Dream Children'

1823

453   If the world were good for nothing else, it is a fine subject for speculation.
William Hazlitt (1778–1830) British essayist.
Characteristics

1824

454   Fleas know not whether they are upon the body of a giant or upon one of ordinary size.
Walter Savage Landor (1775–1864) British poet and writer.
Imaginary Conversations, 'Southey and Porson'

455   Punctuality is the politeness of kings.
Louis XVIII (1755–1824) French king.
Attrib.

1830

456*   We might have been – These are but common words,
And yet they make the sum of life's bewailing.
Letitia Landon (1802–38) British poet and novelist.
Three Extracts from the Diary of a Week

457*   Oh, Vanity of vanities!
How wayward the decrees of Fate are;

How very weak the very wise,
How very small the very great are!
William Makepeace Thackeray (1811–63)
British novelist.
Vanitas Vanitatum

1838

458 The three great elements of modern civilization,
Gunpowder, Printing, and the Protestant
Religion.
Thomas Carlyle (1795–1881) Scottish historian and essayist.
Critical and Miscellaneous Essays, 'The State
of German Literature'

459 Popularity? It's glory's small change.
Victor Hugo (1802–85) French writer.
Ruy Blas, III

1840

460 Nothing great was ever achieved without
enthusiasm.
Ralph Waldo Emerson (1803–82) US poet
and essayist.
Essays, 'Circles'

1841

461 Men talk of killing time, while time quietly kills
them.
Dion Boucicault (Dionysius Lardner Boursiquot; 1820–90) Irish-born US actor and
dramatist.
London Assurance, II:1

1844

462 As she frequently remarked when she made
any such mistake, it would be all the same a
hundred years hence.
Charles Dickens (1812–70) British novelist.
Said by Mrs Squeers
Martin Chuzzlewit, Ch. 9

463 Almost everything that is great has been done
by youth.
Benjamin Disraeli (1804–81) British
statesman.
Coningsby, Bk. III, Ch. 1

1847

464 Revolts, republics, revolutions, most
No graver than a schoolboy's barring out.
Alfred, Lord Tennyson (1809–92) British
poet.
The Princess, Conclusion

1849

465 *Plus ça change, plus c'est la même chose.*
The more things change, the more they stay
the same.
Alphonse Karr (1808–90) French writer.
Les Guêpes, Jan 1849

1850

466* Time is a great teacher, but unfortunately it kill
all its pupils.
Hector Berlioz (1803–69) French composer
Almanach des lettres françaises

467* Some say that the age of chivalry is past, tha
the spirit of romance is dead. The age of chivalry is never past, so long as there is a
wrong left unredressed on earth.
Charles Kingsley (1819–75) British writer.
Life (Mrs C. Kingsley), Vol. II, Ch. 28

468* To be alone is the fate of all great minds – a
fate deplored at times, but still always chosen as the less grievous of two evils.
Arthur Schopenhauer (1788–1860) Germa
philosopher.
Aphorismen zur Lebensweisheit

469* I don't pretend to understand the Universe –
it's a great deal bigger than I am ... People
ought to be modester.
Thomas Carlyle (1795–1881) Scottish histo
rian and essayist.
Attrib.

470 At last awake
From life, that insane dream we take
For waking now.
Robert Browning (1812–89) British poet.
Easter-Day, XIV

471* 'Tis better to have fought and lost,
Than never to have fought at all.
Arthur Hugh Clough (1819–61) British poe
Peschiera

472 One God, one law, one element,
And one far-off divine event,
To which the whole creation moves.
Alfred, Lord Tennyson (1809–92) British
poet.
In Memoriam A.H.H., CXXXI

473 But what am I?
An infant crying in the night:
An infant crying for the light:
And with no language but a cry.
Alfred, Lord Tennyson
In Memoriam A.H.H., LIV

1851

474 Now, what I want is Facts ... Facts alone are
wanted in life.
Charles Dickens (1812–70) British novelist
Hard Times, Bk. I, Ch. 1

475 Remember that the most beautiful things in th
world are the most useless, peacocks and lilies for instance.
John Ruskin (1819–1900) British art critic ar
writer.
The Stones of Venice, Vol. I, Ch. 2

476 The thing-in-itself, the will-to-live, exists whol
and undivided in every being, even in the tini-

est; it is present as completely as in all that ever were, are, and will be, taken together.
Arthur Schopenhauer (1788–1860) German philosopher.
Parerga and Paralipomena

1853

477 Before this strange disease of modern life,
With its sick hurry, its divided aims.
Matthew Arnold (1822–88) British poet and critic.
The Scholar Gipsy

1854

478 Our life is frittered away by detail . . . Simplify, simplify.
Henry David Thoreau (1817–62) US writer.
Walden, 'Where I Lived, and What I Lived For'

479 Time is but the stream I go a-fishing in.
Henry David Thoreau
Walden, 'Where I Lived, and What I Lived For'

1855

480 Ah, but a man's reach should exceed his grasp,
Or what's a heaven for?
Robert Browning (1812–89) British poet.
Andrea del Sarto

1856

481 Since when was genius found respectable?
Elizabeth Barrett Browning (1806–61) British poet.
Aurora Leigh, Bk. VI

482 A great city is that which has the greatest men and women.
Walt Whitman (1819–92) US poet.
Song of the Broad-Axe, 5

1857

483 The world's great men have not commonly been great scholars, nor great scholars great men.
Oliver Wendell Holmes (1809–94) US writer.
The Autocrat of the Breakfast Table, Ch. 6

484 Life isn't all beer and skittles.
Thomas Hughes (1822–96) British novelist.
Tom Brown's Schooldays, Pt. I, Ch. 2

1858

485 Genius (which means transcendent capacity of taking trouble, first of all).
Thomas Carlyle (1795–1881) Scottish historian and essayist.
Frederick the Great, Vol. IV, Ch. 3

486 In these days a man is nobody unless his biography is kept so far posted up that it may be

ready for the national breakfast-table on the morning after his demise.
Anthony Trollope (1815–82) British novelist.
Doctor Thorne, Ch. 25

1859

487 The Wine of Life keeps oozing drop by drop,
The Leaves of Life keep falling one by one.
Edward Fitzgerald (1809–83) British poet.
The Rubáiyát of Omar Khayyám (4th edn.), VIII

488 Ah, my Belovéd, fill the Cup that clears
TO-DAY of past Regrets and Future Fears:
To-morrow! – Why, To-morrow I may be
Myself with Yesterday's Sev'n thousand Years.
Edward Fitzgerald
The Rubáiyát of Omar Khayyám (1st edn.), XX

489 Ah, fill the Cup: – what boots it to repeat
How Time is slipping underneath our Feet:
Unborn TOMORROW, and dead YESTERDAY,
Why fret about them if TODAY be sweet!
Edward Fitzgerald
The Rubáiyát of Omar Khayyám (1st edn.), XXXVII

490 No human being, however great, or powerful, was ever so free as a fish.
John Ruskin (1819–1900) British art critic and writer.
The Two Paths, Lecture V

491 For man is man and master of his fate.
Alfred, Lord Tennyson (1809–92) British poet.
Idylls of the King, 'The Marriage of Geraint'

1860

492* A wanderer is man from his birth.
He was born in a ship
On the breast of the river of Time.
Matthew Arnold (1822–88) British poet and critic.
The Future

493* If God were suddenly condemned to live the life which he has inflicted on men, He would kill Himself.
Alexandre Dumas, fils (1824–95) French writer.
Pensées d'album

494* Life is mostly froth and bubble;
Two things stand like stone,
Kindness in another's trouble,
Courage in your own.
Adam Lindsay Gordon (1833–70) Australian poet.
Ye Wearie Wayfarer, Fytte 8

495* The chess-board is the world; the pieces are the phenomena of the universe; the rules of the game are what we call the laws of Nature. The player on the other side is hidden from us. We know that his play is always fair, just, and patient. But also we know, to our cost, that he

never overlooks a mistake, or makes the smallest allowance for ignorance.
T. H. Huxley (1825–95) British biologist.
Lay Sermons, 'A Liberal Education'

1862

496   The temerity to believe in nothing.
Ivan Turgenev (1818–83) Russian novelist.
Fathers and Sons, Ch. 14

1863

497   To know how to say what others only know how to think is what makes men poets or sages; and to dare to say what others only dare to think makes men martyrs or reformers – or both.
Elizabeth Charles (1828–96) British writer.
Chronicle of the Schönberg-Cotta Family

1865

498   'If everybody minded their own business,' the Duchess said in a hoarse growl, 'the world would go round a deal faster than it does.'
Lewis Carroll (Charles Lutwidge Dodgson; 1832–98) British writer.
Alice's Adventures in Wonderland, Ch. 6

1868

499   It takes people a long time to learn the difference between talent and genius, especially ambitious young men and women.
Louisa May Alcott (1832–88) US novelist.
Little Women, Pt. II

Love and Sex

1819

500   Man's love is of man's life a thing apart,
'Tis woman's whole existence.
Lord Byron (1788–1824) British poet.
Don Juan, I

501   Now hatred is by far the longest pleasure;
Men love in haste, but they detest at leisure.
Lord Byron
Don Juan, XIII

502   Love is my religion – I could die for that.
John Keats (1795–1821) British poet.
Letter to Fanny Brawne, 13 Oct 1819

1822

503   Life may change, but it may fly not;
Hope may vanish, but can die not;
Truth be veiled, but still it burneth;
Love repulsed, – but it returneth!
Percy Bysshe Shelley (1792–1822) British poet.
Hellas, I

1837

504   If there is any country on earth where the course of true love may be expected to run smooth, it is America.
Harriet Martineau (1802–76) British writer.
Society in America, Vol. III, 'Marriage'

1840

505   In the Spring a young man's fancy lightly turns to thoughts of love.
Alfred, Lord Tennyson (1809–92) British poet.
Locksley Hall

1841

506   'There are strings', said Mr Tappertit, 'in the human heart that had better not be wibrated.'
Charles Dickens (1812–70) British novelist.
Barnaby Rudge, Ch. 22

1847

507   O tell her, brief is life but love is long.
Alfred, Lord Tennyson (1809–92) British poet.
The Princess, IV

1855

508   Onaway! Awake, beloved!
Henry Wadsworth Longfellow (1807–82) US poet.
Opening of the song sung by Chibiabos at Hiawatha's wedding feast; best known in the setting by Coleridge-Taylor
The Song of Hiawatha, XI, 'Hiawatha's Wedding-feast'

1859

509   Love's like the measles – all the worse when it comes late in life.
Douglas William Jerrold (1803–57) British dramatist.
Wit and Opinions of Douglas Jerrold, 'A Philanthropist'

1860

510* The way to a man's heart is through his stomach.
Fanny Fern (1811–72) US writer.
Willis Parton

1865

511   All, everything that I understand, I understand only because I love.
Leo Tolstoy (1828–1910) Russian writer.
War and Peace, Bk. VII, Ch. 16

Marriage and the Family

1822

512 A poor relation — is the most irrelevant thing in nature.
Charles Lamb (1775–1834) British essayist.
Last Essays of Elia, 'Poor Relations'

513 Boys are capital fellows in their own way, among their mates; but they are unwholesome companions for grown people.
Charles Lamb
Essays of Elia, 'The Old and the New Schoolmaster'

1823

514 Mid pleasures and palaces though we may roam,
Be it ever so humble, there's no place like home;

. . .

Home, home, sweet, sweet home!
There's no place like home! there's no place like home!
John Howard Payne (1791–1852) US actor and dramatist.
Clari, or the Maid of Milan

1828

515 The majority of husbands remind me of an orangutang trying to play the violin.
Honoré de Balzac (1799–1850) French novelist.
La Physiologie du mariage

1837

516 . . . the early marriages of silly children . . . where . . . every woman is married before she well knows how serious a matter human life is.
Harriet Martineau (1802–76) British writer.
Society in America, Vol. III, 'Marriage'

1847

517 This I set down as a positive truth. A woman with fair opportunities and without a positive hump, may marry whom she likes.
William Makepeace Thackeray (1811–63) British novelist.
Vanity Fair, Ch. 4

1853

518 It is a melancholy truth that even great men have their poor relations.
Charles Dickens (1812–70) British novelist.
Bleak House, Ch. 28

1862

519 For there is no friend like a sister
In calm or stormy weather;
To cheer one on the tedious way,
To fetch one if one goes astray,

To lift one if one totters down,
To strengthen whilst one stands.
Christina Rossetti (1830–74) British poet.
Goblin Market

1870

520 Every woman should marry — and no man.
Benjamin Disraeli (1804–81) British statesman.
Lothair, Ch. 30

Men and Women

1808

521 The extension of women's rights is the basic principle of all social progress.
Fourier, Charles (1772–1837) French social reformer.
Théorie des Quatre Mouvements

1818

522 A woman, especially if she have the misfortune of knowing anything, should conceal it as well as she can.
Jane Austen (1775–1817) British novelist.
Northanger Abbey, Ch. 14

1840

523 There are some meannesses which are too mean even for man — woman, lovely woman alone, can venture to commit them.
William Makepeace Thackeray (1811–63) British novelist.
A Shabby-Genteel Story, Ch. 3

1842

524 How sweet are looks that ladies bend
On whom their favours fall!
Alfred, Lord Tennyson (1809–92) British poet.
Sir Galahad

1843

525 O! men with sisters dear,
O! men with mothers and wives!
It is not linen you're wearing out,
But human creatures' lives!
Thomas Hood (1799–1845) British poet.
The Song of the Shirt

1844

526 What are little boys made of?
Frogs and snails
And puppy-dogs' tails,
That's what little boys are made of.
What are little girls made of?
Sugar and spice
And all that's nice,

That's what little girls are made of.
Nursery Rhymes (J. O. Halliwell)

1847

527 Man is the hunter; woman is his game:
The sleek and shining creatures of the chase,
We hunt them for the beauty of their skins.
Alfred, Lord Tennyson (1809-92) British
poet.
The Princess, V

528 Man for the field and woman for the hearth:
Man for the sword and for the needle she:
Man with the head and woman with the heart:
Man to command and woman to obey;
All else confusion.
Alfred, Lord Tennyson
The Princess, V

1850

529* The fundamental fault of the female character is
that it has no sense of justice.
Arthur Schopenhauer (1788-1860) German
philosopher.
Gedanken über vielerlei Gegenstände, XXVII

530* God made the woman for the man,
And for the good and increase of the world.
Alfred, Lord Tennyson (1809-92) British
poet.
Edwin Morris

1852

531 'Tis strange what a man may do, and a woman
yet think him an angel.
William Makepeace Thackeray (1811-63)
British novelist.
Henry Esmond, Ch. 7

1853

532 I do not ask for my rights. I have no rights; I
have only wrongs.
Caroline Norton (1808-77) British poet and
campaigner for women's rights.
Said when a court upheld her husband's refusal
to maintain her
Remark, Aug 1853

1855

533 God be thanked, the meanest of his creatures
Boasts two soul-sides, one to face the world
with,
One to show a woman when he loves her!
Robert Browning (1812-89) British poet.
One Word More, XVII

1859

534 I expect that Woman will be the last thing civilized by Man.
George Meredith (1828-1909) British
novelist.
The Ordeal of Richard Feverel, Ch. 1

1860

535 I should like to know what is the proper function of women, if it is not to make reasons for
husbands to stay at home, and still stronger
reasons for bachelors to go out.
George Eliot (Mary Ann Evans; 1819-80) British novelist.
The Mill on the Floss, Ch. 6

536* . . . is it to be understood that the principles of
the Declaration of Independence bear no relation to half of the human race?
Harriet Martineau (1802-76) British writer.
Society in America, Vol. III, 'Marriage'

1863

537 I am a source of satisfaction to him, a nurse, a
piece of furniture, a *woman* – nothing more.
Sophie Tolstoy (1844-1919) Russian writer.
A Diary of Tolstoy's Wife, 1860-1891

1865

538* It is only rarely that one can see in a little boy
the promise of a man, but one can almost always see in a little girl the threat of a
woman.
Alexandre Dumas, fils (1824-95) French
writer.
Attrib.

539 With many women I doubt whether there be
any more effectual way of touching their hearts
than ill-using them and then confessing it. If
you wish to get the sweetest fragrance from
the herb at your feet, tread on it and bruise it.
Anthony Trollope (1815-82) British novelist.
Miss Mackenzie, Ch. 10

1867

540 To employ women and children unduly is simply to run into debt with Nature.
The Times, 4 Mar 1867

541 Women – one half the human race at least –
care fifty times more for a marriage than a
ministry.
Walter Bagehot (1826-77) British economist
and journalist.
The English Constitution, 'The Monarchy'

1868

542 Housekeeping ain't no joke.
Louisa May Alcott (1832-88) US novelist.
Little Women, Pt. I

543 . . . girls are so queer you never know what
they mean. They say No when they mean Yes,
and drive a man out of his wits for the fun of it
. . .
Louisa May Alcott
Little Women, Pt. II

1869

544 The most important thing women have to do is to stir up the zeal of women themselves.
John Stuart Mill (1806–73) British philosopher.
Letter to Alexander Bain, 14 July 1869

Morality, Vices, and Virtues

1817

545 Nothing can permanently please, which does not contain in itself the reason why it is so, and not otherwise.
Samuel Taylor Coleridge (1772–1834) British poet.
Biographia Literaria, Ch. 14

546 I am certain of nothing but the holiness of the heart's affections and the truth of imagination – what the imagination seizes as beauty must be truth – whether it existed before or not.
John Keats (1795–1821) British poet.
Letter to Benjamin Bailey, 22 Nov 1817

1819

547 Though sages may pour out their wisdom's treasure,
There is no sterner moralist than Pleasure.
Lord Byron (1788–1824) British poet.
Don Juan, III

548 Agree to a short armistice with truth.
Lord Byron
Don Juan, III

549 The love of liberty is the love of others; the love of power is the love of ourselves.
William Hazlitt (1778–1830) British essayist.
The Times, 1819

550 'Beauty is truth, truth beauty,' – that is all
Ye know on earth, and all ye need to know.
John Keats (1795–1821) British poet.
Ode on a Grecian Urn

1824

551 Goodness does not more certainly make men happy than happiness makes them good.
Walter Savage Landor (1775–1864) British poet and writer.
Imaginary Conversations, 'Lord Brooke and Sir Philip Sidney'

1827

552 Murder considered as one of the Fine Arts.
Thomas De Quincey (1785–1859) British writer.
Essay title

553 To a shower of gold most things are penetrable.
Thomas Carlyle (1795–1881) Scottish historian and essayist.
History of the French Revolution, Pt. I, Bk. III, Ch. 7

1839

554 The greatest offence against virtue is to speak ill of it.
William Hazlitt (1778–1830) British essayist.
On Cant and Hypocrisy

1840

555 The reward of a thing well done is to have done it.
Ralph Waldo Emerson (1803–82) US poet and essayist.
Essays, 'New England Reformers'

1842

556 My strength is as the strength of ten,
Because my heart is pure.
Alfred, Lord Tennyson (1809–92) British poet.
Sir Galahad

1847

557 Sorrow and silence are strong, and patient endurance is godlike.
Henry Wadsworth Longfellow (1807–82) US poet.
Evangeline

558 That a lie which is all a lie may be met and fought with outright,
But a lie which is part a truth is a harder matter to fight.
Alfred, Lord Tennyson (1809–92) British poet.
The Grandmother

1850

559* There are three kinds of lies: lies, damned lies and statistics.
Benjamin Disraeli (1804–81) British statesman.
Autobiography (Mark Twain)

560* Know how sublime a thing it is
To suffer and be strong.
Henry Wadsworth Longfellow (1807–82) US poet.
The Light of Stars

561* Honesty is the best policy; but he who is governed by that maxim is not an honest man.
Richard Whately (1787–1863) British churchman.
Apophthegms

1851

562 Better sleep with a sober cannibal than a
drunken Christian.
Herman Melville (1819–91) US novelist.
Moby Dick, Ch. 3

1852

563 What men call social virtues, good fellowship,
is commonly but the virtue of pigs in a litter,
which lie close together to keep each other
warm. It brings men together in crowds and
mobs in bar-rooms and elsewhere, but it does
not deserve the name of virtue.
Henry David Thoreau (1817–62) US writer.
Journal, 1852

1860

564 If you would hit the mark, you must aim a little
above it;
Every arrow that flies feels the attraction of
earth.
Henry Wadsworth Longfellow (1807–82)
US poet.
Elegiac Verse

565 Let us all be happy, and live within our means,
even if we have to borrer the money to do it
with.
Artemus Ward (Charles Farrar Browne; 1834–
67) US humorous writer.
Science and Natural History

566* We cannot kindle when we will
The fire which in the heart resides,
The spirit bloweth and is still,
In mystery our soul abides.
Matthew Arnold (1822–88) British poet and
critic.
Morality

567* Years hence, perhaps, may dawn an age,
More fortunate, alas! than we,
Which without hardness will be sage,
And gay without frivolity.
Matthew Arnold
The Grande Chartreuse

1862

568 Thou shalt not kill; but needst not strive
Officiously to keep alive.
Arthur Hugh Clough (1819–61) British poet.
The Latest Decalogue, 11

569 As for conceit, what man will do any good who
is not conceited? Nobody holds a good opinion of a man who has a low opinion of
himself.
Anthony Trollope (1815–82) British novelist.
Orley Farm, Ch. 22

1864

570 Those who offend us are generally punished for
the offence they give; but we so frequently

miss the satisfaction of knowing that we are
avenged!
Anthony Trollope
The Small House at Allington, Ch. 50

1865

571 But men never violate the laws of God without
suffering the consequences, sooner or later.
Lydia M. Child (1802–80) US abolitionist
campaigner.
The Freedmen's Book, 'Toussaint L'Ouverture'

572 Everything's got a moral, if only you can find it.
Lewis Carroll (Charles Lutwidge Dodgson;
1832–98) British writer.
Alice's Adventures in Wonderland, Ch. 9

1867

573 What's a man's first duty? The answer's brief:
To be himself.
Henrik Ibsen (1828–1906) Norwegian
dramatist.
Peer Gynt, IV:1

574 To kill a human being is, after all, the least in-
jury you can do him.
Henry James (1843–1916) US novelist.
My Friend Bingham

1869

575 The pursuit of perfection, then, is the pursuit of
sweetness and light.... He who works for
sweetness and light united, works to make reason and the will of God prevail.
Matthew Arnold (1822–88) British poet and
critic.
Culture and Anarchy, Ch. 1

Other People

1820

576* The English (it must be owned) are rather a
foul-mouthed nation.
William Hazlitt (1778–1830) British essayist.
On Criticism

577* I found there a country with thirty-two religions
and only one sauce.
Talleyrand (Charles Maurice de Talleyrand-Pér-
igord; 1754–1838) French politician.
Referring to America
Autant en apportent les mots (Pedrazzini)

1821

578 While spewy sands and gravel near London are
enclosed and built on, good lands in other
parts are neglected. These enclosures are a
waste; they are means misapplied; they are a
proof of national decline and not of
prosperity.
William Cobbett (1763–1835) British journalist and writer.
Rural Rides

1822

579   I have been trying all my life to like Scotchmen, and am obliged to desist from the experiment in despair.
Charles Lamb (1775–1834) British essayist.
Essays of Elia, 'Imperfect Sympathies'

1835

580   The French want no-one to be their *superior*. The English want *inferiors*. The Frenchman constantly raises his eyes above him with anxiety. The Englishman lowers his beneath him with satisfaction. On either side it is pride, but understood in a different way.
Alexis de Tocqueville (1805–59) French writer, historian, and politician.
Voyage en Angleterre et en Irlande de 1835, 18 May

1847

581   Italy is a geographical expression.
Clement Metternich (1773–1859) Austrian diplomat and Chancellor.
Letter, 6 Aug 1847

1850

582*   Thirty millions, mostly fools.
Thomas Carlyle (1795–1881) Scottish historian and essayist.
When asked what the population of England was
Attrib.

1862

583   We cannot bring ourselves to believe it possible that a foreigner should in any respect be wiser than ourselves. If any such point out to us our follies, we at once claim those follies as the special evidences of our wisdom.
Anthony Trollope (1815–82) British novelist.
Orley Farm, Ch. 18

Religion

1816

584   If a man could pass through Paradise in a dream, and have a flower presented to him as a pledge that his soul had really been there, and if he found that flower in his hand when he awoke – Aye, and what then?
Samuel Taylor Coleridge (1772–1834) British poet.
Anima Poetae

1820

585   Men will wrangle for religion; write for it; fight for it; anything but – live for it.
Charles Caleb Colton (?1780–1832) British clergyman and writer.
Lacon, Vol. I

1825

586   He who begins by loving Christianity better than Truth will proceed by loving his own sect or church better than Christianity, and end by loving himself better than all.
Samuel Taylor Coleridge (1772–1834) British poet.
Aids to Reflection: Moral and Religious Aphorisms.

1833

587   Lead, kindly Light, amid the encircling gloom,
Lead thou me on;
The night is dark, and I am far from home,
Lead thou me on.
Cardinal Newman (1801–90) British theologian.
Lead Kindly Light

1836

588   You will be damned if you do – And you will be damned if you don't.
Lorenzo Dow (1777–1834) British churchman.
Speaking of Calvinism
Reflections on the Love of God

1840

589*   It established a religion without a prelate, a government without a king.
George Bancroft (1800–91) US historian.
Referring to Calvinism
History of the United States (1834–40), Vol. III

590*   The sedate, sober, silent, serious, sad-coloured sect.
Thomas Hood (1799–1845) British poet.
Referring to the Quakers
The Doves and the Crows

1841

591   All service ranks the same with God –
With God, whose puppets, best and worst,
Are we: there is no last or first.
Robert Browning (1812–89) British poet.
Pippa Passes, Pt. I

592   O come all ye faithful,
Joyful and triumphant,
O come ye, O come ye to Bethlehem.
Frederick Oakeley (1802–80) British churchman.
Translated from the Latin hymn, *Adeste Fideles*
O Come All Ye Faithful

1844

593   The religions we call false were once true.
Ralph Waldo Emerson (1803–82) US poet and essayist.
Essays, 'Character'

1845

594 Vain are the thousand creeds
That move men's hearts: unutterably vain;
Worthless as wither'd weeds.
Emily Brontë (1818–48) British novelist.
Last Lines

1848

595 Once in royal David's city
Stood a lowly cattle shed,
Where a Mother laid her Baby
In a manger for His bed:
Mary was that Mother mild,
Jesus Christ her little Child.
C. F. Alexander (1818–95) British hymn
writer.
Once in Royal David's City

596 *We can believe what we choose. We are answerable for what we choose to believe.*
Cardinal Newman (1801–90) British
theologian.
Letter to Mrs Froude, 27 June 1848

1850

597* If Jesus Christ were to come to-day, people
would not even crucify him. They would ask
him to dinner, and hear what he had to say, and
make fun of it.
Thomas Carlyle (1795–1881) Scottish historian and essayist.
Carlyle at his Zenith (D. A. Wilson)

598* Ride on! ride on in majesty!
In lowly pomp ride on to die.
Henry Hart Milman (1791–1868) British poet
and historian.
Ride On

599 Fight the good fight with all thy might,
Christ is thy strength and Christ thy right,
Lay hold on life, and it shall be
Thy joy and crown eternally.
John Monsell (1811–75) British hymn writer.
Hymn

600* Jesus loves me – this I know,
For the Bible tells me so.
Susan Warner (1819–85) US novelist.
The Love of Jesus

601 Though Rome's gross yoke
Drops off, no more to be endured,
Her teaching is not so obscured
By errors and perversities,
That no truth shines athwart the lies.
Robert Browning (1812–89) British poet.
Christmas Eve, XI

602 Religion . . . is the opium of the people.
Karl Marx (1818–83) German philosopher and
revolutionary.
Criticism of the Hegelian Philosophy of Right,
Introduction

603 And so the Word had breath, and wrought
With human hands the creed of creeds
In loveliness of perfect deeds,

More strong than all poetic thought.
Alfred, Lord Tennyson (1809–92) British
poet.
In Memoriam A.H.H., XXXVI

1852

604 Yes, about ten minutes.
Duke of Wellington (1769–1852) British general and statesman.
Responding to a vicar's query as to whether
there was anything he would like his forthcoming
sermon to be about
Attrib.

1855

605 I embrace the purpose of God and the doom
assigned.
Alfred, Lord Tennyson (1809–92) British
poet.
Maud, III

606 But the churchmen fain would kill their church,
As the churches have kill'd their Christ.
Alfred, Lord Tennyson
Maud, V

1856

607 God will pardon me. It is His trade.
Heinrich Heine (1797–1856) German poet
and writer.
Journal (Edmond and Charles Goncourt), 23 Feb
1863

1859

608 If thou shouldst never see my face again,
Pray for my soul. More things are wrought by
prayer
Than this world dreams of.
Alfred, Lord Tennyson (1809–92) British
poet.
Idylls of the King, 'The Passing of Arthur'

1860

609* Whatever a man prays for, he prays for a mira-
cle. Every prayer reduces itself to this: 'Great
God grant that twice two be not four.'
Ivan Turgenev (1818–83) Russian novelist.
Prayer

Science, Medicine, and Technology

1816

610 By machines mankind are able to do that which
their own bodily powers would never effect to
the same extent. Machines are the produce
of the mind of man; and their existence distinguishes the civilized man from the savage.
William Cobbett (1763–1835) British journalist and writer.
Letter to the Luddites of Nottingham

1822

611 In everything that relates to science, I am a whole Encyclopaedia behind the rest of the world.
Charles Lamb (1775–1834) British essayist.
Essays of Elia, 'The Old and the New Schoolmaster'

1827

612 I see no reason to suppose that these machines will ever force themselves into general use.
Duke of Wellington (1769–1852) British general and statesman.
Referring to steam locomotives
Geoffrey Madan's Notebooks (J. Gere)

1836

613 Man is a tool-using animal.
Thomas Carlyle (1795–1881) Scottish historian and essayist.
Sartor Resartus, Bk. I, Ch. 5

1854

614 Where observation is concerned, chance favours only the prepared mind.
Louis Pasteur (1822–95) French scientist.
Said at the inauguration of the Faculty of Science
Address, University of Lille, 7 Dec 1854

1859

615 We will now discuss in a little more detail the struggle for existence.
Charles Darwin (1809–82) British life scientist.
Origin of Species, Ch. 3

616 I have called this principle, by which each slight variation, if useful, is preserved, by the term of Natural Selection.
Charles Darwin
Origin of Species, Ch. 3

617 The expression often used by Mr Herbert Spencer of the Survival of the Fittest is more accurate, and is sometimes equally convenient.
Charles Darwin
Origin of Species, Ch. 3

1860

618 And, in conclusion, I would like to ask the gentleman . . . whether the ape from which he is descended was on his grandmother's or his grandfather's side of the family.
Samuel Wilberforce (1805–73) British churchman.
Speech, 30 June 1860

619 I asserted — and I repeat — that a man has no reason to be ashamed of having an ape for his grandfather. If there were an ancestor whom I should feel shame in recalling it would rather be a *man*— a man of restless and versatile intellect — who, not content with an equivocal

success in his own sphere of activity, plunges into scientific questions with which he has no real acquaintance, only to obscure them by an aimless rhetoric, and distract the attention of his hearers from the real point at issue by eloquent digressions and skilled appeals to religious prejudice.
T. H. Huxley (1825–95) British biologist.
Replying to Bishop Wilberforce in the debate on Darwin's theory of evolution at the meeting of the British Association at Oxford. No transcript was taken at the time; the version above is commonly quoted. After hearing Wilberforce's speech, and before rising himself, Huxley is said to have remarked, 'The Lord has delivered him into my hands!'
Speech, 30 June 1860

1864

620 The question is this: Is man an ape or an angel? I, my lord, am on the side of the angels.
Benjamin Disraeli (1804–81) British statesman.
Speech, 25 Nov 1864

1869

621 The highest wisdom has but one science – the science of the whole – the science explaining the whole creation and man's place in it.
Leo Tolstoy (1828–1910) Russian writer.
War and Peace, Bk.V, Ch. 2

622 Our body is a machine for living. It is organized for that, it is its nature. Let life go on in it unhindered and let it defend itself, it will do more than if you paralyse it by encumbering it with remedies.
Leo Tolstoy
War and Peace, Bk. X, Ch. 29

Wealth and Poverty

1816

623 Business, you know, may bring money, but friendship hardly ever does.
Jane Austen (1775–1817) British novelist.
Emma, Ch. 34

1829

624 To be poor and independent is very nearly an impossibility.
William Cobbett (1763–1835) British journalist and writer.
Advice to Young Men

1831

625 Respectable means rich, and decent means poor. I should die if I heard my family called decent.
Thomas Love Peacock (1785–1866) British novelist.
Crotchet Castle, Ch. 3

1850

626 Annual income twenty pounds, annual expenditure nineteen nineteen six, result happiness.
Annual income twenty pounds, annual expenditure twenty pounds ought and six, result
misery.
Charles Dickens (1812–70) British novelist.
David Copperfield, Ch. 12

1851

627 Wealth is like sea-water; the more we drink, the
thirstier we become; and the same is true of
fame.
Arthur Schopenhauer (1788–1860) German
philosopher.
Parerga and Paralipomena

Work and Occupations

1831

628 Ours is composed of the scum of the earth.
Duke of Wellington (1769–1852) British
general.
Referring to the British army
Remark, 4 Nov 1831

1837

629 Medical men all over the world having merely
entered into a tacit agreement to call all sorts
of maladies people are liable to, in cold
weather, by one name; so that one sort of treatment may serve for all, and their practice
thereby be greatly simplified.
Jane Welsh Carlyle (1801–66) The wife of
Thomas Carlyle.
Letter to John Welsh, 4 Mar 1837

1839

630 A man willing to work, and unable to find work,
is perhaps the saddest sight that fortune's inequality exhibits under the sun.
Thomas Carlyle (1795–1881) Scottish historian and essayist.
Chartism

1840

631* There is no class of men whose rewards are so
disproprotionate to their usefulness to the
community.
Lord John Russell (1792–1878) British
statesman.
Referring to schoolmasters
Attrib.

1854

632 There are now-a-days professors of philosophy
but not philosophers.
Henry David Thoreau (1817–62) US writer.
Walden, 'Economy'

633 As for doing good, that is one of the profes-
sions which are full.
Henry David Thoreau
Walden, 'Economy'

1859

634 The ugliest of trades have their moments of
pleasure. Now, if I were a grave-digger, or even
a hangman, there are some people I could
work for with a great deal of enjoyment.
Douglas William Jerrold (1803–57) British
dramatist.
Wit and Opinions of Douglas Jerrold, 'Ugly
Trades'

635 No *man*, not even a doctor, ever gives any
other definition of what a nurse should be than
this — 'devoted and obedient.' This definition
would do just as well for a porter. It might
even do for a horse. It would not do for a
policeman.
Florence Nightingale (1820–1910) British
nurse.
Notes on Nursing

Sayings of the Time

1820

636 Imitation is the sincerest form of flattery.
Charles Caleb Colton (?1780–1832) British
clergyman and writer.
Lacon, Vol. I

637* Publish and be damned!
Duke of Wellington (1769–1852) British general and statesman.
On being offered the chance to avoid mention in
the memoirs of Harriette Wilson by giving her
money
Attrib.

1826

638 The Last of the Mohicans.
James Fenimore Cooper (1789–1851) US
novelist.
Title of Novel

1831

639 Only one man ever understood me. . . . And he
didn't understand me.
Hegel (1770–1831) German philosopher.
Said on his deathbed
Famous Last Words (B. Conrad)

1838

640 Monday's child is fair of face,
Tuesday's child is full of grace,
Wednesday's child is full of woe,
Thursday's child has far to go,
Friday's child is loving and giving,
Saturday's child works hard for his living,

And the child that is born on the Sabbath day
Is bonny and blithe, and good and gay.
Traditions of Devonshire (A. E. Bray)

1843

641 'God bless us every one!' said Tiny Tim, the
last of all.
Charles Dickens (1812–70) British novelist.
A Christmas Carol

1844

642 All for one, and one for all.
Alexandre Dumas, père (1802–70) French
novelist and dramatist.
The Three Musketeers

1849

643 Tinker,
Tailor,
Soldier,
Sailor,
Rich man,
Poor man,
Beggarman,
Thief.
Popular Rhymes and Nursery Tales (J. O.
Halliwell)

1850

644* I have no pain, dear mother, now;
But oh! I am so dry:
Just moisten poor Jim's lips once more;
And, mother, do not cry!
Edward Farmer (1809–76) British writer.
The Collier's Dying Child

645* 'But the Emperor has nothing on at all!' cried a
little child.
Hans Christian Andersen (1805–75) Danish writer.
The Emperor's New Clothes

646* The Ugly Duckling.
Hans Christian Andersen
Story title

647 I am well aware that I am the 'umblest person
going . . . .My mother is likewise a very 'umble
person. We live in a numble abode.
Charles Dickens (1812–70) British novelist.
Said by Uriah Heep
David Copperfield, Ch. 16

648 Some circumstantial evidence is very strong, as
when you find a trout in the milk.
Henry David Thoreau (1817–62) US writer.
Journal, 1850

1854

649 Beware of all enterprises that require new
clothes.
Henry David Thoreau (1817–62) US writer.
Walden, 'Economy'

1855

650 Come into the garden, Maud,
For the black bat, night, has flown,
Come into the garden, Maud,
I am here at the gate alone.
Alfred, Lord Tennyson (1809–92) British
poet.
Maud, I

1856

651 If suffer we must, let's suffer on the heights.
Victor Hugo (1802–85) French writer.
Contemplations, 'Les Malheureux'

1860

652* All generalizations are dangerous, even this
one.
Alexandre Dumas, fils (1824–95) French
writer.
Attrib.

653* The shades of night were falling fast,
As through an Alpine village passed
A youth, who bore, 'mid snow and ice,
A banner with the strange device,
Excelsior!
Henry Wadsworth Longfellow (1807–82)
US poet.
Opening of a poem best known as a Victorian
drawing-room ballad, and the butt of many music-
hall jokes. Excelsior means 'higher' (Latin)
Excelsior

1864

654 The formula 'Two and two make five' is not
without its attractions.
Fedor Mikhailovich Dostoevsky (1821–
81) Russian novelist.
Notes from the Underground

1865

655 The Owl and the Pussy-Cat went to sea
In a beautiful pea-green boat,
They took some honey, and plenty of money,
Wrapped up in a five-pound note.
Edward Lear (1812–88) British artist and
writer.
The Owl and the Pussy-Cat

1870

656 I'm the king of the castle,
Get down you dirty rascal.
Brand's Popular Antiquities

With Hindsight

20th century

657 Albert was merely a young foreigner, who suf-

fered from having no vices, and whose only claim to distinction was that he had happened to marry the Queen of England.
Lytton Strachey (1880–1932) British writer.
Queen Victoria, Ch. 5

658 Yet her conception of God was certainly not orthodox. She felt towards Him as she might have felt towards a glorified sanitary engineer; and in some of her speculations she seems hardly to distinguish between the Deity and the Drains.
Lytton Strachey
Eminent Victorians, 'Florence Nightingale'

659 He was what I often think is a dangerous thing for a statesman to be — a student of history; and like most of those who study history, he learned from the mistakes of the past how to make new ones.
A. J. P. Taylor (1906–90) British historian.
Referring to Napoleon III
The Listener, 6 June 1963

660 No writer before the middle of the 19th century wrote about the working classes other than as grotesque or as pastoral decoration. Then when they were given the vote certain writers started to suck up to them.
Evelyn Waugh (1903–66) British novelist.
Interview
Paris Review, 1963

11

The Age of Imperialism (1870–1913)

Although not formally proclaimed until 1871, the Prussian-dominated German empire was forged by the military defeat of France in the Franco-Prussian War (1870). Brash and confident, the new German empire epitomized the imperialism that dominated European politics in this period. Most of the European powers, ambitious for prestige and new trading outlets for their rapidly developing industries, acquired colonies in other continents. From 1880 to 1912 most of Africa was partitioned; by 1913 the European powers ruled most of the world. The greatest of these European empires was British, although her lead in industrial production was now challenged – and, by 1913, surpassed – by Germany. This aggressive economic competition was reflected in the political relations between the powers and inevitably in preparations for the next war; indeed, the first of the alliances that operated in World War I was established as early as 1879.

This period was also remarkable for two other major developments – one technological and the other political. The internal-combustion engine brought the car and aeroplane into people's lives, while the radio made instant communication possible between the ends of the earth. The political consequence of this advance of technology in the imperialist framework was the emergence of socialism; an inevitable reaction against the exploitation of the masses by the industrial barons, it was confined at first to a few revolutionaries. However, before long socialist ideas took root in many countries to form the basis of the political party of the working classes.

Politics, Government, and World Events

1870
---

1 The Chancellor of the Exchequer is a man whose duties make him more or less of a taxing machine. He is intrusted with a certain amount of misery which it is his duty to distribute as fairly as he can.
Robert Lowe (1811–92) British lawyer and politician.
Speech, House of Commons, 11 Apr 1870

1872
---

2 We will not go to Canossa.
Bismarck (1815–98) German statesman.
A declaration of his anti-Roman Catholic policy; the Emperor Henry IV had submitted to Pope Gregory VII at Canossa, N. Italy, in 1077
Speech, Reichstag, 14 May 1872

3 The wish to spread those opinions that we hold conducive to our own welfare is so deeply rooted in the English character that few of us can escape its influence.
Samuel Butler (1835–1902) British writer.
Erewhon, Ch. 20

4 It would be better that England should be free than that England should be compulsorily sober.
William Connor Magee (1821–91) British clergyman.
Speech on the Intoxicating Liquor Bill, House of Lords, 2 May 1872

1874
---

5 . . . a great master of gibes and flouts and jeers.
Benjamin Disraeli (1804–81) British statesman.
Referring to Lord Salisbury
Speech, House of Commons, 5 Aug 1874

1876
---

6 Let the Turks now carry away their abuses in the only possible manner, namely by carrying off themselves. Their Zaptiehs and their Mudirs, their Bimbashis and their Yuzbachis, their Kaimakans and their Pashas, one and all, bag and baggage, shall, I hope, clear out from the province they have desolated and profaned.
William Ewart Gladstone (1809–98) British statesman.
Reaction to the massacres of Bulgarians committed by Turkish Bashi-Bazouks (irregular troops)
The Bulgarian Horrors and the Question of the East (pamphlet, 6 Sept 1876)

7 The healthy bones of a single Pomeranian grenadier.
Bismarck (1815–98) German statesman.
A price too high for Germany to pay regarding the Eastern Question
Speech, Reichstag, 5 Dec 1876

8 I am dead: dead, but in the Elysian fields.
Benjamin Disraeli (1804–81) British statesman.
Said on his move to the House of Lords
Attrib.

9 One good turn deserves another.
Caption to a cartoon after Disraeli had become Earl of Beaconsfield; Queen Victoria had been proclaimed Empress of India on 1 May 1876
Punch, 16 Aug 1876

1877
---

10 Gladstone, like Richelieu, can't write. Nothing can be more unmusical, more involved or more uncouth than all his scribblement.
Benjamin Disraeli (1804–81) British statesman.
Letter, 3 Oct 1877

11 Many, if not most, of our Indian wars have had their origin in broken promises and acts of injustice on our part.
Rutherford B. Hayes (1822–93) US president.
Message to Congress, 4 Dec 1877

12 Men are made by nature unequal. It is vain, therefore, to treat them as if they were equal.
J. A. Froude (1818–94) British historian.
Short Studies on Great Subjects, 'Party Politics'

1878
---

13 An honest broker.
Bismarck (1815–98) German statesman.
His professed role in the diplomacy of 1878, including the Congress of Berlin
Speech, Reichstag, 19 Feb 1878

14 Lord Salisbury and myself have brought you back peace – but a peace I hope with honour.
Benjamin Disraeli (1804–81) British statesman.
Speech, House of Commons, 16 July 1878

15 A sophistical rhetorician inebriated with the exuberance of his own verbosity.
Benjamin Disraeli
Referring to Gladstone
Speech, 27 July 1878

16 We don't want to fight, but, by jingo if we do,
We've got the ships, we've got the men, we've got the money too.
We've fought the Bear before, and while Britons shall be true,
The Russians shall not have Constantinople.
George William Hunt (c. 1829–1904) British writer.
We Don't Want to Fight

17 The state is not 'abolished', it withers away.
Friedrich Engels (1820–95) German communist.
Anti-Dühring

18 I always voted at my party's call,
And I never thought of thinking for myself at all.
W. S. Gilbert (1836–1911) British dramatist.
HMS Pinafore, I

19 Horny-handed sons of toil.
Denis Kearney (1847–1907) US trade-union leader.
Speech, San Francisco, c. 1878

1879

20 I am tired and sick of war. Its glory is all moonshine . . . War is hell.
General William Sherman (1820–91) US general.
Attrib. in address, Michigan Military Academy, 19 June 1879

1880

21 Force is not a remedy.
John Bright (1811–89) British radical politician.
Speech, Birmingham, 16 Nov 1880

22 When a man takes a farm from which another has been evicted, you must show him . . . by leaving him severely alone, by putting him into a moral Coventry, by isolating him from his kind as if he were a leper of old – you must show him your detestation of the crimes he has committed.
Charles Stewart Parnell (1846–91) Member of Parliament and champion of Irish Home Rule.
The first person to be so treated was a Captain Boycott – hence the verb, 'to boycott'
Speech, Ennis, 19 Sept 1880

23* He speaks to Me as if I was a public meeting.
Victoria (1819–1901) Queen of the United Kingdom.
Referring to Gladstone
Collections and Recollections (G. W. E. Russell), Ch. 14

24* Walk wide o' the Widow at Windsor,
For 'alf o' Creation she owns:
We have bought 'er the same with sword an' the flame,
An' we've salted it down with our bones.
Rudyard Kipling (1865–1936) Indian-born British writer.
Referring to Queen Victoria
The Widow at Windsor

1881

25 The danger is not that a particular class is unfit to govern. Every class is unfit to govern.
Lord Acton (1834–1902) British historian.
Letter to Mary Gladstone, 1881

26 No, it is better not. She will only ask me to take a message to Albert.
Benjamin Disraeli (1804–81) British statesman.
On his deathbed, declining an offer of a visit from Queen Victoria

27 . . . a man who, with all his great qualities, was unable to decide a general principle of action, or to ensure that when decided on it should be carried out by his subordinates.
Marquess of Salisbury (1830–1903) British statesman.
Referring to Benjamin Disraeli
Chapters of Autobiography (A. J. Balfour)

28* A balanced state of well-modulated dissatisfaction.
Eduard, Count von Taaffe (1833–95) Austrian Prime Minister (1868–70, 1879–93).
Referring to his policy towards nationalistic tensions within the Austro-Hungarian Empire
Remark

29* It was a brilliant affair; water flowed like champagne.
William M. Evarts (1818–1901) US lawyer and statesman.
Describing a dinner given by US President Rutherford B. Hayes (1877–81), an advocate of temperance
Attrib.

30 Log-cabin to White House.
W. M. Thayer (1820–98) US writer.
The title of his biography of James Garfield, 20th US president (1881), who was assassinated soon after taking office

---

1882

31 Argue as you please, you are nowhere, that grand old man, the Prime Minister, insists on the other thing.
Lord Northcote (1818–87) British statesman.
Referring to Gladstone: the phrase, and its acronym GOM, became his nickname – temporarily reversed to MOG ('Murderer of Gordon') in 1885, after the death of General Gordon at Khartoum
Speech, Liverpool, 12 Apr 1882

32 Bow, bow, ye lower middle classes!
Bow, bow, ye tradesmen, bow, ye masses!
W. S. Gilbert (1836–1911) British dramatist.
Iolanthe, I

33 The House of Peers, throughout the war,
Did nothing in particular,
And did it very well.
W. S. Gilbert
Iolanthe, II

34 I often think it's comical
How Nature always does contrive
That every boy and every gal
That's born into the world alive
Is either a little Liberal
Or else a little Conservative!
W. S. Gilbert
Iolanthe, II

35 The majority has the might – more's the pity –

but it hasn't right . . . The minority is always
right.
Henrik Ibsen (1828–1906) Norwegian
dramatist.
An Enemy of the People, IV

36 The worst enemy of truth and freedom in our
society is the compact majority. Yes, the
damned, compact, liberal majority.
Henrik Ibsen
An Enemy of the People, IV

1883

37 Lord Salisbury constitutes himself the spokesman of a class, of the class to which he himself belongs, who 'toil not neither do they
spin'.
Joseph Chamberlain (1836–1914) British
politician.
Referring to the aristocracy
Speech, Birmingham, 30 Mar 1883

38 We the English seem, as it were, to have conquered and peopled half the world in a fit of
absence of mind.
John Robert Seeley (1834–95) British
historian.
The Expansion of England, I

39 The philosophers have only interpreted the
world in various ways; the point is to change it.
Karl Marx (1818–83) German philosopher and
revolutionary.
Theses on Feuerbach

40 All I know is that I am not a Marxist.
Karl Marx
Attrib.

41 Eena, meena, mina, mo,
Catch a nigger by his toe;
If he hollers, let him go,
Eena, meena, mina, mo.
Games and Songs of American Children
(Newell)

1884

42 The Empire is a Commonwealth of Nations.
Earl of Rosebery (1847–1929) British
statesman.
Speech, Adelaide, 18 Jan 1884

43 For the purposes of recreation he has selected
the felling of trees, and we may usefully remark that his amusements, like his politics, are
essentially destructive . . . The forest laments
in order that Mr Gladstone may perspire.
Randolph Churchill (1849–95) British
politician.
Speech, Blackpool, 24 Jan 1884

44 The liberty the citizen enjoys is to be measured
not by the governmental machinery he lives
under, whether representative or other, but by
the paucity of restraints it imposes on him.
Herbert Spencer (1820–1903) British
philosopher.
Man versus the State

1885

45 The G.O.M., when his life ebbs out,
Will ride in a fiery chariot,
And sit in state
On a red-hot plate
Between Pilate and Judas Iscariot.
Anonymous
Gladstone, known as the Grand Old Man, was
blamed for the death of General Gordon at
Khartoum
The Faber Book of English History in Verse
(Kenneth Baker)

46 No man has a right to fix the boundary of the
march of a nation; no man has a right to say
to his country – thus far shalt thou go and no
further.
Charles Stewart Parnell (1846–91) Irish
politician.
Speech at Cork, 21 Jan 1885

47 The public be damned. I am working for my
stockholders.
William Henry Vanderbilt (1821–85) US
railroad chief.
Refusing to speak to a reporter, who was seeking to find out his views on behalf of the public

48 Three acres and a cow.
Jesse Collings (1831–1920) British politician.
Slogan used in his land-reform propaganda

1886

49 Ulster will fight; Ulster will be right.
Randolph Churchill (1849–95) British
politician.
Letter, 7 May 1886

50 All the world over, I will back the masses
against the classes.
William Ewart Gladstone (1809–98) British
statesman.
Speech, Liverpool, 28 June 1886

51 An old man in a hurry.
Randolph Churchill (1849–95) British
politician.
Referring to Gladstone
Speech, June 1886

52 Give me your tired, your poor,
Your huddled masses yearning to breathe
free,
The wretched refuse of your teeming shore,
Send these, the homeless, tempest-tossed to
me,
I lift my lamp beside the golden door!
Emma Lazarus (1849–87) US poet and
philanthropist.
Used as an inscription on the Statue of Liberty
The New Colossus

53 Dialect words – those terrible marks of the
beast to the truly genteel.
Thomas Hardy (1840–1928) British novelist.
The Mayor of Casterbridge, Ch. 20

1887

54 Power tends to corrupt, and absolute power

corrupts absolutely. Great men are almost always bad men . . . There is no worse heresy than that the office sanctifies the holder of it.
Lord Acton (1834–1902) British historian.
Often misquoted as 'Power corrupts . . .'
Letter to Bishop Mandell Creighton, 5 Apr 1887

1888

55 We are part of the community of Europe and we must do our duty as such.
Marquess of Salisbury (1830–1903) British statesman.
Speech, Caernarvon, 11 Apr 1888

56 I haven't got time to be tired.
Wilhelm I (1797–1888) King of Prussia and Emperor of Germany.
Said during his last illness

57 Eight little whores, with no hope of Heaven,
Gladstone may save one, then there'll be seven.
Seven little whores begging for a shilling,
One stays in Heneage Court, then there's a killing.

Six little whores, glad to be alive,
One sidles up to Jack, then there are five.
Four and whore rhyme aright, so do three and me.
I'll set the town alight, ere there are two.

Two little whores, shivering with fright,
Seek a cosy doorway, in the middle of the night.
Jack's knife flashes, then there's but one.
And the last one's ripest for Jack's idea of fun.
Anonymous
Referring to the Whitechapel Murders (1888) – a series of savage murders of about six prostitutes in the Whitechapel area of London. The murderer, who was never caught, was nicknamed 'Jack the Ripper' because of the extensive mutilation of most of the corpses
The Faber Book of English History in Verse (Kenneth Baker)

58 I'm not a butcher,
I'm not a Yid,
Nor yet a foreign skipper,
But I'm your own light-hearted friend,
Yours truly, Jack the Ripper.
Anonymous
The Faber Book of English History in Verse (Kenneth Baker)

59 Jack the Ripper's dead,
And lying in his bed.
He cut his throat
With Sunlight Soap.
Jack the Ripper's dead.
Anonymous
The Faber Book of English History in Verse (Kenneth Baker)

1889

60 The Austrian Government . . . is a system of despotism tempered by casualness.
Victor Adler (1852–1918) Austrian socialist.
Speech, International Socialist Congress, Paris, 17 July 1889

61 The people's flag is deepest red;
It shrouded oft our martyred dead,
And ere their limbs grew stiff and cold,
Their heart's blood dyed its every fold.
　Then raise the scarlet standard high!
　Within its shade we'll live or die.
　Tho' cowards flinch and traitors sneer,
　We'll keep the red flag flying here.
James Connell (1852–1929) British socialist.
Traditionally sung at the close of annual conferences of the British Labour Party
The Red Flag, in *Songs that made History* (H. E. Piggot), Ch. 6

1890

62 Dropping the pilot.
John Tenniel (1820–1914) British illustrator and cartoonist.
Caption of a cartoon; the cartoon refers to Bismarck's resignation portraying him as a ship's pilot walking down the gangway of the ship while Wilhelm II watches from the deck
Punch, 29 Mar 1890

63 The white man knows how to make everything, but he does not know how to distribute it.
Sitting Bull (c. 1834–90) US Sioux Indian chief.
Attrib.

1891

64 I will not accept if nominated, and will not serve if elected.
William Sherman (1820–91) US general.
Replying to a request that he accept the Republican presidential nomination
Attrib.

65 Democracy means simply the bludgeoning of the people by the people for the people.
Oscar Wilde (1854–1900) Irish-born British dramatist.
The Soul of Man under Socialism

1892

66 The danger to the country, to Europe, to her vast Empire, which is involved in having all these great interests entrusted to the shaking hand of an old, wild, and incomprehensible man of 82½, is very great!
Victoria (1819–1901) Queen of the United Kingdom.
Reaction to Gladstone's fourth and last appointment as prime minister, 1892
Letter to Lord Lansdowne, 12 Aug 1892

67 Lizzie Borden took an axe
And gave her mother forty whacks;

When she saw what she had done
She gave her father forty-one!
Anonymous
On 4 Aug 1892 in Fall River, Massachusetts, Lizzie Borden was acquitted of the murder of her stepmother and her father

---

1893

68　It is only when you get to see and realize what India is – that she is the strength and the greatness of England – it is only then that you feel that every nerve a man may strain, every energy he may put forward, cannot be devoted to a nobler purpose than keeping tight the cords that hold India to ourselves.
George Curzon (1859–1925) British politician.
Speech, Southport, 15 Mar 1893

69　Between complete Socialism and Communism there is no difference whatever in my mind. Communism is in fact the completion of Socialism; when that ceases to be militant and becomes triumphant, it will be communism.
William Morris (1834–96) English Utopian socialist.
Lecture to the Hammersmith Socialist Society, 1893

70　O beautiful for spacious skies,
For amber waves of grain,
For purple mountain majesties
Above the fruited plain!
America! America!
God shed His grace on thee
And crown thy good with brotherhood
From sea to shining sea!
Katharine Lee Bates (1859–1929) US writer and poet.
America the Beautiful

1894

71　Before Irish Home Rule is conceded by the Imperial Parliament, England as the predominant member of the three kingdoms will have to be convinced of its justice and equity.
Lord Rosebery (1847–1929) British statesman.
Speech, House of Lords, 11 Mar 1894

72　The majestic egalitarianism of the law, which forbids rich and poor alike to sleep under bridges, to beg in the streets, and to steal bread.
Anatole France (Jacques Anatole François Thibault; 1844–1924) French writer.
The Red Lily, Ch. 7

1895

73　The duty of an opposition is to oppose.
Randolph Churchill (1849–95) British politician.
Lord Randolph Churchill (W. S. Churchill)

1896

74　Parliaments are the great lie of our time.
Konstantin Pobedonostsev (1827–1907) Russian jurist and Procurator of the Holy Synod.
Moskovskii Sbornik

75　I shall maintain the principle of autocracy just as firmly and unflinchingly as it was upheld by my own ever to be remembered dead father.
Nicholas II (1868–1918) Tsar of Russia.
Declaration to representatives of Tver, 17 Jan 1896

76　The German Empire has become a world empire.
Wilhelm II (1859–1941) King of Prussia and Emperor of Germany.
Speech, Berlin, 18 Jan 1896

77　We have stood alone in that which is called isolation – our splendid isolation, as one of our colonial friends was good enough to call it.
George Joachim Goschen (1831–1907) British politician.
Speech, Lewes, 26 Feb 1896

78　East and west on fields forgotten
Bleach the bones of comrades slain,
Lovely lads and dead and rotten;
None that go return again.
A. E. Housman (1859–1936) British scholar and poet.
A Shropshire Lad, 'The Welsh Marches'

79　Written by office boys for office boys.
Marquess of Salisbury (1830–1903) British statesman.
Reaction to the launch of the *Daily Mail*, 1896
Northcliffe, an Intimate Biography (Hamilton Fyfe), Ch. 4

1897

80　Move Queen Anne? Most certainly not! Why it might some day be suggested that *my* statue should be moved, which I should much dislike.
Victoria (1819–1901) Queen of the United Kingdom.
Said at the time of her Diamond Jubilee (1897), when it was suggested that the statue of Queen Anne should be moved from outside St. Paul's
Men, Women and Things (Duke of Portland), Ch. 5

81　The British soldier can stand up to anything except the British War Office.
George Bernard Shaw (1856–1950) Irish dramatist and critic.
The Devil's Disciple, II

82　It is by the goodness of God that in our country we have those three unspeakably precious things: freedom of speech, freedom of conscience, and the prudence never to practise either of them.
Mark Twain (Samuel Langhorne Clemens; 1835–1910) US writer.
Following the Equator, heading of Ch. 20

1898

83 If there is ever another war in Europe, it will come out of some damned silly thing in the Balkans.
Bismarck (1815–98) German statesman.
Remark to Ballen, shortly before Bismarck's death

84 Whatever happens, we have got
The Maxim Gun, and they have not.
Hilaire Belloc (1870–1953) French-born British poet.
Referring to African natives
The Modern Traveller

85 Don't cheer, boys; the poor devils are dying.
John Woodward Philip (1840–1900) US naval officer.
Restraining his victorious crew during the naval battle off Santiago in the Spanish-American War
Attrib.

86 *J'accuse.*
I accuse.
Emile Zola (1840–1902) French novelist.
Title of an open letter to the French President, denouncing the French army's conduct in the Dreyfus affair – a major political scandal in France that centred on the false conviction (1894) of Albert Dreyfus, a Jewish army officer, for betraying state secrets
L'Aurore, 13 Jan 1898

87 Truth is on the march; nothing can stop it now.
Emile Zola
Referring to the Dreyfus affair
Attrib.

88 I know not whether Laws be right,
Or whether Laws be wrong;
All that we know who lie in gaol
Is that the wall is strong;
And that each day is like a year,
A year whose days are long.
Oscar Wilde (1854–1900) Irish-born British dramatist.
The Ballad of Reading Gaol, V:1

1899

The Boer War (1899–1902)

The result of tensions between British and Boer (Afrikaner) settlers in southern Africa, the war was initially a success for the Boers. Large numbers of British reinforcements then forced them to adopt guerilla tactics. The British, under Lord Kitchener, responded by devastating the countryside and rounding up the population into concentration camps, where some 20 000 Boer women and children died. Finally brought to acknowledge defeat, the Boers' republics were annexed by Britain.

89 Please understand that there is no one depressed in *this* house; we are not interested in the possibilities of defeat; they do not exist.
Victoria (1819–1901) Queen of the United Kingdom.
Referring to the Boer War; said to Balfour
Life of Salisbury (Lady G. Cecil)

90 I thought he was a young man of promise; but it appears he was a young man of promises.
Arthur Balfour (1848–1930) British statesman.
Said of Winston Churchill on his entry into politics, 1899
Winston Churchill (Randolph Churchill), Vol. I

91 Conspicuous consumption of valuable goods is a means of reputability to the gentleman of leisure.
Thorstein Bunde Veblen (1857–1929) US social scientist.
The Theory of the Leisure Class

1900s

92 The Admiral of the Atlantic salutes the Admiral of the Pacific.
Wilhelm II (1859–1941) King of Prussia and Emperor of Germany.
Telegram sent to Czar Nicholas II during a naval exercise
The Shadow of the Winter Palace (E. Crankshaw)

93 And when we open our dykes, the waters are ten feet deep.
Wilhelmina (1880–1962) Queen of the Netherlands.
Replying to a boast by Wilhelm II of Germany that his guardsmen were all seven feet tall
Attrib.

1900

94 It is beginning to be hinted that we are a nation of amateurs.
Earl of Rosebery (1847–1929) British statesman.
Rectorial Address, Glasgow, 16 Nov 1900

95* Take up the White Man's burden –
And reap his old reward:
The blame of those ye better,
The hate of those ye guard.
Rudyard Kipling (1865–1936) Indian-born British writer.
The White Man's Burden

96* The radical invents the views. When he has worn them out, the conservative adopts them.
Mark Twain (Samuel Langhorne Clemens; 1835–1910) US writer.
Notebooks

1901

97 When was a war not a war? When it was carried on by methods of barbarism.
Henry Campbell-Bannerman (1836–1908) British statesman.
Referring to the Boer War
Speech, National Reform Union Dinner, 14 June 1901

98 There is a homely adage which runs 'Speak softly and carry a big stick, you will go far'.
Theodore Roosevelt (1858–1919) US Republican president.
Speech, Minnesota State Fair, 2 Sept 1901

99 You have to clean your plate.
Lord Rosebery (1847–1929) British statesman.
Said to the Liberal Party
Speech, Chesterfield, 16 Dec 1901

100 'My country, right or wrong' is a thing that no patriot would think of saying, except in a desperate case. It is like saying 'My mother, drunk or sober.'
G. K. Chesterton (1874–1936) British writer.
The Defendant

101 The time's come: there's a terrific thundercloud advancing upon us, a mighty storm is coming to freshen us up.... It's going to blow away all this idleness and indifference, and prejudice against work.... I'm going to work, and in twenty-five or thirty years' time every man and woman will be working.
Anton Chekhov (1860–1904) Russian dramatist.
Three Sisters, I

102 To disarm the strong and arm the weak would be to change the social order which it's my job to preserve. Justice is the means by which established injustices are sanctioned.
Anatole France (Jacques Anatole François Thibault; 1844–1924) French writer.
Crainquebille

1902

103 Perhaps it is God's will to lead the people of South Africa through defeat and humiliation to a better future and a brighter day.
Jan Smuts (1870–1950) South African statesman and general.
Speaking to Boer delegates at the peace conference that ended the Boer War
Speech, Vereeniging, 31 May 1902

104 Three words made peace and union in South Africa: 'methods of barbarism'.
Louis Botha (1862–1919) South African statesman.
Life of Campbell-Bannerman (J. A. Spender)

105 The rights and interests of the laboring man will be protected and cared for, not by the labor agitators, but by the Christian men to whom God in His infinite wisdom has given control of the property interests of the country.
George Baer (1842–1914) American railroad magnate.
Written during the Pennsylvania miners' strike
Letter to the press, Oct 1902

106 The first requisite of a good citizen in this Republic of ours is that he shall be able and willing to pull his weight.
Theodore Roosevelt (1858–1919) US Republican president.
Speech, New York, 11 Nov 1902

107 Remember that you are an Englishman, and have consequently won first prize in the lottery of life.
Cecil Rhodes (1853–1902) South African statesman.
Dear Me (Peter Ustinov), Ch. 4

108 So little done, so much to do.
Cecil Rhodes
Attrib.

109 ...militarism...is one of the chief bulwarks of capitalism, and the day that militarism is undermined, capitalism will fail.
Helen Keller (1880–1968) US writer and lecturer.
The Story of My Life

1903

110 ...content to follow mechanically the lead given by their fathers. They worked shorter hours, and they exerted themselves less to obtain new practical ideas than their fathers had done, and thus a part of England's leadership was destroyed rapidly. In the 'nineties it became clear that in the future Englishmen must take business as seriously as their grand fathers had done, and as their American and German rivals were doing: that their training for business must be methodical, like that of their new rivals, and not merely practical, on lines that had sufficed for the simpler world of two generations ago: and lastly that the time had passed at which they could afford merely to teach foreigners and not learn from them in return.
Alfred Marshall (1842–1924) British economist.
Referring to British manufacturers
Memorandum; White Paper, 1908

111 In an English ship, they say, it is poor grub, poor pay, and easy work; in an American ship, good grub, good pay, and hard work. And this is applicable to the working populations of both countries.
Jack London (1876–1916) US novelist.
The People of the Abyss, Ch. 20

112 A man who is good enough to shed his blood for the country is good enough to be given a square deal afterwards. More than that no man

is entitled to, and less than that no man shall have.
Theodore Roosevelt (1858–1919) US Republican president.
Speech at the Lincoln Monument, Springfield, Illinois, 4 June 1903

113 Give women the vote, and in five years there will be a crushing tax on bachelors.
George Bernard Shaw (1856–1950) Irish dramatist.
Man and Superman, Preface

114 Titles distinguish the mediocre, embarrass the superior, and are disgraced by the inferior.
George Bernard Shaw
Man and Superman, 'Maxims for Revolutionists'

115* Democracy substitutes election by the incompetent many for appointment by the corrupt few.
George Bernard Shaw
Man and Superman, 'Maxims for Revolutionists'

116* Liberty means responsibility. That is why most men dread it.
George Bernard Shaw
Man and Superman, 'Maxims for Revolutionists'

117 I am a gentleman. I live by robbing the poor.
George Bernard Shaw
Man and Superman

118 Kings are not born, they are made by artificial hallucination.
George Bernard Shaw
Man and Superman

1904
---

119 Provided that the City of London remains as at present, the Clearing-house of the World.
Joseph Chamberlain (1836–1914) British politician.
Speech, Guildhall, London, 19 Jan 1904

120 The day of small nations has long passed away. The day of Empires has come.
Joseph Chamberlain
Speech, Birmingham, 12 May 1904

121 You cannot feed the hungry on statistics.
David Lloyd George (1863–1945) British Liberal statesman.
Advocating Tariff Reform
Speech, 1904

122 In the Western hemisphere the adherence of the United States to the Monroe Doctrine may force the United States, however reluctantly, in flagrant cases of wrongdoing or impotence, to the exercise of an international police power.
Theodore Roosevelt (1858–1919) US Republican president.
Message to Congress, 6 Dec 1904

123 We are all Socialists now.
William Harcourt (1827–1904) British statesman.
Attrib.

1905
---

124 'It is my duty to warn you that it will be used against you,' cried the Inspector, with the magnificent fair play of the British criminal law.
Arthur Conan Doyle (1856–1930) British writer.
The Dancing Men

1906
---

125 I am a Catholic. As far as possible I go to Mass every day. As far as possible I kneel down and tell these beads every day. If you reject me on account of my religion, I shall thank God that he has spared me the indignity of being your representative.
Hilaire Belloc (1870–1953) French-born British poet.
Said in his first election campaign
Speech, Salford, 1906

126 It cannot in the opinion of His Majesty's Government be classified as slavery in the extreme acceptance of the word without some risk of terminological inexactitude.
Winston Churchill (1874–1965) British statesman.
Speech, House of Commons, 22 Feb 1906

127 When a liberal is abused, he says: Thank God they didn't beat me. When he is beaten, he thanks God they didn't kill him. When he is killed, he will thank God that his immortal soul has been delivered from its mortal clay.
Lenin (Vladimir Ilich Ulyanov; 1870–1924) Russian revolutionary leader.
Lenin heard this characterization at a meeting, and repeated it with approval
The Government's Falsification of the Duma and the Tasks of the Social-Democrats, 'Proletary', Dec 1906

128 Lenin's method leads to this: the party organization at first substitutes itself for the party as a whole. Then the central committee substitutes itself for the party organization, and finally a single dictator substitutes himself for the central committee.
Leon Trotsky (Lev Davidovich Bronstein; 1879–1940) Russian revolutionary.
The Communist Parties of Western Europe (N. McInnes), Ch. 3

1907
---

129 The Tsar is not treacherous but he is weak. Weakness is not treachery, but it fulfils all its functions.
Wilhelm II (1859–1941) King of Prussia and Emperor of Germany.
Comment written on a despatch from the German ambassador to Russia, 16 Mar 1907
Referring to Nicholas II

130 Mr Balfour's Poodle.
David Lloyd George (1863–1945) British Liberal statesman.
Referring to the House of Lords and its in-built

Conservative majority; said in reply to a claim that it was 'the watchdog of the nation'
Remark, House of Commons, 26 June 1907

131 Property is organised robbery.
George Bernard Shaw (1856–1950) Irish dramatist and critic.
Major Barbara, Preface

132 Alcohol is a very necessary article . . . It enables Parliament to do things at eleven at night that no sane person would do at eleven in the morning.
George Bernard Shaw
Major Barbara, II

133 He knows nothing; and he thinks he knows everything. That points clearly to a political career.
George Bernard Shaw
Major Barbara, III

1908

134 In England, Justice is open to all, like the Ritz hotel.
James Mathew (1830–1908) British judge.
Also attrib. to Lord Darling
Miscellany-at-Law (R. E. Megarry)

135 America is God's Crucible, the great Melting-Pot where all the races of Europe are melting and re-forming!
Israel Zangwill (1864–1926) British writer.
The Melting Pot, I

The Suffragettes

The Women's Social and Political Union was founded in 1903 by Emmeline Pankhurst to campaign for female suffrage in parliamentary elections. Its protest activities steadily increased in militancy, but were called off on the outbreak of World War I. *See also* Attitudes: Men and Women.

136 Votes for Women.
Slogan

137 We are not ashamed of what we have done, because, when you have a great cause to fight for, the moment of greatest humiliation is the moment when the spirit is proudest.
Christabel Pankhurst (1880–1958) British suffragette.
Speech, Albert Hall, London, 19 Mar 1908

138 We have taken this action, because as women . . . we realize that the condition of our sex is so deplorable that it is our duty even to break the law in order to call attention to the reasons why we do so.
Emmeline Pankhurst (1858–1928) British suffragette.
Speech in court, 21 Oct 1908
Shoulder to Shoulder (ed. Midge Mackenzie)

139* . . . if civilisation is to advance at all in the future, it must be through the help of women,
women freed of their political shackles, women with full power to work their will in society. It was rapidly becoming clear to my mind that men regarded women as a servant class in the community, and that women were going to remain in the servant class until they lifted themselves out of it.
Emmeline Pankhurst
My Own Story

140* Women had always fought for men, and for their children. Now they were ready to fight for their own human rights. Our militant movement was established.
Emmeline Pankhurst
My Own Story

141* Here's to the lot of them, murderer, thief, Forger and lunatic too, Sir –
Infants, and those who get parish relief, And women, it's perfectly true, Sir –
Please to take note, they are in the same boat:
They have not a chance of recording the vote.
H. Crawford
Referring to the women's suffrage movement
In the Same Boat

142* I see some rats have got in; let them squeal, it doesn't matter.
David Lloyd George (1863–1945) British Liberal statesman.
Said when suffragettes interrupted a meeting
The Faber Book of English History in Verse (Kenneth Baker)

1909

143 There are no credentials They do not even need a medical certificate. They need not be sound either in body or mind. They only require a certificate of birth – just to prove that they are first of the litter. You would not choose a spaniel on these principles.
David Lloyd George
Referring to members of the House of Lords
Budget Speech, 1909

144 A fully equipped Duke costs as much to keep up as two Dreadnoughts, and Dukes are just as great a terror, and they last longer.
David Lloyd George
Speech, Limehouse, 30 July 1909

145 Assassination is the extreme form of censorship.
George Bernard Shaw (1856–1950) Irish dramatist and critic.
The Shewing-Up of Blanco Posnet, 'The Limits of Toleration'

1910

146 Wait and see.
Herbert Henry Asquith (1852–1928) British statesman.
In various speeches, 1910

147 Compromise used to mean that half a loaf was better than no bread. Among modern states-

men it really seems to mean that half a loaf is better than a whole loaf.
G. K. Chesterton (1874–1936) British writer.
What's Wrong with the World

148* Have you heard? The Prime Minister has resigned and Northcliffe has sent for the King.
Said by a member of Lord Northcliffe's staff; at the height of his career, Northcliffe owned, among other newspapers, *The Times*, *The Observer*, the *Daily Mail*, the *Daily Mirror*, and the *London Evening News*
Northcliffe, An Intimate Biography (Hamilton Fyfe)

149* Land of Hope and Glory, Mother of the Free,
How shall we extol thee, who are born of thee?
Wider still and wider shall thy bounds be set;
God who made thee mighty, make thee mightier yet.
A. C. Benson (1862–1925) British writer.
Land of Hope and Glory

150 And this is good old Boston,
The home of the bean and the cod,
Where the Lowells talk only to Cabots,
And the Cabots talk only to God.
John Collins Bossidy (1860–1928) US writer.
The Lowells and the Cabots were prominent families in Boston society
Toast at Holy Cross Alumni dinner, 1910

1911

151 I would make great sacrifices to preserve peace. . . . But if a situation were to be forced upon us, in which peace could only be preserved by the surrender of the great and beneficent position Britain has won by centuries of heroism and achievement . . . I say emphatically that peace at that price would be a humiliation intolerable for a great country like ours to endure.
David Lloyd George (1863–1945) British Liberal statesman.
British Documents (Gooch and Temperley), Vol. VII

152 If, therefore, war should ever come between these two countries, which Heaven forbid! it will not, I think, be due to irresistible natural laws, it will be due to the want of human wisdom.
Bonar Law (1858–1923) British statesman.
Referring to the UK and Germany
Speech, House of Commons, 27 Nov 1911

153 We can now look forward with something like confidence to the time when war between civilized nations will be considered as antiquated as a duel.
George Peabody Gooch (1873–1968) English historian and Liberal MP.
History of Our Time

154 I hope to see the day when the American flag will float over every square foot of the British

North American possessions clear to the North Pole.
James Beauchamp Clark (1850–1921) Speaker of US House of Representatives.
Speech, House of Representatives, June 1911

1912

155 In private conversation he tries on speeches like a man trying on ties in his bedroom to see how he would look in them.
Lionel Curtis (1872–1955) British writer.
Referring to Winston Churchill
Letter to Nancy Astor, 1912

156 The only tyrannies from which men, women and children are suffering in real life are the tyrannies of minorities.
Theodore Roosevelt (1858–1919) US Republican president.
Speech, 22 Mar 1912

157 Well, I have one consolation, No candidate was ever elected ex-president by such a large majority!
William Howard Taft (1857–1930) US statesman.
Referring to his disastrous defeat in the 1912 presidential election
Attrib.

158 Great God! this is an awful place.
Captain Robert Falcon Scott (1868–1912) British explorer.
Referring to the South Pole
Journal, 17 Jan 1912

159 Had we lived, I should have had a tale to tell of the hardihood, endurance, and courage of my companions which would have stirred the heart of every Englishman. These rough notes and our dead bodies must tell the tale.
Captain Robert Falcon Scott
Scott's second expedition (1910–12) to the Antarctic, which reached the South Pole, ended in disaster when all its members perished in blizzards, only a few miles from safety
Message to the Public

160 I am just going outside and may be some time.
Captain Lawrence Oates (1880–1912) British soldier and explorer.
Said before leaving the tent and vanishing into the blizzard on the ill-fated Antarctic expedition (1910–12); Oates was afraid that his lameness would slow down the others
Journal (R. F. Scott), 17 Mar 1912

161 Hereabouts died a very gallant gentleman, Captain L. E. G. Oates of the Inniskilling Dragoons. In March 1912, returning from the Pole, he walked willingly to his death in a blizzard, to try and save his comrades, beset by hardships.
E. L. Atkinson (1882–1929) British naval officer.
Epitaph on memorial in the Antarctic

162 Well: while was fashioning
This creature of cleaving wing,
The Immanent Will that stirs and urges
everything

Prepared a sinister mate
For her – so gaily great –
A Shape of Ice, for the time far and
dissociate.

And as the smart ship grew
In stature, grace, and hue,
In shadowy silent distance grew the Iceberg
too.
Thomas Hardy (1840–1928) British novelist.
Referring to the 'Titanic', a luxury passenger
ship, thought to be unsinkable because of its
special design. It struck an iceberg on its maiden
voyage and sank, causing the loss of 1513 lives
The Convergence of the Twain

1913

163 I want to take this occasion to say that the
United States will never again seek one addi-
tional foot of territory by conquest.
Woodrow Wilson (1856–1924) US
statesman.
Speech, Mobile, 27 Oct 1913

164 Do not hit at all if it can be avoided, but never
hit softly.
Theodore Roosevelt (1858–1919) US Republican president.
Autobiography

165 So greatly did she care for freedom that she
died for it. So dearly did she love women that
she offered her life as their ransom. That is
the verdict given at the great Inquest on the
Nation on the death of Emily Wilding Davison.
Christabel Pankhurst (1880–1958) British
suffragette.
Emily Davison threw herself under the King's
horse in protest at the imprisoning of
suffragettes
The Suffragette, 13 June 1913

166 Booth died blind and still by faith he trod,
Eyes still dazzled by the ways of God.
Vachel Lindsay (1879–1931) US poet.
Referring to William Booth, the founder of the
Salvation Army, who died in 1912
General William Booth Enters Heaven

Attitudes

Art, Literature, and Music

1871

167 The Fleshly School of Poetry.
Robert Williams Buchanan (1841–1901)
British poet and writer.
Referring to Swinburne, William Morris, D. G.
Rossetti, etc.
Title of article in the *Contemporary Review*, Oct
1871

1873

168 Culture is the passion for sweetness and light,
and (what is more) the passion for making
them prevail.
Matthew Arnold (1822–88) British poet and
critic.
Literature and Dogma, Preface

1877

169 The song that we hear with our ears is only the
song that is sung in our hearts.
Ouida (Marie Louise de la Ramée; 1839–1908)
British novelist.
Wisdom, Wit and Pathos, 'Ariadne'

170 I have seen, and heard, much of Cockney impu-
dence before now; but never expected to hear
a coxcomb ask two hundred guineas for
flinging a pot of paint in the public's face.
John Ruskin (1819–1900) British art critic and
writer.
On Whistler's painting 'Nocturne in Black and
Gold'
Letter, 18 June 1877

1879

171 It takes a great deal of history to produce a lit-
tle literature.
Henry James (1843–1916) US novelist.
Life of Nathaniel Hawthorne, Ch. 1

172 He was unperfect, unfinished, inartistic; he was
worse than provincial – he was parochial.
Henry James
Referring to Thoreau
Life of Nathaniel Hawthorne, Ch. 4

1881

173 A sonnet is a moment's monument, –
Memorial from the Soul's eternity
To one dead deathless hour.
Dante Gabriel Rossetti (1828–82) British
painter and poet.
The House of Life, Introduction

174 Books are good enough in their own way, but
they are a mighty bloodless substitute for life.
Robert Louis Stevenson (1850–94) Scottish writer.
Virginibus Puerisque

1883

175 A master is dead. Today we sing no more.
Johannes Brahms (1833–97) German
composer.
Stopping a choral rehearsal on hearing of the
death of Wagner
Brahms (P. Latham)

176 Three hours a day will produce as much as a
man ought to write.
Anthony Trollope (1815–82) British novelist.
Autobiography, Ch. 15

1884

177* A good man fallen among Fabians.
Lenin (Vladimir Ilich Ulyanov; 1870–1924) Russian revolutionary leader.
Referring to Bernard Shaw
Attrib.

178 Make 'em laugh; make 'em cry; make 'em wait.
Charles Reade (1814–84) British novelist and dramatist.
Advice to an aspiring writer
Attrib.

1885

179 Listen! There never was an artistic period.
There never was an Art-loving nation.
James Whistler (1834–1903) US painter.
Attrib.

1887

180 When all is said and done, no literature can outdo the cynicism of real life; you won't intoxicate with one glass someone who has already drunk up a whole barrel.
Anton Chekhov (1860–1904) Russian dramatist.
Letter, 1887

1888

181 A criticism of life under the conditions fixed for such a criticism by the laws of poetic truth and poetic beauty.
Matthew Arnold (1822–88) British poet and critic.
Essays in Criticism, Second Series, 'The Study of Poetry'

182* The difference between genuine poetry and the poetry of Dryden, Pope, and all their school, is briefly this: their poetry is conceived and composed in their wits, genuine poetry is conceived and composed in the soul.
Matthew Arnold
Thomas Gray

183 What is poetry? The suggestion, by the imagination, of noble grounds for the noble emotions.
John Ruskin (1819–1900) British art critic and writer.
Modern Painters, Vol. III

184 The only obligation to which in advance we may hold a novel, without incurring the accusation of being arbitrary, is that it be interesting.
Henry James (1843–1916) US novelist.
Partial Portraits, 'The Art of Fiction'

185 It is very simple. The artists retired. The British remained.
James Whistler (1834–1903) US painter.
Explaining his resignation as president of the Royal Society of British Artists
Whistler Stories (D. Seitz)

1890s

186 Our mistake, you see, was to write interminable large operas, which had to fill an entire evening . . . And now along comes someone with a one- or two-act opera without all that pompous nonsense . . . that was a happy reform.
Giuseppe Verdi (1813–1901) Italian composer.
Referring to Mascagni

1891

187 There is no such thing as a moral or an immoral book. Books are well written, or badly written.
Oscar Wilde (1854–1900) Irish-born British dramatist.
The Picture of Dorian Gray, Preface

188 All Art is quite useless.
Oscar Wilde
The Picture of Dorian Gray, Preface

189 Art is the most intense mode of individualism that the world has known.
Oscar Wilde
The Soul of Man Under Socialism

190 Art never expresses anything but itself.
Oscar Wilde
The Decay of Lying

191* Genius does what it must, and Talent does what it can.
Owen Meredith (Robert Bulwer-Lytton, 1st Earl of Lytton; 1831–91) British statesman and poet.
Last Words of a Sensitive Second-rate Poet

1896

192 NINA. Your play's hard to act, there are no living people in it.
TREPLEV. Living people! We should show life neither as it is nor as it ought to be, but as we see it in our dreams.
Anton Chekhov (1860–1904) Russian dramatist.
The Seagull, I

1897

193 A work that aspires, however humbly, to the condition of art should carry its justification in every line.
Joseph Conrad (Teodor Josef Konrad Korzeniowski; 1857–1924) Polish-born British novelist.
The Nigger of the Narcissus, Preface

1898

194 Art is not a handicraft, it is the transmission of feeling the artist has experienced.
Leo Tolstoy (1828–1910) Russian writer.
What is Art?, Ch. 19

1900s

195 I have already heard it. I had better not go: I

will start to get accustomed to it and finally like it.
Nikolai Rimsky-Korsakov (1844–1908) Russian composer.
Referring to music by Debussy
Conversations with Stravinsky (Robert Craft and Igor Stravinsky)

196 To be played with both hands in the pocket.
Erik Satie (1866–1925) French composer.
Direction on one of his piano pieces
The Unimportance of Being Oscar (O. Levant)

197 *Hugo – hélas!*
André Gide (1869–1951) French novelist.
Replying to an inquiry as to whom he considered the finest poet of the 19th century.
André Gide–Paul Valéry Correspondence 1890–1942

198 ... poetry, 'The Cinderella of the Arts.'
Harriet Monroe (1860–1936) US poet and editor.
Famous American Women (Hope Stoddard), 'Harriet Monroe'

199 Out of the quarrel with others we make rhetoric; out of the quarrel with ourselves we make poetry.
W. B. Yeats (1865–1939) Irish poet.
Essay

1900

200 Something that everybody wants to have read and nobody wants to read.
Mark Twain (Samuel Langhorne Clemens; 1835–1910) US writer.
Definition of a classic of literature
Speech at Nineteenth Century Club, New York, 20 Nov 1900

201 The play was a great success, but the audience was a disaster.
Oscar Wilde (1854–1900) Irish-born British dramatist.
Referring to a play that had recently failed
Attrib.

202 One would have to have a heart of stone to read the death of Little Nell without laughing.
Oscar Wilde
Lecturing upon Dickens
Lives of the Wits (H. Pearson)

203 The last gentleman in Europe.
Ada Beddington Leverson (1862–1933) British writer.
Said of Oscar Wilde
Letters to the Sphinx (Wilde), 'Reminiscences', 2

1901

204 It does not follow ... that the right to criticize Shakespeare involves the power of writing better plays. And in fact ... I do not profess to write better plays.
George Bernard Shaw (1856–1950) Irish dramatist and critic.
Three Plays for Puritans, Preface

1902

205 Art is ruled uniquely by the imagination.
Benedetto Croce (1866–1952) Italian philosopher.
Esthetic, Ch. 1

1903

206 Every man's work, whether it be literature or music or pictures or architecture or anything else, is always a portrait of himself.
Samuel Butler (1835–1902) British writer.
The Way of All Flesh, Ch. 14

207 Well, not bad, but there are decidedly too many of them, and they are not very well arranged. I would have done it differently.
James Whistler (1834–1903) US painter.
His reply when asked if he agreed that the stars were especially beautiful one night
Attrib.

1905

208 A good novel tells us the truth about its hero; but a bad novel tells us the truth about its author.
G. K. Chesterton (1874–1936) British writer.
Heretics, Ch. 15

209 The artistic temperament is a disease that afflicts amateurs.
G. K. Chesterton
Heretics, Ch. 17

1906

210 The day is coming when a single carrot, freshly observed, will set off a revolution.
Paul Cézanne (1839–1906) French postimpressionist painter.
Attrib.

211 The profession of letters is, after all, the only one in which one can make no money without being ridiculous.
Jules Renard (1894–1910) French writer.
Journal

212 Popular poets are the parish priests of the Muse, retailing her ancient divinations to a long since converted public.
George Santayana (1863–1952) US philosopher.
The Life of Reason, 'Reason in Art'

1907

213 With the single exception of Homer, there is no eminent writer, not even Sir Walter Scott, whom I can despise so entirely as I despise Shakespeare when I measure my mind against his ... It would positively be a relief to me to dig him up and throw stones at him.
George Bernard Shaw (1856–1950) Irish dramatist and critic.
Dramatic Opinions and Essays, Vol. 2

1909

214 Mr Shaw is (I suspect) the only man on earth
who has never written any poetry.
G. K. Chesterton (1874–1936) British writer.
Referring to George Bernard Shaw
Orthodoxy, Ch. 3

1911

215 "Music" she said dreamily, and such is the
force of habit that "I don't" she added, "know
anything about music really, but I know what I
like."
Max Beerbohm British writer.
Zuleika Dobson

216 Wonderful women! Have you ever thought how
much we all, and women especially, owe to
Shakespeare for his vindication of women in
these fearless, high-spirited, resolute and intel-
ligent heroines?
Ellen Terry (1847–1928) British actress.
Four Lectures on Shakespeare, 'The Triumphant
Women'

217 Words as is well known, are great foes of
reality.
Joseph Conrad (Teodor Josef Konrad
Korzeniowski; 1857–1924) Polish-born British
novelist.
Under Western Eyes

1912

218 When a man is in doubt about this or that in his
writing, it will often guide him if he asks himself how it will tell a hundred years hence.
Samuel Butler (1835–1902) British writer.
Notebooks

219 Sherard Blaw, the dramatist who had discovered himself, and who had given so ungrudg-
ingly of his discovery to the world.
Saki (Hector Hugh Munro; 1870–1916) British
writer.
The Unbearable Bassington, Ch. 13

1913

220 He could not think up to the height of his own
towering style.
G. K. Chesterton (1874–1936) British writer.
Speaking of Tennyson
The Victorian Age in Literature, Ch. 3

221 I like to write when I feel spiteful: it's like hav-
ing a good sneeze.
D. H. Lawrence (1885–1930) British novelist.
Letter to Lady Cynthia Asquith, Nov 1913

Daily Life

1870s

222 Father, dear father, come home with me now,

The clock in the steeple strikes one.
Henry Clay Work (1832–84) US songwriter.
A temperance song
Come Home, Father

1870

223 Of all noxious animals, too, the most noxious is
a tourist. And of all tourists the most vulgar,
ill-bred, offensive and loathsome is the British
tourist.
Francis Kilvert (1840–79) British diarist and
clergyman.
Diary, 5 Apr 1870

1871

224 It is a fine thing to be out on the hills alone. A
man can hardly be a beast or a fool alone on a
great mountain.
Francis Kilvert
Diary, 29 May 1871

1880

225* The smoke of their foul dens
Broodeth on Thy Earth as a black pestilence,
Hiding the kind day's eye. No flower, no
grass there groweth.
Only their engines' dung which the fierce fur-
nace throweth.
Wilfred Scawen Blunt (1840–1922) British
poet.
Describing a northern town
Satan Absolved: a Victorian Mystery

226 A population sodden with drink, steeped in
vice, eaten up by every social and physical
malady, these are the denizens of Darkest
England amidst whom my life has been spent.
William Booth (1829–1912) British preacher
and founder of the Salvation Army.
In Darkest England, and the Way Out

1887

227 London, that great cesspool into which all the
loungers of the Empire are irresistibly
drained.
Arthur Conan Doyle (1856–1930) British
writer.
A Study in Scarlet

1892

228 It is my belief, Watson, founded upon my experience, that the lowest and vilest alleys of
London do not present a more dreadful record
of sin than does the smiling and beautiful
countryside.
Arthur Conan Doyle
Copper Beeches

1893

229 The English country gentleman galloping after a

fox — the unspeakable in full pursuit of the uneatable.
Oscar Wilde (1854–1900) Irish-born British dramatist.
A Woman of No Importance, I

1895

230 Really, if the lower orders don't set us a good example, what on earth is the use of them?
Oscar Wilde
The Importance of Being Earnest, I

1896

231 On Wenlock Edge the wood's in trouble;
His forest fleece the Wrekin heaves;
The gale, it plies the saplings double,
And thick on Severn snow the leaves.
A. E. Housman (1859–1936) British scholar and poet.
A Shropshire Lad, 'The Welsh Marches'

232 Loveliest of trees, the cherry now
Is hung with bloom along the bough,
And stands about the woodland ride
Wearing white for Eastertide.
A. E. Housman
A Shropshire Lad, '1887'

1900

233* This is the weather the cuckoo likes,
And so do I;
When showers betumble the chestnut spikes,
And nestlings fly:
And the little brown nightingale bills his best,
And they sit outside at 'The Travellers' Rest'.
Thomas Hardy (1840–1928) British novelist.
Weathers

1902

234 His Lordship may compel us to be equal up-stairs, but there will never be equality in the servants' hall.
J. M. Barrie (1860–1937) British novelist and dramatist.
The Admirable Crichton, I

1910

235* They are only ten.
Lord Northcliffe (1865–1922) Irish-born Brit-ish newspaper proprietor.
Rumoured to have been a notice to remind his staff of his opinion of the mental age of the gen-eral public
Attrib.

236 Common people do not pray; they only beg.
George Bernard Shaw (1856–1950) Irish dramatist and critic.
Misalliance

237* Come, Come, Come and have a drink with me

Down at the old 'Bull and Bush'.
Harry Tilzer (Albert von Tilzer; 1878–1956) British songwriter.
The Old Bull and Bush

238 Dirty British coaster with a salt-caked smoke stack,
Butting through the Channel in the mad March days,
With a cargo of Tyne coal,
Road-rail, pig-lead,
Firewood, iron-ware, and cheap tin trays.
John Masefield (1878–1967) British poet.
Cargoes

1911

239 Will anyone, a hundred years from now, con-sent to live in the houses the Victorians built, travel by their roads or railways, value the furnishings they made to live among or es-teem, except for curious or historial reasons, their prevalent art and the clipped and limited literature that satisfied their souls?
H. G. Wells (1866–1946) British writer.
The New Machiavelli

1913

240 I have to live for others and not for myself; that's middle class morality.
George Bernard Shaw (1856–1950) Irish dramatist and critic.
Pygmalion

Death

1875

241 Sin brought death, and death will disappear with the disappearance of sin.
Mary Baker Eddy (1821–1910) US religious leader.
Science and Health, with Key to the Scriptures

1886

242 The thought of suicide is a great source of com-fort: with it a calm passage is to be made across many a bad night.
Friedrich Wilhelm Nietzsche (1844–1900) German philosopher.
Jenseits von Gut und Böse (trans. *Beyond Good and Evil*)

1887

243 Under the wide and starry sky
Dig the grave and let me lie.
Glad did I live and gladly die,
— And I laid me down with a will.
This is the verse you grave for me:
'Here he lies where he longed to be;
Home is the sailor, home from sea,

And the hunter home from the hill.'
Robert Louis Stevenson (1850–94) Scottish writer.
Underwoods, Bk. I, 'Requiem'

1902

244 Our civilization is founded on the shambles, and every individual existence goes out in a lonely spasm of helpless agony.
William James (1842–1910) US psychologist and philosopher.
Varieties of Religious Experience

1910

245 Death destroys a man, the idea of Death saves him.
E. M. Forster (1879–1970) British novelist.
Howards End, Ch. 27

Education, Knowledge, and Learning

1872

246 Some who had received a liberal education at the Colleges of Unreason, and taken the highest degrees in hypothetics, which are their principal study.
Samuel Butler (1835–1902) British writer.
Erewhon, Ch. 9

247 It is the province of knowledge to speak and it is the privilege of wisdom to listen.
Oliver Wendell Holmes (1809–94) US writer.
The Poet at the Breakfast Table, Ch. 10

1879

248* It is the customary fate of new truths to begin as heresies and to end as superstitions.
T. H. Huxley (1825–95) British biologist.
The Coming of Age of the Origin of Species

1881

249 Give me the young man who has brains enough to make a fool of himself!
Robert Louis Stevenson (1850–94) Scottish writer.
Virginibus Puerisque

1886

250 I never heard tell of any clever man that came of entirely stupid people.
Thomas Carlyle (1795–1881) Scottish historian and essayist.
Speech, Edinburgh, 2 Apr 1886

251 I am too much of a sceptic to deny the possibility of anything.
T. H. Huxley (1825–95) British biologist.
Letter to Herbert Spencer, 22 Mar 1886

1891

252 There is no sin except stupidity.
Oscar Wilde (1854–1900) Irish-born British dramatist.
The Critic as Artist, Pt. 2

1892

253 Music-hall songs provide the dull with wit, just as proverbs provide them with wisdom.
W. Somerset Maugham (1874–1965) British novelist.
A Writer's Notebook

1893

254 Metaphysics is the finding of bad reasons for what we believe upon instinct; but to find these reasons is no less an instinct.
F. H. Bradley (1846–1924) British philosopher.
Appearance and Reality, Preface

255* Research! A mere excuse for idleness; it has never achieved, and will never achieve any results of the slightest value.
Benjamin Jowett (1817–93) British theologian.
Unforgotten Years (Logan Pearsall Smith)

1894

256 Oxford had not taught me, nor had any other place or person, the value of liberty as an essential condition of excellence in human things.
William Ewart Gladstone (1809–98) British statesman.
Gladstone graduated from Oxford in 1831
Note

257 A blind man in a dark room – looking for a black hat – which isn't there.
Lord Bowen (1835–94) British judge.
Characterization of a metaphysician
Attrib.

258 Language grows out of life, out of its needs and experiences . . . *Language* and *knowledge* are indissolubly connected; they are interdependent. Good work in language presupposes and depends on a real knowledge of things.
Annie Sullivan (1866–1936) US teacher of the handicapped.
Speech, American Association to Promote the Teaching of Speech to the Deaf, July 1894

1902

259 We are thinking beings, and we cannot exclude the intellect from participating in any of our functions.
William James (1842–1910) US psychologist and philosopher.
Varieties of Religious Experience

1904

260 LIBOV ANDREEVNA. Are you still a student? TROFIMOV. I expect I shall be a student to the end of my days.
Anton Chekhov (1860–1904) Russian dramatist.
The Cherry Orchard, I

261 Paradoxes are useful to attract attention to ideas.
Mandell Creighton (1843–1901) British churchman.
Life and Letters

1905

262 There is no such thing on earth as an uninteresting subject; the only thing that can exist is an uninterested person.
G. K. Chesterton (1874–1936) British writer.
Heretics, Ch. 1

263 The word 'orthodoxy' not only no longer means being right; it practically means being wrong.
G. K. Chesterton
Heretics, Ch. 1

264 The philosopher is Nature's pilot. And there you have our difference; to be in hell is to drift; to be in heaven is to steer.
George Bernard Shaw (1856–1950) Irish dramatist and critic.
Man and Superman

1906

265 They know enough who know how to learn.
Henry Brooks Adams (1838–1918) US historian.
The Education of Henry Adams

266 *Logic, n.* The art of thinking and reasoning in strict accordance with the limitations and incapacities of the human understanding.
Ambrose Bierce (1842–?1914) US writer and journalist.
The Devil's Dictionary

267 *Ignoramus, n.* A person unacquainted with certain kinds of knowledge familiar to yourself, and having certain other kinds that you know nothing about.
Ambrose Bierce
The Devil's Dictionary

1907

268 Nobody can say a word against Greek: it stamps a man at once as an educated gentleman.
George Bernard Shaw (1856–1950) Irish dramatist and critic.
Major Barbara, I

1909

269 Nothing would more effectively further the development of education than for all flogging

pedagogues to learn to educate with the head instead of with the hand.
Ellen Key (Karolina Sofia Key; 1849–1926) Swedish writer.
The Century of the Child, Ch. 3

1911

270 We were taught as the chief subjects of instruction Latin and Greek. We were taught very badly because the men who taught us did not habitually use either of these languages.
H. G. Wells (1866–1946) British writer.
The New Machiavelli, Bk. I., Ch. 3

271 Americans have a perfect right to exist. But he did often find himself wishing Mr. Rhodes had not enabled them to excercise that right at Oxford.
Max Beerbohm (1872–1956) British writer.
Zuleika Dobson

1913

272 An idea does not pass from one language to another without change.
Miguel de Unamuno y Jugo (1864–1936) Spanish writer.
The Tragic Sense of Life

History

1895

273 History is past politics, and politics present history.
John Robert Seeley (1834–95) British historian.
Quoting the historian E. A. Freeman
The Growth of British Policy

1903

274 My argument is that War makes rattling good history; but Peace is poor reading.
Thomas Hardy (1840–1928) British novelist.
The Dynasts, II:5

1904

275 One step forward, two steps back . . . It happens in the lives of individuals, and it happens in the history of nations and in the development of parties.
Lenin (Vladimir Ilich Ulyanov; 1870–1924) Russian revolutionary leader.
One Step Forward, Two Steps Back

1905

276 Progress, far from consisting in change, depends on retentiveness. Those who cannot remember the past are condemned to repeat it.
George Santayana (1863–1952) US philosopher.
The Life of Reason

1909

277 It is impossible to write ancient history because we do not have enough sources, and impossible to write modern history because we have far too many.
Charles Pierre Péguy (1873–1914) French writer.
Clio

1910

278* The past is the only dead thing that smells sweet.
Edward Thomas (1878–1917) British poet.
Early One Morning

279* Historians are like deaf people who go on answering questions that no one has asked them.
Leo Tolstoy (1828–1910) Russian writer.
A Discovery of Australia, 'Being an Historian' (Manning Clark)

280* There is always something rather absurd about the past.
Max Beerbohm (1872–1956) British writer.
1880

Human Nature

1873

281 Ask yourself whether you are happy, and you cease to be so.
John Stuart Mill (1806–73) British philosopher.
Autobiography, Ch. 5

1880

282 To show pity is felt as a sign of contempt because one has clearly ceased to be an object of *fear* as soon as one is pitied.
Friedrich Wilhelm Nietzsche (1844–1900) German philosopher.
The Wanderer and His Shadow

1881

283 There is no duty we so much underrate as the duty of being happy.
Robert Louis Stevenson (1850–94) Scottish writer.
Virginibus Puerisque

1882

284 He who does not need to lie is proud of not being a liar.
Friedrich Wilhelm Nietzsche (1844–1900) German philosopher.
Nachgelassene Fragmente

1883

285 I teach you the Superman. Man is something that is to be surpassed.
Friedrich Wilhelm Nietzsche
Thus Spake Zarathustra

1886

286 Wild animals never kill for sport. Man is the only one to whom the torture and death of his fellow-creatures is amusing in itself.
J. A. Froude (1818–94) British historian.
Oceana, Ch. 5

1887

287 She likes stories that make her cry – I think we all do, it's so nice to feel sad when you've nothing particular to be sad about.
Annie Sullivan (1866–1936) US teacher of the handicapped.
Referring to Helen Keller
Letter, 12 Dec 1887

1889

288 It is impossible to enjoy idling thoroughly unless one has plenty of work to do.
Jerome K. Jerome (1859–1927) British humorist.
Idle Thoughts of an Idle Fellow

1891

289 There's a sucker born every minute.
Phineas Barnum (1810–91) US showman.
Attrib.

290 It is only shallow people who do not judge by appearances.
Oscar Wilde (1854–1900) Irish-born British dramatist.
The Picture of Dorian Gray, Ch. 2

291 A man who knows the price of everything and the value of nothing.
Oscar Wilde
Describing a cynic
Lady Windermere's Fan, III

292 The man who sees both sides of a question is a man who sees absolutely nothing at all.
Oscar Wilde
The Critic as Artist, Pt. 2

1893

293 From forty to fifty a man is at heart either a stoic or a satyr.
Arthur Pinero (1855–1934) British dramatist.
The Second Mrs Tanqueray, I

1894

294 Economy is going without something you do

want in case you should, some day, want something you probably won't want.
Anthony Hope (Sir Anthony Hope Hawkins; 1863–1933) British novelist.
The Dolly Dialogues

295   Adam was but human – this explains it all. He did not want the apple for the apple's sake, he wanted it only because it was forbidden.
Mark Twain (Samuel Langhorne Clemens; 1835–1910) US writer.
Pudd'nhead Wilson's Calendar, Ch. 2

1895

296   Other people are quite dreadful. The only possible society is oneself.
Oscar Wilde (1854–1900) Irish-born British dramatist.
An Ideal Husband, III

1896

297   Malt does more than Milton can
To justify God's ways to man.
A. E. Housman (1859–1936) British scholar and poet.
A Shropshire Lad, 'The Welsh Marches'

298   Two men look out through the same bars:
One sees the mud, and one the stars.
Frederick Langbridge (1849–1923) British religious writer.
A Cluster of Quiet Thoughts

1897

299   Man is the only animal that blushes. Or needs to.
Mark Twain (Samuel Langhorne Clemens; 1835–1910) US writer.
Following the Equator, heading of Ch. 27

1899

300   Two may talk together under the same roof for many years, yet never really meet; and two others at first speech are old friends.
Mary Catherwood (1847–1901) US writer.
Mackinac and Lake Stories, 'Marianson'

1900

301   You shall judge of a man by his foes as well as by his friends.
Joseph Conrad (Teodor Josef Konrad Korzeniowski; 1857–1924) Polish-born British novelist.
Lord Jim, Ch. 34

1902

302*   Justice is being allowed to do whatever I like. Injustice is whatever prevents my doing it.
Samuel Butler (1835–1902) British writer.
Notebooks

1903

303   A good man can be stupid and still be good. But a bad man must have brains.
Maxim Gorky (Aleksei Maksimovich Peshkov; 1868–1936) Russian writer.
The Lower Depths

304   A lifetime of happiness: no man alive could bear it: it would be hell on earth.
George Bernard Shaw (1856–1950) Irish dramatist and critic.
Man and Superman, I

305   It was remarked to me by the late Mr Charles Roupell . . . that to play billiards well was a sign of an ill-spent youth.
Herbert Spencer (1820–1903) British philosopher.
Life and Letters of Spencer (Duncan), Ch. 20

1905

306   Happiness is a mystery like religion, and should never be rationalized.
G. K. Chesterton (1874–1936) British writer.
Heretics, Ch. 7

307   Happiness is the only sanction of life; where happiness fails, existence remains a mad and lamentable experiment.
George Santayana (1863–1952) US philosopher.
The Life of Reason

1906

308   I have always found that the man whose second thoughts are good is worth watching.
J. M. Barrie (1860–1937) British novelist and dramatist.
What Every Woman Knows, III

1909

309   The madman is not the man who has lost his reason. The madman is the man who has lost everything except his reason.
G. K. Chesterton (1874–1936) British writer.
Orthodoxy, Ch. 1

310*   The ignorant man always adores what he cannot understand.
Cesare Lombroso (1853–1909) Italian criminologist.
The Man of Genius, Pt. III, Ch. 3

1910

311*   When people do not respect us we are sharply offended; yet deep down in his heart no man much respects himself.
Mark Twain (Samuel Langhorne Clemens; 1835–1910) US writer.
Notebooks

1911

312   You cannot make a man by standing a sheep on its hind legs. But by standing a flock of sheep

in that position you can make a crowd of men.
Max Beerbohm (1872–1956) British writer.
Zuleika Dobson, Ch. 9

1912

313 Man is the only animal that can remain on friendly terms with the victims he intends to eat until he eats them.
Samuel Butler (1835–1902) British writer.
Notebooks

314 I wanted the experience of war. I thought there would be no more wars.
Joyce Cary (1888–1957) British novelist.
Reason for going to the Balkan War in 1912

1913

315 Conscience is the internal perception of the rejection of a particular wish operating within us.
Sigmund Freud (1856–1939) Austrian psychoanalyst.
Totem and Taboo

Humour

1876

316 A different taste in jokes is a great strain on the affections.
George Eliot (Mary Ann Evans; 1819–80) British novelist.
Daniel Deronda

1880

317 He played the King as though under momentary apprehension that someone else was about to play the ace.
Eugene Field (1850–95) US poet and journalist.
Referring to Creston Clarke's performance in the role of King Lear
Attrib.

1881

318 I will not go down to posterity talking bad grammar.
Benjamin Disraeli (1804–81) British statesman.
Remark made when correcting proofs of his last parliamentary speech, 31 Mar 1881
Disraeli (Blake), Ch. 32

1900s

319 I do love cricket – it's so very English.
Sarah Bernhardt (Sarah Henriette Rosine Bernard; 1844–1923) French actress.
On seeing a game of football
Nijinsky (R. Buckle)

320 Men will confess to treason, murder, arson,

false teeth, or a wig. How many of them will own up to a lack of humour?
Frank More Colby (1865–1925) US editor.
Essays, I

1904

321 My way of joking is to tell the truth. It's the funniest joke in the world.
George Bernard Shaw (1856–1950) Irish dramatist and critic.
John Bull's Other Island, II

1910

322 Candidates should not attempt more than six of these.
Hilaire Belloc (1870–1953) French-born British poet.
Suggested addition to the Ten Commandments
Attrib.

1912

323 He uses statistics as a drunken man uses lamp-posts – for support rather than illumination.
Andrew Lang (1844–1912) Scottish writer and poet.
Treasury of Humorous Quotations

Life

1870

324 When a man fell into his anecdotage it was a sign for him to retire from the world.
Benjamin Disraeli (1804–81) British statesman.
Lothair, Ch. 28

1873

325 Everything must be taken seriously, nothing tragically.
Louis Adolphe Thiers (1797–1877) French statesman and historian.
Speech, French National Assembly, 24 May 1873

1874

326 Our ingress into the world
Was naked and bare;
Our progress through the world
Is trouble and care.
Henry Wadsworth Longfellow (1807–82) US poet.
Tales of A Wayside Inn, 'The Student's Tale'

327 Ships that pass in the night, and speak each other in passing;
Only a signal shown and a distant voice in the darkness;
So on the ocean of life we pass and speak one another,

Only a look and a voice; then darkness again
and a silence.
Henry Wadsworth Longfellow
*Tales of a Wayside Inn, 'The Theologian's Tale.
Elizabeth'*

328   For life is but a dream whose shapes return,
Some frequently, some seldom, some by night
And some by day.
James Thomson (1834–82) British poet.
The City of Dreadful Night, I

1875

329   A place for everything, and everything in its
place.
Samuel Smiles (1812–1904) British writer.
Thrift, Ch. 5

1880

330   A day less or more
At sea or ashore,
We die – does it matter when?
Alfred, Lord Tennyson (1809–92) British
poet.
The Revenge, XI

1882

331   Fools are in a terrible, overwhelming majority,
all the wide world over.
Henrik Ibsen (1828–1906) Norwegian
dramatist.
An Enemy of the People, IV

1884

332   Take the saving lie away from the average man
and straight away you take away his
happiness.
Henrik Ibsen
The Wild Duck, V

333   I had never had a piece of toast
Particularly long and wide,
But fell upon the sanded floor,
And always on the buttered side.
James Payn (1830–98) British writer and
editor.
Chambers's Journal, 2 Feb 1884

1885

334   Not, I'll not, carrion comfort, Despair, not feast
on thee;
Not untwist – slack they may be – these last
strands of man
In me or, most weary, cry *I can no more.* I
can;
Can something, hope, wish day come, not
choose not to be.
Gerard Manley Hopkins (1844–99) British
Jesuit and poet.
Carrion Comfort

1888

335   It matters not how strait the gate,
How charged with punishments the scroll,
I am the master of my fate:
I am the captain of my soul.
William Ernest Henley (1849–1903) British
writer.
Echoes, IV, 'Invictus. In Mem. R.T.H.B.'

1889

336   The past was nothing to her; offered no lesson
which she was willing to heed. The future was
a mystery which she never attempted to pen-
etrate. The present alone was significant...
Kate Chopin (1851–1904) US writer.
The Awakening, Ch. 15

337   There are some people who leave impressions
not so lasting as the imprint of an oar upon
the water.
Kate Chopin
The Awakening, Ch. 34

1890

338   ...we could never learn to be brave and patient, if there were only joy in the world.
Helen Keller (1880–1968) US writer and
lecturer.
Atlantic Monthly (May 1890)

339   Nature is usually wrong.
James Whistler (1834–1903) US painter.
The Gentle Art of Making Enemies

1891

340   There is only one thing in the world worse than
being talked about, and that is not being
talked about.
Oscar Wilde (1854–1900) Irish-born British
dramatist.
The Picture of Dorian Gray, Ch. 1

341   I can sympathize with everything, except
suffering.
Oscar Wilde
The Picture of Dorian Gray, Ch. 3

342   We are all in the gutter, but some of us are
looking at the stars.
Oscar Wilde
Lady Windermere's Fan, III

1892

343   They are not long, the days of wine and roses.
Ernest Dowson (1867–1900) British lyric
poet.
*Vitae Summa Brevis Spem Nos Vetat Incohare
Longam*

1895

344 In matters of grave importance, style, not
sincerity, is the vital thing.
Oscar Wilde (1854–1900) Irish-born British
dramatist.
The Importance of Being Earnest, III

1896

345 It's deadly commonplace, but, after all, the
commonplaces are the great poetic truths.
Robert Louis Stevenson (1850–94) Scottish writer.
Weir of Hermiston, Ch. 6

346 Wealth I ask not; hope nor love,
Nor a friend to know me;
All I seek, the heaven above
And the road below me.
Robert Louis Stevenson
Songs of Travel, 'The Vagabond'

1897

347 Man has been endowed with reason, with the
power to create, so that he can add to what
he's been given. But up to now he hasn't been
a creator, only a destroyer. Forests keep dis-
appearing, rivers dry up, wild life's become
extinct, the climate's ruined and the land grows
poorer and uglier every day.
Anton Chekhov (1860–1904) Russian
dramatist.
Uncle Vanya, I

1898

348 I remember my youth and the feeling that will
never come back any more – the feeling that
I could last for ever, outlast the sea, the earth,
and all men; the deceitful feeling that lures
us on to perils, to love, to vain effort – to
death . . .
Joseph Conrad (Teodor Josef Konrad
Korzeniowski; 1857–1924) Polish-born British
novelist.
Youth

1902

349 Life is the art of drawing sufficient conclusions
from insufficient premises.
Samuel Butler (1835–1902) British writer.
Notebooks

350 Life is one long process of getting tired.
Samuel Butler
Notebooks

351 All progress is based upon a universal innate
desire on the part of every organism to live beyond its income.
Samuel Butler
Notebooks

1903

352 In heaven an angel is nobody in particular.
George Bernard Shaw (1856–1950) Irish
dramatist and critic.
Man and Superman, 'Maxims for Revolutionists

353 Live all you can; it's a mistake not to. It doesn't
so much matter what you do in particular, so
long as you have your life. If you haven't had
that what *have* you had?
Henry James (1843–1916) US novelist.
The Ambassadors, Bk. V, Ch. 2

354 The follies which a man regrets most in his life
are those which he didn't commit when he
had the opportunity.
Helen Rowland (1876–1950) US writer.
Reflections of a Bachelor Girl

1904

355 We must be thoroughly democratic and pa-
tronise everybody without distinction of class.
George Bernard Shaw (1856–1950) Irish
dramatist and critic.
John Bull's Other Island

1905

356 As enunciated today, 'progress' is simply a
comparative of which we have not settled the
superlative.
G. K. Chesterton (1874–1936) British writer
Heretics, Ch. 2

357 A life of pleasure requires an aristocratic setting to make it interesting.
George Santayana (1863–1952) US
philosopher.
Life of Reason, 'Reason in Society'

1906

358 Mankind is not a tribe of animals to which we
owe compassion. Mankind is a club to which
we owe our subscription.
G. K. Chesterton (1874–1936) British writer.
Daily News, 10 Apr 1906

359 Life is made up of sobs, sniffles and smiles,
with sniffles predominating.
O. Henry (William Sydney Porter; 1862–1910)
US short-story writer.
The Gifts of the Magi

360 The moral flabbiness born of the bitch-goddess
Success.
William James (1842–1910) US psychologist
and philosopher.
Letter to H. G. Wells, 11 Sept 1906

1908

361 The most important thing in the Olympic
Games is not winning but taking part . . . The

essential thing in life is not conquering but
fighting well.
Pierre de Coubertin (1863–1937) French educator and sportsman.
Speech, Banquet to Officials of Olympic Games,
London, 24 July 1908

1909

362 Reason is itself a matter of faith. It is an act of
faith to assert that our thoughts have any relation to reality at all.
G. K. Chesterton (1874–1936) British writer.
Orthodoxy, Ch. 3

363 All conservatism is based upon the idea that if
you leave things alone you leave them as they
are. But you do not. If you leave a thing
alone you leave it to a torrent of change.
G. K. Chesterton
Orthodoxy, Ch. 7

1910

364 One sees great things from the valley; only
small things from the peak.
G. K. Chesterton
The Hammer of God

365* Everything great in the world is done by neurotics; they alone founded our religions and created our masterpieces.
Marcel Proust (1871–1922) French novelist.
The Perpetual Pessimist (Sagittarius and
George)

1911

366 The dullard's envy of brilliant men is always assuaged by the suspicion that they will come to
a bad end.
Max Beerbohm (1872–1956) British writer.
Zuleika Dobson

367 In the Country of the Blind the One-eyed Man
is King.
H. G. Wells (1866–1946) British writer.
The Country of the Blind

1912

368 All that the young can do for the old is to shock
them and keep them up to date.
George Bernard Shaw (1856–1950) Irish
dramatist and critic.
Fannie's First Play

369 Business underlies everything in our national
life, including our spiritual life. Witness the fact
that in the Lord's Prayer the first petition is
for daily bread. No one can worship God or
love his neighbour on an empty stomach.
Woodrow Wilson (1856–1924) US
statesman.
Speech, New York, 1912

1913

370 May God deny you peace but give you glory!
Miguel de Unamuno y Jugo (1864–1936)
Spanish writer.
Closing words
The Tragic Sense of Life

1915

371* Life is just one damned thing after another.
Elbert Hubbard (1856–1915) US writer.
A Thousand and One Epigrams

Love and Sex

1880s

372 Daisy, Daisy, give me your answer, do!
I'm half crazy, all for the love of you!
It won't be a stylish marriage,
I can't afford a carriage,
But you'll look sweet upon the seat
Of a bicycle made for two!
Harry Dacre (19th century) British songwriter.
Daisy Bell

1887

373 It seems to me that he has never loved, that he
has only imagined that he has loved, that
there has been no real love on his part. I even
think that he is incapable of love; he is too
much occupied with other thoughts and ideas
to become strongly attached to anyone
earthly.
Anna Dostoevsky (1846–1918) Russian diarist and writer.
Dostoevsky Portrayed by His Wife

1893

374 Young men make great mistakes in life; for one
thing, they idealize love too much.
Benjamin Jowett (1817–93) British
theologian.
Letters of B. Jowett (Abbott and Campbell)

1895

375 When a man is in love he endures more than at
other times; he submits to everything.
Friedrich Wilhelm Nietzsche (1844–1900)
German philosopher.
The Antichrist

1903

376 'Tis better to have loved and lost than never to
have lost at all.
Samuel Butler (1835–1902) British writer.
The Way of All Flesh, Ch. 77

1905

377 We don't believe in rheumatism and true love until after the first attack.
Marie Ebner von Eschenbach (1830–1916) Austrian writer.
Aphorism

1910

378* But Love has pitched his mansion in
The place of excrement.
W. B. Yeats (1865–1939) Irish poet.
Crazy Jane Talks with the Bishop

379* A pity beyond all telling
Is hid in the heart of love.
W. B. Yeats
The Pity of Love

380* It doesn't matter what you do in the bedroom as long as you don't do it in the street and frighten the horses.
Mrs Patrick Campbell (Beatrice Stella Tanner; 1865–1940) British actress.
The Duchess of Jermyn Street (Daphne Fielding), Ch. 2

381 But oh, the farmyard world of sex!
Harley Granville-Barker (1877–1946) British actor and dramatist.
The Madras House, IV

1912

382 God is Love – I dare say. But what a mischievous devil Love is!
Samuel Butler (1835–1902) British writer.
Notebooks

Marriage and the Family

1881

383 Marriage is a step so grave and decisive that it attracts light-headed, variable men by its very awfulness.
Robert Louis Stevenson (1850–94) Scottish writer.
Virginibus Puerisque

1900

384 I married beneath me – all women do.
Nancy Astor (1879–1964) American-born British politician.
Dictionary of National Biography

1903

385 It takes a woman twenty years to make a man of her son, and another woman twenty minutes to make a fool of him.
Helen Rowland (1876–1950) US writer.
Reflections of a Bachelor Girl

386 If you strike a child, take care that you strike it in anger, even at the risk of maiming it for life.

A blow in cold blood neither can nor should be forgiven.
George Bernard Shaw (1856–1950) Irish dramatist and critic.
Man and Superman, 'Maxims for Revolutionist'

387 It is a woman's business to get married as soon as possible, and a man's to keep unmarried as long as he can.
George Bernard Shaw
Man and Superman

388 There is only one person an English girl hates more than she hates her elder sister; and that is her mother.
George Bernard Shaw
Man and Superman

1909

389 At every step the child should be allowed to meet the real experiences of life; the thorns should never be plucked from his roses.
Ellen Key (Karolina Sofia Key; 1849–1926) Swedish writer.
The Century of the Child, Ch. 3

390 Physically there is nothing to distinguish human society from the farm-yard except that children are more troublesome and costly than chickens and women are not so completely enslaved as farm stock.
George Bernard Shaw (1856–1950) Irish dramatist and critic.
Getting Married, Preface

1910

391 Many a man in love with a dimple makes the mistake of marrying the whole girl.
Stephen Leacock (1869–1944) English-born Canadian economist and humorist.
Literary Lapses

392 The Western custom of one wife and hardly any mistresses.
Saki (Hector Hugh Munro; 1870–1916) British writer.
Reginald in Russia

1911

393 Love is moral even without legal marriage, but marriage is immoral without love.
Ellen Key (Karolina Sofia Key; 1849–1926) Swedish writer.
The Morality of Woman and Other Essays, 'The Morality of Woman'

Men and Women

1870

394 The Queen is most anxious to enlist every one who can speak or write to join in checking this mad, wicked folly of 'Woman's Rights', with all its attendant horrors, on which her poor feeb

ble sex is bent, forgetting every sense of
womanly feeling and propriety.
Victoria (1819–1901) Queen of England.
Letter to Sir Theodore Martin, 29 May 1870

1877

395   Taste is the feminine of genius.
Edward Fitzgerald (1809–83) British poet.
Letter to J. R. Lowell, Oct 1877

1881

396   *Declaration of Sentiments:* . . . We hold these
truths to be self-evident: that all men and
women are created equal . . .
Elizabeth Stanton (1815–1902) US
suffragette.
History of Woman Suffrage (with Susan B.
Anthony and Mathilda Gage), Vol. I

397   Womanhood is the great fact in her life;
wifehood and motherhood are but incidental
relations.
Elizabeth Stanton
History of Woman Suffrage (with Susan B.
Anthony and Mathilda Gage), Vol. I

398   Man is a creature who lives not upon bread
alone, but principally by catchwords; and the
little rift between the sexes is astonishingly
widened by simply teaching one set of catchwords to the girls and another to the boys.
Robert Louis Stevenson (1850–94) Scottish writer.
Virginibus Puerisque

1883

399   The really original woman is the one who first
imitates a man.
Italo Svevo (Ettore Schmitz; 1861–1928) Italian writer.
A Life, Ch. 8

1887

400   She-who-must-be-obeyed.'
H. Rider Haggard (1856–1925) British
novelist.
She

1888

401   The silliest woman can manage a clever man;
but it needs a very clever woman to manage
a fool.
Rudyard Kipling (1865–1936) Indian-born
British writer.
Plain Tales from the Hills, 'Three and – an Extra'

402   A woman despises a man for loving her, unless
she returns his love.
Elizabeth Drew Stoddard (1823–1902) US
novelist and poet.
Two Men, Ch. 32

1890s

403   Men their rights and nothing more; women
their rights and nothing less.
Susan B. Anthony (1820–1906) US editor.
The Revolution, Motto

404   The prolonged slavery of women is the darkest
page in human history.
Elizabeth Stanton (1815–1902) US
suffragette.
History of Woman Suffrage (with Susan B.
Anthony and Mathilda Gage), Vol. I

1890

405   The superiority of one man's opinion over another's is never so great as when the opinion
is about a woman.
Henry James (1843–1916) US novelist.
The Tragic Muse, Ch. 9

1891

406   Women represent the triumph of matter over
mind, just as men represent the triumph of
mind over morals.
Oscar Wilde (1854–1900) Irish-born British
dramatist.
The Picture of Dorian Gray, Ch. 4

1895

407   God created woman. And boredom did indeed
cease from that moment – but many other
things ceased as well! Woman was God's *second* mistake.
Friedrich Wilhelm Nietzsche (1844–1900)
German philosopher.
The Antichrist

408   All women become like their mothers. That is
their tragedy. No man does. That's his.
Oscar Wilde (1854–1900) Irish-born British
dramatist.
The Importance of Being Earnest, I

1897

409   . . . there never will be complete equality until
women themselves help to make laws and
elect lawmakers.
Susan B. Anthony (1820–1906) US editor.
In *The Arena*, (May 1897) 'The Status of
Women, Past, Present and Future'

410   A woman can become a man's friend only in
the following stages – first an acquaintance,
next a mistress, and only then a friend.
Anton Chekhov (1860–1904) Russian
dramatist.
Uncle Vanya, II

1898

411   Where young boys plan for what they will

achieve and attain, young girls plan for whom they will achieve and attain.
Charlotte Perkins Gilman (1860–1935) US writer.
Women and Economics, Ch. 5

1900s

412 ... the emancipation of women is practically the greatest egoistic movement of the nineteenth century, and the most intense affirmation of the right of the self that history has yet seen ...
Ellen Key (Karolina Sofia Key; 1849–1926) Swedish writer.
The Century of the Child, Ch. 2

1902

413 A homely face and no figure have aided many women heavenward.
Minna Antrim (1861–?) US writer.
Naked Truth and Veiled Allusions

1903

414 ... while there is more drinking, there is less drunkenness than formerly, and that the increase in drinking is to be laid mainly to the account of the female sex. This latter phase seems to be one of the unexpected results of the emancipation of women.
Charles Booth (1840–1916) British sociologist.
Life and Labour in London

1906

415 It's a sort of bloom on a woman. If you have it, you don't need to have anything else; and if you don't have it, it doesn't much matter what else you have.
J. M. Barrie (1860–1937) British novelist and dramatist.
Referring to 'charm'
What Every Woman Knows, I

416 If men knew how women pass their time when they are alone, they'd never marry.
O. Henry (William Sydney Porter; 1862–1910) US short-story writer.
The Four Million Memoirs of a Yellow Dog

1910s

417 When the Himalayan peasant meets the he-bear in his pride,
He shouts to scare the monster, who will often turn aside.
But the she-bear thus accosted rends the peasant tooth and nail
For the female of the species is more deadly than the male.
Rudyard Kipling (1865–1936) Indian-born British writer.
The Female of the Species

418 It's nothing to be born ugly. Sensibly, the ugly woman comes to terms with her ugliness and exploits it as a grace of nature.
Colette (Sidonie-Gabrielle C.; 1873–1954) French novelist.
Journey for Myself

1910

419 Scarce, sir. Mighty scarce.
Mark Twain (Samuel Langhorne Clemens; 1835–1910) US writer.
Responding to the question 'In a world without women what would men become?'
Attrib.

1911

420 You will find that the woman who is really kind to dogs is always one who has failed to inspire sympathy in men.
Max Beerbohm (1872–1956) British writer.
Zuleika Dobson, Ch. 6

Morality, Vices, and Virtues

1871

421 The highest possible stage in moral culture is when we recognize that we ought to control our thoughts.
Charles Darwin (1809–82) British life scientist.
Descent of Man, Ch. 4

1873

422 The eternal *not ourselves* that makes for righteousness.
Matthew Arnold (1822–88) British poet and critic.
Literature and Dogma, Ch. 8

1874

423 To be discontented with the divine discontent, and to be ashamed with the noble shame, is the very germ and first upgrowth of all virtue.
Charles Kingsley (1819–75) British writer.
Health and Education

1881

424 The cruellest lies are often told in silence.
Robert Louis Stevenson (1850–94) Scottish writer.
Virginibus Puerisque

425 To travel hopefully is a better thing than to arrive, and the true success is to labour.
Robert Louis Stevenson
Virginibus Puerisque

1886

426   Morality in Europe today is herd-morality.
      Friedrich Wilhelm Nietzsche (1844–1900)
      German philosopher.
      *Jenseits von Gut und Böse (trans. Beyond
      Good and Evil)*

1889

427   Much truth is spoken, that more may be
      concealed.
      Lord Darling (1849–1936) British judge.
      Scintillae Juris

1891

428   As long as war is regarded as wicked, it will
      always have its fascination. When it is looked
      upon as vulgar, it will cease to be popular.
      Oscar Wilde (1854–1900) Irish-born British
      dramatist.
      The Critic as Artist, Pt. 2

429   A little sincerity is a dangerous thing, and a
      great deal of it is absolutely fatal.
      Oscar Wilde
      The Critic as Artist, Pt. 2

1892

430   If your morals make you dreary, depend upon it,
      they are wrong.
      Robert Louis Stevenson (1850–94) Scot-
      tish writer.
      Across the Plains

1893

431   It is the restrictions placed on vice by our so-
      cial code which makes its pursuit so pecu-
      liarly agreeable.
      Kenneth Grahame (1859–1932) Scottish
      writer.
      Pagan Papers

1895

432   Be modest! It is the kind of pride least likely to
      offend.
      Jules Renard (1894–1910) French writer.
      Journal

1898

433   When a stupid man is doing something he is
      ashamed of, he always declares that it is his
      duty.
      George Bernard Shaw (1856–1950) Irish
      dramatist and critic.
      Caesar and Cleopatra, III

1901

434   No people do so much harm as those who go
      about doing good.
      Mandell Creighton (1843–1901) British
      churchman.
      Life

1902

435   Some men love truth so much that they seem
      to be in continual fear lest she should catch a
      cold on overexposure.
      Samuel Butler (1835–1902) British writer.
      Notebooks

436   There is no worse lie than a truth misunder-
      stood by those who hear it.
      William James (1842–1910) US psychologist
      and philosopher.
      The Varieties of Religious Experience

437   It does not matter much what a man hates, pro-
      vided he hates something.
      Samuel Butler (1835–1902) British writer.
      Notebooks

438   It is the function of vice to keep virtue within
      reasonable bounds.
      Samuel Butler
      Notebooks

1903

439   Pleasure after all is a safer guide than either
      right or duty.
      Samuel Butler
      The Way of All Flesh, Ch. 19

440   The advantage of doing one's praising for one-
      self is that one can lay it on so thick and ex-
      actly in the right places.
      Samuel Butler
      The Way of All Flesh, Ch. 34

441   Half the vices which the world condemns most
      loudly have seeds of good in them and require
      moderate use rather than total abstinence.
      Samuel Butler
      The Way of All Flesh

1905

442   Charity is the power of defending that which we
      know to be indefensible. Hope is the power of
      being cheerful in circumstances which we
      know to be desperate.
      G. K. Chesterton (1874–1936) British writer.
      Heretics, Ch. 12

443   Self-denial is not a virtue; it is only the effect of
      prudence on rascality.
      George Bernard Shaw (1856–1950) Irish
      dramatist and critic.
      Man and Superman, 'Maxims for Revolutionists'

444   Vice is waste of life. Poverty, obedience and
      celibacy are the canonical vices.
      George Bernard Shaw
      Man and Superman

445   Self-sacrifice enables us to sacrifice

Other people without blushing.
George Bernard Shaw
Man and Superman

446 It is dangerous to be sincere unless you are
also stupid.
George Bernard Shaw
Man and Superman

1906

447 *Saint, n.* a dead sinner revised and edited.
Ambrose Bierce (1842–?1914) US writer and
journalist.
The Devil's Dictionary

1907

448 Matilda told such Dreadful Lies
It made one Gasp and Stretch one's Eyes.
For every time she shouted "Fire"
They only answered "Little Liar"
And therefore when her Aunt returned
Matilda, and the House, were Burned.
Hilaire Belloc (1870–1953) French-born Brit-
ish poet.
Cautionary Tales

449 Morals are an acquirement — like music, like a
foreign language, like piety, poker, paralysis —
no man is born with them.
Mark Twain (Samuel Langhorne Clemens;
1835–1910) US writer.
Seventieth Birthday

1908

450 Not only is suicide a sin, it is the sin. It is the
ultimate and absolute evil, the refusal to take
the oath of loyalty to life. The man who kills
a man, kills a man. The man who kills himself
kills all men; as far as he is concerned he
wipes out the world.
G. K. Chesterton (1874–1936) British writer.
Orthodoxy

1909

451 There is false modesty, but there is no false
pride.
Jules Renard (1894–1910) French writer.
Journal

452 Corporal punishment is as humiliating for him
who gives it as for him who receives it; it is
ineffective besides. Neither shame nor physical
pain have any other effect than a hardening
one . . .
Ellen Key (Karolina Sofia Key; 1849–1926)
Swedish writer.
The Century of the Child. Ch. 8

1911

453 The belief in a supernatural source of evil is not

necessary; men alone are quite capable of ev-
ery wickedness.
Joseph Conrad (Teodor Josef Konrad
Korzeniowski; 1857–1924) Polish-born British
novelist.
Under Western Eyes

454 All a man can betray is his conscience.
Joseph Conrad
Under Western Eyes

Other People

1870

455 America is a country of young men.
Ralph Waldo Emerson (1803–82) US poet
and essayist.
Society and Solitude, 'Old Age'

1891

456 Asia is not going to be civilized after the meth-
ods of the West. There is too much Asia and
she is too old.
Rudyard Kipling (1865–1936) Indian-born
British writer.
Life's Handicap, 'The Man Who Was'

1893

457 MRS ALLONBY. They say, Lady Hunstanton, that
when good Americans die they go to Paris.
LADY HUNSTANTON. Indeed? And when bad
Americans die, where do they go to?
LORD ILLINGWORTH. Oh, they go to America.
Oscar Wilde (1854–1900) Irish-born British
dramatist.
A Woman of No Importance, I

1906

458 There are few more impressive sights in the
world than a Scotsman on the make.
J. M. Barrie (1860–1937) British novelist and
dramatist.
What Every Woman Knows, II

459 You've forgotten the grandest moral attribute of
a Scotsman, Maggie, that he'll do nothing
which might damage his career.
J. M. Barrie
What Every Woman Knows, II

1907

460 Cusins is a very nice fellow, certainly: nobody
would ever guess that he was born in
Australia.
George Bernard Shaw (1856–1950) Irish
dramatist and critic.
Major Barbara, I

461* The law of dislike for the unlike will always prevail. And whereas the unlike is normally situ-
ated at a safe distance, the Jews bring the
unlike into the heart of *every milieu,* and must

there defend a frontier line as large as the world.
Israel Zangwill (1864–1926) British writer.
Speeches, Articles and Letters, 'The Jewish Race'

1912

462 The English have no respect for their language, and will not teach their children to speak it . . . It is impossible for an Englishman to open his mouth, without making some other Englishman despise him.
George Bernard Shaw (1856–1950) Irish dramatist and critic.
Pygmalion, Preface

Religion

1872

463 While to deny the existence of an unseen kingdom is bad, to pretend that we know more about it than its bare existence is no better.
Samuel Butler (1835–1902) British writer.
Erewhon, Ch. 15

1875

464 The prayer that reforms the sinner and heals the sick is an absolute faith that all things are possible to God – a spiritual understanding of Him, an unselfed love.
Mary Baker Eddy (1821–1910) US religious leader.
Science and Health, with Key to the Scriptures

465 Christian Science explains all cause and effect as mental, not physical.
Mary Baker Eddy
Science and Health, with Key to the Scriptures

466 Sickness, sin and death, being inharmonious, do not originate in God, nor belong to His government.
Mary Baker Eddy
Science and Health, with Key to the Scriptures

1876

467 An honest God is the noblest work of man.
Robert G. Ingersoll (1833–99) US lawyer and agnostic.
Gods

1882

468 I have been into many of the ancient cathedrals – grand, wonderful, mysterious. But I always leave them with a feeling of indignation because of the generations of human beings who have struggled in poverty to build these altars to the unknown god.
Elizabeth Stanton (1815–1902) US suffragette.
Diary

469 God is dead: but considering the state the species Man is in, there will perhaps be caves, for ages yet, in which his shadow will be shown.
Friedrich Wilhelm Nietzsche (1844–1900) German philosopher.
Die Fröhliche Wissenschaft, Bk. III

470 The Christian resolution to find the world ugly and bad has made the world ugly and bad.
Friedrich Wilhelm Nietzsche
Die Fröhliche Wissenschaft, Bk. III

1892

471 No Jew was ever fool enough to turn Christian unless he was a clever man.
Israel Zangwill (1864–1926) British writer.
Children of the Ghetto, Ch. 1

1893

472 I fled Him, down the nights and down the days;
I fled Him, down the arches of the years;
I fled Him, down the labyrinthine ways
Of my own mind; and in the mist of tears
I hid from Him, and under running laughter.
Francis Thompson (1859–1907) British poet.
The Hound of Heaven

473 If you don't find a God by five o'clock this afternoon you must leave the college.
Benjamin Jowett (1817–93) British theologian.
Responding to a young student's assertion that he could find no evidence for a God
Attrib.

1895

474 I call Christianity the one great curse, the one enormous and innermost perversion, the one great instinct of revenge, for which no means are too venomous, too underhand, too underground and too petty – I call it the one immortal blemish of mankind.
Friedrich Wilhelm Nietzsche (1844–1900) German philosopher.
The Antichrist

1902

475 To be at all is to be religious more or less.
Samuel Butler (1835–1902) British writer.
Notebooks

1903

476 A local cult called Christianity.
Thomas Hardy (1840–1928) British novelist.
The Dynasts, I:6

1905

477 Carlyle said that men were mostly fools. Christianity, with a surer and more reverend realism, says that they are all fools.
G. K. Chesterton (1874-1936) British writer.
Heretics, Ch. 12

1906

478 *Pray, v.* To ask that the rules of the universe be annulled on behalf of a single petitioner, confessedly unworthy.
Ambrose Bierce (1842-?1914) US writer and journalist.
The Devil's Dictionary

1909

479 A Christian is a man who feels
Repentance on a Sunday
For what he did on Saturday
And is going to do on Monday.
Thomas Russell Ybarra (1880-   ) Venezuelan-born US writer.
The Christian

1910

480 Even in the valley of the shadow of death, two and two do not make six.
Leo Tolstoy (1828-1910) Russian writer.
Refusing to reconcile himself with the Russian Orthodox Church as he lay dying

1912

481 Whether you think Jesus was God or not, you must admit that he was a first-rate political economist.
George Bernard Shaw (1856-1950) Irish dramatist and critic.
Androcles and the Lion, Preface, 'Jesus as Economist'

1913

482 At bottom God is nothing more than an exalted father.
Sigmund Freud (1856-1939) Austrian psychoanalyst.
Totem and Taboo

483 For an idea ever to be fashionable is ominous, since it must afterwards be always old-fashioned.
George Santayana (1863-1952) US philosopher.
Winds of Doctrine, 'Modernism and Christianity'

Science, Medicine, and Technology

1871

484 We must, however, acknowledge, as it seems to me, that man with all his noble qualities, still bears in his bodily frame the indelible stamp of his lowly origin.
Charles Darwin (1809-82) British life scientist.
Closing words
Descent of Man, Ch. 21

1872

485 There are no such things as applied sciences, only applications of science.
Louis Pasteur (1822-95) French scientist.
Address, 11 Sept 1872

1875

486 Mr. Darwin . . . has failed to hold definitely before his mind the principle that the difference of sex, whatever it may consist in, must itself be subject to natural selection and to evolution.
Antoinette Brown Blackwell (1825-1921) US feminist writer.
The Sexes Throughout Nature

1876

487 Mr Watson, come here; I want you.
Alexander Graham Bell (1847-1922) Scottish scientist.
The first telephone conversation, 10 Mar 1876, in Boston
Attrib.

1882

488 Do you really believe that the sciences would ever have originated and grown if the way had not been prepared by magicians, alchemists, astrologers and witches whose promises and pretensions first had to create a thirst, a hunger, a taste for *hidden* and *forbidden* powers? Indeed, infinitely more had to be *promised* than could ever be fulfilled in order that anything at all might be fulfilled in the realms of knowledge.
Friedrich Wilhelm Nietzsche (1844-1900) German philosopher.
The Gay Science

1885

489 Psychology has a long past, but only a short history.
Hermann Ebbinghaus German psychologist.
Summary of Psychology

1894

490 Science is nothing but trained and organized common sense, differing from the latter only as a veteran may differ from a raw recruit: and its methods differ from those of common sense only as far as the guardsman's cut and thrust

differ from the manner in which a savage wields his club.
T. H. Huxley (1825–95) British biologist.
Collected Essays, 'The Method of Zadig'

491 The great tragedy of Science – the slaying of a beautiful hypothesis by an ugly fact.
T. H. Huxley
Collected Essays, 'Biogenesis and Abiogenesis'

1903

492* The airplane stays up because it doesn't have the time to fall.
Orville Wright (1871–1948) US aviator.
Explaining the principles of powered flight
Attrib.

1912

493 I like mathematics because it is *not* human and has nothing particular to do with this planet or with the whole accidental universe – because, like Spinoza's God, it won't love us in return.
Bertrand Russell (1872–1970) British philosopher.
Letter to Lady Ottoline Morrell, Mar 1912

1914

494* The universe ought to be presumed too vast to have any character.
C. S. Peirce (1839–1914) US physicist.
Collected Papers, VI

495 You cannot endow even the best machine with initiative. The jolliest steam-roller will not plant flowers.
Walter Lippmann (1889–1974) US editor and author.
A Preface to Politics

Wealth and Poverty

1872

496 It has been said that the love of money is the root of all evil. The want of money is so quite as truly.
Samuel Butler (1835–1902) British writer.
Erewhon, Ch. 20

1879

497 Poverty is an anomaly to rich people. It is very difficult to make out why people who want dinner do not ring the bell.
Walter Bagehot (1826–77) British economist and journalist.
Literary Studies, II

1880s

498 As I walk along the Bois Bou-long,

With an independent air,
You can hear the girls declare,
'He must be a millionaire',
You can hear them sigh and wish to die,
You can see them wink the other eye
At the man who broke the Bank at Monte Carlo.
Fred Gilbert (1850–1903) British songwriter.
The Bois de Boulogne was a fashionable recreational area on the outskirts of Paris
The Man who Broke the Bank at Monte Carlo (song)

1885

499 I have had no real gratification or enjoyment of any sort more than my neighbor on the next block who is worth only half a million.
William Henry Vanderbilt (1821–85) US railway chief.
Famous Last Words (B. Conrad)

1889

500 It is easy enough to say that poverty is no crime. No; if it were men wouldn't be ashamed of it. It is a blunder, though, and is punished as such. A poor man is despised the whole world over.
Jerome K. Jerome (1859–1927) British humorist.
Idle Thoughts of an Idle Fellow

1891

501 As for the virtuous poor, one can pity them, of course, but one cannot possibly admire them.
Oscar Wilde (1854–1900) Irish-born British dramatist.
The Soul of Man under Socialism

1905

502 Lack of money is the root of all evil.
George Bernard Shaw (1856–1950) Irish dramatist and critic.
Man and Superman, 'Maxims for Revolutionists.'

503 The universal regard for money is the one hopeful fact in our civilization. Money is the most important thing in the world. It represents health, strength, honour, generosity and beauty.
George Bernard Shaw
Major Barbara, Preface

504 I am a millionaire. That is my religion.
George Bernard Shaw
Major Barbara

505 CUSINS. Do you call poverty a crime?
UNDERSHAFT. The worst of all crimes. All the other crimes are virtues beside it.
George Bernard Shaw
Major Barbara

1906

506 *Money, n.* A blessing that is of no advantage to us excepting when we part with it.
Ambrose Bierce (1842-?1914) US writer and journalist.
The Devil's Dictionary

1910s

507 I must say I hate money but it's the lack of it I hate most.
Katherine Mansfield (1888-1923) New-Zealand-born British writer.
Katherine Mansfield (Anthony Alpers)

1910

508 The very poor are unthinkable and only to be approached by the statistician and the poet.
E. M. Forster (1879-1970) British novelist.
Howards End

1911

509 To be clever enough to get all that money, one must be stupid enough to want it.
G. K. Chesterton (1874-1936) British writer.
The Innocence of Father Brown

1914

510 The rich are the scum of the earth in every country.
G. K. Chesterton
The Flying Inn

Work and Occupations

1872

511 Any officer who shall behave in a scandalous manner, unbecoming the character of an officer and a gentleman shall . . . be cashiered.
Anonymous
The words 'conduct unbecoming the character of an officer' are a direct quotation from the Naval Discipline Act (10 Aug 1860), Article 24
Articles of War (1872), *Disgraceful Conduct*, 79

1881

512 Man is so made that he can only find relaxation from one kind of labour by taking up another.
Anatole France (Jacques Anatole François Thibault; 1844-1924) French writer.
The Crime of Sylvestre Bonnard

1882

513 Politics is perhaps the only profession for which no preparation is thought necessary.
Robert Louis Stevenson (1850-94) Scottish writer.
Familiar Studies of Men and Books, 'Yoshida-Torajiro'

1886

514 In the philosopher there is nothing whatever impersonal; and, above all, his morality bears decided and decisive testimony to *who he is* — that is to say, to the order of rank in which the innermost drives of his nature stand in relation to one another.
Friedrich Wilhelm Nietzsche (1844-1900) German philosopher.
Jenseits von Gut und Böse

1890

515* It's Tommy this, an' Tommy that, an' 'Chuck him out, the brute!'
But it's 'Saviour of 'is country' when the guns begin to shoot.
Rudyard Kipling (1865-1936) Indian-born British writer.
Tommy

1891

516 There is much to be said in favour of modern journalism. By giving us the opinions of the uneducated, it keeps us in touch with the ignorance of the community.
Oscar Wilde (1854-1900) Irish-born British dramatist.
The Critic as Artist, Pt. 2

1893

517 I doubt if the philosopher lives, or ever has lived, who could know himself to be heartily despised by a street boy without some irritation.
T. H. Huxley (1825-95) British biologist.
Evolution and Ethics

1898

518 I hesitate to say what the functions of the modern journalist may be; but I imagine that they do not exclude the intelligent anticipation of facts even before they occur.
Lord Curzon (1859-1925) British politician.
Speech, House of Commons, 29 Mar 1898

1899

519 I wish to preach, not the doctrine of ignoble ease, but the doctrine of the strenuous life.
Theodore Roosevelt (1858-1919) US Republican president.
Speech, Chicago, 10 Apr 1899

1900

520 Work is the curse of the drinking classes.
Oscar Wilde (1854-1900) Irish-born British dramatist.
Attrib.

1903

521 When work is a pleasure, life is a joy! When work is a duty, life is slavery.
Maxim Gorky (Aleksei Maksimovich Peshkov; 1868–1936) Russian writer.
The Lower Depths

522 He who can, does. He who cannot, teaches.
George Bernard Shaw (1856–1950) Irish dramatist and critic.
Man and Superman, 'Maxims for Revolutionists'

1905

523 Everybody hates house-agents because they have everybody at a disadvantage. All other callings have a certain amount of give and take; the house-agent simply takes.
H. G. Wells (1866–1946) British writer.
Kipps, Bk. III, Ch. 1

1914

524 Optimistic lies have such immense therapeutic value that a doctor who cannot tell them convincingly has mistaken his profession.
George Bernard Shaw (1856–1950) Irish dramatist and critic.
Misalliance, Preface

Sayings of the Time

1871

525 Dr Livingstone, I presume?
Henry Morton Stanley (1841–1904) British explorer.
On finding David Livingstone at Ujiji on Lake Tanganyika, Nov 1871
How I found Livingstone, Ch. 11

1878

526 Beauty is altogether in the eye of the beholder.
Margaret Wolfe Hungerford (c. 1855–97) Irish novelist.
Also attributed to the US soldier and writer Lew Wallace (1827–1905)
Molly Bawn

1892

527 You know my method. It is founded upon the observance of trifles.
Arthur Conan Doyle (1856–1930) British writer.
The Boscombe Valley Mystery

528 It is an old maxim of mine that when you have excluded the impossible, whatever remains, however improbable, must be the truth.
Arthur Conan Doyle
The Beryl Coronet

529 Castles in the air – they're so easy to take refuge in. So easy to build, too.
Henrik Ibsen (1828–1906) Norwegian dramatist.
The Master Builder, III

530 Though I've belted you an' flayed you,
By the livin' Gawd that made you,
You're a better man than I am, Gunga Din!
Rudyard Kipling (1865–1936) Indian-born British writer.
Gunga Din

531 If you can keep your head when all about you
Are losing theirs and blaming it on you.
Rudyard Kipling
If

532 If you can talk with crowds and keep your virtue,
Or walk with Kings – nor lose the common touch,
If neither foes nor loving friends can hurt you,
If all men count with you, but none too much;
If you can fill the unforgiving minute
With sixty seconds' worth of distance run,
Yours is the Earth and everything that's in it,
And – which is more – you'll be a Man my son!
Rudyard Kipling
If

1893

533 'Excellent!' I cried. 'Elementary,' said he.
Arthur Conan Doyle (1856–1930) British writer.
Watson talking to Sherlock Holmes; Holmes's reply is often misquoted as 'Elementary my dear Watson'
The Crooked Man

1900s

534 She's only a bird in a gilded cage.
A. J. Lamb (1870–1928) British songwriter.
Song title

535 Once a jolly swagman camped by a billabong,
Under the shade of a coolibah tree,
And he sang as he sat and waited for his billy-boil,
'You'll come a-waltzing, Matilda, with me.'
Andrew Barton Paterson (1864–1941) Australian journalist and poet.
Waltzing Matilda

536 Where are the boys of the Old Brigade?
Frederic Edward Weatherly (1848–1929) British lawyer and songwriter.
The Old Brigade

537 Every day, in every way, I am getting better and better.
Emile Coué (1857–1920) French doctor.
Formula for a cure by autosuggestion

1900

538 I shall tell you a tale of four little rabbits whose

names were Flopsy, Mopsy, Cottontail and
Peter.
Beatrix Potter (1866–1943) British children's
writer.
The Tale of Peter Rabbit

1905

539   We seek him here, we seek him there,
Those Frenchies seek him everywhere.
Is he in heaven? – Is he in hell?
That damned elusive Pimpernel?
Baroness Orczy (1865–1947) British
novelist.
The Scarlet Pimpernel, Ch. 12

1908

540   The clever men at Oxford
Know all that there is to be knowed.
But they none of them know one half as much
As intelligent Mr Toad.
Kenneth Grahame (1859–1932) Scottish
writer.
The Wind in the Willows, Ch. 10

1910

541* There's a breathless hush in the Close
tonight –
Ten to make and the match to win –
. . .
The sand of the desert is sodden red, –
Red with the wreck of a square that broke; –
The gatling's jammed and the colonel dead,
And the regiment blind with the dust and
smoke.
The river of death has brimmed its banks
And England's far and honour a name.
But the voice of a schoolboy rallies the ranks:
'Play up! play up! and play the game!'
Henry John Newbolt (1862–1938) British
poet.
Vitaī Lampada

542   It's 'Damn you, Jack – I'm all right!' with you
chaps.
David Bone (1874–1959) British sea captain
and writer.
The Brassbounder, Ch. 3

543* Oh, East is East, and West is West, and never
the twain shall meet.
Rudyard Kipling (1865–1936) Indian-born
British writer.
The Ballad of East and West

1911

544   There's a one-eyed yellow idol to the north of
Khatmandu,
There's a little marble cross below the town;
There's a broken-hearted woman tends the
grave of Mad Carew
And the Yellow God forever gazes down.
J. Milton Hayes (1884–1940) British writer.
The Green Eye of the Yellow God

With Hindsight

20th century

545   So they told me how Mr Gladstone read Homer
for fun, which I thought served him right.
Winston Churchill (1874–1965) British
statesman.
My Early Life, Ch. 2

546   They improvidentially piped growing volumes of
sewage into the sea, the healing virtues of
which were advertised on every railway
station.
Robert Cecil (1913–   ) British writer.
Referring to seaside resorts
Life in Edwardian England

547   Virtue consisted in avoiding scandal and vene-
real disease.
Robert Cecil
Life in Edwardian England

548   Physics becomes in those years the greatest
collective work of science – no, more than
that, the great collective work of art of the
twentieth century.
Jacob Bronowski (1908–74) British scientist
and writer.
Referring to the period around the turn of the
century marked by the elucidation of atomic
structure and the development of the quantum
theory
The Ascent of Man, Ch. 10

549   To give an accurate and exhaustive account of
that period would need a far less brilliant pen
than mine.
Max Beerbohm (1872–1956) British writer.
1880

<h1 style="text-align: center">12</h1>

The World Wars (1914—45)

On 28 June 1914 the assassination of the heir to the Austro-Hungarian throne triggered a system of alliances that quickly plunged the whole of Europe into war. This was greeted with enthusiasm in many quarters: both sides expected it to be short and glorious, with everybody home by Christmas. The reality was very different. Such military developments as the machine gun, and the enormous power of the artillery, gave defensive warfare a decisive advantage. The war soon became a contest of attrition with enormous loss of life, especially in the trench warfare on the Western Front. It ended in 1918, after slaughter on a scale hitherto unknown. The strain of the war led to the collapse of the Austrian, German, and Russian monarchies, the last being replaced by the world's first communist state. Europe was now economically exhausted, with the old order totally shattered. Even the victorious British servicemen who had survived the war returned bitter and disillusioned to a country that was supposed to be 'fit for heroes'.

Economic recovery was slow and partial; what improvement there had been was destroyed in 1929 by the Wall Street Crash and the subsequent Great Depression. The USA retreated into isolationism and experimented with prohibition. In the USSR, Stalin, who succeeded Lenin in 1924, brutally imposed his vision of socialism on a reluctant nation. Other countries succumbed to the extreme right, with its cult of the militant dictator: Mussolini, Franco, Salazar, and Hitler. Hitler's combination of ethnic nationalism, antisemitism, and fascism was especially well-received in Germany, where the harshness of the Versailles peace settlement in 1919 accentuated economic hardship and stirred the martial aspirations of the failed Prussian imperialists. After gaining power in 1933, the Nazis attempted to turn their vision of world domination into reality. When appeasement had failed, Britain and France had no alternative but to deliver the ultimatum that led to World War II (1939—45).

Germany's initial successes led to the fall of France and the occupation of nearly the whole of Europe by the Nazis. Britain, expelled ignominiously from France at Dunkirk (June 1940), prepared to defend itself from an invasion that never came. Instead Hitler, his Luftwaffe badly damaged by the RAF in the Battle of Britain, launched an attack on the Soviet Union (June 1941). In December 1941 the Japanese attacked the Americans in Pearl Harbor, thereby joining the conflict on the side of the Axis Powers and forcing the USA to become one of the Allies. By June 1944 Anglo-American forces were ready to invade Europe; in May 1945, two days after Berlin had fallen to the Russians, Germany surrendered. The result of the conflict was the death of some 25 million combatants and civilians, the extermination of 6 million Jews by the Nazis, the ruin of Germany for the second time in a generation, and the devastation of most of Europe.

Politics, Government, and World Events

1914

1   Liberty does not consist in mere declarations of the rights of man. It consists in the translation of those declarations into definite action.
Woodrow Wilson (1856–1924) US statesman.
Speech, 4 July 1914

2   We sauntered through the crowd to Trafalgar Square where Labour, socialist, pacifist demonstrators — with a few trade union flags — were gesticulating from the steps of the monuments to a mixed crowd of admirers, hooligan warmongers and merely curious holidaymakers. It was an undignified and futile exhibition, this singing of the Red Flag and passing of well-worn radical resolutions in favour of universal peace.
Beatrice Webb (1858–1943) British economist and writer.
Referring to an anti-war demonstration, 2 Aug 1914
Diary, 4 Aug 1914; war was declared on Germany at 11 p.m.

3   The lamps are going out over all Europe; we shall not see them lit again in our lifetime.
Lord Grey (1862–1933) British statesman.
Remark made on 3 Aug 1914, the eve of World War I

4   We draw the sword with a clear conscience and with clean hands.
Wilhelm II (1859–1941) King of Prussia and Emperor of Germany.
Speech, Berlin, 4 Aug 1914

5   You will be home before the leaves have fallen from the trees.
Wilhelm II
Said to troops leaving for the Front, Aug 1914
August 1914 (Barbara Tuchman), Ch. 9

6   When you march into France, let the last man on the right brush the Channel with his sleeve.
Alfred Graf von Schlieffen (1833–1913) German general.
Referring to the Schlieffen plan – a German plan of attack
August 1914 (Barbara Tuchman), Ch. 2

7   When the war broke out she took down the signed photograph of the Kaiser and, with some solemnity, hung it in the menservants' lavatory; it was her one combative action.
Evelyn Waugh (1903–66) British novelist.
Vile Bodies, Ch. 3

8   The United States must be neutral in fact as well as in name during these days that are to try men's souls. We must be impartial in thought as well as in action.
Woodrow Wilson (1856–1924) US statesman.
Message to the Senate, 19 Aug 1914

9   It is my Royal and Imperial Command that you . . . exterminate first the treacherous English, and . . . walk over General French's contemptible little Army.
Wilhelm II (1859–1941) King of Prussia and Emperor of Germany.
Referring to the British Expeditionary Force; veterans of this force became known as 'Old Contemptibles'
The Times, 1 Oct 1914

10   We shall never sheathe the sword which we have not lightly drawn until Belgium receives in full measure all and more than all that she has sacrificed, until France is adequately secured against the menace of aggression, until the rights of the smaller nationalities of Europe are placed upon an unassailable foundation, and until the military domination of Prussia is wholly and finally destroyed.
Herbert Henry Asquith (1852–1928) British statesman.
Speech, Guildhall, 9 Nov 1914

11   The maxim of the British people is 'Business as usual'.
Winston Churchill (1874–1965) British statesman.
Speech, Guildhall, 9 Nov 1914

12   I don't mind your being killed, but I object to your being taken prisoner.
Lord Kitchener (1850–1916) British field marshal.
Said to the Prince of Wales (later Edward VIII) when he asked to go to the Front
Journal (Viscount Esher), 18 Dec 1914

13   Your country needs YOU.
British recruiting poster featuring Lord Kitchener

14   If Kitchener was not a great man, he was, at least, a great poster.
Margot Asquith (1865–1945) The second wife of Herbert Asquith.
Kitchener: Portrait of an Imperialist (Sir Philip Magnus), Ch. 14

15*   We Don't Want To Lose You But We Think You Ought To Go.
Paul Alfred Rubens (1875–1917) British dramatist and songwriter.
Title of patriotic music-hall song

16*   Good-bye Piccadilly, Farewell Leicester Square; It's a long, long way to Tipperary, but my heart's right there!
Harry Williams (1874–1924) British songwriter.
Written with Jack Judge (1878–1938)
It's a Long Way to Tipperary

17   It's often safer to be in chains than to be free.
Franz Kafka (1883–1924) Czech novelist.
The Trial, Ch. 8

18*   The old Lie: *Dulce et decorum est Pro patria mori.*
Wilfred Owen (1893–1918) British poet.
Dulce et decorum est

19   My pacifism is not based on any intellectual

theory but on a deep antipathy to every form of cruelty and hatred.
Albert Einstein (1879–1955) German-born US physicist.
Said on the outbreak of World War I
Attrib.

20* Above all I am not concerned with Poetry. My subject is War, and the pity of War. The Poetry is in the pity.
Wilfred Owen (1893–1918) British poet.
Poems, Preface

21* The pallor of girls' brows shall be their pall;
Their flowers the tenderness of patient minds,
And each slow dusk a drawing-down of blinds.
Wilfred Owen
Anthem for Doomed Youth

22* Red lips are not so red
As the stained stones kissed by the English dead.
Wilfred Owen
Greater Love

23* Dead battles, like dead generals, hold the military mind in their dead grip.
Barbara W. Tuchman (1912–89) US editor and writer.
August 1914, Ch. 2

1915

24 No nation is fit to sit in judgement upon any other nation.
Woodrow Wilson (1856–1924) US statesman.
Address, Apr 1915

25* Once lead this people into war and they'll forget there ever was such a thing as tolerance.
Woodrow Wilson
Mr Wilson's War (John Dos Passos), Pt. III, Ch. 2

26 There is such a thing as a man being too proud to fight.
Woodrow Wilson
Address to foreign-born citizens, 10 May 1915

27 LUDENDORFF. The English soldiers fight like lions.
HOFFMANN. True. But don't we know that they are lions led by donkeys.
Max Hoffmann (1869–1927) German general.
The Donkeys (A. Clark)

28 In Flanders fields the poppies blow
Between the crosses, row on row,
That mark our place.
John McCrae (1872–1918) Canadian poet and doctor.
In Flanders Fields, 'Ypres Salient', 3 May 1915

29 There is no room in this country for hyphenated Americanism.
Theodore Roosevelt (1858–1919) US president.
Speech, New York, 12 Oct 1915

30* War knows no power. Safe shall be my going,
Secretly armed against all death's endeavour;
Safe though all safety's lost; safe where men fall;

And if these poor limbs die, safest of all.
Rupert Brooke (1887–1915) British poet.
Safety

31 If I should die, think only this of me:
That there's some corner of a foreign field
That is forever England.
Rupert Brooke
The Soldier

32 I realize that patriotism is not enough. I must have no hatred or bitterness towards anyone.
Edith Cavell (1865–1915) British nurse.
Before her execution by the Germans in 1915

33 Smile at us, pay us, pass us; but do not quite forget.
For we are the people of England, that never have spoken yet.
G. K. Chesterton (1874–1936) British writer.
The Secret People

34 Don't talk to me about naval tradition. It's nothing but rum, sodomy, and the lash.
Winston Churchill (1874–1965) British statesman.
Former Naval Person (Sir Peter Gretton), Ch. 1

1916

35 All dressed up, with nowhere to go.
William Allen White (1868–1944) US writer.
Referring to the Progressive Party, after Theodore Roosevelt's withdrawal from the 1916 US Presidential election

36 America cannot be an ostrich with its head in the sand.
Woodrow Wilson (1856–1924) US statesman.
Speech, Des Moines, 1 Feb 1916

37 Jellicoe was the only man on either side who could lose the war in an afternoon.
Winston Churchill (1874–1965) British statesman.
Referring to Admiral Jellicoe, who commanded the British fleet at the Battle of Jutland (31 May 1916)
The Observer, 'Sayings of the Week', 13 Feb 1927

38 He kept us out of war!
Martin H. Glynn (1891–1924) Governor of New York State.
Referring to President Wilson
Speech, Democratic Convention, St Louis, 15 June 1916

39 What should I do? I think the best thing is to order a new stamp to be made with my face on it.
Charles (1887–1922) Emperor of Austria.
On hearing of his accession to emperor
Anekdotenschatz (H. Hoffmeister)

40 Be the Emperor, be Peter the Great, John the Terrible, the Emperor Paul —crush them all under you — Now don't you laugh, naughty one — but I long to see you so with those men

who try to govern *you* and it must be the contrary.
Alexandra (1872–1918) Empress-Consort of Russia
Letter (in English) to Nicholas II, 27 Dec 1916

41   Ireland is the old sow that eats her farrow.
James Joyce (1882–1941) Irish novelist.
A Portrait of the Artist as a Young Man, Ch. 5

42   This war, like the next war, is a war to end war.
David Lloyd George (1863–1945) British statesman.
Referring to the popular opinion that World War I would be the last major war

43*   O Death, where is thy sting-a-ling-a-ling,
O Grave, thy victoree?
The bells of hell go ting-a-ling-a-ling
For you but not for me.
Anonymous
Song of World War I

44   What's the use of worrying?
It never was worth while,
So, pack up your troubles in your old kit-bag,
And smile, smile, smile.
George Asaf (George H. Powell; 1880–1951) US songwriter.
Pack up Your Troubles in Your Old Kit-bag

45   I have a rendezvous with Death
At some disputed barricade.
Alan Seeger (1888–1916) US poet.
I Have a Rendezvous with Death

46   *Ils ne passeront pas.*
They shall not pass.
Marshal Pétain (1856–1951) French marshal.
Attrib; probably derived from General R.-G. Nivelle's Order of the Day, '*Vous ne les laisserez pas passer*' (June 1916). It is also attributed to the Spanish politician Dolores Ibarruri in the Spanish Civil War.

47   I had always to remember that I could have lost the war in an afternoon.
Lord Jellicoe (1859–1935) British admiral.
Referring to the Battle of Jutland

48   Formerly, a nation that broke the peace did not trouble to try and prove to the world that it was done solely from higher motives ... *Now war has a bad conscience.* Now every nation assures us that it is bleeding for a human cause, the fate of which hangs in the balance of its victory.... No nation dares to admit the guilt of blood before the world.
Ellen Key (Karolina Sofia Key; 1849–1926) Swedish writer.
War, Peace, and the Future, Preface

49   Everything, everything in war is barbaric ... But the worst barbarity of war is that it forces men collectively to commit acts against which individually they would revolt with their whole being.
Ellen Key
War, Peace, and the Future, Ch. 6

<hr/>

1917

50   The first casualty when war comes is truth.
Hiram Warren Johnson (1866–1945) US politician.
Speech, US Senate, 1917

51   The world must be made safe for democracy.
Woodrow Wilson (1856–1924) US statesman.
Address to Congress, asking for a declaration of war 2 Apr 1917

52   Lafayette, we are here!
C. E. Stanton (1859–1933) US colonel.
The Marquis de Lafayette (1757–1834) aided the colonists in the US War of Independence
Address at Lafayette's grave, Paris, 4 July 1917

53*   Deleted by French censor.
James Gordon Bennett (1841–1918) US newspaper owner and editor.
Used to fill empty spaces in his papers during World War I when news was lacking
Americans in Paris (B. Morton)

54   Now all roads lead to France
And heavy is the tread
Of the living; but the dead
Returning lightly dance.
Edward Thomas (1878–1917) British poet.
Roads

55   The Church should be no longer satisfied to represent only the Conservative Party at prayer.
Agnes Maude Royden (1887–1967) British Congregationalist minister.
Speech, London, 16 July 1917

56   America ... is the prize amateur nation of the world. Germany is the prize professional nation.
Woodrow Wilson (1856–1924) US statesman.
Speech, Aug 1917
Mr Wilson's War (John Dos Passos), Pt. III, Ch. 13

57   His Majesty's Government views with favour the establishment in Palestine of a national home for the Jewish people ...
Arthur Balfour (1848–1930) British statesman.
The so-called 'Balfour Declaration'
Letter to Lord Rothschild, 2 Nov 1917

58   The Germans turned upon Russia the most grisly of all weapons. They transported Lenin in a sealed truck like a plague bacillus from Switzerland to Russia.
Winston Churchill (1874–1965) British statesman.
The World Crisis

59   The proper memory for a politician is one that knows when to remember and when to forget.
John Morley (1838–1923) British statesman.
Recollections

The Russian Revolution (1917)

By 1900, Russia was almost alone among European powers in having a strong monarchy; there had been hardly any erosion of the Tsar's autocratic power or indeed any reform at all. Socially, economically, and politically Russia was far behind the rest of Europe. The revolutionary disturbances that had occurred throughout the 19th century culminated in Bloody Sunday (22 January, 1905). As a result of this uprising a parliament was established in 1906; thereafter the Tsar ruled by an ever-weakening mixture of autocratic repression and grudging social and political reform. In Feburary 1917, after the strain of two and a half years of war, the system collapsed. Strikes in the capital and mutinies in the army quickly escalated, forcing the Tsar to abdicate. Although a provisional government attempted to fill the political vacuum, the continuing instability played into the hands of the Bolsheviks, led by Lenin. In the revolution of October 1917 the Bolsheviks finally seized power. During the ensuing years they consolidated their power over the whole country, internal opposition and foreign-backed counter-revolutionaries being defeated by the Red Army in a civil war (1918–21). By 1922 the Soviet Union was firmly established as the world's first communist state.

60 **Peace, Bread and Land.**
Slogan of workers in Petrograd (St Petersburg) during the February Revolution

61 **Dear comrades, soldiers, sailors and workers! I am happy to greet in you the victorious Russian Revolution!**
Lenin (Vladimir Ilich Ulyanov; 1870–1924) Russian revolutionary leader.
Speech, Finland Station (Petrograd), 16 Apr 1917

62 **All Power to the Soviets!**
Slogan of workers in Petrograd (St Petersburg) during the October Revolution

63 **The substitution of the proletarian for the bourgeois state is impossible without a violent revolution.**
Lenin (Vladimir Ilich Ulyanov; 1870–1924)
State and Revolution, Ch. 1

64 **In a state worthy of the name there is no liberty. The people want to exercise power but what on earth would they do with it if it were given to them?**
Lenin
The State and Revolution

65 **If it were necessary to give the briefest possible definition of imperialism we should have to say that imperialism is the monopoly stage of capitalism.**
Lenin
Imperialism, the Highest Stage of Capitalism, Ch. 7

66 **We shall now proceed to construct the socialist order.**
Lenin
First words to the Congress of Soviets after the capture of the Winter Palace, 26 Oct 1917

67 **Ten Days that Shook the World.**
John Reed (1887–1920) American journalist.
Referring to the Bolshevik Revolution in Russia (Nov 1917)
Book title

68 **Neither can you expect a revolution, because there is no new baby in the womb of our society. Russia is a collapse, not a revolution.**
D. H. Lawrence (1885–1930) British novelist.
Phoenix, 'The Good Man'

69* **Patriotism to the Soviet State is a revolutionary duty, whereas patriotism to a bourgeois State is treachery.**
Leon Trotsky (Lev Davidovich Bronstein; 1879–1940) Russian revolutionary.
Disputed Barricade (Fitzroy Maclean)

70 **So long as the state exists there is no freedom. When there is freedom there will be no state.**
Lenin (Vladimir Ilich Ulyanov; 1870–1924) Russian revolutionary leader.
The State and Revolution, Ch. 5

71 **The 23rd of February was International Woman's Day . . . It had not occurred to anyone that it might become the first day of the revolution.**
Leon Trotsky (Lev Davidovich Bronstein; 1879–1940) Russian revolutionary.
History of the Russian Revolution, Pt. I, Ch. 7

72 **Under socialism *all* will govern in turn and will soon become accustomed to no one governing.**
Lenin (Vladimir Ilich Ulyanov; 1870–1924) Russian revolutionary leader.
The State and Revolution, Ch. 6

1918

73 *Per ardua ad astra.*
Through endeavour to the stars.
Anonymous
Motto of the Royal Air Force

74 **What we demand in this war is nothing peculiar to ourselves. It is that the world be made fit and safe to live in.**
Woodrow Wilson (1856–1924) US statesman.
Preamble to his 'Fourteen Points' for ensuring world peace
Speech to Congress, 8 Jan 1918

75 **Self-determination is not a mere phrase. It is an imperative principle which statesmen will henceforth ignore at their peril.**
Woodrow Wilson
Speech to Congress, 11 Feb 1918

76 **My home policy? I wage war. My foreign policy? I wage war. Always, everywhere, I wage war . . . And I shall continue to wage war until the last quarter of an hour.**
Georges Clemenceau (1841–1929) French statesman.
Speech, Chamber of Deputies, 8 Mar 1918

77 **A mademoiselle from Armenteers,
She hasn't been kissed for forty years,**

Hinky, dinky, par-lee-voo.
Edward Rowland (20th century) British songwriter.
Armentières was completely destroyed (1918) in World War I
Mademoiselle from Armentières (song)

78 Every position must be held to the last man: there must be no retirement. With our backs to the wall, and believing in the justice of our cause, each one of us must fight on to the end.
Earl Haig (1861–1928) British general.
Order to the British Army, 12 Apr 1918

79 Come on, you sons of bitches! Do you want to live for ever?
Dan Daly (20th century) Sergeant in the US Marines.
Exhorting his men at Belleau Wood, June 1918
Attrib.

80 My centre is giving way, my right is in retreat; situation excellent. I shall attack.
Marshal Foch (1851–1929) French soldier.
Message sent during the second battle of the Marne, 1918
Biography of Foch (Aston), Ch. 13

81 'Good morning; good morning!' the general said
When we met him last week on our way to the line.
Now the soldiers he smiled at are most of 'em dead,
And we're cursing his staff for incompetent swine.
Siegfried Sassoon (1886–1967) British poet.
The General

82 If I were fierce and bald and short of breath,
I'd live with scarlet Majors at the Base,
And speed glum heroes up the line to death.
Siegfried Sassoon
Base Details

83 Man, it seemed, had been created to jab the life out of Germans.
Siegfried Sassoon
Memoirs of an Infantry Officer, Pt. I, Ch. 1

84 Who will remember, passing through this gate
The unheroic dead who fed the guns?
Who shall absolve the foulness of their fate –
Those doomed, conscripted, unvictorious ones?
Siegfried Sassoon
On Passing the New Menin Gate

85 And when the war is done and youth stone dead
I'd toddle safely home and die – in bed.
Siegfried Sassoon
Base Details

86 I am making this statement as a wilful defiance of military authority because I believe that the War is being deliberately prolonged by those who have the power to end it.
Siegfried Sassoon
Memoirs of an Infantry Officer, Pt. X, Ch. 3

87* I could not give my name to aid the slaughter in this war, fought on both sides for grossly material ends, which did not justify the sacrifice

of a single mother's son. Clearly I must continue to oppose it, and expose it, to all whom I could reach with voice or pen.
Sylvia Pankhurst (1882–1960) British suffragette.
The Home Front, Ch. 25

88 Madam, I am the civilization they are fighting to defend.
Heathcote William Garrod (1878–1960) British classical scholar.
Replying to criticism that he was not fighting to defend civilization, during World War I
Oxford Now and Then (D. Balsdon)

89 They died to save their country and they only saved the world.
Hilaire Belloc (1870–1953) French-born British poet.
The English Graves

90* The shrill demented choirs of wailing shells
And buglers calling for them from sad shires.
Wilfred Owen (1893–1918) British poet.
Anthem for Doomed Youth

91 With proud thanksgiving, a mother for her children,
England mourns for her dead across the sea.
Laurence Binyon (1869–1943) British poet.
In response to the slaughter of World War I
Poems For the Fallen

92 They shall grow not old, as we that are left grow old:
Age shall not weary them, nor the years condemn.
At the going down of the sun and in the morning
We will remember them.
Laurence Binyon
Poems For the Fallen

93 Sire you no longer have an army.
Wilhelm Groener (1867–1939) German general.
Said to the Emperor Wilhelm II of Germany, 9 Nov 1918

94 As an English General has very truly said, 'The German army was stabbed in the back'.
Paul von Hindenburg (1847–1934) German Field Marshal and President.
Referring to Germany's defeat in World War I; it is not known whom Hindenburg was quoting
Statement to a Reichstag Committee, 18 Nov 1918

95 When the days of rejoicing are over,
When the flags are stowed safely away,
They will dream of another wild 'War to End Wars'
And another wild Armistice day.

But the boys who were killed in the trenches,
Who fought with no rage and no rant,
We left them stretched out on their pallets of mud
Low down with the worm and the ant.
Robert Graves (1895–1985) British poet and novelist.
Armistice Day, 1918

96* The war we have just been through, though it was shot through with terror, is not to be compared with the war we would have to face next time.
Woodrow Wilson (1856–1924) US statesman.
Mr Wilson's War (John Dos Passos), Pt. V, Ch. 22

97 The British flag has never flown over a more powerful or a more united empire . . . Never did our voice count for more in the councils of nations; or in determining the future destinies of mankind.
George Nathaniel Carson (1859–1925) British politician.
Speech, House of Lords, 18 Nov 1918

98 What is our task? To make Britain a fit country for heroes to live in.
David Lloyd George (1863–1945) British statesman.
Speech, 24 Nov 1918

99 The Germans, if this Government is returned, are going to pay every penny; they are going to be squeezed, as a lemon is squeezed – until the pips squeak. My only doubt is not whether we can squeeze hard enough, but whether there is enough juice.
Eric Campbell Geddes (1875–1937) British politician.
Speech, Cambridge, 10 Dec 1918

100 A lot of hard-faced men who look as if they had done very well out of the war.
Stanley Baldwin (1867–1947) British statesman.
Referring to the first House of Commons elected after World War I (1918)
Economic Consequences of the Peace (J. M. Keynes), Ch. 5

1919

101 There is nothing that war has ever achieved that we could not better achieve without it.
Havelock Ellis (1859–1939) British sexologist.
The Philosophy of Conflict

102 It is far easier to make war than to make peace.
Georges Clemenceau (1841–1929) French statesman.
Speech, 14 July 1919

103 We are all Home Rulers today.
The Times, 26 Mar 1919

104 I never met anyone in Ireland who understood the Irish question, except one Englishman who had only been there a week.
Keith Fraser (1867–1935) British politician.
Speech, House of Commons, May 1919

105 There is no right to strike against the public safety by anybody, anywhere, any time.
Calvin Coolidge (1872–1933) US president.
Referring to the Boston police strike
Remark, 14 Sept 1919

106 He was the Messiah of the new age, and his crucifixion was yet to come.
George Edward Slocombe (1894–1963) British journalist.
Referring to Woodrow Wilson and his visit to the Versailles conference
Mirror to Geneva

107 Of all tyrannies in history the Bolshevik tyranny is the worst, the most destructive, the most degrading
Winston Churchill (1874–1965) British statesman.
Speech, London, 11 Apr 1919

108 A democracy is a state which recognises the subjecting of the minority to the majority.
Lenin (Vladimir Ilich Ulyanov; 1870–1924) Russian revolutionary leader.
The State and The Revolution

109 I have seen the future and it works.
Lincoln Steffens (1866–1936) US journalist.
Speaking to Bernard Baruch after visiting the Soviet Union, 1919
Autobiography, Ch. 18

1920

110 Russia will certainly inherit the future. What we already call the greatness of Russia is only her pre-natal struggling.
D. H. Lawrence (1885–1930) British novelist.
Phoenix, Preface, 'All Things are Possible' by Leo Shostov

111 Communism is Soviet power plus the electrification of the whole country.
Lenin (Vladimir Ilich Ulyanov; 1870–1924) Russian revolutionary leader.
Political slogan of 1920, promoting the programme of electrification

112 Labour is not fit to govern.
Winston Churchill (1874–1965) British statesman.
Election speech, 1920

113 One to mislead the public, another to mislead the Cabinet, and the third to mislead itself.
Herbert Henry Asquith (1852–1928) British statesman.
Explaining why the War Office kept three sets of figures
The Price of Glory (Alastair Horne), Ch. 2

114 A man may build himself a throne of bayonets, but he cannot sit on it.
Dean Inge (1860–1954) British churchman.
Wit and Wisdom of Dean Inge (ed. Marchant)

115 The enemies of Freedom do not argue; they shout and they shoot.
Dean Inge
The End of an Age, Ch. 4

116 Those only can care intelligently for the future of England to whom the past is dear.
Dean Inge
Assessments and Anticipations

117 There died a myriad,
And of the best, among them,
For an old bitch gone in the teeth,

For a botched civilization
Ezra Pound (1885–1972) US poet.
Hugh Selwyn Mauberley

118　Died some, pro patria,
non 'dulce' non 'et decor'
Ezra Pound
Hugh Selwyn Mauberley

119　The earth is still bursting with the dead bodies
of the victors.
George Bernard Shaw (1856–1950) Irish
dramatist and critic.
Heartbreak House, Preface

120　Peace is not only better than war, but infinitely
more arduous.
George Bernard Shaw
Heartbreak House (Preface)

121　Truth telling is not compatible with the defence
of the realm.
George Bernard Shaw
Heartbreak House

1921

122　They are the only people who like to be told
how bad things are – who like to be told the
worst.
Winston Churchill (1874–1965) British
statesman.
Speech, 1921

123　I have gone to war too . . . I am going to fight
capitalism even if it kills me. It is wrong that
people like you should be comfortable and well
fed while all around you people are starving.
Sylvia Pankhurst (1882–1960) British
suffragette.
The Fighting Pankhursts (David Mitchell)

124　I am signing my death warrant.
Michael Collins (1890–1922) Irish nationalist.
Said on signing the agreement with Great Britain,
1921, that established the Irish Free State; he
was assassinated in an ambush some months
later
Peace by Ordeal (Longford), Pt. 6, Ch. 1

125　It is the government that should ask me for a
pardon.
Eugene Victor Debs (1855–1926) US trade
unionist, socialist, and pacifist.
When released from prison (1921) on the orders
of President Harding after being jailed for sedi-
tion (1918)
The People's Almanac (D. Wallechinsky)

1922

126　America has all that Russia has not. Russia has
things America has not. Why will America not
reach out a hand to Russia, as I have given
my hand?
Isadora Duncan (1878–1927) US dancer.
Speaking in support of Russia following the 1917
Revolution
Speech, Symphony Hall, Boston, 1922

127　The rogue elephant among British prime
ministers.
Dr Kenneth Morgan (1934–　) British
historian.
Referring to Lloyd George
Life of David Lloyd George

128　Count not his broken pledges as a crime
He MEANT them, HOW he meant them – at
the time.
Kensal Green
Referring to David Lloyd George
The Faber Book of English History in Verse
(Kenneth Baker)

129　I have many times asked myself whether there
can be more potent advocates of peace upon
earth through the years to come than this
massed multitude of silent witnesses to the
desolation of war.
George V (1865–1936) King of the United
Kingdom.
Referring to the massed World War I graves in
Flanders, 1922
Silent Cities (ed. Gavin Stamp)

130　*Il Duce ha sempre ragione.*
The Duce is always right.
Fascist Slogan

131　I could have transformed this grey assembly
hall into an armed camp of Blackshirts, a
bivouac for corpses. I could have nailed up the
doors of Parliament.
Benito Mussolini (1883–1945) Italian
dictator.
Referring to the Fascist march on Rome, which
had resulted in Mussolini becoming prime minister (31 Oct 1922)
Speech, Chamber of Deputies, 16 Nov 1922

1923

132　"Liberty Mr Gumboil?" he said, "you don't
suppose any serious minded person imagines a
revolution is going to bring liberty do you?"
Aldous Huxley (1894–1964) British novelist.
Antic Hay

133　All those who are not racially pure are mere
chaff.
Adolf Hitler (1889–1945) German dictator.
Mein Kampf

134　The broad mass of a nation . . . will more easily
fall victim to a big lie than to a small one.
Adolf Hitler
Mein Kampf

135　Only constant repetition will finally succeed in
imprinting an idea on the memory of the
crowd.
Adolf Hitler
Mein Kampf

136　The greater the lie, the greater the chance that
it will be believed.
Adolf Hitler
Mein Kampf

137 Germany will be either a world power or will
     not be at all.
     Adolf Hitler
     Mein Kampf

138 Look at that man's eyes. You will hear more of
     him later.
     Bonar Law (1858–1923) British statesman.
     Referring to Mussolini
     Attrib.

139 It is fitting that we should have buried the Un-
     known Prime Minister by the side of the Un-
     known Soldier.
     Herbert Henry Asquith (1852–1928) British
     statesman.
     Said at Bonar Law's funeral, 5 Nov 1923
     Attrib.

140 Of all the politicians I ever saw
     The least significant was Bonar Law.
     Unless it was MacDonald, by the way:
     Or Baldwin – it's impossible to say.
     Hilaire Belloc (1870–1953) French-born Brit-
     ish poet.
     The Faber Book of English History in Verse
     (Kenneth Baker)

141 Not even a public figure. A man of no experi-
     ence. And of the utmost insignificance.
     Lord Curzon (1859–1925) British politician.
     Referring to Stanley Baldwin on his appointment
     as Prime Minister
     Curzon: The Last Phase (Harold Nicolson)

142 You may be the most liberal Liberal English-
     man, and yet you cannot fail to see the categor-.
     ical difference between the responsible and
     the irresponsible classes.
     D. H. Lawrence (1885–1930) British novelist.
     Kangaroo, Ch. 1

143 The inevitability of gradualness.
     Sydney Webb (1859–1947) British
     economist.
     Presidential Address to Labour Party Confer-
     ence, 1923

1924

144 Today 23 years ago dear Grandmama died. I
     wonder what she would have thought of a
     Labour Government.
     George V (1865–1936) King of the United
     Kingdom
     On the formation of the first Labour Government
     Diary, 22 Jan 1924

145 Well, what are you socialists going to do about
     me?
     George V
     To Ramsay MacDonald at his first meeting as
     prime minister
     Attrib.

146 Under capitalism we have a state in the proper
     sense of the word, that is, a special machine
     for the suppression of one class by another.
     Lenin (Vladimir Ilich Ulyanov; 1870–1924) Rus-
     sian revolutionary leader.
     The State and Revolution, Ch. 5

147 A Social-Democrat must never forget that the
     proletariat will inevitably have to wage a
     class struggle for Socialism even against the
     most democratic and republican bourgeoisie
     and petty bourgeoisie.
     Lenin
     The State and Revolution, Ch. 10

148 It is true that liberty is precious – so precious
     that it must be rationed.
     Lenin
     Attrib.

149 The state is an instrument in the hands of the
     ruling class for suppressing the resistance of
     its class enemies.
     Joseph Stalin (J. Dzhugashvili; 1879–1953)
     Soviet statesman.
     Stalin's Kampf (ed. M. R. Werner)

150 It was the supreme expression of the medioc-
     rity of the apparatus that Stalin himself rose
     to his position.
     Leon Trotsky (Lev Davidovich Bronstein;
     1879–1940) Russian revolutionary.
     My Life, Ch. 40

151 Their worst misfortune was his birth; their next
     worst – his death.
     Winston Churchill (1874–1965) British
     statesman.
     Referring to Lenin
     The World Crisis

152 The first time you meet Winston you see all his
     faults and the rest of your life you spend in
     discovering his virtues.
     Lady Constance Lytton (1869–1923) British
     suffragette.
     Referring to Winston Churchill
     Edward Marsh (Christopher Hassall), Ch. 7

153 The customer is always right.
     H. Gordon Selfridge (1857–1947) US-born
     businessman.
     Slogan adopted at his shops

154 The so-called white races are really pinko-gray.
     E. M. Forster (1879–1970) British novelist.
     A Passage to India, Ch. 7

155 The foundation of the government of a nation
     must be built upon the rights of the people, but
     the administration must be entrusted to
     experts.
     Sun Yat-sen (1867–1925) Chinese revolution-
     ary leader.
     The Three Principles of the People

156* This is virgin territory for whorehouses.
     Al Capone (1899–1947) Italian-born US
     gangster.
     Talking about suburban Chicago
     The Bootleggers (Kenneth Allsop), Ch. 16

1925

157* Is it possible that my people live in such awful
     conditions? . . . I tell you, Mr Wheatley, that if

I had to live in conditions like that I would be a revolutionary myself.
George V (1865–1936) King of the United Kingdom.
On being told Mr Wheatley's life story
The Tragedy of Ramsay MacDonald (L. MacNeill Weir), Ch. 16

158 They hired the money, didn't they?
Calvin Coolidge (1872–1933) US president.
Referring to the war debts incurred by England and others

159 The business of America is business.
Calvin Coolidge
Speech, Washington, 17 Jan 1925

1926

160 Constitutional Government is being attacked ... The general strike is a challenge to Parliament, and is the road to anarchy and ruin.
Stanley Baldwin (1867–1947) British politician and prime minister.
The British Gazette, 6 May 1926

161 Not a penny off the pay; not a minute on the day.
A. J. Cook (1885–1931) British trade-union leader.
Slogan used in the miners' strike, 1926

162 That's what you are. That's what you all are. All of you young people who served in the war. You are a lost generation.
Gertrude Stein (1874–1946) US writer.
A Moveable Feast (E. Hemingway)

1927

163 Nation shall speak peace unto nation.
Montague John Rendall (1862–1950) British schoolmaster.
Motto of BBC, 1927

164 Every man has a House of Lords in his own head. Fears, prejudices, misconceptions – those are the peers, and they are hereditary.
David Lloyd George (1863–1945) British Liberal statesman.
Speech, Cambridge, 1927

165 A sad day this for Alexander
And many another dead commander.
Jealousy's rife in heroes' hall –
Winston Churchill has bluffed them all.
Kensal Green
The Faber Book of English History in Verse (Kenneth Baker)

166 The most conservative man in the world is the British Trade Unionist when you want to change him.
Ernest Bevin (1881–1951) British trade-union leader and politician.
Speech, Trade Union Congress, 8 Sept 1927

167 I do not choose to run for President in 1928.
Calvin Coolidge (1872–1933) US president.
Announcement in 1927

168 Gentlemen, it was necessary to abolish the fez, which sat on the heads of our nation as an emblem of ignorance, negligence, fanaticism and hatred of progress and civilization, to accept in its place the hat, the headgear worn by the whole civilized world.
Kemal Ataturk (1880–1938) Founder of the Turkish Republic.
Speech, Turkish Assembly, Oct 1927

169 Communism is like prohibition, it's a good idea but it won't work.
Will Rogers (1879–1935) US actor and humorist.
Autobiography, Nov 1927

170 Nature has no cure for this sort of madness, though I have known a legacy from a rich relative work wonders.
F. E. Smith (1872–1930) British lawyer and politician.
Referring to Communism
Law, Life and Letters (1927), Vol. II

1928

171* Freedom of the press in Britain is freedom to print such of the proprietor's prejudices as the advertisers don't object to.
Hannen Swaffer (1879–1962) British journalist.
Attrib.

172 God forbid that any book should be banned. The practice is as indefensible as infanticide.
Rebecca West (Cicely Isabel Fairfield: 1892–1983) British novelist and journalist.
The Strange Necessity, 'The Tosh Horse'

173 Nonconformity and lust stalking hand in hand through the country, wasting and ravaging.
Evelyn Waugh (1903–66) British novelist.
Decline and Fall, Pt. I, Ch. 5

174 Our country has deliberately undertaken a great social and economic experiment, noble in motive and far-reaching in purpose.
Herbert Hoover (1874–1964) US president.
Referring to Prohibition
Letter to W.H. Borah, 28 Feb 1928

175 In a country economically backward, the proletariat can take power earlier than in countries where capitalism is advanced.
Leon Trotsky (Lev Davidovich Bronstein: 1879–1940) Russian revolutionary.
Permanent Revolution

1929

176 Moving through the silent crowd
Who stand behind dull cigarettes,
These men who idle in the road,
I have the sense of falling light.

They lounge at corners of the street
And greet friends with a shrug of the shoulder
And turn their empty pockets out,
The cynical gestures of the poor.
Stephen Spender (1909–) British poet.
Unemployed

177 There is in our hands as citizens an instrument to mould the minds of the young and to create

great and good and noble citizens for the future.
Edward Shortt (1862–1935) Home Secretary (1919–22); President of the British Board of Film Censors (1929–35).
Referring to the British Board of Film Censors
Remark, 1929

178 ...I have no fears for the future of our country. It is bright with hope.
Herbert Hoover (1874–1964) US president.
Inaugural address, 4 Mar 1929

179 He is the apostle of class-hatred, the founder of a Satanic anti-religion, which resembles some religions in its cruelty, fanaticism and irrationality.
Dean Inge (1860–1954) British churchman.
Referring to Karl Marx
Assessments and Anticipations

1930

180 When a great many people are unable to find work, unemployment results.
Calvin Coolidge (1872–1933) US president.
City Editor

181 Democracy is only an experiment in government, and it has the obvious disadvantage of merely counting votes instead of weighing them.
Dean Inge (1860–1954) British churchman.
Possible Recovery?

182 The disastrous element in the Labour party is its intellectuals.
George Norman Clark (1890–1979) British historian.
A Man of the Thirties (A. L. Rowse)

183* He therefore was at strenuous pains
To atrophy his puny brains
And registered success in this
Beyond the dreams of avarice
Till when he had at last become
Blind, paralytic, deaf and dumb
Insensible and cretinous
He was admitted ONE OF US.
Hilaire Belloc (1870–1953) French-born British poet.
The Statesman

184 In a free society the state does not administer the affairs of men. It administers justice among men who conduct their own affairs.
Walter Lippmann (1889–1974) US editor and writer.
An Enquiry into the Principles of a Good Society

185 The working of great institutions is mainly the result of a vast mass of routine, petty malice, self interest, carelessness, and sheer mistake. Only a residual fraction is thought.
George Santayana (1863–1952) US philosopher.
The Crime of Galileo

186 The hardest thing in the world to understand is income tax.
Albert Einstein (1879–1955) German-born US physicist.
Attrib.

187 They can't collect legal taxes from illegal money.
Al Capone (1899–1947) Italian-born US gangster.
Objecting to the US Bureau of Internal Revenue claiming large sums in unpaid back tax
Capone (J. Kobler)

188 For us, the tasks of education in socialism were closely integrated with those of fighting. Ideas that enter the mind under fire remain there securely and for ever.
Leon Trotsky (Lev Davidovich Bronstein; 1879–1940) Russian revolutionary.
My Life, Ch. 35

189 If we had more time for discussion we should probably have made a great many more mistakes.
Leon Trotsky
My Life

190* An ally has to be watched just like an enemy.
Leon Trotsky
Expansion and Coexistence (A. Ulam)

191 Today violence is the rhetoric of the period.
José Ortega y Gasset (1883–1955) Spanish philosopher.
The Revolt of the Masses

192 Revolution is not the uprising against pre-existing order, but the setting-up of a new order contradictory to the traditional one.
José Ortega y Gasset
The Revolt of the Masses, Ch. 6

193* Fascism means war.
John St Loe Strachey (1901–63) British politician.
Slogan, 1930s

194 All wars are planned by old men
In council rooms apart.
Grantland Rice (1880–1954) US sportswriter.
Two Sides of War

195 When we, the Workers, all demand: 'What are we fighting for?...
Then, then we'll end that stupid crime, that devil's madness – War.
Robert William Service (1874–1958) Canadian poet.
Michael

196 That all men are equal is a proposition to which, at ordinary times, no sane individual has ever given his assent.
Aldous Huxley (1894–1964) British novelist and essayist.
Proper Studies

197 A politician is a person with whose politics you don't agree; if you agree with him he is a statesman.
David Lloyd George (1863–1945) British statesman.
Attrib.

198 With us the Leader and the Idea are one, and every party member has to do what the Leader orders.
Adolf Hitler (1889–1945) German dictator.
Remark, 21 May 1930, in conversation with Otto Strasser (as recounted by Strasser)
Hitler and Stalin: Parallel Lives (Alan Bullock), Ch.5

199 Let them especially put their demands in such a way that Great Britain could say that she supported both sides.
Ramsey MacDonald (1866–1937) British statesman.
Referring to France and Germany
The Origins of the Second Word War (A. J. P. Taylor), Ch. 3

200 Those who can win a war well can rarely make a good peace and those who could make a good peace would never have won the war.
Winston Churchill (1874–1965) British statesman.
My Early Life, Ch. 26

201 Which brings me to my conclusion upon Free Will and Predestination, namely – let the reader mark it – that they are identical.
Winston Churchill
My Early Life, Ch. 3

202 Everyone threw the blame on me. I have noticed that they nearly always do. I suppose it is because they think I shall be able to bear it best.
Winston Churchill
My Early Life, Ch. 17

203 The loss of India would mark and consummate the downfall of the British Empire.
Winston Churchill
Speech to Indian Empire Society, London, 12 Dec 1930

204 When they circumcised Herbert Samuel they threw away the wrong bit.
David Lloyd George (1863–1945) British statesman.
Attrib. in *The Listener*, 7 Sept 1978

1931

205 Democracy means government by the uneducated, while aristocracy means government by the badly educated.
G. K. Chesterton (1874–1936) British writer.
New York Times, 1 Feb 1931

206 There is just one rule for politicians all over the world. Don't say in Power what you say in Opposition: if you do you only have to carry out what the other fellows have found impossible.
John Galsworthy (1867–1933) British novelist.
Maid in Waiting

207 What the proprietorship of these papers is aiming at is power, and power without responsibility – the prerogative of the harlot through the ages.
Stanley Baldwin (1867–1947) British statesman.
Attacking the press barons Lords Rothermere and Beaverbrook. It was first used by Kipling.

When the Duke of Devonshire heard of the speech he is said to have remarked 'Good God, that's done it. He's lost us the tarts' vote'.
Speech, election rally, 18 Mar 1931

208 India is a geographical term. It is no more a united nation than the Equator.
Winston Churchill (1874–1965) British statesman.
Speech, Royal Albert Hall, 18 Mar 1931

209 Liberty is the hardest test that one can inflict on a people. To know how to be free is not given equally to all men and all nations.
Paul Valéry (1871–1945) French poet and writer.
Reflections on the World Today, 'On the Subject of Dictatorship'

210 Insurrection is an art, and like all arts it has its laws.
Leon Trotsky (Lev Davidovich Bronstein; 1879–1940) Russian revolutionary.
History of the Russian Revolution, Pt. III, Ch. 6

211 Revolutions are always verbose.
Leon Trotsky
History of the Russian Revolution, Pt. II, Ch. 12

212 The fundamental premise of a revolution is that the existing social structure has become incapable of solving the urgent problems of development of the nation.
Leon Trotsky
History of the Russian Revolution, Pt. III, Ch. 6

213 The revolution does not choose its paths: it made its first steps towards victory under the belly of a Cossack's horse.
Leon Trotsky
History of the Russian Revolution, Pt. I, Ch. 7

214 From being a patriotic myth, the Russian people have become an awful reality.
Leon Trotsky
History of the Russian Revolution, Pt. III, Ch. 7

215 To slacken the tempo . . . would mean falling behind. And those who fall behind get beaten . . . We are fifty or a hundred years behind the advanced countries. We must make good this distance in ten years. Either we do it, or they crush us.
Joseph Stalin (J. Dzhugashvili; 1879–1953) Soviet statesman.

1932

216 Happy Days Are Here Again.
Jack Yellen (1892–) US lyricist.
Used by Roosevelt as a campaign song in 1932
Song title

217 The forgotten man at the bottom of the economic pyramid.
Franklin D. Roosevelt (1882–1945) US president.
Speech on radio, 7 Apr 1932

218 I pledge you, I pledge myself, to a new deal for the American people.
Franklin D. Roosevelt
Speech accepting nomination for presidency, Chicago, 2 July 1932

219   Let me assert my firm belief that the only thing
we have to fear is fear itself.
Franklin D. Roosevelt
Speech, 2 July 1932

220   If human beings could be propagated by cutting, like apple trees, aristocracy would be biologically sound.
J. B. S. Haldane (1892–1964) British
geneticist.
The Inequality of Man, title essay

221   I think it is well also for the man in the street to
realise that there is no power on earth that
can protect him from being bombed. Whatever
people may tell him, the bomber will always
get through, and it is very easy to understand
that, if you realise the area of space.
Stanley Baldwin (1867–1947) British
statesman.
Speech, House of Commons, 10 Nov 1932

222   The essential thing is the formation of the political will of the nation: that is the starting point
for political action.
Adolf Hitler (1889–1945) German dictator.
Speech, Düsseldorf, 27 Jan 1932

223   War alone brings up to their highest tension all
human energies and imposes the stamp of nobility upon the peoples who have the courage to make it.
Benito Mussolini (1883–1945) Italian
dictator.
Encyclopedia Italiane

224   Fascism is not an article for export.
Benito Mussolini
Report in the German press, 1932

225   The only defence is in offence, which means
that you have to kill more women and children
more quickly than the enemy if you want to
save yourselves.
Stanley Baldwin (1867–1947) British
statesman.
Speech, Nov 1932

226   In England we have come to rely upon a comfortable time lag of fifty years or a century in-
tervening between the perception that
something ought to be done and a serious attempt to do it.
H. G. Wells (1866–1946) British writer.
The Work, Wealth and Happiness of Mankind

1933

227   Patriotism is easy to understand in America; it
means looking out for yourself while looking
out for your country.
Calvin Coolidge (1872–1933) US president.
Attrib.

228   Something must be done.
Duke of Windsor (1894–1972) King of the
United Kingdom; abdicated 1936.
Said while visiting areas of high unemployment in
South Wales during the 1930s
Attrib.

229   Fascism is a religion; the twentieth century will
be known in history as the century of Fascism.
Benito Mussolini (1883–1945) Italian
dictator.
On Hitler's seizing power
Sawdust Caesar (George Seldes), Ch. 24

230   That this house will in no circumstances fight
for its King and country.
Anonymous
Motion passed at the Oxford Union, 9 Feb 1933

231   Our movement took a grip on cowardly Marxism and from it extracted the meaning of socialism. It also took from the cowardly middle-
class parties their nationalism. Throwing both
into the cauldron of our way of life there
emerged, as clear as a crystal, the synthesis –
German National Socialism.
Hermann Goering (1893–1946) German
leader.
Speech, Berlin, 9 Apr 1933

232   What progress we are making. In the Middle
Ages they would have burned me. Now they are
content with burning my books.
Sigmund Freud (1856–1939) Austrian
psychoanalyst.
Referring to the public burning of his books in
Berlin
Letter to Ernest Jones, 1933

233   In the field of world policy; I would dedicate
this nation to the policy of the good neighbor.
Franklin D. Roosevelt (1882–1945) US
Democratic president.
First Inaugural Address, 4 Mar 1933

234   You can't adopt politics as a profession and remain honest.
Louis McHenry Howe (1871–1936) US
diplomat.
Speech, Columbia University, 17 Jan 1933

235   A nation is not in danger of financial disaster
merely because it owes itself money.
Andrew William Mellon (1855–1937) US
financier.
Attrib.

236   How could they tell?
Dorothy Parker (1893–1967) US writer.
Reaction to news of the death of Calvin Coo-
lidge, US President 1923–29; also attributed to
H. L. Mencken
You Might As Well Live (J. Keats)

237   This goat-footed bard, this half-human visitor to
our age from the hag-ridden magic and enchanted woods of Celtic antiquity.
John Maynard Keynes (1883–1946) British
economist.
Referring to Lloyd George
Essays and Sketches in Biography

238   As society is now constituted, a literal adherence to the moral precepts scattered
throughout the Gospels would mean sudden
death.
A. N. Whitehead (1861–1947) British
philosopher.
Adventures in Ideas

239   But not even Marx is more precious to us than the truth.
Simone Weil (1909–43) French philosopher.
Oppression and Liberty, 'Revolution Proletarienne'

1934

240   The trouble in modern democracy is that men do not approach to leadership until they have lost the desire to lead anyone.
Lord Beveridge (1879–1963) British economist.
The Observer, 'Sayings of the Week', 15 Apr 1934

241   When you think about the defence of England you no longer think of the chalk cliffs of Dover. You think of the Rhine. That is where our frontier lies to-day.
Stanley Baldwin (1867–1947) British statesman.
Speech, House of Commons, 30 July 1934

242   *Ein Reich, Ein Volk, Ein Führer.*
One Realm, One People, One Leader
Slogan of the Nazi Party; first used at Nuremberg, Sept 1934

243   He looks as if he had been weaned on a pickle.
Alice Roosevelt Longworth (1884–1980) US hostess.
Referring to Calvin Coolidge, US president 1923–29
Crowded Hours

1935

244   The government burns down whole cities while the people are forbidden to light lamps.
Mao Tse-Tung (1893–1976) Chinese communist leader.
Attrib.

245   I am not and never have been, a man of the right. My position was on the left and is now in the centre of politics.
Oswald Mosley (1896–1980) British politician.
The Times, 26 Apr 1968

246*   *Kraft durch Freude.*
Strength through joy.
Robert Ley (1890–1945) German Nazi.
German Labour Front slogan

247   In starting and waging a war it is not right that matters, but victory.
Adolf Hitler (1889–1945) German dictator.
The Rise and Fall of the Third Reich (W. L. Shirer), Ch. 16

248   The keystone of the Fascist doctrine is its conception of the State, of its essence, its functions, and its aims. For Fascism the State is absolute, individuals and groups relative.
Benito Mussolini (1883–1945) Italian dictator.
Fascism, Doctrine and Institutions

249   I should be pleased, I suppose, that Hitler has carried out a revolution on our lines. But they are Germans. So they will end by ruining our idea.
Benito Mussolini
Benito Mussolini (C. Hibbert), Pt. II, Ch. 1

250   We cannot change our policy now. After all, we are not political whores.
Benito Mussolini
Hitler (Alan Bullock), Ch. 8

251   The former allies had blundered in the past by offering Germany too little, and offering even that too late, until finally Nazi Germany had become a menace to all mankind.
Allan Nevins (1890–1971) US historian.
Current History, May 1935

252   I have seldom spoken with greater regret, for my lips are not yet unsealed. Were these troubles over I would make a case, and I guarantee that not a man would go into the Lobby against us.
Stanley Baldwin (1867–1947) British statesman.
Referring to the Abyssinian crisis; usually misquoted as 'My lips are sealed'
Speech, House of Commons, 10 Dec 1935

253   ... a bore, a bounder and a prig. He was intoxicated with his own youth and loathed any milieu which he couldn't dominate. Certainly he had none of a gentleman's instincts, strutting about Peace Conferences in Arab dress.
Henry Channon (1897–1958) British writer.
Referring to T. E. Lawrence
Diary, 25 May 1935

254   There are those who have tried to dismiss his story with a flourish of the Union Jack, a psycho-analytical catchword or a sneer; it should move our deepest admiration and pity. Like Shelley and like Baudelaire, it may be said of him that he suffered, in his own person, the neurotic ills of an entire generation.
Christopher Isherwood (1904–86) British novelist.
Referring to T. E. Lawrence
Exhumations

255   We believe in a League system in which the whole world should be ranged against an aggressor.
Clement Attlee (1883–1967) British statesman and Labour prime minister.
Speech, House of Commons, 11 Mar 1935

256*   Sit down, man. You're a bloody tragedy.
James Maxton (1885–1946) Scottish Labour leader.
Said to Ramsay MacDonald when he made his last speech in Parliament
Attrib.

257   Politics and the fate of mankind are shaped by men without ideals and without greatness. Men who have greatness within them don't go in for politics.
Albert Camus (1913–60) French existentialist writer.
Notebooks, 1935–42

258 After I am dead the boy will ruin himself in twelve months.
George V (1865–1936) King of the United Kingdom.
Referring to the Prince of Wales, later Edward VIII; said to Stanley Baldwin
Attrib.

259 Revolution by its very nature is sometimes compelled to take in more territory than it is capable of holding. Retreats are possible – when there is territory to retreat from.
Leon Trotsky (Lev Davidovich Bronstein; 1879–1940) Russian revolutionary.
Diary in Exile, 15 Feb 1935

260 The Pope! How many divisions has *he* got?
Joseph Stalin (J. Dzhugashvili; 1879–1953) Soviet statesman.
When urged by Pierre Laval to tolerate Catholicism in the USSR to appease the Pope, 13 May 1935
The Second World War (W. S. Churchill), Vol. I, Ch. 8

1936

261 How is the Empire?
George V (1865–1936) King of the United Kingdom.
Last words
The Times, 21 Jan 1936

262 Bugger Bognor.
George V
His alleged last words, when his doctor promised him he would soon be well enough to visit Bognor Regis

263 Spirits of well-shot woodcock, partridge, snipe Flutter and bear him up the Norfolk sky.
John Betjeman (1906–84) British poet.
Death of King George V

264 A democracy must remain at home in all matters which affect the nature of her institutions ... We do not want the racial antipathies or national antagonisms of the Old World translated to this continent, as they will should we become a part of European politics. The people of this country are overwhelmingly for a policy of neutrality.
William Edgar Borah (1865–1940) US senator.
Radio broadcast, 22 Feb 1936

265 To attempt to export revolution is nonsense.
Joseph Stalin (J. Dzhugashvili; 1879–1953) Soviet statesman.
Remark, 1 Mar 1936, to Roy Howard (US newspaper owner)

266 Peace is indivisible.
Maxim Litvinov (1876–1951) Russian statesman.
Speech to the League of Nations, 1 July 1936

267 Revolution is delightful in the preliminary stages. So long as it's a question of getting rid of the people at the top.
Aldous Huxley (1894–1964) British novelist and essayist.
Eyeless in Gaza

268 I go the way that Providence dictates with the assurance of a sleepwalker.
Adolf Hitler (1889–1945) German dictator.
Referring to his successful re-occupation of the Rhineland, despite advice against the attempt
Speech, Munich, 15 Mar 1936

269 They will conquer, but they will not convince.
Miguel de Unamuno y Jugo (1864–1936) Spanish writer.
Referring to the Franco rebels
Attrib.

270 It is better to be the widow of a hero than the wife of a coward.
Dolores Ibarruri (1895–1989) Spanish politician.
Speech, Valencia, 1936

271 It is better to die on your feet than to live on your knees.
Dolores Ibarruri
Speech, Paris, 3 Sept 1936

272 Fire – without hatred.
Antonio Rivera (d. 1936) Spanish Nationalist hero.
Giving the order to open fire at the siege of the Alcázar
The Siege of the Alcázar (C. Eby)

273 This Berlin–Rome connection is not so much a diaphragm as an axis, around which can revolve all those states of Europe with a will towards collaboration and peace.
Benito Mussolini (1883–1945) Italian dictator.
Speech, Milan, 1 Nov 1936

274 Guns will make us powerful; butter will only make us fat.
Hermann Goering (1893–1946) German leader.
Radio broadcast, 1936

275 Before the organization of the Blackshirt movement free speech did not exist in this country.
Oswald Mosley (1896–1980) British politician.
Selections from the *New Statesman, This England*, Pt. I

276 Practical men, who believe themselves to be quite exempt from any intellectual influences, are usually the slaves of some defunct economist. Madmen in authority, who hear voices in the air, are distilling their frenzy from some academic scribbler of a few years back.
John Maynard Keynes (1883–1946) British economist.
The General Theory of Employment, Interest and Money, Bk. VI, Ch. 24

277* If he became convinced tomorrow that coming out for cannibalism would get him the votes he so sorely needs, he would begin fattening a missionary on the White House backyard come Wednesday.
H. L. Mencken (1880–1956) US journalist.
Referring to Franklin Roosevelt
Franklin D. Roosevelt, A Profile (ed. W. E. Leuchtenburg)

278 One of the great attractions of patriotism — it fulfils our worst wishes. In the person of our nation we are able, vicariously, to bully and to cheat. Bully and cheat, what's more, with a feeling that we are profoundly virtuous.
Aldous Huxley (1894–1964) British novelist.
Eyeless in Gaza

279 Lloyd George could not see a belt without hitting below it.
Margot Asquith (1865–1945) The second wife of Herbert Asquith.
The Autiobiography of Margot Asquith

280 His modesty amounts to a deformity.
Margot Asquith
Referring to her husband
Autobiography

281 My Lord Archbishop, what a scold you are
And when a man is down, how bold you are,
Of Christian charity how scant you are
You auld Lang Swine, how full of cant you are!
Anonymous
Archbishop Lang was one of the chief opponents of Edward VIII's marriage to Mrs Wallis Simpson
The Faber Book of English History in Verse (Kenneth Baker)

282 Well, Mr Baldwin! *this* is a pretty kettle of fish!
Queen Mary (1867–1953) Consort of George V.
Referring to the abdication of Edward VIII
Life of Queen Mary (James Pope-Hennessy)

283 Our cock won't fight.
Lord Beaverbrook (1879–1964) Canadian-born British newspaper proprietor.
Said to Churchill during the abdication crisis, 1936
Edward VIII (Frances Donaldson), Ch. 22

284 I have found it impossible to carry the heavy burden of responsibility and to discharge my duties as King as I would wish to do without the help and support of the woman I love.
Duke of Windsor (1894–1972) King of the United Kingdom; abdicated 1936.
Radio broadcast, 11 Dec 1936

285 He will go from resort to resort getting more tanned and more tired.
Westbrook Pegler (1894–1969) US journalist.
On the abdication of Edward VIII
Six Men (Alistair Cooke), Pt. II

286 God grant him peace and happiness but never understanding of what he has lost.
Stanley Baldwin (1867–1947) British politician and prime minister.
Referring to Edward VIII

1937

287 I see one-third of a nation ill-housed, ill-clad, ill-nourished.
Franklin D. Roosevelt (1882–1945) US Democratic president.
Second Inaugural Address, 20 Jan 1937

288 His fame endures; we shall not quite forget
The name of Baldwin till we're out of debt.
Kensal Green
The Faber Book of English History in Verse (Kenneth Baker)

289* Then comes Winston with his hundred-horse-power mind and what can I do?
Stanley Baldwin (1867–1947) British statesman.
Stanley Baldwin (G. M. Young), Ch. 11

290 I often think how much easier the world would have been to manage if Herr Hitler and Signor Mussolini had been at Oxford.
Viscount Halifax (1881–1959) British politician.
Speech, York, 4 Nov 1937

291 *La quinta columna*
The Fifth Column
Emilio Mola (1887–1937) Spanish Nationalist General.
Reply when asked (Oct 1937) which of four Nationalist armies would capture Madrid; Mola was referring to Nationalist elements within the city

292 'Can't' will be the epitaph of the British Empire — unless we wake up in time.
Oswald Mosley (1896–1980) British politician.
Speech, Manchester, 9 Dec 1937

293 Sincerity is all that counts. It's a wide-spread modern heresy. Think again. Bolsheviks are sincere. Fascists are sincere. Lunatics are sincere. People who believe the earth is flat are sincere. They can't all be right. Better make certain first you've got something to be sincere about and with.
Tom Driberg (1905–76) British politician, journalist and author.
Daily Express, 1937

294 So long as men worship the Caesars and Napoleons, Caesars and Napoleons will arise to make them miserable.
Aldous Huxley (1894–1964) British novelist.
Ends and Means

295 The propagandist's purpose is to make one set of people forget that certain other sets of people are human.
Aldous Huxley
The Olive Tree

296 Freedom is the right to tell people what they do not want to hear.
George Orwell (Eric Blair; 1903–50) British novelist.
The Road to Wigan Pier

297 It is brought home to you . . . that it is only because miners sweat their guts out that superior persons can remain superior.
George Orwell
The Road to Wigan Pier, Ch. 2

298 I sometimes think that the price of liberty is not so much eternal vigilance as eternal dirt.
George Orwell
The Road to Wigan Pier, Ch. 4

299 As with the Christian religion, the worst advertisement for Socialism is its adherents.
George Orwell
The Road to Wigan Pier, Ch. 11

300 To the ordinary working man, the sort you would meet in any pub on Saturday night, Socialism does not mean much more than better wages and shorter hours and nobody bossing you about.
George Orwell
The Road to Wigan Pier, Ch. 11

1938

301 In war, whichever side may call itself the victor, there are no winners, but all are losers.
Neville Chamberlain (1869–1940) British statesman.
Speech, Kettering, 3 July 1938

302 Before us stands the last problem that must be solved and will be solved. It is the last territorial claim which I have to make in Europe, but it is the claim from which I will not recede.
Adolf Hitler (1889–1945) German dictator.
Referring to the Sudetenland (Czechoslovakia)
Speech, Berlin, 26 Sept 1938

303 How horrible, fantastic, incredible, it is that we should be digging trenches and trying on gasmasks here because of a quarrel in a faraway country between people of whom we know nothing.
Neville Chamberlain (1869–1940) British statesman.
Referring to Germany's annexation of the Sudetenland
Radio broadcast, 27 Sept 1938

304 I believe it is peace for our time . . . peace with honour.
Neville Chamberlain
Radio broadcast after Munich Agreement, 1 Oct 1938

305 We have sustained a defeat without a war.
Winston Churchill (1874–1965)
Speech, House of Commons, 5 Oct 1938

306 Dictators ride to and fro upon tigers which they dare not dismount. And the tigers are getting hungry.
Winston Churchill
While England Slept

307 Other nations use 'force'; we Britons alone use 'Might'.
Evelyn Waugh (1903–66) British novelist.
Scoop, Bk. II, Ch. 5

308 Every Communist must grasp the truth, 'Political power grows out of the barrel of a gun.'
Mao Tse-Tung (1893–1976) Chinese communist leader.
Selected Works, Vol. II, 'Problems of War and Strategy'

309 And here we are – just as before – safe in our skins;
Glory to God for Munich.
And stocks go up and wrecks
Are salved and politicians' reputations
Go up like Jack-on-the-Beanstalk; only the Czechs
Go down and without fighting.
Louis Macneice (1907–63) Irish-born British poet.
Autumn Journal

1939

310 If we are going in without the help of Russia we are walking into a trap.
David Lloyd George (1863–1945) British Liberal statesman.
Speech, House of Commons, 3 Apr 1939

311 That bastard of the Versailles treaty.
Vyacheslav Mikhailovich Molotov (1890–1986) Soviet statesman.
Referring to Poland

312 The machine is running away with *him* as it ran away with *me*.
Wilhelm II (1859–1941) King of Prussia and Emperor of Germany.
Referring to Hitler
Remark to Sir Robert Bruce-Lockhart and Sir John Wheeler-Bennett, 27 Aug 1939

313 Speak for England.
Leopold Amery (1873–1955) British statesman.
Shouted to Arthur Greenwood, Labour Party spokesman, before he began to speak in a House of Commons debate immediately preceding the declaration of war, 2 Sept 1939

314 When peace has been broken anywhere, the peace of all countries everywhere is in danger.
Franklin D. Roosevelt (1882–1945) US Democratic president.
Radio broadcast, 3 Sept 1939

315 Winston's back.
Referring to Churchill's reappointment as First Lord of the Admiralty; he had previously held the office from 1911 to 1915
Radio message from the Admiralty to all ships of the Royal Navy, 3 Sept 1939

316 I cannot forecast to you the action of Russia. It is a riddle wrapped in a mystery inside an enigma.
Winston Churchill (1874–1965) British statesman.
Radio broadcast, 1 Oct 1939

317 I am reminded of four definitions. A radical is a man with both feet firmly planted – in the air; a conservative is a man with two perfectly good legs who, however, has never learned to walk; a reactionary is a somnambulist walking backwards; a liberal is a man who uses his legs and his hands at the behest of his head.
Franklin D. Roosevelt (1882–1945) US Democratic president.
Radio broadcast, 26 Oct 1939

318 *C'est une drôle de guerre.*
It is a phoney war.
Edouard Daladier (1884–1970) French prime minister.
Speech, Chamber of Deputies, 22 Dec 1939

319 And I said to the man who stood at the gate of
the year: 'Give me a light that I may tread
safely into the unknown'. And he replied: 'Go
out into the darkness and put your hand into
the hand of God. That shall be to you better
than light and safer than a known way.'
Minnie Louise Haskins (1875–1957) US
writer.
Remembered because it was quoted by George
VI in his Christmas broadcast, 1939
The Desert, Introduction

1940

320 The Italians will laugh at me; every time Hitler
occupies a country he sends me a message.
Benito Mussolini (1883–1945) Italian
dictator.
Hitler (Alan Bullock), Ch. 8

321 Hitler has missed the bus.
Neville Chamberlain (1869–1940) British
statesman.
Speech, House of Commons, 4 Apr 1940

322 You have sat too long here for any good you
have been doing. Depart, I say, and let us have
done with you. In the name of God, *go!*
Leopold Amery (1873–1955) British
statesman.
Said to Neville Chamberlain using Cromwell's
words
Speech, House of Commons, May 1940

323* He saw foreign policy through the wrong end of
a municipal drainpipe.
David Lloyd George (1863–1945) British
Liberal statesman.
Referring to Neville Chamberlain
The Fine Art of Political Wit (Harris), Ch. 6

324 The language of priorities is the religion of
Socialism.
Aneurin Bevan (1897–1960) British Labour
politician.
Aneurin Bevan (Vincent Brome), Ch. 1

325* I felt as if I were walking with destiny, and that
all my past life had been but a preparation for
this hour and this trial.
Winston Churchill (1874–1965) British
statesman.
The Gathering Storm, Ch. 38

326 I have nothing to offer but blood, toil, tears and
sweat.
Winston Churchill
On becoming prime minister
Speech, House of Commons, 13 May 1940

327 Victory at all costs, victory in spite of all terror,
victory however long and hard the road may
be; for without victory there is no survival.
Winston Churchill
Speech, House of Commons, 13 May 1940

328 We shall not flag or fail. We shall fight in
France, we shall fight on the seas and oceans,
we shall fight with growing confidence and
growing strength in the air, we shall defend
our island, whatever the cost may be, we shall
fight on the beaches, we shall fight on the
landing grounds, we shall fight in the fields
and in the streets, we shall fight in the hills; we
shall never surrender.
Winston Churchill
Speech, House of Commons, 4 June 1940

329 Our great-grandchildren, when they learn how
we began this war by snatching glory out of
defeat . . . may also learn how the little holiday
steamers made an excursion to hell and came
back glorious.
J. B. Priestley (1894–1984) British novelist.
Referring to the British Expeditionary Force's
evacuation from Dunkirk
Radio broadcast, 5 June 1940

330 This was their finest hour.
Winston Churchill (1874–1965) British
statesman.
Referring to the Dunkirk evacuation
Speech, House of Commons, 18 June 1940

331 The little ships, the unforgotten Homeric cata-
logue of *Mary Jane* and *Peggy IV*, of *Folkes-
tone Belle*, *Boy Billy*, and *Ethel Maud*, of *Lady
Haig* and *Skylark* . . . the little ships of Eng-
land brought the Army home.
Philip Guedalla (1889–1944) British writer.
Referring to the evacuation of Dunkirk
Mr. Churchill

332 Wars are not won by evacuations.
Winston Churchill (1874–1965)
Referring to Dunkirk
Their Finest Hour

333 To all Frenchmen: France has lost a battle but
France has not lost the war.
Charles De Gaulle (1890–1970) French gen-
eral and statesman.
Proclamation, June 1940

334 I, General de Gaulle, now in London, call on all
French officers and men who are at present
on British soil, or who may be in the future . . .
to get in touch with me. Whatever happens
the flame of French resistance must not and
shall not be extinguished.
Charles De Gaulle
Broadcast, 18 June 1940

335 In three weeks England will have her neck
wrung like a chicken.
Maxime Weygand (1867–1965) French
general.
Said at the fall of France
Their Finest Hour (Winston S. Churchill)

336 The battle of Britain is about to begin.
Winston Churchill (1874–1965) British
statesman.
Speech, House of Commons, 1 July 1940

337 To make a union with Great Britain would be
fusion with a corpse.
Marshal Pétain (1856–1951) French marshal.
On hearing Churchill's suggestion for an Anglo-
French union, 1940
Their Finest Hour (Winston S. Churchill), Ch. 10

338   Never in the field of human conflict was so
much owed by so many to so few.
Winston Churchill (1874–1965) British
statesman.
Referring to the Battle of Britain pilots
Speech, House of Commons, 20 Aug 1940

339   The universe is so vast and so ageless that the
life of one man can only be justified by the
measure of his sacrifice.
V. A. Rosewarne (1916–1940) British pilot.
Inscribed on the portrait of the 'Young Airman' in
the RAF Museum
Letter to his mother, 1940

340   It is not the walls that make the city, but the
people who live within them. The walls of
London may be battered, but the spirit of the
Londoner stands resolute and undismayed.
George VI (1895–1952) King of the United
Kingdom.
Radio broadcast to the Empire, 23 Sept 1940

341   Now we can look the East End in the face.
Elizabeth the Queen Mother (1900–   )
The wife of King George VI.
Surveying the damage caused to Buckingham
Palace by a bomb during the Blitz in World War II
Attrib.

342   We are waiting for the long-promised invasion.
So are the fishes.
Winston Churchill (1874–1965) British
statesman.
Radio broadcast to the French people, 21 Oct
1940

343   The best immediate defence of the United
States is the success of Great Britain defending
itself.
Franklin D. Roosevelt (1882–1945) US
Democratic president.
At press conference, 17 Dec 1940
Their Finest Hour (Winston S. Churchill), Ch. 28

344   We must be the great arsenal of democracy.
Franklin D. Roosevelt (1882–1945) US
Democratic president.
Broadcast address to Forum on Current Prob-
lems, 29 Dec 1940

345* The Americans cannot build aeroplanes. They
are very good at refrigerators and razor blades.
Hermann Goering (1893–1946) German
leader.
Assurance to Hitler
America (Alistair Cooke)

346   There are not enough prisons and concentration camps in Palestine to hold all the Jews
who are ready to defend their lives and
property.
Golda Meir (1898–1978) Russian-born Israeli
stateswoman.
Speech, 2 May 1940

1941

347   We look forward to a world founded upon four
essential human freedoms. The first is freedom of speech and expression — everywhere

in the world. The second is freedom of every person to worship God in his own way —
everywhere in the world. The third is freedom
from want . . . everywhere in the world. The
fourth is freedom from fear . . . anywhere in the
world.
Franklin D. Roosevelt (1882–1945) US
Democratic president.
Speech to Congress, 6 Jan 1941

348   The tasks of the party are . . . to be cautious
and not allow our country to be drawn into conflicts by warmongers who are accustomed to
have others pull the chestnuts out of the fire
for them.
Joseph Stalin (J. Dzhugashvili; 1879–1953)
Soviet statesman.
Speech, 8th Congress of the Communist Party,
6 Jan 1941

349   The crafty, cold-blooded, black-hearted Italian.
Winston Churchill (1874–1965) British
statesman.
Referring to Benito Mussolini
Radio broadcast, 9 Feb 1941

350   Give us the tools, and we will finish the job.
Winston Churchill
Referring to Lend-lease, which was being legis-
lated in the USA
Radio broadcast, 9 Feb 1941

351   We have finished the job, what shall we do with
the tools?
Haile Selassie (1892–1975) Emperor of
Ethiopia.
Telegram sent to Winston Churchill, mimicking
his 'Give us the tools, and we will finish the job'
Ambrosia and Small Beer, Ch. 4 (Edward
Marsh)

352   This whipped jackal . . . is frisking up by the
side of the German tiger.
Winston Churchill (1874–1965) British
statesman.
Referring to Mussolini
Speech, House of Commons, Apr 1941

353   Like German opera, too long and too loud.
Evelyn Waugh (1903–66) British novelist.
Giving his opinions of warfare after the Battle of
Crete, 1941
Attrib.

354   When Barbarossa commences, the world will
hold its breath and make no comment.
Adolf Hitler (1889–1945) German dictator.
Referring to the planned invasion of the USSR,
Operation Barbarossa, which began on 22
June 1941
Attrib.

355   If we see that Germany is winning the war we
ought to help Russia, and if Russia is winning
we ought to help Germany, and in that way
let them kill as many as possible.
Harry S. Truman (1884–1972) US
statesman.
New York Times, 24 July 1941, when Russia
was invaded by Germany

356   You do your worst, and we will do our best.
Winston Churchill (1874–1965) British statesman.
Addressed to Hitler
Speech, 14 July 1941

357   Do not despair
For Johnny head-in-air;
He sleeps as sound
As Johnny underground.
John Sleigh Pudney (1909–77) British poet and writer.
For Johnny

358   Do not let us speak of darker days; let us rather speak of sterner days. These are not dark days: these are great days — the greatest days our country has ever lived.
Winston Churchill (1874–1965) British statesman.
Address, Harrow School, 29 Oct 1941

359   Probably the Battle of Waterloo *was* won on the playing-fields of Eton, but the opening battles of all subsequent wars have been lost there.
George Orwell (Eric Blair; 1903–50) British novelist.
The Lion and the Unicorn, 'England, Your England'

360   Praise the Lord and pass the ammunition!
Howell Maurice Forgy (1908–83) US naval lieutenant.
Remark made during the Japanese attack on Pearl Harbor, 7 Dec 1941
Attrib. in *The Los Angeles Times*

361   A date that shall live in infamy.
Franklin D. Roosevelt (1882–1945) US president.
Referring to 7 Dec 1941, when Japan attacked Pearl Harbor
Message to Congress, 8 Dec 1941

362   I fear we have only awakened a sleeping giant, and his reaction will be terrible.
Isoroku Yamamoto (1884–1943) Japanese admiral.
Said after the Japanese attack on Pearl Harbor, 1941

363   When you have to kill a man it costs nothing to be polite.
Winston Churchill (1874–1965) British statesman.
Justifying the fact that the declaration of war against Japan was made in the usual diplomatic language
The Grand Alliance

364   When I warned them that Britain would fight on alone whatever they did, their Generals told their Prime Minister and his divided Cabinet: 'In three weeks England will have her neck wrung like a chicken.'
Some chicken! Some neck!
Winston Churchill
Referring to the French Government
Speech, Canadian Parliament, 30 Dec 1941

365   The high sentiments always win in the end, the leaders who offer blood, toil, tears and sweat always get more out of their followers than those who offer safety and a good time. When it comes to the pinch, human beings are heroic.
George Orwell (Eric Blair; 1903–50) British novelist.
The Art of Donald McGill

1942

366   War is not an adventure. It is a disease. It is like typhus.
Antoine de Saint-Exupéry (1900–44) French novelist and aviator.
Flight to Arras

367   The soldier's body becomes a stock of accessories that are not his property.
Antoine de Saint-Exupéry
Flight To Arras

368   I shall return.
Douglas MacArthur (1880–1964) US general.
Message (11 Mar 1942) on leaving for Australia from Corregidor Island (Philippines), which he had been defending against the Japanese

369   Defeat of Germany means the defeat of Japan, probably without firing a shot or losing a life.
Franklin D. Roosevelt (1882–1945) US president.
The Hinge of Fate (Winston S. Churchill), Ch. 25

370*   I have only one purpose, the destruction of Hitler, and my life is much simplified thereby. If Hitler invaded Hell I would make at least a favourable reference to the Devil in the House of Commons.
Winston Churchill (1874–1965) British statesman.
The Grand Alliance

371   A revolutionary France would always rather win a war with General Hoche than lose it with Marshal Soubise.
Charles De Gaulle (1890–1970) French general and statesman.
Speech, London, 1 Apr 1942

372*   I herewith commission you to carry out all preparations with regard to . . . a *total solution* of the Jewish question, in those territories of Europe which are under German influence.
Hermann Goering (1893–1946) German leader.
The Rise and Fall of the Third Reich (William Shirer)

373   I think if the people of this country can be reached with the truth, their judgment will be in favor of the many, as against the privileged few.
Eleanor Roosevelt (1884–1962) US writer and lecturer.
Ladies' Home Journal

374   We all know that books burn — yet we have the greater knowledge that books cannot be killed by fire. People die, but books never die. No

man and no force can abolish memory . . . In this war, we know, books are weapons.
Franklin D. Roosevelt (1882–1945) US president.
Message to American Booksellers Association, 23 Apr 1942

375 Never before have we had so little time in which to do so much.
Franklin D. Roosevelt
Radio broadcast, 23 Feb 1942

376 The century on which we are entering – the century which will come out of this war – can be and must be the century of the common man.
Henry Wallace (1888–1965) US economist and politician.
Speech, 'The Price of Free World Victory', 8 May 1942

377 I have not become the King's First Minister in order to preside over the liquidation of the British Empire.
Winston Churchill (1874–1965) British statesman.
Speech, Mansion House, 10 Nov 1942

378 Before Alamein we never had a victory. After Alamein we never had a defeat.
Winston Churchill
The Hinge of Fate, Ch. 33

379 This is not the end. It is not even the beginning of the end. But it is, perhaps, the end of the beginning.
Winston Churchill
Referring to the Battle of Egypt
Speech, Mansion House, 10 Nov 1942

380 The Almighty in His infinite wisdom did not see fit to create Frenchmen in the image of Englishmen.
Winston Churchill
Speech, House of Commons, 10 Dec 1942

381 The object of government in peace and in war is not the glory of rulers or of races, but the happiness of the common man.
Lord Beveridge (1879–1963) British economist.
Social Insurance

382 In place of the conception of the Power-State we are led to that of the Welfare-State.
William Temple (1881–1944) British churchman.
Citizen and Churchman, Ch. 11

1943

383* In defeat unbeatable; in victory unbearable.
Winston Churchill (1874–1965) British statesman.
Referring to Viscount Montgomery
Ambrosia and Small Beer (E. Marsh), Ch. 5

384 You may take the most gallant sailor, the most intrepid airman, or the most audacious soldier,

put them at a table together – what do you get? *The sum of their fears.*
Winston Churchill
Talking about the Chiefs of Staffs system, 16 Nov 1943
The Blast of War (H. Macmillan), Ch. 16

385 Don't let's be beastly to the Germans.
Noël Coward (1899–1973) British dramatist.
Title of song

386 Politics is the art of preventing people from taking part in affairs which properly concern them.
Paul Valéry (1871–1945) French poet and writer.
Tel quel

387 Freedom is an indivisible word. If we want to enjoy it, and fight for it, we must be prepared to extend it to everyone, whether they are rich or poor, whether they agree with us or not, no matter what their race or the colour of their skin.
Wendell Lewis Willkie (1892–1944) US lawyer and businessman.
One World, Ch. 13

1944

388 It was very successful, but it fell on the wrong planet.
Wernher von Braun (1912–77) German-born US rocket engineer.
Referring to the first V2 rocket to hit London during World War II
Attrib.

389 Liberty is so much latitude as the powerful choose to accord to the weak.
Judge Learned Hand (1872–1961) US judge.
Speech, University of Pennsylvania Law School, 21 May 1944

390 The eyes of the world are upon you. The hopes and prayers of liberty-loving people everywhere march with you.
Dwight D. Eisenhower (1890–1969) US general and statesman.
Order to his troops, 6 June 1944 (D-Day)

391 Older men declare war. But it is youth that must fight and die.
Herbert Clark Hoover (1874–1964) US statesman.
Speech, Republican Convention, Chicago, 27 June 1944

392* They're overpaid, overfed, oversexed and over here.
Tommy Trinder (1909–89) British entertainer.
Referring to the G.I.s
Attrib.

393 Our ships have been salvaged and are retiring at high speed toward the Japanese fleet.
W. C. Halsey (1882–1959) US admiral.
Following Japanese claims that most of the American Third Fleet had been sunk or were retiring
Radio message, Oct 1944

394 Dear Ike, Today I spat in the Seine.
General George Patton (1885–1945) US
general.
Message sent to Eisenhower reporting his cross-
ing of the Seine in World War II
The American Treasury (C. Fadiman)

395 Is Paris burning?
Adolf Hitler (1889–1945) German dictator.
Referring to the liberation of Paris, 1944

1945

396 This war is not as in the past; whoever occupies a territory also imposes on it his own
social system. Everyone imposes his own system as far as his army has power to do so. It
cannot be otherwise.
Joseph Stalin (J. Dzhugashvili; 1879–1953)
Soviet statesman.
Conversations with Stalin (Milovan Djilas)

397 More than an end to war, we want an end to
the beginnings of all wars.
Franklin D. Roosevelt (1882–1945) US
Democratic president.
Speech broadcast on the day after his death (13
Apr 1945)

398 He would rather follow public opinion than lead
it.
Harry Hopkins (1890–1946) US politician.
Referring to Roosevelt
Attrib.

399 In Franklin Roosevelt there died the greatest
American friend we have ever known and the
greatest champion of freedom who has ever
brought help and comfort from the New World
to the Old.
Winston Churchill (1874–1965) British
statesman.
The Second World War

400 This was the Angel of History! We felt its wings
flutter through the room. Was that not the fortune we awaited so anxiously?
Joseph Goebbels (1897–1945) German
politician.
Referring to Roosevelt's death
Diary

401* They entered the war to prevent us from going
into the East, not to have the East come to the
Atlantic.
Hermann Goering (1893–1946) German
leader.
Referring to the war aims of the British in World
War II
Nuremberg Diary (G. M. Gilbert)

402* Now we are all sons of bitches.
Kenneth Bainbridge (1904–   ) US physicist.
After the first atomic test
The Decision to Drop the Bomb

403 We knew the world would not be the same.
J. Robert Oppenheimer (1904–67) US
physicist.
After the first atomic test
The Decision to Drop the Bomb

404 The Bomb brought peace but man alone can
keep that peace.
Winston Churchill (1874–1965) British
statesman.
Speech, House of Commons, 16 Aug 1945

405 At first it was a giant column that soon took the
shape of a supramundane mushroom.
William L. Laurence (1888–1977) US
journalist.
Referring to the explosion of the first atomic
bomb, over Hiroshima, 6 Aug 1945
The New York Times, 26 Sept 1945

406 We have had our last chance. If we do not de-
vise some greater and more equitable system,
Armageddon will be at our door.
Douglas MacArthur (1880–1964) US
General.
Broadcast, 2 Sept 1945

407 War is war. The only good human being is a
dead one.
George Orwell (Eric Blair; 1903–50) British
novelist.
Animal Farm, Ch. 4

408 Peace with Germany and Japan on our terms
will not bring much rest.... As I observed last
time, when the war of the giants is over the
wars of the pygmies will begin.
Winston Churchill (1874–1965) British
statesman.
Triumph and Tragedy, Ch. 25

409 In war, resolution; in defeat, defiance; in vic-
tory, magnanimity; in peace, goodwill.
Winston Churchill
Epigram used by Sir Edward Marsh after World
War II; used as 'a moral of the work' in
Churchill's book
The Second World War

410 In politics, as in grammar, one should be able
to tell the substantives from the adjectives.
Hitler was a substantive; Mussolini only an
adjective. Hitler was a nuisance. Mussolini was
bloody. Together a bloody nuisance.
Salvador de Madariaga y Rogo (1886–
1978) Spanish diplomat and writer.
Attrib.

411 In Germany, the Nazis came for the Communists and I didn't speak up because I was not a
Communist. Then they came for the Jews
and I didn't speak up because I was not a Jew.
Then they came for the trade unionists and I
didn't speak up because I was not a trade
unionist. Then they came for the Catholics and
I was a Protestant so I didn't speak up. Then
they came for me ... By that time there was
no one to speak up for anyone.
Martin Niemöller (1892–1984) German
pastor.
Concise Dictionary of Religious Quotations (W.
Neil)

412 To save your world you asked this man to die:
Would this man, could he see you now, ask
why?
W. H. Auden (1907–73) British poet.
Epitaph for an Unknown Soldier

413* I said that the world must be made safe for at least fifty years. If it was only for fifteen to twenty years then we should have betrayed our soldiers.
Winston Churchill (1874–1965) British statesman.
Closing the Ring, Ch. 20

414* The redress of the grievances of the vanquished should precede the disarmament of the victors.
Winston Churchill
The Gathering Storm, Ch. 3

415 There are few virtues which the Poles do not possess and there are few errors they have ever avoided.
Winston Churchill
Speech, House of Commons, 1945

416* Does that mean that because Americans won't listen to sense, you intend to talk nonsense to them?
John Maynard Keynes (1883–1946) British economist.
Said before a monetary conference, 1944 or 1945

417 The Happy Warrior of Squandermania.
Winston Churchill (1874–1965) British statesman.
Referring to Lloyd George
Attrib.

418 A master of improvised speech and improvised policies.
A. J. P. Taylor (1906–90) British historian.
Referring to Lloyd George
English History 1914–1945

419 Though the Jazz Age continued, it became less and less an affair of youth. The sequel was like a children's party taken over by the elders.
F. Scott Fitzgerald (1896–1940) US novelist.
The Crack-Up

420 Actually I vote Labour, but my butler's a Tory.
Earl Mountbatten of Burma (1900–79) British admiral and statesman.
Said to a Conservative canvasser during the 1945 election

421 This island is almost made of coal and surrounded by fish. Only an organizing genius could produce a shortage of coal and fish in Great Britain at the same time.
Aneurin Bevan (1897–1960) British politician.
Speech, Blackpool, 18 May 1945

422 Man is the only creature that consumes without producing.
George Orwell (Eric Blair; 1903–50) British novelist.
Animal Farm, Ch. 1

423 All animals are equal but some animals are more equal than others.
George Orwell
Animal Farm, Ch. 10

424 We must plan for freedom, and not only for security, if for no other reason than that only freedom can make security secure.
Karl Popper (1902–) Austrian-born British philosopher.
The Open Society and Its Enemies

425 Man is not a solitary animal, and so long as social life survives, self-realization cannot be the supreme principle of ethics.
Bertrand Russell (1872–1970) British philosopher.
History of Western Philosophy, 'Romanticism'

Attitudes

Art, Literature, and Music

1914

426 It is not good enough to spend time and ink in describing the penultimate sensations and physical movements of people getting into a state of rut, we all know them too well.
John Galsworthy (1867–1933) British novelist.
Referring to D. H. Lawrence's *Sons and Lovers*
Letter to Edward Garnett, 13 Apr 1914

427 I think that I shall never see
A poem lovely as a tree.
Alfred Joyce Kilmer (1886–1918) US poet.
Trees

428 Waldo is one of those people who would be enormously improved by death.
Saki (Hector Hugh Munro; 1870–1916) British writer.
Referring to Ralph Waldo Emerson
The Feast of Nemesis

1916

429 They are great parables, the novels, but false art. They are only parables. All the people are *fallen angels* – even the dirtiest scrubs. This I cannot stomach. People are not fallen angels, they are merely people.
D. H. Lawrence (1885–1930) British novelist.
Referring to the novels of Dostoyevsky
Letter to J. Middleton Murry and Katherine Mansfield, 17 Feb 1916

1918

430* His verse exhibits . . . something that is rather like Keats's vulgarity with a Public School accent.
F. R. Leavis (1895–1978) British literary critic.
Referring to Rupert Brooke
New Bearings in English Poetry, Ch. 2

431 Music is the arithmetic of sounds as optics is the geometry of light.
Claude Debussy (1862–1918) French composer.
Attrib.

1919

432 I just keep painting till I feel like pinching. Then
I know it's right.
Pierre Auguste Renoir (1841–1919) French
impressionist painter.
Explaining how he achieved such lifelike flesh
tones in his nudes
Attrib.

433 In a few generations you can breed a
racehorse. The recipe for making a man like
Delacroix is less well known.
Pierre Auguste Renoir
Attrib.

434* Poetry is a comforting piece of fiction set to
more or less lascivious music.
H. L. Mencken (1880–1956) US journalist.
Prejudices, 'The Poet and his Art'

435 When one hears of a poet past thirty-five he
seems somehow unnatural and obscene.
H. L. Mencken
Prejudices

1920

436 I am a man, and alive . . . For this reason I am a
novelist. And being a novelist, I consider myself superior to the saint, the scientist, the
philosopher, and the poet, who are all great
masters of different bits of man alive, but never
get the whole hog.
D. H. Lawrence (1885–1930) British novelist.
Phoenix, 'Why the Novel Matters'

437 Immature poets imitate; mature poets steal.
T. S. Eliot (1888–1965) US-born British poet
and dramatist.
Philip Massinger

438* Never compose anything unless the not composing of it becomes a positive nuisance to
you.
Gustav Holst (1874–1934) British composer.
Letter to W. G. Whittaker

439 Jazz will endure just as long as people hear it
through their feet instead of their brains.
John Philip Sousa (1854–1932) US composer, conductor, and writer.
Attrib.

1922

440 A true poet does not bother to be poetical. Nor
does a nursery gardener scent his roses.
Jean Cocteau (1889–1963) French poet and
artist.
Professional Secrets

441 Literature flourishes best when it is half a trade
and half an art.
Dean Inge (1860–1954) British churchman.
The Victorian Age

1923

442 Words are, of course, the most powerful drug
used by mankind.
Rudyard Kipling (1865–1936) Indian-born
British writer.
Speech, 14 Feb 1923

443 The courage of the poet is to keep ajar the door
that leads to madness.
Christopher Morley (1890–1957) US writer
and journalist.
Inward Ho

444 Poetry is the achievement of the synthesis of
hyacinths and biscuits.
Carl Sandburg (1878–1967) US author and
poet.
Atlantic Monthly

445 A house is a machine for living in.
Le Corbusier (Charles-Édouard Jeanneret;
1887–1965) Swiss-born French architect.
Towards an Architecture

1925

446* Art is not a mirror to reflect the world, but a
hammer with which to shape it.
Vladimir Mayakovsky (1893–1930) Soviet
poet.
The Guardian, 11 Dec 1974

447 Another unsettling element in modern art is that
common symptom of immaturity, the dread of
doing what has been done before.
Edith Wharton (1862–1937) US novelist.
The Writing of Fiction, Ch. 1

448 Trivial personalities decomposing in the eternity
of print.
Virginia Woolf (1882–1941) British novelist.
The Common Reader, 'Jane Eyre'

449 *Middlemarch*, the magnificent book which with
all its imperfections is one of the few English
novels for grown up people.
Virginia Woolf (1882–1941) British novelist.
The Common Reader, 'George Eliot'

450 'It's like the question of the authorship of the
Iliad,' said Mr Cardan. 'The author of that
poem is either Homer or, if not Homer, some-
body else of the same name.'
Aldous Huxley (1894–1964) British novelist.
Those Barren Leaves, Pt. V, Ch. 4

451 Music is not written in red, white and blue. It is
written in the heart's blood of the composer.
Nellie Melba (Helen Porter Mitchell; 1861–
1931) Australian soprano.
Melodies and Memories

452 I don't write modern music. I only write good
music.
Igor Stravinsky (1882–1971) Russian-born
US composer.
To journalists on his first visit to America, 1925

1928

453 A bad book is as much a labour to write as a

good one; it comes as sincerely from the author's soul.
Aldous Huxley (1894–1964) British novelist and essayist.
Point Counter Point

454 My God, what a clumsy *alla patrida* James Joyce is! Nothing but old fags and cabbage stumps of quotations from the Bible and the rest, stewed in the juice of deliberate, journalistic dirty-mindedness.
D. H. Lawrence (1885–1930) British novelist.
Letter to Aldous Huxley

1929

455 I've never been in there . . . but there are only three things to see, and I've seen colour reproductions of all of them.
Harold W. Ross (1892–1951) US journalist.
Referring to the Louvre
A Farewell to Arms (Ernest Hemingway)

456 Until we learn the use of living words we shall continue to be waxworks inhabited by gramophones.
Walter De La Mare (1873–1956) British poet.
The Observer, 'Sayings of the Week', 12 May 1929

457 Literature is strewn with the wreckage of men who have minded beyond reason the opinions of others.
Virginia Woolf (1882–1941) British novelist.
A Room of One's Own

1930

458 As is the case in all branches of art, success depends in a very large measure upon individual initiative and exertion, and cannot be achieved except by dint of hard work.
Anna Pavlova (1881–1931) Russian ballet dancer.
Pavlova: A Biography (ed. A. H. Franks), 'Pages of My Life'

459 Never mind about my soul, just make sure you get my tie right.
James Joyce (1882–1941) Irish novelist.
Responding to the painter Patrick Tuohy's assertion that he wished to capture Joyce's soul in his portrait of him
James Joyce (R. Ellmann)

460 Among the many problems which beset the novelist, not the least weighty is the choice of the moment at which to begin his novel.
Vita Sackville-West (Victoria S.; 1892–1962) British poet and novelist.
The Edwardians, Ch. 1

461 No poet, no artist of any sort, has his complete meaning alone. His significance, his appreciation is the appreciation of his relation to the dead poets and artists.
T. S. Eliot (1888–1965) US-born British poet and dramatist.
Tradition and the Individual Talent

462 The whole of art is an appeal to a reality which is not without us but in our minds.
Desmond MacCarthy (1877–1952) British writer and theatre critic.
Theatre, 'Modern Drama'

463 The ability to simplify means to eliminate the unnecessary so that the necessary may speak.
Hans Hofmann (1880–1966) German-born US painter.
Search for the Real

464* I never realized before that Albert married beneath him.
Noël Coward (1899–1973) British dramatist.
After seeing a certain actress in the role of Queen Victoria
Tynan on Theatre (K. Tynan)

465 It is disappointing to report that George Bernard Shaw appearing as George Bernard Shaw is sadly miscast in the part. Satirists should be heard and not seen.
Robert E. Sherwood (1896–1955) US writer and dramatist.
Reviewing a Shaw play

466 This is not a novel to be tossed aside lightly. It should be thrown with great force.
Dorothy Parker (1893–1967) US writer.
Book review
Wit's End (R. E. Dremman)

467 It is the sexless novel that should be distinguished: the sex novel is now normal.
George Bernard Shaw (1856–1950) Irish dramatist and critic.
Table-Talk of G.B.S.

468 All good writing is *swimming under water* and holding your breath.
F. Scott Fitzgerald (1896–1940) US novelist.
Letter

469 Our American professors like their literature clear and cold and pure and very dead.
Sinclair Lewis (1885–1951) US novelist.
Speech, on receiving the Nobel Prize, 1930

470 There are two motives for reading a book: one, that you enjoy it, the other that you can boast about it.
Bertrand Russell (1872–1970) British philosopher.
The Conquest of Happiness

471 The poet speaks to all men of that other life of theirs that they have smothered and forgotten.
Edith Sitwell (1887–1964) British poet and writer.
Rhyme and Reason

472 Strange how potent cheap music is.
Noël Coward (1899–1973) British dramatist.
Private Lives

473 A good composer does not imitate; he steals.
Igor Stravinsky (1882–1971) Russian-born US composer.
Twentieth Century Music (Peter Yates)

474   Rachmaninov's immortalizing totality was his scowl. He was a six-and-a-half-foot-tall scowl.
Igor Stravinsky
Conversations with Igor Stravinsky (Igor Stravinsky and Robert Craft)

475   Wagner is the Puccini of music.
J. B. Morton (1893–1979) British journalist.
Attrib.

476   Madame, there you sit with that magnificent instrument between your legs, and all you can do is *scratch* it!
Arturo Toscanini (1867–1957) Italian conductor.
Rebuking an incompetent woman cellist; also attributed to Sir Thomas Beecham
Attrib.

477   God tells me how he wants this music played – and you get in his way.
Arturo Toscanini
Etude (Howard Tubman)

1931

478   A best-seller is the gilded tomb of a mediocre talent.
Logan Pearsall Smith (1865–1946) US writer.
Afterthoughts, 'Art and Letters'

1933

479   Even when poetry has a meaning, as it usually has, it may be inadvisable to draw it out . . . Perfect understanding will sometimes almost extinguish pleasure.
A. E. Housman (1859–1936) British scholar and poet.
The Name and Nature of Poetry

480   People are wrong when they say the opera isn't what it used to be. It is what it used to be. That's what's wrong with it.
Noël Coward (1899–1973) British dramatist.
Design for Living

1934

481   It does not matter that Dickens' world is not life-like; it is alive.
Lord Cecil (1902–86) British writer and critic.
Early Victorian Novelists

482   A combination of Little Nell and Lady Macbeth.
Alexander Woollcott (1887–1943) US journalist.
Referring to Dorothy Parker
While Rome Burns

483   Music begins to atrophy when it departs too far from the dance; . . . poetry begins to atrophy when it gets too far from music.
Ezra Pound (1885–1972) US poet.
ABC of Reading, 'Warning'

1935

484*   When I hear anyone talk of Culture, I reach for my revolver.
Hermann Goering (1893–1946) German leader.
Attrib. to Goering but probably said by Hanns Johst

485   Writing free verse is like playing tennis with the net down.
Robert Frost (1875–1963) US poet.
Speech, Milton Academy, 17 May 1935

1936

486   He is all blood, dirt and sucked sugar stick.
W. B. Yeats (1865–1939) Irish poet.
Referring to Wilfred Owen
Letters on Poetry to Dorothy Wellesley, Letter, 21 Dec 1936

487   That was the chief difference between literature and life. In books, the proportion of exceptional to commonplace people is high; in reality, very low.
Aldous Huxley (1894–1964) British novelist.
Eyeless in Gaza

488   For Lawrence, existence was one continuous convalescence; it was as though he were newly reborn from a mortal illness every day of his life.
Aldous Huxley
Referring to D. H. Lawrence
The Olive Tree

489   There are passages in *Ulysses* which can be read only in the toilet – if one wants to extract the full flavour of their content.
Henry Miller (1891–1980) US novelist.
Black Spring

490   You must write for children in the same way as you do for adults, only better.
Maxim Gorky (Aleksei Maksimovich Peshkov; 1868–1936) Russian writer.
Attrib.

1937

491   The higher-water mark, so to speak, of Socialist literature is W. H. Auden, a sort of gutless Kipling.
George Orwell (Eric Blair; 1903–50) British novelist.
The Road to Wigan Pier, Ch. 11

1938

492   A great writer creates a world of his own and his readers are proud to live in it. A lesser writer may entice them in for a moment, but soon he will watch them filing out.
Cyril Connolly (1903–74) British journalist.
Enemies of Promise, Ch. 1

493   An author arrives at a good style when his lan-

guage performs what is required of it without shyness.
Cyril Connolly
Enemies of Promise, Ch. 3

494 For to write good prose is an affair of good manners. It is, unlike verse, a civil art . . . . Poetry is baroque.
W. Somerset Maugham (1874—1965) British novelist.
The Summing Up

495 There is an impression abroad that everyone has it in him to write one book; but if by this is implied a good book the impression is false.
W. Somerset Maugham
The Summing Up

496 It has been said that good prose should resemble the conversation of a well-bred man.
W. Somerset Maugham
The Summing Up

1939

497* At 83 Shaw's mind was perhaps not quite as good as it used to be. It was still better than anyone else's.
Alexander Woollcott (1887—1943) US journalist.
Referring to George Bernard Shaw
While Rome Burns

498 Earth, receive an honoured guest:
William Yeats is laid to rest.
Let the Irish vessel lie
Emptied of its poetry.
W. H. Auden (1907—73) British poet.
In Memory of W. B. Yeats, III

499 No tears in the writer, no tears in the reader.
Robert Frost (1875—1963) US poet.
Collected Poems, Preface

1940

500 Too true, too sincere. The Muse prefers the liars, the gay and warty lads.
W. B. Yeats (1865—1939) Irish poet.
Referring to the poetry of James Reed
The Long Week End (Robert Graves and Alan Hodge)

501 Art is the imposing of a pattern on experience, and our aesthetic enjoyment is recognition of the pattern.
A. N. Whitehead (1861—1947) British philosopher.
Dialogues, 228

502* I enjoyed talking to her, but thought *nothing* of her writing. I considered her 'a beautiful little knitter'.
Edith Sitwell (1887—1964) British poet and writer.
Referring to Virginia Woolf
Letter to G. Singleton

503 It is the logic of our times,
No subject for immortal verse —

That we who lived by honest dreams
Defend the bad against the worse.
C. Day Lewis (1904—72) British poet.
Where are the War Poets?

504 English literature's performing flea.
Sean O'Casey (1884—1964) Irish dramatist.
Referring to P. G. Wodehouse
Attrib.

505 Poetry makes nothing happen, it survives
In the valley of its saying.
W. H. Auden (1907—73) British poet.
In Memory of W. B. Yeats

1941

506 A painter should not paint what he sees, but what will be seen.
Paul Valéry (1871—1945) French poet and writer.
Mauvaises Pensées et Autres

507 What a terrible revenge by the culture of the Negroes on that of the whites.
Ignacy Paderewski (1860—1941) Polish pianist, composer, and statesman.
Referring to jazz
Attrib.

508 Of all the great Victorian writers, he was probably the most antagonistic to the Victorian age itself.
Edmund Wilson (1895—1972) US critic and writer.
Referring to Dickens
The Wound and the Bow, 'The Two Scrooges'

1944

509 The only way for writers to meet is to share a quick pee over a common lamp-post.
Cyril Connolly (1903—74) British journalist.
The Unquiet Grave

1945

510 You can stroke people with words.
F. Scott Fitzgerald (1896—1940) US novelist.
The Crack-up

511 I have only read one book in my life and that is *White Fang*. It's so frightfully good I've never bothered to read another.
Nancy Mitford (1904—73) British writer.
The Pursuit Of Love

512 Music is a beautiful opiate, if you don't take it too seriously.
Henry Miller (1891—1980) US novelist.
The Air Conditioned Nightmare

Daily Life

1917

513 Many a man who thinks to found a home dis-

covers that he has merely opened a tavern for his friends.
Norman Douglas (1868–1952) British novelist.
South Wind, Ch. 24

1920

514* Exercise is bunk. If you are healthy, you don't need it: if you are sick, you shouldn't take it.
Henry Ford (1863–1947) US car manufacturer.
Attrib.

1922

515 Teetotallers lack the sympathy and generosity of men that drink.
W. H. Davies (1871–1940) British poet.
Shorter Lyrics of the 20th Century, Introduction

1925

516 Those comfortably padded lunatic asylums which are known, euphemistically, as the stately homes of England.
Virginia Woolf (1882–1941) British novelist.
The Common Reader, 'Lady Dorothy Nevill'

1930

517* Any time you're Lambeth way,
Any evening, any day,
You'll find us all doin' the Lambeth walk.
Douglas Furber (1885–1961) British songwriter.
Doin' the Lambeth Walk

518* Smokers, male and female, inject and excuse idleness in their lives every time they light a cigarette.
Colette (Sidonie-Gabrielle C.; 1873–1954) French novelist.
Earthly Paradise, 'Freedom'

1932

519 The quality of Mersey is not strained.
Anonymous
Referring to the polluted condition of the River Mersey
Sunday Graphic, 14 Aug 1932

1934

520 The feeling of Sunday is the same everywhere, heavy, melancholy, standing still. Like when they say, 'As it was in the beginning, is now, and ever shall be, world without end.'
Jean Rhys (1894–1979) Dominican-born British novelist.
Voyage in the Dark, Ch. 4

1935

521 The Stately Homes of England

How beautiful they stand,
To prove the upper classes
Have still the upper hand.
Noël Coward (1899–1973) British dramatist.
Operette, 'The Stately Homes of England'

1937

522 Come, friendly bombs, and fall on Slough
It isn't fit for humans now.
There isn't grass to graze a cow
Swarm over, Death!
John Betjeman (1906–84) British poet.
Slough

1938

523 A hundred and fifty accurate reproductions of Anne Hathaway's cottage, each complete with central heating and garage.
Osbert Lancaster (1908–86) British cartoonist.
Pillar to Post, 'Stockbrokers Tudor'

Death

1924

524 What we call mourning for our dead is perhaps not so much grief at not being able to call them back as it is grief at not being able to want to do so.
Thomas Mann (1875–1955) German novelist.
The Magic Mountain

1936

525 Death . . . It's the only thing we haven't succeeded in completely vulgarizing.
Aldous Huxley (1894–1964) British novelist and essayist.
Eyeless in Gaza, Ch. 31

1941

526 It is the only disease you don't look forward to being cured of.
Herman J. Mankiewicz (1897–1953) US journalist and screenwriter.
Referring to death
Citizen Kane

1944

527 Ignore death until the last moment; then when it can't be ignored any longer have yourself squirted full of morphia and shuffle off in a corner.
Aldous Huxley (1894–1964) British novelist and essayist.
Time Must Have A Stop

Education, Knowledge, and Learning

1918

528* An idea isn't responsible for the people who believe in it.
Don Marquis (1878–1937) US journalist.
New York Sun

1920

529* Intelligence is quickness to apprehend as distinct from ability, which is capacity to act wisely on the thing apprehended.
A. N. Whitehead (1861–1947) British philosopher.
Dialogues, 135

530 They go forth into it with well-developed bodies, fairly developed minds, and undeveloped hearts.
E. M. Forster (1879–1970) British novelist.
Referring to public schoolboys going into the world
Abinger Harvest, 'Notes on the English Character'

1921

531 The proper study of mankind is books.
Aldous Huxley (1894–1964) British novelist and essayist.
Chrome Yellow

532 In order to draw a limit to thinking, we should have to be able to think both sides of this limit.
Ludwig Wittgenstein (1889–1951) Austrian philosopher.
Tractatus Logico-Philosophicus, Preface

533 Philosophy is not a theory but an activity.
Ludwig Wittgenstein
Tractatus Logico-Philosophicus, Ch. 4

534 Whereof one cannot speak, thereon one must remain silent.
Ludwig Wittgenstein
Tractatus Logico-Philosophicus, Ch. 7

1922

535 The refined punishments of the spiritual mode are usually much more indecent and dangerous than a good smack.
D. H. Lawrence (1885–1930) British novelist.
Fantasia of the Unconscious, Ch. 4

536 The tendency of the casual mind is to pick out or stumble upon a sample which supports or defines its prejudices, and then to make it representative of a whole class.
Walter Lippmann (1889–1974) US editor and writer.
Public Opinion

1923

537 Knowledge can be communicated but not wisdom.
Hermann Hesse (1877–1962) German novelist and poet.
Siddhartha

1924

538 Education is simply the soul of a society as it passes from one generation to another.
G. K. Chesterton (1874–1936) British writer.
The Observer, 'Sayings of the Week', 6 July 1924

1926

539 One does not discover new lands without consenting to lose sight of the shore for a very long time.
André Gide (1869–1951) French novelist.
The Counterfeiters

1927

540 The voice of the intellect is a soft one, but it does not rest till it has gained a hearing.
Sigmund Freud (1856–1939) Austrian psychoanalyst.
The Future of an Illusion

541 Facts do not cease to exist because they are ignored.
Aldous Huxley (1894–1964) British novelist and essayist.
Proper Studies, 'Note on Dogma'

542 If you make people think they're thinking, they'll love you: but if you really make them think, they'll hate you.
Don Marquis (1878–1937) US journalist.
Archy and Mehitabel

1928

543 Silence is as full of potential wisdom and wit as the unhewn marble of great sculpture.
Aldous Huxley (1894–1964) British novelist and essayist.
Point Counter Point

544 It is undesirable to believe a proposition when there is no ground whatever for supposing it true.
Bertrand Russell (1872–1970) British philosopher.
Sceptical Essays

1929

545 Thought must be divided against itself before it can come to any knowledge of itself.
Aldous Huxley (1894–1964) British novelist and essayist.
Do What You Will

546 The safest general characterization of the European philosophical tradition is that it consists of a series of footnotes to Plato.
A. N. Whitehead (1861–1947) British philosopher.
Process and Reality

1930

547* It is a great advantage for a system of philosophy to be substantially true.
George Santayana (1863–1952) US philosopher.
The Unknowable

548 Philosophy, as we use the word, is a fight against the fascination which forms of expression exert upon us.
Ludwig Wittgenstein (1889–1951) Austrian philosopher.
The Blue Book

549* Stupidity does not consist in being without ideas. Such stupidity would be the sweet, blissful stupidity of animals, molluscs and the gods. Human Stupidity consists in having lots of ideas, but stupid ones.
Henry de Montherlant (1896–1972) French novelist.
Notebooks

550* The point of philosophy is to start with something so simple as to seem not worth stating, and to end with something so paradoxical that no one will believe it.
Bertrand Russell (1872–1970) British philosopher.
Logic and Knowledge

551 Do not on any account attempt to write on both sides of the paper at once.
W. C. Sellar (1898–1951) British humorous writer.
1066 And All That, Test Paper 5

1931

552 What is a highbrow? It is a man who has found something more interesting than women.
Edgar Wallace (1875–1932) British thriller writer.
Interview

1935

553* An intellectual is someone whose mind watches itself.
Albert Camus (1913–60) French existentialist writer.
Notebooks, 1935–42

1936

554 The principles of logic and metaphysics are true simply because we never allow them to be anything else.
A. J. Ayer (1910–89) British philosopher.
Language, Truth and Logic

1938

555 The ape-like virtues without which no one can enjoy a public school.
Cyril Connolly (1903–74) British journalist.
Enemies of Promise, Ch. 1

556 My thought is *me*: that is why I can't stop. I exist by what I think . . . and I can't prevent myself from thinking.
Jean-Paul Sartre (1905–80) French writer.
Nausea

1942

557 Disinterested intellectual curiosity is the life blood of real civilisation.
George Macaulay Trevelyan (1876–1962) British historian.
English Social History, Preface

558 Education . . . has produced a vast population able to read but unable to distinguish what is worth reading.
George Macaulay Trevelyan
English Social History, Ch. 18

1944

559 Facts are ventriloquists' dummies. Sitting on a wise man's knee they may be made to utter words of wisdom; elsewhere they say nothing or talk nonsense.
Aldous Huxley (1894–1964) British novelist and essayist.
Time Must Have A Stop

1945

560 If one is too lazy to think, too vain to do a thing badly, too cowardly to admit it, one will never attain wisdom.
Cyril Connolly (1903–74) British journalist.
The Unquiet Grave

History

1916

561 History is more or less bunk. It's tradition. We don't want tradition. We want to live in the present and the only history that is worth a tinker's damn is the history we make today.
Henry Ford (1863–1947) US car manufacturer.
Chicago Tribune, 25 May 1916

1920

562* What we know of the past is mostly not worth knowing. What is worth knowing is mostly uncertain. Events in the past may roughly be divided into those which probably never happened and those which do not matter.
Dean Inge (1860–1954) British churchman.
Assessments and Anticipations, 'Prognostications'

563 The historian must have . . . some conception of

how men who are not historians behave. Other-
wise he will move in a world of the dead.
E. M. Forster (1879–1970) British novelist.
Abinger Harvest, 'Captain Edward Gibbon'

1922

564 'History', Stephen said, 'is a nightmare from
which I am trying to awake'.
James Joyce (1882–1941) Irish novelist.
Ulysses

1925

565 Why doesn't the past decently bury itself, instead of sitting and waiting to be admitted by
the present?
D. H. Lawrence (1885–1930) British novelist.
St. Mawr

1926

566 I do not know which makes a man more conservative – to know nothing but the present,
or nothing but the past.
John Maynard Keynes (1883–1946) British
economist.
The End of Laisser-Faire, I

1933

567 It is not the neutrals or the lukewarm who make
history.
Adolf Hitler (1889–1945) German dictator.
Speech, Berlin, 23 Apr 1933

1935

568 The Common Law of England has been labori-
ously built about a mythical figure – the figure of 'The Reasonable Man'.
A. P. Herbert (1890–1971) British writer and
politician.
Uncommon Law

1936

569 The greater part of what passes for diplomatic
history is little more than the record of what
one clerk said to another clerk.
G. M. Young (1882–1959) British
historian.
Victorian England: Portrait of an Age

1938

570 The attitude of the English . . . toward English
history reminds one a good deal of the attitude
of a Hollywood director toward love.
Margaret Halsey (1910–) US writer.
With Malice Toward Some

1942

571 To a surprising extent the war-lords in shining
armour, the apostles of the martial virtues,

tend not to die fighting when the time comes.
History is full of ignominious getaways by
the great and famous.
George Orwell (Eric Blair; 1903–50) British
novelist.
Who Are the War Criminals?

1945

572 There is no history of mankind, there are only
many histories of all kinds of aspects of
human life. And one of these is the history of
political power. This is elevated into the history of the world.
Karl Popper (1902–) Austrian-born British
philosopher.
The Open Society and Its Enemies

Human Nature

1914

573 The secret of being miserable is to have leisure
to bother about whether you are happy or not.
George Bernard Shaw (1856–1950) Irish
dramatist and critic.
Misalliance, Preface

574 One's religion is whatever he is most interested
in, and yours is Success.
J. M. Barrie (1860–1937) British novelist and
dramatist.
The Twelve-Pound Look

1915

575 Mediocrity knows nothing higher than itself, but
talent instantly recognizes genius.
Arthur Conan Doyle (1856–1930) British
writer.
The Valley of Fear

576 Like all weak men he laid an exaggerated stress
on not changing one's mind.
W. Somerset Maugham (1874–1965) British
novelist.
Of Human Bondage, Ch. 37

1917

577 Happiness is not best achieved by those who
seek it directly.
Bertrand Russell (1872–1970) British
philosopher.
Mysticism and Logic

1918

578 The human face is indeed, like the face of the
God of some Oriental theogony, a whole cluster of faces, crowded together but on different surfaces so that one does not see them all
at once.
Marcel Proust (1871–1922) French novelist.
*À la recherche du temps perdu: À l'ombre des
jeunes filles en fleurs*

579* Happiness is beneficial for the body, but it is grief that develops the powers of the mind.
Marcel Proust
À la recherche du temps perdu: Le Temps retrouvé

1919

580 It takes in reality only one to make a quarrel. It is useless for the sheep to pass resolutions in favour of vegetarianism while the wolf remains of a different opinion.
Dean Inge (1860–1954) British churchman.
Outspoken Essays

581 It is hard to believe that a man is telling the truth when you know that you would lie if you were in his place.
H. L. Mencken (1880–1956) US journalist.
Prejudices

582 I don't owe a penny to a single soul — not counting tradesmen, of course.
P. G. Wodehouse (1881–1975) British humorous novelist.
My Man Jeeves, 'Jeeves and the Hard-Boiled Egg'

1920

583 If I ever felt inclined to be timid as I was going into a room full of people, I would say to myself, 'You're the cleverest member of one of the cleverest families in the cleverest class of the cleverest nation in the world, why should you be frightened?'
Beatrice Webb (1858–1943) British economist and writer.
Portraits from Memory (Bertrand Russell), 'Sidney and Beatrice Webb'

584 Although there exist many thousand subjects for elegant conversation, there are persons who cannot meet a cripple without talking about feet.
Ernest Bramah (1869–1942) British writer.
The Wallet of Kai Lung

585 I can sympathize with people's pains, but not with their pleasures. There is something curiously boring about somebody else's happiness.
Aldous Huxley (1894–1964) British novelist.
Limbo, 'Cynthia'

586 It is the unbroken testimony of all history that alcoholic liquors have been used by the strongest, wisest, handsomest, and in every way best races of all times.
George Edward Bateman Saintsbury (1845–1933) British writer and critic.
Notes on a Cellar-Book

587 My candle burns at both ends;
It will not last the night;
But ah, my foes, and oh my friends —
It gives a lovely light!
Edna St Vincent Millay (1892–1950) US poet.
A Few Figs from Thistles, 'First Fig'

1922

588 War hath no fury like a non-combatant.
C. E. Montague (1867–1928) British editor and writer.
Disenchantment, Ch. 15

589 Never ascribe to an opponent motives meaner than your own.
J. M. Barrie (1860–1937) British novelist and dramatist.
Speech, St Andrews, 3 May 1922

590 Sadness is almost never anything but a form of fatigue.
André Gide (1869–1951) French novelist.
Journals, 1922

1923

591 I have the true feeling of myself only when I am unbearably unhappy.
Franz Kafka (1883–1924) Czech novelist.
Diaries

592 That which you love most in him (a friend) may be clearer in his absence.
Kahil Gibran (1883–1931) Lebanese mystic poet and novelist.
The Prophet

593 Because it is there.
George Mallory (1886–1924) British mountaineer.
Answer to the question 'Why do you want to climb Mt. Everest?'
George Mallory (D. Robertson)

1924

594 A platitude is simply a truth repeated till people get tired of hearing it.
Stanley Baldwin (1867–1947) British statesman.
Attrib.

595 Curious things, habits. People themselves never knew they had them.
Agatha Christie (1891–1976) British detective-story writer.
Witness for the Prosecution

596 It is seldom indeed that one parts on good terms, because if one were on good terms one would not part.
Marcel Proust (1871–1922) French novelist.
À la recherche du temps perdu: La Prisonnière

1925

597* What men value in this world is not rights but privileges.
H. L. Mencken (1880–1956) US journalist.
Minority Report

598 There is no surer way of calling the worst out of anyone than that of taking their worst as being their true selves; no surer way of bringing out the best than by only accepting that as being true of them.
E. F. Benson (1867–1940) British novelist.
Rex

599 The latest definition of an optimist is one who
     fills up his crossword puzzle in ink.
     Clement King Shorter (1857–1926) British
     journalist and critic.
     The Observer, 'Sayings of the Week', 22 Feb
     1925

1926
---

600 The optimist proclaims we live in the best of all
     possible worlds; and the pessimist fears this
     is true.
     James Cabell (1879–1958) US novelist and
     journalist.
     The Silver Stallion

601 All men dream: but not equally. Those who
     dream by night in the dusty recesses of their
     minds wake in the day to find that it was vanity:
     but the dreamers of the day are dangerous
     men, for they may act their dream with open
     eyes, to make it possible.
     T. E. Lawrence (1888–1935) British soldier
     and writer.
     Seven Pillars of Wisdom, Ch. 1

1927
---

602 Faith may be defined briefly as an illogical be-
     lief in the occurrence of the improbable.
     H. L. Mencken (1880–1956) US journalist.
     Prejudices, 'Types of Men'

603* It is easier to fight for one's principles than to
     live up to them.
     Alfred Adler (1870–1937) Austrian
     psychiatrist.
     Alfred Adler (P. Bottome)

1928
---

604 Watch how a man takes praise and there you
     have the measure of him.
     Thomas Burke (1886–1945) British writer.
     T. P.'s Weekly, 8 June 1928

605 Happiness is like coke - something you get as a
     by-product in the process of making some-
     thing else.
     Aldous Huxley (1894–1964) British novelist.
     Point Counter Point

606 It takes two to make a murder. There are born
     victims, born to have their throats cut.
     Aldous Huxley
     Point Counter Point

607 I can't quite explain it, but I don't believe one
     can ever be unhappy for long provided one
     does just exactly what one wants to and when
     one wants to.
     Evelyn Waugh (1903–66) British novelist.
     Decline and Fall, Pt. I, Ch. 5

1929
---

608 Consistency is contrary to nature, contrary to

life. The only completely consistent people
are the dead.
Aldous Huxley (1894–1964) British novelist.
Do What you Will

609 Most of the time we think we're sick, it's all in
     the mind.
     Thomas Wolfe (1900–38) US novelist.
     Look Homeward, Angel, Pt. I, Ch. 1

1930
---

610 Being Southerners, it was a source of shame to
     some members of the family that we had no
     recorded ancestors on either side of the Battle
     of Hastings.
     Harper Lee (1926–   ) US writer.
     To Kill a Mockingbird, Pt. I, Ch. 1

611 One of the things that makes a Negro unpleas-
     ant to white folk is the fact that he suffers
     from their injustice. He is thus a standing re-
     buke to them.
     H. L. Mencken (1880–1956) US journalist.
     Notebooks, 'Minority Report'

612 War will never cease until babies begin to
     come into the world with larger cerebrums and
     smaller adrenal glands.
     H. L. Mencken
     Notebooks, 'Minority Report'

613* Of course I don't believe in it. But I understand
     that it brings you luck whether you believe in
     it or not.
     Niels Bohr (1885–1962) Danish physicist.
     When asked why he had a horseshoe on his wall
     Attrib.

614 It is no good casting out devils. They belong to
     us, we must accept them and be at peace with
     them.
     D. H. Lawrence (1885–1930) British novelist.
     Phoenix, 'The Reality of Peace'

615 It is not the ape, nor the tiger in man that I fear,
     it is the donkey.
     William Temple (1881–1944) British
     churchman.
     Attrib.

616 The aristocratic pleasure of displeasing is not
     the only delight that bad taste can yield. One
     can love a certain kind of vulgarity for its own
     sake.
     Aldous Huxley (1894–1964) British novelist.
     Vulgarity in Literature, Ch. 4

617 Those who believe that they are exclusively in
     the right are generally those who achieve
     something.
     Aldous Huxley
     Proper Studies

618 The megalomaniac differs from the narcissist by
     the fact that he wishes to be powerful rather
     than charming, and seeks to be feared
     rather than loved. To this type belong many
     lunatics and most of the great men of history.
     Bertrand Russell (1872–1970) British
     philosopher.
     The Conquest of Happiness

619 Ambition is the grand enemy of all peace.
John Cowper Powys (1872–1963) British novelist.
The Meaning of Culture

1931

620 Only solitary men know the full joys of friendship. Others have their family – but to a solitary and an exile his friends are everything.
Willa Cather (1873–1947) US writer and poet.
Shadows On the Rock

1932

621 To the Puritan all things are impure, as somebody says.
D. H. Lawrence (1885–1930) British novelist.
Etruscan Places, 'Cerveteri'

1935

622 Nobody speaks the truth when there's something they must have.
Elizabeth Bowen (1899–1973) Irish novelist.
The House in Paris, Ch. 5

623 It is a kind of spiritual snobbery that makes people think that they can be happy without money.
Albert Camus (1913–60) French existentialist writer.
Notebooks, 1935–1942

624* Human kind
Cannot bear very much reality.
T. S. Eliot (1888–1965) US-born British poet and dramatist.
Four Quartets, 'Burnt Norton'

1936

625 Fighting is like champagne. It goes to the heads of cowards as quickly as of heroes. Any fool can be brave on a battle field when it's be brave or else be killed.
Margaret Mitchell (1909–49) US novelist.
Gone with the Wind

1937

626 The more you are in the right the more natural that everyone else should be bullied into thinking likewise.
George Orwell (Eric Blair; 1903–50) British novelist.
The Road to Wigan Pier

627 No one can make you feel inferior without your consent.
Eleanor Roosevelt (1884–1962) US writer and lecturer.
This is My Story

1938

628 Had I been a man I might have explored the Poles or climbed Mount Everest, but as it was my spirit found outlet in the air.
Amy Johnson (1903–41) British flyer.
Myself When Young (ed. Margot Asquith)

629 I'll give you my opinion of the human race . . . Their heart's in the right place, but their head is a thoroughly inefficient organ.
W. Somerset Maugham (1874–1965) British novelist.
The Summing Up

630 You get the impression that their normal condition is silence and that speech is a slight fever which attacks them now and then.
Jean-Paul Sartre (1905–80) French writer.
Nausea

1939

631 It's easy to make a man confess the lies he tells to himself; it's far harder to make him confess the truth.
Geoffrey Household (1900–88) British writer.
Rogue Male

632 Man, unlike any other thing organic or inorganic in the universe, grows beyond his work, walks up the stairs of his concepts, emerges ahead of his accomplishments.
John Steinbeck (1902–68) US novelist.
The Grapes of Wrath, Ch. 14

1940

633 I hate that aesthetic game of the eye and the mind, played by these connoisseurs, these mandarins who 'appreciate' beauty. What *is* beauty, anyway? There's no such thing. I never 'appreciate', any more than I 'like'. I love or I hate.
Pablo Picasso (1881–1973) Spanish painter.
Life with Picasso (Françoise Gilot and Carlton Lake), Ch. 2

634 The moment a man talks to his fellows he begins to lie.
Hilaire Belloc (1870–1953) French-born British poet.
The Silence of the Sea

1941

635 I don't trust him. We're friends.
Bertolt Brecht (1898–1956) German dramatist.
Mother Courage, III

636 The finest plans have always been spoiled by the littleness of those that should carry them out. Even emperors can't do it all by themselves.
Bertolt Brecht
Mother Courage, VI

637 Sentimentality is only sentiment that rubs you up the wrong way.
W. Somerset Maugham (1874–1965) British novelist.
A Writer's Notebook

1942

638 One of the mysteries of human conduct is why adult men and women all over England are ready to sign documents which they do not read, at the behest of canvassers whom they do not know, binding them to pay for articles which they do not want, with money which they have not got.
Gerald Hurst (1877–1957) British writer and judge.
Closed Chapters

1943

639 Wherever an inferiority complex exists, there is a good reason for it. There is always something inferior there, although not just where we persuade ourselves that it is.
Carl Gustav Jung (1875–1961) Swiss psychoanalyst.
Interview, 1943

640 It is such a secret place, the land of tears.
Antoine de Saint-Exupéry (1900–44) French novelist and aviator.
The Little Prince, Ch. 7

1944

641 Imprisoned in every fat man a thin one is wildly signalling to be let out.
Cyril Connolly (1903–74) British journalist.
The Unquiet Grave

1945

642 There are many who dare not kill themselves for fear of what the neighbours might say.
Cyril Connolly
The Unquiet Grave

643 One can present people with opportunities. One cannot make them equal to them.
Rosamond Lehmann (1901–90) British novelist.
The Ballad and the Source

644 Each generation imagines itself to be more intelligent than the one that went before it, and wiser than the one that comes after it.
George Orwell (Eric Blair; 1903–50) British novelist.
Book Review

645 Serious sport has nothing to do with fair play. It is bound up with hatred, jealousy, boastfulness, disregard of all rules and sadistic pleasure in witnessing violence; in other words it is war minus the shooting.
George Orwell
The Sporting Spirit

Humour

1919

646 Impropriety is the soul of wit.
W. Somerset Maugham (1874–1965) British novelist.
The Moon and Sixpence, Ch. 4

1926

647 Comedy, we may say, is society protecting itself – with a smile.
J. B. Priestley (1894–1984) British novelist.
George Meredith

1930

648* I must get out of these wet clothes and into a dry Martini.
Alexander Woollcott (1887–1943) US journalist.
Reader's Digest

1931

649 A comedian can only last till he either takes himself serious or his audience takes him serious.
Will Rogers (1879–1935) US actor and humorist.
Newspaper article, 1931

650* I've been accused of every death except the casualty list of the World War.
Al Capone (1899–1947) Italian-born US gangster.
The Bootleggers (Kenneth Allsop), Ch. 11

1938

651 Early to rise and early to bed makes a male healthy and wealthy and dead.
James Thurber (1894–1961) US humorist.
Fables for Our Time, 'The Shrike and the Chipmunks'

1940

652* There, but for the Grace of God, goes God.
Herman J. Mankiewicz (1897–1953) US journalist and screenwriter.
Said of Orson Welles in the making of *Citizen Kane*. Also attributed to others
The Citizen Kane Book

Life

1915

653 How reconcile this world of fact with the bright world of my imagining? My darkness has been filled with the light of intelligence, and be-

hold, the outer day-light world was stumbling and groping in social blindness.
Helen Keller (1880–1968) US writer and lecturer.
The Cry for Justice (ed. Upton Sinclair)

1916

654 A man travels the world over in search of what he needs and returns home to find it.
George Moore (1852–1933) Irish writer and art critic.
The Brook Kerith, Ch. 11

1917

655 The degree of a nation's civilization is marked by its disregard for the necessities of existence.
W. Somerset Maugham (1874–1965) British novelist.
Our Betters, I

656 The right people are rude. They can afford to be.
W. Somerset Maugham
Our Betters, II

657 There are three ingredients in the good life: learning, earning and yearning.
Christopher Darlington Morley (1890–1957) US writer.
Parnassus on Wheels, Ch. 10

1919

658 The whole of nature is a conjugation of the verb to eat, in the active and the passive.
Dean Inge (1860–1954) British churchman.
Outspoken Essays

659 So many gods, so many creeds,
So many paths that wind and wind,
While just the art of being kind
Is all the sad world needs.
Ella Wheeler Wilcox (1850–1919) US poet.
The World's Need

660 Laugh, and the world laughs with you;
Weep, and you weep alone,
For the sad old earth must borrow its mirth,
But has trouble enough of its own.
Ella Wheeler Wilcox
Solitude

661 The outcome of any serious research can only be to make two questions grow where only one grew before.
Thorstein Bunde Veblen (1857–1929) US social scientist.
The Place of Science in Modern Civilization

1920

662 When a dog bites a man that is not news, but when a man bites a dog that is news.
John B. Bogart (1845–1920) US journalist.
Sometimes attributed to Charles Dana and Amos Cummings
Attrib.

663* People do not live nowadays – they get about ten percent out of life.
Isadora Duncan (1878–1927) US dancer.
This Quarter Autumn, 'Memoirs'

664 Ideal mankind would abolish death, multiply itself million upon million, rear up city upon city, save every parasite alive, until the accumulation of mere existence is swollen to a horror.
D. H. Lawrence (1885–1930) British novelist.
St Mawr

665 Away with all ideals. Let each individual act spontaneously from the for ever incalculable prompting of the creative wellhead within him. There is no universal law.
D. H. Lawrence
Phoenix, Preface to 'All Things are Possible' by Leo Shostov

666 The young man who has not wept is a savage, and the old man who will not laugh is a fool.
George Santayana (1863–1952) US philosopher.
Dialogues in Limbo, Ch. 3

667 Old men are dangerous; it doesn't matter to them what is going to happen to the world.
George Bernard Shaw (1856–1950) Irish dramatist and critic.
Heartbreak House

668 It isn't mere convention. Everyone can see that the people who hunt are the right people and the people who don't are the wrong ones.
George Bernard Shaw
Heartbreak House

669 What is this life if, full of care,
We have no time to stand and stare?
W. H. Davies (1871–1940) British poet.
Leisure

670 But I, being poor, have only my dreams;
I have spread my dreams under your feet;
Tread softly because you tread on my dreams.
W. B. Yeats (1865–1939) Irish poet.
He Wishes for the Cloths of Heaven

671 'I know myself,' he cried, 'but that is all.'
F. Scott Fitzgerald (1896–1940) US novelist.
This Side of Paradise, Bk. II, Ch. 5

672* Be nice to people on your way up because you'll meet 'em on your way down.
Wilson Mizner (1876–1933) US writer and wit.
Also attributed to Jimmy Durante
A Dictionary of Catch Phrases (Eric Partridge)

673 You can measure the social caste of a person by the distance between the husband's and wife's apartments.
Alfonso XIII (1886–1941) Spanish monarch.
Attrib.

1921

674 Oh to be seventy again.
Georges Clemenceau (1841–1929) French
statesman.
Remark on his eightieth birthday, noticing a
pretty girl in the Champs Elysées
Ego 3 (James Agate)

675 You can do anything in this world if you are
prepared to take the consequences.
W. Somerset Maugham (1874–1965) British
novelist.
The Circle

676 As soon as he ceased to be mad he became
merely stupid. There are maladies we must not
seek to cure because they alone protect us
from others that are more serious.
Marcel Proust (1871–1922) French novelist.
*À la recherche du temps perdu: Le Côté de
Guermantes*

677 The world is everything that is the case.
Ludwig Wittgenstein (1889–1951) Austrian
philosopher.
Tractatus Logico-Philosophicus, Ch. 1

1922

678 They say my verse is sad: no wonder;
Its narrow measure spans
Tears of eternity, and sorrow,
Not mine, but man's.
A. E. Housman (1859–1936) British scholar
and poet.
Last Poems, 'Fancy's Knell'

679 Most of one's life . . . is one prolonged effort to
prevent oneself thinking.
Aldous Huxley (1894–1964) British novelist.
Mortal Coils, 'Green Tunnels'

680 The now, the here, through which all future
plunges to the past.
James Joyce (1882–1941) Irish novelist.
Ulysses

681 There is no cure for birth and death save to enjoy the interval.
George Santayana (1863–1952) US
philosopher.
Soliloquies in England, 'War Shrines'

682 Life is a disease, and the only difference between one man and another is the stage of the
disease at which he lives.
George Bernard Shaw (1856–1950) Irish
dramatist and critic.
Back to Methuselah

683 Each has his past shut in him like the leaves of
a book known to him by heart and his friends
can only read the title.
Virginia Woolf (1882–1941) British novelist.
Jacob's Room

1923

684 The place where optimism most flourishes is
the lunatic asylum.
Havelock Ellis (1859–1939) British
sexologist.
The Dance of Life

685 The world continues to offer glittering prizes to
those who have stout hearts and sharp
swords.
F. E. Smith (1872–1930) British lawyer and
politician.
Speech, Glasgow University, 7 Nov 1923

1924

686 What price Glory?
Maxwell Anderson (1888–1959) US
playwright.
Play title

687 It isn't important to come out on top; what matters is to come out alive.
Bertolt Brecht (1898–1956) German
dramatist.
Jungle of Cities

1925

688 We are the hollow men
We are the stuffed men
Leaning together
Headpiece filled with straw.
T. S. Eliot (1888–1965) US-born British poet.
The Hollow Men

689 This is the way the world ends
Not with a bang but a whimper.
T. S. Eliot
The Hollow Men

690 One of those men who reach such an acute
limited excellence at twenty-one that everything
afterward savours of anti-climax.
F. Scott Fitzgerald (1896–1940) US novelist.
The Great Gatsby, Ch. 1

691 Between
Our birth and death we may touch
understanding
As a moth brushes a window with its wing.
Christopher Fry (1907–   ) British dramatist.
The Boy with a Cart

692 I'm afraid of losing my obscurity. Genuineness
only thrives in the dark. Like celery.
Aldous Huxley (1894–1964) British novelist.
Those Barren Leaves, Pt. I, Ch. 1

693 The first rule in opera is the first rule in life: see
to everything yourself.
Nellie Melba (Helen Porter Mitchell; 1861–
1931) Australian soprano.
Melodies and Memories

1926

694 I have learned to live each day as it comes, and
not to borrow trouble by dreading tomorrow. It

is the dark menace of the future that makes cowards of us.
Dorothy Dix (Elizabeth Meriwether Gilmer; 1861–1951) US journalist and writer.
Dorothy Dix, Her Book, Introduction

695* Birth, and copulation, and death.
That's all the facts when you come to brass tacks.
T. S. Eliot (1888–1965) US-born British poet and dramatist.
Sweeney Agonistes, 'Fragment of an Agon'

696 An optimist is a guy that never had much experience.
Don Marquis (1878–1937) US journalist.
Archy and Mehitabel

697 We begin to live when we have conceived life as a tragedy.
W. B. Yeats (1865–1939) Irish poet.
Autobiography

1927

698 My own suspicion is that the universe is not only queerer than we suppose, but queerer than we *can* suppose.
J. B. S. Haldane (1892–1964) British geneticist.
Possible Worlds, 'On Being the Right Size'

699 Life is for each man a solitary cell whose walls are mirrors.
Eugene O'Neill (1888–1953) US dramatist.
Lazarus Laughed

1928

700 There is no substitute for talent. Industry and all the virtues are of no avail.
Aldous Huxley (1894–1964) British novelist.
Point Counter Point

701 Life is perhaps best regarded as a bad dream between two awakenings.
Eugene O'Neill (1888–1953) US dramatist.
Marco Millions

1930

702* Underneath the arches
We dream our dreams away.
Bud Flanagan (Robert Winthrop; 1896–1968) British comedian.
Underneath the Arches

703 The meek do not inherit the earth unless they are prepared to fight for their meekness.
H. J. Laski (1893–1950) British political theorist.
Attrib.

704 No absolute is going to make the lion lie down with the lamb unless the lamb is inside.
D. H. Lawrence (1885–1930) British novelist.
The Later D. H. Lawrence

705 Most of the change we think we see in life
Is due to truths being in and out of favour.
Robert Frost (1875–1963) US poet.
The Black Cottage

706 A single death is a tragedy; a million is a statistic.
Joseph Stalin (J. Dzhugashvili; 1879–1953) Soviet statesman.
Attrib.

707 It is good to know what a man is, and also what the world takes him for. But you do not understand him until you have learnt how he understands himself.
F. H. Bradley (1846–1924) British philosopher.
Aphorisms

708 I never think of the future. It comes soon enough.
Albert Einstein (1879–1955) German-born US physicist.
Interview, 1930

709 The universe begins to look more like a great thought than like a great machine.
James Jeans (1877–1946) British scientist.
The Mysterious Universe

710 From the earliest times the old have rubbed it into the young that they are wiser than they, and before the young had discovered what nonsense this was they were old too, and it profited them to carry on the imposture.
W. Somerset Maugham (1874–1965) British novelist.
Cakes and Ale, Ch. 9

1933

711 Civilization is a method of living, an attitude of equal respect for all men.
Jane Addams (1860–1935) US social worker.
Speech, Honolulu, 1933

712 The modern world . . . has no notion except that of simplifying something by destroying nearly everything.
G. K. Chesterton (1874–1936) British writer.
All I Survey

713 The universe is not hostile, nor yet is it friendly. It is simply indifferent.
John Haynes Holmes (1879–1964) US clergyman.
A Sensible Man's View of Religion

714 The least of things with a meaning is worth more in life than the greatest of things without it.
Carl Gustav Jung (1875–1961) Swiss psychoanalyst.
Modern Man in Search of a Soul

715 Youth is a malady of which one becomes cured a little every day.
Benito Mussolini (1883–1945) Italian dictator.
Said on his 50th birthday

1934

716 Fortunately, in her kindness and patience, Nature has never put the fatal question as to the meaning of their lives into the mouths of

most people. And where no one asks, no one needs to answer.
Carl Gustav Jung (1875–1961) Swiss psychoanalyst.
The Development of Personality

717 Philosophy is the product of wonder.
A. N. Whitehead (1861–1947) British philosopher.
Nature and Life, Ch. 1

1935

718 We live in stirring times – tea-stirring times.
Christopher Isherwood (1904–86) British novelist.
Mr Norris Changes Trains

719 Society goes on and on and on. It is the same with ideas.
Ramsey MacDonald (1866–1937) British statesman and prime minister.
Speech, 1935

1936

720 Time present and time past
Are both perhaps present in time future
And time future contained in time past.
T. S. Eliot (1888–1965) US-born British poet and dramatist.
Four Quartets

721 Optimism is the content of small men in high places.
F. Scott Fitzgerald (1896–1940) US novelist.
The Crack-Up

722 Worldly wisdom teaches that it is better for the reputation to fail conventionally than to succeed unconventionally.
John Maynard Keynes (1883–1946) British economist.
The General Theory of Employment, Interest and Money, Bk. IV, Ch. 12

723 Until you've lost your reputation, you never realize what a burden it was or what freedom really is.
Margaret Mitchell (1909–49) US novelist.
Gone with the Wind

724 Now: heaven knows, anything goes.
Cole Porter (1893–1964) US songwriter.
Anything Goes, title song

1938

725 If there are obstacles, the shortest line between two points may be the crooked one.
Bertolt Brecht (1898–1956) German dramatist.
Galileo

726 Whom the gods wish to destroy they first call promising.
Cyril Connolly (1903–74) British journalist.
Enemies of Promise, Ch. 3

727 I have always disliked myself at any given moment; the total of such moments is my life.
Cyril Connolly
Enemies of Promise, Ch. 18

728 Boys do not grow up gradually. They move forward in spurts like the hands of clocks in railway stations.
Cyril Connolly
Enemies of Promise, Ch. 18

729 The future will one day be the present and will seem as unimportant as the present does now.
W. Somerset Maugham (1874–1965) British novelist.
The Summing Up

730 I know perfectly well that I don't want to do anything; to do something is to create existence – and there's quite enough existence as it is.
Jean-Paul Sartre (1905–80) French writer.

731 When I think of all the books I have read, and of the wise words I have heard spoken, and of the anxiety I have given to parents and grandparents, and of the hopes that I have had, all life weighed in the scales of my own life seems to me preparation for something that never happens.
W. B. Yeats (1865–1939) Irish poet.
Autobiography

1939

732 ANDREA. Unhappy the land that has no heroes.
GALILEO. No, unhappy the land that needs heroes.
Bertolt Brecht (1898–1956) German dramatist.
Galileo, 13

733 Success is relative. It is what we can make of the mess we have made of things.
T. S. Eliot (1888–1965) US-born British poet and dramatist.
The Family Reunion

1940

734* The world is becoming like a lunatic asylum run by lunatics.
David Lloyd George (1863–1945) British Liberal statesman.
The Observer, 'Sayings of Our Times', 31 May 1953

735 Sorrow is tranquillity remembered in emotion.
Dorothy Parker (1893–1967) US writer.
Sentiment

736 One may not regard the world as a sort of metaphysical brothel for emotions.
Arthur Koestler (1905–83) Hungarian-born British writer.
Darkness at Noon, 'The Second Hearing'

737* The future is made of the same stuff as the present.
Simone Weil (1909–43) French philosopher.
On Science, Necessity, and the Love of God

(ed. Richard Rees), 'Some Thoughts on the Love of God'

738* What we must decide is perhaps how we are valuable, rather than how valuable we are.
F. Scott Fitzgerald (1896–1940) US novelist.
The Crack-Up

1942

739 There is but one truly serious philosophical problem, and that is suicide. Judging whether life is, or is not worth living amounts to answering the fundamental question of philosophy.
Albert Camus (1913–60) French existentialist writer.
The Myth of Sisyphus

740 The Future is something which everyone reaches at the rate of sixty minutes an hour, whatever he does, whoever he is.
C. S. Lewis (1898–1963) British academic and writer.
The Screwtape Letters

741 God made everything out of nothing. But the nothingness shows through.
Paul Valéry (1871–1945) French poet and writer.
Mauvaises Pensées et autres

1943

742 One should try everything once, except incest and folk-dancing.
Arnold Bax (1883–1953) British composer.
Farewell to My Youth

743 Scratch a pessimist, and you find often a defender of privilege.
Lord Beveridge (1879–1963) British economist.
The Observer, 'Sayings of the Week', 17 Dec 1943

1944

744 Alone, alone, about the dreadful wood
Of conscious evil runs a lost mankind,
Dreading to find its Father.
W. H. Auden (1907–73) British poet.
For the Time Being, 'Chorus'

745 Life is a maze in which we take the wrong turning before we have learnt to walk.
Cyril Connolly (1903–74) British journalist.
The Unquiet Grave

1945

746 The visible universe was an illusion or, more precisely, a sophism. Mirrors and fatherhood are abominable because they multiply it and extend it.
Jorge Luis Borges (1899–1986) Argentinian writer.
Ficciones, 'Tlön, Uqbar, Orbis Tertius'

Love and Sex

1919

747 ... I don't want to live – I want to love first, and live incidentally ...
Zelda Fitzgerald (1900–48) US writer.
Letter to F. Scott Fitzgerald, 1919

1920

748* You must always be a-waggle with LOVE.
D. H. Lawrence (1885–1930) British novelist.
Bibbles

749 Pornography is the attempt to insult sex, to do dirt on it.
D. H. Lawrence
Phoenix, 'Pornography and Obscenity'

1926

750 Love is also like a coconut which is good while it is fresh, but you have to spit it out when the juice is gone, what's left tastes bitter.
Bertolt Brecht (1898–1956) German dramatist.
Baal

751 We have long passed the Victorian Era when asterisks were followed after a certain interval by a baby.
W. Somerset Maugham (1874–1965) British novelist.
The Constant Wife

1927

752 I'm not sure if a mental relation with a woman doesn't make it impossible to love her. To know the *mind* of a woman is to end in hating her. Love means the pre-cognitive flow ... it is the honest state before the apple.
D. H. Lawrence (1885–1930) British novelist.
Letter to Dr Trigant Burrow, 3 Aug 1927

1928

753 You mustn't think I advocate perpetual sex. Far from it. Nothing nauseates me more than promiscuous sex in and out of season.
D. H. Lawrence
Referring to *Lady Chatterley's Lover*
Letter to Lady Ottoline Morrell, 22 Dec 1928

1929

754 To fear love is to fear life, and those who fear life are already three parts dead.
Bertrand Russell (1872–1970) British philosopher.
Marriage and Morals

755 Of all forms of caution, caution in love is perhaps the most fatal to true happiness.
Bertrand Russell
Marriage and Morals

1934

756 If all the young ladies who attended the Yale promenade dance were laid end to end, no one would be the least surprised.
Dorothy Parker (1893–1967) US writer.
While Rome Burns (Alexander Woollcott)

1936

757 People will insist . . . on treating the *mons Veneris* as though it were Mount Everest.
Aldous Huxley (1894–1964) British novelist.
Eyeless in Gaza, Ch. 30

758 By the time you say you're his,
Shivering and sighing
And he vows his passion is
Infinite, undying –
Lady, make a note of this
One of you is lying.
Dorothy Parker (1893–1967) US writer.
Not So Deep as a Well

759* Love and marriage, love and marriage,
Go together like a horse and carriage.
Sammy Cahn (Samuel Cohen; 1913–   ) US songwriter.
Our Town, 'Love and Marriage'

1940

760 But did thee feel the earth move?
Ernest Hemingway (1899–1961) US novelist.
For Whom the Bell Tolls, Ch. 13

1942

761 You must remember this;
A kiss is just a kiss,
A sigh is just a sigh –
The fundamental things apply
As time goes by.
Herman Hupfeld (20th century) US songwriter.
From the film *Casablanca*
As Time Goes By

1943

762 I know nothing about platonic love except that it is not to be found in the works of Plato.
Edgar Jepson (1863–1938) British novelist.
EGO 5 (James Agate)

Marriage and the Family

1914

763* My father was frightened of his mother. I was frightened of my father, and I'm damned well going to make sure that my children are frightened of me.
George V (1865–1936) King of the United Kingdom (1910–36).
Attrib.

1915

764 Never trust a husband too far, nor a bachelor too near.
Helen Rowland (1876–1950) US writer.
The Rubaiyat of a Bachelor

1920

765* Being a husband is a whole-time job. That is why so many husbands fail. They cannot give their entire attention to it.
Arnold Bennett (1867–1931) British novelist.
The Title, I

766* To marry a man out of pity is folly; and, if you think you are going to influence the kind of fellow who has 'never had a chance, poor devil,' you are profoundly mistaken. One can only influence the strong characters in life, not the weak; and it is the height of vanity to suppose that you can make an honest man of anyone.
Margot Asquith (1865–1945) The second wife of Herbert Asquith.
The Autobiography of Margot Asquith, Ch. 6

1922

767 Always see a fellow's weak point in his wife.
James Joyce (1882–1941) Irish novelist.
Ulysses

768 In fact there was but one thing wrong with the Babbitt house; it was not a home.
Sinclair Lewis (1885–1951) US novelist.
Babbitt, Ch. 2

1925

769* What a marvellous place to drop one's mother-in-law!
Marshal Foch (1851–1929) French soldier.
Remark on being shown the Grand Canyon
Attrib.

1926

770 Now one of the great reasons why so many husbands and wives make shipwreck of their lives together is because a man is always seeking for happiness, while a woman is on a perpetual still hunt for trouble.
Dorothy Dix (Elizabeth Meriwether Gilmer; 1861–1951) US journalist and writer.
Dorothy Dix, Her Book, Ch. 1

1928

771 There are no illegitimate children – only illegitimate parents.
Léon R. Yankwich US lawyer.
Decision, State District Court, Southern District of California, Jun 1928, quoting columnist O. O. McIntyre

1929

72 Marriage is for women the commonest mode of livelihood, and the total amount of undesired sex endured by women is probably greater in marriage than in prostitution.
Bertrand Russell (1872–1970) British philosopher.
Marriage and Morals

1930

73* All the unhappy marriages come from the husbands having brains. What good are brains to a man? They only unsettle him.
P. G. Wodehouse (1881–1975) British humorous novelist.
The Adventures of Sally

74 Who has not watched a mother stroke her child's cheek or kiss her child *in a certain way* and felt a nervous shudder at the possessive outrage done to a free solitary human soul?
John Cowper Powys (1872–1963) British novelist.
The Meaning of Culture

1931

75 Married women are kept women, and they are beginning to find it out.
Logan Pearsall Smith (1865–1946) US writer.
Afterthoughts, 'Other people'

1935

76* Unlike the male codfish which, suddenly finding itself the parent of three million five hundred thousand little codfish, cheerfully resolves to love them all, the British aristocracy is apt to look with a somewhat jaundiced eye on its younger sons.
P. G. Wodehouse (1881–1975) British humorous novelist.
Wodehouse at Work to the End (Richard Usborne), Ch. 5

1938

77 That dear octopus from whose tentacles we never quite escape, nor in our innermost hearts never quite wish to.
Dodie Smith (1896–1990) British dramatist and novelist.
Dear Octopus

1939

78 A loving wife will do anything for her husband except stop criticising and trying to improve him.
J. B. Priestley (1894–1984) British novelist.
Rain on Godshill

1940

779 The concept of two people living together for 25 years without having a cross word suggests a lack of spirit only to be admired in sheep.
A. P. Herbert (1890–1971) British writer and politician.
News Chronicle, 1940

1943

780 There is no finer investment for any community than putting milk into babies.
Winston Churchill (1874–1965) British statesman.
Radio Broadcast, 21 Mar 1943

Men and Women

1918

781 Mother is far too clever to understand anything she does not like.
Arnold Bennett (1867–1931) British novelist.
The Title

1919

782 Because women can do nothing except love, they've given it a ridiculous importance.
W. Somerset Maugham (1874–1965) British novelist.
The Moon and Sixpence, Ch. 41

783 Thousands of American women know far more about the subconscious than they do about sewing.
H. L. Mencken (1880–1956) US journalist.
Prejudices

1920

784* The 'homo' is the legitimate child of the 'suffragette'.
Wyndham Lewis (1882–1957) British novelist.
The Art of Being Ruled, Pt. VIII, Ch. 4

785 The great question . . . which I have not been able to answer, despite my thirty years of research into the feminine soul, is 'What does a woman want'?
Sigmund Freud (1856–1939) Austrian psychoanalyst.
Psychiatry in American Life (Charles Rolo)

786 Women have served all these centuries as looking-glasses possessing the magic and delicious power of reflecting the figure of man at twice its natural size.
Virginia Woolf (1882–1941) British novelist.
A Room of One's Own

1921

787 One realizes with horror, that the race of men is almost extinct in Europe. Only Christ-like heroes and woman-worshipping Don Juans, and rabid equality-mongrels.
D. H. Lawrence (1885–1930) British novelist.
Sea and Sardinia, Ch. 3

788 A woman will always sacrifice herself if you give her the opportunity. It is her favourite form of self-indulgence.
W. Somerset Maugham (1874–1965) British novelist.
The Circle, III

1922

789 To the old saying that man built the house but woman made of it a 'home' might be added the modern supplement that woman accepted cooking as a chore but man has made of it a recreation.
Emily Post (1873–1960) US writer.
Etiquette, Ch. 34

1925

790* How beastly the bourgeois is especially the male of the species.
D. H. Lawrence (1885–1930) British novelist.
How beastly the bourgeois is

1926

791 It is only the women whose eyes have been washed clear with tears who get the broad vision that makes them little sisters to all the world.
Dorothy Dix (Elizabeth Meriwether Gilmer; 1861–1951) US journalist and writer.
Dorothy Dix, Her Book, Introduction

1928

792 Any girl who was a lady would not even think of having such a good time that she did not remember to hang on to her jewelry.
Anita Loos (1891–1981) US novelist.
Gentlemen Prefer Blondes, Ch. 4

793 Instead of this absurd division into sexes they ought to class people as static and dynamic.
Evelyn Waugh (1903–66) British novelist.
Decline and Fall, Pt. III, Ch. 7

1929

794 Why are women . . . so much more interesting to men than men are to women?
Virginia Woolf (1882–1941) British novelist.
A Room of One's Own

795 I would venture to guess that Anon, who wrote so many poems without signing them, was often a woman.
Virginia Woolf
A Room of One's Own

1930

796* There are two kinds of women – goddesses and doormats.
Pablo Picasso (1881–1973) Spanish painter.
Attrib.

797 Certain women should be struck regularly, like gongs.
Noël Coward (1899–1973) British dramatist.
Private Lives

1938

798 Intimacies between women often go backwards, beginning in revelations and ending in small talk without loss of esteem.
Elizabeth Bowen (1899–1973) Irish novelist.
The Death of the Heart

1939

799 I often want to cry. That is the only advantage women have over men – at least they can cry.
Jean Rhys (1894–1979) Dominican-born British novelist.
Good Morning, Midnight, Pt. II

1940

800* Women do not find it difficult nowadays to behave like men; but they often find it extremely difficult to behave like gentlemen.
Compton Mackenzie (1883–1972) British writer.
On Moral Courage

801 Woman's virtue is man's greatest invention.
Cornelia Otis Skinner (1901–79) US stage actress.
Attrib.

1944

802 In the sex-war thoughtlessness is the weapon of the male, vindictiveness of the female.
Cyril Connolly (1903–74) British journalist.
The Unquiet Grave

Morality, Vices, and Virtues

1915

803* Right is more precious than peace.
Woodrow Wilson (1856–1924) US statesman.
Radio Times, 10 Sept 1964

1918

804 As soon as one is unhappy one becomes moral.
Marcel Proust (1871–1922) French novelist.
À la recherche du temps perdu: À l'ombre des jeunes filles en fleurs

1920

805 Justice should not only be done, but should

manifestly and undoubtedly be seen to be done.
Gordon Hewart (1870–1943) British lawyer and politician.
The Chief (R. Jackson)

806* If you do not tell the truth about yourself you cannot tell it about other people.
Virginia Woolf (1882–1941) British novelist.
The Moment and Other Essays

807 An intellectual hatred is the worst.
W. B. Yeats (1865–1939) Irish poet.
A Prayer for My Daughter

1921

808 You can't learn too soon that the most useful thing about a principle is that it can always be sacrificed to expediency.
W. Somerset Maugham (1874–1965) British novelist.
The Circle, III

809 Silence is the most perfect expression of scorn.
George Bernard Shaw (1856–1950) Irish dramatist and critic.
Back to Methuselah

810 The older one grows the more one likes indecency.
Virginia Woolf (1882–1941) British novelist.
Monday or Tuesday

1922

811 Morality which is based on ideas, or on an ideal, is an unmitigated evil.
D. H. Lawrence (1885–1930) British novelist.
Fantasia of the Unconscious, Ch. 7

1923

812 Mr Mercaptan went on to preach a brilliant sermon on that melancholy sexual perversion known as continence.
Aldous Huxley (1894–1964) British novelist and essayist.
Antic Hay, Ch. 18

1925

813 There's nothing so artificial as sinning nowadays. I suppose it once was real.
D. H. Lawrence (1885–1930) British novelist.
St Mawr

814 It is just when opinions universally prevail and we have added lip service to their authority that we become sometimes most keenly conscious that we do not believe a word that we are saying.
Virginia Woolf (1882–1941) British novelist.
The Common Reader

1928

815 Puritanism – The haunting fear that someone, somewhere, may be happy.
H. L. Mencken (1880–1956) US journalist.
A Book of Burlesques

816 The wickedness of the world is so great you have to run your legs off to avoid having them stolen from under you.
Bertolt Brecht (1898–1956) German dramatist.
The Threepenny Opera, I:3

817 Only reason can convince us of those three fundamental truths without a recognition of which there can be no effective liberty: that what we believe is not necessarily true; that what we like is not necessarily good; and that all questions are open.
Clive Bell (1881–1964) British art critic.
Civilization, Ch. 5

818 We have, in fact, two kinds of morality side by side; one which we preach but do not practise, and another which we practise but seldom preach.
Bertrand Russell (1872–1970) British philosopher.
Sceptical Essays

1930

819 The propriety of some persons seems to consist in having improper thoughts about their neighbours.
F. H. Bradley (1846–1924) British philosopher.
Aphorisms

820 Tact consists in knowing how far we may go too far.
Jean Cocteau (1889–1963) French poet and artist.
In *Treasury of Humorous Quotations*

821 Hypocrisy is the most difficult and nerve-racking vice that any man can pursue; it needs an unceasing vigilance and a rare detachment of spirit. It cannot, like adultery or gluttony, be practised at spare moments; it is a whole-time job.
W. Somerset Maugham (1874–1965) British novelist.
Cakes and Ale, Ch. 1

822 Suspicion of one's own motives is especially necessary for the philanthropist.
Bertrand Russell (1872–1970) British philosopher.
The Conquest of Happiness

823* There are no whole truths; all truths are half-truths. It is trying to treat them as whole truths that plays the devil.
A. N. Whitehead (1861–1947) British philosopher.
Dialogues, 16

1932

824 Never forget that two blacks do not make a white.
George Bernard Shaw (1856–1950) Irish dramatist and critic.
The Adventures of the Black Girl in her Search for God

825 What is moral is what you feel good after, and
what is immoral is what you feel bad after.
Ernest Hemingway (1899–1961) US
novelist.
Death in the Afternoon

1935

826 Jealousy is no more than feeling alone among
smiling enemies.
Elizabeth Bowen (1899–1973) Irish novelist.
The House in Paris

1938

827 Perfection has one grave defect; it is apt to be
dull.
W. Somerset Maugham (1874–1965) British
novelist.
The Summing Up

1939

828 Whenever there are tremendous virtues it's a
sure sign something's wrong.
Bertolt Brecht (1898–1956) German
dramatist.
Mother Courage

1941

829 The quality of moral behaviour varies in inverse
ratio to the number of human beings involved.
Aldous Huxley (1894–1964) British novelist
and essayist.
Grey Eminence, Ch. 10

1942

830 The truth that makes men free is for the most
part the truth which men prefer not to hear.
Herbert Sebastian Agar (1897–1980) US
writer.
A Time for Greatness

831 The only truths which are universal are those
gross enough to be thought so.
Paul Valéry (1871–1945) French poet and
writer.
Mauvaises Pensées et autres

832 Real nobility is based on scorn, courage, and
profound indifference.
Albert Camus (1913–60) French existentialist
writer.
Notebooks

Other People

1919

833 Sometimes people call me an idealist. Well,
that is the way I know I am an American.
America is the only idealistic nation in the
world.
Woodrow Wilson (1856–1924) US
statesman.
Speech, Sioux Falls, 8 Sept 1919

1920

834* Frenchmen drink wine just like we used to drink
water before Prohibition.
Ring Lardner Jnr (1885–1933) American
humorist.
Wit's End (R. E. Drennan)

835 The English people on the whole are surely the
nicest people in the world, and everyone
makes everything so easy for everybody else,
that there is almost nothing to resist at all.
D. H. Lawrence (1885–1930) British novelist.
Dull London

1922

836 In other countries, art and literature are left to a
lot of shabby bums living in attics and feeding
on booze and spaghetti, but in America the
successful writer or picture-painter is indistinguishable from any other decent business
man.
Sinclair Lewis (1885–1951) US novelist.
Babbitt, Ch. 14

837 Trust the man who hesitates in his speech and
is quick and steady in action, but beware of
long arguments and long beards.
George Santayana (1863–1952) US
philosopher.
Soliloquies in England, 'The British Character'

838 England is the paradise of individuality, eccen-
tricity, heresy, anomalies, hobbies, and
humours.
George Santayana
Soliloquies in England, 'The British Character'

1923

839 The very best that is in the Jewish blood: a
faculty for pure disinterestedness, and warm,
physically warm love, that seems to make the
corpuscles of the blood glow.
D. H. Lawrence (1885–1930) British novelist.
Kangaroo, Ch. 6

1928

840 The American system of rugged individualism.
Herbert Clark Hoover (1874–1964) US
statesman.
Speech, New York, 22 Oct 1928

841 The sound of the English county families baying
for broken glass.
Evelyn Waugh (1903–66) British novelist.
Decline and Fall, Prelude

842 For generations the British bourgeoisie have
spoken of themselves as gentlemen, and by
that they have meant, among other things, a
self-respecting scorn of irregular perquisites. It
is the quality that distinguishes the gentleman from both the artist and the aristocrat.
Evelyn Waugh
Decline and Fall, Pt. I, Ch. 6

43　We can trace almost all the disasters of English history to the influence of Wales.
Evelyn Waugh
Decline and Fall, Pt. I, Ch. 8

44　'The Welsh,' said the Doctor, 'are the only nation in the world that has produced no graphic or plastic art, no architecture, no drama. They just sing,' he said with disgust, 'sing and blow down wind instruments of plated silver.'
Evelyn Waugh
Decline and Fall, Pt. I, Ch. 8

1929

45　America is the only nation in history which miraculously has gone directly from barbarism to degeneration without the usual interval of civilization.
Georges Clemenceau (1841–1929) French statesman.
Attrib.

46　Long Island represents the American's idea of what God would have done with Nature if he'd had the money.
Peter Fleming (1907–71) British writer.
Letter to his brother Rupert, 29 Sept 1929

47　America . . . where law and customs alike are based on the dreams of spinsters.
Bertrand Russell (1872–1970) British philosopher.
Marriage and Morals

1930

48*　The English may not like music – but they absolutely love the noise it makes.
Thomas Beecham (1879–1961) British conductor.
The Wit of Music (L. Ayre)

49　That typically English characteristic for which there is no English name – *esprit de corps*.
Frank Ezra Adcock (1886–1968) British classicist.
Presidential address

50　The United States is like a gigantic boiler. Once the fire is lighted under it there is no limit to the power it can generate.
Lord Grey (1862–1933) British statesman.
Their Finest Hour (Winston S. Churchill), Ch. 32

51　Like so many substantial Americans, he had married young and kept on marrying, springing from blonde to blonde like the chamois of the Alps leaping from crag to crag.
P. G. Wodehouse (1881–1975) British humorous novelist.
Wodehouse at Work to the End (Richard Usborne), Ch. 2

52　How appallingly thorough these Germans always managed to be, how emphatic! In sex no less than in war – in scholarship, in science.

Diving deeper than anyone else and coming up muddier.
Aldous Huxley (1894–1964) British novelist.

853　I think it would be a good idea.
Mahatma Gandhi (Mohandas Karamchand Gandhi; 1869–1948) Indian national leader.
On being asked for his view on Western civilization
Attrib.

1931

854　Now Spring, sweet laxative of Georgian strains, Quickens the ink in literary veins, The Stately Homes of England ope their doors To piping Nancy-boys and Crashing Bores.
Roy Campbell (1901–57) South African poet.
The Georgiad

855　There is nothing the matter with Americans except their ideals. The real American is all right; it is the ideal American who is all wrong.
G. K. Chesterton (1874–1936) British writer.
New York Times, 1 Feb 1931

856　There won't be any revolution in America . . . The people are too clean. They spend all their time changing their shirts and washing themselves. You can't feel fierce and revolutionary in a bathroom.
Eric Linklater (1889–1974) Scottish novelist.
Juan in America, Pt. V, Ch. 3

857　That strange blend of the commercial traveller, the missionary, and the barbarian conqueror, which was the American abroad.
Olaf Stapledon (1886–1950) British philosopher and science-fiction writer.
Last and First Men, Ch. 3

1935

858　The Englishman never enjoys himself except for a noble purpose.
A. P. Herbert (1890–1971) British writer and politician.
Uncommon Law

1936

859　An Englishman has to have a Party, just as he has to have trousers.
Bertrand Russell (1872–1970) British philosopher.
Letter to Maurice Amos MP, 16 June 1936

860　In the United States there is more space where nobody is than where anybody is. That is what makes America what it is.
Gertrude Stein (1874–1946) US writer.
The Geographical History of America

1937

861　There can hardly be a town in the South of Eng-

land where you could throw a brick without hitting the niece of a bishop.
George Orwell (Eric Blair; 1903–50) British novelist.
The Road to Wigan Pier, Ch. 7

1938

862   . . . the English think of an opinion as something which a decent person, if he has the misfortune to have one, does all he can to hide.
Margaret Halsey (1910–   ) US writer.
With Malice Toward Some

863   Living in England, provincial England, must be like being married to a stupid but exquisitely beautiful wife.
Margaret Halsey
With Malice Toward Some

864   . . . it takes a great deal to produce ennui in an Englishman and if you do, he only takes it as convincing proof that you are well-bred.
Margaret Halsey
With Malice Toward Some

865   Never judge a country by its politics. After all, we English are quite honest by nature, aren't we?
Alfred Hitchcock (1889–1980) British film director.
The Lady Vanishes

1940

866* There's something Vichy about the French.
Ivor Novello (David Ivor Davies; 1893–1951) British actor, composer, and dramatist.
Ambrosia and Small Beer (Edward Marsh), Ch. 4

867   Long experience has taught me that in England nobody goes to the theatre unless he or she has bronchitis.
James Agate (1877–1947) British theatre critic.
Ego, 6

1941

868   A family with the wrong members in control – that, perhaps, is as near as one can come to describing England in a phrase.
George Orwell (Eric Blair; 1903–50) British novelist.
The Lion and the Unicorn, 'The Ruling Class'

1943

869   There exists in the world today a gigantic reservoir of good will toward us, the American people.
Wendell Lewis Willkie (1892–1944) US lawyer and businessman.
One World, Ch. 10

1945

870   Everything about the behaviour of American society reveals that it is half judaised and half negrified. How can one expect a state like that to hold together?
Adolf Hitler (1889–1945) German dictator.
Attrib.

Religion

1914

871   Even God has been defended with nonsense.
Walter Lippmann (1889–1974) US editor and author.
A Preface to Politics

872   Heaven, as conventionally conceived, is a place so inane, so dull, so useless, so miserable, that nobody has ever ventured to describe a whole day in heaven, though plenty of people have described a day at the seaside.
George Bernard Shaw (1856–1950) Irish dramatist and critic.
Misalliance, Preface

873   God heard the embattled nations shout
Gott strafe England and God save the King.
Good God, said God,
I've got my work cut out.
John Collings Squire (1884–1958) British journalist.
1914

1920

874* It is a mistake to assume that God is interested only, or even chiefly, in religion.
William Temple (1881–1944) British archbishop.
Attrib.

875   Fools! For I also had my hour;
One far fierce hour and sweet;
There was a shout about my ears,
And palms before my feet.
G. K. Chesterton (1874–1936) British writer.
The Donkey

876   Many people believe that they are attracted by God, or by Nature, when they are only repelled by man.
Dean Inge (1860–1954) British churchman.
More Lay Thoughts of a Dean

877   To become a popular religion, it is only necessary for a superstition to enslave a philosophy.
Dean Inge
Outspoken Essays

1921

878   The whole religious complexion of the modern world is due to the absence from Jerusalem of a lunatic asylum.
Havelock Ellis (1859–1939) British sexologist.
Impressions and Comments

879   It has been said that the highest praise of God consists in the denial of Him by the atheist,

who finds creation so perfect that he can dispense with a creator.
Marcel Proust (1871–1922) French novelist.
À la recherche du temps perdu: Le Côté de Guermantes

1925
---

880 I do not consider it an insult but rather a compliment to be called an agnostic. I do not pretend to know where many ignorant men are sure.
Clarence Seward Darrow (1857–1938) US lawyer.
Remark during the trial (1925) of John Scopes for teaching the theory of evolution in school

---
1926
---

881 There's no reason to bring religion into it. I think we ought to have as great a regard for religion as we can, so as to keep it out of as many things as possible.
Sean O'Casey (1884–1964) Irish dramatist.
The Plough and the Stars, I

882 Religion is love; in no case is it logic.
Beatrice Webb (1858–1943) British economist and writer.
My Apprenticeship, Ch. 2

1928
---

883 There is a species of person called a 'Modern Churchman' who draws the full salary of a beneficed clergyman and need not commit himself to any religious belief.
Evelyn Waugh (1903–66) British novelist.
Decline and Fall, Pt. II, Ch. 4

1930

884* I was fired from there, finally, for a lot of things, among them my insistence that the Immaculate Conception was spontaneous combustion.
Dorothy Parker (1893–1967) US writer.
Writers at Work, First Series (Malcolm Cowley)

885 For when the One Great Scorer comes
To write against your name,
He marks — not that you won or lost —
But how you played the game.
Grantland Rice (1880–1954) US sportswriter.
Alumnus Football

886 There once was a man who said 'God
Must think it exceedingly odd
If he finds that this tree
Continues to be
When there's no one about in the Quad.'
Ronald Knox (1888–1957) British Roman Catholic priest.
Attrib.

887 Dear Sir, Your astonishment's odd:
I am always about in the Quad.
And that's why the tree
Will continue to be,

Since observed by Yours faithfully, God.
Anonymous

1933
---

888 He said he was against it.
Calvin Coolidge (1872–1933) US president.
Reply when asked what a clergyman had said regarding sin in his sermon
Attrib.

889 Religion is an illusion and it derives its strength from the fact that it falls in with our instinctual desires.
Sigmund Freud (1856–1939) Austrian psychoanalyst.
New Introductory Lectures on Psychoanalysis, 'A Philosophy of Life'

890 Among all my patients in the second half of life . . . there has not been one whose problem in the last resort was not that of finding a religious outlook on life.
Carl Gustav Jung (1875–1961) Swiss psychoanalyst.
Modern Man in Search of a Soul

1935
---

891 Imagine the Lord talking French! Aside from a few odd words in Hebrew, I took it completely for granted that God had never spoken anything but the most dignified English.
Clarence Shepard Day (1874–1935) US writer.
Life With Father, 'Father interferes'

1936

892* A God who let us prove his existence would be an idol.
Dietrich Bonhoeffer (1906–45) German theologian.
No Rusty Swords

1938
---

893 Religions, which condemn the pleasures of sense, drive men to seek the pleasures of power. Throughout history power has been the vice of the ascetic.
Bertrand Russell (1872–1970) British philosopher.
New York Herald-Tribune Magazine, 6 May 1938

1939
---

894 I feel no need for any other faith than my faith in human beings.
Pearl Buck (1892–1973) US novelist.
I Believe

895 Christianity is the most materialistic of all great religions.
William Temple (1881–1944) British churchman.
Reading in St John's Gospel, Vol. I, Introduction

1941

896 We have no reliable guarantee that the afterlife will be any less exasperating than this one, have we?
Noël Coward (1899–1973) British dramatist.
Blithe Spirit, I

897 Christianity accepted as given a metaphysical system derived from several already existing and mutually incompatible systems.
Aldous Huxley (1894–1964) British novelist.
Grey Eminence, Ch. 3

1944

898 I believe in the Church, One Holy, Catholic and Apostolic, and I regret that it nowhere exists.
William Temple (1881–1944) British churchman.
Attrib.

899 The Church exists for the sake of those outside it.
William Temple
Attrib.

900 Man has learned to cope with all questions of importance without recourse to God as a working hypothesis.
Dietrich Bonhoeffer (1906–45) German theologian.
Letters and Papers from Prison, 8 June 1944

901 Hell is other people.
Jean-Paul Sartre (1905–80) French philosopher and writer.
Huis clos

Science, Medicine, and Technology

1917

902 The true spirit of delight, the exaltation, the sense of being more than Man, which is the touchstone of the highest excellence is to be found in mathematics as surely as in poetry.
Bertrand Russell (1872–1970) British philosopher.
Mysticism and Logic

903 Mathematics, rightly viewed, possesses not only truth by supreme beauty – a beauty cold and austere like that of sculpture.
Bertrand Russell
Mysticism and Logic

904 Pure mathematics consists entirely of assertions to the effect that, if such and such a proposition is true of *anything*, then such and such another proposition is true of that thing. It is essential not to discuss whether the first proposition is really true, and not to mention what the anything is, of which it is supposed to be true.
Bertrand Russell
Mysticism and Logic

1920

905* We have no right to assume that any physical laws exist, or if they have existed up to now, that they will continue to exist in a similar manner in the future.
Max Planck (1858–1947) German physicist.
The Universe in the Light of Modern Physics

906 We haven't the money, so we've got to think.
Ernest Rutherford (1871–1937) British physicist.
Attrib.

1923

907 The machine threatens all achievement.
Rainer Maria Rilke (1875–1926) Austrian poet.
Die Sonette an Orpheus, II, 10

1924

908 Shelley and Keats were the last English poets who were at all up to date in their chemical knowledge.
J. B. S. Haldane (1892–1964) British geneticist.
Daedalus or Science and the Future

909 Einstein – the greatest Jew since Jesus. I have no doubt that Einstein's name will still be remembered and revered when Lloyd George, Foch and William Hohenzollern share with Charlie Chaplin that ineluctable oblivion which awaits the uncreative mind.
J. B. S. Haldane
'William Hohenzollern' was Emperor Wilhelm II of Germany
Daedalus or Science and the Future

1925

910 Mathematics is thought moving in the sphere of complete abstraction from any particular instance of what it is talking about.
A. N. Whitehead (1861–1947) British philosopher.
Science and the Modern World

911 It requires a very unusual mind to undertake the analysis of the obvious.
A. N. Whitehead
Science and the Modern World

1926

912 After all, science is essentially international, and it is only through lack of the historical sense that national qualities have been attributed to it.
Marie Curie (1867–1934) Polish chemist.
Memorandum, 'Intellectual Co-operation'

913 Mystics always hope that science will some day overtake them.
Booth Tarkington (1869–1946) US novelist.
Looking Forward to the Great Adventure

1927

914 Man is slightly nearer to the atom than the stars. From his central position he can survey the grandest works of Nature with the astronomer, or the minutest works with the physicist.
Arthur Eddington (1882–1944) British astronomer.
Stars and Atoms

1928

915 Electrical force is defined as something which causes motion of electrical charge; an electrical charge is something which exerts electric force.
Arthur Eddington
The Nature of the Physical World

916 If all the arts aspire to the condition of music, all the sciences aspire to the condition of mathematics.
George Santayana (1863–1952) US philosopher.
The Observer, 'Sayings of the Week', 4 Mar 1928

1930

917* God is subtle but he is not malicious.
Albert Einstein (1879–1955) German-born US physicist.
Inscribed over the fireplace in the Mathematical Institute, Princeton; it refers to Einstein's objection to the quantum theory
Albert Einstein (Carl Seelig), Ch. 8

918 God does not play dice.
Albert Einstein
Einstein's objection to the quantum theory, in which physical events can only be known in terms of probabilities. It is sometimes quoted as 'God does not play dice with the Universe'
Albert Einstein, Creator and Rebel (B. Hoffman), Ch. 10

919 As far as the laws of mathematics refer to reality, they are not certain, and as far as they are certain, they do not refer to reality.
Albert Einstein
The Tao of Physics (F. Capra), Ch. 2

920* It did not last: the Devil howling 'Ho! Let Einstein be!' restored the status quo.
John Collings Squire (1884–1958) British journalist.
Answer to Pope's Epitaph for Newton
Epigrams, 'The Dilemma'

921 A science which hesitates to forget its founders is lost.
A. N. Whitehead (1861–1947) British philosopher.
Attrib.

922 The evolution of the human race will not be accomplished in the ten thousand years of tame animals, but in the million years of wild animals, because man is and will always be a wild animal.
Charles Darwin (1887–1962) British life scientist.
The Next Ten Million Years, Ch. 4

923 Life exists in the universe only because the carbon atom possesses certain exceptional properties.
James Jeans (1877–1946) British scientist.
The Mysterious Universe, Ch. 1

924 Science should leave off making pronouncements: the river of knowledge has too often turned back on itself.
James Jeans
The Mysterious Universe, Ch. 5

1932

925 The time of our Ford.
Aldous Huxley (1894–1964) British novelist.
Brave New World, Ch. 3

926 That is how the atom is split. But what does it mean? To us who think in terms of practical use it means — Nothing!
Ritchie Calder (1898–   ) US engineer and sculptor.
The Daily Herald, 27 June 1932

927 When we have found how the nucleus of atoms are built-up we shall have found the greatest secret of all — except life. We shall have found the basis of everything — of the earth we walk on, of the air we breathe, of the sunshine, of our physical body itself, of everything in the world, however great or however small — except life.
Ernest Rutherford (1871–1937) British physicist.
Passing Show 24

928 The term Science should not be given to anything but the aggregate of the recipes that are always successful. All the rest is literature.
Paul Valéry (1871–1945) French poet and writer.
Moralités

1933

929 Her own mother lived the latter years of her life in the horrible suspicion that electricity was dripping invisibly all over the house.
James Thurber (1894–1961) US humorist.
My Life and Hard Times, Ch. 2

930 Numbers constitute the only universal language.
Nathaniel West (1903–40) US novelist and scriptwriter.
Miss Lonelyhearts

1936

931 Is ditchwater dull? Naturalists with microscopes have told me that it teems with quiet fun.
G. K. Chesterton (1874–1936) British writer.
The Spice of Life

1938
---

932 I believe my theory of relativity to be true. But it will only be proved for certain in 1981, when I am dead.
Albert Einstein (1879–1955) German-born US physicist.
Einstein: A Study in Simplicity

1940

933* Modern Physics is an instrument of Jewry for the destruction of Nordic science . . . True physics is the creation of the German spirit.
Rudolphe Tomaschek (20th century) German scientist.
The Rise and Fall of the Third Reich (W. L. Shirer), Ch. 8

1944

934* Medicine is a noble profession but a damn bad business.
Humphrey Rolleston (1862–1944) British physician.
Attrib.

Wealth and Poverty

1915
---

935 Money is like a sixth sense without which you cannot make a complete use of the other five.
W. Somerset Maugham (1874–1965) British novelist.
Of Human Bondage, Ch. 51

1920
---

936 The surest way to ruin a man who doesn't know how to handle money is to give him some.
George Bernard Shaw (1856–1950) Irish dramatist and critic.
Heartbreak House

1921
---

937 As long as men are men, a poor society cannot be too poor to find a right order of life, nor a rich society too rich to have need to seek it.
R. H. Tawney (1880–1962) British economist and historian.
The Acquisitive Society

1923
---

938 "To make money", said Mr. Porteous, "one must be really interested in money."
Aldous Huxley (1894–1964) British novelist.
Antic Hay

1925
---

939 It is only the poor who pay cash, and that not

from virtue, but because they are refused credit.
Anatole France (Jacques Anatole François Thibault; 1844–1924) French writer.
A Cynic's Breviary (J. R. Solly)

1930

940* The rich man has his motor car,
His country and his town estate.
He smokes a fifty-cent cigar
And jeers at Fate.
F. P. Adams (1881–1960) US journalist.
The Rich Man

941 Yet though my lamp burns low and dim,
Though I must slave for livelihood —
Think you that I would change with him?
You bet I would!
F. P. Adams
The Rich Man

942 For one person who dreams of making fifty thousand pounds, a hundred people dream of being left fifty thousand pounds.
A. A. Milne (1882–1956) British writer.
If I May, 'The Future'

1932
---

943 God shows his contempt for wealth by the kind of person he selects to receive it.
Austin O'Malley (1858–1932) US writer.
Attrib.

1934
---

944 People don't resent having nothing nearly as much as too little.
Ivy Compton-Burnett (1892–1969) British novelist.
A Family and a Fortune

1937
---

945 I believe the power to make money is a gift of God.
J. D. Rockefeller (1839–1937) US oil magnate.
Attrib.

1940

946* If you can actually count your money you are not really a rich man.
J. Paul Getty (1892–1976) US oil magnate.
Gossip (A. Barrow)

947 One can never be too thin or too rich.
Duchess of Windsor (Wallis Warfield Simpson; 1896–1986) The wife of the Duke of Windsor (formerly Edward VIII).
Attrib.

Work and Occupations

1919

948 The mystic sees the ineffable, and the psycho-
pathologist the unspeakable.
W. Somerset Maugham (1874–1965) British
novelist.
The Moon and Sixpence, Ch. 1

949* He is the only man who is for ever apologizing
for his occupation.
H. L. Mencken (1880–1956) US journalist.
Referring to the businessman
Prejudices, 'Types of Men'

1920

950* Journalists say a thing that they know isn't
true, in the hope that if they keep on saying it
long enough it will be true.
Arnold Bennett (1867–1931) British novelist.
The Title, II

951 You cannot hope
to bribe or twist,
thank God! the
British journalist.

But, seeing what
the man will do
unbribed, there's
no occasion to.
Humbert Wolfe (1886–1940) British poet.
The Uncelestial City, Bk. I, 'Over the Fire'

952 The army ages men sooner than the law and
philosophy; it exposes them more freely to
germs, which undermine and destroy, and it
shelters them more completely from thought,
which stimulates and preserves.
H. G. Wells (1866–1946) British writer.
Bealby, Pt. VIII, Ch. 1

953 Philosophers are as jealous as women. Each
wants a monopoly of praise.
George Santayana (1863–1952) US
philosopher.
Dialogues In Limbo

1921

954 It is very unfair to expect a politician to live in
private up to the statements he makes in
public.
W. Somerset Maugham (1874–1965) British
novelist.
The Circle

955 A doctor who doesn't say too many foolish
things is a patient half-cured, just as a critic is
a poet who has stopped writing verse and a
policeman a burglar who has retired from
practice.
Marcel Proust (1871–1922) French novelist.
*À la recherche du temps perdu: Le Côté de
Guermantes*

956 My doctor said to me afterwards, "When you
were ill you behaved like a true philosopher.

Every time you came to yourself you made a
joke." I never had a compliment that pleased
me more.
Bertrand Russell (1872–1970) British
philosopher.
Letter to Jean Nichol, 2 Oct 1921

1923

957 You sought the last resort of feeble minds with
classical educations. You became a
schoolmaster.
Aldous Huxley (1894–1964) British novelist
and essayist.
Antic Hay

1926

958 Its primary office is the gathering of news. At
the peril of its soul it must see that the supply is not tainted. Neither in what it gives, nor
in what it does not give, nor in the mode of
presentation, must the unclouded face of
truth suffer wrong. Comment is free but facts
are sacred.
C. P. Scott (1846–1932) British journalist.
Manchester Guardian, 6 May 1926

1927

959 The work of a Prime Minister is the loneliest job
in the world.
Stanley Baldwin (1867–1947) British
statesman.
Speech, 9 Jan 1927

1930

960* A musicologist is a man who can read music
but can't hear it.
Thomas Beecham (1879–1961) British
conductor.
Beecham Remembered (H. Procter-Gregg)

961 Soldiers are citizens of death's grey land,
Drawing no dividend from time's tomorrows.
Siegfried Sassoon (1886–1967) British poet.
Dreamers

962 If Max gets to Heaven he won't last long. He
will be chucked out for trying to pull off a
merger between Heaven and Hell . . . after having secured a controlling interest in key sub-
sidiary companies in both places, of course.
H. G. Wells (1866–1946) British writer.
Referring to Lord Beaverbrook
Beaverbrook (A. J. P. Taylor)

963 By working faithfully eight hours a day you may
eventually get to be a boss and work twelve
hours a day.
Robert Frost (1875–1963) US poet.
Attrib.

1931

964 A reporter is a man who has renounced every-

thing in life but the world, the flesh, and the devil.
David Murray (1888–1962) British journalist.
The Observer, 'Sayings of the Week', 5 July 1931

1935

965 There's no better way of exercising the imagination than the study of law. No poet ever interpreted nature as freely as a lawyer interprets truth.
Jean Giraudoux (1882–1944) French dramatist.
Tiger at the Gates, I

966* There is dignity in work only when it is work freely accepted.
Albert Camus (1913–60) French existentialist writer.
Notebooks, 1935–42

1938

967 Literature is the art of writing something that will be read twice; journalism what will be grasped at once.
Cyril Connolly (1903–74) British journalist.
Enemies of Promise, Ch. 3

968 As repressed sadists are supposed to become policemen or butchers so those with irrational fear of life become publishers.
Cyril Connolly
Enemies of Promise, Ch. 3

969 Life is too short to do anything for oneself that one can pay others to do for one.
W. Somerset Maugham (1874–1965) British novelist.
The Summing Up

970 I don't think the profession of historian fits a man for psychological analysis. In our work we have to deal only with simple feelings to which we give generic names such as Ambition and Interest.
Jean-Paul Sartre (1905–80) French writer.
Nausea

1939

971 So, perhaps, I may escape otherwise than by death the last humiliation of an aged scholar, when his juniors conspire to print a volume of essays and offer it to him as a sign that they now consider him senile.
Robin George Collingwood (1889–1943) British philosopher and archaeologist.
Autobiography

1940

972* What do you want to be a sailor for? There are greater storms in politics than you'll ever find

at sea. Piracy, broadsides, blood on the deck – you'll find them all in politics.
David Lloyd George (1863–1945) British statesman.
Remark to Julian Amery
The Observer, 2 Jan 1966

Sayings of the Time

1914

973 *L'acte gratuit.*
The unmotivated action.
André Gide (1869–1951) French novelist.
Les Caves du Vatican

1920

974* Any colour, so long as it's black.
Henry Ford (1863–1947) US car manufacturer.
Referring to the colour options offered for the Model-T Ford car
Attrib.

1924

975 They're changing guard at Buckingham Palace
Christopher Robin went down with Alice.
Alice is marrying one of the guard.
'A soldier's life is terrible hard,'
Says Alice.
A. A. Milne (1882–1956) British writer.
When We Were Very Young, 'Buckingham Palace'

1926

976 I am a Bear of Very Little Brain, and long words Bother me.
A. A. Milne (1882–1956) British writer.
Winnie-the-Pooh, Ch. 4

1927

977 You ain't heard nothin' yet, folks.
Al Jolson (Asa Yoelson; 1886–1950) US actor and singer.
In the film *The Jazz Singer*, July 1927
The Jazz Singer

1929

978 I'm singin' in the rain, just singin' in the rain;
What a wonderful feeling, I'm happy again.
Arthur Freed (1894–1973) US film producer and songwriter.
From the musical, *Hollywood Revue of 1929*
Singing in the Rain

979 All Quiet on the Western Front.
Erich Maria Remarque (1898–1970) German novelist.
Title of novel

1930

980 Very flat, Norfolk.
Noël Coward (1899–1973) British dramatist.
Private Lives

981* Poor Little Rich Girl.
Noël Coward
Title of song

1932

982 I want to be alone.
Greta Garbo (1905–90) Swedish-born US film star.
Words spoken by Garbo in the film *Grand Hotel*, and associated with her for the rest of her career.

1935

983 However, one cannot put a quart in a pint cup.
Charlotte Perkins Gilman (1860–1935) US writer.
The Living of Charlotte Perkins Gilman

1936

984* I murdered my grandmother this morning.
Franklin D. Roosevelt (1882–1945) US president.
His habitual greeting to any guest at the White House he suspected of paying no attention to what he said
Ear on Washington (D. McClellan)

1937

985 How to Win Friends and Influence People.
Dale Carnegie (1888–1955) US lecturer and writer.
Book title

1938

986 Last night I dreamt I went to Manderley again.
Daphne Du Maurier (1907–89) British novelist.
Rebecca, Ch. 1

987* Music, Maestro, Please.
Herb Magidson (20th century) US songwriter.
Song title

988 You can fool too many of the people too much of the time.
James Thurber (1894–1961) US humorist.
Fables for Our Time, 'The Owl Who Was God'

1941

989 What they could do with round here is a good war.
Bertolt Brecht (1898–1956) German dramatist.
Mother Courage, I

1942

990 Play it, Sam. Play 'As Time Goes By.'
Ingrid Bergman (1915–82) Swedish film star.
Hence the imaginary quotation 'Play it again, Sam' attributed to Bergman's co-star, Humphrey Bogart
Casablanca

1944

991 Don't eat too many almonds; they add weight to the breasts.
Colette (Sidonie-Gabrielle C.; 1873–1954) French novelist.
Gigi

Hindsight

992 He did not care in which direction the car was travelling, so long as he remained in the driver's seat.
Lord Beaverbrook (1879–1964) Canadian-born British newspaper proprietor.
Referring to Lloyd George
New Statesman, 14 June 1963

993 Marxian Socialism must always remain a portent to the historians of Opinion – how a doctrine so illogical and so dull can have exercised so powerful and enduring an influence over the minds of men, and, through them, the events of history.
John Maynard Keynes (1883–1946) British economist.
The End of Laisser-Faire, III

994 Communism continued to haunt Europe as a spectre – a name men gave to their own fears and blunders. But the crusade against Communism was even more imaginary than the spectre of Communism.
A. J. P. Taylor (1906–90) British historian.
The Origins of the Second World War, Ch. 2

995 Lenin was the first to discover that capitalism 'inevitably' caused war; and he discovered this only when the First World War was already being fought. Of course he was right. Since every great state was capitalist in 1914, capitalism obviously 'caused' the First World War; but just as obviously it had 'caused' the previous generation of Peace.
A. J. P. Taylor
The Origins of the Second World War, Ch. 6

996 A racing tipster who only reached Hitler's level of accuracy would not do well for his clients.
A. J. P. Taylor
The Origins of the Second World War, Ch. 7

997 When I look back on all these worries I remember the story of the old man who said on his deathbed that he had had a lot of trouble in his life, most of which had never happened.
Winston Churchill (1874–1965) British statesman.
Their Finest Hour

998 The nation had the lion's heart. I had the luck to give the roar.
Winston Churchill
Said on his 80th birthday

999 Hitler showed surprising loyalty to Mussolini, but it never extended to trusting him.
Alan Bullock (1914–) British academic and historian.
Hitler, A Study in Tyranny, Ch. 11

1000 The people Hitler never understood, and whose actions continued to exasperate him to the end of his life, were the British.
Alan Bullock
Hitler, A Study in Tyranny, Ch. 8

13

The Post-War World

World War II marked the eclipse of Europe as the centre of world politics. The USSR held the land its army had occupied during the war, dividing Germany and establishing puppet regimes in Eastern Europe; and the West European states, exhausted economically by the war, had to be supported by the USA. By 1950 two rival power blocs had formed, dominated by the USA and USSR and characterized by their respective capitalist and communist economic systems.

One feature of their confrontation was completely new: the USA's development of an atomic bomb and its use against Japan in 1945 showed that, for the first time, human conflict had the capacity to wreck the Earth. In 1949 the USSR acquired its own atomic bomb and the threat of nuclear war was the underlying factor in the 'Cold War' that dominated international relations for the next forty years. This threat – elevated into a doctrine of 'mutually assured destruction' – produced a system of diplomacy geared to its avoidance. Because of the danger, the USA and USSR mostly exercised their rivalry indirectly by supporting and influencing smaller states or groups within states, especially in the Third World. In one of the few direct confrontations, the Cuban missile crisis (1962), nuclear war seemed close.

This system lasted until the end of the 1980s, when the communist bloc collapsed. The inadequacies of Soviet-style communism as an economic and social system were becoming ever harder to disguise by the early 1980s. From 1985 Mikhail Gorbachov tried to implement reform and end the Cold War, but the forces and ambitions he released proved impossible to contain. The puppet communist regimes in Eastern Europe collapsed in 1989–90, with Germany being reunited; and, after the failure of a coup by reactionary elements in 1991, not only did Soviet communism collapse but the Soviet Union itself split into its component republics. The end of the Cold War was widely hailed as an opportunity for a peaceful 'New World Order'; but the new problems posed by these radical changes – and the resurrection of old problems such as ethnic hatreds in the Balkans – made such hopes seem premature.

Two other features characterized the Post-War World: a proliferation of new states outside Europe; and rapid technological change. In 1945 the United Nations was founded with 51 members; by 1990 its membership had more than trebled to 158. Most of these new states resulted from the dismantling of the West European nations' colonial empires; they were always underdeveloped, often poor, and – especially in Africa – encumbered with artificial frontiers that did not reflect tribal geography. The continuing problems of these countries, often intensified by rapidly growing populations, gradually assumed a greater importance in world politics.

Technological change after 1945 proceeded at a pace unknown hitherto. Developments in science, materials, manufacturing techniques, transport, communication and information technology, medicine, and agriculture transformed economic and everyday life in the advanced countries. One area that did not fulfil its early promise was nuclear power: unforeseen difficulties and expense as well as concern about its harmful by-products slowed its development. This last is part of a wider phenomenon: a concern about the effect of man's activities on the balance of the Earth's natural systems. This and the decline in demand for human labour in manufacturing constituted some of the problems that faced what was by 1992 increasingly being called 'the Post-Industrial Society'.

Politics, Government, and World Events

1946

1 An iron curtain has descended across the Continent.
Winston Churchill (1874–1965) British statesman.
The phrase 'iron curtain' was originally coined by Joseph Goebbels
Address, Westminster College, Fulton, USA, 5 Mar 1946

2 We are the masters at the moment – and not only for the moment, but for a very long time to come.
Lord Shawcross (1902–87) British politician and lawyer.
Sometimes misquoted as, 'We are the masters now!'
House of Commons, 2 Apr 1946

3 Our hospital organization has grown up with no plan, with no system; it is unevenly distributed over the country . . . I would rather be kept alive in the efficient if cold altruism of a large hospital than expire in a gush of warm sympathy in a small one.
Aneurin Bevan (1897–1960) British politician.
Introducing the National Health Service Bill
Speech, House of Commons, 30 Apr 1946

4 I stuffed their mouths with gold!
Aneurin Bevan
Explaining how he persuaded doctors not to oppose the introduction of the National Health Service
Attrib.

5 We must build a kind of United States of Europe.
Winston Churchill (1874–1965) British statesman.
Speech, Zurich, 19 Sept 1946

6 Our agenda is now exhausted. The secretary general is exhausted. All of you are exhausted. I find it comforting that, beginning with our very first day, we find ourselves in such complete unanimity.
Paul Henri Spaak (1899–1972) Belgian statesman.
Concluding the first General Assembly meeting of the United Nations

7 Since wars begin in the minds of men, it is in the minds of men that the defences of peace must be constructed.
Anonymous
Constitution of UNESCO

8 The atom bomb is a paper tiger which the United States reactionaries use to scare people.
Mao Tse-Tung (1893–1976) Chinese communist leader.
Interview, Aug 1946

9 I am against government by crony.
Harold L. Ickes (1874–1952) US politician.
Comment on his resignation as Secretary of the Interior (1946) after a dispute with President Truman

10 EQUALITY . . . is the thing. It is the only true and central premise from which constructive ideas can radiate freely and be operated without prejudice.
Mervyn Peake (1911–68) British novelist.
Titus Groan, 'The Sun goes down again'

1947

11 Let us not be deceived – we are today in the midst of a cold war.
Bernard Baruch (1870–1965) US financier and presidential adviser.
Speech, South Carolina Legislature, 16 Apr 1947

12 The tragedy of the Police State is that it always regards all opposition as a crime, and there are no degrees.
Lord Vansittart (1881–1957) British politician.
Speech, House of Lords, June 1947

13 No annihilation without representation.
Arnold Toynbee (1889–1975) British historian.
Urging the need for a greater British influence in the UN

14 Wars, conflict, it's all business. One murder makes a villain. Millions a hero. Numbers sanctify.
Charlie Chaplin (Sir Charles Spencer C.; 1889–1977) British film actor.
Monsieur Verdoux

15 There are three groups that no British Prime Minister should provoke: the Vatican, the Treasury and the miners.
Stanley Baldwin (1867–1947) British statesman.
A similar remark is often attributed to Harold Macmillan in 1960
Attrib.

16 I would rather be an opportunist and float than go to the bottom with my principles round my neck.
Stanley Baldwin
Attrib.

1948

17 There is only a certain sized cake to be divided up, and if a lot of people want a larger slice they can only take it from others who would, in terms of real income, have a smaller one.
Stafford Cripps (1889–1952) British politician.
Speech, Trade Union Congress, 7 Sept 1948

18 I like old Joe Stalin. He's a good fellow but he's a prisoner of the Politburo. He would make

certain agreements but they won't let him keep
them.
Harry S. Truman (1884–1972) US
statesman.
News Review, 24 June 1948

19 All human beings are born free and equal in
dignity and rights.
Anonymous
Universal Declaration of Human Rights (1948),
Article 1

20 The House of Lords must be the only institution
in the world which is kept efficient by the persistent absenteeism of most of its members.
Herbert Samuel (1870–1963) British
statesman.
News Review, 5 Feb 1948

21 I will shake my little finger — and there will be
no more Tito. He will fall.
Joseph Stalin (J. Dzhugashvili; 1879–1953)
Soviet statesman.
Said to Khrushchev
Attrib.

22 I have never seen a human being who more
perfectly represented the modern conception of
a robot.
Winston Churchill (1874–1965) British
statesman.
Referring to the Soviet statesman Molotov
The Second World War

23 Wars come because not enough people are
sufficiently afraid.
Hugh Schonfield (1901–   ) British writer and
editor.
The News Review, 26 Feb 1948

1949

24 No attempt at ethical or social seduction can
eradicate from my heart a deep burning hatred
for the Tory Party . . . So far as I am concerned they are lower than vermin.
Aneurin Bevan (1897–1960) British politician.
Speech, Manchester, 4 July 1949

25 If ever he went to school without any boots it
was because he was too big for them.
Ivor Bulmer-Thomas (1905–   ) British writer
and politician.
Referring to Harold Wilson
Remark, Conservative Party Conference, 1949

26 Now we are in a period which I can character-
ize as a period of cold peace.
Trygve Lie (1896–1968) Norwegian lawyer.
The Observer, 'Sayings of the Week', 21 Aug
1949

27 Hansard is history's ear, already listening.
Herbert Samuel (1870–1963) British
statesman.
Speech, Dec 1949

28 Those who have had no share in the good fortunes of the mighty often have a share in their
misfortunes.
Bertolt Brecht (1898–1956) German
dramatist.
The Caucasian Chalk Circle

29 No one can guarantee success in war, but only
deserve it.
Winston Churchill (1874–1965) British
statesman.
Their Finest Hour

30 Big Brother is watching you.
George Orwell (Eric Blair; 1903–50) British
novelist.
Nineteen Eighty-Four

31 War is Peace, Freedom is Slavery, Ignorance is
Strength.
George Orwell
Nineteen Eighty-Four

32 Doublethink means the power of holding two
contradictory beliefs in one's mind simulta-
neously, and accepting both of them.
George Orwell
Nineteen Eighty-Four

33 Who controls the past controls the future. Who
controls the present controls the past.
George Orwell
Nineteen Eighty-Four

1950s

34 He is not only a bore but he bores for England.
Malcolm Muggeridge (1903–90) British
writer and editor.
Referring to Sir Anthony Eden
Newstatesmanship (E. Hyams), 'Boring for
England'

35 He is a man suffering from petrified
adolescence.
Aneurin Bevan (1897–1960) British politician.
Referring to Winston Churchill
Aneurin Bevan (Vincent Brome), Ch. 11

36 A desiccated calculating machine.
Aneurin Bevan
Referring to Hugh Gaitskell
Hugh Gaitskell (W. T. Rodgers)

37 Its relationship to democratic institutions is that
of the death watch beetle — it is not a Party, it
is a conspiracy.
Aneurin Bevan
Referring to the Communist Party
Tribune

38 'War is the continuation of politics'. In this
sense war is politics and war itself is a political
action.
Mao Tse-Tung (1893–1976) Chinese communist leader.
Quotations from Chairman Mao Tse-Tung, Ch.
5

39 We are advocates of the abolition of war, we do
not want war; but war can only be abolished
through war, and in order to get rid of the
gun it is necessary to take up the gun.
Mao Tse-Tung
Quotations from Chairman Mao Tse-Tung, Ch.
5

40 Politics is a blood sport.
Aneurin Bevan (1897–1960) British politician.
My Life with Nye (Jennie Lee)

41 We're not a family; we're a firm.
George VI (1895–1952) King of the United Kingdom.
Our Future King (Peter Lane)

1950

42 Perhaps it is better to be irresponsible and right than to be responsible and wrong.
Winston Churchill (1874–1965) British statesman.
Party Political Broadcast, London, 26 Aug 1950

43 When old settlers say 'One has to understand the country', what they mean is, 'You have to get used to our ideas about the native.' They are saying, in effect, 'Learn our ideas, or otherwise get out; we don't want you.'
Doris Lessing (1919–) British novelist.
Referring specifically to South Africa
The Grass is Singing, Ch. 1

44 When a white man in Africa by accident looks into the eyes of a native and sees the human being (which it is his chief preoccupation to avoid), his sense of guilt, which he denies, fumes up in resentment and he brings down the whip.
Doris Lessing
The Grass is Singing, Ch. 8

45 In our time, political speech and writing are largely the defence of the indefensible.
George Orwell (Eric Blair; 1903–50) British novelist.
Politics and the English Language

1951

46 My policy is to be able to take a ticket at Victoria Station and go anywhere I damn well please.
Ernest Bevin (1881–1951) British trade-union leader and politician.
The Spectator, 20 Apr 1951

47 The wrong war, at the wrong place, at the wrong time, and with the wrong enemy.
Omar Nelson Bradley (1893–1981) US general.
Said in evidence to a Senate inquiry, May 1951, over a proposal by MacArthur that the Korean war should be extended into China

48 I didn't fire him because he was a dumb son of a bitch, although he was, but that's not against the law for generals. If it was, half to three-quarters of them would be in gaol.
Harry S. Truman (1884–1972) US statesman.
Referring to General MacArthur
Plain Speaking (Merle Miller)

49 Whose finger do you want on the trigger?
Daily Mirror, 21 Sept 1951

50 Our great democracies still tend to think that a stupid man is more likely to be honest than a clever man, and our politicians take advantage of this prejudice by pretending to be even more stupid than nature has made them.
Bertrand Russell (1872–1970) British philosopher.
New Hopes for a Changing World

51 When the rich wage war it is the poor who die.
Jean-Paul Sartre (1905–80) French writer.
The Devil and the Good Lord

52 Communism is the corruption of a dream of justice.
Adlai Stevenson (1900–65) US statesman.
Speech, 1951

53 What is a rebel? A man who says no.
Albert Camus (1913–60) French existentialist writer.
The Rebel

54 I am not made for politics because I am incapable of wishing for, or accepting the death of my adversary.
Albert Camus
The Rebel

55 All modern revolutions have ended in a reinforcement of the power of the State.
Albert Camus
The Rebel

56 The future is the only kind of property that the masters willingly concede to slaves.
Albert Camus
The Rebel

57 The slave begins by demanding justice and ends by wanting to wear a crown. He must dominate in his turn.
Albert Camus
The Rebel

58 There will soon be only five kings left – the Kings of England, Diamonds, Hearts, Spades and Clubs.
Farouk I (1920–65) The last king of Egypt.
Remark made to Lord Boyd-Orr

59 I hate the idea of causes, and if I had to choose between betraying my country and betraying my friend, I hope I should have the guts to betray my country.
E. M. Forster (1879–1970) British novelist.
Two Cheers for Democracy, 'What I Believe'

60 The French will only be united under the threat of danger. Nobody can simply bring together a country that has 265 kinds of cheese.
Charles De Gaulle (1890–1970) French general and statesman.
Speech, 1951

1952

61 The way to win an atomic war is to make certain it never starts.
Omar Nelson Bradley (1893–1981) US general.
The Observer, 'Sayings of the Week', 20 Apr 1952

62 McCarthyism is Americanism with its sleeves rolled.
Joseph R. McCarthy (1908–57) US senator.
Speech, 1952

63 I cannot and will not cut my conscience to fit this year's fashions, even though I long ago came to the conclusion that I was not a political person and could have no comfortable place in any political group.
Lillian Hellman (1905–84) US dramatist.
Letter to the US House of Representatives Committee on Un-American Activities, *The Nation*, 31 May 1952

64 Let's talk sense to the American people. Let's tell them the truth, that there are no gains without pains.
Adlai Stevenson (1900–65) US statesman.
Speech, Chicago, 26 July 1952

65 Man has wrested from nature the power to make the world a desert or to make the deserts bloom. There is no evil in the atom, only in men's souls.
Adlai Stevenson
Speech, 18 Sept 1952

66 The buck stops here.
Harry S. Truman (1884–1972) US statesman.
Describing a sign kept on his desk during his term as president (1945–53)
Speech, National War College, 19 Dec 1952

67 I will undoubtedly have to seek what is happily known as gainful employment, which I am glad to say does not describe holding public office.
Dean Acheson (1893–1971) US lawyer and statesman.
Remark made on leaving his post as secretary of state, 1952; he subsequently returned to private legal practice

68 My definition of a free society is a society where it is safe to be unpopular.
Adlai Stevenson (1900–65) US statesman.
Speech, Detroit, Oct 1952

69 Nothing is news until it has appeared in *The Times*.
Ralph Deakin (1888–1952) Foreign News Editor of *The Times*.
Attrib.

1953

70 We know what happens to people who stay in the middle of the road. They get run over.
Aneurin Bevan (1897–1960) British politician.
The Observer, 'Sayings of the Week', 9 Dec 1953

71 Whatever America hopes to bring to pass in this world must first come to pass in the heart of America.
Dwight D. Eisenhower (1890–1969) US general and statesman.
Inaugural address, 1953

72 There is one thing about being President — nobody can tell you when to sit down.
Dwight D. Eisenhower
The Observer, 'Sayings of the Week', 9 Aug 1953

73 The countries of western Europe are no longer in a position to protect themselves individually.
Konrad Adenauer (1876–1967) West German chancellor.
Speech, May 1953

74 As far as I knew, he had never taken a photograph before, and the summit of Everest was hardly the place to show him how.
Edmund Hillary (1919–   ) New Zealand mountaineer.
Referring to Tenzing Norgay, his companion on the conquest of Mt Everest
High Adventure

75 The party is the rallying-point for the best elements of the working class.
Joseph Stalin (J. Dzhugashvili; 1879–1953) Soviet statesman.
Attrib.

76 REPORTER. If Mr Stalin dies, what will be the effect on international affairs?
EDEN. That is a good question for you to ask, not a wise question for me to answer.
Anthony Eden (1897–1977) British statesman.
Interview on board the *Queen Elizabeth*, 4 Mar 1953; Stalin died the next day

77 . . . that great lover of peace, a man of giant stature who moulded, as few other men have done, the destinies of his age.
Jawaharlal Nehru (1889–1964) Indian statesman.
Referring to Stalin
Obituary tribute, Indian Parliament, 9 Mar 1953

78 For many years I thought what was good for our country was good for General Motors, and vice versa.
Charles Erwin Wilson (1890–1961) US engineer.
Testimony to the Senate Armed Services Committee, 15 Jan 1953

79 It will be said of this generation that it found England a land of beauty and left it a land of beauty spots.
Cyril Joad (1891–1953) British philosopher, writer, and broadcaster.
The Observer, 'Sayings of Our Times', 31 May 1953

1954

80 You have a row of dominoes set up; you knock over the first one, and what will happen to the last one is that it will go over very quickly.
Dwight D. Eisenhower (1890–1969) US general and statesman.
The so-called 'domino effect'; said during the Battle of Dien Bien Phu, in which the French were defeated by the communist Viet-Minh
Press conference, 7 Apr 1954

81   To jaw-jaw is better than to war-war.
Winston Churchill (1874–1965) British statesman.
Speech, Washington, 26 June 1954

82*   An appeaser is one who feeds a crocodile – hoping that it will eat him last.
Winston Churchill
Attrib.

83   All diplomacy is a continuation of war by other means.
Chou En Lai (1898–1976) Chinese statesman.

1955

84   The best prime minister we have.
R. A. Butler (1902–82) British politician.
A common misquotation; in fact, Butler simply answered 'Yes' to the question 'Would you say that this is the best prime minister we have?' Referring properly to Anthony Eden, the epithet is sometimes applied to Harold Macmillan.
Interview, London Airport, Dec 1955

85   Not a gentleman; dresses too well.
Bertrand Russell (1872–1970) British philosopher.
Referring to Anthony Eden
Six Men (A. Cooke)

86   The word 'revolution' is a word for which you kill, for which you die, for which you send the labouring masses to their death, but which does not possess any content.
Simone Weil (1909–43) French philosopher.
Oppression and Liberty, 'Reflections Concerning the Causes of Liberty and Social Oppression'

1956

87   Everybody is always in favour of general economy and particular expenditure.
Anthony Eden (1897–1977) British statesman.
Speech, June 1956

88   We must face the fact that the United Nations is not yet the international equivalent of our own legal system and the rule of law.
Anthony Eden
Speech, House of Commons, 1 Nov 1956

89   We are not at war with Egypt. We are in an armed conflict.
Anthony Eden
Referring to the Suez crisis
Speech, House of Commons, 4 Nov 1956

90   During the last few weeks I have felt that the Suez Canal was flowing through my drawing room.
Clarissa Eden (1920–85) Wife of Anthony Eden.
Attrib.

91   Russian communism is the illegitimate child of Karl Marx and Catherine the Great.
Clement Attlee (1883–1967) British statesman.
Speech, 11 Apr 1956

92   Every year humanity takes a step towards Communism. Maybe not you, but at all events your grandson will surely be a Communist.
Nikita Khrushchev (1894–1971) Soviet statesman.
Said to Sir William Hayter

93   We will bury you.
Nikita Khrushchev
Said at a reception at the Kremlin, 26 Nov 1956

94   With the publication of his Private Papers in 1952, he committed suicide 25 years after his death.
Lord Beaverbrook (1879–1964) British newspaper owner and politician.
Referring to Earl Haig, British commander in chief in World War I
Men and Power

95   The worst government is the most moral. One composed of cynics is often very tolerant and human. But when fanatics are on top there is no limit to oppression.
H. L. Mencken (1880–1956) US journalist.
Notebooks, 'Minority Report'

96   An aristocracy in a republic is like a chicken whose head has been cut off: it may run about in a lively way, but in fact it is dead.
Nancy Mitford (1904–73) British writer.
Noblesse Oblige

97   The official world, the corridors of power, the dilemmas of conscience and egotism – she disliked them all.
C. P. Snow (1905–80) British novelist.
Homecomings, Ch. 22

98   Jam today, and men aren't at their most exciting: Jam tomorrow, and one often sees them at their noblest.
C. P. Snow
The Two Cultures and the Scientific Revolution, 4

1957

99   There is no reason to attack the monkey when the organ-grinder is present.
Aneurin Bevan (1897–1960) British politician.
The 'monkey' was Selwyn Lloyd; the 'organ-grinder' was Harold Macmillan
Remark, House of Commons, 16 May 1957

100   Democracy means government by discussion but it is only effective if you can stop people talking.
Clement Attlee (1883–1967) British statesman.
Speech, Oxford, 14 June 1957

101   Surely the right course is to test the Russians, not the bombs.
Hugh Gaitskell (1906–63) British politician.
Observer, 'Sayings of the Week', 23 June 1957

102   Most of our people have never had it so good.
Harold Macmillan (1894–1986) British statesman.
Speech, Bedford Football Ground, 20 July 1957

103   If you carry this resolution and follow out all its implications and do not run away from it you

will send a Foreign Minister, whoever he may be, naked into the conference chamber.
Aneurin Bevan (1897–1960) British politician.
Opposing a motion advocating unilateral nuclear disarmament
Speech, Labour Party Conference, 3 Oct 1957

104 The only inequalities that matter begin in the mind. It is not income levels but differences in mental equipment that keep people apart, breed feelings of inferiority.
Jacquetta Hawkes (1910–) British archeologist.
New Statesman, Jan 1957

1958

105 *Algérie Française.*
Algeria is French.
Slogan of the opponents of Algerian independence

106 When you're abroad you're a statesman: when you're at home you're just a politician.
Harold Macmillan (1894–1986) British statesman.
Speech, 1958

107 Introducing Super-Mac.
Vicky (Victor Weisz; 1913–66) German-born British cartoonist.
Cartoon caption depicting Harold Macmillan as Superman
Evening Standard, 6 Nov 1958

108 It's a recession when your neighbour loses his job; it's a depression when you lose your own.
Harry S. Truman (1884–1972) US statesman.
The Observer, 'Sayings of the Week', 6 Apr 1958

109 A politician is a man who understands government, and it takes a politician to run a government. A statesman is a politician who's been dead ten or fifteen years.
Harry S. Truman
New York World Telegram and Sun, 12 Apr 1958

110 The British, being brought up on team games, enter their House of Commons in the spirit of those who would rather be doing something else. If they cannot be playing golf or tennis, they can at least pretend that politics is a game with very similar rules.
Cyril Northcote Parkinson (1919–) British historian and writer.
Parkinson's Law, Ch. 2

111 No one can go on being a rebel too long without turning into an autocrat.
Lawrence Durrell (1912–90) British novelist.
Balthazar, II

112 More die in the United States of too much food than of too little.
John Kenneth Galbraith (1908–) US economist.
The Affluent Society, Ch. 9

113 Few things are as immutable as the addiction of

political groups to the ideas by which they have once won office.
John Kenneth Galbraith
The Affluent Society, Ch. 13

114 The Rise of the Meritocracy.
Michael Young (1915–) British political writer.
Book title

1959

115 Churchill on top of the wave has in him the stuff of which tyrants are made.
Lord Beaverbrook (1879–1964) Canadian-born British newspaper proprietor.
Politicians and the War

116 It takes twenty years or more of peace to make a man, it takes only twenty seconds of war to destroy him.
Baudouin I (1930–) King of Belgium.
Speech, US Congress, 12 May 1959

117 In a civil war, a general must know — and I'm afraid it's a thing rather of instinct than of practice — he must know exactly when to move over to the other side.
Henry Reed (1914–86) British poet and dramatist.
Not a Drum was Heard: The War Memoirs of General Gland

1960s

118 All wars are popular for the first thirty days.
Arthur Schlesinger Jnr (1917–) US historian, educator, and author.
Attrib.

119 The military don't start wars. The politicians start wars.
William Westmorland (1914–) US army officer.
Attrib.

120 It is worse than immoral, it's a mistake.
Dean Acheson (1893–1971) US lawyer and statesman.
Describing the Vietnam war
Quoted by Alistair Cooke in his radio programme *Letter from America*

121 You may reasonably expect a man to walk a tightrope safely for ten minutes; it would be unreasonable to do so without accident for two hundred years.
Bertrand Russell (1872–1970) British philosopher.
On the subject of nuclear war between the USA and the USSR
The Tightrope Men (D. Bagley)

122 What a genius the Labour Party has for cutting itself in half and letting the two parts writhe in public.
Cassandra (William Neil Cannon; 1910–67) Irish journalist.
The Daily Mirror

123   Equality of opportunity means equal opportunity to be unequal.
Iain Macleod (1913–70) British politician.
Way Of Life (John Boyd Carpenter)

124   An independent is a guy who wants to take the politics out of politics.
Adlai Stevenson (1900–65) US statesman.
The Art Of Politics

1960

125*   Classical physics has been superseded by quantum theory: quantum theory is verified by experiments. Experiments must be described in terms of classical physics.
C. F. von Weizsäcker (1912–   ) German physicist and philosopher.
Attrib.

126   One does not arrest Voltaire.
Charles De Gaulle (1890–1970) French general and statesman.
Explaining why he had not arrested Jean-Paul Sartre for urging French soldiers in Algeria to desert
Attrib.

127   We stand today on the edge of a new frontier.
John Fitzgerald Kennedy (1917–63) US statesman.
Said on his nomination as Presidential candidate
Speech, Democratic Party Convention, 15 July 1960

128   Do you realize the responsibility I carry? I'm the only person standing between Nixon and the White House.
John Fitzgerald Kennedy
Said to Arthur Schlesinger, 13 Oct 1960; Richard Nixon was the Republican candidate in the 1960 US Presidential election
A Thousand Days (Arthur M. Schlesinger, Jnr)

129   There are some of us ... who will fight, fight, fight, and fight again to save the party we love.
Hugh Gaitskell (1906–63) British politician.
After his policy for a nuclear deterrent had been defeated
Speech, Labour Party Conference, Scarborough, 3 Oct 1960

130   The wind of change is blowing through this continent. Whether we like it or not, this growth of national consciousness is a political fact.
Harold Macmillan (1894–1986) British statesman.
Speech, South African Parliament, 3 Feb 1960

131   Macmillan seemed, in his very person, to embody the national decay he supposed himself to be confuting. He exuded a flavour of mothballs.
Malcolm Muggeridge (1903–90) British writer and editor.
Tread Softly For You Tread on My Jokes, 'England, whose England'

132   Politicians are the same everywhere. They promise to build bridges even where there are no rivers.
Nikita Khrushchev (1894–1971) Soviet statesman.
Attrib., Oct 1960

133   The statesmen of the world who boast and threaten that they have Doomsday weapons are far more dangerous, and far more estranged from 'reality', than many of the people on whom the label 'psychotic' is affixed.
R. D. Laing (1927–89) British psychiatrist.
The Divided Self, Preface

134   The expression 'positive neutrality' is a contradiction in terms. There can be no more positive neutrality than there can be a vegetarian tiger.
V. K. Krishna Menon (1897–1974) Indian barrister and writer.
The New York Times, 18 Oct 1960

135   The one class you *do* not belong to and are not proud of at all is the lower-middle class. No one ever describes himself as belonging to the lower-middle class.
George Mikes (1912–87) Hungarian-born British writer and humorist.
How to be Inimitable

136   The nobility of England, my lord, would have snored through the Sermon on the Mount.
Robert Bolt (1924–   ) British playwright.
A Man for All Seasons

137   You don't set a fox to watching the chickens just because he has a lot of experience in the hen house.
Harry S. Truman (1884–1972) US statesman.
Referring to Vice-President Nixon's nomination for President
Speech, 30 Oct 1960

138   There are three groups that no prime minister should provoke: the Treasury, the Vatican, and the National Union of Mineworkers.
Harold Macmillan (1894–1986) British statesman.
First used by Stanley Baldwin
Attrib.

139*   A coloured man can tell, in five seconds dead, whether a white man likes him or not. If the white man *says* he does, he is instantly – and usually quite rightly – mistrusted.
Colin MacInnes (1914–76) British novelist.
England, Half English, 'A Short Guide for Jumbles'

1961

140   A revolution is not a bed of roses. A revolution is a struggle to the death between the future and the past.
Fidel Castro (1926–   ) Cuban statesman.
Speech, Havana, Jan 1961 (2nd anniversary of the Cuban Revolution)

141 The Irish don't know what they want and are
prepared to fight to the death to get it.
Sidney Littlewood (1895–1967) President of
The Law Society.
Speech, 13 Apr 1961

142 I think it is about time we pulled our fingers out
... The rest of the world most certainly does
not owe us a living.
Prince Philip (1921–   ) The consort of
Queen Elizabeth II.
Speech, London, 17 Oct 1961

143 And so, my fellow Americans: ask not what
your country can do for you – ask what you
can do for your country. My fellow citizens of
the world: ask not what America will do for
you, but what together we can do for the freedom of man.
John Fitzgerald Kennedy (1917–63) US
statesman.
Inaugural address, 20 Jan 1961

144 I believe that this nation should commit itself to
achieving the goal, before this decade is out,
of landing a man on the Moon and returning
him safely to earth.
John Fitzgerald Kennedy
Supplementary State of the Union Message, 25
May 1961

145 We must use time as a tool, not as a couch.
John Fitzgerald Kennedy
The Observer, 'Sayings of the Week', 10 Dec
1961

146 The worse I do, the more popular I get.
John Fitzgerald Kennedy
Referring to his popularity following the 'Bay of
Pigs', an abortive US-supported invasion of
Cuba by Cuban exiles
The People's Almanac (D. Wallechinsky)

147 I can't see that it's wrong to give him a little
legal experience before he goes out to practice
law.
John Fitzgerald Kennedy
On being criticized for making his brother Robert
attorney general
Nobody Said It Better (M. Ringo)

148 When you are skinning your customers you
should leave some skin on to grow, so that you
can skin them again.
Nikita Khrushchev (1894–1971) Soviet
statesman.
Speech to British industrialists, May 1961

149 A politician rises on the backs of his friends ...
but it is through his enemies he will have to
govern afterwards.
Richard Hughes (1900–76) British writer.
The Fox in the Attic

150 I'd like to see the government get out of war
altogether and leave the whole feud to private
industry.
Joseph Heller (1923–   ) US novelist.
Catch 22

151 But bombs *are* unbelievable until they actually
fall.
Patrick White (1912–90) British-born Australian novelist.
Riders in the Chariot, I:4

152 No Jewish blood runs among my blood,
but I am as bitterly and hardly hated
by every anti-semite
as if I were a Jew. By this
I am a Russian.
Yevgeny Yevtushenko (1933–   ) Russian
poet.
Babi Yar

1962

153 The House of Lords is the British Outer Mon-
golia for retired politicians.
Tony Benn (1925–   ) British politician.
Speech, 11 Feb 1962

154 Great Britain has lost an Empire and has not
yet found a role.
Dean Acheson (1893–1971) US lawyer and
statesman.
Speech, Military Academy, West Point, 5 Dec
1962

155 You won't have Nixon to kick around any more,
gentlemen. This is my last Press Conference.
Richard Milhous Nixon (1913–   ) US
president.
Press conference, after losing the election for
the governorship of California, 2 Nov 1962

156 I guess this is the week I earn my salary.
John Fitzgerald Kennedy (1917–63) US
statesman.
Comment made during the Cuban missile crisis
Nobody Said It Better (M. Ringo)

157 Arms alone are not enough to keep the peace –
it must be kept by men.
John Fitzgerald Kennedy
The Observer, 'Sayings of the Decade', 1962

158 She would rather light candles than curse the
darkness, and her glow has warmed the
world.
Adlai Stevenson (1900–65) US statesman.
Referring to Eleanor Roosevelt, who had recently
died. She was the wife of President Franklin D.
Roosevelt and chairman (1946–51) of the UN
commission on human rights
Address, United Nations General Assembly, 9
Nov 1962

159 They talk about who won and who lost. Human
reason won. Mankind won.
Nikita Khrushchev (1894–1971) Soviet
statesman.
Referring to the Cuban missile crisis
Speech, Nov 1962

160 I want to be the white man's brother, not his
brother-in-law.
Martin Luther King (1929–68) US civil-rights
leader.
New York Journal-American, 10 Sept 1962

161 Since a politician never believes what he says,
he is surprised when others believe him.
Charles De Gaulle (1890–1970) French general and statesman.
Attrib.

162 They really are bad shots.
Charles De Gaulle
Remark after narrowly escaping death in an assassination attempt
Ten First Ladies of the World (Pauline Frederick)

163 A small acquaintance with history shows that
all Governments are selfish and the French
Governments more selfish than most.
David Eccles (1904–   ) British politician.
The Observer, 'Sayings of the Year', 29 Dec
1962

164 The collection of prejudices which is called political philosophy is useful provided that it is
not called philosophy.
Bertrand Russell (1872–1970) British
philosopher.
Remark, 1962

165 Greater love hath no man than this, that he lay
down his friends for his life.
Jeremy Thorpe (1929–   ) British politician.
After Macmillan's 1962 Cabinet reshuffle
The Pendulum Years (Bernard Levin), Ch. 12

166 Members rise from CMG (known sometimes in
Whitehall as 'Call me God') to the KCMG
('Kindly Call me God') to ... The GCMG ('God
Calls me God').
Anthony Sampson (1926–   ) British writer
and journalist.
Anatomy of Britain, Ch. 18

167 It is better for aged diplomats to be bored than
for young men to die.
Warren Austin (1877–1962) US politician and
diplomat.
When asked if he got tired during long debates
at the UN
Attrib.

1963
---

168 I wish I could bring Stonehenge to Nyasaland
to show there was a time when Britain had a
savage culture.
Hastings Banda (1906–   ) Malawi
statesman.
The Observer, 'Sayings of the Week', 10 Mar
1963

169 If we cannot now end our differences, at least
we can help make the world safe for diversity.
John Fitzgerald Kennedy (1917–63) US
statesman.
Speech, American University (Washington, DC),
10 June 1963

170 All free men, wherever they may live, are citizens of Berlin. And therefore, as a free man, I
take pride in the words *Ich bin ein Berliner.*
John Fitzgerald Kennedy
Speech, City Hall, West Berlin, 26 June 1963

171 Human salvation lies in the hands of the creatively maladjusted.
Martin Luther King (1929–68) US civil-rights
leader.
Strength to Love

172 If a man hasn't discovered something that he
would die for, he isn't fit to live.
Martin Luther King
Speech, Detroit, 23 June 1963

173 I have a dream that one day this nation will rise
up, live out the true meaning of its creed: we
hold these truths to be self-evident, that all
men are created equal.
Martin Luther King
King used the words 'I have a dream' in a number of speeches
Speech, Washington, 27 Aug 1963

174 A constant effort to keep his party together,
without sacrificing either principle or the essentials of basic strategy, is the very stuff of political leadership. Macmillan was canonised
for it.
Harold Wilson (1916–   ) British statesman.
Final Term: The Labour Government 1974–76

175 A great party is not to be brought down because of a scandal by a woman of easy virtue
and a proved liar.
Lord Hailsham (1907–   ) British politician.
Referring to the Profumo affair
BBC interview, 13 June 1963

176 There is something utterly nauseating about a
system of society which pays a harlot 25
times as much as it pays its Prime Minister,
250 times as much as it pays its Members of
Parliament, and 500 times as much as it
pays some of its ministers of religion.
Harold Wilson (1916–   ) British statesman.
Referring to Christine Keeler
Speech, House of Commons, June 1963

177 He would, wouldn't he?
Mandy Rice-Davies (1944–   ) British call
girl.
Referring to Lord Astor, when told that he had
repudiated her evidence at the trial of Stephen
Ward, 29 June 1963

178 The members of our secret service have apparently spent so much time looking under the
beds for Communists, they haven't had time to
look in the bed.
Michael Foot (1913–   ) British politician and
journalist.
Referring to the Profumo affair
Attrib.

179 The United States has to move very fast to even
stand still.
John Fitzgerald Kennedy (1917–63) US
statesman.
The Observer, 'Sayings of the Week', 21 July
1963

180 We are redefining and we are restating our socialism in terms of the scientific revolution ...
the Britain that is going to be forged in the
white heat of this revolution will be no place for

restrictive practices or out-dated methods on either side of industry.
Harold Wilson (1916–) British statesman.
Speech, Labour Party Conference, 1 Oct 1963

181 After half a century of democratic advance, the whole process has ground to a halt with a 14th Earl.
Harold Wilson
Referring to the 4th Earl of Home who, after the retirement of Harold Macmillan, was chosen to be the new prime minister by 'a process of consultation'. Lord Home renounced his peerage and became Sir Alec Douglas-Home.
Speech, Manchester, 19 Oct 1963

182 As far as the 14th Earl is concerned, I suppose Mr Wilson, when you come to think of it, is the 14th Mr Wilson.
Alec Douglas-Home (1903–) British statesman.
Television interview, 21 Oct 1963

183 He is used to dealing with estate workers. I cannot see how anyone can say he is out of touch.
Caroline Douglas-Home (1937–) Daughter of Alec Douglas-Home.
When asked about her father's suitability for his new role as prime minister
Daily Herald, 21 Oct 1963

184 A piece of each of us died at that moment.
Michael J. Mansfield (1903–) US senator.
Referring to the assassination (22 Nov 1963) of President Kennedy
Speech, Senate, 24 Nov 1963

185 Christ in this country would quite likely have been arrested under the Suppression of Communism Act.
Joost de Blank (1908–68) Dutch-born British churchman.
Referring to South Africa
The Observer, 'Sayings of the Week', 27 Oct 1963

186 I myself have become a Gaullist only little by little.
Charles De Gaulle (1890–1970) French general and statesman.
The Observer, 'Sayings of the Year', 29 Dec 1963

187 Treaties are like roses and young girls – they last while they last.
Charles De Gaulle
Attrib.

188 The great nations have always acted like gangsters, and the small nations like prostitutes.
Stanley Kubrick (1928–) US film director.
The Guardian, 5 June 1963

189 In Western Europe there are now only small countries – those that know it and those that don't know it yet.
Théo Lefèvre (1914–73) Belgian statesman.
Speech

190 Democracy can't work. Mathematicians, peasants, and animals, that's all there is – so democracy, a theory based on the assumption that mathematicians and peasants are equal,

can never work. Wisdom is not additive; its maximum is that of the wisest man in a given group.
Robert Heinlein (1907–88) US science-fiction writer.
Glory Road, Ch. 20

191 Every communist has a fascist frown, every fascist a communist smile.
Muriel Spark (1918–) British novelist.
The Girls of Slender Means, Ch. 4

192 Power corrupts, but lack of power corrupts absolutely.
Adlai Stevenson (1900–65) US statesman.
Speech, Jan 1963

193 Everybody should have an equal chance – but they shouldn't have a flying start.
Harold Wilson (1916–) British statesman.
The Observer, 'Sayings of the Year', 1963

194 All terrorists, at the invitation of the Government, end up with drinks at the Dorchester.
Hugh Gaitskell (1906–63) British politician.
Letter to The Guardian, 23 Aug 1977 (Dora Gaitskell)

1964

195 There are two problems in my life. The political ones are insoluble and the economic ones are incomprehensible.
Alec Douglas-Home (1903–) British statesman.
Speech, Jan 1964

196 This Administration here and now declares unconditional war on poverty in America.
Lyndon B. Johnson (1908–73) US president.
State of the Union message, 8 Jan 1964

197 For Hon. Members opposite the deterrent is a phallic symbol. It convinces them that they are men.
George Wigg (1900–76) British politician.
The Observer, 'Sayings of the Week', 8 Mar 1964

198 One fifth of the people are against everything all the time.
Robert Kennedy (1925–68) US politician.
Speech, May 1964

199 The great society is a place where men are more concerned with the quality of their goods than the quantity of their goods.
Lyndon B. Johnson (1908–73) US president.
Speech, 22 May 1964

200 I would remind you that extremism in the defence of liberty is no vice. And let me remind you also that moderation in the pursuit of justice is no virtue!
Barry Goldwater (1904–) US politician.
Speech, San Francisco, 17 July 1964

201 If the British public falls for this, I say it will be stark, staring bonkers.
Lord Hailsham (1907–) British politician.
Referring to Labour policy in the 1964 general-election campaign
Press conference, Conservative Central Office, 12 Oct 1964

202 I am going to build the kind of nation that President Roosevelt hoped for, President Truman worked for and President Kennedy died for.
Lyndon B. Johnson (1908–73) US president.
The Sunday Times, 27 Dec 1964

203 A Royal Commission is a broody hen sitting on a china egg.
Michael Foot (1913–) British politician and journalist.
Speech, House of Commons, 1964

204 My government will protect all liberties but one – the liberty to do away with other liberties.
Gustavo Diaz Ordaz (1911–) President of Mexico (1964–1970).
Inaugural speech

205 I can honestly say that I was never affected by the question of the success of an undertaking. If I felt it was the right thing to do, I was for it regardless of the possible outcome.
Golda Meir (1898–1978) Russian-born Israeli stateswoman.
Golda Meir: Woman with a Cause (Marie Syrkin)

1965

206 The vote is the most powerful instrument ever devised by man for breaking down injustice and destroying the terrible walls which imprison men because they are different from other men.
Lyndon B. Johnson (1908–73) US president.
Address on signing Voting Rights Bill, Washington D.C., 6 Aug 1965

207 It is a great shock at the age of five or six to find that in a world of Gary Coopers you are the Indian.
James Baldwin (1924–87) US writer.
Speech, Cambridge Union, 17 Feb 1965

208 If only I had known, I should have become a watchmaker.
Albert Einstein (1879–1955) German-born US physicist.
Reflecting on his role in the development of the atom bomb
New Statesman, 16 Apr 1965

209 If someone puts his hand on you, send him to the cemetery.
Malcolm X (1925–65) US black leader.
Malcolm X Speaks

210 A week is a long time in politics.
Harold Wilson (1916–) British statesman.
First said in 1965 or 1966, and repeated on several occasions
Attrib.

211 To be absolutely honest, what I feel really bad about is that I don't feel worse. There's the ineffectual liberal's problem in a nutshell.
Michael Frayn (1933–) British journalist and writer.
The Observer, 8 Aug 1965

212 I believe in the armed struggle as the only solution for those people who fight to free themselves, and I am consistent with my beliefs.

Many will call me an adventurer – and that I am, only one of a different sort: one of those who risks his skin to prove his platitudes.
Che Guevara (Ernesto G.; 1928–67) Argentine-born revolutionary.
On leaving Cuba to join guerrillas in the Bolivian jungle
Last letter to his parents (1965)

213 Simply a radio personality who outlived his prime.
Evelyn Waugh (1903–66) British novelist.
Referring to Winston Churchill
Evelyn Waugh (Christopher Sykes)

1966

214 I respect only those who resist me; but I cannot tolerate them.
Charles De Gaulle (1890–1970) French general and statesman.
New York Times magazine, 12 May 1966

215 The House of Lords, an illusion to which I have never been able to subscribe – responsibility without power, the prerogative of the eunuch throughout the ages.
Tom Stoppard (1937–) Czech-born British dramatist.
Lord Malquist and Mr Moon, Pt. VI, Ch. 1

216 Catholics and Communists have committed great crimes, but at least they have not stood aside, like an established society, and been indifferent. I would rather have blood on my hands than water like Pilate.
Graham Greene (1904–91) British novelist.
The Comedians, Pt. III, Ch. 4

1967

217 You've got to forget about this civilian. Whenever you drop bombs, you're going to hit civilians.
Barry Goldwater (1904–) US politician.
Speech, New York, 23 Jan 1967

218 . . . if there was one word I would use to identify modern socialism, it was 'Science'.
Harold Wilson (1916–) British statesman.
Speech, 17 June 1967

219 From now, the pound is worth 14 per cent or so less in terms of other currencies. It does not mean, of course, that the pound here in Britain, in your pocket or purse or in your bank, has been devalued.
Harold Wilson
Speech after devaluation of the pound, 20 Nov 1967

220 The House of Lords is like a glass of champagne that has stood for five days.
Clement Attlee (1883–1967) British statesman.
Attrib.

221 A riot is at bottom the language of the unheard.
Martin Luther King (1929–68) US civil-rights leader.
Chaos or Community, Ch. 4

222   Patriots always talk of dying for their country and never of killing for their country.
Bertrand Russell (1872–1970) British philosopher.
The Autobiography of Bertrand Russell

223   I was obviously destined to go down and down when in 1958 my father and brother died within ten days of each other and I became an Earl... Life is much easier, being an Earl. It has changed me a lot. I'm much nastier now.
Earl of Arran (1938–) British publisher.
The Sunday Times, 15 Jan 1967

1968

224   There are times in politics when you must be on the right side and lose.
John Kenneth Galbraith (1908–) US economist.
The Observer, 'Sayings of the Week', 11 Feb 1968

225   In the service of the people we followed such a policy that socialism would not lose its human face.
Alexander Dubček (1921–92) Czech statesman.
Often misquoted as 'Communism with a human face'
Rudé Právo, 19 July 1968 (a resolution by the party group in the Ministry of Foreign Affairs, on 14 March 1968, referred to Czechoslovak foreign policy acquiring 'its own defined face')

226   ...when internal and external forces that are hostile to socialism try to turn the development of some socialist country towards the restoration of a capitalist regime, when socialism in that country and the socialist community as a whole is threatened...
Leonid Brezhnev (1906–82) Soviet statesman.
The 'Brezhnev doctrine', used to justify the USSR's intervention in Czechoslovakia, stated the circumstances when the USSR had a right to intervene in the internal affairs of another socialist state

227   The monarchy is part of the fabric of the country. And, as the fabric alters, so the monarchy and its people's relations to it alters.
Prince Philip (1921–) The consort of Queen Elizabeth II.
Television interview, 20 Mar 1968

228   Let us begin by committing ourselves to the truth, to see it like it is and to tell it like it is, to find the truth, to speak the truth and live with the truth. That's what we'll do.
Richard Milhous Nixon (1913–) US president.
Nomination acceptance speech, Miami, 8 Aug 1968

229   To win in Vietnam, we will have to exterminate a nation.
Benjamin Spock (1903–) US paediatrician and psychiatrist.
Dr Spock on Vietnam, Ch.7

230   One of those ideas was that man was not born to go down on his belly before the state.
Alan Paton (1903–88) South African novelist.
Speech at the last meeting of the South African Liberal party, 1968; referring to the party's principles

231   I suffer from an incurable disease – colour blindness.
Joost de Blank (1908–68) Dutch-born British churchman.
Attrib.

232   As I look ahead, I am filled with foreboding. Like the Roman, I seem to see 'the River Tiber foaming with much blood'.
Enoch Powell (1912–) British politician.
Referring to the effects of immigration; Powell was quoting the Roman poet Virgil (*Aeneid*, Bk.VI)
Speech, Birmingham, 20 Apr 1968

233   Remember this, Griffin. The revolution eats its own. Capitalism re-creates itself.
Mordecai Richler (1931–) Canadian novelist.
Cocksure, Ch. 22

1969

234   That's one small step for man, one giant leap for mankind.
Neil Armstrong (1930–) US astronaut.
Said on stepping onto the moon. Often quoted as 'small step for a man...' (which is probably what he intended)
Remark, 21 July 1969

235   This is the greatest week in the history of the world since the creation.
Richard Milhous Nixon (1913–) US president.
Said when men first landed on the moon
Attrib., 24 July 1969

236   As far as criticism is concerned, we don't resent that unless it is absolutely biased, as it is in most cases.
John Vorster (Balthazar Johannes V.; 1915–83) South African politician.
The Observer, 'Sayings of the Week', 9 Nov 1969

237* The coach has turned into a pumpkin and the mice have all run away.
Lady Bird Johnson (1912–) Wife of Lyndon B. Johnson, US president.
Said after Lyndon Johnson gave up the presidency
The Vantage Point (Lyndon B. Johnson)

238   By yesterday morning British troops were patrolling the streets of Belfast. I fear that once Catholics and Protestants get used to our presence they will hate us more than they hate each other.
Richard Crossman (1907–74) British politician.
British troops were sent to Northern Ireland in 1969, originally to protect the Catholic minority
Diaries, 17 Aug 1969

239   The conventional army loses if it does not win. The guerrilla wins if he does not lose.
Henry Kissinger (1923–) German-born US politician and diplomat.
Foreign Affairs, XIII (Jan 1969), 'The Vietnam Negotiations'

240   You took my freedom away a long time ago and you can't give it back because you haven't got it yourself.
Alexander Solzhenitsyn (1918–) Soviet-born novelist.
The First Circle, Ch. 17

241   You only have power over people so long as you don't take *everything* away from them. But when you've robbed a man of everything he's no longer in your power – he's free again.
Alexander Solzhenitsyn
The First Circle, Ch. 17

1970s

242   The U.S. has broken the second rule of war. That is, don't go fighting with your land army on the mainland of Asia. Rule One is don't march on Moscow. I developed these two rules myself.
Lord Montgomery (1887–1976) British field marshal.
Referring to the Vietnam war
Montgomery of Alamein (Chalfont)

243   This universal, obligatory force-feeding with lies is now the most agonizing aspect of existence in our country – worse than all our material miseries, worse than any lack of civil liberties.
Alexander Solzhenitsyn (1918–) Soviet-born novelist.
Letter to Soviet Leaders, 6

244   If people behaved in the way nations do they would all be put in straitjackets.
Tennessee Williams (1911–83) US dramatist.
BBC interview

1970

245   One man's wage rise is another man's price increase.
Harold Wilson (1916–) British statesman.
The Observer, 'Sayings of the Week', 11 Jan 1970

246   The House of Lords is a perfect eventide home.
Mary Stocks (1891–1975) British politician and writer.
Remark, Oct 1970

247   It is time for the great silent majority of Americans to stand up and be counted.
Richard Milhous Nixon (1913–) US president.
Election speech, Oct 1970

248   We are all the President's men.
Henry Kissinger (1923–) German-born US politician and diplomat.
Referring to the invasion of Cambodia
The Sunday Times Magazine, 4 May 1975

249   We had no use for the policy of the Gospels: if someone slaps you, just turn the other cheek. We had shown that anyone who slapped us on our cheek would get his head kicked off.
Nikita Khrushchev (1894–1971) Soviet statesman.
Khrushchev Remembers, Vol. II

250*   People don't seem to realize that it takes time and effort and preparation to think. Statesmen are far too busy making speeches to think.
Bertrand Russell (1872–1970) British philosopher.
Kenneth Harris Talking To, 'Bertrand Russell' (Kenneth Harris)

251   I have come to the conclusion that politics are too serious a matter to be left to the politicians.
Charles De Gaulle (1890–1970) French general and statesman.
Attrib.

252   In order to become the master, the politician poses as the servant.
Charles De Gaulle
Attrib.

1971

253   You cannot shake hands with a clenched fist.
Indira Gandhi (1917–84) Indian stateswoman.
Press conference, New Delhi, 19 Oct 1971

254   I'd much rather have that fellow inside my tent pissing out, than outside my tent pissing in.
Lyndon B. Johnson (1908–73) US president.
When asked why he retained J. Edgar Hoover at the FBI
Guardian Weekly, 18 Dec 1971

255   I would rather be British than just.
Ian Paisley (1926–) Northern Irish politician.
The Sunday Times, 12 Dec 1971

256   Inflation in the Sixties was a nuisance to be endured, like varicose veins or French foreign policy.
Bernard Levin (1928–) British journalist.
The Pendulum Years, 'Epilogue'

257   We intend to remain alive. Our neighbors want to see us dead. This is not a question that leaves much room for compromise.
Golda Meir (1898–1978) Russian-born Israeli stateswoman.
Reader's Digest (July 1971), 'The Indestructible Golda Meir'

258   Politics is the art of the possible.
R. A. Butler (1902–82) British politician.
Often attrib. to Butler but used earlier by others, including Bismarck
The Art of the Possible, Epigraph

259   I was a man who was lucky enough to have discovered a political theory, a man who was caught up in the whirlpool of Cuba's political crisis long before becoming a fully fledged Communist . . . discovering Marxism . . . was like finding a map in the forest.
Fidel Castro (1926–) Cuban statesman.
Speech, Chile, 18 Nov 1971

260 No-one ever mentions these millions of women. I declare that I am one of them. I declare that I have had an abortion.
Part of a statement, signed by 343 French women headed by Simone de Beauvoir, marking the beginning of the campaign for free legal abortion on demand in France
Le Nouvel Observateur, 5 Apr 1971

261 There they were, all the lovely sisters, giggling and shivering and bawdy and prim and I turned and turned again, gloating at the numbers before and behind my motley, frost-defying sex. Because sex is all we really had in common.
Jill Tweedie (1936–) British writer and journalist.
Reporting the first large Women's Liberation demonstration, 6 Mar 1971
Telegraph Weekend Magazine, Mar 1991

262 If you feed people just with revolutionary slogans they will listen today, they will listen tomorrow, they will listen the day after tomorrow, but on the fourth day they will say 'To hell with you!'
Nikita Khrushchev (1894–1971) Soviet statesman.
Attrib.

1972
---

263 I think that everyone will concede that – today of all days – I should begin by saying, 'My husband and I'.
Elizabeth II (1926–) Queen of the United Kingdom.
On the celebration of her silver wedding anniversary
Speech, Guildhall, 2 Nov 1972

264 Censorship is more depraving and corrupting than anything pornography can produce.
Tony Smythe (1938–) Chairman of the National Council for Civil Liberties, Great Britain.
The Observer, 'Sayings of the Week', 18 Sept 1972

265 Nothing and no one can destroy the Chinese people. They are relentless survivors. They are the oldest civilized people on earth. Their civilization passes through phases but its basic characteristics remain the same. They yield, they bend to the wind, but they never break.
Pearl Buck (1892–1973) US novelist.
China, Past and Present, Ch. 1

266 I'm not hard – I'm frightfully soft. But I will not be hounded.
Margaret Thatcher (1925–) British stateswoman.
Daily Mail, 1972

267 It's not the voting that's democracy; it's the counting.
Tom Stoppard (1937–) Czech-born British dramatist.
Jumpers

268 The defiance of established authority, religious and secular, social and political, as a world-wide phenomenon may well one day be ac-counted the outstanding event of the last decade.
Hannah Arendt (1906–75) German-born US philosopher and historian.
Crises of the Republic, 'Civil Disobedience'

1973
---

269 No wonder Harold is back in form – every Labour politician feels more at home attacking his own party's politics.
Referring to Harold Wilson
Cartoon caption, *Punch*, 31 Jan 1973

270 It is the unpleasant and unacceptable face of capitalism but one should not suggest that the whole of British industry consists of practices of this kind.
Edward Heath (1916–) British statesman.
Referring to the Lonrho Affair, a scandal involving financial dealings in the City
Speech, House of Commons, 15 May 1973

271 This is a very fine country to be acutely ill or injured in, but take my advice and do not be old and frail or mentally ill here – at least not for a few years. This is definitely not a good country to be deaf or blind in either.
Keith Joseph (1918–) British politician.
The Observer, 'Sayings of the Week', 1 July 1973

272 There will be no whitewash in the White House.
Richard Milhous Nixon (1913–) US president.
Referring to the Watergate scandal
Statement, 17 Apr 1973

273 I am not a crook.
Richard Milhous Nixon
Attrib., 17 Nov 1973

274* Would you buy a second-hand car from this man?
Mort Sahl (1927–) US political comedian.
Referring to President Nixon
Attrib.

275 If sunbeams were weapons of war, we would have had solar energy long ago.
George Porter (1920–) British chemist.
Remark, Aug 1973

276 I am MacWonder one moment and MacBlunder the next.
Harold Macmillan (1894–1986) British statesman.
Daily Telegraph, 15 Nov 1973

277 A statesman is a politician who places himself at the service of the nation. A politician is a statesman who places the nation at his service.
Georges Pompidou (1911–74) French statesman.
The Observer, 'Sayings of the Year', 30 Dec 1973

278 I do not intend to prejudge the past.
William Whitelaw (1918–) British politician.
Said on arriving in Ulster as Minister for Northern Ireland
The Times, 3 Dec 1973

279 If I had to give a definition of capitalism I would say: the process whereby American girls turn into American women.
Christopher Hampton (1946–) British writer and dramatist.
Savages, Sc. 16

280 A just society would be one in which liberty for one person is constrained only by the demands created by equal liberty for another.
Ivan Illich (1926–) Austrian sociologist.
Tools for Conviviality

1974

281 If you want to see the acceptable face of capitalism, go out to an oil rig in the North Sea.
Edward Heath (1916–) British statesman.
Speech, Edinburgh, 18 Feb 1974

282 I do not mind the Liberals, still less do I mind the Country Party, calling me a bastard. In some circumstances I am only doing my job if they do. But I hope you will not publicly call me a bastard, as some bastards in the Caucus have.
Gough Whitlam (1916–) Australian statesman.
Speech to the Australian Labor Party, 9 June 1974

283 President Nixon's motto was, if two wrongs don't make a right, try three.
Norman Cousins (1915–) US editor and author.
Daily Telegraph, 17 July 1979

284 Our long national nightmare is over. Our constitution works.
Gerald Ford (1913–) US president.
On being sworn in as President after the resignation of Richard Nixon
Speech, 9 Aug 1974

285 It will be years — and not in my time — before a woman will lead the party or become Prime Minister.
Margaret Thatcher (1925–) British stateswoman.
Speech, 1974

286 The charm of Britain has always been the ease with which one can move into the middle class.
Margaret Thatcher
Speech, Oct 1974

287 In our country the lie has become not just a moral category but a pillar of the State.
Alexander Solzhenitsyn (1918–) Soviet-born novelist.
The Observer, 'Sayings of the Year', 29 Dec 1974

288 A committee is an animal with four back legs.
John Le Carré (1931–) British writer.
Tinker, Tailor, Soldier, Spy

1975

289 This going into Europe will not turn out to be

the thrilling mutual exchange supposed. It is more like nine middle-aged couples with failing marriages meeting in a darkened bedroom in a Brussels hotel for a Group Grope.
E. P. Thompson (1924–) British historian.
Sunday Times, 27 Apr 1975

290 Television brought the brutality of war into the comfort of the living room. Vietnam was lost in the living rooms of America — not on the battlefields of Vietnam.
Marshall McLuhan (1911–81) Canadian sociologist.
Montreal *Gazette*, 16 May 1975

291 There exists no politician in India daring enough to attempt to explain to the masses that cows can be eaten.
Indira Gandhi (1917–84) Indian stateswoman.
New York Review of Books, 'Indira's Coup' (Oriana Fallaci)

292 To bear many children is considered not only a religious blessing but also an investment. The greater their number, some Indians reason, the more alms they can beg.
Indira Gandhi
New York Review of Books, 'Indira's Coup' (Oriana Fallaci)

293 I believe the greatest asset a head of state can have is the ability to get a good night's sleep.
Harold Wilson (1916–) British statesman.
The World Tonight, BBC radio, 16 Apr 1975

294 We are not just here to manage capitalism but to change society and to define its finer values.
Tony Benn (1925–) British politician.
Speech, Labour Party Conference, 1 Oct 1975

295 It might be said that it is the ideal of the employer to have production without employees and the ideal of the employee is to have income without work.
E. F. Schumacher (1911–77) German-born economist.
The Observer, 'Sayings of the Week', 4 May 1975

296 War is capitalism with the gloves off.
Tom Stoppard (1937–) Czech-born British dramatist.
Travesties

297 Let our children grow tall, and some taller than others if they have it in them to do so.
Margaret Thatcher (1925–) British stateswoman.
Speech, US tour, 1975

298 We cannot remove the evils of capitalism without taking its source of power: ownership.
Neil Kinnock (1942–) British politician.
Tribune, 1975

299 The ship follows Soviet custom: it is riddled with class distinctions so subtle, it takes a trained Marxist to appreciate them.
Paul Theroux (1941–) US-born writer.
The Great Railway Bazaar, Ch. 30

300 Britain is not a country that is easily rocked by

revolution . . . In Britain our institutions evolve.
We are a Fabian Society writ large.
William Hamilton (1917–   ) Scottish MP.
My Queen and I, Ch. 9

301   An act to render unlawful certain kinds of sex
discrimination and discrimination on the
ground of marriage and establish a Commission
with the function of working towards the elimi-
nation of such discrimination and promoting
equality of opportunity between men and
women generally.
Sex Discrimination Act

1976

302   This is a rotten argument, but it should be good
enough for their lordships on a hot summer
afternoon.
Anonymous
A note on a ministerial brief read out by mistake
in the House of Lords
The Way the Wind Blows (Lord Home)

303   I don't believe in black majority rule ever in
Rhodesia . . . not in a thousand years.
Ian Smith (1919–   ) Rhodesian (Zimbabwe)
politician.
Speech, Mar 1976

304   Britain has lived for too long on borrowed time,
borrowed money and even borrowed ideas.
James Callaghan (1912–   ) British
statesman.
The Observer, 'Sayings of the Week', 3 Oct
1976

305   A lie can be half-way round the world before
the truth has got its boots on.
James Callaghan
Speech, 1 Nov 1976

306   Power is the ultimate aphrodisiac.
Henry Kissinger (1923–   ) German-born US
politician and diplomat.
The Guardian, 28 Nov 1976

307   In so far as socialism means anything, it must
be about the wider distribution of smoked
salmon and caviar.
Richard Marsh (1928–   ) British politician
and businessman.
Remark, Oct 1976

308   There comes a time in every man's life when he
must make way for an older man.
Reginald Maudling (1917–77) British
politician.
Remark made on being replaced in the shadow
cabinet by John Davies, his elder by four years
The Guardian, 20 Nov 1976

309   You cannot control a free society by force.
Robert Mark (1917–   ) British police
commissioner.
The Observer, 'Sayings of the Week', 25 July
1976

310   We thus denounce the false and dangerous
programme of the arms race, of the secret ri-

valry between peoples for military
superiority.
John Paul II (Karol Wojtyla; 1920–   ) Polish
pope.
Said when Archbishop of Kraków
Speech, Dec 1976

311   The Iron Lady of British politics is seeking to
revive the cold war.
Commenting on a speech by Margaret Thatcher
Red Star (newspaper of the Soviet ministry of
defence), 23 Jan 1976

312   Margaret Thatcher's great strength seems to be
the better people know her, the better they
like her. But, of course, she has one great disadvantage – she is a daughter of the people
and looks trim, as the daughters of the people
desire to be. Shirley Williams has such an
advantage over her because she's a member of
the upper-middle class and can achieve that
kitchen-sink-revolutionary look that one cannot
get unless one has been to a really good
school.
Rebecca West (Cicely Isabel Fairfield; 1892–
1983) British novelist and journalist.
Interview,
The Sunday Times, 25 July 1976

313   Once, when a British Prime Minister sneezed,
men half a world away would blow their
noses. Now when a British Prime Minister
sneezes nobody else will even say 'Bless You'.
Bernard Levin (1928–   ) British journalist.
The Times, 1976

1977

314   I let down my friends, I let down my country. I
let down our system of government.
Richard Milhous Nixon (1913–   ) US
president.
The Observer, 'Sayings of the Week', 8 May
1977

315   I have come to regard the law courts not as a
cathedral but rather as a casino.
Richard Ingrams (1937–   ) British editor.
The Guardian, 30 July 1977

316   Whenever you accept our views we shall be in
full agreement with you.
Moshe Dayan (1915–81) Israeli general.
Said to Cyrus Vance during Arab–Israeli
negotiations
The Observer, 'Sayings of the Week', 14 Aug
1977

317   As the Prime Minister put it to me . . . he saw
his role as being that of Moses.
Peter Jay (1937–   ) British economist and
broadcaster.
Referring to a conversation with James
Callaghan
Guardian Weekly, 18 Sept 1977

318   Parliament is the longest running farce in the
West End.
Cyril Smith (1928–   ) British politician.
The Times, 23 Sept 1977

19 Either back us or sack us.
James Callaghan (1912–　) British statesman.
Speech, Labour Party Conference, Brighton, 5 Oct 1977

20 All political lives, unless they are cut off in mid-stream at a happy juncture, end in failure.
Enoch Powell (1912–　) British politician.
Sunday Times, 6 Nov 1977

21 Britain is no longer in the politics of the pendulum, but of the ratchet.
Margaret Thatcher (1925–　) British stateswoman.
Speech, Institute of Public Relations, 1977

22 Much of the world's work, it has been said, is done by men who do not feel quite well. Marx is a case in point.
John Kenneth Galbraith (1908–　) US economist.
The Age of Uncertainty, Ch. 3

1978

23 Like being savaged by a dead sheep.
Denis Healey (1917–　) British politician.
Referring to Geoffrey Howe's attack on his Budget proposals
The Listener, 21 Dec 1978

24 Of course they have, or I wouldn't be sitting here talking to someone like you.
Barbara Cartland (1902–　) British romantic novelist.
When asked in a radio interview whether she thought that British class barriers had broken down
Class (J. Cooper)

25 Not every problem someone has with his girl-friend is necessarily due to the capitalist mode of production.
Herbert Marcuse (1898–1979) German-born US philosopher.
The Listener

26 Labour isn't working.
Caption on a Conservative Party poster, 1978–79

1979

27 I don't think that other people in the world would share the view that there is mounting chaos.
James Callaghan (1912–　) British statesman.
Referring to increasing industrial unrest in Britain; generally misquoted as 'Crisis? What crisis?'
Remark, 10 Jan 1979

28 British management doesn't seem to understand the importance of the human factor.
Charles, Prince of Wales (1948–　) Eldest son of Elizabeth II.
Speech, Parliamentary and Scientific Committee lunch, 21 Feb 1979

29 As a military man who has given half a century of active service, I say in all sincerity that the nuclear arms race has no military purpose. Wars cannot be fought with nuclear weapons; their existence only adds to our perils because of the illusions which they have generated.
Earl Mountbatten of Burma (1900–79) British admiral and statesman.
Speech, Strasbourg, 11 May 1979

330 We are unable to influence events in the way we want because we do not have the power or will to do so.
Nicholas Henderson (1919–　) British diplomat.
Referring to Britain; written on ceasing to be ambassador to France
Letter to the foreign secretary, David Owen, 1979

331 And I don't feel the attraction of the Kennedys at all . . . I don't think they are Christians; they may be Catholics but they are not Christians, in my belief anyway.
Mary McCarthy (1912–89) US novelist.
The Observer, 14 Oct 1979

332 I am a socialist – and I only wish the Labour Party was.
Donald Soper (1903–　) British Methodist minister and writer.
Any Questions, BBC radio, 11 May 1979

333 For us in Russia communism is a dead dog, while, for many people in the West, it is still a living lion.
Alexander Solzhenitsyn (1918–　) Soviet-born novelist.
The Listener, 15 Feb 1979

334 Any woman who understands the problems of running a home will be nearer to understanding the problems of running a country.
Margaret Thatcher (1925–　) British stateswoman.
The Observer, 8 May 1979

335 She is trying to wear the trousers of Winston Churchill.
Leonid Brezhnev (1906–82) Soviet statesman.
Referring to Margaret Thatcher
Speech, 1979

336 Margaret Thatcher is David Owen in drag.
The Rhodesia Herald, 8 Aug 1979

1980

337 It is difficult to go on strike if there is no work in the first place.
Lord George-Brown (1914–85) British statesman.
The Observer, 24 Feb 1980

338 The British civil service . . . is a beautifully designed and effective braking mechanism.
Shirley Williams (1930–　) British politician.
Speech, Royal Institute of Public Administration, 11 Feb 1980

339 She is the Enid Blyton of economics. Nothing
must be allowed to spoil her simple plots.
Richard Holme (1936–) British campaigner
for electoral reform.
Referring to Margaret Thatcher
Speech, Liberal Party Assembly, 10 Sept 1980

340 I love argument, I love debate. I don't expect
anyone just to sit there and agree with me,
that's not their job.
Margaret Thatcher (1925–) British
stateswoman.
The Times, 1980

341 If a woman like Eva Peron with no ideals can
get that far, think how far I can go with all the
ideals that I have.
Margaret Thatcher
The Sunday Times, 1980

342 U-turn if you want to. The lady's not for turning.
Margaret Thatcher
Speech, Conservative Party Conference, 1980

343 She is clearly the best man among them.
Barbara Castle (1910–) British politician.
Referring to Margaret Thatcher
The Castle Diaries

344 You can tell a British workman by his hands.
They are always in his pockets.
Anonymous
Quote Unquote, BBC radio, 26 June 1980

345 Voodoo economics.
George Bush (1924–) US president.
Referring to Ronald Reagan's economic policies
Remark during the 1980 presidential election
campaign

346 Like the sorry tapping of Neville Chamberlain's
umbrella on the cobblestones of Munich.
Ronald Reagan (1911–) US president.
Referring to President Carter's foreign policy

347 Detente is like the race in 'Alice in Wonder-
land' where everyone had to have a prize.
Lord Carrington (1919–) British politician.
Speech, Mar 1980

348 To adopt nuclear disarmament would be akin to
behaving like a virgin in a brothel.
David Penhaligon (1944–86) British
politician.
The Guardian, 1980

349 It could never be a correct justification that, because the whites oppressed us yesterday
when they had power, that the blacks must oppress them today because they have power.
Robert Mugabe (1925–) Zimbabwe
president.
Speech, Mar 1980

350 The soil of our country is destined to be the
scene of the fiercest fight and the sharpest
struggles to rid our continent of the last ves-
tiges of white minority rule.
Nelson Mandela (1918–) South African
lawyer and politician.
Referring to South Africa
Remark, June 1980

351 Men of power have not time to read; yet men
who do not read are unfit for power.
Michael Foot (1913–) British politician and
journalist.
Debts Of Honour

352* The monarchy is the oldest profession in the
world.
Charles, Prince of Wales (1948–) Eldest
son of Elizabeth II.
Attrib.

1981

353 Marxism is like a classical building that followed the Renaissance; beautiful in its way, but
incapable of growth.
Harold Macmillan (1894–1986) British
statesman.
Speech to the Primrose League, 29 Apr 1981

354 If ever there's any emergence of a fourth party
in this country, the task of the Liberal party is
to strangle it at birth.
Cyril Smith (1928–) British politician.
The Guardian, 1981

355 The House of Lords is a model of how to care
for the elderly.
Frank Field (1942–) British politician.
The Observer, 24 May 1981

356 My advice was delicately poised between the
cliché and the indiscretion.
Robert Runcie (1921–) British churchman.
Comment to the press concerning his advice to
the Prince of Wales and Lady Diana Spencer
on their approaching wedding, 13 July 1981

357 I know all about these problems. I grew up in
the thirties with an unemployed father. He
didn't riot. He got on his bike and looked for
work. And he found it!
Norman Tebbit (1931–) British politician.
Speech, Conservative Party Conference, 1981

358 I have never understood why one's affections
must be confined, as once with women, to a
single country.
John Kenneth Galbraith (1908–) US
economist.
A Life in our Times

359 I have always said about Tony that he imma-
tures with age.
Harold Wilson (1916–) British statesman.
Referring to Anthony Wedgwood Benn
The Chariot of Israel

360 A triumph of the embalmer's art.
Gore Vidal (1925–) US novelist.
Referring to Ronald Reagan
The Observer, 26 Apr 1981

1982

361 Giz a job.
Alan Bleasdale (1946–) British playwright
and novelist.
Said by his character Yosser Hughes
Boys From the Blackstuff

362 The British won't fight.
Leopoldo Galtieri (1924–) President of Argentina.
Referring to the Falklands crisis
Remark to Alexander Haig, US Secretary of State, 10 Apr 1982

363 We have suffered the inevitable consequences of a combination of unpreparedness and feeble counsel.
Julian Amery (1919–) British politician.
Referring to Argentina's seizure of the Falkland Islands
Speech, House of Commons, 3 Apr 1982

364 The *Daily Mirror* does not believe that patriotism had to be proved in blood. Especially someone else's blood.
Referring to the Falklands War
The Daily Mirror, Apr 1982

365 I am proud to have a son who died doing the job he loved for the country he loved.
Harry Taylor Father of soldier killed in Falklands war.
Remark, May 1982

366 For the past few months she has been charging about like some bargain-basement Boadicea.
Denis Healey (1917–) British politician.
Referring to Margaret Thatcher
Observer, 'Sayings of the Week', 7 Nov 1982

367 War should belong to the tragic past, to history: it should find no place on humanity's agenda for the future.
John Paul II (Karol Wojtyla; 1920–) Polish pope.
Speech, Coventry, 30 May 1982

368 Let no one expect us to disarm unilaterally. We are not a naive people.
Yuri Andropov (1914–83) Soviet statesman.
Speech, Central Committee of the Soviet Communist Party, 22 Nov 1982

369 In politics, if you want anything said, ask a man; if you want anything done, ask a woman.
Margaret Thatcher (1925–) British stateswoman.
The Changing Anatomy of Britain (Anthony Sampson)

370 Victorian values . . . were the values when our country became great.
Margaret Thatcher
Television interview, 1982

371 We have to believe in free will. We've got no choice.
Isaac Bashevis Singer (1904–91) Polish-born US writer.
The Times, 21 June 1982

1983

72 The longest suicide note in history.
Gerald Kaufman (1930–) British politician.
Referring to the 1983 Labour Party election manifesto
Time of My Life (Denis Healey)

73 Those who prate about Blimpish patriotism in the mode of Margaret Thatcher are also the ones who will take millions off the caring services of this country.
Neil Kinnock (1942–) British politician.
Speech, Labour Party Conference, Brighton, 1983

374 Proportional Representation, I think, is fundamentally counter-democratic.
Neil Kinnock
Marxism Today, 1983

375 It is inconceivable that we could transform this society without a major extension of public ownership.
Neil Kinnock
Marxism Today, 1983

376* She has no imagination and that means no compassion.
Michael Foot (1913–) British politician and journalist.
Referring to Margaret Thatcher
Attrib.

377 I am painted as the greatest little dictator, which is ridiculous — you always take some consultations.
Margaret Thatcher (1925–) British stateswoman.
The Times, 1983

378 Oh. I have got lots of human weaknesses, who hasn't?
Margaret Thatcher
The Times, 1983

379 And what a prize we have to fight for: no less than the chance to banish from our land the dark divisive clouds of Marxist socialism.
Margaret Thatcher
Speech, Scottish Conservative Party Conference, 1983

380 We are the true peace movement.
Margaret Thatcher
The Times, 1983

381 State socialism is totally alien to the British character.
Margaret Thatcher
The Times, 1983

382 Down South where I come from you don't go around hitting too many white keys.
Eubie Blake (1883–1983) US pianist and ragtime composer.
When asked why his compositions contained so many sharps and flats
Attrib.

1984

383 Young people ought not to be idle. It is very bad for them.
Margaret Thatcher (1925–) British stateswoman.
The Times, 1984

384 One nanny said, 'Feed a cold'; she was a neo-Keynesian. Another nanny said, 'Starve a cold'; she was a monetarist.
Harold Macmillan (1894–1986) British statesman.
Maiden speech, House of Lords, 1984

385 Feed the World
Let them know it's Christmas.
Band Aid
Song written to raise money for the relief of famine in Ethiopia
Do They Know It's Christmas?

1985

386 Politics come from man. Mercy, compassion and justice come from God.
Terry Waite (1939–) British churchman.
The Observer, 'Sayings of the Week', 13 Jan 1985

387 I cannot and will not give any undertaking at a time when I, and you, the people, are not free. Your freedom and mine cannot be separated.
Nelson Mandela (1918–) South African lawyer and politician.
Message read by his daughter to a rally in Soweto, 10 Feb 1985

388 We don't want apartheid liberalized. We want it dismantled. You can't improve something that is intrinsically evil.
Desmond Tutu (1931–) South African churchman.
Speech, Mar 1985

389 Go back to your constituencies and prepare for government!
David Steel (1938–) British politician.
Speech, Liberal Party Assembly, 1985

390 The grotesque chaos of a Labour council – a *Labour* council – hiring taxis to scuttle around a city handing out redundancy notices to its own workers.
Neil Kinnock (1942–) British politician.
Referring to Liverpool City Council
Speech, Labour Party Conference, Bournemouth, 1985

391 I'm not interested in the bloody system! Why has he no food? Why is he starving to death?
Bob Geldof (1952–) Irish rock musician.
Interview, Oct 1985

392 Without class differences, England would cease to be the living theatre it is.
Anthony Burgess (John Burgess Wilson; 1917–) British novelist.
Remark, May 1985

393 I think, historically, the term 'Thatcherism' will be seen as a compliment.
Margaret Thatcher (1925–) British stateswoman.
Remark, Oct 1985

1986

394 Democracy is the wholesome and pure air without which a socialist public organisation cannot live a full-blooded life.
Mikhail Gorbachov (1931–) Soviet statesman.
Report to 27th Party Congress, 25 Feb 1986

395 No party has a monopoly over what is right.
Mikhail Gorbachov
Speech, Mar 1986

396 No one can kill Americans and brag about it. No one.
Ronald Reagan (1911–) US president.
Remark, Apr 1986

397 It seems that the British Government sees black people as expendable.
Desmond Tutu (1931–) South African churchman.
Speech, June 1986

398 You won't force South Africans to commit national suicide.
P. W. Botha (1916–) South African president.
Speech, Aug 1986

399 Irish Americans are about as Irish as Black Americans are African.
Bob Geldof (1952–) Irish rock musician.
The Observer, 'Sayings of the Week', 22 Jun 1986

400 Preparing for suicide is not a very intelligent means of defence.
Bruce Kent (1929–) British campaigner for nuclear disarmament.
Speech, Aug 1986

401 The thing I value about Wales and Welsh background is that it has always been a genuinely more classless society than many people present England as being.
Geoffrey Howe (1926–) British politician.
Remark, Nov 1986

402 It was on this issue, the nuclear defence of Britain, on which I left the Labour Party, and on this issue I am prepared to stake my entire political career.
David Owen (1938–) British politician.
Speech, Nov 1986

403 The idea that there is a model Labour voter, a blue-collar council house tenant who belongs to a union and has 2.4 children, a five-year-old car and a holiday in Blackpool, is patronizing and politically immature.
Neil Kinnock (1942–) British politician.
Speech, 1986

404 Selling the family silver.
Harold Macmillan (1894–1986) British statesman.
Referring to privatization of profitable nationalized industries
Speech, House of Lords, 1986

1987

405 I would die for my country ... but I would not let my country die for me.
Neil Kinnock (1942–) British politician.
Speech on nuclear disarmament, 1987

406 She only went to Venice because somebody told her she could walk down the middle of the street.
Neil Kinnock
Referring to Margaret Thatcher, who attended a

meeting in Venice just before the 1987 general election
Speech, Leeds, 9 June 1987

407 Above any other position of eminence, that of Prime Minister is filled by fluke.
Enoch Powell (1912–) British politician.
Remark, Mar 1987

408 I don't mind how much my ministers talk – as long as they do what I say.
Margaret Thatcher (1925–) British stateswoman.
The Times, 1987

409 I am certain that we will win the election with a good majority. Not that I am ever over-confident.
Margaret Thatcher
Evening Standard, 1987

410 I think I have become a bit of an institution – you know, the sort of thing people expect to see around the place.
Margaret Thatcher
Remark, July 1987

411 I am not prepared to accept the economics of a housewife.
Jacques Chirac (1932–) French politician.
Referring to Margaret Thatcher
Remark, July 1987

412 There is no such thing as Society. There are individual men and women, and there are families.
Margaret Thatcher (1925–) British stateswoman.
Woman's Own, 31 Oct 1987

413 I bear no ill-will against those responsible for this. That sort of talk will not bring her back to life. I know there has to be a plan even though we might not understand it. God is good and we shall meet again.
Gordon Wilson Retired businessman.
Speaking of the murder of his daughter, Marie Wilson, in an IRA bombing at the Enniskillen Remembrance Day service, 8 Nov 1987

414 Some comrades apparently find it hard to understand that democracy is just a slogan.
Mikhail Gorbachov (1931–) Soviet statesman.
The Observer, 'Sayings of the Week', 1 Feb 1987

415 Only socialism would put up with it for so long. Capitalism would have gone bankrupt years ago.
Mikhail Gorbachov
Talking of sub-standard workmanship in the Soviet Union
Television documentary, 23 March 1987

416 If freedom were not so economically efficient it certainly wouldn't stand a chance.
Milton Friedman (1912–) US economist.
Remark, Mar 1987

417 The cry of equality pulls everyone down.
Iris Murdoch (1919–) Irish-born British novelist.
Remark, Sept 1987

418 The essence of perestroika lies in the fact that *it unites socialism with democracy* . . . .
Mikhail Gorbachov (1931–) Soviet statesman.
Perestroika

419 Our rockets can find Halley's comet and fly to Venus with amazing accuracy, but side by side with these scientific and technical triumphs is an obvious lack of efficiency in using scientific achievements for economic needs, and many Soviet household appliances are of poor quality.
Mikhail Gorbachov
Perestroika

420 And if the Russian word 'perestroika' has easily entered the international lexicon, this is due to more than just interest in what is going on in the Soviet Union. Now the whole world needs restructuring i.e. progressive development, a fundamental change.
Mikhail Gorbachov
Perestroika

421 Arms control so easily becomes an incantation rather than policy.
Richard Perle US politician.
Remark, Mar 1987

422 People think we do not understand our black and coloured countrymen. But there is a special relationship between us.
Elize Botha Wife of P. W. Botha, South African president.
Remark, May 1987

───────

1988

423 The spread of personal ownership is in harmony with the deepest instincts of the British people. Few changes have done more to create one nation.
Nigel Lawson (1932–) British politician.
Speech, Jan 1988

424 Everything that is most beautiful in Britain has always been in private hands.
Malcolm Rifkind (1946–) British politician.
The Observer, 'Sayings of the Week', 17 Jan 1988

425 It seems that the historic inability in Britain to comprehend Irish feelings and sensitivities still remains.
Charles Haughey (1925–) Irish statesman.
Speech, Feb 1988

426 The United States is the best and fairest and most decent nation on the face of the earth.
George Bush (1924–) US president.
Speech, May 1988

427 His foreparents came to America in immigrant ships. My foreparents came to America in slave ships. But whatever the original ships, we are both in the same boat tonight.
Jesse Jackson (1941–) US politician.
Referring to Michael Dukakis, the Democratic presidential candidate
Speech, Democratic Party Convention, Atlanta, July 1988

428 The Congress will push me to raise taxes and I'll say no, and they'll push, and I'll say no, and they'll push again. And I'll say to them, read my lips, no new taxes.
George Bush (1924–) US president.
Often misquoted as 'Watch my lips'
Speech, Republican Party Convention, New Orleans, Aug 1988

429 The worst fault of the working classes is telling their children they're not going to succeed, saying: "There is a life, but it's not for you".
John Mortimer (1923–) British lawyer and dramatist.
The Observer, 'Sayings of the Week', 5 June 1988

430 Our English countryside is one of the most heavily man-made habitats in Europe. To make it into a green museum would be to belie its whole history.
Nicholas Ridley (1929–) British politician.
Speech, Nov 1988

431 You don't have power if you surrender all your principles — you have office.
Ron Todd (1927–) British trade union leader.
Remark, June 1988

432 The Soviet people want full-blooded and unconditional democracy.
Mikhail Gorbachov (1931–) Soviet statesman.
Speech, July 1988

433 Sanctions are now the only feasible, non-violent way of ending apartheid. The other road to change is covered with blood.
Neil Kinnock (1942–) British politician.
Speech, July 1988

434 You have riches and freedom here but I feel no sense of faith or direction. You have so many computers, why don't you use them in the search for love?
Lech Walesa (1943–) Polish trade unionist and president.
Speech, Dec 1988

1989

435 The author of the Satanic Verses book, which is against Islam, the Prophet and the Koran, and all those involved in its publication who were aware of its content, are sentenced to death. I ask all Moslems to execute them wherever they find them.
Ayatollah Ruholla Khomeini (1900–89) Iranian Shiite Muslim leader.
Referring to *The Satanic Verses* (1988), a novel by Salman Rushdie
Speech, 14 Feb 1989

436 I call upon the intellectual community in this country and abroad to stand up for freedom of the imagination, an issue much larger than my book or indeed my life.
Salman Rushdie (1947–) Indian-born British novelist.
Press statement, 14 Feb 1989

437 Socialism with a human face must function

again for a new generation. We have lived in the darkness for long enough.
Alexander Dubček (1921–92) Czech statesman.
Speech, Wenceslas Square, Prague, 24 Nov 1989

438 Green politics is not about being far left or far right, but far-sighted.
David Icke (1952–) British broadcaster and former Green Party spokesman.
Speech, Green Party Conference, Sept 1989

439 Simply having a convention which says you must not make species extinct does not make a blind bit of difference.
Prince Philip (1921–) The consort of Queen Elizabeth II.
Referring to the UN treaty on world conservation, Mar 1989
The Sunday Correspondent, 31 Dec 1989

1990

440 I have cherished the ideal of a democratic and free society in which all persons live together in harmony and with equal opportunites . . . if needs be, it is an ideal for which I am prepared to die.
Nelson Mandela (1918–) South African lawyer and politician.
Speech, 11 Feb 1990, after his release from prison. Mandela was reiterating his words at his trial in 1964

441 The cricket test — which side do they cheer for?
Norman Tebbit (1931–) British politician.
Referring to immigrants
Los Angeles Times, Apr 1990

442 Britain does not wish to be ruled by a conglomerate in Europe which include Third World nations such as the Greeks and Irish, nor for that matter the Italians and French, whose standards of political morality are not ours, and never will be.
Alfred Sherman (1919–) British journalist.
The Independent, 10 Aug 1990

443 It is rather like sending your opening batsmen to the crease, only for them to find that their bats have been broken before the game by the team captain.
Geoffrey Howe (1926–) British politician.
Referring, on his resignation from the government, to his differences with Margaret Thatcher over European policy; Thatcher had previously likened her position as prime minister to the captaincy of a cricket team
Speech, House of Commons, Nov 1990

444 I fight on, I fight to win.
Margaret Thatcher (1925–) British stateswoman.
Referring to the election for the leadership of the Conservative Party
The Times, 21 Nov 1990

445 Having consulted widely among colleagues I have concluded that the unity of the party and the prospects of victory in a general election

would be better served if I stood down to enable cabinet colleagues to enter the ballot for leadership.
Margaret Thatcher
The Times, 23 Nov 1990

446 It's a funny old world.
Margaret Thatcher
Remark, Nov 1990, after informing the Cabinet of her decision to withdraw from the Conservative Party leadership election

447 When you see the way she was done down, you are bound to think that the people who organized the coup must have had a conscience bypass.
Neil Kinnock (1942–   ) British politician.
Referring to the removal of Margaret Thatcher as leader of the Conservative Party
Attrib. in *The Guardian*, 19 Aug 1991

448 She put back the chance of another woman becoming PM by 50 years – by going over the top, becoming a dictator, having illusions of infallibility, which of course brought her downfall.
Ann Clwyd (1937–   ) British journalist and politician.
Referring to Margaret Thatcher
The Independent, 28 Apr 1992

449 A disease in the family that is never mentioned.
William Trevor (W. T. Cox; 1928–   ) Irish writer.
Referring to the Troubles in Northern Ireland
The Observer, 18 Nov 1990

450 You can call an ecu a pound in Britain. A single currency does not need a single name, but it does need a single value.
Michael Heseltine (1933–   ) British politician.
The Times, 19 Nov 1990

451 This is a day of jubilation, a day of remembrance and gratitude. Our common task now is to establish a new European order.
Hans-Dietrich Genscher (1927–   ) German politician.
Referring to the conclusion of the agreement to reunite East and West Germany
The Independent, 10 Sept 1990

452 The highlights and shadows of our history give us cause to reflect in these days, to reflect on that which was done in the name of Germany. That will not repeat itself.
Hans-Dietrich Genscher
The Independent, 5 Oct 1990

453 I can't remember a time when the world was so strongly together against an action as now.
Margaret Thatcher (1925–   ) British stateswoman.
Referring to the Iraqi invasion of Kuwait
The Times, 7 Aug 1990

454 I will draw a line in the sand.
George Bush (1924–   ) US president.
Referring to the defence of Saudi Arabia by US forces following the Iraqi invasion of Kuwait (1990)
Speech, 1990

455 They will drown in their own blood.
Saddam Hussein (1937–   ) Iraqi dictator.
Referring to the coalition forces assembling in Saudi Arabia to expel the Iraqis from Kuwait
Speech, 1990

456 If Kuwait and Saudi Arabia sold bananas or oranges, the Americans would not go there. They are there because Kuwait is an oil monarchy.
Julius Nyerere (1922–   ) Tanzanian statesman.
Referring to the international response to the Iraqi invasion of Kuwait (Aug 1990)
The Independent, 28 Sept 1990

1991

457 The mother of battles will be our battle of victory and martyrdom.
Saddam Hussein (1937–   ) Iraqi dictator.
Referring to the imminent Gulf War
Speech, 1991

458 Our goal is not the conquest of Iraq. It is the liberation of Kuwait.
George Bush (1924–   ) US president.
Referring to the Gulf War (1991)
The Times, 16 Jan 1991

459 War is never cheap or easy.
George Bush
Referring to the Gulf War (1991)
The Observer, 20 Jan 1991

460 A very great man once said you should love your enemies and that's not a bad piece of advice. We can love them but, by God, that doesn't mean we're not going to fight them.
Norman Schwarzkopf (1934–   ) US general.
Referring to the Gulf War (1991)
The Observer, 3 Feb 1991

461 We're going around, over, through, on top, underneath.
Norman Schwarzkopf
Describing his tactics for attacking the Iraqi army
Press conference, 24 Feb 1991

462 The war wasn't fought about democracy in Kuwait.
George Bush (1924–   ) US president.
Referring to the Gulf War (1991)
The Observer, 14 July 1991

463 This is a historic moment. Russia has entered the family of civilized nations.
Gavriil Popov (1936–   ) Russian economist and politician.
Remark on his election as the first elected mayor of Moscow
The Observer, 16 June 1991

464 The Communist Party, the KGB, and the army – the three ugly sisters – are the instruments of control in the Soviet Union.
Douglas Hurd (1930–   ) British politician.
Referring to an abortive coup in the Soviet Union (Aug 1991)
The Observer, 25 Aug 1991

465 This is a ridiculous country. It can't do anything properly, not even carry out a coup.
Igor Zakharov Russian journalist.
Referring to an abortive coup in the Soviet Union (Aug 1991)
The Observer, 25 Aug 1991

466 Rising unemployment and the recession have been the price that we've had to pay to get inflation down: that is a price well worth paying.
Norman Lamont (1942–) British politician.
The Observer, 19 May 1991

467 People are not willing to be governed by those who do not speak their language.
Norman Tebbit (1931–) British politician.
The Observer, 24 Nov 1991

468 If we had spent £167 million on condoms we wouldn't have had these problems in the first place.
Nicholas Fairbairn (1933–) British politician.
Referring to food aid for Africa
The Observer, 12 May 1991

1992

469 The region is undergoing ethnic cleansing.
Referring to Bosnia-Hercegovina
Serbian radio, reported in *The Times*, 21 May 1992

470 We all know the Iron Curtain has been demolished, but in its place an economic and social curtain might come down.
József Antall (1932–) Hungarian statesman.
The Independent, 29 Oct 1992

471 Reforms mean you can have a big car if you're in the mafia. Reforms mean hard-currency shops for a handful of people who have it. I'm a factory worker. I'll never have a big car or dollars, so reform for me will be when the milk isn't sour, that's all.
Remark by an anonymous Russian woman while queuing for food, reported in *The Times*, 25 Nov 1992

472 Today we have closed the book on apartheid.
F. W. de Klerk (1936–) South African president.
Remark after a referendum of white South Africans had endorsed his government's reform programme
The Independent, 19 Mar 1992

473 That's only fair – it is, after all, their turn.
Paddy Ashdown (Jeremy John Durham A.; 1941–) British politician.
Remark, Mar 1992, on hearing that David Owen had announced his support for the Conservative Party at the coming general election

474 I think Essex Man will vote for a Conservative government.
Margaret Thatcher (1925–) British stateswoman.
Referring to the imminent British general election
The Independent, 2 Apr 1992

475 I'm feeling lucky.
John Major (1943–) British statesman.
Referring to the imminent British general election
The Times, 9 Apr 1992

476 Who am I? Why am I here?
James Stockdale US admiral.
Opening remarks, Oct 1992, in a televised debate for vice-presidential candidates in the 1992 US presidential election. Stockdale was the running mate of H. Ross Perot.

477 My dog Millie knows more about foreign policy than these two bozos.
George Bush (1924–) US president.
Referring to Bill Clinton and Al Gore, his Democratic opponents in the 1992 US presidential election
Speech, Oct 1992

478 It must have been Millie that taught him to roll over and play dead.
Al Gore (1948–) US politician.
Reply to the above, Oct 1992

479 If you'll be my voice today, I'll be yours for the next four years.
Bill Clinton (1946–) US president.
Speech, 3 Nov 1992 (polling day in the 1992 US presidential election), while suffering from laryngitis

480 1992 is not a year I shall look back on with undiluted pleasure. In the words of one of my more sympathetic correspondents, it has turned out to be an 'annus horribilis'.
Elizabeth II (1926–) Queen of the United Kingdom.
Alluding to *Annus Mirabilis* (1667), a poem by John Dryden that celebrated the events of 1665–66
Speech, Guildhall, 24 Nov 1992

Attitudes

Art, Literature, and Music

1946

481 To be a poet is a condition rather than a profession.
Robert Graves (1895–1985) British poet and novelist.
Horizon

482* Painting is a blind man's profession. He paints not what he sees, but what he feels, what he tells himself about what he has seen.
Pablo Picasso (1881–1973) Spanish painter.
Journals (Jean Cocteau), 'Childhood'

1947

483 A work of art has an author and yet, when it is

perfect, it has something which is anonymous about it.
Simone Weil (1909–43) French philosopher.
Gravity and Grace

484   Imagination and fiction make up more than three quarters of our real life.
Simone Weil
Gravity and Grace

1948

485   The idea that it is necessary to go to a university in order to become a successful writer, or even a man or woman of letters (which is by no means the same thing), is one of those phantasies that surround authorship.
Vera Brittain (1893–1970) British writer and feminist.
On Being an Author, Ch. 2

486   The metaphor is probably the most fertile power possessed by man.
José Ortega y Gasset (1883–1955) Spanish philosopher.
The Dehumanization of Art

1949

487   Art is the only thing that can go on mattering once it has stopped hurting.
Elizabeth Bowen (1899–1973) Irish novelist.
The Heat of the Day, Ch. 16

488   Authors are easy to get on with – if you're fond of children.
Michael Joseph (1897–1958) British publisher.
The Observer, 1949

1950s

489   It's either easy or impossible.
Salvador Dali (1904–89) Spanish painter.
Reply when asked if he found it hard to paint a picture
Attrib.

1950

490   Poetry is the language in which man explores his own amazement.
Christopher Fry (1907–   ) British dramatist.
Time, 3 Apr 1950

491   The poet gives us his essence, but prose takes the mould of the body and mind entire.
Virginia Woolf (1882–1941) British novelist.
The Captain's Death Bed, 'Reading'

1951

492   Photography can never grow up if it imitates some other medium. It has to walk alone; it has to be itself.
Berenice Abbott (1898–1991) US photographer.
Infinity, 'It Has to Walk Alone'

493   A writer's ambition should be to trade a hun-

dred contemporary readers for ten readers in ten years' time and for one reader in a hundred years' time.
Arthur Koestler (1905–83) Hungarian-born British writer.
New York Times Book Review, 1 Apr 1951

1952

494   We participate in a tragedy; at a comedy we only look.
Aldous Huxley (1894–1964) British novelist and essayist.
The Devils of Loudon, Ch. 11

495   If people dug up the remains of this civilization a thousand years hence, and found Epstein's statues and that man Ellis, they would think we were just savages.
Doris Lessing (1919–   ) British novelist.
Martha Quest, Pt. I, Ch. 1

496   In recommending a book to a friend the less said the better. The moment you praise a book too highly you awaken resistance in your listener.
Henry Miller (1891–1980) US novelist.
The Books In My Life

497   These poems, with all their crudities, doubts, and confusions, are written for the love of Man and in praise of God, and I'd be a damn' fool if they weren't.
Dylan Thomas (1914–53) Welsh poet.
Collected Poems, Note

1953

498   Literature is the orchestration of platitudes.
Thornton Wilder (1897–1975) US novelist and dramatist.
Time

1954

499   My poems are hymns of praise to the glory of life.
Edith Sitwell (1887–1964) British poet and writer.
Collected Poems, 'Some Notes on My Poetry'

1955

500*   I do not know whether he draws a line himself. But I assume that his is the direction . . . It makes Disney the most significant figure in graphic art since Leonardo.
David Low (1871–1963) New-Zealand-born newspaper cartoonist.
Walt Disney (R. Schickel), Ch. 20

501   The public doesn't want new music: the main thing it demands of a composer is that he be dead.
Arthur Honegger (1892–1955) French composer.
Attrib.

502   I do not mind what language an opera is sung

in so long as it is a language I don't
understand.
Edward Appleton (1892–1965) British
physicist.
The Observer, 'Sayings of the Week,' 28 Aug
1955

1956

503 Why should people go out and pay money to
see bad films when they can stay at home and
see bad television for nothing?
Samuel Goldwyn (Samuel Goldfish; 1882–
1974) Polish-born US film producer.
The Observer, 'Sayings of the Week', 9 Sept
1956

504 Thanks to words, we have been able to rise
above the brutes; and thanks to words, we have
often sunk to the level of the demons.
Aldous Huxley (1894–1964) British novelist
and essayist.
Adonis and the Alphabet of the demons

1957

505 Farce is the essential theatre. Farce refined becomes high comedy: farce brutalized becomes
tragedy.
Gordon Craig (1872–1966) British actor.
The Story of my Days

506 A good many inconveniences attend play-going
in any large city, but the greatest of them is
usually the play itself.
Kenneth Tynan (1927–80) British theatre
critic.
New York Herald Tribune

507 The poet is the priest of the invisible.
Wallace Stevens (1879–1955) US poet.
Opus Posthumous, 'Adagio'

508 ...any authentic work of art must start an argument between the artist and his audience.
Rebecca West (Cicely Isabel Fairfield; 1892–
1983) British novelist and journalist.
The Court and the Castle, Pt. I, Ch. 1

1958

509 The notes I handle no better than many pia-
nists. But the pauses between the notes – ah,
that is where the art resides.
Artur Schnabel (1882–1951) Austrian concert pianist.
Chicago Daily News, 11 June 1958

1960s

510 In England, pop art and fine art stand resolutely
back to back.
Colin MacInnes (1914–76) British novelist.
England, Half English, 'Pop Songs and Teenagers'

511 Since Mozart's day composers have learned

the art of making music throatily and palpitat-
ingly sexual.
Aldous Huxley (1894–1964) British novelist
and essayist.
Along the Road, 'Popular music'

512 Get stewed:
Books are a load of crap.
Philip Larkin (1922–85) British poet.
A Study of Reading Habits

1960

513 Music was invented to confirm human
loneliness.
Lawrence Durrell (1912–90) British novelist.
Clea

514 You may think that one of the ways in which
you can test this book, and test it from the
most liberal outlook, is to ask yourselves the
question when you have read it through:
'Would you approve of your young sons and
daughters – because girls can read as well as
boys – reading this book?' Is it a book you
would have lying around in your own house?
Is it a book you would even wish your wife or
your servants to read?
Mervyn Griffith-Jones (1909–78) British
lawyer.
As counsel for the prosecution in the *Lady Chatterley's Lover* trial

515 More to the point, would you allow your
gamekeeper to read it?
Anonymous
Referring to Mervyn Griffiths-Jones' remark during the *Lady Chatterley's Lover* trial

516 *Lady Chatterley's Lover* is a book that all Chris-
tians might read with profit.
John Robinson (1919–83) Bishop of
Woolwich.
Said in the court case against Penguin Books
Attrib.

1961

517 A novel is a static thing that one moves
through; a play is a dynamic thing that moves
past one.
Kenneth Tynan (1927–80) British theatre
critic.
Curtains

518 William Congreve is the only sophisticated
playwright England has produced; and like
Shaw, Sheridan, and Wilde, his nearest rivals,
he was brought up in Ireland.
Kenneth Tynan
Curtains, 'The Way of the World'

519 No good opera plot can be sensible, for people
do not sing when they are feeling sensible.
W. H. Auden (1907–73) British poet.
Time, 29 Dec 1961

520 My music is best understood by children and animals.
Igor Stravinsky (1882–1971) Russian-born US composer.
The Observer, 'Sayings of the Week', 8 Oct 1961

1962

521 You know, I go to the theatre to be entertained . . . I don't want to see plays about rape, sodomy and drug addiction . . . I can get all that at home.
Peter Cook (1937–) British writer and entertainer.
The Observer, caption to cartoon, 8 July 1962

522 If Botticelli were alive today he'd be working for *Vogue*.
Peter Ustinov (1921–) British actor.
Remark, Oct 1962

1963

523 In free society art is not a weapon . . . Artists are not engineers of the soul.
John Fitzgerald Kennedy (1917–63) US statesman.
Address at Dedication of the Robert Frost Library, 26 Oct 1963

524 When power narrows the areas of man's concern, poetry reminds him of the richness and diversity of his existence.
John Fitzgerald Kennedy
Address at Dedication of the Robert Frost Library, 26 Oct 1963

525 The reason why Absurdist plays take place in No Man's Land with only two characters is primarily financial.
Arthur Adamov (1908–70) Russian-born French dramatist.
Said at the Edinburgh International Drama Conference, 13 Sept 1963

526 I wanted a play that would paint the full face of sensuality, rebellion and revivalism. In South Wales these three phenomena have played second fiddle only to the Rugby Union which is a distillation of all three.
Gwyn Thomas (1913–81) British writer.
Jackie the Jumper (Introduction), 'Plays and Players'

1964

527 The British love permanence more than they love beauty.
Hugh Casson (1910–) British architect.
The Observer, 'Sayings of the Week', 14 June 1964

528 The remarkable thing about Shakespeare is that he is really very good – in spite of all the people who say he is very good.
Robert Graves (1895–1985) British poet and novelist.
Remark, Dec 1964

1965

529 Literature is mostly about having sex and not much about having children; life is the other way round.
David Lodge (1935–) British author.
The British Museum is Falling Down, Ch. 4

1966

530 Poetry is as much a part of the universe as mathematics and physics. It is not a cleverer device or recreation, unless the Eternal is clever.
Edmund Blunden (1896–1974) British poet.
Speech on his election as Professor of Poetry at Oxford University, 1966

531 I put the words down and push them a bit.
Evelyn Waugh (1903–66) British novelist.
Obituary, *New York Times*, 11 Apr 1966

532 We're more popular than Jesus Christ now. I don't know which will go first. Rock and roll or Christianity.
John Lennon (1940–80) British rock musician.
Interview, *Evening Standard*, 4 Mar 1966

1968

533 Musicians don't retire; they stop when there's no more music in them.
Louis Armstrong (1900–71) US jazz trumpeter.
The Observer, 'Sayings of the Week', 21 Apr 1968

534 The novel being dead, there is no point to writing made-up stories. Look at the French who will not and the Americans who cannot.
Gore Vidal (1925–) US novelist.
Myra Breckinridge, Ch. 2

1969

535 One cannot assess in terms of cash or exports and imports an imponderable thing like the turn of a lane or an inn or a church tower or a familiar skyline.
John Betjeman (1906–84) British poet.
On siting a new London airport at Wing
Remark, July 1969

536 We all write poems; it is simply that poets are the ones who write in words.
John Fowles (1926–) British novelist.
The French Lieutenant's Woman, Ch. 19

537 A novelist who writes nothing for 10 years finds his reputation rising. Because I keep on producing books they say there must be something wrong with this fellow.
J. B. Priestley (1894–1984) British novelist.
Remark, Sept 1969

538 No regime has ever loved great writers, only minor ones.
Alexander Solzhenitsyn (1918–) Soviet-born novelist.
The First Circle, Ch. 57

539 Their teacher had advised them not to read Tol-

stoy novels, because they were very long and would easily confuse the clear ideas which they had learned from reading critical studies of him.
Alexander Solzhenitsyn
The First Circle, Ch. 40

1970s

540 The basic difference between classical music and jazz is that in the former the music is always greater than its performance – whereas the way jazz is performed is always more important than what is being played.
André Previn (1929–) German-born conductor.
An Encyclopedia of Quotations about Music (Nat Shapiro)

1970

541 I'd say award winning plays are written only for the critics.
Lew Grade (Lewis Winogradsky; 1906–) British film and television producer.
The Observer, 'Sayings of the Week', 18 Oct 1970

1971

542 Shakespeare – the nearest thing in incarnation to the eye of God.
Laurence Olivier (1907–89) British actor.
Kenneth Harris Talking To, 'Sir Laurence Olivier' (Kenneth Harris)

1972

543 I have nothing to say, I am saying it, and that is poetry.
John Cage (1912–92) US composer.
The Sunday Times (quoted by Cyril Connolly), 10 Sept 1972

544 No one really understood music unless he was a scientist, her father had declared, and not just a scientist, either, oh, no, only the real ones, the theoreticians, whose language was mathematics.
Pearl Buck (1892–1973) US novelist.
The Goddess Abides, Pt. I

545 Skill without imagination is craftsmanship and gives us many useful objects such as wickerwork picnic baskets. Imagination without skill gives us modern art.
Tom Stoppard (1937–) Czech-born British dramatist.
Artist Descending a Staircase

1973

546 I paint objects as I think them, not as I see them.
Pablo Picasso (1881–1973) Spanish painter.
Attrib.

547 The object of art is to give life a shape.
Jean Anouilh (1910–87) French dramatist.
The Rehearsal

548 Rehearsing a play is making the word flesh. Publishing a play is reversing the process.
Peter Shaffer (1926–) British dramatist.
Equus, Note

549 People sometimes divide others into those you laugh at and those you laugh with. The young Auden was someone you could laugh-at-with.
Stephen Spender (1909–) British poet.
Address, W. H. Auden's memorial service, Oxford, 27 Oct 1973

1974

550 All art deals with the absurd and aims at the simple. Good art speaks truth, indeed *is* truth, perhaps the only truth.
Iris Murdoch (1919–) Irish-born British novelist.
The Black Prince, 'Bradley Pearson's Foreword'

551 This music won't do. There's not enough sarcasm in it.
Samuel Goldwyn (Samuel Goldfish; 1882–1974) Polish-born US film producer.
Attrib.

552 Please write music like Wagner, only louder.
Samuel Goldwyn
Instructions to composer for movie score
Attrib.

553 It's only rock 'n' roll
But I like it.
The Rolling Stones British rock band.
It's Only Rock 'n' Roll

554 Writing is like getting married. One should never commit oneself until one is amazed at one's luck.
Iris Murdoch (1919–) Irish-born British novelist.
The Black Prince, 'Bradley Pearson's Foreword'

555 Depending upon shock tactics is easy, whereas writing a good play is difficult. Pubic hair is no substitute for wit.
J. B. Priestley (1894–1984) British novelist.
Outcries and Asides

556 The greater part of critics are parasites, who, if nothing had been written, would find nothing to write.
J. B. Priestley
Outcries and Asides

557 Too many people in the modern world view poetry as a luxury, not a necessity like petrol. But to me it's the oil of life.
John Betjeman (1906–84) British poet.
The Observer, 'Sayings of the Year', 1974

1975

558 Walt Whitman who laid end to end words never

seen in each other's company before outside of a dictionary.
David Lodge (1935–) British author.
Changing Places, Ch. 5

559   I never deliberately set out to shock, but when people don't walk out of my plays I think there is something wrong.
John Osborne (1929–) British dramatist.
Remark, Jan 1975

560   People think that because a novel's invented, it isn't true. Exactly the reverse is the case. Biography and memoirs can never be wholly true, since they cannot include every conceivable circumstance of what happened. The novel can do that.
Anthony Powell (1905–) British novelist.
A Dance to the Music of Time: Hearing Secret Harmonies, Ch. 3

1976

561   Music creates order out of chaos; for rhythm imposes unanimity upon the divergent, melody imposes continuity upon the disjointed, and harmony imposes compatibility upon the incongruous.
Yehudi Menuhin (1916–) US-born British violinist.
The Sunday Times, 10 Oct 1976

562   Poetry is to prose as dancing is to walking.
John Wain (1925–) British novelist and poet.
Talk, BBC radio, 13 Jan 1976

1977

563   We were put to Dickens as children but it never quite took. That unremitting humanity soon had me cheesed off.
Alan Bennett (1934–) British playwright.
The Old Country, II

564   There are many reasons why novelists write, but they all have one thing in common – a need to create an alternative world.
John Fowles (1926–) British novelist.
The Sunday Times Magazine, 2 Oct 1977

565   Asking a working writer what he thinks about critics is like asking a lamp-post how it feels about dogs.
Christopher Hampton (1946–) British writer and dramatist.
The Sunday Times Magazine, 16 Oct 1977

566   It's not a writer's business to hold opinions.
W. B. Yeats (1865–1939) Irish poet.
Speaking to playwright, Denis Johnston
The Guardian, 5 May 1977

567   A photograph is not only an image (as a painting is an image), an interpretation of the real; it is also a trace, something directly stencilled off the real, like a footprint or a death mask.
Susan Sontag (1933–) US novelist and essayist.
On Photography

568   I doubt that art needed Ruskin any more than a moving train needs one of its passengers to shove it.
Tom Stoppard (1937–) Czech-born British dramatist.
Times Literary Supplement, 3 June 1977

1978

569   It is not possible for a poet to be a professional. Poetry is essentially an amateur activity.
Lord Barrington (1908–) British barrister and peer.
Speech, House of Lords, 23 Nov 1978

570   The cliché is dead poetry. English, being the language of an imaginative race, abounds in clichés, so that English literature is always in danger of being poisoned by its own secretions.
Gerald Brenan (Edward Fitzgerald Brenan; 1894–1987) British writer.
Thoughts in a Dry Season, 'Literature'

571   Miller is not really a writer but a non-stop talker to whom someone has given a typewriter.
Gerald Brenan
Referring to Henry Miller
Thoughts in a Dry Season, 'Literature'

572   Far too many relied on the classic formula of a beginning, a muddle, and an end.
Philip Larkin (1922–85) British poet.
Referring to modern novels
New Fiction, 15 (Jan 1978)

573   Tragedy is if I cut my finger. Comedy is if I walk into an open sewer and die.
Mel Brooks (Melvyn Kaminsky; 1926–) US film director.
The New Yorker, 30 Oct 1978

1980

574   You see, our fingers are circumcised, which gives it a very good dexterity, you know, particularly in the pinky.
Itzhak Perlman (1945–) Israeli violinist.
Responding to an observation that many great violinists are Jewish
Close Encounters (M. Wallace)

1983

575   What has happened to architecture since the second world war that the only passers-by who can contemplate it without pain are those equipped with a white stick and a dog?
Bernard Levin (1928–) British journalist.
The Times, 1983 can contemplate it . . . with a white stick and a dog

1985

576   Everybody writes a book too many.
Mordecai Richler (1931–) Canadian novelist.
The Observer, 'Sayings of the Week', 9 Jan 1985

1986

577   Like a carbuncle on the face of an old and valued friend.
Charles, Prince of Wales (1948–) Eldest son of Elizabeth II.
Referring to a proposed modern extension to the National Gallery
Speech, 1986

1987

578   ...a jostling scrum of office buildings so mediocre that the only way you ever remember them is by the frustration they induce – like a basketball team standing shoulder to shoulder between you and the Mona Lisa.
Charles, Prince of Wales
Referring to the buildings surrounding St Paul's Cathedral
Speech, London, 1 Dec 1987

579   You have to give this much to the Luftwaffe – when it knocked down our buildings it did not replace them with anything more offensive than rubble. We did that.
Charles, Prince of Wales
The Observer, 'Sayings of the Week', 6 Dec 1987

580   The shelf life of the modern hardback writer is somewhere between the milk and the yoghurt.
John Mortimer (1923–) British lawyer and dramatist.
The Observer, 28 June 1987

1988

581   Art has to move you and design does not, unless it's a good design for a bus.
David Hockney (1937–) British painter, draughtsman, and printmaker.
Remark, Oct 1988

Daily Life

1959

582   Fings Ain't Wot They Used T'Be.
Frank Norman (1931–80) British dramatist and broadcaster.
Title of musical

1960

583   I read the newspaper avidly. It is my one form of continuous fiction.
Aneurin Bevan (1897–1960) British politician.
Remark, Apr 1960

1961

584   A good newspaper, I suppose, is a nation talking to itself.
Arthur Miller (1915–) US dramatist.
Remark, Nov 1961

1962

585   Over increasingly large areas of the United States, spring now comes unheralded by the return of the birds, and the early mornings are strangely silent where once they were filled with the beauty of bird song.
Rachel Carson (1907–64) US biologist.
The Silent Spring

586   It must be generations since anyone but highbrows lived in this cottage...I imagine most of the agricultural labourers round here commute from London.
Anthony Powell (1905–) British novelist.
A Dance to the Music of Time: The Kindly Ones, Ch. 2

587   I will lift up mine eyes unto the pills...It is an age of pills.
Malcolm Muggeridge (1903–90) British writer and editor.
The New Statesman, 3 Aug 1962

588   They're all made out of ticky-tacky, and they all look just the same.
Malvina Reynolds (1900–78) US folksinger and songwriter.
Little Boxes (song describing a housing scheme in the hills south of San Francisco)

1963

589   On the whole I would not say that our Press is obscene. I would say that it trembles on the brink of obscenity.
Lord Longford (1905–) British politician and social reformer.
The Observer, 'Sayings of the Year', 1963

1964

590   The car has become the carapace, the protective and aggressive shell, of urban and suburban man.
Marshall McLuhan (1911–81) Canadian sociologist.
Understanding Media, Ch. 22

1969

591   Clearly, then, the city is not a concrete jungle, it is a human zoo.
Desmond Morris (1928–) British biologist and writer.
The Human Zoo, Introduction

1971

592   Television is an invention that permits you to be entertained in your living room by people you wouldn't have in your home.
David Frost (1939–) British television personality.
Attrib., CBS television, 1971 home

1975

593   The British, he thought, must be gluttons for

satire: even the weather forecast seemed to be some kind of spoof, predicting every possible combination of weather for the next twenty-four hours without actually committing itself to anything specific.
David Lodge (1935–) British author.
Changing Places, Ch. 2

1976

594   It's just like having a licence to print your own money.
Lord Thomson of Fleet (1894–1976) Canadian-born British newspaper proprietor.
Referring to commercial television
Attrib.

1981

595   Football isn't a matter of life and death – it's much more important than that.
Bill Shankly (1914–81) British football manager.
Attrib.

596   *Punch* – the official journal of dentists' waiting rooms.
The Times, 7 Oct 1981

1986

597   I answer 20,000 letters a year and so many couples are having problems because they are not getting the right proteins and vitamins.
Barbara Cartland (1902–) British romantic novelist.
The Observer, 'Sayings of the Week', 31 Aug 1986

598   Blood sport is brought to its ultimate refine-ment in the gossip columns.
Bernard Ingham (1932–) British journalist.
Remark, Dec 1986

599   Many children are suffering from muesli-belt malnutrition.
Professor Vincent Marks British nutritionist.
Remark, June 1986

1988

600   If someone asks for a soft drink at a party, we no longer think he is a wimp.
Edwina Currie (1946–) British politician.
Speech, Dec 1988

Death

1952

601   When you're between any sort of devil and the deep blue sea, the deep blue sea sometimes looks very inviting.
Terence Rattigan (1911–77) British dramatist.
The Deep Blue Sea

602   Do not go gentle into that good night,
Old age should burn and rave at close of day;
Rage, rage, against the dying of the light.
Dylan Thomas (1914–53) Welsh poet.
Do not go gentle into that good night

1959

603   It is. But not as hard as farce.
Edmund Gwenn (1875–1959) British actor.
On his deathbed, in reply to the comment 'It must be very hard'
Time, 30 Jan 1984

1964

604   I am sick of this way of life. The weariness and sadness of old age make it intolerable. I have walked with death in hand, and death's own hand is warmer than my own. I don't wish to live any longer.
W. Somerset Maugham (1874–1965) British novelist.
Said on his ninetieth birthday
Familiar Medical Quotations (M. B. Strauss)

1969

605   I do really think that death will be marvellous . . . If there wasn't death, I think you couldn't go on.
Stevie Smith (Florence Margaret Smith; 1902–71) British poet.
The Observer, 9 Nov 1969

1972

606   Few men of action have been able to make a graceful exit at the appropriate time.
Malcolm Muggeridge (1903–90) British writer and editor.
Chronicles Of Wasted Time

1976

607   It's not that I'm afraid to die. I just don't want to be there when it happens.
Woody Allen (Allen Stewart Konigsberg; 1935–) US film actor.
Without Feathers, 'Death (A Play)'

1978

608   It is important what a man still plans at the end. It shows the measure of injustice in his death.
Elias Canetti (1905–) Bulgarian-born novelist.
The Human Province

Education, Knowledge, and Learning

1947

609 If you educate a man you educate a person, but if you educate a woman you educate a family.
Ruby Manikan Indian Church leader.
The Observer, 'Sayings of the Week', 30 Mar 1947

1949

610 Most people are such fools that it is really no great compliment to say that a man is above the average.
W. Somerset Maugham (1874–1965) British novelist.
A Writer's Notebook

611 We teachers can only help the work going on, as servants wait upon a master.
Maria Montessori (1870–1952) Italian doctor and educationalist.
The Absorbent Mind

612 And if education is always to be conceived along the same antiquated lines of a mere transmission of knowledge, there is little to be hoped from it in the bettering of man's future. For what is the use of transmitting knowledge if the individual's total development lags behind?
Maria Montessori
The Absorbent Mind

1951

613 Spoon feeding in the long run teaches us nothing but the shape of the spoon.
E. M. Forster (1879–1970) British novelist.
Remark, Oct 1951

614 There was never an age in which useless knowledge was more important than in our own.
Cyril Joad (1891–1953) British philosopher, writer, and broadcaster.
Remark, Sept 1951

1952

615 Culture is an instrument wielded by professors to manufacture professors, who when their turn comes will manufacture professors.
Simone Weil (1909–43) French philosopher.
The Need for Roots

1953

616 Our principal writers have nearly all been fortunate in escaping regular education.
Hugh MacDiarmid (Christopher Murray Grieve; 1892–1978) Scottish poet.
The Observer, 'Sayings of the Week', 29 Mar 1953

617 A philosopher of imposing stature doesn't think in a vacuum. Even his most abstract ideas are, to some extent, conditioned by what is or what is not known in the time when he lives.
A. N. Whitehead (1861–1947) British philosopher.
Dialogues

1957

618 Letting a hundred flowers blossom and a hundred schools of thought contend is the policy for promoting the progress of the arts and the sciences and a flourishing socialist culture in our land.
Mao Tse-Tung (1893–1976) Chinese communist leader.
Speech, Peking, 27 Feb 1957

1958

619 It is the tragedy of the world that no one knows what he doesn't know – and the less a man knows, the more sure he is that he knows everything.
Joyce Cary (1888–1957) British novelist.
Art and Reality

1959

620 The intellectuals' chief cause of anguish are one another's works.
Jacques Barzun (1907–) US writer.
The House of Intellect

1960s

621 Our knowledge can only be finite, while our ignorance must necessarily be infinite.
Karl Popper (1902–) Austrian-born British philosopher.
Conjectures and Refutations

1960

622 What was once thought can never be unthought.
Friedrich Dürrenmatt (1921–) Swiss writer.
The Physicists

1961

623 To me education is a leading out of what is already there in the pupil's soul. To Miss Mackay it is a putting in of something that is not there, and that is not what I call education, I call it intrusion.
Muriel Spark (1918–) British novelist.
The Prime of Miss Jean Brodie, Ch. 2

624 Art and religion first; then philosophy; lastly science. That is the order of the great subjects of life, that's their order of importance.
Muriel Spark
The Prime of Miss Jean Brodie, Ch. 2

1962

625 The greater our knowledge increases the more our ignorance unfolds.
John Fitzgerald Kennedy (1917–63) US statesman.
Speech, Rice University, 12 Sept 1962

626 There are no new truths, but only truths that have not been recognized by those who have perceived them without noticing.
Mary McCarthy (1912–89) US novelist.
On the Contrary

1963

627 Nothing in the world is more dangerous than sincere ignorance and conscientious stupidity.
Martin Luther King (1929–68) US civil-rights leader.
Strength To Love

628 It is a good morning exercise for a research scientist to discard a pet hypothesis every day before breakfast. It keeps him young.
Konrad Lorenz (1903–89) Austrian zoologist.
On Aggression, Ch. 2

1964

629 Education is what survives when what has been learnt has been forgotten.
B. F. Skinner (1904–90) US psychologist.
New Scientist, 21 May 1964, 'Education in 1984'

1966

630 The possession of a book becomes a substitute for reading it.
Anthony Burgess (John Burgess Wilson; 1917–) British novelist.
New York Times Book Review

1967

631 The average man's opinions are much less foolish than they would be if he thought for himself.
Bertrand Russell (1872–1970) British philosopher.
Autobiography

1969

632 I have yet to see any problem, however complicated, which, when looked at in the right way, did not become still more complicated.
Poul Anderson
New Scientist, 1969

633 . . . that is what learning is. You suddenly understand something you've understood all your life, but in a new way.
Doris Lessing (1919–) British novelist.
The Four-Gated City

1970

634 You know very well that unless you're a scientist, it's much more important for a theory to be shapely, than for it to be true.
Christopher Hampton (1946–) British writer and dramatist.
The Philanthropist, Sc. 1

1974

635 Every intellectual attitude is latently political.
Thomas Mann (1875–1955) German novelist.
The Observer, 11 Aug 1974

636 For hundreds of pages the closely-reasoned arguments unroll, axioms and theorems interlock. And what remains with us in the end? A general sense that the world can be expressed in closely-reasoned arguments, in interlocking axioms and theorems.
Michael Frayn (1933–) British journalist and writer.
Constructions

637 That's the classical mind at work, runs fine inside but looks dingy on the surface.
Robert T. Pirsig (1928–) US writer.
Zen and the Art of Motorcycle Maintenance, Pt. III, Ch. 25

1975

638 Four times, under our educational rules, the human pack is shuffled and cut — at eleven-plus, sixteen-plus, eighteen-plus and twenty-plus — and happy is he who comes top of the deck on each occasion, but especially the last. This is called Finals, the very name of which implies that nothing of importance can happen after it. The British postgraduate student is a lonely forlorn soul . . . for whom nothing has been real since the Big Push.
David Lodge (1935–) British author.
Changing Places, Ch. 1

639 It is never wise to try to appear to be more clever than you are. It is sometimes wise to appear slightly less so.
William Whitelaw (1918–) British politician.
The Observer, 'Sayings of the Year', 1975

1976

640 A theory can be proved by experiment; but no path leads from experiment to the birth of a theory.
Albert Einstein (1879–1955) German-born US physicist.
The Sunday Times, 18 July 1976

641 Common sense is the collection of prejudices acquired by age eighteen.
Albert Einstein
Scientific American, Feb 1976

1977

642 To read too many books is harmful.
Mao Tse-Tung (1893–1976) Chinese communist leader.
The New Yorker, 7 Mar 1977

1978

643 Intellectuals are people who believe that ideas are of more importance than values. That is to say, their own ideas and other people's values.
Gerald Brenan (Edward Fitzgerald Brenan; 1894–1987) British writer.
Thoughts in a Dry Season, 'Life'

644 The great writers of aphorisms read as if they had all known each other well.
Elias Canetti (1905–) Bulgarian-born novelist.
The Human Province

1979

645 The ratio of literacy to illiteracy is constant, but nowadays the illiterates can read and write.
Alberto Moravia (Alberto Pincherle; 1907–90) Italian novelist.
The Observer, 14 Oct 1979

1980

646 A society in which women are taught anything at all but the management of a family, the care of men and the creation of the future generation is a society which is on the way out.
L. Ron Hubbard (1911–86) US founder of the Church of Scientology.
Questions for Our Time

1982

647 My father still reads the dictionary every day. He says your life depends on your power to master words.
Arthur Scargill (1941–) British trades union leader.
Sunday Times, 10 Jan 1982

1988

648 Universities are the cathedrals of the modern age. They shouldn't have to justify their existence by utilitarian criteria.
David Lodge (1935–) British author.
Nice Work IV

649 Girls and boys grow up more normally together than apart.
Daphne Rae Wife of John Rae, British schoolmaster and writer.
Remark, May 1988

1992

650 Shakespeare is fine for grammar school kids.
Nigel de Gruchy (1943–) British teacher and trade unionist.
The Observer, 5 July 1992

History

1953

651 The past is a foreign country: they do things differently there.
L. P. Hartley (1895–1972) British novelist.
The Go-Between

1960

652 The most persistent sound which reverberates through men's history is the beating of war drums.
Arthur Koestler (1905–83) Hungarian-born British writer.
Janus: A Summing Up, Prologue

1961

653 History is too serious to be left to historians.
Iain Macleod (1913–70) British politician.
The Observer, 'Sayings of the Week', 16 July 1961

654 Human blunders usually do more to shape history than human wickedness.
A. J. P. Taylor (1906–90) British historian.
The Origins of the Second World War, Ch. 10

1962

655 Man is a history-making creature who can neither repeat his past nor leave it behind.
W. H. Auden (1907–73) British poet.
The Dyer's Hand, 'D. H. Lawrence'

656 The anthropologist respects history, but he does not accord it a special value. He conceives it as a study complementary to his own: one of them unfurls the range of human societies in time, the other in space.
Claude Lévi-Strauss (1908–) French anthropologist.
The Savage Mind

1965

657 History gets thicker as it approaches recent times.
A. J. P. Taylor (1906–90) British historian.
English History, 1914–1945, Bibliography

1968

658 History never looks like history when you are living through it. It always looks confusing and messy, and it always feels uncomfortable.
John W. Gardner (1912–) US writer.
No Easy Victories

1971

659 Political history is far too criminal and patho-
logical to be a fit subject of study for the young.
Children should acquire their heroes and vil-
lains from fiction.
W. H. Auden (1907–73) British poet.
A Certain World

660 There are moments in history when brooding
tragedy and its dark shadows can be lightened
by recalling great moments of the past.
Indira Gandhi (1917–84) Indian stateswoman.
Letter to Richard Nixon, 16 Dec 1971

1972

661 A study of history shows that civilizations that
abandon the quest for knowledge are doomed
to disintegration.
Bernard Lovell (1913–) British astronomer
and writer.
The Observer, 'Sayings of the Week', 14 May
1972

Human Nature

1946

662 No, it is not only our fate but our business to
lose innocence, and once we have lost that, it
is futile to attempt a picnic in Eden.
Elizabeth Bowen (1899–1973) Irish novelist.
Orion III (ed. Rosamund Lehmann and others),
'Out of a Book'

1947

663 Gamesmanship or The Art of Winning Games
Without Actually Cheating.
Stephen Potter (1900–69) British writer.
Book title

1950

664 Friendship is unnecessary, like philosophy, like
art . . . . It has no survival value; rather it is
one of those things that give value to survival.
C. S. Lewis (1898–1963) British academic and
writer.
The Four Loves, Friendship

665* The man who is master of his passions is Rea-
son's slave.
Cyril Connolly (1903–74) British journalist.
Turnstile One (ed. V. S. Pritchett)

666 *How to be one up* – how to make the other
man feel that something has gone wrong, however slightly.
Stephen Potter (1900–69) British writer.
Lifemanship, Introduction

667 Most human beings have an almost infinite capacity for taking things for granted.
Aldous Huxley (1894–1964) British novelist
and essayist.
Themes and Variations

668 It is an important general rule always to refer to
your friend's country establishment as a
'cottage'.
Stephen Potter (1900–69) British writer.
Lifemanship, Ch. 2

1951

669 Pray that your loneliness may spur you into
finding something to live for, great enough to
die for.
Dag Hammarskjöld (1905–61) Swedish
diplomat.
Diaries, 1951

1952

670 We all are born mad. Some remain so.
Samuel Beckett (1906–89) Irish novelist and
dramatist.
Waiting for Godot, II

671 Habit is a great deadener.
Samuel Beckett
Waiting for Godot, III

672 Cocaine isn't habit-forming. I should know –
I've been using it for years.
Tallulah Bankhead (1903–68) US actress.
Pentimento (Lillian Hellman), 'Theatre'

1953

673 Sentimentality is a superstructure covering
brutality.
Carl Gustav Jung (1875–1961) Swiss
psychoanalyst.
Reflections

1954

674 Men have never been good, they are not good,
they never will be good.
Karl Barth (1886–1968) Swiss Protestant
theologian.
Time, 12 Apr 1954

675 When people are free to do as they please,
they usually imitate each other.
Eric Hoffer (1902–83) US writer.
The Passionate State of Mind

676 Many things – such as loving, going to sleep
or behaving unaffectedly – are done worst
when we try hardest to do them.
C. S. Lewis (1898–1963) British academic and
writer.
Studies in Medieval and Renaissance Literature

1955

677* We need more understanding of human nature,
because the only real danger that exists is
man himself . . . We know nothing of man, far
too little. His psyche should be studied because we are the origin of all coming evil.
Carl Gustav Jung (1875–1961) Swiss
psychoanalyst.
BBC television interview

1956

678 A single sentence will suffice for modern man: he fornicated and read the papers.
Albert Camus (1913–60) French existentialist writer.
The Fall

679 Style, like sheer silk, too often hides eczema.
Albert Camus
The Fall

680 When a small child... I thought that success spelled happiness. I was wrong. Happiness is like a butterfly which appears and delights us for one brief moment, but soon flits away.
Anna Pavlova (1881–1931) Russian ballet dancer.
Pavlova: A Biography (ed. A. H. Franks), 'Pages of My Life'

1959

681 My problem lies in reconciling my gross habits with my net income.
Errol Flynn (1909–59) Australian actor.
Attrib.

1960s

682 Experience teaches you that the man who looks you straight in the eye, particularly if he adds a firm handshake, is hiding something.
Clifton Fadiman (1904–   ) US writer.
Enter, Conversing

1960

683 Schizophrenia cannot be understood without understanding despair.
R. D. Laing (1927–89) British psychiatrist.
The Divided Self, Ch. 2

1961

684 There was only one catch and that was Catch-22, which specified that a concern for one's own safety in the face of dangers that were real and immediate was the process of a rational mind.
Joseph Heller (1923–   ) US novelist.
Catch-22, Ch. 5

1962

685 Solitude is the playfield of Satan.
Vladimir Nabokov (1899–1977) Russian-born US novelist.
Pale Fire

1965

686 Being a star has made it possible for me to get insulted in places where the average Negro could never hope to get insulted.
Sammy Davis Jnr (1925–80) US singer.
Yes I Can

687 He's a real Nowhere Man,
Sitting in his Nowhere Land,
Making all his nowhere plans for nobody.
Doesn't have a point of view,
Knows not where he's going to,
Isn't he a bit like you and me?
The Beatles British rock band.
Nowhere Man

1966

688 Waits at the window, wearing the face that she keeps in a jar by the door
Who is it for? All the lonely people, where do they all come from?
All the lonely people, where do they all belong?
The Beatles
Eleanor Rigby

1967

689 Madness need not be all breakdown. It may also be break-through. It is potential liberation and renewal as well as enslavement and existential death.
R. D. Laing (1927–89) British psychiatrist.
The Politics of Experience, Ch. 16

690 Schizophrenic behaviour is a special strategy that a person invents in order to live in an unlivable situation.
R. D. Laing
The Politics of Experience

691 Three passions, simple but overwhelmingly strong, have governed my life: the longing for love, the search for knowledge, and unbearable pity for the suffering of mankind.
Bertrand Russell (1872–1970) British philosopher.
The Autobiography of Bertrand Russell, Prologue

692 I discovered to my amazement that average men and women were delighted at the prospect of war. I had fondly imagined what most pacifists contended, that wars were forced upon a reluctant population by despotic and Machiavellian governments.
Bertrand Russell
The Autobiography of Bertrand Russell

1968

693 A man is happy so long as he chooses to be happy and nothing can stop him.
Alexander Solzhenitsyn (1918–   ) Soviet-born novelist.
Cancer Ward

1970s

694 There are only two kinds of people in the world. Those who are nice to their servants and those who aren't.
Duke of Argyll (1937–   )
Attrib.

1970

695 You see, I always divide people into two groups. Those who live by what they know to be a lie, and those who live by what they believe, falsely, to be the truth.
Christopher Hampton (1946–) British writer and dramatist.
The Philanthropist, Sc. 6

696 Of course not. After all, I may be wrong.
Bertrand Russell (1872–1970) British philosopher.
On being asked whether he would be prepared to die for his beliefs
Attrib.

1971

697 A memorandum is written not to inform the reader but to protect the writer.
Dean Acheson (1893–1971) US lawyer and statesman.
Attrib.

1973

698 Man is the only animal that learns by being hypocritical. He pretends to be polite and then, eventually, he *becomes* polite.
Jean Kerr (1923–) US dramatist.
Finishing Touches

1974

699 Happiness is an imaginary condition, formerly often attributed by the living to the dead, now usually attributed by adults to children, and by children to adults.
Thomas Szasz (1920–) US psychiatrist.
The Second Sin

700 The stupid neither forgive nor forget; the naive forgive and forget; the wise forgive but do not forget.
Thomas Szasz
The Second Sin

701 Men are rewarded and punished not for what they do, but rather for how their acts are defined. This is why men are more interested in better justifying themselves than in better behaving themselves.
Thomas Szasz
The Second Sin

1975

702 If you haven't been happy very young, you can still be happy later on, but it's much harder. You need more luck.
Simone de Beauvoir (1908–86) French writer.
The Observer, 'Sayings of the Week', 19 May 1975

703 I've noticed your hostility towards him . . . I ought to have guessed you were friends.
Malcolm Bradbury (1932–) British academic and novelist.
The History Man, Ch. 7

1976

704 It's possible to disagree with someone about the ethics of non-violence without wanting to kick his face in.
Christopher Hampton (1946–) British writer and dramatist.
Treats, Sc. 4

1977

705 Only the man who finds everything wrong and expects it to get worse is thought to have a clear brain.
John Kenneth Galbraith (1908–) US economist.
The Age of Uncertainty

706 . . . he willed that the hearts of Men should seek beyond the world and should find no rest therein; but they should have a virtue to shape their life, amid the powers and chances of the world.
J. R. R. Tolkien (1892–1973) British scholar and writer.
The Silmarillion, Ch. 1

1979

707 We confess our bad qualities to others out of fear of appearing naive or ridiculous by not being aware of them.
Gerald Brenan (Edward Fitzgerald Brenan; 1894–1987) British writer.
Thoughts in a Dry Season

708 Worrying is the most natural and spontaneous of all human functions. It is time to acknowledge this, perhaps even to learn to do it better.
Lewis Thomas (1913–) US pathologist.
More Notes of a Biology Watcher, 'The Medusa and the Snail'

1980

709 People wil not readily bear pain unless there is hope.
Michael Edwards (1930–) South African businessman.
Speech, 2 July 1980

1988

710 Shyness is just egotism out of its depth.
Penelope Keith British actress.
Remark, July 1988

Humour

1947

711 It has been discovered experimentally that you can draw laughter from an audience anywhere in the world, of any class or race, simply by walking on to a stage and uttering the words ''I am a married man''.
Ted Kavanagh (1892–1958) British radio scriptwriter.
News Review, 10 July 1947

1950

712* The coarse joke proclaims that we have here an animal which finds its own animality either objectionable or funny.
C. S. Lewis (1898–1963) British academic and writer.
Miracles

713 As for the Freudian, it is a very low, Central European sort of humour.
Robert Graves (1895–1985) British poet and novelist.
Occupation: Writer

1951

714 A lie is an abomination unto the Lord and a very present help in trouble.
Adlai Stevenson (1900–65) US statesman.
Speech, Jan 1951

1953

715 Check enclosed.
Dorothy Parker (1893–1967) US writer.
Giving her version of the two most beautiful words in the English language
Attrib.

1956

716 Being published by the O.U.P. is rather like being married to a duchess; the honour is almost greater than the pleasure.
G. M. Young (1882–1959) British historian.
Letter to Rupert Hart-Davis, 20 Nov 1956

1960

717 All English shop assistants are Miltonists. All Miltonists firmly believe that 'they also serve who only stand and wait.'
George Mikes (1912–87) Hungarian-born British writer and humorist.
How to be Inimitable

1964

718 All I need to make a comedy is a park, a policeman and a pretty girl.
Charlie Chaplin (Sir Charles Spencer C.; 1889–1977) British film actor.
My Autobiography

719 Thank you, sister. May you be the mother of a bishop!
Brendan Behan (1923–64) Irish playwright.
Said to a nun nursing him on his deathbed
Attrib.

720 She believed in nothing; only her scepticism kept her from being an atheist.
Jean-Paul Sartre (1905–80) French writer.
Words

1965

721 The trouble with Freud is that he never played the Glasgow Empire Saturday night.
Ken Dodd (1931–) British comedian.
Television interview, 1965

1966

722 It is not for nothing that, in the English language alone, to accuse someone of trying to be funny is highly abusive.
Malcolm Muggeridge (1903–90) British writer and editor.
Tread Softly For You Tread on My Jokes

1969

723 Comedy, like sodomy, is an unnatural act.
Marty Feldman (1933–83) British comedian.
The Times, 9 June 1969

1980

724 John Wayne is dead
The hell I am
Anonymous
Inscription on a wall in Bermondsey Antique Market, together with a ghostly denial
Evening Standard, 1980

Life

1946

725 I have recently been all round the world and have formed a very poor opinion of it.
Thomas Beecham (1879–1961) British conductor.
Speech at the Savoy
The News Review, 22 Aug 1946

726 Anything that is worth doing has been done frequently. Things hitherto undone should be given, I suspect, a wide berth.
Max Beerbohm (1872–1956) British writer.
Mainly on the Air

1947

727 Man is condemned to be free.
Jean-Paul Sartre (1905–80) French writer.
Existentialism is a Humanism

728 What a strange thing is memory, and hope; one looks backward, the other forward. The one is of today, the other is the Tomorrow. Memory

is history recorded in our brain, memory is a painter, it paints pictures of the past and of the day.
Grandma Moses (Anna Mary Robertson Moses; 1860–1961) US primitive painter.
Grandma Moses, My Life's History (ed. Aotto Kallir), Ch. 1

1948

729 Without measureless and perpetual uncertainty the drama of human life would be destroyed.
Winston Churchill (1874–1965) British statesman.
The Gathering Storm

730 Man's 'progress' is but a gradual discovery that his questions have no meaning.
Antoine de Saint-Exupéry (1900–44) French novelist and aviator.
The Wisdom of the Sands

1949

731 Hell is oneself;
Hell is alone, the other figures in it
Merely projections. There is nothing to es-
cape from
And nothing to escape to. One is always
alone.
T. S. Eliot (1888–1965) US-born British poet and dramatist.
The Cocktail Party, I:3

732 At fifty everyone has the face he deserves.
George Orwell (Eric Blair; 1903–50) British novelist.
Final entry in his notebook

1950

733 The world is made of people who never quite get into the first team and who just miss the prizes at the flower show.
Jacob Bronowski (1908–74) British scientist and writer.
The Face of Violence, Ch. 6

734 Most people get a fair amount of fun out of their lives, but on balance life is suffering and only the very young or the very foolish imag-
ine otherwise.
George Orwell (Eric Blair; 1903–50) British novelist.
Shooting an Elephant

735 Contemporary man has rationalised the myths, but he has not been able to destroy them.
Octavio Paz (1914–) Mexican author and poet.
The Labyrinth of Solitude

736 The most savage controversies are those about matters as to which there is no good evidence either way.
Bertrand Russell (1872–1970) British philosopher.
Unpopular Essays

737 Facts speak louder than statistics.
Geoffrey Streatfield (1897–1978) British lawyer.
Remark, Mar 1950

1951

738 He who despairs over an event is a coward, but he who holds hopes for the human condition is a fool.
Albert Camus (1913–60) French existentialist writer.
The Rebel

739 Everybody has a right to pronounce foreign names as he chooses.
Winston Churchill (1874–1965) British statesman.
The Observer, 'Sayings of the Week', 5 Aug 1951

1952

740 There are no gains without pains.
Adlai Stevenson (1900–65) US statesman.
Speech, Chicago, 26 July 1952

1954

741 Now all the world she knew is dead
In this small room she lives her days.
The wash-hand stand and single bed
Screened from the public gaze.
John Betjeman (1906–84) British poet.
A Few Late Chrysanthemums, 'House of Rest'

742 Oh, isn't life a terrible thing, thank God?
Dylan Thomas (1914–53) Welsh poet.
Under Milk Wood

743 But there comes a moment in everybody's life when he must decide whether he'll live among human beings or not – a fool among fools or a fool alone.
Thornton Wilder (1897–1975) US novelist and dramatist.
The Matchmaker, IV

1955

744 I will never be an old man. To me, old age is always fifteen years older than I am.
Bernard Baruch (1870–1965) US financier and presidential adviser.
The Observer, 'Sayings of the Week', 21 Aug 1955

745 Many men would take the death-sentence with-
out a whimper to escape the life-sentence which fate carries in her other hand.
T. E. Lawrence (1888–1935) British soldier and writer.
The Mint, Pt. I, Ch. 4

746 A vacuum is a hell of a lot better than some of the stuff that nature replaces it with.
Tennessee Williams (1911–83) US dramatist.
Cat On A Hot Tin Roof

1956

747 The penalty of success is to be bored by people
who used to snub you.
Nancy Astor (1879–1964) American-born
British politician.
Sunday Express, 12 Jan 1956

748 A society made up of individuals who were all
capable of original thought would probably be
unendurable. The pressure of ideas would
simply drive it frantic.
H. L. Mencken (1880–1956) US journalist.
Notebooks, 'Minority Report'

749 Poor old Daddy — just one of those sturdy old
plants left over from the Edwardian Wilderness, that can't understand why the sun isn't
shining any more.
John Osborne (1929–   ) British dramatist.
Look Back in Anger, II:2

750 I never give them hell. I just tell the truth and
they think it is hell.
Harry S. Truman (1884–1972) US
statesman.
Look, 3 Apr 1956

1957

751 Sweet Smell of Success.
Ernest Lehman (1920–   ) US screenwriter.
Novel and film title

1959

752 People are inexterminable — like flies and bed-
bugs. There will always be some that survive
in cracks and crevices — that's us.
Robert Frost (1875–1963) US poet.
The Observer, 29 Mar 1959

753 Being over seventy is like being engaged in a
war. All our friends are going or gone and we
survive amongst the dead and the dying as on a
battlefield.
Muriel Spark (1918–   ) British novelist.
Memento Mori, Ch. 4

1960

754 Not a future. At least not in Europe. America's
different, of course, but America's really only
a kind of Russia. You've no idea how pleasant it is not to have any future. It's like having a
totally efficient contraceptive.
Anthony Burgess (John Burgess Wilson;
1917–   ) British novelist.
Honey for the Bears, Pt. II, Ch. 6

755 Nobody hears old people complain because
people think that's all old people do. And that's
because old people are gnarled and sagged
and twisted into the shape of a complaint.
Edward Albee (1928–   ) US dramatist.
The American Dream

756 All evil comes from the old. They grow fat on
ideas and young men die of them.
Jean Anouilh (1910–87) French dramatist.
Catch as Catch Can

757 Children have never been very good at listening
to their elders, but they have never failed to
imitate them.
James Baldwin (1924–87) US writer.
Esquire, 1960

758 There is precious little in civilization to appeal
to a Yeti.
Edmund Hillary (1919–   ) New Zealand
mountaineer.
The Observer, 'Sayings of the Week', 3 June
1960

1961

759 Nature is as wasteful of promising young men
as she is of fish spawn.
Richard Hughes (1900–76) British writer.
The Fox in the Attic

760 Stop the World, I Want to Get Off.
Anthony Newley (1931–   ) British actor,
composer, singer, and comedian.
Title of musical (with Leslie Bricusse)

1962

761 The weak have one weapon: the errors of those
who think they are strong.
Georges Bidault (1899–1983) French
statesman.
The Observer, 1962

762 In this unbelievable universe in which we live
there are no absolutes. Even parallel lines,
reaching into infinity, meet somewhere yonder.
Pearl Buck (1892–1973) US novelist.
A Bridge for Passing

763 He who confronts the paradoxical exposes himself to reality.
Friedrich Dürrenmatt (1921–   ) Swiss
writer.
The Physicists

764 How many roads must a man walk down
Before you call him a man?
Bob Dylan (Robert Allen Zimmerman; 1941–
) US popular singer.
Blowin' in the Wind

765 As far as we can discern, the sole purpose of
human existence is to kindle a light in the
darkness of mere being.
Carl Gustav Jung (1875–1961) Swiss
psychoanalyst.
Memories, Dreams, Reflections, Ch. 11

766 There is always inequality in life. Some men are
killed in a war and some men are wounded
and some men never leave the country — Life
is unfair.
John Fitzgerald Kennedy (1917–63) US
statesman.
Speech, 21 Mar 1962

767 The new electronic interdependence recreates
the world in the image of a global village.
Marshall McLuhan (1911–81) Canadian
sociologist.
The Gutenberg Galaxy

768 One of the worst things about life is not how

nasty the nasty people are. You know that already. It is how nasty the nice people can be.
Anthony Powell (1905–) British novelist.
A Dance to the Music of Time: The Kindly Ones, Ch. 4

1963

769 Yes, 'n' how many years can some people exist
Before they're allowed to be free?
Yes, 'n' how many times can a man turn his head,
Pretending he just doesn't see?
The answer, my friend, is blowin' in the wind.
Bob Dylan (Robert Allen Zimmerman; 1941–) US popular singer.
Blowin' in the Wind

770 The war against hunger is truly mankind's war of liberation.
John Fitzgerald Kennedy (1917–63) US statesman.
Speech, World Food Congress, 4 June 1963

771 The supreme reality of our time is . . . the vulnerability of this planet.
John Fitzgerald Kennedy
Speech, Dublin, 28 June 1963

772 Victory has a thousand fathers but defeat is an orphan.
John Fitzgerald Kennedy
Attrib.

773 One starts to get young at the age of sixty and then it is too late.
Pablo Picasso (1881–1973) Spanish painter.
Sunday Times, 20 Oct 1963

1964

774 There is no security in this life. There is only opportunity.
Douglas MacArthur (1880–1964) US general.
MacArthur, His Rendezvous with History (Courtney Whitney)

1965

775 I've looked at life from both sides now
From win and lose and still somehow
It's life's illusions I recall
I really don't know life at all.
Joni Mitchell (1945–) Singer and songwriter.
Both Sides Now

776 How does it feel
To be without a home
Like a complete unknown
Like a rolling stone?
Bob Dylan (Robert Allen Zimmerman; 1941–) US popular singer.
Like a Rolling Stone

777 Every luxury was lavished on you – atheism, breast-feeding, circumcision. I had to make my own way.
Joe Orton (1933–67) British dramatist.
Loot, I

778 In other words, apart from the known and the unknown, what else is there?
Harold Pinter (1930–) British dramatist.
The Homecoming, II

779 A lady asked me why, on most occasions, I wore black. 'Are you in mourning?'
'Yes.'
'For whom are you in mourning?'
'For the world.'
Edith Sitwell (1887–1964) British poet and writer.
Taken Care Of, Ch. 1

780 The only way to succeed is to make people hate you. That way, they remember you.
Joseph von Sternberg (1894–1969) US film director.
Autobiography (Fun in a Chinese Laundry)

781 One of the most obvious facts about grown-ups to a child is that they have forgotten what it is like to be a child.
Randall Jarrell (1914–65) US author.
Third Book of Criticism

782 People talking without speaking,
People listening without hearing,
People writing songs that voices never shared.
Paul Simon (1941–) US singer and songwriter.
Sounds of Silence

1966

783 Longevity is the revenge of talent upon genius.
Cyril Connolly (1903–74) British journalist.
Sunday Times, 19 June 1966

1967

784 What is an adult? A child blown up by age.
Simone de Beauvoir (1908–86) French writer.
La Femme rompue

785 One doesn't recognize in one's life the really important moments – not until it's too late.
Agatha Christie (1891–1976) British detective-story writer.
Endless Night, Bk. II, Ch. 14

786 Two half-truths do not make a truth, and two half-cultures do not make a culture.
Arthur Koestler (1905–83) Hungarian-born British writer.
The Ghost in the Machine, Preface

787 We are effectively destroying ourselves by violence masquerading as love.
R. D. Laing (1927–89) British psychiatrist.
The Politics of Experience, Ch. 13

1968

788 Life was a funny thing that occurred on the way to the grave.
Quentin Crisp (c. 1910–) British model, publicist, and writer.
The Naked Civil Servant

789 The young always have the same problem —
how to rebel and conform at the same time.
They have now solved this by defying their par-
ents and copying one another.
Quentin Crisp
The Naked Civil Servant

790 Years ago a person, he was unhappy, didn't
know what to do with himself — he'd go to
church, start a revolution — *something*. Today
you're unhappy? Can't figure it out? What is
the salvation? Go shopping.
Arthur Miller (1915–) US dramatist.
The Price, I

1969

791 I am a passenger on the spaceship, Earth.
Richard Buckminster Fuller (1895–1983)
US architect and inventor.
Operating Manual for Spaceship Earth

792 The trouble with the world is that the stupid are
cocksure and the intelligent full of doubt.
Bertrand Russell (1872–1970) British
philosopher.
Autobiography

1970

793 In my youth I regarded the universe as an open
book, printed in the language of physical
equations, whereas now it appears to me as a
text written in invisible ink, of which in our
rare moments of grace we are able to decipher
a small fragment.
Arthur Koestler (1905–83) Hungarian-born
British writer.
Bricks to Babel, Epilogue

794 The salvation of mankind lies only in making
everything the concern of all.
Alexander Solzhenitsyn (1918–) Soviet-
born novelist.
Nobel Lecture, 1970

795 Winning isn't everything, but wanting to win is.
Vince Lombardi (1913–70) US football
coach.
Attrib.

1971

796 We must rediscover the distinction between
hope and expectation.
Ivan Illich (1926–) Austrian sociologist.
Deschooling Society, Ch. 7

797 Being seventy is not a sin.
Golda Meir (1898–1978) Russian-born Israeli
stateswoman.
Reader's Digest (July 1971), 'The Indestructible
Golda Meir'

798 Youth is something very new: twenty years ago
no one mentioned it.
Coco Chanel (1883–1971) French dress
designer.
Coco Chanel, Her Life, Her Secrets (Marcel
Haedrich)

1972

799 The only way of finding the limits of the possible is by going beyond them into the
impossible.
Arthur C. Clarke (1917–) British science-
fiction writer.
The Lost Worlds of 2001

800 There is no reason to assume that the universe
has the slightest interest in intelligence — or
even in life. Both may be random accidental
by-products of its operations like the beautiful
patterns on a butterfly's wings. The insect
would fly just as well without them.
Arthur C. Clarke
The Lost Worlds of 2001

1973

801 Every animal leaves traces of what it was; man
alone leaves traces of what he created.
Jacob Bronowski (1908–74) British scientist
and writer.
The Ascent of Man, Ch. 1

802 In a consumer society there are inevitably two
kinds of slaves: the prisoners of addiction and
the prisoners of envy.
Ivan Illich (1926–) Austrian sociologist.
Tools for Conviviality

803 Growing old is like being increasingly penalized
for a crime you haven't committed.
Anthony Powell (1905–) British novelist.
*A Dance to the Music of Time: Temporary
Kings*, Ch. 1

1974

804 At sixteen I was stupid, confused, insecure and
indecisive. At twenty-five I was wise, self-con-
fident, prepossessing and assertive. At forty-
five I am stupid, confused, insecure and indecisive. Who would have supposed that maturity
is only a short break in adolescence?
Jules Feiffer (1929–) US writer, cartoonist,
and humorist.
The Observer, 3 Feb 1974

805 It is the true nature of mankind to learn from
mistakes, not from example.
Fred Hoyle (1915–) British astronomer.
Into Deepest Space

806 We are living beyond our means. As a people
we have developed a life-style that is draining
the earth of its priceless and irreplaceable resources without regard for the future of our
children and people all around the world.
Margaret Mead (1901–78) US
anthropologist.
Redbook, 'The Energy Crisis — Why Our World
Will Never Again Be the Same.'

807 It isn't evil that is ruining the earth, but medioc-
rity. The crime is not that Nero played while
Rome burned, but that he played badly.
Ned Rorem (1923–) US composer and
writer.
The Final Diary

808   A child becomes an adult when he realizes that he has a right not only to be right but also to be wrong.
Thomas Szasz (1920–) US psychiatrist.
The Second Sin

1975

809   We may become the makers of our fate when we have ceased to pose as its prophets.
Karl Popper (1902–) Austrian-born British philosopher.
The Observer, 28 Dec 1975

810   Loneliness and the feeling of being unwanted is the most terrible poverty.
Mother Teresa (Agnes Gonxha Bojaxhui; 1910–) Yugoslavian-born missionary in Calcutta.
Time, 'Saints Among Us', 29 Dec 1975

1976

811   It is not enough to succeed. Others must fail.
Gore Vidal (1925–) US novelist.
Antipanegyric for Tom Driberg (G. Irvine)

1977

812   Life is a tragedy when seen in close-up, but a comedy in long-shot.
Charlie Chaplin (Sir Charles Spencer C.; 1889–1977) British film actor.
The Guardian, Obituary, 28 Dec 1977

813   If we see light at the end of the tunnel it is the light of an oncoming train.
Robert Lowell (1917–77) US poet.
Day by Day

814   I do not keep a diary. Never have. To write a diary every day is like returning to one's own vomit.
Enoch Powell (1912–) British politician.
Sunday Times, 6 Nov 1977

815   A true bond of friendship is usually only possible between people of roughly equal status.
Desmond Morris (1928–) British biologist and writer.
Manwatching, 'Postural Echo'

1978

816   Old age takes away from us what we have inherited and gives us what we have earned.
Gerald Brenan (Edward Fitzgerald Brenan; 1894–1987) British writer.
Thoughts in a Dry Season, 'Life'

1979

817   To be old is to be part of a huge and ordinary multitude ... the reason why old age was venerated in the past was because it was extraordinary.
Ronald Blythe (1922–) British author.
The View in Winter

818   Life is something to do when you can't get to sleep.
Fran Lebowitz (1950–) US writer.
The Observer, 21 Jan 1979

819   Life is what happens to you while you're busy making other plans.
John Lennon (1940–80) British rock musician.
Beautiful Boy

1980

820   Better to enjoy and suffer than sit around with folded arms. You know the only true prayer? Please God, lead me into temptation.
Jennie Lee (1904–88) British politician and writer.
My Life with Nye

821   With lack of sleep and too much understanding I grow a little crazy, I think, like all men at sea who live too close to each other and too close thereby to all that is monstrous under the sun and moon.
William Golding (1911–) British novelist.
Rites of Passage, '&'

822   What a man does defiles him, not what is done by others.
William Golding
Rites of Passage, 'Next Day'

1982

823   When the white man came we had the land and they had the Bibles; now they have the land and we have the Bibles.
Dan George (1899–1982) Canadian Indian chief.
Attrib.

824   We have to believe in free-will. We've got no choice.
Isaac Bashevis Singer (1904–91) Polish-born US writer.
The Times, 21 June 1982

825   Pennies do not come from heaven. They have to be earned here on earth.
Margaret Thatcher (1925–) British stateswoman.
Sunday Telegraph, 1982

826   There is nothing funny or commendable about old age. It is a miserable affliction which brings a sort of imbecility to those who suffer from it and distresses everyone else.
Auberon Waugh (1939–) British novelist and critic.
The Diaries of Auberon Waugh 1976–1985, 'July 21, 1982'

1983

827   Pleasant people are just as real as horrible people.
John Braine (1922–86) British author.
Remark, Apr 1983

1987

828   The issues are the same. We wanted peace on earth, love, and understanding between everyone around the world. We have learned that change comes slowly.
Paul McCartney (1943–   ) British rock musician.
Comparing 1967 and 1987
Remark, June 1987

1988

829   We do not necessarily improve with age: for better or worse we become more like ourselves.
Peter Hall (1930–   ) British theatre director.
The Observer, 'Sayings of the Week', 24 Jan 1988

830   I think your whole life shows in your face and you should be proud of that.
Lauren Bacall (1924–   ) US actress.
Remark, Mar 1988

831   You know, you can only perceive real beauty in a person as they get older.
Anouk Aimee (1932–   ) French actress.
Remark, Aug 1988

832   The British loathe the middle-aged and I await rediscovery at 65, when one is too old to be in anyone's way.
Roy Strong (1935–   ) British art critic.
Remark, Jan 1988

1989

833   Population growth is the primary source of environmental damage.
Jacques Cousteau (1910–   ) French naval officer and underwater explorer.
Remark, Jan 1989

834   You come into the world alone, you go out alone. In between it's nice to know a few people, but being alone is a fundamental quality of human life, depressing as that is.
Helen Mirren (1945–   ) British actress.
Remark, Jan 1989

835   Life is a sexually transmitted disease.
Graffiti, quoted in *Faber Book of Fevers and Frets* (1989)

Love and Sex

1948

836   Oh, love is real enough, you will find it some day, but it has one arch-enemy — and that is life.
Jean Anouilh (1910–87) French dramatist.
Ardèle

1949

837   The moon is nothing

But a circumambulating aphrodisiac
Divinely subsidized to provoke the world
Into a rising birth-rate.
Christopher Fry (1907–   ) British dramatist.
The Lady's Not for Burning

1950s

838   Now the peak of summer's past, the sky is overcast
And the love we swore would last for an age seems deceit.
C. Day Lewis (1904–72) British poet.
Hornpipe

1951

839   Sex is something I really don't understand too hot. You never know *where* the hell you are. I keep making up these sex rules for myself, and then I break them right away.
J. D. Salinger (1919–   ) US novelist.
The Catcher in the Rye, Ch. 9

1955

840   Self-love seems so often unrequited.
Anthony Powell (1905–   ) British novelist.
The Acceptance World

1956

841   'Bed,' as the Italian proverb succinctly puts it, 'is the poor man's opera.'
Aldous Huxley (1894–1964) British novelist and essayist.
Heaven and Hell

1960

842   The Christian view of sex is that it is, indeed, a form of holy communion.
John Robinson (1919–83) Bishop of Woolwich.
Giving evidence in the prosecution of Penguin Books for publishing *Lady Chatterly's Lover*

1964

843   It has to be admitted that we English have sex on the brain, which is a very unsatisfactory place to have it.
Malcolm Muggeridge (1903–90) British writer and editor.
The Observer, 'Sayings of the Decade', 1964

1965

844   This sort of thing may be tolerated by the French, but we are British — thank God.
Lord Montgomery (1887–1976) British field marshal.
Comment on a bill to relax the laws against homosexuals
Daily Mail, 27 May 1965

1966

845 The orgasm has replaced the Cross as the focus of longing and the image of fulfilment.
Malcolm Muggeridge (1903–90) British writer and editor.
The Most of Malcolm Muggeridge, 'Down with Sex'

1968

846 It is better to be unfaithful than faithful without wanting to be.
Brigitte Bardot (1934–   ) French film actress.
Remark, Feb 1968

847 No more about sex, it's too boring.
Lawrence Durrell (1912–90) British novelist.
Tunc

1970

848 Love, love, love – all the wretched cant of it, masking egotism, lust, masochism, fantasy under a mythology of sentimental postures, a welter of self-induced miseries and joys, blinding and masking the essential personal-ities in the frozen gestures of courtship, in the kissing and the dating and the desire, the compliments and the quarrels which vivify its barrenness.
Germaine Greer (1939–   ) Australian-born British writer and feminist.
The Female Eunuch

1972

849 I don't think pornography is very harmful, but it is terribly, terribly boring.
Noël Coward (1899–1973) British dramatist.
Remark, Sept 1972

1974

850 Masturbation: the primary sexual activity of mankind. In the nineteenth century it was a disease; in the twentieth, it's a cure.
Thomas Szasz (1920–   ) US psychiatrist.
The Second Sin

851 Traditionally, sex has been a very private, secretive activity. Herein perhaps lies its powerful force for uniting people in a strong bond. As we make sex less secretive, we may rob it of its power to hold men and women together.
Thomas Szasz
The Second Sin

1976

852 I'll wager you that in 10 years it will be fashionable again to be a virgin.
Barbara Cartland (1902–   ) British romantic novelist.
The Observer, 'Sayings of the Week', 20 June 1976

1986

853 Everywhere I go I see increasing evidence of people swirling about in a human cesspit of their own making.
James Anderton (1932–   ) British Chief Constable of Greater Manchester.
Referring to AIDS
Speech, 11 Dec 1986

1987

854 I said 10 years ago that in 10 years time it would be smart to be a virgin. Now everyone is back to virgins again.
Barbara Cartland (1902–   ) British romantic novelist.
The Observer, 'Sayings of the Week', 12 July 1987

855 You think intercourse is a private act; it's not, it's a social act. Men are sexually predatory in life; and women are sexually manipulative. When two individuals come together and leave their gender outside the bedroom door, then they make love. If they take it inside with them, they do something else, because society is in the room with them.
Andrea Dworkin (1946–   ) US feminist.
Intercourse

856 I know it does make people happy but to me it is just like having a cup of tea.
Cynthia Payne (1934–   ) London housewife.
After her acquittal on a charge of controlling prostitutes in a famous 'sex-for-luncheon-vouchers' case, 8 Nov 1987

857 My message to the businessmen of this country when they go abroad on business is that there is one thing above all they can take with them to stop them catching Aids, and that is the wife.
Edwina Currie (1946–   ) British politician.
Speech, Feb 1987

858 Don't die of ignorance.
Slogan in British government campaign against AIDS, 1987

859 Every time you sleep with a boy you sleep with all his old girlfriends.
Government-sponsored AIDS advertisement, 1987

860 We hope people will learn to love condoms. In the past people like Casanova had lots of fun with their condoms.
David Cox British television producer.
Remark, Mar 1987

1988

861 It could be said that the Aids pandemic is a classic own-goal scored by the human race against itself.
Princess Anne (1950–   ) The Princess Royal, only daughter of Elizabeth II.
Remark, Jan 1988

862 The strongest possible piece of advice I would

give to any young woman is: Don't screw around, and don't smoke.
Edwina Currie (1946–) British politician.
The Observer, 'Sayings of the Week', 3 Apr 1988

1991

863 Love is just a system for getting someone to call you darling after sex.
Julian Barnes (1946–) British novelist.
Talking It Over, Ch. 16

864 As women have known since the dawn of our time, the primary site for stimulation to orgasm centers upon the clitoris. The revolution unleashed by the Kinsey report of 1953 has, by now, made this information available to men who, for whatever reason, had not figured it out for themselves by the more obvious routes of experience and sensitivity.
Stephen Jay Gould (1941–) US geologist and writer.
Bully for Brontosaurus

Marriage and the Family

1949

865 Few misfortunes can befall a boy which bring worse consequences than to have a really affectionate mother.
W. Somerset Maugham (1874–1965) British novelist.
A Writer's Notebook

1950

866 They fuck you up, your mum and dad.
They may not mean to, but they do.
They fill you with the faults they had
And add some extra, just for you.
Philip Larkin (1922–85) British poet.
This be the Verse

867 A group of closely related persons living under one roof; it is a convenience, often a necessity, sometimes a pleasure, sometimes the reverse; but who first exalted it as admirable, an almost religious ideal?
Rose Macaulay (1889–1958) British writer.
The World My Wilderness, Ch. 20

1954

868 There are times when parenthood seems nothing but feeding the mouth that bites you.
Peter De Vries (1910–) US novelist.
Tunnel of Love

869 Marriage isn't a process of prolonging the life of love, but of mummifying the corpse.
P. G. Wodehouse (1881–1975) British humorous novelist.
Bring on the Girls (with Guy Bolton)

1955

870 This man, she reasons, as she looks at her husband, is a poor fish. But he is the nearest I can get to the big one that got away.
Nigel Dennis (1912–89) British writer.
Cards of Identity

1956

871 Most marriages don't add two people together. They subtract one from the other.
Ian Fleming (1908–64) British journalist and author.
Diamonds are Forever

1957

872 "Parents are strange," said Amy, "for their age."
Amanda Vail (Warren Miller; 1921–66) US writer.
Love Me Little

1958

873 It is now known . . . that men enter local politics solely as a result of being unhappily married.
Cyril Northcote Parkinson (1919–) British historian and writer.
Parkinson's Law, Ch. 10

1960

874 A man in love is incomplete until he has married. Then he's finished.
Zsa Zsa Gabor (1919–) Hungarian-born US film star.
Newsweek, 28 Mar 1960

1964

875 Come mothers and fathers
Throughout the land
And don't criticize
What you can't understand.
Bob Dylan (Robert Allen Zimmerman; 1941–) US popular singer.
The Times They Are A-Changin'

876 I'd the upbringing a nun would envy and that's the truth. Until I was fifteen I was more familiar with Africa than my own body.
Joe Orton (1933–67) British dramatist.
Entertaining Mr Sloane, I

1966

877 Happy is the man with a wife to tell him what to do and a secretary to do it.
Lord Mancroft (1917–87) British businessman and writer.
Remark, Dec 1966

1967

878 Possessive parents rarely live long enough to
see the fruits of their selfishness.
Alan Garner (1934–) British writer.
The Owl Service

879 Far from being the basis of the good society,
the family, with its narrow privacy and tawdry
secrets, is the source of all our discontents.
Edmund Leach (1910–89) British social
anthropologist.
In the BBC Reith Lectures for 1967, reprinted in
The Listener

1970

880 Most married couples in the end arrive at toler-
able arrangements for living – arrangements
that may strike others as odd, but which suit
them very well.
John Braine (1922–86) British author.
Remark, June 1970

881 Mother is the dead heart of the family, spending father's earnings on consumer goods to
enhance the environment in which he eats,
sleeps and watches the television.
Germaine Greer (1939–) Australian-born
British writer and feminist.
The Female Eunuch

1972

882 Of course, I do have a slight advantage over
the rest of you. It helps in a pinch to be able to
remind your bride that you gave up a throne
for her.
Duke of Windsor (1894–1972) King of the
United Kingdom (as Edward VIII).
Discussing the maintenance of happy marital
relations
Attrib.

883 I think women are basically quite lazy. Marriage
is still a woman's best investment, because
she can con some man into supporting her for
the rest of his life.
Alan Whicker (1925–) British television
broadcaster and writer.
The Observer, 'Sayings of the Week', 10 Sept
1972

1974

884 If divorce has increased one thousand percent,
don't blame the woman's movement. Blame
our obsolete sex roles on which our marriages
were based.
Betty Friedan (1921–) US writer.
Speech, 20 Jan 1974

1975

885 'We stay together, but we distrust one another.'

'Ah, yes . . . but isn't that a definition of
marriage?'
Malcolm Bradbury (1932–) British academic and novelist.
The History Man, Ch. 3

1977

886 Parents are the bones on which children
sharpen their teeth.
Peter Ustinov (1921–) British actor.
Dear Me

1978

887 Children . . . have no use for psychology. They
detest sociology. They still believe in God,
the family, angels, devils, witches, goblins,
logic, clarity, punctuation, and other such obsolete stuff . . . When a book is boring, they
yawn openly. They don't expect their writer to
redeem humanity, but leave to adults such
childish illusions.
Isaac Bashevis Singer (1904–91) Polish-
born US writer.
Speech on receiving the Nobel Prize for
Literature
The Observer, 17 Dec 1978

1984

888 If men had to have babies they would only ever
have one each.
Diana, Princess of Wales (1961–) Wife of
Prince Charles.
Remark, July 1984

1988

889 Being married six times shows a degree of optimism over wisdom, but I am incorrigibly
optimistic.
Norman Mailer (1923–) US writer.
The Observer, 'Sayings of the Week', 17 Jan
1988

890 When a man opens the car door for his wife,
it's either a new car or a new wife.
Prince Philip (1921–) The consort of
Queen Elizabeth II.
Remark, Mar 1988

891 Kids haven't changed much, but parents seem
increasingly unhappy with the child raising
phase of their lives.
Penelope Leach British writer and child-care
specialist.
Remark, Oct 1988

892 The nice thing about having relatives' kids
around is that they go home.
Cliff Richard (1940–) British pop singer.
Remark, Nov 1988

1991

893 We take the view that the time has now arrived
when the law should declare that a rapist remains a rapist and is subject to the criminal

law, irrespective of his relationship with his victim.
Lord Lane (1918–) British judge and Lord Chief Justice.
Dismissing the appeal of a man who argued, on the 1736 principle of Chief Justice Hale, that he could not be guilty of raping his wife
The Times, 15 Mar 1991

894 Marriage in modern times is regarded as a partnership of equals and no longer one in which the wife must be the subservient chattel of the husband.
Lord Keith of Kinkel (1922–) British judge.
Giving judgment in the House of Lords that rape can occur within marriage
The Independent, 24 Oct 1991

1992

895 Marriage is an insult and women shouldn't touch it.
Jenni Murray (1950–) British broadcaster.
The Independent, 20 June 1992

Men and Women

1946

896 Most women . . . unlike most men, do not expect either now or in the future, to support a married partner or a family of children out of the proceeds of their labour; on the contrary most of them look forward to being themselves supported in the relatively near future.
Royal Commission on Equal Pay

1949

897 One is not born a woman, one becomes one.
Simone de Beauvoir (1908–86) French writer.
Le Deuxième Sexe (trans. The Second Sex)

898 The Professor of Gynaecology began his course of lectures as follows: Gentlemen, woman is an animal that micturates once a day, defecates once a week, menstruates once a month, parturates once a year and copulates whenever she has the opportunity.
W. Somerset Maugham (1874–1965) British novelist.
A Writer's Notebook

1950s

899 Women have always been the guardians of wisdom and humanity which makes them natural, but usually secret, rulers. The time has come for them to rule openly, but together with and not against men.
Charlotte Wolff (1904–86) German-born British writer.
Bisexuality: A Study, Ch. 2

1954

900 The average man is more interested in a woman who is interested in him than he is in a woman – any woman – with beautiful legs.
Marlene Dietrich (Maria Magdalene von Losch; 1904–92) German-born film star.
News item, 13 Dec 1954

1955

901 There is more difference within the sexes than between them.
Ivy Compton-Burnett (1892–1969) British novelist.
Mother and Son

902 Women are most fascinating between the ages of thirty-five and forty, after they have won a few races and know how to pace themselves. Since few women ever pass forty, maximum fascination can continue indefinitely.
Christian Dior (1905–57)
Colliers Magazine, 10 June 1955

1956

903 Women are equal because they are not different any more.
Erich Fromm (1910–80) US writer.
The Art of Loving

904 Why can't a woman be more like a man?
Men are so honest, so thoroughly square;
Eternally noble, historically fair.
Alan Jay Lerner (1918–86) US songwriter.
My Fair Lady, II:4

1957

905 There are only three things to be done with a woman. You can love her, you can suffer for her, or you can turn her into literature.
Lawrence Durrell (1912–90) British novelist.
Justine

906 Every little girl knows about love. It is only her capacity to suffer because of it that increases.
Françoise Sagan (1935–) French writer.
Daily Express

907 Sometimes I think if there was a third sex men wouldn't get so much as a glance from me.
Amanda Vail (Warren Miller; 1921–66) US writer.
Love Me Little, Ch. 6

1958

908 Women want mediocre men, and men are working to be as mediocre as possible.
Margaret Mead (1901–78) US anthropologist.
Quote Magazine, 15 May 1958

909 Women never have young minds. They are born three thousand years old.
Shelagh Delaney (1939–) British dramatist.
A Taste of Honey, I:1

1960s

910 People call me a feminist whenever I express sentiments that differentiate me from a doormat or a prostitute.
Rebecca West (Cicely Isabel Fairfield; 1892–1983) British novelist and journalist.
Attrib.

1964

911 A woman should be an illusion.
Ian Fleming (1908–64) British journalist and author.
Life of Ian Fleming (John Pearson)

1966

912 She takes just like a woman, yes, she does
She makes love just like a woman, yes, she does
And she aches just like a woman
But she breaks just like a little girl.
Bob Dylan (Robert Allen Zimmerman; 1941–) US popular singer.
Just Like a Woman

913 A woman should open everything to a man except her mouth.
Derek Marlowe
A Dandy in Aspic

1967

914 The male is a biological accident: the y (male) gene is an incomplete x (female) gene, that is, has an incomplete set of chromosomes. In other words, the male is an incomplete female, a walking abortion, aborted at the gene stage.
Valerie Solanas (1940–) US writer.
'SCUM' was the Society for Cutting Up Men
SCUM Manifesto

1968

915 The contraceptive pill may reduce the importance of sex not only as a basis for the division of labor, but as a guideline in developing talents and interests.
Caroline Bird (1915–) US writer.
Born Female, Foreword

1970s

916 A woman needs a man like a fish needs a bicycle.
Graffiti

1970

917 Probably the only place where a man can feel really secure is in a maximum security prison, except for the imminent threat of release.
Germaine Greer (1939–) Australian-born British writer and feminist.
The Female Eunuch

918 Women fail to understand how much men hate them.
Germaine Greer
The Female Eunuch

919 Raising a family and doing housework are the common tasks of a society, to be done equally by men and women; along with this equality of shared necessity will come the equal pursuit of work, love, amusement, thought, emotional independence, and any other damn thing that increases life and gives peace and pleasure.
Vivian Gornick
SCUM Manifesto, Introduction (Valerie Solanas)

1972

920 All Berkshire women are very silly. I don't know why women in Berkshire are more silly than anywhere else.
Claude Duveen (1903–) British judge.
Remark, Reading County Court, July 1972

1973

921 I'm furious about the Women's Liberationists. They keep getting up on soapboxes and proclaiming that women are brighter than men. That's true, but it should be kept very quiet or it ruins the whole racket.
Anita Loos (1891–1981) US novelist.
The Observer, 'Sayings of the Year', 30 Dec 1973

1974

922 No woman so naked as one you can see to be naked underneath her clothes.
Michael Frayn (1933–) British journalist and writer.
Constructions

1975

923 If women didn't exist, all the money in the world would have no meaning.
Aristotle Onassis (1906–75) Greek businessman.
Attrib.

924 Our motto: Life is too short to stuff a mushroom.
Shirley Conran (1932–) Designer and journalist.
Superwoman, Epigraph

1977

925 It makes me feel masculine to tell you that I do not answer questions like this without being paid for answering them.
Lillian Hellman (1905–84) US dramatist.
When asked by *Harper's* magazine when she felt most masculine; this question had already been asked of several famous men
Reader's Digest, July 1977

1978

926 Women's Liberation is just a lot of foolishness. It's the men who are discriminated against. They can't bear children. And no one's likely to do anything about that.
Golda Meir (1898–1978) Russian-born Israeli stateswoman.
Attrib.

1981

927 It is men who face the biggest problems in the future, adjusting to their new and complicated role.
Anna Ford British newscaster.
Remark, Jan 1981

928 I do, and I also wash and iron them.
Denis Thatcher (1915–) British businessman, husband of Margaret Thatcher.
Replying to the question 'Who wears the pants in this house?'
Los Angeles Times, 21 Apr 1981

1982

929 The battle for women's rights has been largely won.
Margaret Thatcher (1925–) British stateswoman.
The Guardian, 1982

1984

930 I don't think men and women were meant to live together. They are totally different animals.
Diana Dors (1931–84) British actress.
Attrib.

1985

931 My mother said it was simple to keep a man, you must be a maid in the living room, a cook in the kitchen and a whore in the bedroom. I said I'd hire the other two and take care of the bedroom bit.
Jerry Hall US model and actress.
Remark, Oct 1985

1986

932 Women have smaller brains than men.
Ali Akbar Hashemi Rafsanjani (1934–) Iranian president.
Remark, July 1986

933 One wants to mutter deeply that apart from having two good legs I also have two good degrees and it is just possible that I do know what I'm talking about.
Edwina Currie (1946–) British politician.
Remark, Nov 1986

1987

934 It is ironic that the wife who made Britain great again, and who is the leader of the Western World, has to get her husband to sign her tax form.
Jacqui Lait
Referring to Margaret Thatcher
Speech, Oct 1987

935 You have to admit that most women who have done something with their lives have been disliked by almost everyone.
Françoise Gilot Artist and mistress of Picasso.
Remark, Oct 1987

1988

936 I shrug my shoulders in despair at women who moan at the lack of opportunities and then take two weeks off as a result of falling out with their boyfriends.
Sophie Mirman (1956–) British businesswoman.
On receiving the Business Woman of the Year Award

937 Women are entitled to dress attractively, even provocatively if you like, be friendly with casual acquaintances and still say no at the end of the evening without being brutally assaulted ... This sort of brutal violence, particularly to women, has got to be dealt with severely. You broke her jaw just because she wasn't prepared to go to bed with you.
Richard Rougier (1932–) British judge.
Sentencing an attacker at the Old Bailey
Daily Telegraph, 4 Mar 1988

938 I think a lot of the women's lib movement came from the war. The women who were growing up then are the mothers of today, and I'm sure they've been affected by the fact that their mothers worked then.
Mary Wolfard British radio journalist.
Don't You Know There's a War On? (Jonathan Croall)

939 I don't think a prostitute is more moral than a wife, but they are doing the same thing.
Prince Philip (1921–) The consort of Queen Elizabeth II.
Speech, 6 Dec 1988

1990

940 The most dramatic thing is that, even when you look at women who are working full time outside the home – as full time as their men – when it comes to ironing and cleaning, 60 or 70 per cent of that work is still done by the women.
Malcolm Wicks Director, Family Policy Studies Institute.
Move Over Darling (Kathy Barnby and Loretta Loach)

941 Had I faltered, we would have neither the success nor international reputation we have. Yet when a woman is strong, she is strident. If a man is strong, he's a good guy.
Margaret Thatcher (1925–) British stateswoman.
The Times, 19 Nov 1990

1991

942 We are unimportant. We are here to serve, to
heal the wounds and give love.
Marike de Klerk The wife of F. W. de Klerk,
South African president.
Referring to the role of women
The Observer, 12 May 1991

943 But they underestimate the cumulative effect of
always hearing Stone-Age man, postman,
chairman; of the different reactions you have
to 'landlord' and 'landlady' or 'a bit of a bitch'
and 'a bit of a dog'.
Katherine Whitehorn (1926–) British
journalist.
The Observer, 18 Aug 1991

944 You can now see the Female Eunuch the world
over . . . Wherever you see nail varnish, lip-
stick, brassieres, and high heels, the Eunuch
has set up her camp.
Germaine Greer (1939–) Australian-born
British writer and feminist.
The Female Eunuch (20th anniversary edition)

Morality, Vices, and Virtues

1947

945 Without doubt the greatest injury . . . was done
by basing morals on myth, for sooner or later
myth is recognized for what it is, and disap-
pears. Then morality loses the foundation on
which it has been built.
Herbert Samuel (1870–1963) British
statesman.
Romanes Lecture, 1947

1948

946 It is better to be violent, if there is violence in
our hearts, than to put on the cloak of non-
violence to cover impotence.
Mahatma Gandhi (Mohandas Karamchand
Gandhi; 1869–1948) Indian national leader.
Non-Violence in Peace and War

947 They had been corrupted by money, and he had
been corrupted by sentiment. Sentiment was
the more dangerous, because you couldn't
name its price. A man open to bribes was to be
relied upon below a certain figure, but sentiment might uncoil in the heart at a name, a
photograph, even a smell remembered.
Graham Greene (1904–91) British novelist.
The Heart of the Matter

1949

948 No action is in itself good or bad, but only such
according to convention.
W. Somerset Maugham (1874–1965) British
novelist.
A Writer's Notebook

1950

949 Euthanasia is a long, smooth-sounding word,
and it conceals its danger as long, smooth
words do, but the danger is there, nevertheless.
Pearl Buck (1892–1973) US novelist.
The Child Who Never Grew, Ch. 2

950 Ethical axioms are found and tested not very
differently from the axioms of science. Truth is
what stands the test of experience.
Albert Einstein (1879–1955) German-born
US physicist.
Out of My Later Years

1952

951 It is often easier to fight for principles than to
live up to them.
Adlai Stevenson (1900–65) US statesman.
Speech, New York, 27 Aug 1952

1953

952 What is morality in any given time or place? It
is what the majority then and there happen to
like and immorality is what they dislike.
A. N. Whitehead (1861–1947) British
philosopher.
Dialogues (Lucien Price)

1954

953 Obscenity is what happens to shock some elderly and ignorant magistrate.
Bertrand Russell (1872–1970) British
philosopher.
Look

1955

954 Kill a man, and you are a murderer. Kill millions
of men, and you are a conqueror. Kill everyone, and you are a god.
Jean Rostand (1894–1977) French biologist
and writer.
Pensées d'un biologiste

1956

955 Gluttony is an emotional escape, a sign some-
thing is eating us.
Peter De Vries (1910–) US novelist.
Comfort me with Apples, Ch. 7

1958

956 He who passively accepts evil is as much involved in it as he who helps to perpetrate it.
Martin Luther King (1929–68) US civil-rights
leader.
Stride Towards Freedom

1959

957 Saintliness is also a temptation.
Jean Anouilh (1910–87) French dramatist.
Becket

1960

958 Propaganda is that branch of the art of lying which consists in nearly deceiving your friends without quite deceiving your enemies.
F. M. Cornford (1886–1960) British poet.
New Statesman, 15 Sept 1978

959 Morality's not practical. Morality's a gesture. A complicated gesture learnt from books.
Robert Bolt (1924–) British playwright.
A Man for All Seasons

960 War is, after all, the universal perversion. We are all tainted: if we cannot experience our perversion at first hand we spend our time reading war stories, the pornography of war; or seeing war films, the blue films of war; or titillating our senses with the imagination of great deeds, the masturbation of war.
John Rae (1931–) British schoolmaster and writer.
The Custard Boys, Ch. 6

1961

961 Moral indignation is in most cases 2 percent moral, 48 percent indignation and 50 percent envy.
Vittorio De Sica (1901–74) Italian film director.
The Observer, 1961

962 Only lies and evil come from letting people off.
Iris Murdoch (1919–) Irish-born British novelist.
A Severed Head

1962

963 Righteous people terrify me . . . Virtue is its own punishment.
Aneurin Bevan (1897–1960) British politician.
Aneurin Bevan (Michael Foot), Vol. I

964 Every form of addiction is bad, no matter whether the narcotic be alcohol or morphine or idealism.
Carl Gustav Jung (1875–1961) Swiss psychoanalyst.
Memories, Dreams, Reflections, Ch. 12

965 Punctuality is the virtue of the bored.
Evelyn Waugh (1903–66) British novelist.
Diaries, 'Irregular Notes', 26 Mar 1962

1963

966 The so-called new morality is too often the old immorality condoned.
Lord Shawcross (1902–87) British politician and lawyer.
The Observer, 17 Nov 1963

967 And there isn't any way that one can get rid of the guilt of having a nice body by saying that one can serve society with it, because that would end up with oneself as what? There simply doesn't seem to be any moral place for flesh.
Margaret Drabble (1939–) British novelist.
A Summer Bird-Cage, Ch. 10

1967

968 A leader who doesn't hesitate before he sends his nation into battle is not fit to be a leader.
Golda Meir (1898–1978) Russian-born Israeli stateswoman.
As Good as Golda (ed. Israel and Mary Shenker)

1968

969 Vice is its own reward.
Quentin Crisp (c. 1910–) British model, publicist, and writer.
The Naked Civil Servant

970 Some of the worst men in the world are sincere and the more sincere they are the worse they are.
Lord Hailsham (1907–) British politician.
Speech, Jan 1968

1969

971 I made a remark a long time ago. I said I was very pleased that television was now showing murder stories, because it's bringing murder back into its rightful setting – in the home.
Alfred Hitchcock (1889–1980) British film director.
The Observer, 'Sayings of the Week', 17 Aug 1969

1970

972 Good can imagine Evil; but Evil cannot imagine Good.
W. H. Auden (1907–73) British poet.
A Certain World: A Commonplace Book

973 Few people can be happy unless they hate some other person, nation or creed.
Bertrand Russell (1872–1970) British philosopher.
Attrib.

1971

974 All sin tends to be addictive, and the terminal point of addiction is what is called damnation.
W. H. Auden (1907–73) British poet.
A Certain World

1973

975 Abortion leads to an appalling trivialisation of the act of procreation.
Donald Coggan (1909–) British churchman.
Speech to the Shaftesbury Society, 2 Oct 1973

976 . . . there's no difference between one's killing and making decisions that will send others to

kill. It's exactly the same thing, or even worse.
Golda Meir (1898–1978) Russian-born Israeli stateswoman.
L'Europeo (Oriana Fallaci)

7 It's better to be quotable than to be honest.
Tom Stoppard (1937–) Czech-born British dramatist.
The Guardian

1974

78 It is difficult to be humble. Even if you aim at humility, there is no guarantee that when you have attained the state you will not be proud of the feat.
Bonamy Dobrée (1891–1974) British scholar and writer.
John Wesley

79 He led a double life. Did that make him a liar? He did not feel a liar. He was a man of two truths.
Iris Murdoch (1919–) Irish-born British novelist.
The Sacred and Profane Love Machine

1975

30 To keep a lamp burning we have to keep putting oil in it.
Mother Teresa (Agnes Gonxha Bojaxhui; 1910–) Yugoslavian-born missionary in Calcutta.
Time, 'Saints Among Us', 29 Dec 1975

1976

31 I have looked on a lot of women with lust. I've committed adultery in my heart many times.
Jimmy Carter (1924–) US president.
Playboy, Nov 1976

1979

32 It is heartless and it is mindless and it is a lie.
John McGahern (1934–) British writer.
The Pornographer

33 The greatest destroyer of peace is abortion because if a mother can kill her own child what is left for me to kill you and you to kill me? There is nothing between.
Mother Teresa (Agnes Gonxha Bojaxhui; 1910–) Yugoslavian-born missionary in Calcutta.
Nobel Peace Prize Lecture

1980

84 How next to impossible is the exercise of virtue! It requires a constant watchfulness, constant guard.
William Golding (1911–) British novelist.
Rites of Passage, 'Colley's Letter'

1982

985 Moderation is a virtue only in those who are thought to have an alternative.
Henry Kissinger (1923–) German-born US politician and diplomat.
The Observer, 24 Jan 1982

1992

986 I strongly believe there's no subject you can't tackle on television. I'm as moral as Mary Whitehouse. The difference between us is that I think people should know about the world they're living in, but she thinks it should be swept under the carpet.
Julia Smith British television producer.
TV Times, July 1992

Other People

1946

987 An Englishman, even if he is alone, forms an orderly queue of one.
George Mikes (1912–87) Hungarian-born British writer and humorist.
How to be an Alien

988 On the Continent people have good food; in England people have good table manners.
George Mikes
How to be an Alien

989 Continental people have sex life; the English have hot-water bottles.
George Mikes
How to be an Alien

1947

990 The English instinctively admire any man who has no talent and is modest about it.
James Agate (1877–1947) British theatre critic.
Attrib.

1948

991 You must not miss Whitehall. At one end you will find a statue of one of our kings who was beheaded; at the other the monument to the man who did it. This is just an example of our attempts to be fair to everybody.
Edward Appleton (1892–1965) British physicist.
Referring to Charles I and Cromwell
Speech, Stockholm, 1 Jan 1948

992 You never find an Englishman among the underdogs – except in England of course.
Evelyn Waugh (1903–66) British novelist.
The Loved One

1949

993 In Italy for thirty years under the Borgias they had warfare, terror, murder, bloodshed –

they produced Michelangelo, Leonardo da Vinci and the Renaissance. In Switzerland they had brotherly love, five hundred years of democracy and peace, and what did they produce . . . ? The cuckoo clock.
Orson Welles (1915–85) US film actor.
The Third Man peace

1950s

994　God bless the USA, so large,
So friendly, and so rich.
W. H. Auden (1907–73) British poet.
On the Circuit

995　First the sweetheart of the nation, then the aunt, woman governs America because America is a land of boys who refuse to grow up.
Salvador de Madariaga y Rogo (1886–1978) Spanish diplomat and writer.
The Perpetual Pessimist (Sagitarius and George)

1950

996　In America everybody is of the opinion that he has no social superiors, since all men are equal, but he does not admit that he has no social inferiors.
Bertrand Russell (1872–1970) British philosopher.
Unpopular Essays

997　To be an Englishman is to belong to the most exclusive club there is.
Ogden Nash (1902–71) US poet.
England Expects

1953

998　Courtesy is not dead – it has merely taken refuge in Great Britain.
Georges Duhamel (1884–1966) French writer.
The Observer, 'Sayings of Our Times', 31 May 1953

999　The land of my fathers. My fathers can have it.
Dylan Thomas (1914–53) Welsh poet.
Referring to Wales
Dylan Thomas (John Ackerman)

1954

1000　To Americans English manners are far more frightening than none at all.
Randall Jarrell (1914–65) US author.
Pictures from an Institution, Pt. I, Ch. 5

1001　I like the English. They have the most rigid code of immorality in the world.
Malcolm Bradbury (1932–　) British academic and novelist.
Eating People is Wrong, Ch. 5

1002　America is a large, friendly dog in a very small room. Every time it wags its tail it knocks over a chair.
Arnold Toynbee (1889–1975) British historian.
Broadcast news summary, 14 July 1954

1955

1003　. . . an impotent people,
Sick with inbreeding,
Worrying the carcase of an old song.
R. S. Thomas (1913–　) Welsh poet.
Welsh Landscape

1956

1004　An Englishman's way of speaking absolutely classifies him
The moment he talks he makes some other Englishman despise him.
Alan Jay Lerner (1918–86) US songwriter.
My Fair Lady, I:1

1005　A cynic is a man who, when he smells flowers looks around for a coffin.
H. L. Mencken (1880–1956) US journalist.
Attrib.

1957

1006　The thing that impresses me most about America is the way parents obey their children.
Duke of Windsor (1894–1972) King of the United Kingdom (as Edward VIII).
Look, 5 Mar 1957

1958

1007　There are still parts of Wales where the only concession to gaiety is a striped shroud.
Gwyn Thomas (1913–81) British writer.
Punch, 18 June 1958

1959

1008　Latins are tenderly enthusiastic. In Brazil they throw flowers at you. In Argentina they throw themselves.
Marlene Dietrich (Maria Magdalene von Losch; 1904–92) German-born film star.
Newsweek, 24 Aug 1959

1960s

1009　Other people have a nationality. The Irish and the Jews have a psychosis.
Brendan Behan (1923–64) Irish playwright.
Richard's Cork Leg, I

1010　The English and Americans dislike only *some* Irish – the same Irish that the Irish themselves detest, Irish writers – the ones that *think*.
Brendan Behan
Richard's Cork Leg, I

1011　The United States, I believe, are under the impression that they are twenty years in advance of this country; whilst, as a matter of

actual verifiable fact, of course, they are just about six hours behind it.
Harold Hobson (1904–) British theatre critic and writer.
The Devil in Woodford Wells, Ch. 8

1012 England is . . . a country infested with people who love to tell us what to do, but who very rarely seem to know what's going on.
Colin MacInnes (1914–76) British novelist.
England, Half English, 'Pop Songs and Teenagers'

1960

1013 An American is either a Jew, or an anti-Semite, unless he is both at the same time.
Jean-Paul Sartre (1905–80) French writer.
Altona

1961

1014 Venice is like eating an entire box of chocolate liqueurs at one go.
Truman Capote (1924–84) US novelist.
Remark, Nov 1961

1015 Damn you, England. You're rotting now, and quite soon you'll disappear.
John Osborne (1929–) British dramatist.
Letter in *Tribune*, Aug 1961

1016 The difference between our decadence and the Russians' is that while theirs is brutal, ours is apathetic.
James Thurber (1894–1961) US humorist.
Remark, Feb 1961

1017 We are all American at puberty; we die French.
Evelyn Waugh (1903–66) British novelist.
Diaries, 'Irregular Notes', 18 July 1961

1962

1018 To like an individual because he's black is just as insulting as to dislike him because he isn't white.
e. e. cummings (1894–1962) US poet.
Attrib.

1019 The immense popularity of American movies abroad demonstrates that Europe is the unfinished negative of which America is the proof.
Mary McCarthy (1912–89) US novelist.
On the Contrary

1020 When an American heiress wants to buy a man, she at once crosses the Atlantic. The only really materialistic people I have ever met have been Europeans.
Mary McCarthy
On the Contrary

1965

1021 The English are polite by telling lies. The Americans are polite by telling the truth.
Malcolm Bradbury (1932–) British academic and novelist.
Stepping Westward, Bk. II, Ch. 5

1022 To eat well in England you should have breakfast three times a day.
W. Somerset Maugham (1874–1965) British novelist.
Attrib.

1968

1023 The most dangerous thing in the world is to make a friend of an Englishman, because he'll come sleep in your closet rather than spend 10s on a hotel.
Truman Capote (1924–84) US novelist.
Remark, Mar 1968

1024 There are many things in life more worthwhile than money. One is to be brought up in this our England which is still the envy of less happy lands.
Lord Denning (1899–) British judge.
The Observer, 'Sayings of the Week', 4 Aug 1968

1969

1025 Scratch an American and you get a Seventh Day Adventist every time.
Lord Hailsham (1907–) British politician.
Remark, June 1969

1026 A Jewish man with parents alive is a fifteen-year-old boy, and will remain a fifteen-year-old boy till they die.
Philip Roth (1933–) US novelist.
Portnoy's Complaint

1970

1027 We may be a small island, but we are not a small people.
Edward Heath (1916–) British statesman.
Speech, June 1970

1972

1028 Pass a law to give every single wingeing bloody Pommie his fare home to England. Back to the smoke and the sun shining ten days a year and shit in the streets. Yer can have it.
Thomas Keneally (1935–) Australian novelist.
The Chant of Jimmy Blacksmith

1974

1029 Pessimism is a luxury that a Jew never can allow himself.
Golda Meir (1898–1978) Russian-born Israeli stateswoman.
The Observer, 'Sayings of the Year', 29 Dec 1974

1030 A lot of men who have accepted – or had imposed upon them in boyhood – the old English public school styles of careful modesty in speech, with much understatement, have behind their masks an appalling and impregnable conceit of themselves. If they do not

blow their own trumpets it is because they feel you are not fit to listen to the performance.
J. B. Priestley (1894–1984) British novelist.
Outcries and Asides

1975

1031 Americans have been conditioned to respect newness, whatever it costs them.
John Updike (1932–) US novelist.
A Month of Sundays, Ch. 18

1032 The Japanese have perfected good manners and made them indistinguishable from rudeness.
Paul Theroux (1941–) US-born writer.
The Great Railway Bazaar, Ch. 2

1977

1033 All races have produced notable economists, with the exception of the Irish who doubtless can protest their devotion to higher arts.
John Kenneth Galbraith (1908–) US economist.
The Age of Uncertainty, Ch. 1

1034 The problem with Ireland is that it's a country full of genius, but with absolutely no talent.
Hugh Leonard (1926–) Irish dramatist.
Interview, *The Times*, Aug 1977

1035 The national dish of America is menus.
Robert Robinson (1927–) British writer and broadcaster.
BBC television programme, *Robinson's Travels*, Aug 1977

1036 I believe that the Jews have made a contribution to the human condition out of all proportion to their numbers: I believe them to be an immense people. Not only have they supplied the world with two leaders of the stature of Jesus Christ and Karl Marx, but they have even indulged in the luxury of following neither one nor the other.
Peter Ustinov (1921–) British actor.
Dear Me, Ch. 19

1978

1037 I find it hard to say, because when I was there it seemed to be shut.
Clement Freud (1924–) British politician and broadcaster.
On being asked for his opinion of New Zealand. Similar remarks have been attributed to others
BBC radio, 12 Apr 1978

1988

1038 America is not a blanket woven from one thread, one color, one cloth.
Jesse Jackson (1941–) US politician.
Speech, Democratic Party Convention, Atlanta, July 1988

Religion

1948

1039 Religion
Has made an honest woman of the supernatural,
And we won't have it kicking over the traces again.
Christopher Fry (1907–) British dramatist.
The Lady's Not for Burning, II

1040 If a Jew is fascinated by Christians it is not because of their virtues, which he values little, but because they represent anonymity, humanity without race.
Jean-Paul Sartre (1905–80) French writer.
Anti-Semite and Jew

1949

1041 The dogma of the Ghost in the Machine.
Gilbert Ryle (1900–76) British philosopher.
The Concept of Mind, Ch. 1

1042 'God knows how you Protestants can be expected to have any sense of direction,' she said. 'It's different with us. I haven't been to mass for years, I've got every mortal sin on my conscience, but I know when I'm doing wrong. I'm still a Catholic.
Angus Wilson (1913–91) British novelist.
The Wrong Set, 'Significant Experience'

1950s

1043 Becoming an Anglo-Catholic must surely be a sad business — rather like becoming an amateur conjurer.
John St Loe Strachey (1901–63) British politician.
The Coming Struggle for Power, Pt. III, Ch. 11

1950

1044 One cannot really be a Catholic and grown-up.
George Orwell (Eric Blair; 1903–50) British novelist.
Collected Essays

1953

1045 There are many who stay away from church these days because you hardly ever mention God any more.
Arthur Miller (1915–) US dramatist.
The Crucible, I

1954

1046 There seems to be a terrible misunderstanding on the part of a great many people to the effect that when you cease to believe you may cease to behave.
Louis Kronenberger (1904–80) US writer and literary critic.
Company Manners

1047 To perceive Christmas through its wrapping becomes more difficult with every year.
Elwyn Brooks White (1899–1985) US journalist and humorist.
The Second Tree from the Corner

1956

1048 It is now quite lawful for a Catholic woman to avoid pregnancy by a resort to mathematics, though she is still forbidden to resort to physics and chemistry.
H. L. Mencken (1880–1956) US journalist.
Notebooks, 'Minority Report'

1049 God is the immemorial refuge of the incompetent, the helpless, the miserable. They find not only sanctuary in His arms, but also a kind of superiority, soothing to their macerated egos; He will set them above their betters.
H. L. Mencken
Notebooks, 'Minority Report'

1957

1050 Operationally, God is beginning to resemble not a ruler but the last fading smile of a cosmic Cheshire cat.
Julian Huxley (1887–1975) British biologist.
Religion without Revelation, Ch. 3

1958

1051 It is the final proof of God's omnipotence that he need not exist in order to save us.
Peter De Vries (1910–) US novelist.
The Mackerel Plaza, Ch. 2

1961

1052 Those who marry God . . . can become domesticated too – it's just as humdrum a marriage as all the others.
Graham Greene (1904–91) British novelist.
A Burnt-Out Case, Ch. 1

1053 Your cravings as a human animal do not become a prayer just because it is God whom you must ask to attend to them.
Dag Hammarskjöld (1905–61) Swedish diplomat.
Markings

1962

1054 To die for a religion is easier than to live it absolutely.
Jorge Luis Borges (1899–1986) Argentinian writer.
Labyrinthes

1055 Forgive, O Lord, my little jokes on Thee
And I'll forgive Thy great big one on me.
Robert Frost (1875–1963) US poet.
In the Clearing, 'Cluster of Faith'

1963

1056 If the concept of God has any validity or use, it

can only be to make us larger, freer, and more loving. If God cannot do this, then it is time we got rid of Him.
James Baldwin (1924–87) US writer.
The Fire Next Time

1965

1057 The most odious of concealed narcissisms – prayer.
John Fowles (1926–) British novelist.
The Aristos

1058 God can stand being told by Professor Ayer and Marghanita Laski that He doesn't exist.
J. B. Priestley (1894–1984) British novelist.
The Listener, 1 July 1965, 'The BBC's Duty to Society'

1970

1059 Meditation is not a means to an end. It is both the means and the end.
Jiddu Krishnamurti (1895–1986) Indian Hindu philosopher.
The Penguin Krishnamurti Reader

1060 There's a Bible on that shelf there. But I keep it next to Voltaire – poison and antidote.
Bertrand Russell (1872–1970) British philosopher.
Kenneth Harris Talking To, 'Bertrand Russell' (Kenneth Harris)

1974

1061 If you talk to God, you are praying; if God talks to you, you have schizophrenia. If the dead talk to you, you are a spiritualist; if God talks to you, you are a schizophrenic.
Thomas Szasz (1920–) US psychiatrist.
The Second Sin

1062 He no play-a da game. He no make-a da rules!
Earl Butz (1909–) US politician.
Referring to the Pope's strictures against contraception
Remark, 1974

1975

1063 In general the churches, visited by me too often on weekdays . . . bore for me the same relation to God that billboards did to Coca-Cola: they promoted thirst without quenching it.
John Updike (1932–) US novelist.
A Month of Sundays, Ch. 2

1977

1064 The idea that He would take his attention away from the universe in order to give me a bicycle with three speeds is just so unlikely I can't go along with it.
Quentin Crisp (c. 1910–) British model, publicist, and writer.
The Sunday Times, 18 Dec 1977

1065 It is no accident that the symbol of a bishop is

a crook, and the sign of an archbishop is a
double-cross.
Dom Gregory Dix (1901–52) British monk.
Letter to *The Times*, 3 Dec 1977 (Francis Bown)

1981

1066 If this is God's world there are no unimportant
people.
George Thomas (1909–) British politician.
Remark, in a television interview

1983

1067 The purpose of population is not ultimately
peopling earth. It is to fill heaven.
Graham Leonard (1921–) British
churchman.
Said during a debate on the Church and the
Bomb
Speech, General Synod of the Church of
England, 10 Feb 1983

1985

1068 It's not an accident that when God became
'man' He chose to be a male. There's no doubt
that He could have chosen to be a woman if
He'd wanted to.
Graham Leonard
Arguing against women priests in the Church of
England
The Sunday Times, 22 Dec 1985

1986

1069 What sort of God are we portraying and believing in if we insist on what I will nickname 'the
divine laser beam' type of miracle as the
heart and basis of the Incarnation and
Resurrection?
David Jenkins (1925–) British churchman.
Speech, July 1986

1070 Organized religion is making Christianity political rather than making politics Christian.
Laurens Van der Post (1906–) South African novelist.
The Observer, 'Sayings of the Week', 9 Nov
1986

1987

1071 If I really believed that the Church of England
came out of the loins of Henry VIII I could be
as free as I liked about making changes, but I
do not believe that.
Peter Boulton (1925–) British churchman.
Remark, Mar 1987

1072 Beware when you take on the Church of God.
Others have tried and have bitten the dust.
Desmond Tutu (1931–) South African
churchman.
Speech, Apr 1987

1988

1073 We must reject a privatization of religion which
results in its reduction to being simply a matter of personal salvation.
Robert Runcie (1921–) British churchman.
The Observer, 'Sayings of the Week', 17 Apr
1988

1074 If women in the priesthood has come as a result of women's liberation, then I think it is
satanic.
William Pwaisiho
Daily Telegraph, Aug 1988

1075 Christ called as his Apostles only men. He did
this in a totally free and sovereign way.
John Paul II (Karol Wojtyla; 1920–) Polish
pope.
Speech, Sept 1988

1989

1076 It's just called 'The Bible' now. We dropped the
word 'Holy' to give it a more mass-market
appeal.
An editor at Hodder & Stoughton, quoted in *The
Daily Telegraph*, 30 Dec 1989

1991

1077 I see it as an elderly lady, who mutters away to
herself in a corner, ignored most of the time.
George Carey (1935–) British churchman.
Referring to the Church of England
Reader's Digest, Mar 1991

1078 The idea that only a male can represent Christ
at the altar is a most serious heresy.
George Carey
Reader's Digest, Apr 1991

1992

1079 My fear will be that in 15 years time Jerusalem,
Bethlehem, once centres of strong Christian
presence, might become a kind of Walt Disney
Theme Park.
George Carey
The Observer, 12 Jan 1992

1080 The Vatican is an oppressive regime which, like
a bat, fears the light.
Leonardo Boff (1938–) Brazilian theologian.
Said on leaving the Roman Catholic church
The Observer, 5 July 1992

Science, Medicine, and Technology

1946

1081 MASTER. They split the atom by firing particles at
it, at 5,500 miles a second.
BOY. Good heavens. And they only split it?
Will Hay (1888–1949) British comedian.
The Fourth Form at St Michael's

1947

1082 The physicists have known sin; and this is a knowledge which they cannot lose.
J. Robert Oppenheimer (1904–67) US physicist.
Lecture, Massachusetts Institute of Technology, 25 Nov 1947

1949

1083 When you are courting a nice girl an hour seems like a second. When you sit on a red-hot cinder a second seems like an hour. That's relativity.
Albert Einstein (1879–1955) German-born US physicist.
News Chronicle, 14 Mar 1949

1950

1084 Science without religion is lame, religion without science is blind.
Albert Einstein
Out of My Later Years

1085 The whole of science is nothing more than a refinement of everyday thinking.
Albert Einstein
Out of My Later Years

1951

1086 By his very success in inventing labour-saving devices modern man has manufactured an abyss of boredom that only the privileged classes in earlier civilisations have ever fathomed.
Lewis Mumford (1895–1990) US social philosopher.
The Conduct of Life

1952

1087 There is no evil in the atom; only in men's souls.
Adlai Stevenson (1900–65) US statesman.
Speech, Hartford, Connecticut, 18 Sept 1952

1953

1088 Factual evidence can never 'prove' a hypothesis; it can only fail to disprove it, which is what we generally mean when we say, somewhat inexactly, that the hypothesis is 'confirmed' by experience.
Milton Friedman (1912–) US economist.
Essays in Positive Economics

1955

1089 From an evolutionary point of view, man has stopped moving, if he ever did move.
Pierre Teilhard de Chardin (1881–1955) French Jesuit and palaeontologist.
The Phenomenon of Man, Postscript

1957

1090 Science must begin with myths, and with the criticism of myths.
Karl Popper (1902–) Austrian-born British philosopher.
British Philosophy in the Mid-Century (ed. C. A. Mace)

1958

1091 Don't tell me that man doesn't belong out there. Man belongs wherever he wants to go; and he'll do plenty well when he gets there.
Wernher von Braun (1912–77) German-born US rocket engineer.
Referring to space flights

1961

1092 Show me a sane man and I will cure him for you.
Carl Gustav Jung (1875–1961) Swiss psychoanalyst.
Attrib. in The Observer, 19 July 1975

1962

1093 When I find myself in the company of scientists, I feel like a shabby curate who has strayed by mistake into a drawing-room full of dukes.
W. H. Auden (1907–73) British poet.
The Dyer's Hand

1094 As cruel a weapon as the cave man's club, the chemical barrage has been hurled against the fabric of life.
Rachel Carson (1907–64) US biologist.
The Silent Spring

1095 The true men of action in our time, those who transform the world, are not the politicians and statesmen, but the scientists. Unfortunately, poetry cannot celebrate them, because their deeds are concerned with things, not persons and are, therefore, speechless.
W. H. Auden (1907–73) British poet.
The Dyer's Hand

1096 The content of physics is the concern of physicists, its effect the concern of all men.
Friedrich Dürrenmatt (1921–) Swiss writer.
The Physicists

1963

1097 Our scientific power has outrun our spiritual power. We have guided missiles and misguided men.
Martin Luther King (1929–68) US civil-rights leader.
Strength to Love

1098 We have genuflected before the god of science only to find that it has given us the atomic

bomb, producing fears and anxieties that science can never mitigate.
Martin Luther King
Strength through Love, Ch. 13

1964

1099 People must understand that science is inherently neither a potential for good nor for evil. It is a potential to be harnessed by man to do his bidding.
Glenn T. Seaborg (1912–) US physicist.
Associated Press interview with Alton Blakeslee, 29 Sept 1964

*1100 Science has 'explained' nothing; the more we know the more fantastic the world becomes and the profounder the surrounding darkness.
Aldous Huxley (1894–1964) British novelist and essayist.
Views Of Holland

1967

1101 There are one hundred and ninety-three living species of monkeys and apes. One hundred and ninety-two of them are covered with hair. The exception is a naked ape self-named *Homo sapiens*.
Desmond Morris (1928–) British biologist and writer.
The Naked Ape, Introduction

1968

1102 Already for thirty-five years he had not stopped talking and almost nothing of fundamental value had emerged.
James Dewey Watson (1928–) US geneticist.
Referring to Francis Crick, with whom Watson had discovered the structure of DNA
The Double Helix, Ch. 8

1969

1103 Machines from the Maxim gun to the computer, are for the most part means by which a minority can keep free men in subjection.
Kenneth Clark (1903–83) British art historian.
Civilisation

1970

*1104 The emergence of intelligence, I am convinced, tends to unbalance the ecology. In other words, intelligence is the great polluter. It is not until a creature begins to manage its environment that nature is thrown into disorder.
Clifford D. Simak (1904–88) US journalist.
Shakespeare's Planet

1105 Freud is the father of psychoanalysis. It has no mother.
Germaine Greer (1939–) Australian-born British writer and feminist.
The Female Eunuch

1972

1106 Any sufficiently advanced technology is indistinguishable from magic.
Arthur C. Clarke (1917–) British science-fiction writer.
The Lost Worlds of 2001

1973

1107 That is the essence of science: ask an impertinent question, and you are on the way to the pertinent answer.
Jacob Bronowski (1908–74) British scientist and writer.
The Ascent of Man, Ch. 4

1108 When a distinguished but elderly scientist states that something is possible, he is almost certainly right. When he states that something is impossible, he is very probably wrong.
Arthur C. Clarke (1917–) British science-fiction writer.
Profiles of the Future

1974

1109 Traditional scientific method has always been at the very *best*, 20-20 hindsight. It's good for seeing where you've been.
Robert T. Pirsig (1928–) US writer.
Zen and the Art of Motorcycle Maintenance, Pt. III, Ch. 24

1110 Formerly, when religion was strong and science weak, men mistook magic for medicine; now, when science is strong and religion weak, men mistake medicine for magic.
Thomas Szasz (1920–) US psychiatrist.
The Second Sin

1978

1111 Out of all possible universes, the only one which can exist, in the sense that it can be known, is simply the one which satisfies the narrow conditions necessary for the development of intelligent life.
Bernard Lovell (1913–) British astronomer and writer.
In the Centre of Immensities

1979

1112 Space isn't remote at all. It's only an hour's drive away if your car could go straight upwards.
Fred Hoyle (1915–) British astronomer.
The Observer, 9 Sept 1979

1982

1113 Science may be described as the art of systematic over-simplification.
Karl Popper (1902–) Austrian-born British philosopher.
Remark, Aug 1982

1983

1114 It is, of course, a bit of a drawback that science was invented after I left school.
Lord Carrington (1919–) British statesman.
The Observer, 23 Jan 1983

1986

1115 Should we force science down the throats of those that have no taste for it? Is it our duty to drag them kicking and screaming into the twenty-first century? I am afraid that it is.
George Porter (1920–) British chemist.
Speech, Sept 1986

1988

1116 Had we gone the way of France and got 60 per cent of our electricity from nuclear power, we should not have environmental problems.
Margaret Thatcher (1925–) British stateswoman.
Speech, Oct 1988

Wealth and Poverty

1946

1117 A rich man is one who isn't afraid to ask the salesman to show him something cheaper.
Anonymous
Ladies Home Journal, Jan 1946

1948

1118 Increase of material comforts, it may be generally laid down, does not in any way whatsoever conduce to moral growth.
Mahatma Gandhi (Mohandas Karamchand Gandhi; 1869–1948) Indian national leader.
Obituary, *News Chronicle*

1956

1119 Who Wants to Be a Millionaire? I don't.
Cole Porter (1893–1964) US songwriter.
Who Wants to be a Millionaire?, title song

1958

1120 In the affluent society no useful distinction can be made between luxuries and necessaries.
John Kenneth Galbraith (1908–) US economist.
The Affluent Society, Ch. 21

1121 Wealth has never been a sufficient source of honour in itself. It must be advertised, and the normal medium is obtrusively expensive goods.
John Kenneth Galbraith
The Affluent Society, Ch. 7

1122 Wealth is not without its advantages, and the case to the contrary, although it has often been made, has never proved widely persuasive.
John Kenneth Galbraith
The Affluent Society, Ch. 1

1961

1123 Money, it turned out, was exactly like sex, you thought of nothing else if you didn't have it and thought of other things if you did.
James Baldwin (1924–87) US writer.
Nobody Knows My Name

1124 For every talent that poverty has stimulated, it has blighted a hundred.
John W. Gardner (1912–) US writer.
Excellence

1125 If a free society cannot help the many who are poor it cannot save the few who are rich.
John Fitzgerald Kennedy (1917–63) US statesman.
Speech, 20 Jan 1961

1962

1126 People who are much too sensitive to demand of cripples that they run races ask of the poor that they get up and act just like everyone else in society.
Michael Harrington (1928–) US socialist and writer.
The Other America

1967

1127 I don't know how much money I've got . . . I did ask the accountant how much it came to. I wrote it down on a bit of paper. But I've lost the bit of paper.
John Lennon (1940–80) British rock musician.
The Beatles (Hunter Davies)

1968

1128 To some extent, if you've seen one city slum you've seen them all.
Spiro Agnew (1918–) US politician.
Election speech, Detroit, 18 Oct 1968

1973

1129 The heart of the matter, as I see it, is the stark fact that world poverty is primarily a problem of two million villages, and thus a problem of two thousand million villagers.
E. F. Schumacher (1911–77) German-born economist.
Small is Beautiful, A Study of Economics as if People Mattered, Ch. 13

1975

1130 . . . the poor are our brothers and sisters. . . .

people in the world who need love, who need care, who have to be wanted.
Mother Teresa (Agnes Gonxha Bojaxhui; 1910–) Yugoslavian-born missionary in Calcutta.
Time, 'Saints Among Us', 29 Dec 1975

1980

1131 The rich hate signing cheques. Hence the success of credit cards.
Graham Greene (1904–91) British novelist.
Dr. Fischer of Geneva

1132 No one would have remembered the Good Samaritan if he'd only had good intentions. He had money as well.
Margaret Thatcher (1925–) British stateswoman.
Television interview, 1980

1981

1133 They gave me star treatment because I was making a lot of money. But I was just as good when I was poor.
Bob Marley (1945–81) Jamaican reggae singer.
The Radio Times, 18 Sept 1981

1983

1134 This is not for me. The honour is for the poor.
Mother Teresa (Agnes Gonxha Bojaxhui; 1910–) Yugoslavian-born missionary in Calcutta.
Said on receiving the Order of Merit, 24 Nov 1983
The Sunday Times, 3 Dec 1989

1985

1135 The trouble with the profit system has always been that it was highly unprofitable to most people.
Elwyn Brooks White (1899–1985) US journalist and humorist.
Attrib.

1987

1136 The working classes are never embarrassed by money – only the absence of it.
Ken Livingstone (1945–) British politician.
Speech, Sept 1987

1988

1137 It does seem to be true that the more you get the more you spend. It is rather like being on a golden treadmill.
Charles Allsop (1940–) Commodities broker.
Remark, Dec 1988

Work and Occupations

1946

1138 Today we have naming of parts. Yesterday, We had daily cleaning. And tomorrow morning
We shall have what to do after firing. But today, Today we have naming of parts.
Henry Reed (1914–86) British poet and dramatist.
Naming of Parts

1951

1139 I was born at the age of twelve on a Metro-Goldwyn-Mayer lot.
Judy Garland (Frances Gumm; 1922–69) US film star.
The Observer, 'Sayings of the Week', 18 Feb 1951

1953

1140 The physician can bury his mistakes, but the architect can only advise his client to plant vines.
Frank Lloyd Wright (1869–1959) US architect.
New York Times Magazine, 4 Oct 1953

1956

1141 An actor's a guy who, if you ain't talking about him, ain't listening.
Marlon Brando (1924–) US film star.
The Observer, 'Sayings of the Year', Jan 1956

1958

1142 The rise in the total of those employed is governed by Parkinson's Law and would be much the same whether the volume of work were to increase, diminish or even disappear.
Cyril Northcote Parkinson (1919–) British historian and writer.
Parkinson's Law, Ch. 1

1143 Work expands so as to fill the time available for its completion.
Cyril Northcote Parkinson
Parkinson's Law, Ch. 1

1144 The development of industry has created many new sources of danger. Occupational diseases are socially different from other diseases, but not biologically.
Henry E. Sigerist (1891–1957)
Journal of the History of Medicine and Allied Sciences, 13:214, 1958

1960

1145 You ask me what it is I do. Well actually, you know,
I'm partly a liaison man and partly P.R.O.
Essentially I integrate the current export drive

And basically I'm viable from ten o'clock till five.
John Betjeman (1906–84) British poet.
Executive

1146 An artist is someone who produces things that people don't need to have but that he — for *some reason* — thinks it would be a good idea to give them.
Andy Warhol (Andrew Warhola; 1926–87) US pop artist.
From A to B and Back Again, 'Atmosphere'

1147 I remain just one thing, and one thing only — and that is a clown.
It places me on a far higher plane than any politician.
Charlie Chaplin (Sir Charles Spencer C.; 1889–1977) British film actor.
The Observer, 'Sayings of the Week', 17 June 1960

1961

1148 A psychiatrist is a man who goes to the Folies-Bergère and looks at the audience.
Mervyn Stockwood (1913–) British churchman.
Remark, Oct 1961

1149 A judge is not supposed to know anything about the facts of life until they have been presented in evidence and explained to him at least three times.
Hubert Lister Parker (1900–72) Lord Chief Justice of England.
The Observer, 'Sayings of the Week', 12 Mar 1961

1963

1150 Work is much more fun than fun.
Noël Coward (1899–1973) British dramatist.
Remark, June 1963

1964

1151 Once a newspaper touches a story, the facts are lost forever, even to the protagonists.
Norman Mailer (1923–) US writer.
The Presidential Papers

1152 I have nothing against undertakers personally. It's just that I wouldn't want one to bury my sister.
Jessica Mitford (1917–) British writer.
Attrib. in *Saturday Review*, 1 Feb 1964

1967

1153 Journalism is the only job that requires no degrees, no diplomas and no specialised knowledge of any kind.
Patrick Campbell (1913–80) British humorous writer and editor.
My Life and Easy Times

1154 Do they merit vitriol, even a drop of it? Yes, because they corrupt the young, persuading them that the mature world, which produced

Beethoven and Schweitzer, sets an even higher value on the transient anodynes of youth than does youth itself... They are the Hollow Men. They are electronic lice.
Anthony Burgess (John Burgess Wilson; 1917–) British novelist.
Referring to disc jockeys
Punch, 20 Sept 1967

1970s

1155 The only place where success comes before work is a dictionary.
Vidal Sassoon (1928–) British hair stylist.
Quoting one of his teachers in a BBC radio broadcast

1970

1156 No brilliance is needed in the law. Nothing but common sense, and relatively clean finger nails.
John Mortimer (1923–) British lawyer and dramatist.
A Voyage Round My Father, I

1974

1157 Publication is the male equivalent of childbirth.
Richard Acland (1906–) British politician and writer.
The Observer, 'Sayings of the Week', 19 May 1974

1158 Some breakfast food manufacturer hit upon the simple notion of emptying out the leavings of carthorse nosebags, adding a few other things like unconsumed portions of chicken layer's mash, and the sweepings of racing stables, packing the mixture in little bags and selling them in health food shops.
Frank Muir (1920–) British writer and broadcaster.
Upon My Word!

1159 Psychiatrists classify a person as neurotic if he suffers from his problems in living, and a psychotic if he makes others suffer.
Thomas Szasz (1920–) US psychiatrist.
The Second Sin

1975

1160 The best careers advice to give to the young is 'Find out what you like doing best and get someone to pay you for doing it.'
Katherine Whitehorn (1926–) British journalist.
The Observer, 1975

1976

1161 I think it's good for a writer to think he's dying; he works harder.
Tennessee Williams (1911–83) US dramatist.
The Observer, 'Sayings of the Week', 31 Oct 1976

1978

1162 Poets and painters are outside the class system, or rather they constitute a special class of
their own, like the circus people and the
gipsies.
Gerald Brenan (Edward Fitzgerald Brenan;
1894–1987) British writer.
Thoughts in a Dry Season, 'Writing'

1163 We are closer to the ants than to the butter-
flies. Very few people can endure much leisure.
Gerald Brenan
Thoughts in a Dry Season

1979

1164 I used to say that politics was the second lowest profession and I have come to know that it
bears a great similarity to the first.
Ronald Reagan (1911–) US president.
The Observer, 13 May 1979

1165 I should have worked just long enough to dis-
cover that I didn't like it.
Paul Theroux (1941–) US-born writer.
The Observer Magazine, 1 Apr 1979

1981

1166 The affluent society has made everyone dislike
work, and come to think of idleness as the
happiest life.
Geoffrey Keynes (1887–) British surgeon
and literary scholar.
The Observer, 25 Oct 1981

1167 Politicians can forgive almost anything in the
way of abuse; they can forgive subversion, revolution, being contradicted, exposed as liars,
even ridiculed, but they can never forgive being ignored.
Auberon Waugh (1939–) British novelist
and critic.
The Observer, 11 Oct 1981

1982

1168 Nowadays there are no serious philosophers
who are not looking forward to the pension to
which their involvement with the subject en-
titles them.
Anthony Quinton (1925–) British
philosopher.
Thoughts and Thinkers

1983

1169 The police are the only 24-hour social service
in the country.
Commander Alex Marnoch
Remark, Feb 1983

1984

1170 If I had been someone not very clever, I would

have done an easier job like publishing. That's
the easiest job I can think of.
A. J. Ayer (1910–89) British philosopher.
Remark, Sept 1984

1985

1171 The schoolteacher is certainly underpaid as a
childminder, but ludicrously overpaid as an
educator.
John Osborne (1929–) British dramatist.
The Observer, 'Sayings of the Week', 21 July
1985

1172 All politicians have vanity. Some wear it more
gently than others.
David Steel (1938–) British politician.
Remark, July 1985

1986

1173 To finish is both a relief and a release from an
extraordinarily pleasant prison.
Robert Burchfield (1923–) New Zealand
editor.
On completing the supplements to the Oxford
English Dictionary, Sept 1986

1989

1174 To the average British farmer, organic farming
is about as relevant as caviar and a flight on
Concorde.
Oliver Walston (1941–)
Speech, Jan 1989

1990

1175 I do not think British industry has made any
recognition whatsoever of the social revolution
of the 1980s and 1990s. Two out of every
three families are dual-career families, but industry has not designed itself in any way to
help women – or, indeed, men who have working wives – to cope with the new family
circumstance.
Cary Cooper (1940–) British psychologist.
Move Over Darling (Kathy Barnby and Loretta
Loach)

Sayings of the Time

1950s

1176 SIXTY HORSES WEDGED IN A CHIMNEY
The story to fit this sensational headline has
not turned up yet.
J. B. Morton (1893–1979) British journalist.
The Best of Beachcomber, 'Mr Justice Cockle-
carrot: Home Life'

1951

1177 Angry Young Man.
Leslie Paul (1905–85) British writer.
Book title

1955

1178 I never said, 'I want to be alone.' I only said, 'I want to be *left* alone.' There is all the difference.
Greta Garbo (1905–90) Swedish-born US film star.
Garbo (John Bainbridge)

1960

1179 Shoot all the bluejays you want, if you can hit 'em, but remember it's a sin to kill a mockingbird.
Harper Lee (1926–) US writer.
To Kill a Mockingbird, Pt. II, Ch. 10

1962

1180 Who's Afraid of Virginia Woolf?
Edward Albee (1928–) US dramatist.
Play title

1181 It is hard to tell where the MCC ends and the Church of England begins.
J. B. Priestley (1894–1984) British novelist.
New Statesman, 20 July 1962, 'Topside Schools'

1967

1182 Sergeant Pepper's Lonely Hearts Club Band.
The Beatles British rock band.
Album title

1969

1183 I'll make him an offer he can't refuse.
Mario Puzo (1920–) US novelist.
The Godfather, Ch. 1

1973

1184 All the faces here this evening seem to be bloody Poms.
Charles, Prince of Wales (1948–) Eldest son of Elizabeth II.
Remark at Australia Day dinner, 1973

1975

1185 Don't mention the war.
John Cleese (1939–) British comedian.
Fawlty Towers (BBC television programme, 1975) (with Connie Booth)

1977

1186 May the Force be with you.
George Lucas (1945–) US film director.
Star Wars

1978

1187 The opera isn't over till the fat lady sings.
Dan Cook US journalist.
Washington Post, 13 June 1978

1979

1188 Pretentious? *Moi?*.
John Cleese (1939–) British comedian.
Fawlty Towers (BBC television programme, 1979) (with Connie Booth)

1189 Far out in the uncharted backwaters of the unfashionable end of the Western Spiral arm of the Galaxy lies a small unregarded yellow sun.
Orbiting this at a distance of roughly ninety-two million miles is an utterly insignificant little blue green planet whose ape-descended life forms are so amazingly primitive that they still think digital watches are a pretty neat idea.
Douglas Adams (1952–) British writer.
The Hitch Hiker's Guide to the Galaxy, Introduction

1980

1190 I tend to believe that cricket is the greatest thing that God ever created on earth . . . certainly greater than sex, although sex isn't too bad either.
Harold Pinter (1930–) British dramatist.
The Observer, 5 Oct 1980

1991

1191 It was the wrong kind of snow.
Terry Worrall British railway manager.
Explaining why British Rail's anti-snow measures had not worked
The Observer, 17 Feb 1991

With Foresight

1192 Boast not thyself of tomorrow; for thou knowest not what a day may bring forth.
Bible: Proverbs
27:1

1193 If you want a picture of the future, imagine a boot stamping on a human face – for ever.
George Orwell (Eric Blair; 1903–50) British novelist.
Nineteen Eighty-Four

1194 I have a vision of the future, chum.
The workers' flats in fields of soya beans
Tower up like silver pencils.
John Betjeman (1906–84) British poet.

1195 The future is made of the same stuff as the present.
Simone Weil (1909–43) French philosopher.
On Science, Necessity, and the Love of God (ed. Richard Rees), 'Some Thoughts on the Love of God'

1196 The Earth is just too small and fragile a basket for the human race to keep all its eggs in.
Robert Heinlein (1907–88) US science-fiction writer.
Speech to the US Naval Academy, 1973

1197 The only good thing about Hammerfall, women's lib was dead milliseconds after Hammerstrike.
Larry Niven (1938–) US science-fiction writer.
'Hammerfall' was a fictional collision in the late 1970s between the Earth and a large comet that destroyed civilization
Lucifer's Hammer, Pt. III (with Jerry Pournelle)

1198 This is the way the world ends
Not with a bang but a whimper
T. S. Eliot (1888–1965) US-born British poet and dramatist.
The Hollow Men

Keyword Index

A

abandon A. hope, all ye who enter — 6:123
abideth now a. faith, hope, charity — 3:95
abilities From each according to his a. — 10:127
Great a. are not requisite for an Historian — 8:361
ability a.,...is capacity to act wisely — 12:529
distressed by his want of a. — 2:41
One should oblige everyone to...one's a. — 8:380
abolished The state is not 'a.', it withers away — 11:17
war can only be a. through war — 13:39
abortion A....an appalling trivialisation of...procreation — 13:975
The greatest destroyer of peace is a. — 13:983
abroad an honest man sent to lie a. for...his country — 7:414
know something of his own country...before he goes a. — 8:469
absence clearer in his a. — 12:592
in a fit of a. of mind — 11:38
absolute For Fascism the State is a. — 12:248
The sovereign is a. — 8:164
absolutism A. tempered by assassination — 10:42
abstinence vices...require moderate use rather than total a. — 11:441
abstract a. reasoning concerning quantity or number — 8:342
absurd All art deals with the a. — 13:550
I have...taken his side when a. men have condemned him — 8:349
something rather a. about the past — 11:280
There is nothing so a. — 4:95
absurdist why A. plays take place in No Man's Land — 13:525
abuse If it is a. — 8:427
the more dangerous the a. — 8:181
Whipping and a. are like laudanum — 10:138
abusive to accuse someone of trying to be funny is highly a. — 13:722
Academe And seek for truth in the groves of A. — 4:40
accent a. of one's birthplace lingers — 8:376
accept I will not a. if nominated — 11:64
acceptable the a. face of capitalism — 13:281
accidentally A. — 10:83
accord My cousin Francis and I are in perfect a. — 7:5
accuse A. not Nature, she hath done her part — 8:378
I a. — 11:86
accused Never make a defence...before you be a. — 7:113
accustomed become a. to no one governing — 12:72
I will start to get a. to it — 11:195
ace someone else was about to play the a. — 11:317
achieve those who a. something — 12:617
To a. great things — 8:463
acquire poor men and rich may possess what they rightly a. — 5:9
act last a. crowns the play — 7:179
acting The danger chiefly lies in a. well — 8:557
action Liberty of a. — 8:131
lust in a. — 7:325
man...unable to decide a general principle of a. — 11:27
No a. is in itself good or bad — 13:948
The true men of a....are...scientists — 13:1095
The unmotivated a. — 12:973
actor An a.'s a guy who — 13:1141
Adam A. was but human — 11:295
When A. delved — 6:49
addiction a. of political groups to ideas — 13:113
Every form of a. is bad — 13:964
prisoners of a. and...prisoners of envy — 13:802
the terminal point of a. is...damnation — 13:974

adjectives to tell the substantives from the a. — 12:410
administration a. must be entrusted to experts — 12:155
admiral good to kill an a. — 8:136
salutes the A. of the Pacific — 11:92
admire one cannot possibly a. them — 11:501
The English instinctively a. — 13:990
admiring the cure for a. the House of Lords — 10:236
adolescence a man suffering from petrified a. — 13:35
maturity is only a short break in a. — 13:804
Adonais I weep for A. — 10:269
adores he a. his maker — 10:104
The ignorant man always a. — 11:310
adorned as a bride a. for her husband — 3:124
adrenal larger cerebrums and smaller a. glands — 12:612
Adullam retired into...his political Cave of A. — 10:234
adult A child becomes an a. when — 13:808
What is an a. — 13:784
adultery I've committed a. in my heart — 13:981
thou shalt not commit a. — 1:40
advanced years behind the a. countries — 12:215
advantage a. of time and place...is half a victory — 7:61
The a. of doing one's praising — 11:440
advantages Wealth is not without its a. — 13:1122
advertised Wealth...must be a. — 13:1121
advertisement the worst a. for Socialism is its adherents — 12:299
advertisers as the a. don't object to — 12:171
advice a....poised between the cliché — 13:356
woman seldom asks a. — 8:515
advocate the soul of a martyr with the intellect of an a. — 10:184
Aesculapius we owe a cock to A. — 2:6
affairs tide in the a. of men — 7:277
affections different taste in jokes is a...strain on the a. — 11:316
affluent the a. society — 13:1120
The a. society...made everyone dislike work — 13:1166
afford purest treasure mortal times a. — 7:267
afraid A. of Virginia Woolf — 13:1180
be not a. to do thine office — 7:22
Africa more familiar with A. than my own body — 13:876
something new out of A. — 4:66
When a white man in A. — 13:44
afterlife that the a. will be any less exasperating — 12:896
afternoon could lose the war in an a. — 12:37
I could have lost the war in an a. — 12:47
against He said he was a. it — 12:888
This is a. fighting ever hereafter — 7:128
Agamemnon's Many brave men...before A. time — 2:82
age A child blown up by a. — 13:784
a. of chivalry is gone — 9:10
A. shall not weary them — 12:92
A. will bring all things — 8:484
an a. in which useless knowledge — 13:614
Crabbed a. and youth — 7:273
do not necessarily improve with a. — 13:829
no a. between ten and three and twenty — 7:196
nothing in thy youth, how canst thou find any thing in thine a. — 1:77
not of an a., but for all time — 7:176
Old a....gives us what we have earned — 13:816
old a. is...older than I am — 13:744
Our parents' a....has produced us — 4:12
what a. takes away — 9:167
When men grow virtuous in their old a. — 8:453
when Mozart was my a. — 8:670
Years hence, perhaps, may dawn an a. — 10:567

aged a. diplomats...bored than for young men to die 13:167
agenda Our a. is now exhausted 13:6
agent prime a. of all human perception 10:359
ages His acts being seven a. 7:274
aggregate the a. of the recipes 12:928
aggressor whole world should be ranged against an a. 12:255
agnostic rather a compliment to be called an a. 12:880
agony a lonely spasm of helpless a. 11:244
agreeable I do not want people to be very a. 9:146
agreement My people and I have come to an a. 8:178
  Whenever you accept our views we shall be in full a. 13:316
agricultural the a. labourers...commute from London 13:586
Aids A. pandemic is a classic own-goal 13:861
  to stop them catching A. 13:857
air my spirit found outlet in the a. 12:628
  to the Germans that of the a. 9:39
airplane The a. stays up because it doesn't have the time to
  fall 11:492
Alamein Before A. we never had a victory 12:378
alarm The tocsin you hear today is not an a. but an alert 9:17
Albert A. was merely a young foreigner 10:657
  ask me to take a message to A. 11:26
  that A. married beneath him 12:464
alcohol A....enables Parliament to do things at eleven 11:132
alcoholic a. liquors have been used by the...best races 12:586
ale no more cakes and a. 7:362
ale-house jangled in every a. and tavern 7:32
alert The tocsin you hear today is not an alarm but an a. 9:17
Alexander If I were not A. 2:12
Algérie A. Française 13:105
alien State socialism is totally a. 13:381
alive Bliss was it in that dawn to be a. 9:208
  needst not strive...to keep a. 10:568
  not one will still be a. in a hundred years' time 2:49
  We intend to remain a. 13:257
  what matters is to come out a. 12:687
all a. for one, and one for a. 10:642
  a. our yesterdays 7:287
  Damn you, Jack – I'm a. right 11:542
allegiance Not bound to swear a. to any master 4:15
allies former a. had blundered 12:251
ally An a. has to be watched 12:190
almonds Don't eat too many a. 12:991
alone All we ask is to be let a. 10:192
  And we are left, or shall be left, a. 9:64
  I want to be a. 12:982
  'I want to be a..' 13:1178
  No poet...has...meaning a. 12:461
  To be a. is the fate of all great minds 10:468
  woe to him that is a. when he falleth 1:69
  You come into the world a. 13:834
Alpha A. and Omega 3:120
altars struggled in poverty to build these a. 11:468
alternative a need to create an a. world 13:564
am I a. that I a. 1:35
  in the infinite I A. 10:359
  I think therefore I a. 7:304
amateur America...is the prize a. nation 12:56
amateurs a disease that afflicts a. 11:209
  nation of a. 11:94
ambition A. is the grand enemy of all peace 12:619
  A. should be made of sterner stuff 7:358
  A writer's a. should be 13:493
  Every man has...an a. to be a wag 8:442
  Let not A. mock 8:627
  What argufies pride and a. 8:322
America A....based on the dreams of spinsters 12:847
  A. cannot be an ostrich 12:36
  A.!.../God shed His grace on thee 11:70
  A....has gone directly from barbarism to degeneration 12:845
  A. is a country of young men 11:455
  A. is a large, friendly dog 13:1002
  A. is just ourselves 10:250
  A. is...the great Melting-Pot 11:135
  A. is the only idealistic nation 12:833
  A....is the prize amateur nation 12:56
  A.'s really only a kind of Russia 13:754
  ask not what A. will do for you 13:143

declares unconditional war on poverty in A. 13:196
elected a vestryman by the people of any parish in A. 8:261
first come to pass in the heart of A. 13:71
His foreparents came to A. 13:427
most memorable epoch in the history of A. 8:205
The business of A. is business 12:159
the greatest that we owe to the discovery of A. 10:340
The national dish of A. 13:1035
to be willing to grant A. independence 8:235
Vietnam was lost in the living rooms of A. 13:290
what makes A. what it is 12:860
when we think of thee, O A. 8:202
Why will A. not reach out...to Russia 12:126
woman governs A. 13:995
You cannot conquer A. 8:221
American A. continents,...not to be considered as subjects
  for future colonization 10:20
  A. heiress wants to buy a man 13:1020
  A. society...half judaised and half negrified 12:870
  A. system of rugged individualism 12:840
  An A. is either a Jew, or an anti-Semite 13:1013
  I am not a Virginian, but an A. 8:191
  I am willing to love all mankind, *except an A.* 8:228
  If I were an A., as I am an Englishman 8:223
  Let's talk sense to the A. people 13:64
  Long Island represents the A.'s idea 12:846
  Scratch an A. 13:1025
  the A. abroad 12:857
  the A. flag will float over...the British North A. possessions
  11:154
  the greatest A. friend we have ever known 12:399
  Thirteen States..., concur in erecting one great A. system
  8:257
  We are all A. at puberty 13:1017
  whereby A. girls turn into A. women 13:279
Americanism hyphenated A. 12:29
  McCarthyism is A. 13:62
Americans A. have a perfect right to exist 11:271
  A. have been conditioned to respect newness 13:1031
  A....very good at refrigerators 12:345
  because A. won't listen to sense 12:416
  No one can kill A. and brag 13:396
  the matter with A. 12:855
  when good A. die they go to Paris 11:457
ammunition Praise the Lord and pass the a. 12:360
am'rous dire offence from a. causes springs 8:489
analysed Everything has been discussed and a. 8:346
analysis historian fits a man for psychological a. 12:970
anarchy grieved under a *democracy*, call it a. 7:152
ancestor I am my own a. 9:99
ancestors a. on either side of the Battle of Hastings 12:610
  when his half-civilized a. were hunting the wild boar 10:436
ancient with the a. is wisdom 1:61
anecdotage man fell into his a. 11:324
angel A. of Death has been abroad 10:153
  A. of the Lord came down 8:593
  in action, how like an a. 7:240
  In heaven an a. is nobody in particular 11:352
  This was the A. of History 12:400
angels a little lower than the a. 6:18
  fools rush in where a. fear to tread 8:337
  I...am on the side of the a. 10:620
  Not Angles, but a. 5:3
  People are not fallen a. 12:429
  the tongues of men and of a. 3:95
anger A. is one of the sinews of the soul 7:259
  Grief and disappointment give rise to a. 8:550
  he that is slow to a. is better than the mighty 1:83
Angles Not A., but angels 5:3
Angli the *Saxones, A.,* and *lutae* 5:1
Anglo-Catholic Becoming an A. must...be a sad business
  13:1043
angry A. Young Man 13:1177
  The man who gets a....in the right way...is commended 2:65
animal Man is a gaming a. 10:403
  man is and will always be a wild a. 12:922
  Man is an intellectual a. 10:363
  man is...a religious a. 9:196

artistic a. temperament...afflicts amateurs   11:209
There never was an a. period   11:179
artists A. are not engineers of the soul   13:523
Great a. have no country   10:302
The a. retired. The British remained   11:185
art-loving an A. nation   11:179
arts If all the a. aspire to the condition of music   12:916
rustics...bringing up their...offspring to the liberal a.   6:17
secret of the a. is to correct nature   8:276
ashamed not a. of having been in love   8:482
to see them not a.   8:400
We are not a. of what we have done   11:137
Asia There is too much A.   11:456
the Sultan were driven, bag and baggage. into the heart of A.   10:14
ask a., and it shall be given   3:129
To labour and not a. for any reward   7:349
asks where no one a., no one needs to answer   12:716
aspires a....to the condition of art   11:193
ass An unlettered king is a crowned a.   6:133
every a. thinks he may kick at him   8:307
assassination A....the extreme form of censorship   11:145
Absolutism tempered by a.   10:42
A. has never changed   10:232
assemblance Care I for the...a. of a man   7:232
assertions Pure mathematics consists entirely of a.   12:904
asset the greatest a. a head of state can have   13:293
associate good must a.   8:177
assure a. him that he'd live tomorrow   7:392
astonished a. at my own moderation   8:187
asunder let not man put a.   3:73
asylum the absence from Jerusalem of a lunatic a.   12:878
world is...like a lunatic a.   12:734
asylums lunatic a....the stately homes   12:516
atheism a., breast-feeding, circumcision   13:777
miracle to convince a.   7:400
atheist an a. if the king were   8:590
he was no a.   8:42
scepticism kept her from being an a.   13:720
Athens a new A. might be created in the land of the Franks   5:7
A. arose   10:16
men of A....ye are too superstitious   3:47
Atlantic The Admiral of the A.   11:92
to have the East come to the A.   12:401
atom carbon a. possesses certain exceptional properties   12:923
how the a. is split   12:926
nearer to the a. than the stars   12:914
The a. bomb is a paper tiger   13:8
There is no evil in the a.   13:1087
They split the a. by firing particles at   13:1081
atomic The way to win an a. war   13:61
atoms fortuitous concurrence of a.   10:166
atone a. for the sins of your fathers   4:14
atrophy Music begins to a.   12:483
attack love until after the first a.   11:377
situation excellent. I shall a.   12:80
attainments rare a....but...can she spin   7:346
attention a. to the inside...contempt for the outside   8:344
take his a. away from the universe   13:1064
attorney the gentleman is an a.   8:643
attraction Every arrow...feels the a. of earth   10:564
attractively Women are entitled to dress a.   13:937
audacity a. of elected persons   10:164
Auden A. was someone you could laugh-at-with   13:549
W. H. A., a sort of gutless Kipling   12:491
audience the a. was a disaster   11:201
Augustus said of A. that he found Rome brick   10:160
Austen Jane A.   10:278
Austerlitz There rises the sun of A.   9:89
Australia guess...he was born in A.   11:460
author bad novel tells us...about its a.   11:208
authority a. be a stubborn bear   7:102
A. forgets a dying king   10:183
Nothing destroyeth a. so much   7:99
purge the land of...false a.   6:36
The defiance of established a.   13:268

authors A. are easy to get on with   13:488
much exposed to a.   10:291
The faults of great a.   9:126
The reciprocal civility of a.   8:288
autocracy maintain the principle of a.   11:75
autocrat be an a.: that's my trade   8:143
avarice rich beyond the dreams of a.   8:628
ave a. atque vale   4:96
avenged the satisfaction of knowing that we are a.   10:570
average no great compliment to say that a man is above the a.   13:610
Take the saving lie away from the a. man   11:332
avoiding Reading...ingenious device for a. thought   10:377
Avon Sweet Swan of A.   7:175
a-waggle You must always be a.   12:748
awake At last a.   10:470
I dream when I am a.   7:303
Onaway! A., beloved   10:508
away the big one that got a.   13:870
awfulness by its very a.   11:383
awoke I a. one morning   9:128
axe his keener eye /The a.'s edge did try   7:137
Lizzie Borden took an a.   11:67
axioms the world can be expressed in...arguments...a. and theorems   13:636
axis This Berlin–Rome connection is...an a.   12:273
aye A., and what then   10:584

B

baa B. b., black sheep   6:56
Babbitt one thing wrong with the B. house   12:768
Babel B.; because the Lord did there confound the language   1:23
the tower of B. should have got language all mixed up   8:165
babies If men had to have b.   13:888
putting milk into b.   12:780
War will never cease until b.   12:612
baby my b. at my breast   4:10
no new b. in the womb of our society   12:68
Babylon B. the great   3:100
By the waters of B. we sit down and weep   8:202
Bach J. S. B.   8:669
bachelor Never trust...a b. too near   12:764
bachelors reasons for b. to go out   10:535
back Either b. us or sack us   13:319
Will ye no come b. again   8:662
backs With our b. to the wall...each...must fight on to the end   12:78
backward In a country economically b., the proletariat can take power earlier   12:175
bad a b. man must have brains   11:303
a b. novel tells us the truth about its author   11:208
a brave b. man   7:163
A truth that's told with b. intent   9:188
Defend the b. against the worse   12:503
never was a b. peace   8:249
nothing either good or b.   7:359
the name of...obstinacy in a b. one   8:556
what I feel really b. about   13:211
When b. men combine   8:177
bag b. and baggage   11:6
the Sultan were driven, b. and baggage, into the heart of Asia   10:14
baggage bag and b.   11:6
the Sultan were driven, bag and b., into the heart of Asia   10:14
balance The b. of power   8:116
balanced b. state of well-modulated dis-satisfaction   11:28
Baldwin not quite forget...B. till we're out of debt   12:288
Balfour Mr B.'s Poodle   11:130
Balkans some damned silly thing in the B.   11:83
ballot The b. is stronger than the bullet   10:163
balm wash the b. from an anointed king   7:70
bananas Kuwait...sold b. or oranges   13:456
bang Not with a b. but a whimper   12:689, 13:1198
banish to b....the dark divisive clouds of Marxist socialism   13:379

It was the b. of times   9:210
Men of few words are the b.   7:234
The b. is the enemy of the good   8:559
the b. of possible worlds   8:470
There died a myriad, /And of the b.   12:117
we live in the b. of all possible worlds   12:600
we will do our b.   12:356
bestial   what remains is b.   7:285
best-seller   A b. is the gilded tomb of a mediocre talent 12:478
Bethlehem   O come ye to B.   10:592
betray   All a man can b. is his conscience   11:454
betrayed   woe unto that man by whom the Son of man is b.
                                                          3:26
betraying   if I had to choose between b. my country and b.
my friend   13:59
better   always...trying to get the b.   10:403
B. than a play   8:14
b. to have no opinion of God   7:403
b. to marry than to burn   3:74
for b. for worse   7:339
I am getting b. and b.   11:537
no b. than you should be   7:249
When you meet someone b....turn your thoughts to
becoming his equal   2:42
You're a b. man than I am, Gunga Din   11:530
bewailing   the sum of life's b.   10:456
Bible   have used the B. as if it was a constable's handbook
                                                          10:110
the B. tells me so   10:600
There's a B. on that shelf there   13:1060
Bibles   they have the land and we have the B.   13:823
bicycle   a b. made for two   11:372
big   B. Brother is watching you   13:30
he was too b. for them   13:25
the b. one that got away   13:870
bike   He got on his b. and looked for work   13:357
billabong   Once a jolly swagman camped by a b.   11:535
billboards   the churches...bore for me the same relation to
God that b. did to Coca-Cola   13:1063
billiards   to play b. well   11:305
biographies   History is the essence of...b.   10:390
biography   a man is nobody unless his b.   10:486
history...the b. of great men   10:392
biological   male is a b. accident   13:914
bird   keep such a b. in a cage   7:101
She's only a b. in a gilded cage   11:534
birds   b....caught in the snare   1:76
I see all the b. are flown   7:120
spring now comes unheralded by the return of the b.   13:585
that make fine b.   2:34
Birmingham   One has no great hopes from B.   10:326
birth   B., and copulation, and death   12:695
no credentials...not even...a certificate of b.   11:143
no cure for b. and death   12:681
birthplace   accent of one's b. lingers   8:376
bishop   a b....must be blameless   3:127
May you be the mother of a b.   13:719
No B., no King   7:86
the symbol of a b. is a crook   13:1065
bisier   he semed b. than he was   6:131
bitch   an old b. gone in the teeth   12:117
bitches   Now we are all sons of b.   12:402
bite   would b. some other of my generals   8:133
bites   dead woman b. not   7:56
when a man b. a dog that is news   12:662
bivouac   an armed camp of Blackshirts, a b. for corpses
                                                          12:131
black   A lady asked me why..., I wore b.   13:779
Any colour, so long as it's b.   12:974
I don't believe in b. majority rule   13:303
looking for a b. hat   11:257
People think we do not understand our b....countrymen 13:422
sees b. people as expendable   13:397
The Ethiopians say that their gods are...b.   2:70
To like an individual because he's b.   13:1018
blacks   two b. do not make a white   12:824
Blackshirt   Before the organization of the B. movement 12:275

Blackshirts   an armed camp of B., a bivouac for corpses
                                                          12:131
blame   Everyone threw the b. on me   12:202
blanket   not a b. woven from one thread, one color, one cloth
                                                          13:1038
blast   The First B. of the Trumpet   7:41
bleed   If you prick us, do we not b.   7:231
blemish   Christianity...the one immortal b. of mankind 11:474
blessed   all generations shall call me b.   3:2
B. are the meek   3:80
b. are the poor in spirit   3:79
b. are they that have not seen, and yet have believed   3:42
b. is he that cometh in the name of the Lord   3:25
b. is the man that endureth temptation   1:89
blessings   all which we behold /Is full of b.   9:163
a world of b. by good Queen Elizabeth   7:40
blind   A b. man in a dark room   11:257
Booth died b.   11:166
Country of the B.   11:367
love is b.   7:316
old, mad, b., despised and dying king   10:4
Painting is a b. man's profession   13:482
wing'd Cupid painted b.   7:315
blindness   the...world was stumbling...in social b.   12:653
bliss   B. was it in that dawn to be alive   9:208
block   a chip of the old b.   8:247
blockhead   No man but a b. ever wrote   8:300
blonde   springing from b. to b. like the chamois of the Alps
                                                          12:851
blood   be his b. on your own conscience   8:30
b. and iron   10:207
B. sport is brought to its ultimate refinement   13:598
b., toil, tears and sweat   12:326
drown in their own b.   13:455
He is all b., dirt and sucked sugar stick   12:486
his b. be on us   3:33
my b. of the new testament   3:27
rather have b. on my hands   13:216
shed his b. for the country   11:112
The b. of the martyrs is the seed of the Church   4:89
the River Tiber foaming with much b.   13:232
thy brother's b. crieth unto me   1:16
trading on the b. of my men   10:256
without shedding of b. is no remission   3:51
your b. of your lives will I require   1:21
bloody   All the faces...seem to be b. Poms   13:1184
not half b. enough   8:45
bloom   It's a sort of b. on a woman   11:415
blow   A b. in cold blood   11:386
Another year! – another deadly b.   9:64
B., b., thou winter wind   7:357
b. the Scots back again into Scotland   7:89
themselves must strike the b.   9:94
bludgeoning   the b. of the people   11:65
blue   The b. ribbon of the turf   10:343
bluffed   Winston Churchill has b. them all   12:165
blunder   poverty...is a b.   11:500
worse than a crime, it is a b.   9:49
blunders   b. usually do more to shape history
than...wickedness   13:654
blushes   Man is the only animal that b.   11:299
Boadicea   some bargain-basement B.   13:366
boar   the b. out of the wood doth waste it   7:6
when his half-civilized ancestors were hunting the wild b.
                                                          10:436
boat   a beautiful pea-green b.   10:655
in the same b....not a chance of recording the vote   11:141
boating   Jolly b. weather   10:348
bodies   many b. of the saints which slept arose   3:39
our dead b. must tell the tale   11:159
well-developed b., fairly developed minds   12:530
body   a sound mind in a sound b.   4:67
b. of a weak and feeble woman   7:65
Happiness is beneficial for the b.   12:579
Man has no B. distinct from his Soul   9:197
mind that makes the b. rich   7:350
more familiar with Africa than my own b.   13:876
Our b. is a machine for living   10:622

take, eat; this is my b.   3:27
your b. is the temple of the Holy Ghost   3:66
Bognor Bugger B.   12:262
boiler The United States is like a gigantic b.   12:850
bomb god of science…has given us the atomic b.   13:1098
bombed no power on earth that can protect him from being b.   12:221
bombs b. *are* unbelievable until they…fall   13:151
Come, friendly b., and fall on Slough   12:522
drop b.…hit civilians   13:217
test the Russians, not the b.   13:101
Bonaparte The three-o'-clock in the morning courage, which B. thought was the rarest   9:209
Bonar Law all the politicians…least significant was B.   12:140
bones Bleach the b. of comrades slain   11:78
O ye dry b.   1:107
The healthy b. of a single Pomeranian grenadier   11:7
bonkers If the British public falls for this…it will be…b.   13:201
bonny Is b. and blithe, and good and gay   10:640
book a b.…sealed with seven seals   3:121
A b. that furnishes no quotations is…a plaything   10:281
A good b. is the best of friends   10:288
A good b. is the precious life-blood   7:183
Another damned, thick, square b.   8:309
any b. should be banned   12:172
Bell, b., and candle   7:351
closed the b. on apartheid   13:472
Everybody writes a b. too many   13:576
he who destroys a good b., kills reason   7:182
I have only read one b.   12:511
little woman who wrote the b.   10:198
moral or an immoral b.   11:187
that everyone has it in him to write one b.   12:495
The possession of a b.   13:630
There are two motives for reading a b.   12:470
There must be a man behind the b.   10:315
When a b. is boring, they yawn openly   13:887
books All b. are divisible into two classes   10:319
be not swallowed up in b.   8:336
between a man of sense and his b.   8:344
B. are a load of crap   13:512
B. are…a mighty bloodless substitute for life   11:174
B. are well written, or badly written   11:187
b. by which the printers have lost   7:222
b. cannot be killed by fire   12:374
B. must follow sciences   7:405
B.…propose to *instruct* or to *amuse*   10:310
b.…written by people who don't understand them   8:292
but b. never die   12:374
Give me b., fruit, French wine and fine weather   10:330
Morality's a gesture…learnt from b.   13:959
proper study of mankind is b.   12:531
the b. of the hour   10:319
the disease of writing b.   8:287
The reading of all good b.   7:181
To read too many b.   13:642
We all know that b. burn   12:374
Whenever b. are burned   10:15
When I think of all the b. I have read   12:731
booksellers b. are generous liberal-minded men   8:640
nor even b. have put up with poets' being second-rate   4:30
boorish the opinionated, the ignorant, and the b.   2:44
boot imagine a b. stamping on a human face   13:1193
Booth B. died blind   11:166
boots before the truth has got its b. on   13:305
If ever he went to school without any b.   13:25
bore a b., a bounder and a prig   12:253
bored aged diplomats to be b.   13:167
Punctuality is the virtue of the b.   13:965
boredom three great evils, b., vice, and poverty   8:641
bores he b. for England   13:34
the *B.* and *Bored*   10:444
boring curiously b. about…happiness   12:585
born a time to be b., and a time to die   1:75
better if neither of us had been b.   9:80
he is not conscious of being b.   8:450
I was b. at the age of twelve   13:1139
joy that a man is b. into the world   3:76

Man was b. free   8:144
natural to die as to be b.   7:206
One is not b. a woman   13:897
Some are b. great   7:282
sucker b. every minute   11:289
to have been b.   7:302
We are all b. mad   13:670
borrow If you don't want to use the army, I should like to b. it   10:204
borrowed Britain has lived…on b. time   13:304
borrower Neither a b. nor a lender be   7:360
borrowing be not made a beggar by banqueting upon b.   1:86
b. dulls the edge of husbandry   7:360
boss working…eight hours a day…get to be a b.   12:963
Boston this is good old B.   11:150
bother long words B. me   12:976
Botticelli If B. were alive today   13:522
bottinney b. means a knowledge of plants   10:372
bottles the English have hot-water b.   13:989
bottom b. of the economic pyramid   12:217
boundary right to fix the b.   11:46
bountiful Lady B.   8:651
bourgeois How beastly the b. is   12:790
bourgeoisie the British b. have spoken of themselves as gentlemen   12:842
bourn from whose b. /No traveller returns   7:208
bow B., b., ye lower middle classes   11:32
I, said the Sparrow, /With my b. and arrow   6:3
bowels in the b. of Christ   7:145
boy And said, What a good b. am I   7:25
every b. and every gal /That's born into the world alive   11:34
He was a b. to the last   10:367
Let the b. win his spurs   6:44
Love is a b.   8:498
rarely…one can see in a little b. the promise of a man   10:538
Shades of the prison-house begin to close /Upon the growing b.   9:199
the b. will ruin himself   12:258
the little b. /Who lives down the lane   6:56
boys As flies to wanton b.   7:210
B. and girls come out to play   8:652
B. are capital fellows in their own way   10:513
B. do not grow up gradually   12:728
Girls and b. grow up more normally together   13:469
Where are the b. of the Old Brigade   11:536
Where…b. plan for what…young girls plan for whom   11:411
Written by office b. for office b.   11:79
brain a Bear of Very Little B.   12:976
Let schoolmasters puzzle their b.   8:351
brains b. enough to make a fool of himself   11:249
our b. as fruitful as our bodies   8:510
What good are b. to a man   12:773
brainsick folly of one b. Pole   7:27
braking British civil service…effective b. mechanism   13:338
brandy I am not well; pray get me…b.   9:29
brass Men's evil manners live in b.   7:375
sounding b.   3:95
brave Any fool can be b. on a battle field   12:625
land of the free, and the home of the b.   9:103
Many b. men…before Agamemnon's time   2:82
we could never learn to be b.…if there were only joy   11:338
bravery man of the greatest honour and b.   6:22
breach Once more unto the b.   6:61
breache lay the b. at their door   8:15
bread b. and circuses   4:24
I am the b. of life   3:109
Jesus took b., and blessed it   3:27
man shall not live by b. alone   3:78
Peace, B. and Land   12:60
that b. should be so dear   10:95
the living b.   3:14
breakfast-table ready for the national b.   10:486
breast charms to soothe a savage b.   8:275
my baby at my b.   4:10
breast-feeding atheism, b., circumcision   13:777
breasts they add weight to the b.   12:991
breath Can storied urn…/Back to its mansion call the fleeting b.   8:319

He reaps the bearded grain at a b. — 10:354
world will hold its b. — 12:354
breathed God...b. into his nostrils — 1:7
breed happy b. of men — 7:69
more careful of the b. of their horses and dogs than of their
children — 8:501
breezes spicy b. /Blow soft o'er Ceylon's isle — 10:405
bribe You cannot hope to b. or twist — 12:951
bride as a b. adorned for her husband — 3:124
It helps...to remind your b. that you gave up a throne for her — 13:882
bridge London B. is broken down — 8:654
brief Out, out, b. candle — 7:287
brigade Forward the Light B. — 10:149
Where are the boys of the Old B. — 11:536
bright b. with hope — 12:178
brightness To pass away ere life hath lost its b. — 10:353
brilliance No b. is needed in the law — 13:1156
brilliant a far less b. pen than mine — 11:549
b. men...will come to a bad end — 11:366
The dullard's envy of b. men — 11:366
Britain a time when B. had a savage culture — 13:168
battle of B. is about to begin — 12:336
B....Fabian Society writ large — 13:300
B. fit country for heroes to live in — 12:98
B. is no longer in the politics of the pendulum — 13:321
B. is not...easily rocked by revolution — 13:300
When B. first, at heaven's command — 8:115
Britannia Rule, B., rule the waves — 8:115
British B. loathe the middle-aged — 13:832
but we are B. – thank God — 13:844
I would rather be B. than just — 13:255
less known by the B. than these selfsame B. Islands — 10:341, 10:341
socialism...alien to the B. character — 13:381
the American flag will float over...the B. North American
possessions — 11:154
The artists retired. The B. remained — 11:185
The B., being brought up on team games — 13:110
The B. love permanence — 13:527
The B. won't fight — 13:362
the magnificent fair play of the B. criminal law — 11:124
the most vulgar,...is the B. tourist — 11:223
when a B. Prime Minister sneezed — 13:313
British Empire 'Can't' will be the epitaph of the B. — 12:292
liquidation of the B. — 12:377
Briton as only a free-born B. can do — 10:108
I glory in the name of B. — 8:139
Britons B. never will be slaves — 8:115
B. were only natives — 4:102
broils never to entangle ourselves in the b. of Europe — 10:19
broken A b. head in Cold Bath Fields — 10:53
bats have been b....by the team captain — 13:443
baying for b. glass — 12:841
broker An honest b. — 11:13
bronchitis nobody goes to the theatre unless he...has b. — 12:867
brothel a sort of metaphysical b. for emotions — 12:736
brothels b. with bricks of Religion — 9:25
brother am I my b.'s keeper — 1:16
Big B. is watching you — 13:30
I want to be the white man's b. — 13:160
brotherhood Freedom! Equality! B. — 9:2
brother-in-law not his b. — 13:160
brotherly let b. love continue — 3:98
brothers the poor are our b. and sisters — 13:1130
brought b. nothing into this world — 3:71
bruise it shall b. thy head — 1:13
sweetest fragrance from the herb...tread on it and b. it — 10:539
Brummell patronized...by B. and the Prince Regent — 9:132
Brussels meeting in a darkened bedroom in a B. hotel — 13:289
brutality Sentimentality is a superstructure covering b. — 13:673
brutes Thanks to words, we have been able to rise above
the b. — 13:504
Brutus Caesar had his B. – Charles the First, his Cromwell — 8:153
bubble Life is mostly froth and b. — 10:494
buck The b. stops here — 13:66

Buckingham changing guard at B. Palace — 12:975
bugger B. Bognor — 12:262
build let us think that we b. for ever — 10:298
The *end* is to b. well — 7:178
builder he can only be a *b*. — 10:308
building Well b. hath three Conditions — 7:178
buildings jostling scrum of office b. — 13:578
Luftwaffe –...knocked down our b. — 13:579
piles of b. now rise up and down — 8:313
built till we have b. Jerusalem — 9:73
bull Down at the old 'B. and Bush' — 11:237
bullet Each b. has got its commission — 8:322
The b. that is to kill me — 9:101
bulrushes an ark of b. — 1:31
bums art and literature are left to a lot of shabby b. — 12:836
bunk History is more or less b. — 12:561
burden Take up the White Man's b. — 11:95
The dreadful b. — 8:543
burial Knight of the Crimean B. Grounds — 10:159
burn better to marry than to b. — 3:74
burned Whenever books are b. — 10:15
burning To keep a lamp b. — 13:980
burnings B. of people — 7:419
bury I come to b. Caesar, not to praise him — 13:93
We will b. you — 12:321
bus Hitler has missed the b. — 1:33
bush the b. burned with fire — 11:387
business a woman's b. to get married — 12:11
B. as usual — 10:623
B....may bring money,...friendship hardly ever does — 11:369
B. underlies everything in our national life — 10:498
If everybody minded their own b. — 13:662
it is...our b. to lose innocence — 10:415
That's the true b. precept — 12:159
The b. of America is b. —
the future Englishmen must take b. as seriously as their
grandfathers had done — 11:110
businessmen My message to the b. of this country — 13:857
busy How doth the little b. bee — 8:637
It is a stupidity...to b. oneself with the correction of the world — 8:446
thou knowest how b. I must be this day — 7:122
butchers Governments needs to have both shepherds and
b. — 8:232
butchery Had any Christian bishop visited that scene of b. — 10:165
butler I vote Labour, but my b.'s a Tory — 12:420
butter b. will only make us fat — 12:274
fine words b. no parsnips — 10:448
buttered I had never had a piece of toast.../But fell...on the
b. side — 11:333
butterfly a man dreaming I was a b. — 2:53
Happiness is like a b. — 13:680
buttress a b. of the church — 10:79
buy American heiress wants to b. a man — 13:1020
would never b. my pictures — 10:301
bypass a conscience b. — 13:447
Byron a more worthless set than B. — 10:284
the words: B. is dead — 10:271

C

Caesar Ave C., morituri te salutant — 4:18
C. had his Brutus – Charles the First, his Cromwell — 8:153
C.'s laurel crown — 9:47
C.'s wife must be above suspicion — 2:51
hast thou appealed unto C. — 3:49
I always remember that I am C.'s daughter — 4:17
I come to bury C. — 4:7
render...unto C. the things which are C.'s — 3:117
that C. might be great — 9:144
Caesars So long as men worship the C. and Napoleons — 12:294
cage keep such a bird in a c. — 7:101
Marriage is like a c. — 7:331
Nor iron bars a c. — 7:119
She's only a bird in a gilded c. — 11:534

chamois springing from blonde to blonde like the c. of the Alps — 12:851

champagne Fighting is like c. — 12:625
like a glass of c. that has stood — 13:220
water flowed like c. — 11:29

chance c. favours only the prepared mind — 10:614
time and c. happeneth to them all — 1:76
We have had our last c. — 12:406

Chancellor C. of the Exchequer — 11:1

change C. is not made without inconvenience — 7:263
If you leave a thing alone you leave it to a torrent of c. — 11:363
Most of the c. we think we see — 12:705
Plus ça c. — 10:465
Popularity?...glory's small c. — 10:459
The more things c. — 10:465
The wind of c. — 13:130

changing Woman is always fickle and c. — 4:77

Channel let the last man...brush the C. with his sleeve — 12:6

chaos The grotesque c. of a Labour council – a *Labour* council — 13:390
the view that there is mounting c. — 13:327

chapel Devil always builds a c. there — 8:594

characteristic typically English c. — 12:849

characters Most women have no c. — 8:517

charge Electrical force...causes motion of electrical c. — 12:915

Charing-Cross the full tide of human existence is at C. — 8:194

chariot a c....of fire — 1:52

charity C. is the power of defending that which we know to be indefensible — 11:442
c. never faileth — 3:95
c. suffereth long, and is kind — 3:95
knowledge puffeth up, but c. edifieth — 3:56
now abideth faith, hope, c. — 3:95
the greatest of these is c. — 3:95

Charles Caesar had his Brutus – C. the First, his Cromwell — 8:153
cast out C. our Norman oppressor — 7:141

Charlie C. is my darling — 8:663

charter This c....constitutes an insult to the Holy See — 6:32

chaste godly poet must be c. himself — 2:25

chastity Give me c. and continence — 5:29

cheap flesh and blood so c. — 10:95
War is never c. or easy — 13:459

check C. enclosed — 13:715

cheek whosoever shall smite thee on thy right c. — 3:83

cheer Don't c., boys; the poor devils are dying — 11:85

cheese 265 kinds of c. — 13:60

chemical c. barrage has been hurled against the fabric of life — 13:1094
Shelley and Keats were...up to date in...c. knowledge — 12:908

cheques The rich hate signing c. — 13:1131

cherish to love and to c. — 7:339

cherry Loveliest of trees, the c. — 11:232

chess-board c. is the world; the pieces...the phenomena of the universe — 10:495

chestnuts warmongers who...have others pull the c. out of the fire — 12:348

chicken a c. in his pot every Sunday — 7:78
England will have her neck wrung like a c. — 12:335
Some c. — 12:364

chickens children are more troublesome and costly than c. — 11:390
Don't count your c. — 2:32
You don't set a fox to watching the c. — 13:137

child A c. becomes an adult when — 13:808
getting wenches with c. — 7:196
give her the living c. — 1:49
If you strike a c. — 11:386
spoil the c. — 8:498
sweetest Shakespeare, Fancy's c. — 7:180
Think no more of it, John; you are only a c. — 6:24
unto us a c. is born — 1:99
when I was a c., I spake as a c. — 3:95
wise father that knows his own c. — 7:332

childbirth the male equivalent of c. — 13:1157

childish I put away c. things — 3:95

childishness second c. — 7:275

children as c. fear to go in the dark — 7:205

c. are more troublesome and costly than chickens — 11:390
C. have never been very good at listening — 13:757
C....have no use for psychology. They detest sociology — 13:887
c., obey your parents — 3:75
C. should acquire...heroes and villains from fiction — 13:659
C. sweeten labours — 7:335
desire not a multitude of unprofitable c. — 1:80
except ye...become as little c. — 3:104
He that loves not his wife and c. — 7:338
in sorrow thou shalt bring forth c. — 1:13
Let our c. grow tall — 13:297
like a c.'s party taken over by the elders — 12:419
make your c. *capable of honesty* is the beginning of education — 10:386
Many c. are suffering from muesli-belt malnutrition — 13:599
Men are but c. of a larger growth — 8:388
more careful of the breed of their horses and dogs than of their c. — 8:501
My music...understood by c. and animals — 13:520
the early marriages of silly c. — 10:516
the Revolution may...devour each of her c. — 9:24
To bear many c. is considered...an investment — 13:292
To employ women and c. unduly — 10:540
to seyn, to syngen and to rede, /As smale c. doon — 6:105
write for c....as you do for adults — 12:490

chimney sixty horses wedged in a c. — 13:1176

chimney-sweepers As c., come to dust — 7:212

Chinese Nothing...can destroy the C. people — 13:265

chip c. of the old block — 8:247

chirche-dore Housbondes at c. — 6:118

chivalry age of c. is gone — 9:10
The age of c. is never past — 10:467

chocolate Venice is like eating...c. liqueurs — 13:1014

choose *We can believe what we c.* — 10:596

chose *plus c'est la même c.* — 10:465

Christ C....would quite likely have been arrested — 13:185
I beseech you, in the bowels of C. — 7:145
only a male can represent C....serious heresy — 13:1078
We're more popular than Jesus C. — 13:532

Christendom Of the two lights of C. — 6:70
wisest fool in C. — 7:100

Christian A C....feels /Repentance on a Sunday — 11:479
Better sleep with a sober cannibal than a drunken C. — 10:562
C. glories in the death of a pagan — 6:6
C. resolution to find the world ugly — 11:470
C. Science explains all cause and effect as mental — 11:465
I die a C. — 7:136
I was born of C. race — 8:458
No Jew was ever fool enough to turn C. — 11:471
The C. religion...cannot be believed by any reasonable person without one — 8:598
The C. religion not only was at first attended with miracles — 8:598

Christianity C. accepted as given a metaphysical system — 12:897
C. is part of the Common Law of England — 7:162
C. is the most materialistic of all great religions — 12:895
C....says that they are all fools — 11:474
C. the one great curse — 11:474
C....the one immortal blemish of mankind — 11:474
local cult called C. — 11:476
loving C. better than Truth — 10:586
Rock and roll or C. — 13:532
single friar who goes counter to all C. — 7:8

Christians these C. love one another — 4:88
they may be Catholics but they are not C. — 13:331

Christ-like C. heroes and woman-worshipping Don Juans — 12:787

Christmas Eating a C. pie — 7:25
For C. comes but once a year — 7:188
Let them know it's C. — 13:385
perceive C. through its wrapping — 13:1047
'Twas the night before C. — 10:333

Christopher C. Robin went down with Alice — 12:975

church an alien C. — 10:96
Beware when you take on the C. of God — 13:1072
custom of the Roman C. — 5:33
he'd go to c., start a revolution – *something* — 13:790

diversion Most sorts of d....are an imitation of fighting 8:402
diversity make the world safe for d. 13:169
divided Obstinate people can be d. into 2:44
  Thought must be d. against itself 12:545
divine The right d. of kings to govern wrong 8:99
  To be discontented with the d. discontent 11:423
  To err is human, to forgive, d. 8:401, 8:547
divines Many a long dispute among d. 8:599
divinity a d. that shapes our ends 7:399
  a piece of d. in us 7:308
  There's such d. doth hedge a king 7:82
divisions How many d. has *he* got 12:260
divorce d....Blame our obsolete sex roles 13:884
do D. as you would be done by 8:553
  D. other men 10:415
  for they know not what they d. 3:35
  I am to d. what I please 8:178
  Nature...hath done her part; D. thou but thine 8:378
  they would d. you 10:415
Dobest Dowel, Dobet and D. 6:119
Dobet Dowel, D. and Dobest 6:119
doctor A d....is a patient half-cured 12:955
doctrine a d. so illogical and so dull 12:993
documents sign d. which they do not read 12:638
dog America is a large, friendly d. 13:1002
  A woman's preaching is like a d.'s walking on his hinder legs 8:521
  The little d. laughed /To see such sport 7:52
  the only passers-by who can contemplate it...are those...with a white stick and a d. 13:575
dogs how much more d. are animated when they hunt in a pack 8:412
  let slip the d. of war 7:77
  like asking a lamp-post...about d. 13:565
  more careful of the breed of their horses and d. than of their children 8:501
  woman who is...kind to d. 11:420
doing Anything that is worth d. 13:726
  Find out what you like d. best and get someone to pay you for d. it 13:1160
  let us not be weary in well d. 3:70
  we learn by d. 2:28
  Whatever is worth d. 8:552
dollar The almighty d....object of universal devotion 10:158
dominion establish...sure English d. in India for all time to come 8:49
dominions The sun does not set in my d. 7:73
dominoes a row of d. set up; you knock over the first 13:80
done Do as you would be d. by 8:553
  d. those things we ought not 8:368
  Justice should...be seen to be d. 12:805
  Let justice be d. 7:44
  the dread of doing what has been d. before 12:447
  thy worldly task hast d. 7:212
  What you do not want d. to yourself 2:61
Don Juans Christ-like heroes and woman-worshipping D. 12:787
donkeys lions led by d. 12:27
Dons If the D. sight Devon 7:64
Doodle Yankee D. came to town 8:212
door I am the d. 3:111
  the judge standeth before the d. 3:64
  world will make a beaten path to his d. 10:432
Dorchester All terrorists...end up with drinks at the D. 13:194
doublethink D....holding two contradictory beliefs 13:32
doubt new Philosophy calls all in d. 7:407
  O thou of little faith, wherefore didst thou d. 3:132
  When a man is in d. about...his writing 11:218
doubts end in d. 7:217
Dove No visit to D. Cottage, Grasmere, is complete 9:215
dove and the d. came in to him 1:20
  the wings of a d. 8:429
Dover It is burning a farthing candle at D. 8:291
  the chalk cliffs of D. 12:241
Dowel D., Dobet and Dobest 6:119
dower forfeited their ancient English d. 9:71
down for coming d. let me shift for myself 7:21
  He that is d. 8:448

Yes, and they went d. very well too 9:11
drainpipe wrong end of a municipal d. 12:323
drains to distinguish between the Deity and the D. 10:658
Drake D. he's in his hammock 7:63
dramatist Sherard Blaw, the d. who had discovered himself 11:219
Drang *Sturm und D.* 8:301
drawing the Suez Canal was flowing through my d. room 13:90
dread the d. of doing what has been done before 12:447
dreadful Other people are quite d. 11:296
Dreadnoughts A...Duke costs as much...as two D. 11:144
dream All men d.: but not equally 12:601
  awakened from the d. of life 10:451
  For life is but a d. 11:328
  Happiness is no vague d. 10:429
  hope is...the d. of those that wake 8:404
  I d. when I am awake 7:303
  I have a d. 13:173
  The young men's vision, and the old men's d. 8:32
  To sleep, perchance to d. 7:209
  warned of God in a d. 3:10
  Where is it now, the glory and the d. 9:196
dreamer this d. cometh 1:29
dreamers the d. of the day are dangerous men 12:601
dreamin' d....o' Plymouth Hoe 7:63
dreaming a man d. I was a butterfly 2:53
  City with her d. spires 10:349
dreams dream our d. away 12:702
  D. and predictions 7:294
  For one person who d. of making fifty thousand pounds 12:942
  I, being poor, have only my d. 12:670
  show life...as we see it in our d. 11:192
  Than this world d. of 10:608
  We are nothing; less than nothing, and d. 10:452
  We are such stuff /As d. are made on 7:174
  what d. may come 7:209
dreamt d. of in your philosophy 7:280
dreary d. intercourse of daily life 9:163
  If your morals make you d. 11:430
dregs the foul d. of his power, the tools of despotism and corruption 8:145
dress The Englishman's d. is like a traitor's body 7:384
dressed All d. up, with nowhere to go 12:35
drink A population sodden with d. 11:226
  D. to me only with thine eyes 7:329
  I commended mirth...to eat...to d., and to be merry 1:71
  let us eat and d.; for tomorrow we...die 1:78
  soft d. at a party 13:600
  woe unto them that...follow strong d. 1:87
drinkers no verse can give pleasure...that is written by d. of water 4:28
drinking D....and making love 8:425
  let me die d. in an inn 6:95
  the increase in d. is to be laid mainly to the account of the female sex 11:414
  'Tis not the d....but the excess 8:312
  Work is the curse of the d. classes 11:520
dripping Constant d. hollows out a stone 4:57
  electricity was d. invisibly 12:929
driver in the d.'s seat 12:992
droit *Dieu et mon d.* 6:27
drôle *une d. de guerre* 12:318
dromedary whose muse on d. trots 10:266
dropsies there were people who died of d. 8:188
drown d. in their own blood 13:455
drug Words are...the most powerful d. 12:442
drum Not a d. was heard 9:76
  Take my d. to England 7:64
drums the beating of war d. 13:652
drunk My mother, d. or sober 11:100
  you won't intoxicate with one glass someone who has...d...a...barrel 11:180
drunken Better sleep with a sober cannibal than a d. Christian 10:562
  He uses statistics as a d. man uses lamp-posts 11:323
drunkenness A branch of the sin of d. 7:193
  there is more drinking...less d. 11:414

dry out of these wet clothes and into a d. Martini — 12:648
O ye d. bones — 1:107
the midst of the sea upon d. ground — 1:38
Dublin D., though…much worse than London — 8:240
Duce The D. is always right — 12:130
duckling The Ugly D. — 10:646
duel war…will be considered as antiquated as a d. — 11:153
Duke A…D. costs as much…as two Dreadnoughts — 11:144
How very mean a thing's a D. — 8:95
dukes a drawing-room full of d. — 13:1093
dulce Died some…/non 'd.' non 'et decor' — 12:118
D. et decorum est — 4:13
dull a doctrine so illogical and so d. — 12:993
Heaven…is a place so inane, so d. — 12:872
He was d. in a new way — 8:299
Music-hall songs provide the d. with wit — 11:253
dullard The d.'s envy of brilliant men — 11:366
dumplings I am the emperor, and I want d. — 10:115
dunces the d. are all in confederacy against him — 8:454
dung no grass there groweth, /Only their engines' d. — 11:225
dusk slow d. a drawing-down of blinds — 12:21
dust As chimney-sweepers, come to d. — 7:212
d. shalt thou eat — 1:13
d. thou art — 1:14
this quintessence of d. — 7:240
duty a stupid man…always declares that it is his d. — 11:433
d. of an opposition — 11:73
England expects every man will do his d. — 9:53
give my d. to the Queen — 8:77
It is my d. to warn you that it will be used against you — 11:124
Patriotism…is a revolutionary d. — 12:69
right of all…d. of some — 9:87
the d. of being happy — 11:283
this is the whole d. of man — 1:95
What's a man's first d. — 10:573
dying Don't cheer, boys; the poor devils are d. — 11:85
For a priest to turn a man when he lies a-d. — 8:592
good for a writer to think he's d. — 13:1161
He had been, he said, a most unconscionable time d. — 8:40
it is not death, but d., which is terrible — 8:318
we survive amongst the dead and the d. as on a battlefield — 13:753
dykes our d.,…are ten feet deep — 11:93
dynamic class people as static and d. — 12:793
play is a d. thing — 13:517

E

ear I took the right sow by the e. — 8:105
jest's prosperity lies in the e. — 7:260
Earl As far as the 14th E. is concerned — 13:182
Life is much easier, being an E. — 13:223
the whole process has ground to a halt with a 14th E. — 13:181
early A useless life is an e. death — 8:480
E. to rise and e. to bed — 12:651
too e. to form a final judgement on the French Revolution — 9:214
earn this is the week I e. my salary — 13:156
earned Old age…gives us what we have e. — 13:816
earning learning, e. and yearning — 12:657
ears e. to hear, let him hear — 3:131
Romans, countrymen, lend me your e. — 4:7
the seven thin e. — 1:30
earth a new heaven and a new e. — 3:124
But did thee feel the e. move — 12:760
E. has not anything to show more fair — 9:130
E. is just too small and fragile a basket — 13:1196
from whose face the e. and the heaven fled — 3:55
God called the dry land E. — 1:2
God created…the e. — 1:1
heaven and e. shall pass away — 3:105
hell upon e….in a melancholy man's heart — 7:298
I will move the e. — 2:79
mine were princes of the e. — 10:436
more things in heaven and e. — 7:280
passenger on the spaceship, E. — 13:791
the cool flowery lap of e. — 10:305
The e. does not argue — 10:428
the e. is free for every son and daughter of mankind — 7:142

the e. is the Lord's, and the fulness — 3:68
the e. of England is in my two hands — 5:12
The meek do not inherit the e. — 12:703
This e. of majesty — 7:69
ease True e. in writing comes from art — 8:279
easeful half in love with e. Death — 10:350
east E. is E., and West is West — 11:543
Now we can look the E. End in the face — 12:341
to have the E. come to the Atlantic — 12:401
to prevent us from going into the E. — 12:401
wise men from the e. — 3:9
easterly praying…for an E. wind — 8:53
Eastertide I love the gay E. — 6:96
easy It's either e. or impossible — 13:489
eat Don't e. too many almonds — 12:991
great ones e. up the little ones — 7:245
I commended mirth…to e.…to drink, and to be merry — 1:71
I could e. one of Bellamy's veal pies — 9:60
if any would not work, neither should he e. — 3:126
let us e. and drink; for tomorrow we…die — 1:78
To e. well in England — 13:1022
eaten daring…to explain…that cows can be e. — 13:291
eating sign something he…use us — 13:955
eats e., sleeps and watches the television — 13:881
Man is the only animal…on friendly terms with the victims…he e. — 11:313
ecclesiastic E. tyranny's the worst — 8:75
echo The sound must seem an e. to the sense — 8:279
economic a great social and e. experiment — 12:174
bottom of the e. pyramid — 12:217
lack of efficiency in using scientific achievements for e. needs — 13:419
economics I am not prepared to accept the e. of a housewife — 13:411
She is the Enid Blyton of e. — 13:339
Voodoo e. — 13:345
economist Jesus was…a first-rate political e. — 11:481
Practical men,…are usually the slaves of some defunct e. — 12:276
economists All races have…e., with the exception of the Irish — 13:1033
economy E. is going without something you do want — 11:294
Everybody is always in favour of general e. — 13:87
ecu can call an e. a pound — 13:450
eczema style…often hides e. — 13:679
Eden a garden eastward in E. — 1:7
futile to attempt a picnic in E. — 13:662
Sir Anthony E. — 13:34
the garden of E. — 1:8
This other E., demi-paradise — 7:69
edge his keener eye /The axe's e. did try — 7:137
We stand today on the e. of a new frontier — 13:127
educate e. a woman you e. a family — 13:609
e. with the head instead of with the hand — 11:269
education a liberal e. at the Colleges of Unreason — 11:246
E….has produced a vast population able to read — 12:558
e. is a leading out of what is…in the pupil's soul — 13:623
E. is…the soul of a society — 12:538
E. is what survives — 13:629
E. made us what we are — 8:350
fortunate in escaping regular e. — 13:616
if e. is…a mere transmission of knowledge — 13:612
make all this fuss about e. — 10:378
make your children capable of honesty is the beginning of e. — 10:386
'Tis e. forms the common mind — 8:339
educations last resort of feeble minds with classical e. — 12:957
Edward King E….made Lord E….Prince of Wales — 6:40
Edwardian plants left over from the E. Wilderness — 13:749
eena E., meena, mina, mo — 11:41
effeminate wanton and e. sound — 6:92
effort What is written without e. — 8:306
efforts One is happy as a result of one's own e. — 10:429
egalitarianism The majestic e. of the law — 11:72
égalité Liberté! É.! Fraternité — 9:2
egg a broody hen sitting on a china e. — 13:203
egotism dilemmas of conscience and e. — 13:97
Egypt We are not at war with E. — 13:89

The fundamental f. of the female character	10:529
worst f. of the working classes	13:429

faults f., do not fear to abandon them | 2:39
If we had no f. of our own | 8:526
When you have f. | 2:39
favour accepts a smaller as a f. | 10:156
every man feel that he is enjoying his special f. | 7:1
Many terms…out of f., will be revived | 4:31
truths being in and out of f. | 12:705
favoured thou that art highly f. | 3:1
favours On whom their f. fall | 10:524
Whether a pretty woman grants or withholds her f. | 4:79
fear concessions of f. | 8:199
do I f. thy nature | 7:244
f. God, and keep his commandments | 1:95
F. no more the heat o' th' sun | 7:212
fools rush in where angels f. to tread | 8:337
freedom from f. | 12:347
Men f. death | 7:205
one has…ceased to be an object of f. as soon as one is pitied | 11:282
only thing we have to f. is f. | 12:219
Perhaps your f. in passing judgement | 7:76
the f. of one evil | 8:536
fears A man who f. suffering | 7:226
man f.…only the stroke of death | 7:204
The sum of their f. | 12:384
feathers not only fine f. | 2:34
February dreadful pictures of January and F. | 10:345
Excepting F. alone /And that has twenty-eight days clear | 7:415
feed F. the World | 13:385
You cannot f. the hungry on statistics | 11:121
feeding Spoon f.…teaches us nothing but the shape of the spoon | 13:613
feel what I f. really bad about | 13:211
feels A really intelligent man f. what other men…know | 8:410
feet An emperor ought at least to die on his f. | 4:20
die on your f. than to live on your knees | 12:271
those f. in ancient time | 9:73
feigning truest poetry is the most f. | 7:170
fell f. among thieves | 3:16
men f. out | 8:369
fellows Boys are capital f. in their own way | 10:513
fellowship such a f. of good knights shall never be together | 6:76
female male and f. created he them | 1:5
see the F. Eunuch the world over | 13:944
the f. of the species is more deadly than the male | 11:417
The fundamental fault of the f. character | 10:529
the increase in drinking is to be laid mainly to the account of the f. sex | 11:414
females No vote can be given by lunatics…f. | 8:160
feminine Taste is the f. of genius | 11:395
Février Generals Janvier and F. | 10:141
few err as grosly as the F. | 8:33
owed by so many to so f. | 12:338
fickle Woman is always f. and changing | 4:77
fiction ancient history,…is no more than accepted f. | 8:362
Children should acquire…heroes and villains from f. | 13:659
one form of continuous f. | 13:583
Poetry is a comforting piece of f. | 12:434
fiddle Hey diddle diddle, /The cat and the f. | 7:52
field A cow is a very good animal in the f. | 8:138
Man for the f. and woman for the hearth | 10:528
shepherds abiding in the f. | 3:5
some corner of a foreign f. | 12:31
fields East and west on f. forgotten | 11:78
Now there are f. where Troy once was | 2:83
fiend forgive the f. for becoming a torrent | 9:100
fierce f. and bald and short of breath | 12:82
fifteen we might more reasonably expect f. years of peace | 9:14
fifth One f. of the people are against everything | 13:198
The F. Column | 12:291
fifty At f. everyone has the face he deserves | 13:732
F.-four forty or fight | 10:98
For one person who dreams of making f. thousand pounds | 12:942

there are f. thousand men slain…, and not one Englishman	8:104

fight a great cause to f. for | 11:137
easier to f. for one's principles | 12:603
Fifty-four forty or f. | 10:98
f., f., f., and f. again | 13:129
F. the good f. with all thy might | 10:599
I f. on, I f. to win | 13:444
I have not yet begun to f. | 8:233
I purpose to f. it out on this line | 10:215
I will not cease from mental f. | 9:73
Our cock won't f. | 12:283
The British won't f. | 13:362
To f. and not to heed the wounds | 7:349
too proud to f. | 12:26
Ulster will f. | 11:49
We don't want to f., but, by jingo if we do | 11:16
We'll f. and we'll conquer | 8:132
we shall f. on the beaches | 12:328
With our backs to the wall…each…must f. on to the end | 12:78
You cannot f. against the future | 10:233
fighting F. is like champagne | 12:625
Most sorts of diversion…are an imitation of f. | 8:402
not conquering but f. well | 11:361
This is against f. ever hereafter | 7:128
What are we f. for | 12:195
fights I can't spare this man; he f. | 10:217
fig leaves they sewed f. together | 1:12
films Why…pay money to see bad f. | 13:503
fine f. feathers that make f. birds | 2:34
In England, pop art and f. art | 13:510
finest their f. hour | 12:330
finger I will shake my little f. – and there will be no more Tito | 13:21
fingers about time we pulled our f. out | 13:142
our f. are circumcised | 13:574
fings F. Ain't Wot They Used T'Be | 13:582
finished it is f. | 3:38
finite Our knowledge can only be f. | 13:621
fire a chariot…of f. | 1:52
All things, oh priests, are on f. | 2:68
a pillar of f. | 1:37
cloven tongues like as of f. | 3:44
F. – without hatred | 12:272
French Guard, fire first | 8:120
Ideas that enter the mind under f. | 12:188
It is with our passions as it is with f. and water | 8:487
that deplorable f. near Fish Street in London | 8:8
the bush burned with f. | 1:33
The f.…walks in a broader gross | 8:9
The f. which in the heart resides | 10:566
two irons in the f. | 7:373
firebell a f. in the night | 10:12
fireside A man may surely be allowed to take a glass of wine by his own f. | 9:125
firm not a family; we're a f. | 13:41
firmness *Commodity, F., and Delight* | 7:178
first many that are f. shall be last | 3:65
The F. Blast of the Trumpet | 7:41
there is no last or f. | 10:591
Who ever loved, that loved not at f. sight | 7:317
firstborn I…will smite all the f. | 1:36
first-rate the powers of a f. man and the creed of a second-rate man | 10:122
fish a great f. to swallow up Jonah | 1:58
No human being,…was ever so free as a f. | 10:490
This man…is a poor f. | 13:870
fishers f. of men | 3:19
fishes f. live in the sea | 7:245
five barley loaves, and two small f. | 3:13
So are the f. | 12:342
fishing Time is but the stream I go a-f. in | 10:479
fist You cannot shake hands with a clenched f. | 13:253
fit It is not f. that you should sit here | 7:157
fitly no one in the realm…f. to come to me | 6:71
fits periodical f. of morality | 10:274
five If you don't find a God by f. o'clock this afternoon | 11:473
practise f. things | 2:60

G

heretic I shall never be a h. 7:2
hero better to be the widow of a h. than the wife of a coward 12:270
heroes Children should acquire...h. and villains from fiction 13:659
fit country for h. to live in 12:98
speed glum h....to death 12:82
Unhappy the land that has no h. 12:732
heroic human beings are h. 12:365
hert Myn h. ys set 6:68
hesitate A leader who doesn't h....is not fit to be a leader 13:968
hesitates A science which h. to forget 12:921
heterodoxy H. or Thy-doxy 10:371
hidden Nature is often h. 7:248
hiding man who looks you...in the eye...h. something 13:682
high civil fury first grew h. 8:369
highbrow What is a h. 12:552
highlights h. and shadows of our history 13:452
highly at no time stand so h. in our estate royal 7:31
Highness His Royal H....prides himself upon...the excellent harvest 9:82
will not fail to attend your H. upon your landing 8:54
hill If the h. will not come to Mahomet 7:98
Tonight the American flag floats from yonder h. 8:220
hills a fine thing to be out on the h. alone 11:224
him he could not avoid making H. set the world in motion 8:588
himself He would kill H. 10:493
hinky H., dinky, par-lee-voo 12:77
historian A good h. is timeless 8:359
A h. is a prophet in reverse 9:143
Great abilities are not requisite for an H. 8:361
h. fits a man for psychological analysis 12:970
The h. must have...some conception of how men...behave 12:563
historians H. are like deaf people 11:279
H. tell the story of the past 10:323
history ancient h....is no more than accepted fiction 8:362
blunders usually do more to shape h. than...wickedness 13:654
deal of h. to produce...literature 11:171
diplomatic h. is...what one clerk said to another clerk 12:569
From today...there begins a new epoch in the h. of the world 9:18
He was...a student of h. 10:659
h....a tableau of crimes and misfortunes 8:363
H. gets thicker 13:657
H. is more or less bunk 12:561
H. is past politics 11:273
H. is philosophy teaching by examples 4:41
H. is too serious 13:653
h. must be false 8:360
h. of England is...the h. of progress 10:393
h....the biography of great men 10:392
h....the register of the...misfortunes of mankind 8:364
If men could learn from h. 10:387
It is impossible to write ancient h. 11:277
longest suicide note in h. 13:372
never looks like h. 13:658
no h.; only biography 10:391
one of these is the h. of political power 12:572
poetry is...more philosophical...than h. 2:31
Political h. is far too criminal...to be...fit...for the young 13:659
The attitude of the English...toward English h. 12:570
the greatest week in the h. of the world 13:235
The h. of all...society is the h. of class struggles 10:117
The h. of the World is the World's court 9:142
the lukewarm who make h. 12:567
The most persistent sound...through men's h. 13:652
This was the Angel of H. 12:400
trace...the disasters of English h. to...Wales 12:843
War makes...good h. 11:274
history-making Man is a h. creature 13:655
hit If you would h. the mark 10:564
never h. softly 11:164
Hitler every time H. occupies a country 12:320
Herr H. and Signor Mussolini had been at Oxford 12:290
H. has carried out a revolution on our lines 12:249

H. has missed the bus 12:321
H. showed surprising loyalty to Mussolini 12:999
H. was a nuisance. Mussolini was bloody one purpose, the destruction of H. 12:410 / 12:370
The people H. never understood 12:1000
tipster who...reached H.'s level of accuracy 12:996
hobgoblin the h. of little minds 10:375
hog he rides like a h. in armour 8:58
Rule all England under a h. 6:82
hoi the multitude, the *h. polloi* 8:56
hold To have and to h. 7:339
holder office sanctifies the h. 11:54
holiday the little h. steamers made an excursion to hell 12:329
holiness put off H. 9:139
the h. of the heart's affections 10:546
hollow We are the h. men 12:688
within the h. crown 6:55
Hollywood the attitude of a H. director toward love 12:570
holy dropped the word 'H.' to give it a more mass-market appeal 13:1076
everything that lives is h. 9:159
h., h., h., is the Lord of hosts 1:96
the H. Roman Empire was neither h., nor Roman, nor an empire 8:169
unite in some h. confederacy 7:26
Holy See This charter...constitutes an insult to the H. 6:32
home Father,...come h. with me now 11:222
For h. is best 7:189
h. his footsteps he hath turn'd 9:169
H. is the sailor, h. from sea 11:243
H. of lost causes 10:230
I can get all that at h. 13:521
Irish H. Rule is conceded 11:71
Many a man who thinks to found a h. 12:513
permits you to be entertained...by people you wouldn't have in your h. 13:592
there's no place like h. 10:514
We are all H. Rulers today 12:103
we come /From God, who is our h. 9:199
homely A h. face...aided many women heavenward 11:413
Homer even excellent H. nods 4:29
Mr Gladstone read H. for fun 11:545
The author of that poem is either H. 12:450
homo The 'h.' is the legitimate child 12:784
honest An h. broker 11:13
An h. God 11:467
an h. man sent to lie abroad for...his country 7:414
give me six lines...by the most h. man 7:258
It's better to be quotable than...h. 13:977
not an h. man 10:561
Though I am not naturally h. 7:374
honestly If possible h., if not, somehow, make money 4:91
honesty H. is the best policy 10:561
make your children *capable of h.* is the beginning of education 10:386
honey a land flowing with milk and h. 1:34
gather h. all the day 8:637
They took some h., and plenty of money 10:655
honi *H. soit qui mal y pense* 6:43
honour All is lost save h. 7:12
could not love thee.../Loved I not H. 7:123
h. all men 3:50
h. is for the poor 13:1134
H. pricks me on 7:353
h. sinks where commerce long prevails 8:150
h. thy father and thy mother 1:40
if I accepted the h....I would not answer for the integrity of my intellect 10:422
man of the greatest h. and bravery 6:22
only h. and life have been spared 7:12
peace I hope with h. 11:14
So h. peereth in the meanest habit 7:350
To h. we call you 8:132
Wealth has never been a sufficient source of h. 13:1121
honourable His designs were strictly h. 8:504
the most h. thing that man...has ever produced 10:311
hook canst thou draw out leviathan with an h. 1:103
hope Abandon h., all ye who enter here 6:123

intoxicate you won't i. with one glass someone who
has...drunk...a...barrel 11:180
intrigue the i. of a Greek of the lower empire 10:185
invasion no stand can be made against i. by an idea 10:379
the long-promised i. 12:342
invent it would be necessary to i. Him 8:612
invention Woman's virtue is man's greatest i. 12:801
inventions All one's i. are true 10:307
investment There is no finer i. 12:780
To bear many children is considered...an i. 13:292
invisible the only evil that walks /I. 8:532
invisibly electricity was dripping i. 12:929
Iraq the conquest of I. 13:458
Ireland I never met anyone in I. who understood the Irish
question 12:104
I. is the old sow 12:41
The moment...I. is mentioned 9:68
The problem with I. 13:1034
Irish All races have...economists, with the exception of the I. 13:1033
as I. as Black Americans 13:399
historic inability in Britain to comprehend I. feelings 13:425
I....devotion to higher arts 13:1033
I. might do very good Service 7:388
That is the I. Question 10:96
The English and Americans dislike only *some* I. 13:1010
The I. and the Jews have a psychosis 13:1009
The I. are a fair people 8:577
The I.,...are needed in this cold age 10:92
The I. don't know what they want 13:141
iron also wash and i. them 13:928
An i. curtain 13:1
blood and i. 10:207
the I. Curtain has been demolished 13:470
The I. Lady of British politics 13:311
irons two i. in the fire 7:373
irrelevant the most i. thing in nature 10:512
irresponsible better to be i. and right 13:42
Islam I. unashamedly came with a sword 5:35
island No man is an I. 7:299
wealth of our i. may be diminished 9:65
islands less known by the British than these selfsame British
I. 10:341
isle this sceptred i. 7:69
isolating by i. him...as if he were a leper 11:22
isolation our splendid i. 11:77
Italia I. farà da se 10:111
Italian imitation of the most fam'd I. masters 8:272
I speak...I. to women, French to men 7:16
The crafty, cold-blooded, black-hearted I. 12:349
Italians The I. will laugh at me 12:320
Italy A man who has not been in I. 8:217
I. a paradise for horses 7:386
I. is a geographical expression 10:581
without Rome I. cannot be constituted 10:197
itch the i. of literature 10:294
Iutae the *Saxones*, *Angli*, and *I.* 5:1

J

jab Man,...had been created to j. the life out of Germans 12:83
Jack Damn you, J. – I'm all right 11:542
J. the Ripper's dead 11:59
Little J. Horner /Sat in the corner 7:25
Two little whores.../J.'s knife flashes 11:57
Yours truly, J. the Ripper 11:58
jackal This whipped j. 12:352
Jackson J. standing like a stone wall 10:195
jam J. today, and men aren't at their most exciting 13:98
James King J. is good and honest 8:65
James Joyce J....Nothing but old fags and cabbage stumps
of quotations 12:454
jangled j. in every ale-house and tavern 7:32
January dreadful pictures of J. and February 10:345
Janvier Generals J. and Février 10:141
Japanese The J. have perfected good manners 13:1032
jaw-jaw To j. is better than to war-war 13:81

jazz J....people hear it through their feet 12:439
The basic difference between classical music and j. 13:540
the J. Age...became less and less an affair of youth 12:419
jealous a j. God 1:40
jealousy J....feeling alone among smiling enemies 12:826
J.'s rife in heroes' hall 12:165
of j.; /It is the green-ey'd monster 7:366
the ear of j. heareth all things 1:91
jeering laughing and j. at everything...strange 8:568
jeers j. at Fate 12:940
Jerusalem J. 9:73
the holy city, new J. 3:124
Till we have built J. 9:73
jest A j.'s prosperity lies in the ear 7:260
Life is a j. 8:460
Jesus If J. Christ were to come to-day 10:597
J. loves me – this I know 10:600
J. was...a first-rate political economist 11:481
when J. was born in Bethlehem of Judaea 3:9
Jew An American is either a J., or an anti-Semite 13:1013
Einstein – the greatest J. since Jesus 12:909
hated /by every anti-semite /as if I were a J. 13:152
Hath not a J. eyes 7:231
I was born of Christian race, /And not a Heathen, or a J. 8:458
No J. was ever fool enough to turn Christian 11:471
Pessimism is a luxury that a J. never can allow himself 13:1029
jewel that most precious j., the Word of God 7:32
jewelry she did not remember...her j. 12:792
Jewish A J. man with parents alive 13:1026
a *total solution* of the J. question 12:372
best that is in the J. blood 12:839
Jewry Modern Physics is an instrument of J. 12:933
Jews King of the J. 3:9
not enough prisons...in Palestine to hold all the J. 12:346
The Irish and the J. have a psychosis 13:1009
the J. bring the unlike into the heart of *every milieu* 11:461
the J. have made a contribution to the human condition 13:1036
jingo We don't want to fight, but, by j. if we do 11:16
Job J. endured everything – until his friends came 10:419
job Being a husband is a whole-time j. 12:765
Giz a j. 13:361
We have finished the j. 12:351
we will finish the j. 12:350
John Hell itself is defiled by...King J. 6:33
J., King and Priest, who dwells in the extreme Orient 6:111
Think no more of it, J.; you are only a child 6:24
Johnny J. head-in-air 12:357
J. underground 12:357
Johnson Dr J.'s morality was as English...as a beefsteak 8:666
That great Cham of literature, Samuel J. 8:289
There is no arguing with J. 8:294
join He's gone to j. the majority 4:38
joined what...God hath j. together 3:73
joke A j.'s a very serious thing 8:440
Housekeeping ain't no j. 10:542
The coarse j. proclaims 13:712
jokes different taste in j. is a...strain on the affections 11:316
Forgive...my little j. on Thee 13:1055
joking My way of j. is to tell the truth 11:321
Jonah a great fish to swallow up J. 1:58
Joseph Here lies J., who failed in everything he undertook 8:264
journal *Punch* – the official j. 13:596
journalism J. is the only job that requires no degrees 13:1153
j.....keeps us in touch with the ignorance of the community 11:516
j. what will be grasped at once 12:967
journalist the functions of the modern j. 11:518
to bribe or twist...the British j. 12:951
journalists J. say a thing that they know isn't true 12:950
joy Strength through j. 12:246
we could never learn to be brave...if there were only j. 11:338
joys For present j. 8:394
Hence, vain deluding J. 7:254
jubilation a day of j....remembrance and gratitude 13:451
Jubilee hurrah! we bring the J. 10:219
judge A j. is not supposed to know 13:1149

K

L

M

macaroni He stuck a feather in his cap /And called it m. 8:212
McCarthyism M. is Americanism 13:62
MacDonald Ramsay M. 12:256
mace that fool's bauble, the m. 7:156
machine a taxing m. 11:1
 cannot endow…m. with initiative 11:495
 Our body is a m. for living 10:622
 the Ghost in the M. 13:1041
 The m. is running away with *him* 12:312
 The m. threatens 12:907
machinery liberty…is to be measured not by the
 governmental m. 11:44
machines M. are the produce of the mind of man 10:610
 M.…keep free men in subjection 13:1103
 no reason…these m. will ever force themselves into general
 use 10:612
Macmillan M. seemed…to embody the national decay 13:131
MacWonder M. one moment and MacBlunder the next 13:276
mad escaped from a m. and savage master 2:54
 half of the nation is m. 8:140
 he ceased to be m. he became merely stupid 12:676
 he first makes m. 2:71
 M., bad, and dangerous to know 9:127
 Men will always be m. 8:619
 We all are born m. 13:670
maddest those who think they can cure them are the the m. 8:619
made My father m.…you…out of nothing 7:35
mademoiselle A m. from Armenteers 12:77
madman The m.…has lost everything except his reason
   11:309
 The m. is not the man who has lost his reason 11:309
madness devil's m. – War 12:195
 Great Wits…to M. near alli'd 8:447
 M. need not be all breakdown 13:689
maestro Music, M., Please 12:987
maggot how to create a m. 7:396
magic men mistook m. for medicine 13:1110
magicians if the way had not been prepared by m. 11:488
magistrate Obscenity…happens to shock some elderly…m.
   13:953
 suppose…the m. corruptible 9:21
magistrates rather than that the sovereigns and m. should
 be destroyed 7:14
 The power of kings and m. 7:144
Magna Charta M. is such a fellow 7:111
magnanimity in victory, m. 12:409
magnificent some m. myth 2:9
 there you sit with that m. instrument between your legs 12:476
magnify my soul doth m. the Lord 3:2
Mahomet If the hill will not come to M. 7:98
maid like a moth, the simple m. 8:516
majesty A sight so touching in its m. 9:130
 Ride on! ride on in m. 10:598
 This earth of m. 7:69
 When I invented the phrase 'His M.'s Opposition' 10:229
majority A m. is always the best repartee 10:106
 Fools are in a terrible…m. 11:331
 He's gone to join the m. 4:38
 I am certain that we will win the election with a good m. 13:409
 No candidate…elected ex-president by such a large m. 11:157
 the damned, compact, liberal m. 11:36
 the great silent m. 13:247
 The m. has the might 11:35
Majors scarlet M. 12:82
make a Scotsman on the m. 11:458
 The white man knows how to m. everything 11:63
maker he adores his m. 10:104
making If you get the English people into the way of m. kings
   10:81
mal *Honi soit qui m. y pense* 6:43
maladies Medical men…call all sorts of m.…by one name
   10:629
 There are m. we must not seek to cure 12:676
male especially the m. of the species 12:790
 In the sex-war thoughtlessness is the weapon of the m. 12:802
 m. and female created he them 1:5

 m. is a biological accident 13:914
 more deadly than the m. 11:417
 only a m. can represent Christ…serious heresy 13:1078
 when God became 'man' He chose to be a m. 13:1068
malicious God is subtle but he is not m. 12:917
malt M. does more than Milton 11:297
malvesye drowned in a barrel of m. 6:77
man a cold, hard, silent, practical m. 10:300
 all animals were created…for the use of m. 10:442
 a m. can die but once 7:202
 a m. has no reason to be ashamed of having an ape for his
 grandfather 10:619
 a m. is always seeking for happiness 12:770
 A m. should…own he has been in the wrong 8:399
 A m. with God 7:393
 apparel oft proclaims the m. 7:238
 behold the m. 3:31
 condition of m. is a condition of war 7:147
 England expects every m. will do his duty 9:53
 Every m. is as Heaven made him 7:252
 Every m. meets his Waterloo 10:182
 figure of 'The Reasonable M.' 12:568
 Go West, young m. 10:225
 hate ingratitude more in a m. 7:363
 I care not whether a m. is Good 9:139
 I myself also am a m. 3:46
 I said to the m. who stood at the gate of the year 12:319
 It is good to know what a m. is 12:707
 It takes…twenty years to make a m. 11:385
 King is but a m. 7:272
 make m. in our own image 1:5
 m. alone leaves traces of what he created 13:801
 M., being reasonable, must get drunk 10:329
 M. belongs wherever he wants to go 13:1091
 M.…can neither repeat his past nor leave it behind 13:655
 M.…can only find relaxation from one…labour by taking up
 another 11:512
 M.…consumes without producing 12:422
 M. delights not me 7:240
 m. fell into his anecdotage 11:324
 M. for the field and woman for the hearth 10:528
 M.…grows beyond his work 12:632
 m. has stopped moving 13:1089
 M. is a history-making creature 13:655
 M. is an intellectual animal 10:363
 M. is…a political animal 2:14
 m. is…a religious animal 9:196
 M. is a social animal 8:387
 M. is a tool-making animal 8:620
 m. is…a wild animal 12:922
 M. is not a solitary animal 12:425
 M. is something that is to be surpassed 11:285
 M. is the hunter 10:527
 M. is the only animal that can remain on friendly terms 11:313
 m. made the town 8:478
 M. proposes 6:125
 m.'s greatest crime 7:302
 M.'s love is of man's life a thing apart 10:500
 m. that hath no music in himself 7:167
 m. that is born of a woman 1:73
 m. that is young in years 7:297
 M. to command and woman to obey 10:528
 M. wants but little 8:473
 M. was born free 8:144
 m. who…had the largest…soul 8:270
 m. with all his noble qualities 11:484
 M. with the head and woman with the heart 10:528
 mean m. is always full of distress 2:40
 My mother said it was simple to keep a m. 13:931
 No m. is an Island 7:299
 Nothing happens to any m. 4:72
 No young m. believes he shall ever die 9:166
 Of M.'s first disobedience 1:111
 On earth there is nothing great but m. 10:382
 One cannot be always laughing at a m. 9:185
 one m. pick'd out of ten thousand 7:239
 One m. shall have one vote 8:239
 one small step for m. 13:234

N

O

P

making p. Christian   13:1070
Men who have greatness...don't go in for p.   12:257
Never judge a country by its p.   12:865
P. are now nothing more than   8:193
p. are too serious...to be left to the politicians   13:251
P. come from man. Mercy   13:386
P. is a blood sport   13:40
P. is not an exact science   10:213
P. is the art of preventing people from taking part   12:386
P. is...the only profession   11:513
p. was the second lowest profession   13:1164
that men enter local p.   13:873
There are times in p.   13:224
the science of p. deals with the government of men   10:88
they can at least pretend that p. is a game   13:110
War is the continuation of p.   10:47, 13:38
polloi   the multitude, the *hoi p*.   8:56
polluter   intelligence is the great p.   13:1104
polonies   My father...deals in nice p.   10:82
polygamy   P. was made a Sin   8:34
Pomeranian   The healthy bones of a single P. grenadier   11:7
pomp   In lowly p. ride on to die   10:598
Pride, p., and circumstance   7:95
solemnized with p. and parade   8:205
Poms   All the faces...seem to be bloody P.   13:1184
pondered   Mary...p. them in her heart   3:7
pontifical   royal power takes all its reputation...from the p.
power   6:25
poodle   Mr Balfour's P.   11:130
poor   A p. man is despised the whole world over   11:500
a p. society cannot be too p.   12:937
as difficult to elevate the p....depress the rich   10:56
ask of the p. that they get up and act   13:1126
cynical gestures of the p.   12:176
decent means p.   10:625
Hard to train to accept being p.   4:92
I, being p., have only my dreams   12:670
If a free society cannot help the...p.   13:1125
it is p. grub, p. pay, and easy work   11:111
Laws grind the p.   8:151
many a p. man...has been relieved and helped by him   6:83
only the p. who pay cash   12:939
p. have no right to the property of the rich   10:208
P. Little Rich Girl   12:981
p. relation   10:512
Resolve not to be p.   8:632
short and simple annals of the p.   8:627
that plenty should attain the p.   10:18
the p. are our brothers and sisters   13:1130
the p....need love,...need care,...have to be wanted   13:1130
To be p. and independent   10:624
very p. are unthinkable   11:508
poorer   for richer for p.   7:339
poorest   p....hath a life to live as the greatest   10:253
p. man may in his cottage bid defiance to...the Crown   8:148
pop   In England, p. art and fine art   13:510
Popery   No P., No Slavery   8:28
Popish   their deliverer from P. tyranny   8:53
poppies   the p. blow   12:28
populace   society distributes itself into Barbarians,
Philistines, and P.   10:250
the p. cannot exact their demands   10:60
this vast residuum we may...give the name of P.   10:253
popular   Nothing can render them p.   8:605
The worse I do, the more p. I get   13:146
We're more p. than Jesus Christ   13:532
popularity   P.?...glory's small change   10:459
P. is a crime   8:540
population   a starving p.   10:96
P. growth...environmental damage   13:833
The purpose of p....is to fill heaven   13:1067
populi   *vox p., vox dei*   5:5
pornography   P. is the attempt to insult sex   12:749
p....it is terribly, terribly boring   13:849
p. of war   13:960
portion   best p. of a good man's life   9:187
portrait   Every man's work...is always a p. of himself   11:206
portraying   What sort of God are we p.   13:1069

possess   poor men and rich may p. what they rightly acquire
                                                             5:9
possession   The p. of a book   13:630
possessions   Not the owner of many p. will you be right to
call happy   4:50
possibility   too much of a sceptic to deny the p. of anything
                                                             11:251
possible   something is p., he is...right   13:1108
the art of the p.   13:258
The only way of finding the limits of the p.   13:799
postchaise   You are forgetting the p.   10:32
posterity   doing something for p.   8:456
Think of your p.   9:43
postgraduate   The British p. student is a lonely forlorn soul
                                                             13:638
potent   how p. cheap music is   12:472
pound   can call an ecu a p.   13:450
the p....in your pocket   13:219
pounds   the p. will take care of themselves   8:626
poverty   crime so shameful as p.   8:625
declares unconditional war on p. in America   13:196
Do you call p. a crime   11:505
For every talent that p. has stimulated   13:1124
generations...have struggled in p. to build these altars   11:468
If p. is the mother of crime, stupidity is its father   8:451
It is easy enough to say that p. is no crime   11:500
Loneliness...is the most terrible p.   13:810
p....is a blunder   11:500
P. is a great enemy to human happiness   8:632
P. is an anomaly to rich people   11:497
The misfortunes of p.   4:93
three great evils, boredom, vice, and p.   8:641
world p. is primarily a problem of two million villages   13:1129
powder   when your p.'s runnin' low   7:64
power   All P. to the Soviets   12:62
All that is literature seeks to communicate p.   10:310
As we make sex less secretive, we may rob it of its p.   13:851
corridors of p.   13:97
don't have p. if you surrender all your principles   13:431
Germany will be...a world p.   12:137
greater the p.   8:181
In a country economically backward, the proletariat can take
p. earlier   12:175
its source of p.: ownership   13:298
Knowledge itself is p.   7:220
life depends on your p. to master words   13:647
love of p. is the love of ourselves   10:549
Men of p. have not time to read   13:351
one of these is the history of political p.   12:572
P....and Liberty...are seldom upon good Terms   8:47
P. corrupts   13:192
p. has been the vice of the ascetic   12:893
p. is apt to corrupt   8:172
P. is the ultimate aphrodisiac   13:306
p. should always be distrusted   8:248
P. tends to corrupt   11:54
p. without responsibility   12:207
royal p. takes all its reputation...from the pontifical p.   6:25
The balance of p.   8:116
the blacks must oppress them today because they have p.
                                                             13:349
The English nation...has successfully regulated the p. of its
kings   8:570
the exercise of an international police p.   11:122
the foul dregs of his p., the tools of despotism and corruption
                                                             8:145
the kingdom of God is not in word, but in p.   3:118
The p. of kings and magistrates   7:144
they...take, who have the p.   9:165
unable to influence events...do not have the p.   13:330
War knows no p.   12:30
When p. narrows the areas of man's concern   13:524
You only have p. over people   13:241
powerful   a more p. or a more united empire   12:97
Guns will make us p.   12:274
powers   a taste for *hidden* and *forbidden* p.   11:488
England is one of the greatest p. of the world   10:177

rights bill of r. is what the people are entitled to | 8:260
government…must be built upon the r. of the people | 12:155
human beings are born free…dignity and r. | 13:19
I do not ask for my r. | 10:532
r. and interests of the laboring man | 11:105
The Sovereign has, under a constitutional monarchy…three r. | 10:237
We come, our country's r. to save | 10:52
women their r. and nothing less | 11:403
Women…were ready to fight for their own human r. | 11:140
ring They now r. the bells | 8:111
riot A r. is at bottom | 13:221
ripe we r. and r. | 7:276
Ripper Jack the R.'s dead | 11:59
Yours truly, Jack the R. | 11:58
rise Early to r. and early to bed | 12:651
Thanks to words, we have been able to r. above the brutes | 13:504
rising r. hope of those stern and unbending Tories | 10:76
Ritz like the R. hotel | 11:134
river build your House of Parliament upon the r. | 10:60
On the breast of the r. of Time | 10:492
the r. of knowledge has too often turned back on itself | 12:924
The vanity of human life is like a r. | 8:452
road All I seek…the r. below me | 11:346
roads all r. lead to France | 12:54
How many r. must a man walk down | 13:764
roam Mid pleasures and palaces though we may r. | 10:514
roar luck to give the r. | 12:998
robbed when you've r. a man of everything | 13:241
robber now Barabbas was a r. | 3:30
Robin Who killed Cock R. | 6:3
robot the modern conception of a r. | 13:22
rock It's only r. 'n' roll | 13:553
R. and roll or Christianity | 13:532
upon this r. I will build my church | 3:23
rod he that spareth his r. hateth his son | 1:79
spare the r. | 8:498
rogues we should indeed be very great r. | 10:187
role he saw his r. as being that of Moses | 13:317
roll R. up that map | 9:57
rolling Like a r. stone | 13:776
Roma R. locuta est | 5:28
Roman noblest R. of them all | 4:9
the Holy R. Empire was neither holy, nor R., nor an empire | 8:169
The Papacy is not other than the Ghost of the deceased R. Empire | 7:153
the R. people had but one neck | 4:19
Romans Friends, R., countrymen, lend me your ears | 4:7
The R. and Greeks found everything human | 2:84
Romanticism R. is…presenting people with the literary works…affording…the greatest…pleasure | 10:277
Romanus Civis R. sum | 10:123
Rome R. has spoken; the case is concluded | 5:28
R.'s gross yoke /Drops off | 10:601
said of Augustus that he found R. brick | 10:160
so much bounden to the See of R. | 7:10
The farther you go from the church of R. | 7:402
without R. Italy cannot be constituted | 10:197
room no r. for them in the inn | 3:4
The perpetual struggle for r. and food | 9:36
Roosevelt the kind of nation that President R. hoped for | 13:202
root love of money is the r. of all evil | 3:97
the r. of all sins | 7:193
rose a r. /By any other name | 7:229
rosebuds Gather ye r. while ye may | 7:330
roses days of wine and r. | 11:343
Nor does a…gardener scent his r. | 12:440
Ring-a-ring o'r. | 8:5
Treaties are like r. and young girls | 13:187
rot we r. and r. | 7:276
rotting Damn you, England. You're r. | 13:1015
Rouen forcing R. into submission by starvation | 6:63
rough-hew R. them how we will | 7:399
round The trivial r., the common task | 10:335
Roundheads R. (Right but Repulsive) | 7:421

Rowley Heigh ho! says R. | 7:41
royal A R. Commission is a broody hen | 13:20
at no time stand so highly in our estate r. | 7:3
Once in r. David's city | 10:59
royalty Prince Henry,…something of r. in his demeanour | 6:8
rub there's the r. | 7:20
rubies her price is far above r. | 1:8
the price of wisdom is above r. | 1:6
rubs sentimentality…r. you up the wrong way | 12:63
rude The right people are r. | 12:65
Rugby R. Union which is a distillation | 13:52
ruin the boy will r. himself | 12:25
ruined Such another victory and we are r. | 2:1
ruining they will end by r. our idea | 12:24
rule A little r., a little sway | 8:45
he must r. the roast everywhere | 10:7
I don't believe in black majority r. | 13:30
Irish Home R. is conceded | 11:7
R. all England under a hog | 6:8
safer to obey than to r. | 6:6
The first r. in opera is the first r. in life | 12:69
rulers We are all Home R. today | 12:10
Women…natural, but usually secret, r. | 13:89
rules R. and models destroy genius and art | 10:29
r. of the game are what we call the laws of Nature | 10:49
the r. of the universe be annulled | 11:47
ruleth the cry of him that r. among fools | 1:6
ruling The state is an instrument…of the r. class | 12:14
rum r., sodomy, and the lash | 12:3
rumour Where r. of oppression and deceit | 8:47
runners like r. hand on the torch of life | 4:5
running drive out nature with a pitchfork…she'll be constantly r. back | 4:4
The machine is r. away with *him* | 12:31
rushing a r. mighty wind | 3:4
Ruskin I doubt that art needed R. | 13:56
Russia For us in R. communism is a dead dog | 13:33
going in without the help of R. | 12:31
R. has entered the family of civilized nations | 13:46
R. is a collapse, not a revolution | 12:6
the greatness of R. is only her pre-natal struggling | 12:11
Why will America not reach out…to R. | 12:12
Russian greet in you the victorious R. Revolution | 12:6
Scratch the R. and…find the Tartar | 9:19
the R. people have become | 12:21
Russians our decadence and the R.' | 13:101
test the R., not the bombs | 13:10
rut people getting into a state of r. | 12:42

S

Sabbath the child that is born on the S. day /Is bonny and blithe, and good and gay | 10:64
sack Either back us or s. us | 13:31
sacrifice A woman will always s. herself | 12:78
s.…of the devil's leavings | 8:45
this war…which did not justify the s. of a single mother's son | 12:8
sacrificed the most useful thing about a principle…s. to expediency | 12:80
sad Becoming an Anglo-Catholic must…be a s. business | 13:104
being kind /Is all the s. world needs | 12:65
sadists repressed s.…become policemen or butchers | 12:96
sadness S.…a form of fatigue | 12:59
safe make the world s. for diversity | 13:10
safer s. to obey than to rule | 6:6
safety Safe though all s.'s lost | 12:3
sage without hardness will be s. | 10:56
said Nothing has yet been s. that's not been s. before | 4:3
sailor how a carter, a common s., a beggar is still…an Englishman | 8:57
Tinker, /Tailor, /Soldier, /S. | 10:64
sailors Dear comrades, soldiers, s. and workers | 12:6
saint I consider myself superior to the s., the scientist | 12:43
S., n. a dead sinner | 11:44
saintliness S. is also a temptation | 13:95

shambles   Our civilization is founded on the s.   11:244

shame   expense of spirit in a waste of s.   7:325
  Neither s. nor physical pain have any...effect   11:452

shape   hearts of Men...should have a virtue to s. their life   13:706

shapely   it's...more important for a theory to be s., than...true   13:634

share   s. in the good fortunes of the mighty   13:28

sharp   those who have stout hearts and s. swords   12:685

Shaw   Bernard S.   11:177
  George Bernard S. is sadly miscast   12:465
  Mr S....has never written any poetry   11:214
  S.'s mind...was still better than anyone else's   12:497

she   s. is my country still   8:149
  S.-who-must-be-obeyed   11:400

sheathe   never s. the sword   12:10

Sheba   the queen of S.   1:50

shed   s....for the remission of sins   3:27

shedding   without s. of blood is no remission   3:51

sheep   Baa, baa, black s.   6:56
  good shepherd giveth his life for the s.   3:112
  like lost s.   8:367
  make a man by standing a s.   11:312
  savaged by a dead s.   13:323
  the wolf in the s.'s clothing   2:33
  useless for the s. to pass resolutions in favour of vegetarianism   12:580

Shelley   S. and Keats were...up to date in...chemical knowledge   12:908
  the right sphere for S.'s genius   10:299

shells   shrill demented choirs of wailing s.   12:90

shepherd   I am the good s.   3:112

shepherds   Governments needs to have both s. and butchers   8:232
  s. abiding in the field   3:5
  s. watch'd their flocks   8:593

Sherard   S. Blaw, the dramatist who had discovered himself   11:219

shift   for coming down let me s. for myself   7:21

ship   as the smart s. grew...grew the Iceberg too   11:162
  places his s. alongside that of an enemy   9:52
  The s. follows Soviet custom   13:299
  They did not,...so much as sink...one s.   7:67

ships   Heart of oak are our s.   8:132
  little s. of England brought the Army home   12:331
  S. that pass in the night   11:327
  We've got the s., we've got the men, we've got the money too   11:16

shipwreck   husbands and wives make s. of their lives   12:770

shit   the sun shining ten days a year and s. in the streets   13:1028

shock   deliberately set out to s.   13:559

shocks   s. /That flesh is heir to   7:209

shoemaker   I take my shoes from the s.   8:608

shook   Ten Days that S. the World   12:67

shoot   It is not the business of generals to s. one another   9:110
  S., if you must, this old gray head   10:199

shooting   war minus the s.   12:645

shop   All English s. assistants are Miltonists   13:717
  A man must keep a little back s.   7:265

shopkeepers   A nation of s.   8:210
  England is a nation of s.   9:63, 9:192

shopping   Today you're unhappy?...Go s.   13:790

shore   waves make towards the pebbled s.   7:211

short   it will take a while long to make it s.   10:321
  Life is too s. to do anything...one can pay others to do   12:969
  s. and simple annals of the poor   8:627
  the life of man, solitary, poor, nasty, brutish, and s.   7:149

shortage   a s. of coal and fish...at the same time   12:421

shorter   not had the time to make it s.   8:366

shot   had them all s.   10:248

shots   God is on the side...of the best s.   8:441
  They really are bad s.   13:162

should   no better than you s. be   7:249

shoulders   it is by standing on the s. of giants   8:614

shuffled   s. off this mortal coil   7:209
  the human pack is s. and cut   13:638

shut   when I was there it seemed to be s.   13:1037

shyness   S. is just egotism out of its depth   13:710

sick   A person seldom falls s.   10:430
  so many poor s. people in the streets full of sores   8:4
  The prayer that...heals the s.   11:464
  We have on our hands a s. man   10:140

sickness   in s. and in health   7:339
  Love is a s.   7:328
  s. enlarges the dimensions of a man's self   10:404
  S., sin and death...do not originate in God   11:466

side   passed by on the other s.   3:16
  Time is on our s.   10:233

sides   Do not...write on both s. of the paper   12:551

sighs   S. are the natural language of the heart   8:271

sight   we walk by faith, not by s.   3:69
  Who ever loved, that loved not at first s.   7:317

sightless   clapped the glass to his s. eye   9:41

sights   few more impressive s. in the world   11:458

sign   s. of an ill-spent youth   11:305

signal   I really do not see the s.   9:40

signifying   S. nothing   7:287

signing   I am s. my death warrant   12:124

silence   S. is as full of potential wisdom   12:543
  S. is the best tactic   8:373
  S. is the...perfect expression of scorn   12:809
  Sorrow and s. are strong   10:557
  The cruellest lies are...told in s.   11:424
  the impression that their normal condition is s.   12:630

silent   the great s. majority   13:247
  thereon one must remain s.   12:534

silk   s., too often hides eczema   13:679

silly   some damned s. thing in the Balkans   11:83

silver   Selling the family s.   13:404

simple   A s. race   9:124
  short and s. annals of the poor   8:627

simplify   ability to s. means   12:463
  S., s.   10:478

simplifying   s. something by destroying nearly everything   12:712

sin   A branch of the s. of drunkenness   7:193
  All s. tends to be addictive   13:974
  a more dreadful record of s. than...countryside   11:228
  A private s. is not so prejudicial   7:377
  Be a sinner and s. strongly   7:391
  Being seventy is not a s.   13:797
  he that is without s....let him first cast a stone   3:94
  if we say that we have no s., we deceive   3:63
  it is no s. to s. in secret   8:524
  it's a s. to kill a mockingbird   13:1179
  no s. but to be rich   7:411
  no s. except stupidity   11:252
  Sickness, s. and death...do not originate in God   11:466
  S. brought death   11:241
  which taketh away the s. of the world   3:12

sincere   It is dangerous to be s. unless   11:446
  Some of the worst men in the world are s.   13:970

sincerity   A little s. is a dangerous thing   11:429
  S. is all that counts...modern heresy   12:293
  style, not s., is the vital thing   11:344

sinecure   a widow...is a kind of s.   8:511

sinews   Anger is one of the s. of the soul   7:259

sinful   Popular stage-plays are s., heathenish   7:200

sing   The Welsh...just s.   12:844
  we s. no more   11:175

singed   s. the Spanish king's beard   7:59

singin'   s. in the rain   12:978

single   a s. man in possession of a good fortune must be in want of a wife   9:179

sinning   nothing so artificial as s. nowadays   12:813

sins   atone for the s. of your fathers   4:14
  shed...for the remission of s.   3:27

sirens   Blest pair of S.   8:267

sister   no friend like a s.   10:519

sisters   all the lovely s.   13:261
  little s. to all the world   12:791
  O! men with s. dear   10:525

sit   I will s. down now   10:68
  nobody can tell you when to s. down   13:72
  say what you have to say, and then s. down   10:7

our love...of the mind does not make us s. 2:5

soldier Every French s. carries in his cartridge-pouch 9:79
in the s. is flat blasphemy 7:94
strength and majesty the British s. fights 9:92
The s.'s body...a stock of accessories 12:367
The summer s. and the sunshine patriot 8:253
Tinker, /Tailor, /S., /Sailor 10:643

soldiers Dear comrades, s., sailors and workers 12:61
English s. fight like lions 12:27
S. are citizens of death's grey land 12:961
when staring at our s. drilling in Berlin 8:579

solitary Life is for each man a s. cell 12:699
Man is not a s. animal 12:425
Only s. men know the full joys of friendship 12:620

solitude In s. alone can he know true freedom 7:265
In s. /What happiness 8:379
so companionable as s. 10:424
S. is the playfield of Satan 13:685

solution total s. of the Jewish question 12:372

some I...may be s. time 11:160
You can fool s. of the people all the time 10:188

someone I wouldn't be...talking to s. like you 13:324

something S. must be done 12:228

son the earth is free for every s. and daughter of mankind 7:142
woman, behold thy s. 3:36

sonatas The s. of Mozart are unique 8:671

song the s. that is sung in our hearts 11:169
Who loves not wine, woman and s. 7:184

sonnet s. is a moment's monument 11:173

sons I have a wife, I have s. 4:76
my four s. who cease not to persecute me 6:20
Now we are all s. of bitches 12:402
S. of Belial had a Glorious Time 8:35

sophistry it can contain nothing but s. and illusion 8:342

sorcery false enchantments and s. 6:64

sorrow in s. thou shalt bring forth children 1:13
S. and silence are strong 10:557
S. is tranquillity remembered in emotion 12:735
s. makes us wise 10:421
Tears of eternity and s. 12:678
There is no greater s. 6:108

sorrows When s. come, they come not single spies 7:278

sought Love s. is good 7:321
Pleasure is...seldom found where it is s. 8:419

soul Anger is one of the sinews of the s. 7:259
Artists are not engineers of the s. 13:523
a...s. like season'd timber 7:379
become a living s. 9:134
education is a leading out of what is...in the pupil's s. 13:623
Education is...the s. of a society 12:538
I am positive I have a s. 8:606
I am the captain of my s. 11:335
Impropriety is the s. of wit 12:646
In mystery our s. abides 10:566
Man has no Body distinct from his S. 9:197
my s. doth magnify the Lord 3:2
Never mind about my s....get my tie right 12:49
passion in the human s. 8:282
possessive outrage done to a free solitary human s. 12:774
The British postgraduate student is a lonely forlorn s. 13:638
The dark night of the s. 7:227
the...essence of a human s. 10:292
the largest and most comprehensive s. 8:270
the s. of a martyr with the intellect of an advocate 10:184
The S. that rises with us, our life's Star 9:199

souls a follower of hounds to become a shepherd of s. 6:10
the s. of five hundred...Newtons 9:200
The s. of women are so small 8:507

soul-sides the meanest of his creatures /Boasts two s. 10:533

sound full of s. and fury 7:287
The most persistent s....through men's history 13:652
The s. must seem an echo to the sense 8:279
The s. of the English county families 12:841
the trumpet shall s. 3:53

sounding s. brass 3:95

sounds Music is the arithmetic of s. 12:431

sour How s. sweet music is 7:268

I am sure the grapes are s. 2:35
when the milk isn't s. 13:471

South hardly be a town in the S. of England 12:861

South Africa God's will to lead...S. Africa through defeat and humiliation 11:103
Three words made peace and union in S. 11:104

South Africans You won't force S. 13:398

sovereign A Subject and a S. are clean different things 7:135
he will have no s. 7:111
The S. has, under a constitutional monarchy...three rights 10:237
The s. is absolute 8:164
When I forget my s. 8:230

sovereigns rather than that the s. and magistrates should be destroyed 7:14

Soviet Communism is S. power plus the electrification 12:111
S. people want full-blooded...democracy 13:432
The ship follows S. custom 13:299

Soviets All Power to the S. 12:62

sow Ireland is the old s. 12:41
I took the right s. by the ear 8:105
that man hath the s. by the right ear 7:15

soweth whatsoever a man s., that shall he also reap 3:70

space In the United States there is more s. 12:860
range of human societies in time, the other in s. 13:656
S. isn't remote at all 13:1112

spaceship passenger on the s., Earth 13:791

span Life's short s. forbids us...far-reaching hopes 4:64

Spaniards the S. seem wiser than they are 7:385
time to win this game, and to thrash the S. 7:62

spaniel the cur dog of Britain and s. of Spain 8:101

Spanish I speak S. to God 7:16
singed the S. king's beard 7:59

spare I can't this man; he fights 10:217
S. all I have 8:650
s. the rod 8:498
Woodman, s. that tree 10:407

spareth he that s. his rod hateth his son 1:79

sparrow I, said the S., /With my bow and arrow 6:3

sparrowhawks S., Ma'am 10:133

sparrows one of the s....flew...through the hall 5:24

spasm a lonely s. of helpless agony 11:244

spat Today I s. in the Seine 12:394

speak I didn't s. up 12:411
province of knowledge to s. 11:247
some...s...before they think 8:327
S. softly and carry a big stick 11:98
s. to God as if men were listening 4:83
When I think, I must s. 7:343
Whereof one cannot s. 12:534

speaking An Englishman's way of s. 13:1004
People talking without s. 13:782

spectator a S. of mankind 8:455

spectre A s. is haunting Europe – the s. of communism 10:116
Communism continued to haunt Europe as a s. 12:994

speculation If the world were good for...s. 10:453

speech freedom of s. and expression 12:347
freedom of s., freedom of conscience, and the prudence never to practise...them 11:82
let thy s. be short 1:85
S. was given to man to disguise his thoughts 10:397
The true use of s. 8:421

speeches he tries on s. like a man trying on ties 11:155
Many have been the wise s. of fools 7:223
solved by s. and majority votes 10:207
Statesmen are far too busy making s. 13:250

spending Getting and s. 9:172
Riches are for s. 7:412

spice Sugar and s. /And all that's nice 10:526

spices our ancestors who were given so much to eat s. 8:310

spies sorrows...come not single s. 7:278

spin rare attainments...but...can she s. 7:346

spinning from eternity s. the thread of your being 4:73

spires City with her dreaming s. 10:349

spirit and an haughty s. before a fall 1:82
Give me the s. 7:232
into thy hands I commend my s. 3:40
my s. found outlet in the air 12:628

my s. hath rejoiced in God my Saviour 3:2
s. of the Londoner stands resolute 12:340
the meanest...deeds require s. and talent 8:472
the s....is willing 3:59
the S. of God moved upon...the waters 1:1
Th' expense of s. in a waste of shame 7:325
spiritualist   If the dead talk to you, you are a s. 13:1061
spiteful   I like to write when I feel s. 11:221
splendid   our s. isolation 11:77
split   They s. the atom by firing particles at 13:1081
spoil   s. the child 8:498
spoke   s. among your wheels 7:417
spokesman   Lord Salisbury constitutes himself the s. 11:37
spontaneous   set a high value on s. kindness 8:428
the Immaculate Conception was s. combustion 12:884
Worrying is the most natural and s. of...functions 13:708
spoof   even the weather forecast seemed to be some kind of s. 13:593
spoon   And the dish ran away with the s. 7:52
S. feeding...teaches us nothing but the shape of the s. 13:613
spoons   let us count our s. 8:558
the faster we counted our s. 10:431
sport   Blood s. is brought to its ultimate refinement 13:598
kill us for their s. 7:210
Serious s. has nothing to do with fair play 12:645
to make s. for our neighbours 9:155
spotless   s. reputation 7:267
spots   or the leopard his s. 1:90
spring   In the S. a young man's fancy 10:505
s. now comes unheralded by the return of the birds 13:585
spur   Fame is the s. 7:306
spurs   Let the boy win his s. 6:44
spurts   They move forward in s. 12:728
squandermania   The Happy Warrior of S. 12:417
square   Shed his blood...given a s. deal 11:112
squares   city is arrayed in s. just like a chess-board 6:38
squeezed   The Germans,...are going to be s., as a lemon 12:99
squire   Bless the s. and his relations 10:101
stabbed   The German army was s. in the back 12:94
stage   All the world's a s. 7:274
no man dies for love, but on the s. 8:486
this great s. of fools 7:288
we go quite off this s. 8:317
stagecoach   You will hear more good things on...a s. from London to Oxford 10:362
stage-plays   Popular s. are sinful, heathenish 7:200
stags   he loved the s. as...though he had been their father 5:14
stairs   walks up the s. of his concepts 12:632
Stalin   If Mr S. dies 13:76
I like old Joe S. 13:18
stamp   the indelible s. of his lowly origin 11:484
to order a new s....with my face on it 12:39
stand   a firm place to s. 2:79
at no time s. so highly in our estate royal 7:31
Here s. I. I can do no other 7:7
no time to s. and stare 12:669
S. your ground...if they mean to have a war, let it begin here 8:201
They also serve who only s. and wait 8:582
We s. today on the edge of a new frontier 13:127
standard   a s. of rebellion 8:52
star   Being a s. has made it possible 13:686
s. treatment...I was just as good when I was poor 13:1133
The Soul that rises with us, our life's S. 9:199
Twinkle, twinkle, little s. 9:205
we have seen his s. in the east 3:9
stare   no time to stand and s. 12:669
Stark   Tonight the American flag floats from yonder hill or Molly S. sleeps a widow 8:220
starry   the s. heaven above me 8:481
Under the wide and s. sky 11:243
stars   he made the s. also 1:3
I'll hold my head so high it'll strike the s. 4:27
One sees the mud, and one the s. 11:298
some of us are looking at the s. 11:342
strives to touch the s. 7:224
Tempt not the s. 7:301

Through endeavour to the s. 12:73
star-spangled   'Tis the s. banner 9:103
starts   make certain it never s. 13:61
starvation   forcing Rouen into submission by s. 6:63
starve   His taxes...s. the poor souls 9:37
Let not poor Nelly s. 8:41
starving   all around you people are s. 12:123
state   a s. in the proper sense of the word 12:146
For Fascism the S. is absolute 12:248
I am the S. 8:90
In a free society the s....administers justice among men 12:184
man was not born to go down on his belly before the s. 13:230
O Lord, to what a s....those who love Thee 7:394
Our object in the construction of the s. 2:7
reinforcement of the power of the S. 13:55
So long as the s. exists there is no freedom 12:70
Star for every S. 10:202
S. socialism is totally alien 13:381
the lie has become...a pillar of the S. 13:287
The S., in choosing men...takes no notice of their opinions 7:126
The s. is an instrument...of the ruling class 12:149
The s. is not 'abolished', it withers away 11:17
the s....Man is in 11:469
The worth of a S. 10:181
stately   lunatic asylums...the s. homes 12:516
S. Homes of England ope their doors 12:854
The S. Homes of England 12:521
states   S., like men, have their growth,..., their decay 10:21
United S. of Europe 13:5
statesman   abroad you're a s. 13:106
A s. is a politician who 13:277
A s. is a politician who's been dead 13:109
definition of a constitutional s. 10:122
if you agree with him he is a s. 12:197
statesmen   an imperative principle which s....ignore at their peril 12:75
S. are far too busy making speeches 13:250
s....estranged from reality 13:133
static   class people as s. and dynamic 12:793
novel is a s. thing 13:517
stations   always know our proper s. 10:101
statistics   Facts speak louder than s. 13:737
He uses s. as a drunken man uses lamp-posts 11:323
lies, damned lies and s. 10:559
s., born to consume resources 4:61
You cannot feed the hungry on s. 11:121
statue   that my s. should be moved, which I should much dislike 11:80
stature   man of giant s. 13:77
status   restored the s. quo 12:920
steal   thou shalt not s. 1:40
stealing   hanged for s. horses 8:48
steals   A good composer...s. 12:473
steel   the cold s. 10:210
steeple   clock in the s. strikes one 11:222
stem   a rod out of the s. of Jesse 1:100
step   a s. from the sublime to the ridiculous 9:90
one small s. for man 13:234
One s. forward, two steps back 11:275
only the first s....is difficult 8:658
stern   rising hope of those s. and unbending Tories 10:76
stick   if we praise ourselves fearlessly, something will always s. 7:364
Speak softly and carry a big s. 11:98
sticks   it is always said of slander that something always s. 7:364
still   a s. small voice 1:51
sting   O death, where is thy s. 3:53
stinking   found Paris s. and left it sweet 10:160
stockholders   The public be damned. I am working for my s. 11:47
stoic   man is...either a s. or a satyr 11:293
stomach   An army marches on its s. 9:105
No one can worship God...on an empty s. 11:369
The way to a man's heart is through his s. 10:510
use a little wine for thy s.'s sake 3:52
stomachs   Napoleon's armies used to march on their s. 9:212

T

U

W

Give me books, fruit, French w. and fine weather 10:330
new w. into old bottles 3:58
the w. is in, the wit is out 7:187
Truth comes out in w. 4:36
use a little w. for thy stomach's sake 3:52
Who loves not w., woman and song 7:184
w. is a mocker 1:84

wings man with w....might...overcome the resistance of the
air 6:129
the seraphims: each one had six w. 1:96
the w. of a dove 8:429

winners In war...there are no w. 12:301

winning not w. but taking part 11:361
W. isn't everything, but wanting to win is 13:795

Winston The first time you meet W. 12:152
W.'s back 12:315
W. with his hundred-horse-power mind 12:289

winter got through the perils of w. till at least the seventh of
May 10:345
the furious w.'s rages 7:212
w. of our discontent 6:81

wisdom follies as the special evidences of our w. 10:583
If one is too lazy to think...never attain w. 12:560
in much w. is much grief 1:63
Knowledge can be communicated but not w. 12:537
privilege of w. to listen 11:247
proverbs provide them with w. 11:253
Silence is...full of potential w. 12:543
The highest w. has but one science 10:621
The only infallible criterion of w. 9:202
the price of w. is above rubies 1:62
Vain w. all, and false philosophy 8:325
want of human w. 11:152
w....a pure influence flowing from the glory of the 1:67
w....cometh by opportunity of leisure 1:66
W. in minds attentive 8:357
w. is more moving than any motion 1:67
W. is not additive 13:190
w. of the crocodiles 7:250
with how little w. the world is governed 7:134
with the ancient is w. 1:61

wise all the w. men promised has not happened 10:31
A w. man will make more opportunities 7:219
How very weak the very w. 10:457
Many have been the w. speeches of fools 7:223
more of the fool than of the w. 7:246
No man...so w. as Thurlow looked 8:242
sorrow makes us w. 10:421
The only wretched are the w. 8:330
the w. forgive 13:700
To be w. and love 7:322

wisely deserves the name of happy who knows how to use
the gods' gifts w. 4:50

Wiseman Mr Worldly W. 8:649

wiser Be w. than other people 8:341
foreigner should...be w. than ourselves 10:583
The French are w. than they seem 7:385
the old have rubbed it into the young that they are w. 12:710
w. to-day than...yesterday 8:399

wish Conscience is...rejection of a...w. 11:315
Justice is the...perpetual w. 5:2
The w. to spread those opinions that we hold 11:3

wished consummation devoutly to be w. 7:209

wit An ounce of a man's own w. 8:439
Impropriety is the soul of w. 12:646
men of w. can so hardly use that gift 7:48
Music-hall songs provide the dull with w. 11:253
Pubic hair is no substitute for w. 13:555
To the Greeks the Muse gave native w. 2:67
True w. is nature to advantage dress'd 8:437
wine is in, the w. is out 7:187

witch not only suspected but pronounced for a w. 7:131
thou shalt not suffer a w. to live 1:42

witches My question is not whether there be w. or nay 7:184

withers The state is not 'abolished', it w. away 11:17

witness thou shalt not bear false w. 1:40

witnesses this massed multitude of silent w. to...war 12:129

wits Great W....to Madness near alli'd 8:447

their poetry is conceived and composed in their w. 11:182

witty Anger makes dull men w. 7:355
Pretty w. Nell 8:3
stumbling on something w. 9:185

wives husbands and w. make shipwreck of their lives 12:770
O! men with mothers and w. 10:525
W. are young men's mistresses 7:334

woe Wednesday's child is full of w. 10:640
w. to him that is alone when he falleth 1:69
W. to the vanquished 4:65
w. unto them that...follow strong drink 1:87

wolf The boy cried 'W., w.!' 2:36
the w. in the sheep's clothing 2:33

woman all the keys should hang from the belt of one w. 6:47
another w. becoming PM 13:448
Any w. who understands the problems of running a home 13:334
a w. is on a...hunt for trouble 12:770
a w....ought to lay aside...modesty with her skirt 7:311
A w. should be an illusion 13:911
A w. should open everything 13:913
a w.'s reason 7:342
A w. will always sacrifice herself 12:788
a w. yet think him an angel 10:531
body of a weak and feeble w. 7:65
chosen to be a w. if He'd wanted to 13:1068
Christ-like heroes and w.-worshipping Don Juans 12:787
educate a w. you educate a family 13:609
Every old w. with a wrinkled face 7:131
every w. is at heart a rake 8:518
Every w. is infallibly to be gained 8:520
Frailty, thy name is w. 7:344
God made the w. for the man 10:530
hell a fury like a w. scorned 8:514
I am a...w. – nothing more 10:537
I am a w.? When I think, I must speak 7:343
If a w. like Eva Peron with no ideals 13:341
International W.'s Day 12:71
It is a great glory in a w. 2:55
It's a sort of bloom on a w. 11:415
I would...guess that Anon...was often a w. 12:795
Man for the field and w. for the hearth 10:528
No one delights more in vengeance than a w. 4:78
nor w. neither 7:240
No w. so naked as...underneath her clothes 13:922
Once a w. has given you her heart 8:513
one can...see in a little girl the threat of a w. 10:538
One is not born a w. 13:897
One tongue is sufficient for a w. 8:509
only three things to be done with a w. 13:905
She makes love just like a w. 13:912
the help and support of the w. I love 12:284
The really original w....imitates a man 11:399
the rib...made he a w. 1:10
the w. who is really kind to dogs 11:420
To know the *mind* of a w. 12:752
What does a w. want 12:785
who can find a virtuous w. 1:81
Who loves not wine, w. and song 7:184
Why can't a w. be more like a man 13:904
w. alone, can...commit them 10:523
w., behold thy son 3:36
w. governs America 13:995
W. is always fickle and changing 4:77
w. is an animal that 13:898
w. is his game 10:527
w. needs a man 13:916
w. seldom asks advice 8:515
W.'s virtue is man's greatest invention 12:801
w.'s whole existence 10:500
W. to bear rule...is repugnant to Nature 7:340
W. was God's *second* mistake 11:407
W. will be the last thing civilized by Man 10:534

womanhood W. is the great fact in her life 11:397

womb no new baby in the w. of our society 12:68
teeming w. of royal kings 7:69

women A homely face...aided many w. heavenward 11:413
All Berkshire w. are very silly 13:920

Y

Z

Name Index

K

L